THE FERNANDO CORONIL READER

THE FERNANDO CORONIL READER

THE STRUGGLE

FOR LIFE

IS THE MATTER

Fernando Coronil

Julie Skurski, Gary Wilder,
Laurent Dubois, Paul Eiss,
Edward Murphy, Mariana Coronil,
and David Pedersen, editors

DUKE UNIVERSITY PRESS · DURHAM AND LONDON · 2019

For previously published chapters, see credits on page 467.
Designed by Amy Ruth Buchanan
Typeset in Quadraat Pro
by Westchester Publishing Services

Library of Congress Cataloging-in-Publication Data
Names: Coronil, Fernando, [date] author. | Skurski,
Julie, [date] editor. | Wilder, Gary, [date] editor. Title:
The Fernando Coronil reader : the struggle for life is the
matter / Fernando Coronil ; Julie Skurski, Gary Wilder,
Laurent Dubois, Paul Eiss, Edward Murphy, Mariana
Coronil, David Pederson, editors. Description:
Durham : Duke University Press, 2019. | Includes
bibliographical references and index. Identifiers: LCCN
2018044270 (print)
LCCN 2019000355 (ebook)
ISBN 9781478004592 (ebook)
ISBN 9781478003670 (hardcover)
ISBN 9781478003960 (pbk.)
Subjects: LCSH: Ethnohistory—LatinAmer ica.|
Ethnology—LatinAmer ica.|LatinAmer ica—Politics
and government—1980– | Developing countries—
Politics and government. | Postcolonialism.
Classification: LCC gn345.2 (ebook) | LCC gn345.2 .c67
2019 (print) | DDC 305.800098—dc23
LC recordavailableathttps:// lccn.loc.gov/2018044270

Cover art: Fernando Coronil, La Sabana, Venezuela.
Photo by Mariana Coronil.

CONTENTS

Introduction: Transcultural Paths and Utopian Imaginings
MARIANA CORONIL, LAURENT DUBOIS, JULIE SKURSKI,
AND GARY WILDER 1

■ **Part I. Labyrinths of Critique: The Promise of Anthrohistory**

Introduction DAVID PEDERSEN 47

1   Pieces for Anthrohistory: A Puzzle to Be Assembled
Together 53

2   Transculturation and the Politics of Theory:
Countering the Center, Cuban Counterpoint 69

3   Foreword to *Close Encounters of Empire* 118

4   Perspectives on Tierney's *Darkness in El Dorado* 123

5   The Future in Question: History and Utopia in Latin
America (1989–2010) 128

■ **Part II. Geohistorical States: Latin American Counterpoint**

Introduction EDWARD MURPHY 165

6   Dismembering and Remembering the Nation:
The Semantics of Political Violence in Venezuela 171
Coauthored with Julie Skurski

7   Transitions to Transitions: Democracy and Nation
in Latin America 231

8   Venezuela's Wounded Bodies: Nation and Imagination
during the 2002 Coup 250

9   Oilpacity: Secrets of History in the Coup against
Hugo Chávez 262

10 Crude Matters: Seizing the Venezuelan Petro-state
    in Times of Chávez 266

■ Part III. Beyond Occidentalism, Beyond Empire

Introduction PAUL EISS 309

11 Occidentalism 315

12 Beyond Occidentalism: Toward Nonimperial
    Geohistorical Categories 323

13 Listening to the Subaltern: The Poetics of Neocolonial
    States 368

14 Smelling Like a Market 385

15 Latin American Postcolonial Studies and Global
    Decolonization 399

16 After Empire: Reflections on Imperialism
    from the Américas 425

Credits 457

Index 459

Introduction: Transcultural Paths and Utopian Imaginings MARIANA CORONIL, LAURENT DUBOIS, JULIE SKURSKI, AND GARY WILDER

■ Shortly before his untimely death in 2011, Fernando Coronil captured the core ethic of his practice as a thinker: "the struggle for life is the matter." The search to find and communicate "historical truth," he wrote, implied "struggling against the forces that limit life, the source and aim of history, an elusive marvel." The pursuit of that "marvel" shaped his many interventions, offering a powerful history of the present that always insisted on the possibility of new ways of seeing and thinking, and therefore of new worlds.[1]

The essays gathered in this collection were written between 1991 and 2011. An innovative and coherent body of work, they illuminate the intellectual conjuncture in which they were written while speaking directly to many of our most pressing analytic and political challenges. Through empirically rich and conceptually sophisticated analyses of history, culture, and practice, Coronil examined the forces that sought to delimit and foreclose alternative futures. Yet his work also identified openings for alternatives, reminding us of the unwritten and unknown that could always be ahead. He was fascinated by the search for a utopian project grounded in this world, by how struggles for alternative futures always take place under conditions that can then themselves give rise to as yet unimagined possibilities.

In this search and struggle he found allies in poetry and novels; Nicolás Guillén, Jorge Luis Borges, and Alejo Carpentier were among the touchstones to whom he returned constantly in his teaching and writing. Braided through his rigorous political and economic analyses are reflections on magic, marvels, myths, illusion, imagination, poetics, voyages, and labyrinths. It is not incidental that the epigraph to The Magical State, his masterly 1997 book on oil wealth, nationalist ideology, and state power in Venezuela,

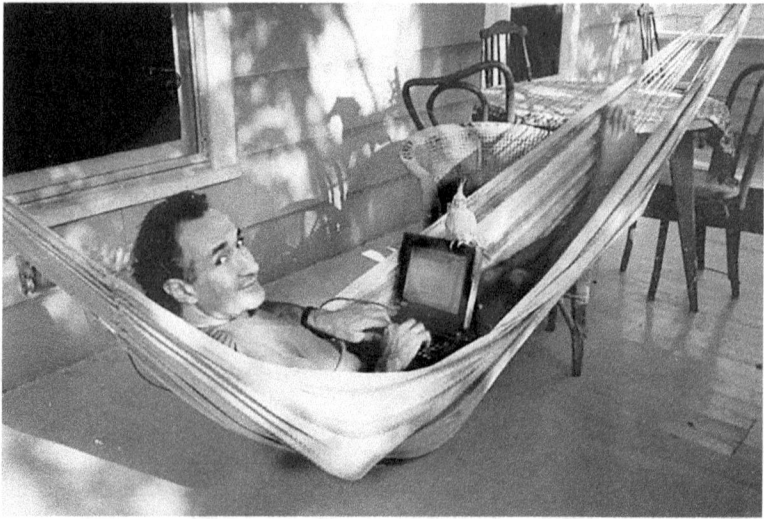

Figure I.1. Fernando preferred to write in a hammock wherever he was—
here, at his home in Ann Arbor, Michigan. Photo by Julie Skurski.

is drawn from the poet Derek Walcott: "For every poet it is always morning in the world, and History is a forgotten insomniac night. History and
elemental awe are always our early beginning, because the fate of poetry is
to fall in love with the world in spite of History."[2]

This love for the world in spite of history's depredations deeply informed
Coronil's life and work. He was a fierce critic, generous reader, and open-
minded thinker. He delighted in unforeseen difficulties, unexpected surprises, and unsettling realities. Although situated firmly on the anti-imperial
Left, his thinking was free from theoretical dogma and political orthodoxy.
Coronil was as interested in *how* we know what we know, reflecting critically
on taken-for-granted categories and frameworks, as he was in producing
new knowledge. His analyses, which typically tacked between the concrete and conceptual, always started from complex historical situations.
Rather than use worldly examples to demonstrate the truth of theoretical principles, he allowed worldly complexity to present real dilemmas, to
raise pressing questions, which displaced inherited categories and frameworks. Coronil constantly called into question academic common sense,
disciplinary divisions, and the false binaries that have limited scholarly
debates: empirical versus theoretical, material versus cultural, local versus
global, universal versus particular, practical politics versus political imagi-

Figure I.2. At his home in Caracas, Venezuela.

nation, poetry and art versus scholarship, scholarship versus advocacy. Drawing on a multitude of inspirations and sources, he sought constantly to find a space beyond these binaries from which to critically analyze and engage the world.

Coronil gave profound importance to the intrinsic relations between form and content, means and ends, an individual's concrete location and their intellectual insights. Those who knew him as a colleague and teacher came to see that there was an underlying connection between what he said and how he acted, between his politics and his ethics, between the kind of work he produced and the kind of person he was. Coronil was an engaged intellectual and internationally known public commentator on the political situation in Venezuela and Latin America. He was an enthusiastic interlocutor who cherished collective projects and delighted in productive disagreement. He was a committed teacher and mentor who invariably treated younger scholars as collaborators; disciplinary parochialism and professional productivism were anathema to him. Throughout, he brought boundless vitality, imagination, and humor to his undertakings and relations. This book is an invitation to think with Fernando Coronil about the central forces shaping our present and the prospect of a different and better world.

Figures I.3 and I.4. Portrait of Fernando by the Ecuadorian artist Oswaldo Guayasamín, painted as a gift to Fernando's family in thanks for their support during his exile. Self-portrait by Fernando when he was a teenager.

Futures Present

It is telling that the last essay Coronil wrote was entitled "The Future in Question," for it crystallizes many of the approaches and questions that preoccupied him throughout his life. In it he analyzes the complexities of Latin America while viewing the world from the perspective of the Global South; he reflects deeply on politics without being bound by conventional binaries; he pays equal attention to material conditions and utopian imaginings. The essay demonstrates how Coronil engaged simultaneously with Marxism, critical theory, and postcolonialism without subscribing to any of their orthodoxies. We see him forcefully challenge Western hegemony while endorsing struggles and envisioning futures that cross identitarian divisions. It stands as a testament to Coronil's enduring contemporaneity, a charter for why he needs to be read now.

"The Future in Question" analyzes the leftward shift among Latin American governments whose beginning Coronil dates from the electoral defeat of Augusto Pinochet in Chile in the 1989 referendum. He frames his analysis with a central paradox: Latin American leftists were increasingly animated by a renewed commitment to fundamentally change society in the service of postcapitalist futures even as they were less certain than ever about what such a future might look like. Given the failure of both capitalist and existing socialist development models to realize "universal equality" and "general well-being," the Latin American Left, according to Coronil, no longer knew "*what* to desire." This "crisis of futurity," he explains, was marked by a temporal disjuncture between a long-term utopianism fueled by belief in an alternative future and a short-term pragmatism plagued by the sense of an inescapable and ever-extending present. The result, he shows, was a constant tension between radical political imaginaries and everyday accommodations with neoliberal economic arrangements.[3]

This is the kind of paradox that Coronil skillfully identified and engaged throughout his work. It is geographically situated and of global importance. It can be only grasped through empirical examination and theoretical reflection. It calls for close attention to present conditions and requires a longer historical perspective. It entails systemic processes and conjunctural shifts. It must be explained in relation to material, political, and ideological conditions. The paradox is both conceptually challenging and politically urgent. And it invites us to unthink a whole range of conventional (leftist) political assumptions.

For Coronil, this inability to envision the alternative future for which one was already struggling marked a crisis of political imagination that was rooted in a contradictory geopolitical situation. If the Latin American Left no longer knew what to desire, this was not simply a matter of bad thinking, political weakness, or hypocrisy. It expressed a real predicament that confronted states critical of transnational capitalism across the Global South. Coronil explains that their ongoing reliance on ground rent from primary products and their vulnerability to the international financial system has left them nominally politically independent but economically dependent. Under such conditions, any attempts to develop long-term transformative projects are obstructed by the short-term imperative to maximize income and seek comparative advantage in the existing global marketplace. This means that "in a perverse twist of fate, in pursuit of fortune, leftist states may be doing the work of capital." The very capacity to imagine a radically different future is undermined by this sense of being trapped within an endlessly extending present.[4]

The hope of bringing about fundamental change is often displaced by the debilitating sense that human society cannot be improved. This double vision generates a split world that appears to oscillate between the malleable landscape of utopian imaginaries and the immutable ground of recalcitrant histories. From the fissure between these worlds there emanate contradictory dispositions and incentives that stretch the present forward and push the desired future toward an uncertain horizon: "On the one hand, the future enters the public stage as an open horizon of expectation, as potentiality, offering a hopeful sense of possibility that is characteristic of liminal phases in revolutions. On the other, the future imposes its presence as a receding historical horizon, a future in doubt, inducing a sense of despondency that is typical of periods of decline or historical depression."[5]

When Coronil proposes that the future is *in question*, then, he is not only observing that the Left does not know what kind of future to wish for. He is also indicating that under existing global arrangements, Latin America's very material survival is threatened and, moreover, that people's faith in futurity itself, their sense that a truly different future is possible, has eroded. Yet he does not himself reproduce the political despondency that he identifies, accounts for, and takes seriously. On the contrary, he observes that "although the future is not open, it offers openings."[6]

In this spirit, Coronil examines the dynamic field of Latin American politics to identify an emergent set of political logics and practices that might indeed ground a renewed leftist project for Latin America. He thus points to the pluralization of political actors and imaginaries; the eclipse of a single, class-based revolutionary subject; and the end of the assumption that radical social transformation must always be mediated by the state. He emphasizes the importance of difference as a political value and the integration of indigenous and diasporic epistemologies and cosmologies into radical political projects. He points to a new commitment to multiclass alliances, an expansive vision of plurinationality, and democracy as an indispensable means and end of socialist struggle. It is precisely because the existing models for progressive futures have failed so thoroughly, according to Coronil, that leftist movements in Latin America came to question the old party politics and inherited Marxist orthodoxies, conventional assumptions about Left versus Right, reform versus revolution, means versus ends, and realism versus utopianism.

By situating this crisis of futurity within a broader imperial framework, Coronil refuses liberal pieties (often favored by Latin American elites) about progress through economic development. Yet he also resists the temptation, increasingly common in poststructural and postcolonial analyses, to simply unmask this progressivist ideology. Beyond merely identifying this impasse, he seeks to understand how the leftward turn in Latin America, however contradictory, may have created new openings that compel us to reconsider our political categories. He does so by paying close attention to the relation between shifting contingencies and emergent possibilities in specific places. He identifies with these radical possibilities while refusing orthodox Marxist doctrines about economic determinism, class universalism, and historical stages. Like Stuart Hall's, Coronil's is a Marxism "without guarantees." He thus resists the poststructuralist and postcolonial tendency to posit an epistemological equivalence between liberalism and Marxism.[7]

Coronil's ability in "The Future in Question" to identify an impasse on the Left, to account for it structurally and conjuncturally while remaining unapologetically attuned to and aligned with emergent emancipatory possibilities, is precisely what distinguished Coronil as a critical thinker. He writes, "Although the final destination may not be clear, the sense of direction is: toward justice, equality, freedom, diversity, and social and ecological harmony. The Left has no map, but it has a compass."[8]

Unlike many of his critical contemporaries, and in contrast to much current academic discourse, Coronil both insisted that the future could not be known *and* boldly named that which a Left should desire: universal equality, democracy, diversity, justice, freedom, "general well-being in ever more domains, ever more comprehensively," and "the pursuit of an alternative social order guided by the indigenous concept of el *buen vivir*— living well." On the one hand, he reminds us that, "as a political project, the pursuit of well being for all—and all now includes non-human entities—is now less than ever the monopoly of the 'West,' of its dominant conceptions and logics. In effect, these struggles in Latin America are part of a decolonizing process that challenges the ethnocentrism of Western modernity and opens up spaces for other imaginaries based on different histories, epistemologies, aesthetics, and ethics." On the other hand, he does not insist on a categorical distinction between Latin America and the "West." Indeed, he suggests that new utopian "imaginaries now unite South and North in a politics that fuses the pursuit of well-being and sheer global survival."[9]

Ultimately, Coronil desired a transformative political project that would overcome the false opposition between universality and particularity: "Carried along by winds of history that fan old flames and rouse new struggles, Latin America has become a diverse fabric of collective utopian dreams. The dialogue between past and future informing current struggles has, despite constraints, challenged place-bound, parochial conceptions of universality and has generated global exchanges about reimagined worlds." Engaging with "different cosmologies," he suggests, makes it possible "to recognize particulars in universals and universals in particulars." This would then be the basis of a new "planetary universality." Coronil is not naïve about this prospect: "Of course, given the unequal structures of power within which this leftward turn has taken place, it is possible that its new imaginings may be co-opted or crushed. . . . Politics will remain a battle of desire waged on an uneven terrain." Yet he concludes by affirming that "as long as people find themselves without a safe and dignified home in the world, utopian dreams will continue to proliferate, energizing struggles to build a world made of many worlds, where people can dream their futures without fear of waking up."[10]

Hemispheric Itinerary: Enter the (Cold War) Labyrinth

Whatever the topic, Coronil's thinking was always profoundly refracted through his own political present and his extraordinary hemispheric itinerary. His singular perspective was rooted in his experiences, beginning as a young student activist engaged with the swirling world of politics in Venezuela and Latin America more broadly. To introduce his work is to tell his story, and vice versa. As he certainly would have reminded us, to tell any individual's story is to relay the material and cultural conditions in which they lived, learned, argued, and dreamed.

Coronil understood himself as having been formed by his extended family and its rich network of friends and colleagues. Over the years he reflected on their efforts to create what they saw as a modern nation, and these relationships informed his work. He was born in Caracas in November 1944, and his life was shaped by the social vision and achievements of his parents, both of whom were physicians who took an active role in building Venezuela's medical and social welfare systems during periods of dramatic social transformation. While neither was a member of the established economic elite, his parents became members of an emerging professional elite that was socially respected and internationally connected. From markedly different backgrounds, they became a pioneering example of a couple who shared their professions as well as their ethics of secularism, nonpartisanship, and socially responsible medicine.

In many respects, Coronil's critical and global orientations were shaped by his mother, Lya Ímber Barú, with whom he was very close. A Russian

Figure I.5. With his mother, Lya Ímber, in Caracas. Photo by Julie Skurski.

Jewish immigrant from Odessa, Ukraine, whose family fled pogroms in 1920 to seek refuge in Romania (then Moldova), she arrived in Venezuela with her family (her father, Nahum Ímber, an agronomist; her mother, Ana Barú; and younger sister, Sofía) in 1930, after a difficult ten years in Romania where anti-Semitic repression was on the rise. Part of a wave of European refugees, they sought to establish a new life in the Americas. Uncertain of what it might offer, they imagined tropical abundance, freedom from repression, and an egalitarian sense of possibility. Venezuela was then an agrarian country with limited educational and medical systems, ruled by one of the continent's most repressive dictators, Juan Vicente Gómez (1908–35). But when Lya's family arrived, political opposition had begun to coalesce. At a time of rising oil income and urbanization, new initiatives to establish health and educational institutions became possible.

Though Lya was sixteen and spoke no Spanish when they arrived, she quickly enrolled in the Central University's school of medicine, and in 1936 she became the first woman to graduate from medical school in Venezuela. It was there that she met her future husband, Fernando's father, Fernando Rubén Coronil. Lya did her residency in pediatrics under the mentorship of professors, trained in France, whose holistic concept of childhood oriented her clinical work and pedagogic activity. She treated children's health as a social issue requiring social policies on national and international scales.[11] From 1965 on, her international activity intensified, along with her public role as a moral critic of Venezuela's oil income-fueled economic expansion.[12]

Lya and Fernando Rubén married in 1938. While their backgrounds differed, their respective families were remarkably accepting of a marriage that challenged the norms of each of their communities: Jewish and Catholic, recent immigrant European and established Venezuelan. Fernando Rubén's father, Domingo Antonio Coronil, was a mestizo of humble origins who had come to Caracas as a young man from the southern state of Guyana. He entered law school, became a law professor, and, though marginal to the social and economic elite, quickly rose within the political elite as the personal lawyer of the dictator General Juan Vicente Gómez, who was adept at incorporating talented professionals into his regime. Gómez made him his trusted representative (he referred to Coronil as "my eyes") following his seizure of power in 1908.[13]

Domingo Antonio married Adela Ravelo, the daughter of immigrants from the Canary Island, and had ten children: three boys (including Fernando's father, Fernando Rubén) and seven girls. When Domingo Antonio died in 1925, his family had limited means, for he had refrained from the standard practice of personal enrichment through government office. Fernando Rubén, then a teenager, managed the family's modest coffee hacienda after his father's death, while his mother and sisters sewed items to sell to sustain the family. Eventually, he attended the university, where he specialized in surgery.[14]

Following Gómez's death in 1935, rising oil income and democratizing initiatives allowed for the expansion of medical institutions.[15] Fernando Rubén was a proponent of public healthcare, and his life work centered on developing the Hospital Vargas as a teaching and research institution that promoted attention to the whole patient. In his medical practice, where he often performed surgery for free, he had a devoted following from all social classes. An elegant and charming man, he inspired generations of physicians while keeping himself outside the fray of party politics. Like other doctors of his generation, he was widely read; he could readily recite poems, discuss world history, or name Venezuela's rivers.

Being raised by socially concerned professionals who maintained their independence from political party affiliation deeply shaped Fernando, as well as his older sister, María Elena, who became a psychologist.[16] While close to his grandparents and cousins on both sides, Fernando was especially influenced by his mother's younger sister, his aunt Sofía, and her husband, the acclaimed Venezuelan author Guillermo Meneses. Closely entwined with his parents' lives, they brought to his family a cosmopolitan perspective as well as personal connections to European and Latin American artists and writers. They lived for years in Paris, which was then the center of the Latin American intellectual community.[17] The Coronil family's visits to Paris, where his aunt and uncle were deeply engaged with the intelligentsia, left Fernando with a lifelong passion for contemporary art. His deep interest in Venezuelan self-taught artists and his desire to learn from artists and writers about different ways to see the world grew out of his lasting relationship with his aunt and uncle.

Fernando attended high school from 1958 to 1962 during a tumultuous period for Venezuela and the hemisphere. In January 1958, a civic-military alliance overthrew the U.S.-backed Pérez Jiménez dictatorship. The newly elected President Rómulo Betancourt, leader of the social-democratic Acción Democrática party, made a pact before taking office with the Social Christian party that marginalized leftist parties from power and promoted an anticommunist agenda.[18] Unlike many students of his social class, Fernando attended a public high school with a diverse student body, Liceo Andrés Bello (as had his father). Here he formed lasting friendships with students of nonelite origins. Many participated with him in student politics, which at that time were closely connected to national politics, given that political parties sponsored electoral slates for student government. Like his parents, Coronil did not join a party, but he was elected president of the student federation on a slate composed primarily of Communist Youth members.

Fernando's position in student government placed him in a high-profile public position at a moment of remarkable political turmoil. Much of the populace in Caracas held deep antipathy toward the United States at the time. The overthrow of Guatemala's President Jacobo Arbenz in 1954 with backing from the Central Intelligence Agency, along with U.S. support for dictatorial regimes in the region, including those of the Dominican Republic, Haiti, Cuba, Guatemala, El Salvador, Honduras and Venezuela, had aligned the United States with antidemocratic forces. When U.S. Vice President Richard Nixon visited Venezuela in May 1958, he was shocked to encounter massive popular protest against his presence.

To the distress of the United States, Venezuela's interim government had sent arms to Castro's guerrilla forces then fighting Fulgencio Batista, in a gesture of antidictatorial solidarity that reflected historic ties among exile

PLANCHA 5

POR EL LOGRO DE LOS MAXIMOS ANHELOS ESTUDIANTILES

Sec. General: LUISA BARROSO
Sup: MARIA A. ESPINOZA

¡¡POR EL PSICO PEDAGOGICO!!

PRESIDENTE
FERNANDO CORONIL
Sup: MIRNA GUERRA

EXPERIENCIA
EFICACIA
DINAMISMO

Sec. de Reivindicaciones:
WINSTON PERAZA
Sup: IVAN GONZALEZ

¡¡POR GRADUACION
GRATUITA!!

Sec. Cultura: ANTONIO OLIVIERI
Sup: NELSON SCORZA

¡¡POR EL SABADO LABISTA!!

Sec. Deportes: DOMINGO PINTO
Sup: ESTHER CAPRILES

¡¡POR LA UNION DEL PARQUE
CARABOBO!!

Sec. Femenina: LUZ M. PEÑALVER
Sup: SONIA SUAREZ

Sec. Relaciones: Alejandro Mesuti
Sup: MARIANELA RUIZ

Sec. Finanzas: RAISA GARCIA
Sup: IRIS ASCANIO

Sec. Actas y Correspondencia:
RUBEN GUEVARA
Sup: RAFAEL PORTE

Figure I.6. Campaign poster for election to the high school student federation. The slogan of Fernando's slate: "For the fulfilment of students' highest aspirations. Experience, Effectiveness, Dynamism."

Figure I.7. Speech delivered as president of the student federation at the Liceo Andrés Bello.

groups in the greater Caribbean. After Batista's overthrow in January 1959, Castro visited Venezuela to thank the country for its support and to promote his message of hemispheric independence. The teenage Coronil was among the massive crowd, which included university and political leaders, who welcomed the Cuban revolutionary. Castro delivered speeches that wove together the histories of the countries, linked the ideas of their independence leaders Simón Bolívar and José Martí, and pointed toward a future of Latin American liberation during what was a defining moment in a newly divided political arena.[19] However, President-elect Betancourt (1959–64) was closely aligned with the United States. U.S. President John F. Kennedy would soon present him as a counter to Castro, casting his regime as a model for the combination of electoral democracy and capitalism the United States sought to promote in Latin America through the Alliance for Progress (1961). Under Betancourt, Venezuela led the campaign to expel Cuba from the Organization of American States and severed diplomatic relations with Cuba (1961).

These dramatic political events profoundly shaped Coronil's understanding of history, bringing into focus the connection between national and international representations of freedom. The debates surrounding U.S. interventions led him to a question that would preoccupy him in the future: who tells the story and from what perspective? During the Bay of Pigs invasion by U.S.-backed Cuban exiles (April 1961), the news media provided misleading accounts of the success of the attack. Coronil and his fellow students listened to shortwave radio broadcasts from Cuba on the defeat of the invading troops by military and civilian forces and created posters with news summaries mounted on boards in front of their school. In this heavily transited neighborhood, crowds gathered to read the reports and debate their implications for Venezuela. The posters did not only challenge official media; they criticized Betancourt's relationship with the United States and his claim to represent a Latin American path to sovereignty.

Coronil's political actions in this volatile period unsettled local authorities. The fact that a member of a respected family with which Betancourt had personal ties was publicly critical of the government was galling. As antigovernment protests increased, the authorities began to pay closer attention to his activities. At one point when the police came looking for him at his high school, fellow students directed him to hide in the girls' bathroom. Following that incident, he slept at friends' houses for a period. As street demonstrations intensified, Coronil's father was once called to the morgue to identify a body thought to be his son's. Although it was not Fernando, his parents were shaken by the mounting dangers just when he planned to pursue university studies. Hoping to protect him from state repression in this highly charged atmosphere, his parents obtained a sabbatical to London. While there, Fernando connected with members of the Latin American intelligentsia who were attempting to reimagine the region's political future.

Despite this political engagement, when Coronil entered Stanford University in 1963 he began a premedical curriculum, as he intended to follow in his parents' path as a physician. However, when he encountered the array of courses offered by a liberal arts education, which differed from Latin America's system of early professional study, he changed paths and immersed himself in history, literature, and social theory. He majored in Social Thought and Institutions, an interdisciplinary honors program centered on theme-based seminars that presaged his future intellectual orientation.

Early in his studies at Stanford, where he was intellectually engaged but ill at ease in its monochromatic atmosphere, Coronil attended a talk on Cuba by members of a group that had challenged the U.S. travel ban. At the event, a fellow student and activist on U.S.-Latin American relations, Fred Goff (future founder of the magazine NACLA Report on the Americas), introduced him to Julie Skurski, a fellow student. Raised on the West Coast by leftist parents of working-class immigrant origins who had been active in the labor movement, she had long been interested in Latin America. At Stanford she pursued studies on the region, majoring in history, and became involved in the civil rights and antiwar movements.[20] Although Fernando and Julie were from markedly different social and national backgrounds, they shared many convictions, aesthetics, and hopes. While undergraduates they began a relationship that shaped both of them over the course of their forty-six years together. They explored work and life, with their thinking and writing intertwined, as they sought to find the humor in everyday life and the poetry in the political.

In the context of growing national upheaval and counterculture questionings in the United States, they looked to graduate studies in anthropology as a path to studying social transformation and political imaginaries. They entered the doctoral program in anthropology at Cornell University in late 1967 to study with Victor Turner, a British social anthropologist of Africa who pioneered the integration of social and symbolic processes. They also worked closely with Terence Turner (no relation), a young scholar of lowland Brazilian indigenous peoples, myth and poetics, and social theory. As members of the Turners' innovative joint seminar on symbolic processes, in which Victor Turner developed his theories of liminality and communitas, and Terence Turner developed an innovative theory of Kayapó myth and a critique of Talcott Parsons's systems theory, the couple encountered exciting new work that addressed the production of meaning as part of social practice. When Victor and Terence Turner were recruited by the University of Chicago, they took with them Coronil, Skurski, and Anthony Seeger (who, like his uncle Pete Seeger, was an accomplished musician), where they began studies in the fall of 1968.

This was an explosive time in the United States and the world. There were uprisings met by violent repression in Mexico City, Paris, Prague, Northern Ireland, and Chicago; Malcom X, Martin Luther King Jr., and Robert Kennedy were assassinated; the Vietnam Tet Offensive, antiwar movement, Black Power movement, and urban rebellions exploded; and the feminist movement challenged notions of the political. As protests against imperialism, racism, and patriarchy expanded, so did critiques of the dominant social theories and disciplinary premises that held sway at the University of Chicago. Fernando and Julie joined the emerging challenges to British structural functionalism, American symbolic anthropology, and modernization theory (of which the prominent University of Chicago professors Clifford Geertz and Lloyd Fallers, founding members of the Committee on New Nations, were leading proponents[21]), village studies, and Parsons's systems theory. These frameworks had buttressed the prevailing theoretical division between the cultural and the social, their ahistorical conceptualization, and the exclusion of power relations from both realms.[22]

Coronil was critical of the dominant depoliticized conception of culture as well as of the role that modernization theory played in legitimating U.S. power in Latin America. He began to craft an intellectual approach to social inquiry that could relate the material and the symbolic, social relations and cultural processes, and anthropology and history. These efforts were nourished by his continuing dialogue with Terence Turner's work. Long before the studies of Michel Foucault and Edward Said appeared in the U.S. academy, Coronil was thinking through the question of how to confront the relationship between imperial arrangements and knowledge production. For example, in a paper written for Victor Turner's seminar, he used Turner's ideas of communitas and liminality to analyze the Cuban Revolution's literacy campaign that upended social hierarchies, mobilized urban youth, and transformed subjectivities. He sought to craft an integrated approach in which culture, politics, and history were grasped together and to introduce a dynamic concept of culture into the study of political conflict and social transformation. These intellectual developments estranged him from Victor Turner and placed him in an uneasy relationship with the University of Chicago's dominant strain of culturalism. Increasingly he looked to history for intellectual resources. There he found support from John Coatsworth, a Marxist-influenced economic historian of Latin America, and Bernard S. Cohn, a pioneering historical anthropologist of India whose critique of colonial sources anticipated the Subaltern Studies movement.

Coronil and Skurski developed dissertation proposals on the dynamics of the Cuban Revolution. During this period, Cuba had become a focal point for an international anti-imperialist intelligentsia, highlighted by the Tricontinental Conference held in 1966 in Havana, and the formation of the Non-Aligned Movement. While Cuba was a hub for this activity, the U.S. trade embargo restricted communication with the island, and lack of scholarly studies limited the possibilities for conducting research there. The Cuban state welcomed solidarity groups and permitted closely controlled visits. But it was suspicious of academics and allowed research only by those who arrived with formal government invitations.

In an effort to obtain such an invitation to do research in Cuba, Fernando and Julie traveled to the Cuban Embassy in Mexico City. This ultimately futile effort led to their involvement in a serious car crash (with Fernando's uncle at the wheel) that would alter both the course of their lives and their understanding of state power. In the convoluted aftermath of the crash (with Julie hospitalized), Fernando was jailed as the falsely accused driver of the car, then imprisoned in Mexico City under charges of international drug dealing. The subsequent fictions and negotiations required to obtain his release and their departure from the country provided a stunning lesson on the hidden relations between state officials and powerful local figures, and on the state's capacity to create appearances for national and international publics.

After Coronil was depicted in the Mexican press as a drug dealer, he and Skurski left for Venezuela. This sequence of bizarre events brought home the depth of their commitment to each other personally and the importance of legal recognition by state and medical authorities. In an improvised wedding marked by comedic turns of events, they married in September 1969 in a city clerk's office. With characteristic calm and understanding, Fernando's mother hastily organized a reception at his home for extended family and friends who had not yet met Fernando's spouse.

On their return to Chicago they received welcome news: through the mediation of a Venezuelan friend of Fernando's parents (the leftist intellectual Inocente Palacios), who had contacts with Cuban leaders dating from his period of exile, Carlos Rafael Rodríguez, a respected leader of the Cuban regime, had offered them an invitation to do research there.[23] Thus, the long-established Venezuelan practice of using personal connections had worked, while conventional efforts had not. They had already arranged to travel to Cuba with the Venceremos Brigade,[24] and the invitation from the Cuban government would allow them to remain there to do anthropological fieldwork. The more than four hundred members of the Third Venceremos Brigade converged in St. Johns, Canada, from where they traveled on a Cuban cargo ship to Cuba. There they spent several weeks on the Isla de la Juventud (Isle of Youth, formerly the Isle of Pines) tending citrus trees (fruit was an export crop) and attending talks, including memorable presentations by Vietnamese female guerrillas. After the rest of the Brigade returned to the United States, Coronil and Skurski remained in Cuba, hosted in hotels by the government.

In the context of U.S. pressure on the Cuban regime and the international outcry over U.S. social scientists' counterinsurgency research projects, Coronil and Skurski told Cuban authorities that their proposed research topics were open to revision. Officials asked them to study the agricultural brigade Columna Juvenil del Centenario (Centennial Youth Column; CJC), at the suggestion of Rodríguez, who believed that young anthropologists could help understand the difficulties of "integrating" youth from rural and low-income backgrounds into the revolutionary project. When they explained that they expected to do participant observation, they were told that it would just be a matter of time before the required permits were issued.

Their stay in Cuba coincided with a period of deep shifts in economic and cultural life there, now referred to as "la Década Gris" (the Gray Decade, also known as "el Quinquenio Gris," or the Gray Five Years). This was a time of heightened Sovietization and state repression that had a lasting impact on policies of social control, racial relations, and intellectual activity. The consequences of this grim period only became public years later and have been little studied. Coronil and Skurski had arrived in Cuba shortly after the official failure of the Ten Million Tons Harvest in 1970, a two-year push to achieve the largest sugar harvest in history, one that Castro promised would allow Cuba to achieve economic autonomy.[25] This productivist project, which fused notions of revolutionary sacrifice and the creation of a "new man," aimed to expand the neglected sugar industry, despite sugar's identification with colonialism. The campaign entailed the semi-militarization of society and deeply disrupted economic and state activities. However, given Castro's extraordinary ability to create a narrative of revolutionary triumph over a past of colonial submission, much of the population was mobilized for this effort, and many people enthusiastically placed faith in the promised future. Paradoxically, the project led to a greater economic and ideological reliance on the Soviet Union. Among its consequences, determinist Soviet Marxism was imposed on the educational system and its curriculum, while the philosophy department of the University of Havana (where Gramscian Marxism had been taught) and the journal Pensamiento Crítico were shut down. Many Cuban intellectuals lost their posts or had no outlet for their work during this decade.

These forms of silencing were linked to Castro's public break with leading international intellectuals—notably, the anthropologist Oscar Lewis and French theorists whose books were critical of the regime's anti-democratic aspects.[26] The arrest of the prizewinning Cuban poet Herberto Padilla and his public confession as a counter-revolutionary in April 1971 had the greatest impact on the national and international scene. Padilla's detention and Soviet-style self-criticism prompted public letters of concern to Castro from a wide range of international leftist intellectuals, primarily from Latin America and Europe (including Jean-Paul Sartre, Simone de Beauvoir, Italo Calvino, Carlos Fuentes, Gabriel García Márquez, and Mario Vargas Llosa). Several of these critics broke relations with the regime.[27] In angry response, Castro denounced the "shameless pseudo-leftists" who sought glory living in Paris, London, or Rome. He declared that only "truly revolutionary" intellectuals would serve as judges or receive prizes in Cuba and announced that the country's doors were henceforth shut to the "bourgeois libelers" of the Revolution.[28]

Given the silence of the Cuban press, Coronil and Skurski learned about these events secondhand. Since they were unable to interpret the veiled references in official statements or to identify the officials who were orchestrating this repressive cultural policy, their status as foreign researchers in Cuba was uncertain.[29] The sudden shift from the triumphalist heroic discourse presented to the Venceremos Brigade to the embattled atmosphere of la Década Gris, marked by food shortages and growing skepticism, confronted them with an opaque reality. A transformative friendship with a young Afro-Cuban filmmaker, Sara Gómez, the only female director at the Instituto Cubano del Arte e Industria Cinematográficos, changed their perspective. She introduced them to a circle of intellectuals and artists who identified with the revolution yet were critical of its growing centralization, dogmatism, and blindness to racial and patriarchal hierarchies. This was a profoundly influential friendship for both of them.

In her open-ended films, Gómez documented the everyday lives of working-class people in their discussions about the changes brought by the revolutionary process. During the same period that Antonio Gramsci's thought was being erased from the university, Frantz Fanon's thought was being marginalized, and feminism was being equated with women's advancement, Gómez made cinematic works that in contemporary terms would be called intersectional. Her documentary work on grassroots life was revolutionary in ways that challenged the government's statist orientation.[30] "I am not a Fidelista," she said, critiquing the top-down, male-centered, culturally and politically white project of the Cuban Revolution.

During this period, cultural repression extended beyond intellectual censorship. Measures taken against gay people, banned from teaching and in earlier years forcibly detained, received some international attention. Less publicly known were the policies that restricted Afro-Cuban religions. Practitioners were stigmatized as "antisocial" and their beliefs as primitive atavisms that were supposed to disappear under the revolution. When radio broadcasts as well as police actions cast these practitioners as criminals, they were obliged to conceal their affiliation. If their beliefs became known, they could be denied membership in the Communist Party, and their avenues of professional advancement could be blocked.[31] Like all such policies in Cuba, they were applied unevenly, and there were individual exceptions.

Coronil and Skurski took part in gatherings at Gómez's apartment while she was conducting research on Afro-Cuban life and cultural practices for her planned feature length film De cierta manera (One Way or Another).[32] As these topics were not addressed at that time in the social sciences, they had limited knowledge of Afro-Cuban history or religion when they accompanied friends to religious ceremonies (primarily Santería or Yoruba) in people's houses. They were cautioned not to talk to anyone about these gatherings, as they could cause problems for themselves and others. They learned that these African-derived and Cuban transculturated practices were fundamental to the lives of working people of all origins and races, many of whom, such as their interlocutor Oriol Bustamante—founding member of the Conjunto Folklórico Nacional—viewed Cuban history from a subaltern perspective. These experiences provided an enormous chal-

lenge to the standard class- and state-centered studies of Cuba in which
race, religion, and ethnicity were absent or present in the form of statistics.
As lived alternative perspectives, they were formative for what became lasting concerns in Coronil's work: Eurocentric narratives of the past and the
future and their forms of silencing; the epistemological basis of these narratives; and the processes of transculturation through which Latin American societies have been forged.

This was the context in which Coronil and Skurski attempted to conduct research on the CJC. But their efforts stalled, as they were allowed to
make only an officially accompanied visit with leaders and members of the
brigade in Camagüey.[33] After many months, they were called to meet with
officials at the Central Committee who informed them they would not be
able to do fieldwork because the government was revising its policy on foreign researchers. They were asked to leave the country. Nevertheless, this
period in Cuba profoundly shaped Coronil's perspective on leftist politics,
race and history, the state, personalism, and the politics of knowledge.
It also marked the beginning of a larger saga that compelled Coronil and
Skurski to shift their research topic, led to Coronil's deportation from the
United States and the couple's return to Venezuela, and obstructed Coronil's
career.

Once obliged to leave Cuba, Coronil needed to renew his Venezuelan
passport but could do so only through the Swiss Embassy. When his mother,
Lya, learned this after she fortuitously phoned the couple from Switzerland,
where she was staying at the home of the former president (and Fernando's
former nemesis) Rómulo Betancourt, she asked Betancourt to send a new
passport to the embassy. Strangely, on the same day as his mother's call,
the U.S. Federal Bureau of Investigation (FBI), which had been trying to
locate the couple when they did not return to the United States with the
Venceremos Brigade, learned that he was in Cuba. It then placed his name,
as a subversive agent, on a list of persons to be denied entry to the United
States, a fact he learned only years later through FBI files the couple obtained through the Freedom of Information Act.

The couple left for Paris, from where they planned to renew Coronil's
student visa and return to the United States to formulate a new research
project. After spending months in the austere conditions of embattled Havana, they were shocked to find themselves amid refined consumer displays and mildly inquisitive French intellectuals. When Coronil sought to
renew his student visa at the U.S. embassy, he nonchalantly walked past
anti–Vietnam War demonstrators throwing balloons filled with red paint—

not a cause for concern after his experiences of protest in Caracas—and distracted U.S. officials quickly stamped his visa. When they later flew to New York, he was able to pass through immigration control without questions. His name was apparently not listed in the infamous Blue Book used in the pre-digital age to keep track of travelers who were to be stopped at the border. Enormously relieved, they continued to California to visit Skurski's family in Oakland.

Coronil then took a brief trip to Caracas to see his family before the couple returned to the University of Chicago. While in Caracas he met with friends from the Movimiento al Socialismo, an independent socialist party founded by leftists who had broken with the Cuban government. As it turned out, his every move was reported to U.S. authorities. On his return trip to California he was detained in transit by immigration control at the airport in Miami and refused entry to the United States. Without being told why, he was placed in an off-site Immigration and Naturalization Service (INS) detention center, an old motel run by Cuban exiles, where he lacked the rights of a person legally on U.S. soil.[34]

A juridical world of Kafkaesque fictions and imaginings drew the couple ever deeper into an opaque realm of unknown accusations and futile demands. During his three days of detention the INS officers focused on examining his passport rather than questioning him. As Coronil later learned, they were convinced that he had altered his passport to remove the stamps of countries where he had traveled, including Cuba. They were building a case that he was an international communist agent. Confident that the confusion would be cleared up, Coronil phoned the Venezuelan consul in Miami, a family friend, to inform him of his situation. Despite his request to keep this quiet, the consul promptly called Coronil's father, who was then physician to President Rafael Caldera's wife. The president requested immediate action from the Venezuelan ambassador in Washington, instructing him to "treat Coronil as if he were my son." However, these and subsequent diplomatic pressures had limited effect. Coronil was allowed to travel to California to join Skurski, but his legal status was unchanged. The INS considered him technically "offshore" at the Port of San Francisco.

Coronil sought to obtain a hearing from the INS so he could contest whatever mysterious charges they had against him. During this period of legal limbo, the couple lived in a co-op in Berkeley and participated in the escalating demonstrations against the secret bombings in Laos and Cambodia. Coronil's requests for a hearing went unanswered after submitting a dossier on his life as an upstanding citizen, on the advice of his American Civil Liberties Union lawyer. The agency claimed that revealing the charges against him would endanger the security of the U.S. government. In frustration, his lawyer commented, "They're treating your case as if you'd flown a U-2 spy plane over the Pentagon."[35] Soon Coronil received a letter from the INS instructing him to report to the San Francisco airport within forty-eight hours with no more than forty-four pounds of luggage. He was to be deported. However, only days before, his mother had had a chance social encounter with a New York corporate lawyer, Jay Shaffron, who worked with oil companies in Venezuela. Alarmed when he learned that Lya's son had "problems" with the INS, he contacted his friend, Secretary of State George Schultz, and obtained a stay of deportation order. Coronil received the two letters at the same time.

The deportation order cited an article that dated from the Immigration Act of 1918, a product of the first Red Scare when categories of people vaguely defined as anarchists and subversives were excluded from entry into the United States.[36] Shaffron offered to take over Coronil's case. He advised him to remain in the United States until it was resolved, because the law made no exceptions for those married to U.S. citizens, and deportation under it would result in permanent exclusion. Yet despite his extensive efforts over the following months, the INS did not relent. Coronil and Skurski spent much of this period in Chicago, where they sought support from the University of Chicago and approval for new dissertation projects. Although the university took no steps to aid him, his adviser Terence Turner wrote in his support. Eventually Shaffron was able to negotiate one concession: if Coronil left the United States, he would be allowed to return only once—to defend his doctoral dissertation. In 1972, worn out by this state security nightmare, the couple moved to Venezuela, where they lived for the next seven years.

This experience of being caught up in the twisted works of a powerful but dysfunctional bureaucratic, legal, and intelligence apparatus deeply informed Coronil's thinking. In subsequent research, he approached the state as a complex and contradictory web of institutions and actors.

His expulsion from the United States made his future as an academic difficult to imagine. The U.S. Embassy signaled that he was being monitored in Venezuela. Nevertheless, Coronil and Skurksi began a new life as engaged anthropologists.[37] With the aid of a Venezuelan government grant and a cohort of supportive social scientists and historians, they began to research the impact of industrial development projects and ideology

Figure I.8. Fieldwork on the auto industry: business conference, Caracas, 1975.

initiated during Venezuela's oil boom period under the presidency of Carlos Andrés Pérez (1974–79).

During this period, a new vision of Venezuela's future as an industrial,
economically independent, and globally influential power burst onto the
national scene. The mirage of wildly accelerating and amplifying development was not simply a state construct. Global, private sector, and popular
actors participated in promoting the vision. Coronil and Skurski focused
on the automobile industry—specifically, the auto parts sector—because
it occupied a key ideological space in the imagined creation of a national
bourgeoisie capable of stimulating modern heavy industry and its related
businesses. The projected goal was to manufacture a Venezuelan car, including the engine, rather than to simply assemble on Venezuelan soil vehicles
made by multinationals. They explored connections among state planners,
small manufacturers, and major national investors through intersecting
boards of directors, as well as kinship ties. At a time before anthropologists regularly produced ethnographies of the state, Coronil and Skurski's

work brought out the concealed presence of diversified economic groups based in prominent families that had long-standing connections to the state and to multinational capital.[38] Following the Middle East oil crisis of 1973 and efforts of international financial institutions to redirect the flood of petrodollars to metropolitan economies, Venezuela experienced an oil boom. In this context, Coronil undertook long-term research into how petrodollars and their materialization transformed Venezuela's political, economic, and cultural relations. Deeply attached to his country of origin, he intended to pursue an academic career in Venezuela. He was undeterred by the fact that some established intellectuals there regarded his work as overly empirical and insufficiently theoretical at a time when Nicos Poulantzas's structural Marxist approach dominated discussions.

During their years living in Caracas, Coronil and Skurski became more richly involved with life in their new home. The birth of their daughter Mariana Adela, along with bringing them great joy, deepened their family ties as well as their understanding of Venezuelan society. They also developed friendships with a number of self-taught artists (misleadingly labeled *ingenuos*, or "naïve"). At the same time that they researched automobile parts firms across the country, they established connections with creative artists and thinkers, some of whom lived in desolate towns spawned by the oil industry. These artists reflected on subjects that included ecological devastation, the solitude of oil towns, the veneration of Simón Bolívar, and the beauty of the land and the cosmos. Their explorations into villages and rural areas, as well as the barrios of Caracas, informed Coronil's effort to understand the hidden dimensions of the petro-state and to listen to the views of those seen as marginal to its projects. Coronil and Skurski organized an exhibition at the Museum of Contemporary Art, directed by Fernando's aunt Sofía Ímber, titled "Artistas al Margen" (Artists on the Margins). It was the first exhibition of its kind at that institution, and their essays for the catalogue challenged prevailing theories in the art world that viewed these kinds of producers as "intuitive" and unselfconscious rather than as proper artists.

In the midst of their varied engagements, which also included university teaching and work at the Central University of Venezuela's Centro de Estudios para el Desarrollo (Center for Development Studies; CENDES), Coronil was stunned to receive a letter from the U.S. Embassy, at the end of Jimmy Carter's presidency, stating that the unspecified charges against him had been dropped. He was free to return to the United States. He and Skurski decided to return to the University of Chicago to complete their doctoral dissertations and rejoin academic discussions in the United States.

Figure I.9. With the Venezuelan artist Rafael Vargas, who, decades earlier, migrated to work in the oil industry in Cabimas, Zulia. Photo by Julie Skurski.

Figure I.10. Visit with rural artists in Falcón State, Venezuela. Photo by Julie Skurski.

Figure I.11. Fernando and Julie with the painter Emerio Dario Lunar at his home in Cabimas, with an oil pump in the background.

Figure I.12. With Elsa Morales, artist and friend, in Caracas, 1993. Photo by Julie Skurski.

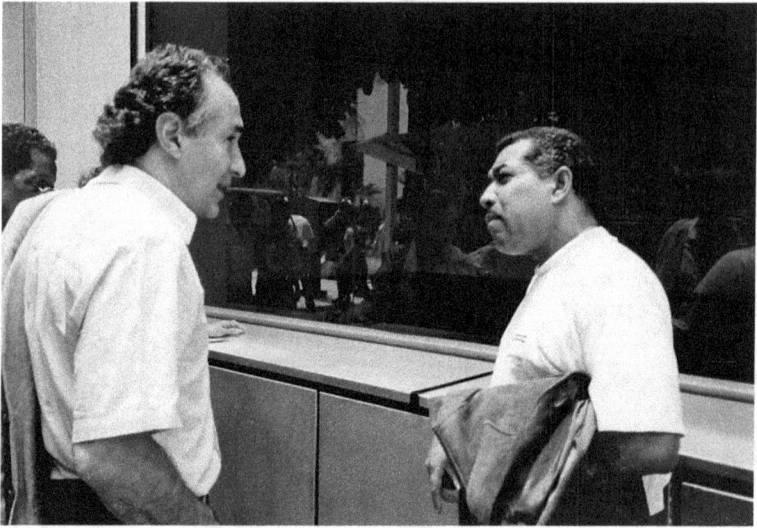

Figure I.13. Debating politics with painter Rafael Castillo Arnal in downtown Caracas, 2000. Photo by Julie Skurski.

Figure I.14. Painting by Castillo Arnal on bills of Venezuelan currency that depict a masked protester, Simón Bolívar with a machete, and an indigenous woman. The work is dedicated to Fernando, acknowledging his efforts to promote the artist's work internationally.

After moving back to Chicago, Coronil tragically lost his mother, Lya, while soon after the couple joyously welcomed their second daughter, Andrea Lya, to the family. During this period, John and Jean Comaroff joined the anthropology faculty, helping to change its primary emphasis on American symbolic anthropology. Their friendship, along with the continuing intellectual support of the historical anthropologist Bernard S. Cohn and the historian John Coatsworth, shaped Coronil's work in important ways. Terence Turner's support remained constant. Coronil's dissertation, "The Black Eldorado: Money, Fetishism, Capitalism and Democracy in Venezuela" (1987), at the time an anomaly in the University of Chicago's Anthropology Department, pioneered coming shifts in the discipline more broadly toward global and state issues.

Anthrohistory and Anthroheresy

Following his extended graduate studies, interrupted by state interventions, Coronil forged a new path as a historical anthropologist of the state. During a postdoc at the Helen Kellogg Institute for International Studies at Notre Dame University (directed by the Argentine sociologist Guillermo O'Donnell), amid scholars focused on regime types and transitions, Coronil developed the concept of the "magical state."[39] He was then delighted to receive a Society of Fellows postdoc in 1988 at the University of Michigan. He quickly became integrated into the stimulating intellectual life of the university, and with the backing of faculty from both departments, he was offered a tenure-track position in the Anthropology Department and the History Department, where he spent much of his career.

While he and his family were in Venezuela for a year of research, they witnessed the rapid deterioration of the party system, rising protests, and the violently repressed social uprising against International Monetary Fund measures that occurred on February 27–March 2, 1989. Coronil and Skurski carried out research on the protests and the ensuing military massacre that became known as the Caracazo, which they lived through with their daughters. They wrote an article on this unprecedented event, included in this volume, "Dismembering and Remembering the Nation," that located the discussion of political violence within an analysis of economic and political policies and the discourse of civilization and progress.[40]

The University of Michigan was an important center of interdisciplinary efforts to rethink the human sciences in the wake of the epistemological decentering prompted by the linguistic turn, postcolonial studies, critical race

studies, feminist theory, and Foucauldian attention to power-knowledge relations. Coronil and Skurski were active participants in the interdisciplinary
faculty seminar Comparative Studies of Social Transformation (1987–2001),
a generative working group that invited path-breaking thinkers, including
Stuart Hall.[41] At the university, Coronil devoted his greatest efforts and imagination to the development of the unique doctoral program in anthropology
and history.[42] The program, which he directed and reorganized following
the departure of founding members,[43] became a noted center for debates
in critical anthropology, poststructuralist theory, Marxian cultural studies,
postcolonial theory, and studies of empire.[44] His pedagogical approach
profoundly shaped the intellectual development of several generations
of students in the program, many of whom became lasting friends. He
worked collectively with them, engaging them as he would colleagues, discussing with them as colleagues, and concluding conferences with parties
at their home where everyone was encouraged to dance.[45]

Coronil's book *The Magical State* was profoundly shaped by his participation in the debates of this generative period. This book traces how twentieth-
century state formation in Venezuela was mediated through the state's claim
to stewardship over natural wealth. It demonstrates the historical process by
which oil income from ground rent became central to the state's fetishistic,
or "magical," capacity to represent the people (*el pueblo*) and direct national
progress. Through its hidden capture and rematerialization of international rents, the state appeared as endowed with independent powers, the
magician at center stage.

At a time when postmodernist currents in the social sciences had severed
representations from material processes and granted them free-floating
agency, Coronil built on the work of Marx, Gramsci, Hall, Raymond Williams,
Walter Benjamin, and others to study the materiality of representations.
While the notion of agency in the social sciences was becoming identified
with human intentionality, he asked whether a powerful commodity such as
oil could be seen as exercising agency within larger structural processes. In a
period in which poststructuralist interest in the fragment left aside questions
of broader connections, and in which globalization became equated with
free-flowing movement, he asked how boundaries and hierarchies were
being remade on the global level, including within and among subaltern
states.

A pioneering work of anthrohistory, *The Magical State* integrates political economy and political ideology, state policy and representational prac-

tices, material life and cultural processes, and national and global relations into a single historical inquiry. It is a work of ethnographic history and historical sociology and an anthropology of the state in the Global South. Through the examination of historical conjunctures in a succession of regimes, it includes topics that range from political coups, oil policy, and infrastructure displays to presidential campaigns, industrial programs, political scandals, and presidential performances. By taking up issues then seen by many as outmoded (such as nature as well as development economics), the work combines a discursively informed approach with the analysis of state performances and representations and the study of systemic political and economic processes.

Drawing on Henri Lefebvre's theorization of space (along with Doreen Massey, David Harvey, and Edward Soja), Coronil analyzes how the dynamics of state power in Latin America can be adequately understood only by attending to the historical relationships among nature, value, and space at different scales. Arguing that Marx neglected to analyze Nature in his own tripartite theory of value—focusing on the capital-labor relation—his work begins from the premise that the possibilities of countries in the Global South are often tied to their role as providers of primary products. An examination of modernity in and from the Global South, it questions the universalizing developmentalism of both modernization theory and reductionist Marxism. At the same time, it challenges narrow and descriptive tendencies within both cultural anthropology and conventional history that obstruct the structural understanding of large-scale and long-term processes. Like his last essay, "The Future in Question," *The Magical State* points beyond a set of false oppositions that continue to govern much social inquiry.

Views from the South

Coronil developed his synthetic theoretical approach to the Global South while participating in transnational networks that brought together diverse intellectual communities. The discussions he was engaged in provide an essential framework for understanding the generative essays he wrote beginning in the 1990s, as well as two additional projects that he undertook. He was a member of the Darkness in El Dorado Task Force of the American Anthropological Association (AAA), an ethics inquiry into the controversy over the anthropologist Napoleon Chagnon's work in the

Amazon and Patrick Tierney's denunciatory book of 2000 (two articles on the debate are in this volume). He also began work on a new book project, *Crude Matters*, that sought to analyze the failed coup against President Hugo Chávez in 2002 (two articles on the coup and two draft book chapters are included in this collection).

Coronil participated in the Latin American modernity/coloniality group (*modernidad/colonialidad*) from its founding meeting in 1998. This itinerate think tank first met in Caracas at an event organized by the Venezuelan social theorist Edgardo Lander. Its leading voices initially included the Peruvian theorist Aníbal Quijano, Enrique Dussel, and Walter Mignolo.[46] The group grew into a network of thinkers from diverse approaches, including liberation theology, postcolonial theory, cultural studies, and political economy, who sought to integrate Latin American critical theories with developments in European and U.S. critical thought. Coronil played an important role in developing the group's critique of Eurocentrism, its role in forming the modern world, and its theorization of coloniality in the Americas. In essays on occidentalism and Latin American postcolonialism that drew on Quijano's concept of "the coloniality of power," Coronil argued that the Iberian imperial projects, with their racial hierarchies and labor regimes, were constitutive of modernity and capitalism, not their antecedents. He contended that the making of the modern world could be understood only in relation to European imperial expansion from the fifteenth century on and to the continuing cultural logic of coloniality.[47] Understood as the "dark side of modernity," in Mignolo's term, coloniality's logic has worked through institutions ranging from the church to the social sciences, negating alternative epistemologies and violently reordering social worlds.

Coronil helped link the group's challenge to develop decolonial thinking to the controversy in the AAA and at the University of Michigan concerning Chagnon's work in Venezuela and Brazil.[48] He was asked to join the AAA Ethics Committee's El Dorado Task Force, in light of his work on the Venezuelan state, to examine contentious accusations Tierney made in his flawed book. Coronil offered an independent voice in a conflict polarized around a misleading "science versus anti-science" clash in which evolutionary and biomedical schools of thought lined up against sectors of cultural anthropology. As he pointed out, the debate largely overlooked the long-standing critiques of Chagnon's projects set forth by anthropologists in Brazil and Venezuela and marginalized the views of affected Yanomami people. In this controversy, Coronil felt that disciplinary and legal concerns had taken precedence over issues of the politics of knowledge and the ethics of research.[49] In an instantiation of the coloniality of power, Yanomami villagers had been viewed by some evolutionary scientists as if they were representatives of the human past, geographically isolated from social and genetic change. Treated as an Amazonian natural resource, they had unknowingly provided raw materials, including their DNA and genealogical information, for scientific research in U.S. centers that was unrelated to their health needs and that violated their concepts of the body, illness, and death.

Coronil was alarmed that the University of Michigan administration and the Anthropology Department had immediately defended the work of Chagnon and Dr. James Neel, the prominent University of Michigan human geneticist under whom he initially worked, by presenting one-sided arguments and ignoring scholarly discussion. In response, and with support from the Provost, he organized a symposium on the controversy through the anthrohistory program.[50] Initially, he was at odds with figures in the Anthropology Department and the University of Michigan administration. But following the symposium, the Provost's Office quietly retracted the university's original statement supporting Neel and Chagnon and issued a statement of support for scholarly debate.[51]

During this period, Coronil was suddenly drawn into an event that would be momentous for Venezuela's history and for his own work. On April 11–13, 2002, there was a brief, failed coup against Hugo Chávez, followed by his unprecedented return to power due to divisions in the opposition and a massive popular outpouring of support.[52] Given the dramatic unfolding of events and his own work on coups and presidentialism, Coronil dropped a project he was developing on Cuba and undertook research on the events surrounding the coup. It had occurred in the context of mass mobilization by opposition groups, many of which had close ties to the administration of President George W. Bush, and of statements by officials in the Bush government that were overtly hostile to Chávez. Yet what had happened during the coup, and why, was far from clear.

Coronil spent the next few years grappling with this increasingly complex project as troubling changes taking place in Venezuela confronted him with ever deeper questions. He first planned to structure his analysis as a microchronology of the 2002 coup and its aftermath. He envisioned a book of broad public interest that would identify the behind-the-scenes promoters of the coup, who were likely to include certain U.S. officials and Venezuelan business figures. Yet as he followed leads and conducted interviews with figures from all sides of the event, including imprisoned military officers and the powerful Venezuelan media entrepreneur Gustavo Cisneros (rumored to be a coup backer), the contradictory accounts and layers of obfuscation compelled him to redefine the project.

Given the shifts in oil policy, state structure, and Chávez's discourse that followed the coup, Coronil saw the event as a turning point for the regime.[53] During his year as a Cisneros Fellow at Harvard University's Rockefeller Center in 2004–2005, he broadened his research for this project. While there he organized an issue of the magazine ReVista (2008) for which a politically diverse set of petroleum industry experts responded to questions on oil policy. Some argued that Chávez had single-handedly realigned legal relations with multinational oil companies by again allowing joint ventures. They viewed this action as effectively reducing national sovereignty and denationalizing the oil industry (see "Oilpacity" in this volume). While extending oil-funded social programs and radicalizing his rhetoric, Chávez, who then renamed the Bolivarian Revolution "Socialism of the Twenty-First Century," had tied the country's future to the goal of dramatically increasing oil exports. The petro-state's scope had intensified without alternative proposals from any sector.[54] In his discussion of this process, Coronil uses the concept of "oilpacity" to capture the viscous quality of state-society relations whereby oil is visible primarily as a source of state income, while the organization of state-capital relations shaping the oil sector's links to the nation and to the global arena are obscured.

Crude Matters seeks to address the coup as a conjuncture of multiscale relations, forces, and actors in which contending projects, ideologies, and interests struggled for control. Refusing to limit the book to the conspiratorial maneuverings and personality clashes that consumed writings on the Chávez presidency, Coronil focuses on debates about Nature and issues of secrecy, truth, and knowledge. In this work he seeks both to reconstruct what happened over the course of a few days in April 2002 (still the subject of heated disagreements) and to analyze broader structural forces at work. At the same time, he asks how one can construct a history that is woven around narratives of secrets and rendered through masking.

Coronil developed these dimensions of the book project following his move from the University of Michigan to a position as Presidential Professor in the Anthropology Program at the Graduate Center of the City University of New York (CUNY) in 2008. There, he and Skurski, who also obtained an appointment in anthropology, found a stimulating network

Figure I.15. Looking at the sea from his house in the coastal village La Sabana. Photo by Mariana Coronil.

of scholars, including former students and colleagues from the University of Michigan.[55] With the engaged orientation of the Graduate Center and the possibilities offered by working in New York (which Fernando called the only city in the United States where he did not feel like a foreigner), he expanded the range of his work and flourished, even as he was anguished by Venezuela's signs of coming crisis.

Resisting the pressures of political polarization, Coronil reflected on the possibilities and limitations in a neoliberal world for a certain kind of revolutionary tradition in the Global South. He struggled to find a way to rigorously engage the tensions and contradictions of the Chávez project while pursuing his critique of U.S. imperialism and neoliberal capitalism. What options are available for a self-proclaimed anticapitalist state project? How could a vision of hope for the future inform practice under these conditions?[56]

By including these draft chapters of Coronil's unfinished work, we invite readers into an ongoing engagement with his critical and open-ended analysis of Latin American and global futures. His insights are especially valuable at a moment when many currents of postcolonial theory have become preoccupied with cultural incommensurability, Marxists still tend to regard the world through a metropolitan lens, and metropolitan critical theory has renounced the task of naming the future it desires.

Coronil was a gifted practitioner within the Latin American tradition of essay writing. His innovative pieces—on issues such as political futurity, Occidentalism, transculturation, anthrohistory, oilpacity, postcoloniality, subalternity, and imperial formations—ranged from the development of concepts that he addressed in *The Magical State* to programmatic discussions that engaged concepts at higher levels of abstraction. This collection gathers together some of his most important interventions into three sections organized according to thematic focus.

The first, "Labyrinths of Critique," presents key reflections and interventions on the practice of what Coronil called "anthrohistory." The second contains a series of critical essays on "Thinking from Latin America," which showcases his work on Venezuela, including two chapters from *Crude Matters*. Finally, the third, "Beyond Occidentalism, Beyond Empire," foregrounds his interventions into thinking about empire and its epistemological legacies. As editors, we had to make difficult decisions to exclude some wonderful essays. However, we feel that the pieces gathered here compose a powerful body of work that is greater than the sum of its parts. We regard this volume as a worthy companion to *The Magical State*, and we urge readers to consider these two works in relation to each other.

We might read Coronil as reflecting on the ongoing dilemmas he faced when he wrote in "The Future in Question":

> Under leftist rulers, political contests over different visions of society have stimulated public debate but have also tended to polarize political discourse, turning often useful simplifications into flat caricatures that block rather than stimulate understanding. In the context of heated political confrontations, this flattening of reason and heightening of emotions have affected political representations both in Latin America and abroad. . . . The demonization of the Left cannot be countered by its deification; the reduction of politics to a battle between Good and Evil must be challenged by accounts that develop the public's capacity to make sense of the world and of the history that produces it. If the mainstream media numbs people, we need accounts that help un-numb them.

His distinctive mode of critical engagement can be understood in terms of this effort to unnumb the public, neither deifying leftist leaders nor reducing politics to ahistorical confrontations between Good and Evil, "to avoid flat dichotomies, or at least turn them into meaningful distinctions" that might help us better understand the specific "conditions of possibility of historical change facing each [Latin American] nation."[57]

Conditions have worsened and possibilities have diminished for the Left in Latin America and beyond since Coronil's passing. At a moment in which the old axes of political differentiation no longer obtain, whether in the North or the South, his insistence on the need for conjunctural analysis from a systemic perspective has never been more urgent. Given the resurgence of neoliberal dogma after the financial crisis of 2008; the worldwide move toward authoritarian statism; and the upsurge of mass movements, both reactionary and progressive, against the existing order, Coronil's work appears more contemporary than ever. Those aspects of his work that might have seemed untimely in the 1980s and 1990s today provide a valuable framework for examining present predicaments. Some of the most urgent political and exciting intellectual work in contemporary scholarship is unfolding around confrontations concerning natural resources, capitalist imperatives, state sovereignty, and public welfare. There is a pressing need to realign Marxian and postcolonial modes of critique in ways that refuse orthodoxies, avoid flattened dichotomies, and resist Manichean oppositions. Assaulted by all manner of crude matters, the public is numbed. The future is in question. The way forward will certainly be precarious.

Coronil's writings remind us that any path toward an alternative future will have to be provisional and dialogical, democratic and plurinational, nourished by political imagination and utopian longing, mindful that means and ends must align. If intellectual work is to play a role in such an undertaking, and Coronil believed it could, it would have to be based on his insight that critical thinking is a process without limit, "an open-ended space oriented toward making sense of the world. . . . [I]t is openness to possibilities, it interprets being, what was and is, as forms of becoming. Through its recognition that what can be inhabits what is, it pursues knowledge for a world that can become home to multiple worlds. . . . Assembled as a labyrinth whose exits become entrances into an expanding labyrinth, its arrivals are points of departure and its answers pose new questions."[58]

His insistence on an open future is clear in his call for the "pursuit of knowledge for free people, who . . . will continue to struggle for aims we now can barely imagine." His critical practice was unapologetically utopian and grounded in the world. It was oriented toward a new "planetary universality" based in social equality, human differences, and respect for nonhuman life, in the service of a world of many worlds, nourished by the prospect of "living well." Fernando Coronil's writings and example may help us make our way on this tightrope stretched between the imperative to envision and the impossibility of foreseeing a radically alternative future.[59]

Notes

1 Coronil, "Pieces for Anthrohistory," this volume, 55. Subsequent citations to this essay also give page numbers for this volume.

2 Coronil, *The Magical State*, xi.

3 Coronil, "The Future in Question," this volume, 128–162. Subsequent citations to this essay also give page numbers for this volume.

4 Coronil, "The Future in Question," 153.

5 Coronil, "The Future in Question," 132.

6 Coronil, "The Future in Question," 154.

7 Hall, "The Problem of Ideology."

8 Coronil, "The Future in Question," 154.

9 Coronil, "The Future in Question," 158.

10 Coronil, "The Future in Question," 158.

11 In the 1950s and '60s she held directive positions at the Children's Hospital and the Sociedad de Médicos and was a director of the Consejo Venezolano de Niños. For a discussion of the institutions Lya Ímber helped found or direct and her international activities, see Torres, *Lya Ímber de Coronil*, 51–62, 77–88. For her publications and official positions, see http://www.fundacionbengoa.org/personalidades/lya_imber_coronil.asp.

12 Among many posts, she was a vice president of UNICEF (1972–74), and in 1981 she was the first woman to be elected to Venezuela's National Academy of Medicine.

13 Coronil served as Minister of Finance, Senator, head of Congress, ambassador to Colombia, and diplomatic representative for oil company negotiations. His position as a thirty-third degree Freemason further cemented his standing as a respected figure and facilitated his international connections.

14 Of their sisters, the eldest was a French instructor and founder of a trade school for low-income girls; another became a doctor; and the youngest, "la Nena," founded the Ballet of Caracas. Of the two brothers, one became a lawyer and the other, a surgeon.

15 As founder of its Department of Experimental Surgery, he undertook innovative transplant research, was elected to the Venezuelan Academy of Medicine, and helped found an experimental medical school; see González Luque, "La escuela de medicina 'José María Vargas,'" 1.

16 During the dictatorship of Marcos Pérez Jiménez (1952–58), his parents were
expelled from public positions. He recalled that when he was a child his parents
hid a labor leader active in the clandestine struggle in their house, a fact he was
told never to mention.

17 They founded an experimental arts magazine, and their home was a gathering place for people in the arts during Coronil's youth. His aunt Sofía helped
bring art works by European and Venezuelan artists to the Central University
of Venezuela and became a leading television commentator, turning toward
politics with her second husband, Carlos Rangel. She founded the Museo de
Arte Contemporáneo Sofía Ímber, which opened in 1974, and directed it until
2001, when President Hugo Chávez abruptly fired her and removed her name
from the institution: see Arroyo Gil, *La señora Ímber*.

18 The "Pacto de Punto Fijo" was a de facto agreement that excluded leftist parties
from participating in cabinet level posts. Over time, this "pacted democracy"
became increasingly patronage-based and exclusionary.

19 For Castro's itinerary and reception, see http://www.fidelcastro.cu/en/viajes
/venezuela-1959.

20 She worked with the Congress of Racial Equality on voter registration in 1965 in
the town of Marianna, Florida, a stronghold of the Ku Klux Klan.

21 Gilman, *Mandarins of the Future*, 316.

22 In this context, Victor Turner moved toward performance studies and universalizing humanism, changing his appointment to the Committee on Social
Thought, while Terence Turner undertook the study of Marx's theory of value
and its relevance for non-class-based societies.

23 Rodríguez, an economist and lawyer, and prior leader of the Cuban Communist
Party, was an important intellectual figure in the Cuban government and one of
the few leaders who had been prominent during the prerevolutionary period.

24 Founded in 1969 by members of Students for a Democratic Society in support
of the Cuban Revolution, the group recruited volunteers of diverse racial and
class origins to do agricultural work and learn about Cuban and international
revolutionary struggles. The brigade was heavily surveilled by the FBI and
infiltrated by COINTELPRO, a secret counterintelligence program designed to
disrupt New Left, civil rights, and black militant organizations: see Cunningham, *There's Something Happening Here*, 36–38.

25 The harvest reached 8.5 million tons. While it was the largest in history, it
was deemed a failure. The lack of adequate refinery capacity, skilled person-
nel, cane cutters, and transportation made it impossible for the goal to be
fulfilled.

26 Lewis, known for his oral histories of poor people in Mexico and Puerto Rico
and for his controversial concept of the "culture of poverty," was invited by
Castro to undertake a study of former residents of slums in Havana based on
the expectation he would find that the socialist revolution had transformed

their culture. Lewis's "Project Cuba," which trained Cuban students in research techniques, was abruptly terminated in June 1970 when Lewis and his wife and co-author, Ruth Lewis, were expelled from the country and their remaining materials were confiscated. Ruth Lewis posthumously published three volumes based on their joint research. The Polish-French journalist K. S. Karol published *The Guerrillas in Power*, and René Dumont, noted French agronomist and proponent of citizen participation, published *Is Cuba Socialist?* in 1970, prompting Castro's denunciation of these authors and signaling the growing estrangement of the French intelligentsia.

27 Fornet, *El 71*, documents the critical international and national events that took place in 1971. It marks a breakthrough in scholarship published in Cuba.

28 For an account of Padilla's behavior and Castro's reaction, see http://www .nexos.com.mx/?p=11664. For Castro's speech, see http://www.cuba.cu /gobierno/discursos/1971/esp/f300471e.html. For a collection of documents and publications concerning the case, see Casal, *El Caso Padilla*.

29 As invitees of the Cuban government, they were housed in hotels, first at the Habana Libre (formerly the Havana Hilton), then mainly a residence for political exiles, and for most of their stay at the Hotel Vedado.

30 Gómez's short films, most of which were never shown, were neither stories of the heroic proletariat and peasantry, nor of the conflicted bourgeoisie. They presented working and primarily black "marginal" people debating projects, performing music, and recounting their history. She also placed herself and her black middle-class family under the gaze of her unwavering critical eye. On her exploration of working women involved in the sugar harvest, *Mi Aporte* (My Contribution), see Alvarez Ramírez, "El Aporte de Sara Gómez."

31 This was a problem for those who took part in many religions and associations, including the Freemasons. However, followers of Afro-Cuban practices were more severely limited than others.

32 The film explores the strained relationship of a couple whose class, race, gender, religious, and political identifications conflicted at the height of the revolution's demands. Released in 1977, it was unfinished at the time of Gómez's untimely death in 1974, at thirty-one, from asthma. Two noted filmmakers completed it; the film has belatedly received attention, as has Gómez's body of work, for its innovative combination of documentary and fictional components and its radical insistence on presenting full characters struggling with conflicts rather than giving viewers a "happy end" resolution of them. For a nuanced discussion of the film as a feminist work, see Rich, One Way or Another." (Rich makes mistaken assertions about Afro-Cuban religions that reflect the limited material available in 1978, when the article was written.)

33 They later learned that participant observation was not an accepted practice and that Rodríguez's support for their work undoubtedly had met with strong opposition.

34 The INS, formerly an autonomous agency within the U.S. Department of Justice, was organized after 2003 into several agencies within the Department of Homeland Security.

35 This quotation and other uncited quotations later in the introduction come from Skurski's recollection of the period.

36 For the political context, including anarchist attacks, labor unrest, race riots, and anti-Bolshevism, in which the Immigration Law was passed and amended to include anti-radical categories, see http://law.jrank.org/pages/9705/Red -Scare.html. For the political exclusion clauses in an early version of the law, see https://www.loc.gov/law/help/statutes-at-large/65th-congress/session-2 /c65s2ch186.pdf.

37 At a cocktail party in Caracas, the U.S. ambassador commented to Josefina, "Mademoiselle," Fernando's aunt, "I hear your nephew is coming back to Venezuela. Tell him to be a good boy."

38 This research led to the publication of their co-written article "Reproducing Dependency: Auto Industry Policy and Petrodollar Circulation in Venezuela" (1982), which was an early effort to understand the complexity of the Venezuelan state. The essay examined the disjunction between the state's self-representation in official programs and the practices through which elite Venezuelan families with old wealth influenced policy and multinationals established a network of connections with state figures and entrepreneurs.

39 Coronil's "The Magical State: History and Illusion in the Appearance of Venezuelan Democracy" (working paper, October 1988) critiqued Bonapartism as applied to Latin America through a discussion of several coups in Venezuela, understood as a neocolonial rentier state.

40 Given their interest in understanding violence in its social, discursive, and colonial dimensions, with the support of Raymond Grew, of the journal *Comparative Studies in Society and History*, they organized a conference, "States of Violence," which led to an edited volume by the same name: see Coronil and Skurski, *States of Violence*.

41 Among the founders of the seminar were Geoff Eley, Terence McDonald, Ronald Suny, and Sherry Ortner. For a list of papers, see https://quod.lib.umich .edu/b/bhlead/umich-bhl-2011120?view=text. Coronil first presented "Beyond Occidentalism: Toward Postimperial Geohistorical Categories" as a Comparative Study of Social Transformations working paper in 1992.

42 The doctoral program is connected to the Anthropology and History departments but has its own requirements, admissions, affiliated faculty, core seminar, student fellowships, and meeting space.

43 They included Ann Laura Stoler, Brinkley Messick, Nick Dirks, and E. Valentine Daniels.

44 For an innovative discussion of the debates and questions nourished by the doctoral program in anthropology and history, see Murphy et al., *Anthrohistory*.

45 Most of the co-editors of the volume are graduates of the anthrohistory program. Skurski was its associate director under David W. Cohen, the dedicated director of the program who succeeded Coronil.

46 The group met at frequent conferences in Latin America and the United States over the course of the first decade of the twenty-first century and produced many publications. Among its central participants were Catherine Walsh, Javier Sanjinés, and Arturo Escobar. For a chronology of conferences and list of publications, see http://www.ceapedi.com.ar/encuentro2012/encuentro_3.htm.

47 This argument converged with those of the anthropologists Sidney Mintz and Michel-Rolph Trouillot, among others.

48 For an archive of documents and sources concerning the "Darkness in El Dorado" controversy, see the website AnthroNiche, organized by Douglas W. Hume, at http://anthroniche.com/darkness-in-el-dorado-controversy. For an informative exchange among central figures, see Borofsky, *Yanomami*.

49 In an effort to counter this tendency, members of the task force, including Coronil and Turner, took part in an unprecedented meeting of Yanomami village leaders in the Venezuelan Amazon to discuss the past research projects and their current health needs.

50 For statements by participants in the conference, see https://quod.lib.umich .edu/j/jii/4750978.0009.104/--production-of-knowledge-indigenous-peoples ?rgn=main;view=fulltext.

51 For a discussion of the controversy at the University of Michigan, including a history of the expeditions to obtain Yanomami biological materials and kinship information, see Skurski, "Past Warfare."

52 On April 12, with Chávez out of power and contradictory accounts of the unfolding events, Coronil was invited to PBS *NewsHour* to comment on the upheaval, along with a mainstream analyst of Latin America. At a moment in which U.S. officials and media figures were claiming that Chávez had resigned amid popular rejection of his rule, Coronil cited the electoral foundations of Chávez's support and argued in defense of constitutional mechanisms of change.

53 Before the coup, employees of the state oil company Petróleos de Venezuela (PDVSA) had gone on strike, and after the coup the opposition almost toppled him through a crippling oil company lockout and a business strike in 2002. These events helped cement the fierce polarization that marked the country for years.

54 The political theorist Edgardo Lander, initially a supporter of Chávez's project, published critiques of the regime's heightened oil dependency and its turn toward ecologically destructive mining under Chávez's successor Nicolás Maduro. For a discussion of the constitutional crisis and its link to the intensification of extractivism, see Lander and Arconada Rodríguez, "Venezuela."

55 At the CUNY Graduate Center, they included Katherine Verdery, with whom he worked closely. Gary Wilder, with whom he shared a deep concern for interdisciplinary and Global South issues, joined the Graduate Center soon after.

56 As Lander observes with anguish in an interview, the international Left has shown an unwillingness to engage in critical discussion of Chavismo, given its focus on imperial attacks, thus weakening its voice when the crisis of the Maduro government became glaring: see Lander, "Ante la crisis de Venezuela la izquierda carece de crítica."

57 Coronil, "The Future in Question," 137.

58 Coronil, "Pieces for Anthrohistory," 53–54.

59 Coronil, "Pieces for Anthrohistory," 56.

Bibliography

Alvarez Ramírez, Sandra. "El Aporte de Sara Gómez." In *Afrocubanas: Historia, pensamiento y prácticas culturales*, ed. Daisy Rubiera Castillo and Inés María Martiatu Terry, 324–32. Havana: Ciencias Sociales, 2011.

Arroyo Gil, Diego. *La señora Ímber: Genio y figura*. Caracas: Planeta Venezolana, 2016.

Borofsky, Robert. *Yanomami: The Fierce Controversy and What We Can Learn from 2005*. Berkeley: University of California Press, 2005.

Casal, Lourdes, ed. *El Caso Padilla: Literatura y revolución en Cuba*. Miami: Universal, 1971.

Coronil, Fernando. *The Magical State: Nature, Money, and Modernity in Venezuela*. Chicago: University of Chicago Press, 1997.

Coronil, Fernando, and Julie Skurski, eds. *States of Violence*. Ann Arbor: University of Michigan Press, 2006.

Cunningham, David. *There's Something Happening Here: The New Left, the Klan, and FBI Counterintelligence*. Berkeley: University of California Press, 2004.

Fornet, Jorge. *El 71: Anatomía de una crisis*. Havana: Letras Cubanas, 2013.

Gilman, Nils. *Mandarins of the Future: Modernization Theory in Cold War America*. Baltimore, MD: Johns Hopkins University Press, 2007.

González Luque, Ángel. "La escuela de medicina 'José María Vargas': Breve introducción histórica." *Dermatología venezolana* 40, no. 2 (2002): 55–59.

Hall, Stuart. "The Problem of Ideology: Marxism without Guarantees." *Journal of Communication Inquiry* 10, no. 2 (1986): 28–44.

Lander, Edgardo. "Ante la crisis de Venezuela la izquierda carece de crítica." *Red Filosófica del Uruguay*, April 1, 2017. https://redfilosoficadeluruguay.wordpress .com/2017/04/01/edgardo-lander-ante-la-crisis-de-venezuela-la-izquierda -carece-de-critica.

Lander, Edgardo, and Santiago Arconada Rodríguez. "Venezuela: Un barril de pólvora." *Nueva Sociedad*, no. 269, May–June 2017, http://nuso.org.

Murphy, Edward, David William Cohen, Chandra D. Bhimull, Fernando Coronil, Monica Eileen Patterson, and Julie Skurski, eds. *Anthrohistory: Unsettling Knowledge, Questioning Discipline*. Ann Arbor: University of Michigan Press, 2011.

Rich, B. Ruby. "One Way or Another: Sara Gómez and the Cuban Experience" (1978). In *Theories and Memories of the Feminist Film Movement*, 92–102. Durham, NC: Duke University Press, 1998.

Skurski, Julie. "Past Warfare: Ethics, Knowledge, and the Yanomami Controversy." In *Anthrohistory: Unsettling Knowledge, Questioning Discipline*, ed. Edward Murphy, David William Cohen, Chandra D. Bhimull, Fernando Coronil, Monica Eileen Patterson, and Julie Skurski, 121–39. Ann Arbor: University of Michigan Press, 2011.

Torres, Ana Teresa. *Lya Ímber de Coronil*. Caracas: El Nacional, 2010.

LABYRINTHS OF CRITIQUE

THE PROMISE OF ANTHROHISTORY

Part I. Labyrinths of Critique: The Promise of Anthrohistory

Introduction DAVID PEDERSEN

■   During the winter of 2008, Fernando Coronil composed "Pieces for Anthrohistory: A Puzzle to Be Assembled Together." He circulated many drafts to friends, completing it for publication in the 2011 edited book *AnthroHistory: Unsettling Knowledge, Questioning Discipline.*[1] The essay appeared as the culmination of twenty-two chapters in that collection (see the introduction). It stands here as the opening one in this volume. Like other famous theses that go to eleven or eighteen, though not ninety-five, Coronil's theses may be appreciated for their poetic and aphoristic rendering of a resolutely practical orientation and project. He names this heartfelt venture "anthrohistory," acknowledging in the first footnote to the essay that it, "as Juliette's Romeo or Quijote's Dulcinea . . . [,] is an idealized hyper-real subject." Coronil reflects more on this comparison: "Perhaps love holds not just an ideal reality, but the impetus to make it real. As in any romance, readers can treat 'anthrohistory' in this text as a space-holder for a love of their own" (306).

"Pieces for Anthrohistory" (hereafter, "Pieces") offers a passionate base note for understanding Fernando's life work. We borrow the first sentence of Thesis Eight for this book's title: "The struggle for life is the matter." This is the object and purpose at the center of "Pieces." The essay helps explain Fernando's abiding interest in Cuba; his studies of the Venezuelan state; his defiance of colonial and imperial relations; and the manner of critical knowledge production that he honed as a Venezuelan-born, U.S. university-based professor in the academic disciplines of anthropology and history. As a practical orientation, "Pieces" defines all at once a unique combination of inquiry, explanation, critique, and presentation. It has ethico-political and aesthetic implications and carries significant ontological and epistemological import.

In this prefatory essay, I draw out these propositions, especially the latter two, by considering some qualities of "Pieces" and linking them with several essays that preceded its publication and one that appeared after "Pieces," which are included in this opening section of this book under the title "Labyrinths of Critique."

The theses begin with a recognition of anthrohistory's emergence both from within and in opposition to the dominant "history, premises, and politics of Western knowledge," especially the two academic disciplines that make up its name. While keeping this in focus, Coronil figuratively pulls back and broadens the field of view to show anthrohistory as a fully planetary endeavor that emerges from and encompasses, but also goes beyond, the disciplinary-specific conditions of its formation: "Of this world, but not at home in it, anthrohistory resists being disciplined in existing institutions or contained by definitions."[2] He concludes the third thesis with a programmatic statement that reiterates anthrohistory's immanently critical stance: "Brushing history against the brain, its task is to examine what has been recorded and uncover what has been silenced, bringing to light possible histories."

Coronil follows this opening sequence with eight subsequent theses that creatively explore in more detail what such a project entails, including what should be presupposed about the world—or worlds, as Coronil acknowledges in the second footnote—how best to inquire into these worlds, and inseparably, why, and to what ends.

Overall, the eleven theses contain multiple and extended footnotes that offer evidence and explicit recognition of the influences behind each of them. One can read "Pieces" lineally by thesis-number progression, appreciating its closed rhetorical logic, and in a more capacious way by following up each note, the notes' references, and potentially beyond. Coronil alludes to this combined shape when he writes as a note to his "Notes," "Imagine these notes as endnotes within notes, in counterpoint to each piece. They can be read as footnotes, or as beginning notes, all at once, or next to the eleven pieces—as side notes" (306).

This open and expansive modality, expressed with the footnote gesture, as well as the multiple references to Jorge Luis Borges's literary explorations, and especially the playful exemplification in Thesis Seven, point out that Coronil presupposes something like an infinite continuum of relations in which the practice of anthrohistory unfolds. There is no temporal or spatial unit, no form, that cannot be further divided or placed within a yet more encompassing whole, including that whole itself. As he writes in Thesis Five, "Anthrohistory seeks to produce representations of the world as fragments of an unfolding totality, itself a fragment of other totalities. Any totality is partial" (303). This secular reverence for infinitude is a first ontological presupposition for anthrohistory.[3]

As the opening three theses illustrated through their simultaneous shift in point of view, level of focus, and overall framing, whatever something is in its fullest sense (such as anthrohistory) includes the composite of relations out of which it congealed, in which it develops, and that contribute to its capacities—and that it can react back on like an external entity. Coronil expresses this inherently dynamic and relational understanding of part and open whole, of form, content, and meaning, in Thesis Six, explaining that "points on a map make a point. Like lines in a play, they become meaningful by being joined to each other by the authors and publics who join them. These lines form not just texts about the world, but the texture of the world. They represent an external reality from within it" (303). This privileging of representational relations rather than discrete things is a second ontological stance with respect to anthrohistory's worlds.

Given these premises—infinitely open wholes composed of infinitely divisible parts of wholes—Coronil proposes a uniquely appropriate method of inquiry. He writes that anthrohistory is an "ensemble of practices for examining human practices through ever changing prisms" and takes "form as a never-ending puzzle whose pieces are crafted and pieced together by these practices" (302). I take this to mean that anthrohistory's manner of inquiry entails using different optics capable of dispersing, deviating, displacing, or rotating what passes through them. This suggests a technique of inquiry predicated on moving about, varying the angles, positions and surfaces of the optics in order to look at, around, through, and beyond phenomena, bringing out various qualities and constitutive relations, like white light dispersed into a spectrum of visible and invisible electromagnetic radiation, at once particles and waves.

One effect of such inquiry is to show the partiality of any single perspective or angle and, in the process, produce more inclusive, multidimensional, even contradiction-laden accounts of whatever is under study, including the larger determinative whole of which it is a part. Coronil uses the example of maps to develop this epistemological implication and its inseparable political consequences. He begins Thesis Five with a quote from Adrienne Rich that he develops: "'If a place on the map is also a place in history' any representation simultaneously encloses time and space." Coronil continues the theme in Thesis Six, noting that the truth of maps "is measured by their exactitude as models of the world they image, but it is realized by the world they help create. The point of a map defines its points" (303).

As the essay's opening epigraph from Borges and its reference to labyrinths encapsulates, "Pieces" presupposes an infinite continuum of relations and calls for multiplex inquiry into the appearance of borders, boundaries, and qualities of stasis. A sense of movement is entailed with finding and making connections that are otherwise difficult to immediately perceive. Metaphorically, the critical project that "Pieces" describes is much like moving through a labyrinth.

In his introduction to the Duke University Press edition of Fernando Ortiz's *Cuban Counterpoint*, "Transculturation and the Politics of Theory: Countering the Center, Cuban Counterpoint," Coronil inquires into the reciprocal interaction of Ortiz's book with the larger and also highly uneven imperial conditions of its formation and circulation. In this way, it exemplifies aspects of the part-whole relationship explored in "Pieces." For Fernando, the book was an example of engaged inquiry, at once public and scholarly, written from and with respect to a peripheral locus (Cuba) that was relationally connected, however unevenly, with dominant metropolitan centers that historically had imported Cuban tobacco and sugar and continued to house prominent academic disciplines (anthropology). Like Fernando's own life and writings, it was a work that traversed multiple hierarchies and boundaries.[4]

Coronil emphasized that Ortiz developed the term "counterpoint" as a way to grasp the co-determination of opposites. Joined with this conceptualization, Ortiz then proposed "transculturation" as a way to describe the interaction of such opposing entities not as discrete and separate but, rather, as forming and changing in relation to the larger whole of which they both were an expression of and an influence on. Mirroring this approach, Coronil explores how particular features of Ortiz's life and work were shaped by the larger wholes within which they developed. He concludes the essay following a similar logic, showing how Bronisław Malinowski's appreciation for Ortiz and his perspective on anthropology more generally changed in relation to broader historical circumstances. In both instances, some qualities and aspects of each scholar's works and perspectives were amplified while others were diminished. Coronil's essay uncovered this process, much in the way that this kind of inquiry is outlined in "Pieces."

Coronil's writings show him to be an inspired stickler for suitable titles and a creative wrangler of keywords. For Coronil, concepts really matter. Reality is not just conceptualized reality. It also is part of the concepts themselves. This is especially apparent in the preface that he contributed to the book *Close Encounters*, edited by Gilbert Joseph and Catherine LeGrand. Coronil's preface is a clever study of dominant categories and their adequacy. As with optics and maps in "Pieces," Coronil recognizes that terms such as "postcolonial," "political economy," "culture," and "materiality" express aspects or qualities of a larger open whole as much as separate and discrete objects. Following a thesis-like progression, Coronil reworks a series of categorical distinctions to show the shared content of the supposed oppositions, much in the way that Ortiz defined such reciprocal transformation as "transculturation." Coronil's goal is to bring together and transform a field of inquiry and, by extension, go as much as possible beyond it.

In his short essay that reflects on the controversy surrounding the publication of Patrick Tierney's book *Darkness in El Dorado*, Coronil again takes the approach of critically examining the emergence of a dominant formation or understanding and the ways that this process occludes much of the form's enabling conditions. By moving between parts and their larger but less visible wholes, Coronil discloses the structural inequalities masked by metropolitan perspectives and the ruse of a fact-value distinction that hides the political and ethical stakes of inquiry.

Coronil wrote "The Future in Question: History and Utopia in Latin America (1989–2010)" several years after "Pieces." The essay reflects Coronil's relational approach to part and whole and the task of disclosing what is concealed in dominant representations by multiply reworking these form-content relationships according to different viewpoints, levels of focus, and geohistorical frame, as outlined in "Pieces." He brings this perspective explicitly to temporal dimensions of life in Latin America, showing that past, present, and future each refer to aspects of the same, unfinished whole. By moving across this content, Coronil seeks to keep alive future possibilities as they are present in both the past and the present. Cast in terms of dreams, desires, and counterpoints, Cuban and otherwise, Coronil writes:

> Of course, given the unequal structures of power within which this leftward turn has taken place, it is possible that its new imaginings may be co-opted or crushed. But given that these imaginaries now unite South and North in a politics that fuses the pursuit of well-being and sheer

global survival, it is likely that a counterpoint between the embers of the past and the poetry of the future will continue to conjure up images of worlds free from the horrors of history. Politics will remain a battle of desires waged on an uneven terrain. But as long as people find themselves without a safe and dignified home in the world, utopian dreams will continue to proliferate, energizing struggles to build a world made of many worlds, where people can dream their futures without fear of waking up.[5]

This is the poetic and political promise of Anthrohistory.

Notes

1 Fernando Coronil, "Pieces for Anthrohistory: A Puzzle to Be Assembled Together," in *AnthroHistory: Unsettling Knowledge, Questioning Discipline*, ed. Chandra Bhimull, David William Cohen, Fernando Coronil, Edward L. Murphy, Monica Patterson, and Julie Skurski, eds., 301–16 (Ann Arbor: University of Michigan Press). Hereafter, page numbers are cited in parentheses in the text. The true breadth of Fernando's circulation of "Pieces" in its many iterations gradually became clear to me through conversations with people who attended a memorial celebration of his life in 2013, organized by Richard Turits, Coronil's friend and colleague in the Department of History at the University of Michigan.

2 From the habitual perspective of any single academic discipline, Coronil's audacious opening gesture may prompt a feeling of disorientation and falling, similar to the way that the "dolly zoom" achieved this effect in Alfred Hitchcock's *Vertigo*.

3 During one conversation in the early 1990s, Fernando said that, in his experience, he had not found many contemporary scholars who really took infinity seriously, or even the impossibly large whole that would include all human social and cultural life on the planet, not limited to just its biological aspects, and include as well its future possibilities. To make the point, Fernando enjoyed naming earthly capitalism as no more than offensive flatulence in the larger cosmos and musing about the fantastic redemptive promise of a simultaneous orgasm among all capable species on the planet.

4 Coronil's friend and colleague at the University of Michigan, Rebecca Scott, teasingly referred to *Cuban Counterpoint*'s author as "Fernando's Ortiz."

5 Fernando Coronil, "The Future in Question," this volume, 128–162.

1 Pieces for Anthrohistory: A Puzzle to Be Assembled Together

IN HOMAGE TO MARX'S
AND BENJAMIN'S THESES ELEVEN

> There are many people adept in those diverse disciplines, but
> few capable of imagination—fewer still capable of subordinating
> imagination to a rigorous and systematic plan. The plan is so vast
> that the contribution of each writer is infinitesimal.
> —Jorge Luis Borges, "Tlön, Uqbar, Orbis Tertius"

1

The chief defect of all hitherto existing academic disciplines is that they conceptualize discipline as their mode of being, seldom as an object for being. Taking into account perspectives from borders and margins, since the 1980s several scholarly fields have developed critical evaluations of the history, premises, and politics of Western knowledge—its teleological narratives, disciplinary classifications, and complicity with eurocentrism, racism, sexism, elitism, and other modalities of dominative knowledge. As the offspring of these fields, anthrohistory shares with them genealogies, concerns, and products. As an academic project devoted to producing knowledge betwixt and between disciplines, anthrohistory seeks to educate scholars in anthropology and history by transgressing their limits and tending to their impact. Insofar as it is capable of subordinating imagination to a rigorous and systematic plan, it becomes a questioning discipline that undisciplines the disciplines and educates the educator. Through this critical practice, discipline is subordinated to its object.

2

Growing out of disciplines implicated in Western understandings of the world and dominion over it, anthrohistory, like kindred critical ventures, occupies an open-ended space oriented toward making sense of the world and of sense making. In its openness to possibilities, it interprets being, what was and what is, as forms of becoming. Through its recognition that what can be inhabits what is, it pursues knowledge for a world that can become home to multiple worlds.

3

Of this world but not at home in it, anthrohistory resists being disciplined in existing institutions or contained by definitions. As long as this planet is not home for all, this project must roam as an exile, witnessing what has been made of it and reflecting on the work to make it habitable. For to the extent that winning entails domination, no one—not even plants—can be safe from the enemy, for who would inherit the earth's energy and care for our collective legacy? Brushing history against the brain, its task is to examine what has been recorded and uncover what has been silenced, bringing to light possible histories.

4

As an ensemble of practices for examining human practices through ever changing prisms, anthrohistory acquires form as a never-ending puzzle whose pieces are crafted and pieced together by these practices. Assembled as a labyrinth whose exits become entrances into an expanding labyrinth, its arrivals are points of departure and its answers pose new questions.

5

"If a place on the map is also a place in history," any representation simultaneously encloses time and space. There is no space outside time or time without space; together they form the medium through which our world is constituted and brought into awareness. At a specific scale, a map represents a place in space at a moment in time, whether a grain of sand or a whole country. Just as in an account of the cosmos "the paltry fifty millennia of homo sapiens" could be a single point, in a chronicle of the battle of Borodino Napoleon's head cold and the action of a "most humble soldier" could mark two significant moments. Macrohistory and microhistory are two scales of the same history. Anthrohistory seeks to produce representations of the world as fragments of an unfolding totality, itself a fragment of other totalities. Any totality is partial.

6

Points on maps make a point. Like lines in a play, they become meaningful by being joined to each other by the authors and publics who join them. These lines form not just texts about the world, but the texture of the world. They represent an external reality from within it. Their truth is measured by their exactitude as models of the world they image, but it is realized by the world they help create. The point of a map defines its points. Our journey is guided by a compass; our destination defines our destiny.

7

Imagine a discussion about truth in a Jorge Luis Borges story written by Italo Calvino and illustrated by M. C. Escher. In a magnificent square called "Paris 1945–2000," Jean-Paul Sartre, Claude Lévi-Strauss, and Jacques Derrida argue in French about how best to explain human history through forms of reasoning associated with "dialectical materialism," "structuralism," and "poststructuralism." Through a crack in its foundation, a path suddenly opens into a larger square called "Europe," where Kant, Hegel, and Marx animatedly discuss the nature of universal history in German while Heidegger listens. Unbeknownst to them, "Europe," their assumed center of world history, is located atop a grain of sand, minutely drawn by William Blake's mind. Trapped in a convent built upon Aztec ruins located inside this granule, Sor Juana Inés de la Cruz reflects on faith through Christian, Muslim, and Buddhist theologies. From one of the convent's secret doors, a labyrinthine path one hundred years long leads us to an elongated islet, "Saint Domingue, 1791–1820," where the rebel Boukman, a slave who had learned from his African ancestors the power of spirits and plants, places his faith in Legba to battle for freedom, and Ti Noel, a freed slave oppressed under Henry Christophe's kingdom in independent Haiti familiar with Boukman's rebellion and with the Declaration of the Rights of Man and Citizen, at the end of his life comes to declare war against all masters. From a telescope 10 (500)n times more powerful than the Palomar Observatory located in a star of another universe, we could retrace all their words and deeds, backward or forward, floating as cosmic dust, long after their authors died. And if we look for certain words with care, we may be able even to find those brought together by Alejo Carpentier in a historical novel and read that in a place called *The Kingdom of This World*, where each individual life came to be valued as a precious universe, historical truth was discovered to be fundamentally practical, a matter of struggling against the forces that limit life, the source and aim of history, an elusive marvel.

8

The struggle for life is the matter. We can find its germinations and ruins in fields, those expanding spaces where social activity continuously unfolds, and archives, the ever more varied containers of its readable traces and signs. Both are formed through the myriad classificatory and discriminatory procedures that shape lives and select significance. Through "fieldwork" and "archival research," the disciplines of anthropology and history construct their objects. In pursuit of its object, non-dominative knowledge excavates deep within and beyond given fields and archives. Brushing history against the brain, as if mining for life's gems, from the debris this practice of survival creates its own library, organized less as a Museum of Knowledge than as a Practical Workshop: photos, musical tapes, poems, films, field notes, books, newspapers, artifacts kept digitally in data banks or located in crates thrown all over the floor in constant use in pursuit of knowledge for free people, who therefore will continue to struggle for aims we now can barely imagine. Honoring those oppressed in the past by standing for freedom in the present, we can perhaps envisage a future unburdened by origins, free to abandon images that sustained past struggles—a future perfect released from the burden of the past. By this novel time, images that Walter Benjamin conjured up to inspire our struggles, whether of a dark past ("the hatred and the spirit of sacrifice" of enslaved ancestors) or of a bright future (the dream of "liberated grandchildren") will become historical dust, the taken-for-granted soil of new social landscapes, except perhaps for a few tattered relics kept by historians or antiquarians. Recognizing in lives built amid "wreckage upon wreckage" the stronger love that holds together what has been broken, we could then be moved by a "structure of political thought" that, in the yearning words of a historian of longing, "will recognize what has been made out on the margins; and then, recognizing it, refuse to celebrate it; a politics that will, watching this past, say 'So What?' and consign it to the dark." As our struggle is endless, the poet reminds us that "irony is the struggle to struggle."

9

Synchrony and diachrony
Are modes of holding
Space in time or
Time in space. It
all depends on
the eyes of the beholder
Who, What,
holds the beholder?

10

The poetry of
the present
holds
the prose of
the future

And vice versa.
So much, as much,
depends on
Words as Deeds.

11

It's about people making it.

Notes

Epigraph: Borges (1964: 72).

These pieces are constructed in playful counterpoint to Karl Marx's "Theses on Feuerbach" and Walter Benjamin's "Theses on the Philosophy of History," accompanied by Fernando Ortiz's *Cuban Counterpoint*.

1

1.1 In this volume we use the terms "anthrohistory" and "anthrohistorians" because this is how we came to identify ourselves in our regular activities at the University of Michigan. As far as I know, a similar term, "anthrohistorical," was first used by Paul Friedrich in his *Princes of Naranja: An Essay in Anthrohistorical Method* (1986). Just like Juliet's Romeo or Don Quixote's Dulcinea, my anthrohistory here is an idealized, hyperreal subject; perhaps love holds not just an ideal reality but the impetus to make it real. As in any romance, readers can treat "anthrohistory" in this text as a space holder for a love of their own. If love of the general is realized through love of particulars—for me the central lesson of seeing the "personal" as "political"—these pieces for anthrohistory may work for other projects as well. Upon reading a draft of this paper, Javier Sanjines, a member of a Latin American group also involved in decolonizing projects, commented that much of what I say here about anthrohistory applies to this group. Perhaps the core of this general project is the recognition of mutuality and reciprocity among living beings and the ethical obligations entailed in acknowledging this collective interdependence. If we come to "work and toil for people we will never know, as Ti Noel realized at the end of Carpentier's novel *The Kingdom of This World* (1957), it is because we are sustained by the work and toil, and by the love, of others.

In recognition of this entangled gift, I dedicate these pieces to the memory of Lya Ímber de Coronil, my mother, Venezuela's first female doctor who dedicated her life to public health, and to Bellas for their care.

1.2　The major scholarly fields involved in the critical movement associated with intellectual turns in the 1980s are social and cultural history; cultural anthropology; linguistics; literary theory; critical geography; British and U.S. cultural studies; microhistory; feminist, gay, and queer studies; the German school Kultur-Gesellschaft-Alltag; and postcolonial and subaltern studies in their hegemonic, as well as Latin American and African, modalities.

1.3　I use the word "movement" following David William Cohen's suggestion that the category "social movement" serves to examine the development of "historical anthropology." Coinciding with this notion, in internal discussions among a group of scholars and activists united by a decolonizing project centering on Latin America, Walter Mignolo has argued for the value of thinking of ourselves as a "social movement" that seeks to overcome Western separations between the knowing subject and its object as well as academia and society.

1.4　My use of "borders" and "betwixt and between" here intends to suggest the potentiality inhering in liminal social spaces, as explored in the works of Victor Turner (1967), Gloria Anzaldúa (1987), and Walter Mignolo (2000), among others.

1.5　The notion of "undisciplining the disciplines" is inspired by the work of the network of Latin American scholars and activists associated with the decolonizing project mentioned earlier, guided by Aníbal Quijano (1993) and Enrique Dussel (1998), as well as by the work of kindred thinkers, such as Boaventura de Sousa Santos (1995) and Franz Hinkelammert (2006); for a collection of essays on this topic, see the books edited on this topic by Santiago Castro-Gómez and Eduardo Mendieta (1998) as well as those by Catherine Walsh (2002) and Edgardo Lander (2000).

1.6　In the 1990s, the Gulbenkian Commission celebrated the "opening" of the social sciences and the blurring of the disciplinary boundaries separating the social sciences, the humanities, and the natural sciences (Wallerstein et al. 1996). I think it is evident that the disciplines now are more self-aware and open; they certainly have assimilated terms and concepts from each other. Yet professional interests, market pressures, and conservative politics, in my view, are normalizing these changes and leading to a closing of the social sciences. Michael Buroway's (2005) insightful critique of the Gulbenkian report is also an indictment of the conformism affecting academic disciplines a few years after its publication. Given the growing corporatization of the universities (see the January 2008 issue of *Anthropology News*) I fear that the promotion of interdisciplinarity at the present time is too often cast instrumentally as the pursuit of established objectives through the interaction among given disciplines, rather than as a genuine expansion of the horizons of knowledge through the questioning of assumptions, boundaries, and ends.

1.7 The current "privatization of knowledge" in multiple forms, including the concentration of knowledge production in research centers in universities located in metropolitan centers increasingly subjected to corporate pressures, is a general phenomenon that affects all academic programs, including anthrohistory.

1.8 Critical praxis should be distinguished from the conventional pragmatism that focuses on efficient means to achieve given ends. Marx's claim that we must prove the truth of "human thinking" through transformative practice is far from narrowly instrumental, for it entails the constant redefinition of ends through practical activity. If human beings are both the creators and creatures of their circumstances, a critical praxis entails the ongoing and mutual formation of means and ends as part of the permanent exchange between people and their circumstances. Just as "the educator must be educated," ends must be defined as well as realized by means, and means must prefigure ends. Ends and means mediate each other.

1.9 Marx's thesis eleven (1978) asserts, "The philosophers have only interpreted the world: the point, however, is to change it." As his work shows, radically interpreting the world not only is necessary for transforming it but already changes it.

1.10 Benjamin's thesis eleven (1986) argues for a view of development based on the realization of labor and nature rather than on their exploitation, as proposed by German social democracy's technocratic view of progress. Labor and nature are the twin factors that make up the comparative advantage of the Global South and help structure its ongoing subordination as a region not despite but through the mediation of high-modernist enclaves located in its midst of, and connected economically and culturally to, metropolitan centers. The increasingly evident negative effects of the global exploitation of labor and nature, as it leads to persisting poverty and inequality worldwide, as well as to the destruction of the planet, may open spaces for global alliances toward alternative visions of development. This requires, as Arturo Escobar (1995) has suggested, a negation of development as commonly understood in the modern period, but also, as Enrique Dussel (1998) proposes, the pursuit of a vision of "transmodernity" that recognizes in modernity the ground upon which to construct a more just, harmonious, and plural world; transmodernity involves not a rejection of modernity but its transformation.

2

2.1 There is a vast literature on the complicity between Western academic disciplines and Western dominion. In my view, its fundamental contribution has been to illuminate the connection between the fragmentation of the world into seemingly independent and unequal entities and the reification of knowledge into separate disciplines, each concerned with bounded units. Serious intellectual projects should challenge boundaries that blind us to the processes that have made the world at once interconnected and fragmented. Far from the egotistic "diversity" celebrated by the free market, the Zapatista ideal of a world that can hold multiple worlds is only possible under conditions of inclusive global solidarity and deep democracy.

3

3.1 The concept of knowledge in exile builds on Edward Said's work and renders homage to his memory.

3.2 The warning that not even the dead will be safe so long as the enemy remains victorious comes from Walter Benjamin's thesis six. Much of contemporary history has been shaped by the control through networks of elites, corporations, and states of hydrocarbon energy that belong to humanity, our collective inheritance of organic life in the planet. The hidden struggle over oil and other natural resources in the making of modern history makes particularly evident that what Michel-Rolph Trouillot (1995) called the "silences of the past" extends widely into the present, defining its delusory clarity. (My current book project, *Crude Matters*, centers on the exploration of the opacity of the present through research on the 2002 coup d'état against Hugo Chávez's petro-state and its aftermath.)

4

4.1 The image of a labyrinth whose exits open into another labyrinth comes from Jorge Luis Borges's stories; this image inspired Jacques Derrida's deconstructive work. My use of the notion of a puzzle to be assembled together comes from Subcomandante Marcos (1997), who used it as a metaphor in an article on global capitalism published in *Le Monde Diplomatique*. I use it to evoke a performative epistemology and representational strategy.

5

5.1 The citation about the map comes from Adrienne Rich's "Notes toward a Theory of Location," as cited in my "Beyond Occidentalism: Towards Nonimperial Geohistorical Categories" (1996).

5.2 The citation about an account of the cosmos as "a point" is itself an unreferenced citation of a "modern biologist" in Walter Benjamin's thesis eighteen.

5.3 The reference to the need to include Napoleon's head cold and the actions of humble soldiers in accounts of the battle of Borodino comes from Carlo Ginzburg's comments on Tolstoy's *War and Peace* as an inclusive model of microhistory in "Microhistory: Two or Three Things I Know about It" (1993).

6.1 This reflection about maps as metaphors for positivist science is inspired by Jorge Luis Borges's short story "On Exactitude in Science" (1975). Showing the uselessness of a map that coincides with the empire point by point, his story suggests that any representation is partial in two senses: incomplete and partisan. Its exactitude, and thus the exactitude of science, depends not on its correspondence to reality, but on its significance. If one treats maps not just as objects that represent the world but that perform representing it, their point centers on the effects of their representations—on how they connect their producers and users to the world. Critical knowledge production is not a matter of "filling gaps" so as to make representations more complete (as in much of historical and anthropological work; I owe this insight to David Pedersen), but of creating useful knowledge—producing maps that can guide us toward, and define, desirable ends.

7.1 This piece refers to real figures in imagined situations, except for Ti Noel, an actual character in Carpentier's *The Kingdom of This World* (1957), a novel about the Haitian revolution centering on the life of a common man, Ti Noel, subjected to different forms of oppression under various masters during this revolutionary period.

7.2 Claude Lévi-Strauss's critique of humanism and discussion of multiple temporal scales in *The Savage Mind* (1966) paralyzed Jean-Paul Sartre's effort to write a grand theory of history in *Critique of Dialectical Reason* (1976). In turn, Jacques Derrida undermined Lévi-Strauss's structuralism by questioning the necessarily assumed foundations of any structuralism. (For illuminating discussions, see Gikandi 2005 and Young 1990.) Since any paradigm involves the acceptance, even if tactical, of unproven premises, truth lies on faith, as Sor Juana Inés de la Cruz suspected long ago.

7.3 In the first thesis of his "Theses on the Philosophy of History" (1986), Benjamin criticizes the determinism of historical materialism, yet in the others he endorses an open-ended historical materialism. Sartre's struggle to reconcile these two viewpoints was deeply affected by Lévi-Strauss's critique of his humanism and Eurocentrism.

7.4 The notion that one can see the universe in a grain of sand comes from William Blake (1982), but it derives from medieval theology and cosmologies of nature. Extrapolating from an insight by Nicos Poulantzas (1978: 14) on nation-state formation, this piece suggests that any point anywhere, at any scale (a grain of sand, a square, a nation, an island, a convent), involves the territorialization of a history and the historicization of a territory. Treating such concepts as the "universe" and a "grain of sand" as metaphors for the relationship between wholes and parts, in a discussion of Cuban historiography I suggested that in order to see the universe in a grain of sand one must also see a grain of sand in the universe (Coronil 2003). Yet this programmatic assertion leaves uncharted the hard analytical task of integrating different temporal and spatial scales and finding adequate modalities for representing such visions.

7.5   The image of recovered histories from another star comes from Calvino's *Mt. Palomar* (1985), with gratitude to Genese Sodikoff, who brought his stories to my attention and whose own work on Madagascar, by connecting footprints of laborers in forest preserves to the workings of global capital, shows the complex interweaving of parts and wholes at different scales, as well as the possibility of developing an exemplary narrative to represent this process.

7.6   The notion of multiple universes comes from recent work by physicists on the nature of reality. The figure of 10 to the 500th degree mentioned here represents the number of solutions allegedly credited to string theory—the theory that one metalaw applies to the "multiverse," an entity composed of zillions of universes within which ours is only a granule. It will probably be a while before the social sciences feel at home in Albert Einstein's relative world. At that future time, Mikhail Bakhtin's "chronotrope," inspired by Einstein, will be seen as a pioneering ancestor, but at least for a while, Isaac Newton's notion of absolute space and time probably will continue to define our earthly three-dimensional reality.

8

8.1   The goal of challenging what he called "non-dominative knowledge" comes from Edward Said's sustained critique of the complicity between power and knowledge.

8.2   Critical of German social democracy's notion of progress for being forgetful of past struggles, Benjamin proposed that struggles for a better future should be guided not by images of "liberated grandchildren" but by "hatred" or the "spirit of sacrifice" (1986: 260; thesis twelve). I thank Janam Mukherjee for clarifying my reading of Benjamin. In light of the failure of the revolutions of 1848, Marx invoked a poetics of the future as a guide to radical change. A poetics of the present informs Ortiz's work on Cuba, as well as Derek Walcott's (1998) notion that the love that puts together a broken vase is stronger than the love that created it. Despite their differences, there is an intimate affinity among Benjamin's call to recognize the struggles of the past, Walcott's appreciation of love in the present, Marx's poetics of the future, and Caroline Steedman's (1986) desire to free the present from the burden of the past.

8.3   My word "ruin" here is itself a ruin taken from dialogues with Javier Sanjines, Ann Stoler, and Nicholas Dirks, as well as from Trouillot's (1995) evocation of Haiti's Sans Souci (both the palace and Jean-Baptiste Sans Souci), Benjamin's image of the wreckages of history, and Constantin-François Volnay's recognition of imperial spoils in *Les Ruines, ou Méditations sur le révolutions des empires* (1791).

8.4 A vision of the past as a piling of "wreckage upon wreckage" comes from Benjamin's thesis nine. The quote about transcending the past (ending with a provocative "So what?") comes from the conclusion of Steedman's extraordinary account of working-class longing, *Landscape for a Good Woman* (1986).

8.5 A conception of "struggle" as a quotidian disposition defines an ethical-political position that seeks to find plenitude within history, not outside it. Wrestling against what holds people down may guide scholarly work away from narrow careerism, detached curiosity, antiseptic scientism, abstract aestheticism, or a value-free social science restricted to evaluating means, not ends. If "rationality" is to have any connection with reason, then ends, not just means, have to be subjected to reasonable scholarly examination rather than exiled to the realm of personal preferences. As Trouillot argues in *Silencing the Past* (1995), representations of the horrors of the past lack "authenticity" if they do not engage the horrors of the present. Yet, as Dan Birchok writes me from the midst of his mine-filled fieldwork, "But at the same time, a certain kind of constructive unpurposefulness is also an important part of this endeavor. Too much purpose ruins the opportunities to draw new maps. Perhaps too much purpose is what makes it so difficult to subordinate imagination to a plan (to paraphrase your opening quote)." Perhaps the realization that the blood of the world is on our pages—my reading of Paul Eiss (2011)—would enable us to connect plan and freedom, purpose and imagination in writing our pages.

8.6 The citation about the irony of struggling to struggle comes from Joshua Edwards's "Small Islands Are Largely Themselves, Aphorisms and Poems (Erasures)" (2007).

9

9.1 From its origins to the present, anthropology has confronted the complex problem of integrating different units of analysis at different scales. Perhaps a symptom of the difficulty of relating them to one another is a tendency to define these units as if they were self-contained and to examine them in terms of such binaries such as past and present, diachrony and synchrony, events and structure, society and culture, the material and the ideal, the global and local, and other such polarities. This tendency is present in both British and U.S. anthropology—for instance, in discussions of "social structure and social organization" (Raymond Firth), "process and structure" (Max Gluckman), structure and contingency in "social dramas" (Victor Turner), and "culture" and "society" as treated in the United States by major figures (e.g., Franz Boas, Ruth Benedict, Margaret Mead, David Schneider, Clifford

Geertz, and Marshall Sahlins). While Sahlins's early work, with its focus on material production, privileges "society," his later work treats "culture" as a determining structure; it seems to argue that events make history, but under cultures not of their own choosing. William Sewell (2005) treats Geertz as a theoretician of synchrony and Sahlins as a theoretician of the "event," yet in both cases structures explain events but are not explained by previous events; in this respect, history remains a mystery.

It is revealing that one of the most influential anthropologists of the twentieth century centered his work on the rejection of "history." For Claude Lévi-Strauss, structures define primitive or "cold" societies; events, modern or "hot" societies. In the former, events are turned into structures; in the latter, structures generate events. By freezing history, cold societies reveal the logic of "savage thought," but this thought turns out to be not a particular mode of thinking but the transhistorical structures of a universal Mind. Given the fundamental ahistoricism of his structures, in a pioneering critique of Lévi-Strauss, Octavio Paz (1967) referred to his work as Kantianism without a subject or a transcendental objectivism. Attempts to introduce a temporal dimension in these structures, as in Jean Piaget's genetic structuralism, reveal the difficulty of overcoming the subject-object duality once this duality is posited as a starting point, as with Kant. The reification into polarities of the distinctions between subject and object and diachrony and synchrony was insightfully challenged rather early in the twentieth century in Russia by Volosinov and Bakhtin, who focused their critique on Ferdinand de Saussure's agentless structuralism and Vossler's and Humboldt's voluntaristic subjectivism. As Raymond Williams (1989) noted, their work had little impact on Western social thought, which in an unfortunate fateful turn has come to be framed by the reified polarities defined by Saussure.

The ideas expressed here in poetic verse benefited by the sensibility of Christina Lazaridi and Nomi Stone; my gratitude.

9.2   While mainstream anthropology has often treated "history" (as what happened) as a messy force that disorders "culture," historians since the 1980s, affected by the linguistic turn, have treated "culture" (as an analytical construct of the Geertzian variety) as a meaningful system that helps examine difference not just among different societies separated by space but of the same society at different times.

9.3   Marxists interested in historical change, less prone to restrict social agency to individuals (except for analytical Marxists who favor methodological individualism), have focused on the connection between "objective" conditions and "subjective" meaning (Jean-Paul Sartre) or on the relation among different "structures" or "instances of society" (Louis Althusser). In Sartre's grand historical narrative, totality is an encompassing and evolving historical process defined by universal politics; in Althusser's grand structuralism, totality is a hierarchical system discerned by science. In both cases, even if at any one point historical outcomes can result from individual agency or be dominated by superstructural instances, it is the economy, or the principle of value, that "in the last instance" asserts itself in time—that is, that determines the direction of history.

9.4 Dipesh Chakrabarty (2000) has recently expanded his compelling critique of historiography by making a distinction between the time of History and the times of God and exploring the workings of different historicities in different social formations. His discussion reflects a productive tension of South Asian subaltern scholarship between finely grained historical studies and sharp categorical distinctions between the West, as the home of modernity, and the rest, as the home of difference. A view of capitalist modernity—narrated in the time of history—as a heterogeneous global process shows how diverse historicities and agents are frequently entangled in the same region, even in the home of capital, making it possible, for instance, for Mr. Henry Ford to organize his River Rouge factory according to the logic of capital and yet claim that God "runs his business." For a lucid argument about capitalism as a heterogeneous formation—as "a 'one' that is a 'many'"—that builds on a critical engagement with the work of David Harvey and Chakrabarty, see the work of Vinay Gidwani (2008). In my own work I have sought to examine capitalism as a global process that takes different forms in distinct locations and to view modernity as involving the counterpointal formation of its dominant and subaltern modalities. This view of modernity as a partial totality always in the making allows for the examination of forms of negation and difference not subsumed by capital or defined in relation to it.

9.5 The body of work that Sherry Ortner (1984) famously discussed as practice theory sought to resolve the structure/event conundrum through the analysis of the practical interactions of social agents. Yet the tendency to view society as a sum of self-constituted parts, rather than as a constantly changing ensemble of mutually formed relations, inhibits even interactional perspectives from grasping the ongoing formation of the interacting agents. For instance, while Eric Wolf (1982) famously argued for an interactional view and criticized conceptions of societies as "billiard balls"—as bounded units clashing with one another—his own work presented global capitalism as a self-fashioned overwhelming ball that crushed other societies. The "West" has been shaped not just by capitalist social relations but by a cosmological order that privileges a metaphysics of external relations among independent individuals, often related to one another through the figure of the contract and seen as motivated by relentless pursuit of personal gain. This worldview is so hegemonic that it renders it difficult to imagine different social logics as well as alternative social orders.

9.6   Here this holding together of the knower and the known treats the Heisenberg "uncertainty principle" as a norm not just about knowing but about caring.

10

Many of the notes of other pieces apply to this piece, particularly 9.2–5. As these notes explain, "poetry of the future" refers to Marx's notion of desired futures in the 18th *Brumaire of Louis Bonaparte*. In *The Great Transformation*, Karl Polanyi (1944) suggests that unknown futures are first imagined by poetry, not prose. Yet for Bakhtin, prose, as the medium of heterogeneous voices, not poetry, holds the potential of change through dialogue among diverse subjects. But perhaps the political use of poetry under Stalin affected his conception of poetry as monological. As the poetry of Walt Whitman and Pablo Neruda make evident, poetry, like prose, can imaginatively express not just a single authorial voice but the diverse voices of a multiple humanity.

References

Anzaldúa, Gloria. 1987. *Borderlands: The New Mestiza; La Frontera*. San Francisco, CA: Spiters-Aunt Lute.

Benjamin, Walter. 1986. "Theses on the Philosophy of History." In *Critical Theory since 1965*, ed. Hazard Adams and Leroy Searle, 680–85. Tallahassee: Florida State University Press.

Blake, William. 1982. *The Complete Poetry and Prose of William Blake*. New York: Anchor Books.

Borges, Jorge Luis. 1964. Tlön, Uqbar, Orbis Tertius. In *Labyrinths: Selected Stories and Other Writings*, ed. Donald A. Yates and James E. Irby, 68–81. New York: New Directions.

Borges, Jorge Luis. 1975. "On Exactitude in Science." In *A Universal History of Infamy*, 131. London: Penguin.

Buroway, Michael. 2005. "Provincializing the Social Sciences." In *The Politics of Method in the Social Sciences*, ed. George Steinmetz, 508–26. Durham, NC: Duke University Press.

Calvino, Italo. 1985. *Mr. Palomar*. San Diego, CA: Harcourt Brace Jovanovich.

Carpentier, Alejo. 1957. *The Kingdom of this World*. New York: Farrar, Straus, and Giroux.

Castro-Gómez, Santiago, and Eduardo Mendieta, eds. 1998. *Teorías sin disciplina: Latinoamericanismo, postcolonialidad y globalización en debate*. Mexico City: Miguel Angel Porrúa.

Chakrabarty, Dipesh. 2000. *Provincializing Europe*. Chicago: University of Chicago Press.

Coronil, Fernando. 1996. "Beyond Occidentalism: Towards Nonimperial Geo-historical Categories." *Cultural Anthropology* 11: 51–87.

Coronil, Fernando. 2000. "Towards a Critique of Globalcentrism: Speculations on Capitalism's Nature." *Public Culture* 12: 351–75.

Coronil, Fernando. 2003. "Epílogo: El Universo en un grano de arena, un grano de arena en el universo." In *Sociedad, cultura y vida cotidiana en Cuba, 1878–1917*, ed. José Amador, 290–305. Havana: Centro Marinello.

Coronil, Fernando. 2004. "Latin American Postcolonial Studies and Global Decolonisation." In *Postcolonial Literary Studies*, ed. Neil Lazarus, 221–41. London: Cambridge University Press.

Dussel, Enrique. 1998. "Beyond Eurocentrism: The World System and the Limits of Modernity." In *The Cultures of Globalization*, ed. Fredric Jameson and Masao Miyoshi, 8–31. Durham, NC: Duke University Press.

Edward, Joshua. 2007. "Small Islands Are Largely Themselves, Aphorisms and Poems (Erasures)." Poem presented in the seminar "What's Left in Latin America," University of Michigan, Ann Arbor, winter.

Eiss, Paul. "Notes on the Difficulty of Studying El Pueblo." In Edward Murphy et. al., eds., *Anthrohistory: Unsettling Knowledge, Questioning Discipline*, 37–47. Ann Arbor: University of Michigan Press, 2011.

Escobar, Arturo. 1995. *Encountering Development: The Making and Unmaking of the Third World*. Princeton, NJ: Princeton University Press.

Friedrich, Paul. 1986. *Princes of Naranja: An Essay in Anthrohistorical Method*. Austin: University of Texas Press.

Gidwani, Viney. 2008. *Capital Interrupted: Agrarian Development and the Politics of Work in India*. Minneapolis: University of Minnesota Press.

Gikandi, Simon. 2005. "Poststructuralism and Postcolonial Discourse." In *Postcolonial Literary Studies*, ed. Neil Lazarus, 97–119. London: Cambridge University Press.

Ginzburg, Carlo. 1993. "Microhistory: Two or Three Things I Know about It." *Critical Inquiry* 20: 10–35.

Hinkelammert, Franz J. 2006. *El sujeto de la ley: El retorno del sujeto reprimido*. Caracas: Fundación Editorial El Perro y la Rana.

Lévi-Strauss, Claude. 1966. *The Savage Mind*. Chicago: University of Chicago Press.

Marcos, Subcomandante. 1997. "La 4e guerre mondiale a commencé." *Le Monde Diplomatique*, 1 August, 4–5.

Marx, Karl. 1978. "Theses on Feuerbach" (1888). In *The Marx and Engels Reader*, 2nd ed., ed. Robert C. Tucker, 143–46. New York: W. W. Norton.

Mignolo, Walter. 2000. *Local Histories/Global Designs: Coloniality, Subaltern Knowledge, and Border Thinking*. Princeton, NJ: Princeton University Press.

Ortiz, Fernando. 1995. *Cuban Counterpoint: Tobacco and Sugar*. Durham, NC: Duke University Press.

Ortner, Sherry B. 1984. "Theory and Anthropology Since the Sixties." *Comparative Study in Society and History* 26(1): 126–66.

Paz, Octavio. 1967. *Claude Lévi-Strauss o el nuevo festín de Esopo*. Mexico City: Joaquín Mortiz.

Polanyi, Karl. 1944. *The Great Transformation: The Political and Economic Origins of Our Time*. New York: Farrar & Reinhart.

Poulantzas, Nicos. 1978. *State, Power, Socialism*. London: New Left Books.

Quijano, Aníbal. "Modernity, Identity and Utopia in Latin America." *boundary 2* 20(3): 140–55.

Said, Edward. 2000. *Reflections on Exile and Other Essays*. Cambridge, MA: Harvard University Press.

Santos, Boaventura de Sousa. 1995. *Toward a New Common Sense: Law, Science and Politics in the Paradigmatic Transition*. New York: Routledge.

Sartre, Jean-Paul. *Critique of Dialectical Reason: Theory of Practical Ensembles*, trans. Alan Sheridan-Smith, ed. Jonathan Rée. London: New Left Books.

Sewell, William H., Jr. 2005. *Logics of History: Social Theory and Social Transformation*. Chicago: University of Chicago Press.

Steedman, Carolyn Kay. 1986. *Landscape for a Good Woman. A Story of Two Lives*. New Brunswick, NJ: Rutgers University Press.

Trouillot, Michel-Rolph. 1995. *Silencing the Past: Power and the Production of History*. Boston: Beacon.

Turner, Victor. 1967. *The Forest of Symbols: Aspects of Ndembu Ritual*. Ithaca, NY: Cornell University Press.

Volnay, Constantin-François. 1791. *Les Ruines, ou Méditation sur les révolutions des Empires*. Paris: Desenne.

Walcott, Derek. 1998. "The Antilles: Fragments of Epic Memory." In *What the Twilight Says: Essays*, 65–85. London: Faber and Faber.

Wallerstein, Immanuel, et al. 1996. *Open the Social Sciences: Report of the Gulbenkian Commission on the Restructuring of the Social Sciences*. Stanford, CA: Stanford University Press.

Walsh, Catherine, Freya Schiwy, and Santiago Castro-Gómez, eds. 2002. *Interdisciplinar las ciencias sociales*. Quito: Universidad Andian/Abya Yala.

Williams, Raymond. 1989. *The Politics of Modernism: Against the New Conformists*. London: Verso.

Wolf, Eric. 1982. *Europe and the People without History*. Berkeley: University of California Press.

Young, Robert. 1990. *White Mythologies: Writing History and the West*. New York: Routledge.

2 Transculturation and the Politics of Theory:
Countering the Center, Cuban Counterpoint

Un solo palo no hace monte.
—Cuban proverb

For without exception, the cultural treasures he surveys have an
origin which he cannot contemplate without horror. They owe their
existence not only to the efforts of the great minds and talents of
those who created them, but also to the anonymous toil of their
contemporaries. And just as such a document is not free of barba-
risms, barbarism taints also the manner in which it was transmit-
ted from owner to owner.
—Walter Benjamin

Las obras literarias no están fuera de las culturas sino que las
coronan y en la medida en que estas culturas son invenciones secu-
lares y multitudinarias hacen del escritor un productor que trabaja
con las obras de innumerables hombres. Un compilador, hubiera
dicho Roa Bastos. El genial tejedor, en el vasto taller histórico de la
sociedad americana.
—Ángel Rama

When *Cuban Counterpoint: Tobacco and Sugar* (1940) was published in Cuba,
Fernando Ortiz (1881–1969) had established himself as one of the country's
most influential public intellectuals. Like so many Latin American and Caribbean men of his position and generation, Fernando Ortiz had left his
native land to receive a European education. When he returned to Cuba,
where he remained until his death, he dedicated his life to the study of

---

This piece was originally published as the introduction to Fernando Ortiz, *Cuban Counterpoint:
Tobacco and Sugar*, ed. Fernando Coronil. Durham, NC: Duke University Press, 1995.

its popular traditions. Taking Cuba as his central concern, he addressed issues of national culture and colonialism, supported democratic institutions, promoted cultural organizations and journals, and authored works in areas ranging from criminology to ethnology. In *Cuban Counterpoint*'s prologue, Herminio Portell Vilá, a Cuban historian, insists that there is actually no need to introduce an outstanding work by this prominent author and expresses gratitude that he has been allowed to link his name to that of Don Fernando Ortiz.

Perhaps in Portell Vilá's insistence one may detect a critical commentary on the introduction of the book, authored by the most renowned anthropologist of the time, Bronisław Malinowski. A Polish émigré to England, Malinowski was a leading figure in defining anthropology as a scientific discipline and in conceptualizing fieldwork as the core of its method. In his introduction, Malinowski, then at Yale University, enthusiastically praises Ortiz's ethnographic skills and unabashedly presents the book as an outstanding example of functionalism, the theory of social integration with which Malinowski was closely aligned. He notes in particular his admiration for Ortiz's neologism "transculturation" and vows to employ it himself in his subsequent work: "I promised its author that I would appropriate the new expression for my own use, acknowledging its paternity, and use it constantly and loyally whenever I had occasion to do so" (1947: ix). Before his death in 1942, Malinowski wrote a number of papers and prepared two books, published posthumously. In these works he only used "transculturation" twice.

While I too recognize the privilege of introducing a book that speaks for itself, I acknowledge that, in the words of an earlier contrapuntal author, we necessarily read it "not just as we please, but under circumstances not chosen by ourselves" (Marx 1963: 15). It is difficult to assess the impact of ideas, to trace their origins and circulation, the paths through which they enter disciplinary canons and collective understandings, and the contexts that mark their reception by different publics. It is undeniable that Ortiz's greatest work has received exceptional international recognition; his book was translated into English in 1947, and in 1954 Columbia University, on the occasion of its two-hundredth anniversary, conferred on Ortiz an honorary doctorate. Yet my sense is that, given the conditions shaping its international reception, Ortiz's book has been read in ways that have overlooked aspects of its significance and have left its critical potential undeveloped. By offering a reading of selected sections of the book and of Malinowski's introduction, this essay seeks to enter into a dialogue with these texts, not so much to introduce the book as to make its introduction ultimately unnecessary.

"A written preface," writes Gayatri Spivak in her introductory essay to *Of Grammatology*, "provisionally localizes the place where, between reading and reading, book and book, the inter-inscribing of 'reader(s),' 'writer(s),' and language is forever at work" (Derrida 1974: xii). A reader of Ortiz's *Cuban Counterpoint: Tobacco and Sugar* can readily understand the notion that "the return to the book is also the abandoning of the book" (Spivak quoting Derrida in Derrida 1974: xii), that each reader and each reading of the same book opens up a different book. As Spivak suggests, "The preface, by daring to repeat the book and reconstitute it at another register, merely enacts what is already the case: the book's repetitions are always other than the book. There is, in fact, no 'book' other than these ever-different repetitions" (Spivak 1974: xii). Ortiz would have welcomed a perspective that, while respecting the integrity of a cultural text, recognizes its provisionality and inconclusiveness, the contrapuntal play of text against text and of reader against author. If, indeed, a counterpoint among reader, writer, and language is forever at work, my text pays tribute to Ortiz by engaging in this transcultural exchange, as Ortiz's book does, in counterpoint with the historical conditions of its own making.

Conditions of Reception

The publication of Ortiz's book in 1940 occurred at a time of international and domestic upheaval that frames the concerns of the text and helps explain its allegorical character. Fascism had begun to engulf Western Europe and to challenge the principles, already shaken by World War I, considered fundamental to "Western civilization." In Cuba, the strongman Fulgencio Batista, who controlled the state through intermediaries, gained widespread support and was elected president of the country. By the time Ortiz received his honorary doctorate in 1954, the United States had emerged as the dominant global power and the arbiter of Latin American affairs, and Batista had returned to the presidency of Cuba in 1952 by way of a coup. Batista's dictatorship, backed by the United States, came to an end in 1959 when a guerrilla-led revolution overthrew him and led to the first socialist regime in the Americas.

Cuban Counterpoint has circulated, until recent years, in a world divided into socialist and capitalist camps and modern and backward nations. For Third World nations—and this seemingly indispensable category was also born in the 1940s—socialism and capitalism have commonly been regarded as competing strategies to achieve modernity. While in the Third World, socialism and capitalism have offered competing images of the future, they have shared the assumption that the future, whatever its particular political or economic form, must of necessity be "modern." Ortiz's book did not quite fit the terms of this polarized debate. It was unconventional in form and content, did not express explicitly the wisdom of the times or reiterate prevailing currents of thought, and it proposed neither unambiguous solutions nor a blueprint for the future. Rather than straightforwardly offering an argument, it worked tangentially through poetic allusion, brief theoretical comments, and a detailed historical interpretation.

Half a century later, this edition of *Cuban Counterpoint* addresses a world where cultural differences and political inequalities cannot be mapped in terms of old polarities. The Second World has drastically contracted and transformed, while the First World is decentering and diversifying. Third World "development" programs of neoliberal design are accelerating the fractures within and among the nations of the "periphery." A number of intimately related processes, in which globalizing forms of capital accumulation and communication are met both with transnationalizing and reconfigured nationalist responses, have unsettled certainties associated with the belief in modernity.

Particularly in those intellectual fields shaped by feminist theory, Gramscian Marxism, and poststructuralism, an attempt has been made to develop new perspectives and to bring excluded problems under critical observation. In certain respects, these efforts have helped counter the silencing and stereotyping of subaltern collectivities and revealed their role in the making and the contestation of histories and cultures long represented from the homogenizing perspective of those who hold dominant power. This new edition of *Cuban Counterpoint* enters the space opened by these collective achievements; as an example of engaged cultural analysis, it may contribute to expanding it.

Modernity and Postmodernity:
A Counterpoint from the Margins

Cuban Counterpoint examines the significance of tobacco and sugar for Cuban history in two complementary sections written in contrasting styles. The first, titled "Cuban Counterpoint," is a relatively brief allegorical tale of Cuban history narrated as a counterpoint between tobacco and sugar. The second,

"The Ethnography and Transculturation of Havana Tobacco and the Beginnings of Sugar in America," is a historical essay that adheres loosely to the conventions of the genre. It is divided into two brief theoretical chapters and ten longer historical ones that discuss sociological and historical aspects of the evolution of sugar and tobacco production. Although each chapter can be read as a unit, together they present Ortiz's understanding of Cuban history.[1] Through their counterpoint, the two sections reinforce each other. While each is complex, they place different demands upon the reader. The historical essay is imposing and requires the reader to assimilate a vast amount of information. The brief allegorical essay poses a more unusual challenge: it reads almost too easily.

The allegorical essay seems to pull us in two directions at once. It is as if, through his playful evocation of the pleasures associated with sugar's and tobacco's consumption, Ortiz wishes to seduce us into enjoying the text with sensuous abandon. And yet it is also as if, through the unfolding dramatic plot that compellingly recounts a story of colonial domination, Ortiz wishes us to read this text in the same way that he reads tobacco and sugar: as complex hieroglyphs that elude definitive decoding. Through the interplay of these two readings the essay may seem at once to stand by itself and to call for continuing reinterpretation.

At a time when debates about postmodernity and modernity affect the climate of discussion about Latin America, there may be a desire to receive *Cuban Counterpoint* as a postmodern text on the basis of its unusual formal organization and its evident distance from positivism. There is a certain risk in this appropriation, however, for it is likely to deflect attention from the book's significance as a historical interpretation that seeks to integrate, through innovative methods of investigation and narration, the interplay of cultural forms and material conditions. In my view, Ortiz's analysis of the complex articulation of stabilizing and disruptive forces throughout Cuban history both questions prevailing assumption about the existence of separate "premodern" and "modern" domains and demystifies certain pretensions of modernity itself. In this respect, we may wish to see *Cuban Counterpoint* as offering a historical analysis that can contribute to the understanding of Latin America's deepening social crisis and the emergence of a world at once increasingly interrelated and fractured.

From my position as a Venezuelan anthropologist working in the United States, I wish to approach *Cuban Counterpoint* as a valuable book for these difficult times. I take this text as an invitation to question the conceits of modernity and postmodernity alike. Ortiz shows that the constitution of the modern world has entailed the clash and disarticulation of peoples and civilizations together with the production of images of integrated cultures, bounded identities, and inexorable progress. His counterpoint of cultures makes evident that in a world forged by the violence of conquest and colonization, the boundaries defining the West and its Others, white and dark, man and woman, and high and low are always at risk. Formed and transformed through dynamic processes of transculturation, the landscape of the modern world must constantly be stabilized and represented, often violently, in ways that reflect the play of power in society. If a postmodern vision offers the image of fragmentary cultural formations unmoored from social foundations as an alternative to the modernist representation of integrated cultures rooted in bounded territories, Ortiz's perspective suggests that the formation of this vision be understood in relation to the changing geopolitics of empires. Ortiz invites us to understand the micro-stories of postmodernity and the master narratives of modernity in relation to their respective conditions of possibility, rather than regarding one as epistemologically superior and thus trading the certainties of one age for those of another.

Cuban Counterpoint helps show the play of illusion and power in the making and unmaking of cultural formations. If the self-fashioning of sovereign centers entails the making of dependent peripheries, Ortiz celebrates the self-fashioning of these peripheries, the counterpoint through which people turn margins into centers and make fluidly coherent identities out of fragmented histories. Like other Caribbean thinkers who left their homelands and figure as foundational figures of postcolonial discourse, Fernando Ortiz struggled against Eurocentrism, although within the political and cultural confines of his nation and of reformist nationalist thought. While Ortiz clearly valorizes forms of sociality embedded in certain traditions and is hesitant with respect to the specific form of the future, he does not root identity in the past. His utopia involves less of a rupture with the present than Frantz Fanon's, but like Fanon, Ortiz uses binary oppositions (black and white, West and non-West) in a way that recognizes the experiential value of these terms for people subject to imperial domination but that also refuses to imprison an emancipatory politics in them. His allegorical essay recognizes the play of desire in the construction of colonial oppositions, vividly revealing how the colonial encounter forged cognitive categories as well as structures of sentiment. Ortiz treats binary oppositions not as fixities, but as hybrid and productive, reflecting their transcultural formation and their transitional value in the flow of Cuban history.[2]

Against the imperial alchemy that turns a Western particularity into a model of universality, *Cuban Counterpoint* calls attention to the play of globally interconnected particularities. Given Malinowski's role in establishing the centrality of anthropology as a Western discipline of otherness, there is a certain irony in the counterpoint that occurs between Malinowski and Ortiz. If Malinowski was the metropolitan ethnographer whose "magic" was most responsible for creating the concept of cultures as islands standing outside the currents of history,[3] Ortiz, constructing a perspective from the periphery, viewed cultural boundaries as artifices of power traced precariously on the sands of history.

Ortiz's playful treatment of cultural forms as fluid and unstable in *Cuban Counterpoint* explains the temptation to see him as a postmodern ethnographer *avant la lettre*.[4] Yet we should not forget the significance, in Ortiz's life work, of his critique of Eurocentric categories, his respect for the integrity, however precariously ambivalent, of subaltern cultures, and the attentiveness with which he studied the material constraints within which people make their cultures. I believe Ortiz would endorse Marshall Sahlins's warning concerning certain currents in postmodern ethnography:

> Everyone hates the destruction rained upon the peoples by the planetary conquests of capitalism. But to indulge in what Stephen Greenblatt calls the "sentimental pessimism" of collapsing their lives within a global vision of domination, in subtle intellectual ideological ways makes the conquest complete. Nor should it be forgotten that the West owes its own sense of cultural superiority to an invention of the past so flagrant that it should make natives blush to call other peoples culturally counterfeit. (Sahlins 1993: 381)

In Ortiz's works the concept of "transculturation" is used to apprehend at once the destructive and constructive moments in histories affected by colonialism and imperialism. Through his critical valorization of popular creativity, Ortiz shows how the social spaces where people are coerced to labor and live are also made habitable by them, how in effect power resides not only in the sugar mill but in the rumba. As a liberal democrat who had seen the failure of liberal democracy in Cuba and elsewhere, Ortiz could find little hope in a democratic option for Cuba in 1940. He probably found even less promise in Marxism, given its formulaic application in Cuba. If Ortiz's distrust of theory is related to Antonio Gramsci's "pessimism of the intellect," his analysis of popular culture reflects its counterpart, "the optimism of the will." This optimism takes as its central object the life-affirming creativity with which Cuban popular sectors countered their violent history. As if inspired by Cuban popular tradition, Ortiz offered *Cuban Counterpoint* as his own response to the critical circumstances of his time.

After the revolution in 1959, many professionals left Cuba, but Ortiz remained, conducting research on Cuban culture until his death in 1969. Now, when the promise of a democratic society appears as a receding mirage and the market parading as Freedom haunts much of the world, we may wish to remember how Ortiz found strength in Cuban popular traditions and recognized in them exemplary forms of sociality and creativity.[5]

The Caribbean, formed by a history of colonialism and neocolonialism, cannot be studied without addressing the geopolitics of empires. *Cuban Counterpoint* offers a glimpse into this story that demystifies its ruling fantasies—notions of the authentic native, of separate pure cultures, of a superior Western modernity.[6] Listening to the dialogue between Malinowski and Ortiz today may allow us to participate in their understanding of this history and to trace links between the politics of social theory and the geopolitics of empire. My discussion of these texts is organized into three parts. First, I discuss some of the personal, cultural, and political circumstances in which the book was produced. Second, I offer a reading of the book which centers on its first part.[7] Third, I discuss the politics of theory, through an examination of the counterpoint between Malinowski and Ortiz, and argue for the need to distinguish between theory production and canon formation.

Circumstances

Cuban Counterpoint was published when sixty-year-old Fernando Ortiz was at the height of his creative activity and Cuba was at the end of a tumultuous decade marked by numerous ruptures: domestic upheavals arbitrated by the United States; sharp swings in its U.S.-dependent economy; the collapse of a revolutionary civilian regime in 1933; and the consolidation of the army's power under Fulgencio Batista.

Born in Cuba in 1881 to a Cuban mother and Spanish father, Ortiz spent his youth in Minorca, Spain, where he completed high school. While he went to Cuba in 1895 to study law, the turbulent conditions created by the War of Independence led him to return to Spain to complete his studies. In 1900 he obtained a bachelor's degree in law (*licenciatura*) in Barcelona and the next year a doctorate in Madrid. He returned to Cuba briefly in 1902 but left again to serve as Cuba's consul in Italy and Spain until 1906, when he was appointed public prosecutor for the city of Havana. He resigned from this position in 1916 when he was elected to a seven-year term in Cuba's House of Representatives. Throughout his life he combined academic pursuits with public service. He served several terms in Congress, where he sought to implement liberal political reforms, and in 1923 he headed the Committee of National Civic Restoration, created to combat the rampant corruption of the period.

During the short-lived revolutionary government led by Ramón Grau San Martín in 1933, which the United States refused to recognize, Ortiz was invited to join the cabinet and to offer a plan of reconciliation. While he did not join the regime, he made a proposal for national political unity built on the participation of major groups in Grau's government.[8] The plan was accepted by all; even Sumner Welles, the U.S. ambassador hostile to Grau, found it a "reasonable compromise" (Aguilar 1972: 189). But Ortiz's formula ultimately failed "because of mutual suspicion and past resentment and the internal fragmentation of almost every group involved." With the loss of support for the civilian revolution, the military, headed by Batista, gained control of the state. Unable to rule without U.S. support, Grau went into exile in January 1934. Batista then ruled Cuba by way of puppet presidents until 1940, when he was elected president. This defeat of domestic progressive forces took place at the same time as the Spanish Republic's demise and the advance of fascism in Europe. Concerned with these developments, Ortiz organized La Alianza Cubana por un Mundo Libre (The Cuban Alliance for a Free World) in 1941.

Written in this political context, Cuban Counterpoint was the product of a career that sought, from multiple angles, to interpret Cuban society, analyze the sources of its "backwardness," and valorize the distinctive aspects of its culture. His scholarly work was marked at once by a continuity of concerns and a shift in perspectives. Ortiz's first book, Los negros brujos (1906), was a treatise of criminal anthropology focused on Afro-Cubans, their "superstitions," and their deviance. Framed by evolutionary positivist theories ascendant at the time and adhering to the biological reductionism of the Italian criminologist Cesare Lombroso, who prefaced the book, it analyzed the conditions that promoted the criminality and "backward" beliefs among practitioners of brujería (sorcery) in Cuba. Illustrated with photos of the heads of Afro-Cuban criminals, it exemplified the biological notion of race widely accepted in Europe and the United States and the assumption that those of African descent were a source of social disruption and stagnation.[9]

However, by 1910 Ortiz had begun to develop a sociological approach to race, one that emphasized cultural rather than biological factors as the basis of social progress. Concerned as before with Cuba's "backwardness," Ortiz felt Cubans must recognize their inferiority if they were to advance: "We are inferior, and our great inferiority consists, without doubt, in not acknowledging it, even though we frequently mention it" (Ortiz 1910: 27). But he explained that this inferiority was not due to "our race . . . but our sense of life, our civilization is much inferior to the civilization of England, of America, of the countries that today rule the world." He argued that Cubans could be civilized or uncivilized, like all men, "like those who are victorious, like those more backward ones who still splash around in the mud of barbarism" (Ortiz 1910: 28). Distancing himself from biological essentialism, he argued that people were physically alike; what Cubans needed, he argued, was "not a brain to fill the skull, but ideas to flood it and to wipe out its drowsiness. . . . We only lack one thing: civilization."[10] The "civilization" that Cubans needed, however, was European. Ortiz, in effect, transcoded biological signs into cultural signs, adopting at this time a racially marked evaluation of civilizing progress.[11]

The cause of Cuba's backwardness, of the corruption of its politicians, of the precariousness of its institutions was attributed to the influence of the sugar industry by the historian Ramiro Guerra y Sánchez in his highly influential *Azúcar y población en las Antillas* (1927), published at a time of heightened authoritarianism under President Gerardo Machado. This study profoundly affected a generation of intellectuals involved in the struggle for political reform and honesty in public life. In Guerra y Sánchez's analysis, Afro-Cubans figured as victims of the giant sugar factories that dominated the Cuban economy rather than as a source of Cuban culture.

For this reason, it is likely that Oswald Spengler's widely read work *The Decline of the West* (1918, translated into Spanish in 1923) exercised a greater influence on Ortiz. Its depiction of multiple paths leading toward historical development encouraged many Latin American intellectuals during the interwar period to view their societies as occupying not a lower stage in the unilineal development of Western civilization, but a unique position in a different historical pattern, one informed by its greater spiritual qualities and by the revitalizing mixture of races (Skurski 1994). Latin America no longer had to be seen as an incomplete version of Europe, but as an alternative to it.

The journal *Revista de Occidente*, founded by the Spanish philosopher José Ortega y Gasset in 1923, made German philosophy and historiography available to a generation of Cuban intellectuals, for whom it provided intellectual resources with which to redefine Cuban identity (González Echevarría 1977: 52–60). According to the Cuban novelist Alejo Carpentier, the journal became "our guiding light." It helped forge new links between Cuba and Spain, like the Spanish-Cuban Cultural Institute over which Ortiz presided (González Echevarría 1977: 53). Spain, because of its own marginality within Europe, became a conduit for German thought, especially that of Spengler, which provided a compelling vision of historical diversity. As González Echevarría suggests,

> Spengler offers a view of Universal history in which there is no fixed center, and where Europe is simply one more culture. From this arises a relativism in morals and values: no more acculturation of blacks, no need to absorb European civilization. Spengler provided the philosophical ground on which to stake the autonomy of Latin American culture and deny its filial relation to Europe. (González Echevarría 1977: 56)[12]

The shift in Ortiz's evaluation of the Afro-Cuban population and his concern for establishing the foundations of Cuban nationhood can be better understood in the light of this influence. Ortiz's alternative conception of Latin American development revalorizes popular and regional cultures but maintains a modified evolutionary framework (evidenced, for example, in his conception of cultural stages presented in the introduction to the second half of *Cuban Counterpoint*). Thus, while he keeps a notion of levels of cultural development, and in this respect, reproduces certain biases concerning primitive and advanced civilizations, he significantly revalorizes contemporary Latin American cultures. Thus, in his *Africanía de la música folklórica en Cuba*, he seeks to establish the universal value of African and Afro-Cuban music, and to relativize European music as the standard of accomplishment. Ironically, to achieve this aim, Ortiz invokes the authoritative words of a European intellectual, Marcel Mauss: "Our European music is but *a* case of music, it is not *the* music" (Ortiz [1950] 1965: 331; my translation).

Cuban Counterpoint, like Guerra y Sánchez's book, was published in the context of a strongman's consolidation. But Ortiz's book, in contrast, is a highly metaphorical interpretation of Cuban history. Its framework is not positivist, but literary, and it is modeled after the work not of Lombroso, Guerra y Sánchez, or even Spengler, but of the medieval Spanish poet Juan Ruiz, the archpriest of Hita.

The core of Ortiz's book is its first section. It creates a playful counterpoint between sugar and tobacco that is modeled, according to Ortiz, on Ruiz's allegorical poem "Pelea que ovo Don Carnal con Doña Cuaresma," and inspired by Cuban popular traditions: the antiphonal liturgy prayers of both whites and blacks, the erotic controversy in dance measures of the rumba, and the versified counterpoint of *guajiros* and the Afro-Cuban *curros* (Ortiz 1947: 4).[13] While Ruiz set Carnival and Lent in a contest against each other, Ortiz engaged sugar and tobacco in a theatrical interaction structured around their contrasting attributes.

Ortiz's use of allegory not only draws on this long-established literary form, but speaks as well to an allegorical literary tradition influential in Latin America's republican era. In the foundational novels of the nascent republics, as Doris Sommer argues, national political conflicts and the romantic ties of a couple from differing origins mirror each other, charting a resolution to divisions in the polity and family through the formation of desire for the nation (Sommer 1991).[14] As icons of opposing regions and ways of life, the pair integrates the fractured social collectivity.

In *Cuban Counterpoint*, Ortiz offers an interpretation of Cuba's social evolution narrated through the actions of sugar and tobacco, products he introduces as "the two most important figures in the history of Cuba" (1947: 4). Throughout the book he emphasizes their contrasting properties:

> Sugar cane lives for years, the tobacco plant only a few months. . . . The one is white, the other dark. Sugar is sweet and odorless; tobacco bitter and aromatic. Always in contrast! Food and poison, waking and drowsing, energy and dream, delight of the flesh and delight of the spirit, sensuality and thought, the satisfaction of an appetite and the contemplation of a moment's illusion, calories of nourishment and puffs of fantasy, undifferentiated and commonplace anonymity from the cradle and aristocratic individuality recognized wherever it goes, medicine and magic, reality and deception, virtue and vice. Sugar is she; tobacco is he. Sugar cane was the gift of the gods, tobacco of the devils; she is the daughter of Apollo, he is the offspring of Persephone. (1947: 6)

He also establishes their profound impact on Cuban society and culture:

> In the economy of Cuba there are also striking contrasts on the cultivation, the processing, and the human connotations of the two products. Tobacco requires delicate care, sugar can look after itself; the one requires continual attention, the other involves seasonal work; intensive versus

extensive cultivation; steady work on the part of a few, intermittent jobs for many; the immigration of whites on the one hand, the slave trade on the other; liberty and slavery; skilled and unskilled labor; hands versus arms; men versus machines; delicacy versus brute force. The cultivation of tobacco gave rise to the small holding; that of sugar brought about the great land grants. In their industrial aspects tobacco belongs to the city, sugar to the country. Commercially the whole world is in the market for our tobacco, while our sugar has only a single market. Centripetence and centrifugence. The native versus the foreigner. National sovereignty as against colonial status. The proud cigar band as against the lowly sack. (1947: 6–7)[15]

The contrasts of tobacco and sugar thread throughout the book and present themselves as a series of oppositions. However, they have unexpected alignments that destabilize notions of fixed polarity: indigenous-foreign; dark-light; tradition-modernity; unique-generic; quality-quantity; masculine-feminine; artisan production-mass production; seasonal time-mechanical time; independent producers-monopoly production; generates middle classes-polarizes classes; "native" autonomy-Spanish absolutism; national independence-foreign intervention; world market-U.S. market.

These contrasts, while first described in Lombrosian fashion as deriving from the "biological distinction" between tobacco and sugar (1947: 4), unfold not as fixed qualities but as themselves hybrid products. While tobacco is seen as male, its biological variety is seen as female. Tobacco is variously linked to the native (as an indigenous plant), to the European (as cultivated by white smallholders), to the uniquely Cuban (as a transcultural product); it is related to the satanic, to the sacred, and to the magical. Although in its finished form it is an icon of Cuba's identity, it symbolizes foreign capital's control as well. Linked to the violent history of indigenous, white colonist, and slave labor, tobacco has become a unique Cuban creation, leading Ortiz to call it "mulatto." Similarly, sugar's contrasts also change, as both a modernizing and an enslaving force identified with foreign domination as well as with Afro-Cuban labor. Their qualities are contradictory and multiple, carrying with them the marks of their shifting histories. In an encompassment of diverse attributes typical of the baroque, tobacco and sugar incorporate multiple meanings and transform their identities. As paradigmatic metaphors, they acquire new meanings by being placed within a syntagmatic structure through which they express a changing historical flow.

Yet this apparent mutability, which historicizes racial categories and productive relations, is stabilized by Ortiz's tendency to naturalize gender and to use common values associated with the masculine and the feminine as standards for valorization.[16] Tobacco tends to be masculine and to represent the more desirable features in Cuban culture; sugar, in contrast, stands for the feminine and represents the most destructive features of foreign capitalism. Quality and uniqueness become, in this alignment, strongly associated with masculinity and the national, whereas quantity and homogeneity are, in seeming paradox linked to femininity and the international. Yet this paradox points to his representation of the character of capitalism on the periphery. While capitalism is powerful and therefore masculine, capitalism in the periphery is dependent and therefore feminine. As a dependent fragment in an expanding system of international capitalist relations, Cuba appears as feminized even as it is modernized, neocolonized rather than developed. The feminine becomes the sign of weakness and of seduction. As a result, Cuba, as a ground for national identity, appears contradictorily as essential and as constructed, as a metaphysical entity and as a historical product.

As metaphorical constructs condensing a multiplicity of meanings, tobacco and sugar stand for themselves, as agricultural products, as well as for their changing conditions of production. Tobacco represents a native plant from which is made a product of great individuality and uniqueness, but also relations of production marked by domestic control over the labor process, individual craftsmanship, and the flexible rhythms of seasonal time. Sugar, on the other hand, represents not only a generic product derived from an imported plant, but also stands for industrial capitalist relations of production that reduce people to commodities, homogenize social relations and products, and subject labor to the impersonal discipline of machine production and to the fixed routines of mechanical time.

Symbols both of commodities and of productive relations, tobacco and sugar become defined reflexively by the conditions of production that they represent. This reciprocal interplay between products and their generative historical contexts constitutes a second counterpoint. As both products come under the impact of the capitalist forces, they become less differentiated, and their attributes converge. They represent not only distinctive qualities or identities, but also their mutability under changing conditions.

Thus, the social identities of tobacco and sugar emerge from the interplay between their biological makeup and their productive relations. Except for certain aspects of their gendering, there is little that remains essential about them, for their biological attributes are mediated by human activity and modified by evolving patterns of production and consumption. Thus, in the last pages of the book's allegorical section, just when Ortiz identifies sugar with Spanish absolutism and tobacco with Cuban nationalism, he clarifies: "But today, unfortunately, this capitalism which is not Cuban by birth or by inclination, is reducing everything to the same common denominator" (1947: 71). He returns to this idea in the conclusion of this section: "We have seen the fundamental differences that existed between them (tobacco and sugar) from the beginning until machines and capitalism gradually ironed out these differences, dehumanized their economy, and made their problems more and more similar" (1947: 93).

The playful construction of contrasts between tobacco and sugar meets its counter in the sobering image of capital's growing domination of Cuban society. As Ortiz states in the conclusion of the book, in the face of this domination "many peoples and nations may find in tobacco their only temporary refuge for their oppressed personalities" (1947: 309). Yet Ortiz's work offers no predictions and seeks no closure.[17] Instead, the first section suggests a utopian solution in the form of a fairy tale. Asserting that "there was never any enmity between sugar and tobacco," Ortiz constructs a historical possibility that envisions the marriage, à la family romance, of Cuba's central actors, much as he had proposed a unifying alliance to resolve the political crisis of 1933:

> Therefore it would be impossible for the rhymesters of Cuba to write a "Controversy between Don Tobacco and Doña Sugar," as the roguish archpriest would have liked. Just a bit of friendly bickering, which should end, like the fairy tales, in marrying and living happily ever after. The marriage of tobacco and sugar, and the birth of alcohol, conceived of the unholy ghost, the devil, who is the father of tobacco, in the sweet womb of wanton sugar. The Cuban Trinity: tobacco, sugar and alcohol. (1947: 93)

It is poetic justice that in the end, tobacco and sugar, these impersonators who had taken the license to borrow so many human attributes, reciprocate by becoming models of the generative powers of the Cuban people.

This utopian allegory, however, bears the marks of its intellectual origins within an elite discourse of reformist nationalism. It conjures up the "unity of a collectivity" (Jameson 1981: 291) by means of a trope of the liberal imagination with deep roots in Latin American fiction: a fruitful marriage, compromise and fusion, rather than conflict or transformation.

Ortiz envisioned national unity attained by making the productive relations established under colonialism the basis of Cuban culture. Yet alcohol, like tobacco and sugar, could not escape the expanding grip of monopoly capital or stimulate more than a transient illusion of community within a fractured nation. Ortiz's utopia was imagined within the confining landscape of a neo-colonial commodity-producing society, revealing, once again, how utopia and ideology set the limits of each other in the battle over history.

Transculturation

This suggestion of utopia is followed by a sober second section where Ortiz presents an amply documented study of the evolution of tobacco and sugar production in Cuba. The historical discussion begins with an unusual introduction of seven pages divided into two chapters. The first, titled "On Cuban Counterpoint," is a two paragraph chapter in which he explains that the second section is intended to give the preceding "schematic essay" supporting evidence. Yet he warns against a simplistic reading of the first section: "[The first section] makes no attempt to exhaust the subject nor does it claim that the economic, social, and historical contrasts pointed out between the two great products of Cuban industry are all as absolute and clear-cut as they would sometimes appear. The historic evolution of economic-social phenomena is extremely complex, and the variety of factors that determine them cause them to vary greatly in the course of their development" (1947: 97).

The second chapter is titled "On the Social Phenomenon of 'Transculturation' and Its Importance in Cuba." As if to mark his distaste for "theory," Ortiz begs the reader's permission for introducing the neologism "transculturation." His introduction of this term comes in two parts. First, he explains that he is "employing for the first time" the term "transculturation," and invites others to follow him: "I venture to suggest that it might be adopted in sociological terminology, to a great extent at least, as a substitute for the term acculturation, whose use is now spreading." He explains that acculturation is being used to describe the process of transition from one culture to another and its manifold social repercussions, but asserts that transculturation is a more fitting term. Transculturation provides a larger conceptual framework within which to place the unpredictable features of Cuban society; it helps us understand "the highly varied phenomena that have come about in Cuba as a result of the extremely complex transmutations of culture that have taken place here, and without a knowledge of which it is impossible to understand the evolution of the Cuban folk, either in the economic or in the institutional, legal, ethical, religious, artistic, linguistic, psychological, sexual, or other aspects of its life" (1947: 98).

Making his strongest claim, Ortiz asserts, "The real history of Cuba is the history of its intermeshed transculturations." Whose transculturation makes up "the real history of Cuba"—that of tobacco and sugar? But sugar and tobacco now recede to the background of the narrative. Ortiz instead reviews the array of "human groups" that have populated the island over its history, from Indians to contemporary immigrants. He gives close attention to the violent conditions in which African slaves were forced to become part of these vast processes:

> There was. . . . the transculturation of a steady human stream of African Negroes coming from all the coastal regions of Africa along the Atlantic from Senegal, Guinea, the Congo, and Angola and as far away as Mozambique on the opposite shore of that continent. All of them snatched from their original social groups, their own cultures destroyed and crushed under the weight of the cultures in existence here, like sugar cane ground in the rollers of the mill.

Following the forced African migration "began the influx of Jews, French, Anglo-Saxons, Chinese, and the peoples from the four quarters of the globe. They were all coming to a new world, all on the way to a more or less rapid process of transculturation" (1947: 102). According to Ortiz,

> There was no more important human factor in the evolution of Cuba than these continuous, radical, contrasting geographic transmigrations economic and social, of the first settlers, the perennially transitory nature of their objectives, and their unstable life in the land where they were living, in perpetual disharmony with the society from which they drew their living. Men, economies, cultures, ambitions were all foreigners here, provisional, changing, "birds of passage" over the country at its cost, against its wishes, and without its approval. (1947: 101)

After making this point, Ortiz elaborates the concept of transculturation by contrasting it to the English term "acculturation." Evidently referring to the way the concept has been actually used in anthropological studies (rather than to the way it has been formally defined), he argues that acculturation implies the acquisition of a culture in a unidirectional process. Instead, transculturation suggests two phases: the loss or uprooting of a culture ("deculturation") and the creation of a new culture ("neoculturation"). He thus places emphasis on both the destruction of cultures and on the creativity of cultural unions. Giving credit to Malinowski's school for this idea, he says that cultural unions, like genetic unions between individuals, lead to offspring that partake of elements of both sources and yet are different from them.[18]

Ortiz insists that the concept of transculturation is indispensable for an understanding of Cuba, "whose history, more than that of any other country of America, is an intense, complex, unbroken process of transculturation of human groups, all in a state of transition" (1947: 103). Yet far from restricting this term to Cuba, he argues that, for analogous reasons, transculturation is fundamental for understanding the history of "America in general." He left it for others to apply this concept to societies in which native peoples remained an important sector of the population. It was through his analysis, more than through his brief formal definition, that Ortiz showed his understanding of transculturation.

Counterfetishism

While in the first section of *Cuban Counterpoint* we are told that "the most important personages of Cuban history" are sugar and tobacco, in the second section we learn that "the real history of Cuba" is made up of "the intermeshed transmigrations of people." What is the significance of this apparent contradiction, of this shift from commodities to people as the central characters of Cuban history?

Perhaps it is related to the strange effect the book produces upon its readers. The more Ortiz tells us about tobacco and sugar, the more we feel we learn about Cubans—their culture, musicality, humor, uprootedness; their baroque manner of refashioning their identities by integrating the fractured meanings of multiple cultures. Imperceptibly, we likewise begin to understand the social forces that have conditioned the ongoing construction of Cuban identities within the context of colonial and neocolonial relations. How is it that a book about two commodities produces this effect?

The mystery of this effect, and the apparent contradiction between these two views, is perhaps resolved by realizing that Ortiz treats tobacco and sugar as highly complex metaphorical constructs that represent at once material things and human actors. Moreover, by showing how these things/actors are defined by their social intercourse under specific conditions, he illuminates the forces shaping the lives of the real actors of Cuban history—of Africans

"like sugar cane ground in the rollers of the mill," or of Cuban national-
ists turned into interventionists, like the tobacco of the foreign-controlled
cigarette industry.

Ortiz, in my view, uses the fetish power of commodities as a poetic
means to understand the society that produces them.[19] Without making
reference to Marx, he shows how the appearance of commodities as independent entities—as potent agents in their own right—conceals their origins in conflictual relations of production and confirms a commonsense
perception of these relations as natural and necessary. The meaningful
misrepresentation that occurs when social relations appear encoded as the
attribute not of people, but of things, transforms commodities into opaque
hieroglyphs, whose mysterious power derives from their ability to misrepresent and conceal reality, and whose multiple meanings can only be deciphered through social analysis.

By constructing a playful masquerade of tobacco and sugar, Ortiz links
the fetish to the poetic and transgressive possibilities of the carnivalesque.
Using the idiom of fetishized renderings of Cuban culture, he presents a
counterfetishistic interpretation that challenges essentialist understandings of Cuban history. In this respect, his work resonates with Walter Benjamin's treatment of fetishism. Unlike other members of the Frankfurt
School, who were primarily concerned with demystifying the fetish in the
service of reality, Benjamin sought to apprehend how the fetish commands
the imagination, at once revealing and appreciating its power of mystification. By treating tobacco and sugar not as things but as social actors, Ortiz in
effect brings them back to the social world that creates them—re-socializes
them, as it were—and in so doing illuminates the society that has given rise
to them. The relationships concealed through the real appearance of commodities as independent forces become visible once commodities are treated
as what they are: social things impersonating autonomous actors.

As the narrative unfolds, tobacco and sugar indeed become historical
personages; they appear as social actors with political preferences, personal passions, philosophical orientations, and even sexual proclivities. It
becomes clear that tobacco and sugar, far from mere things, are changing figures defined by their intercourse with surrounding social forces. By turning
them into full-fledged social actors, Ortiz has shown that they can appear as
autonomous agents only because they are in fact social creatures—that is,
the products of human interaction within the context of capitalist relations
of production. Like Marx (1981: 969), who by personifying Madame la Terre

and Monsieur le Capital in *Capital* highlighted their fetishization in capitalist society, Ortiz simultaneously presents sugar and tobacco as consummate impersonators and unmasks them.

The book's conclusion makes this clear. It follows an account of how Havana tobacco was accepted in Europe and its cigars "became the symbol of the triumphant capitalist bourgeoisie" and how the democratic cigarette eventually replaced the cigar, affecting in turn how these commodities were produced: "But cigars and cigarettes are now being made by machines just as economy, politics, government, and ideas are being revised by machines. It may be that many peoples and nations now dominated by the owners of machines can find in tobacco their only temporary refuge for their oppressed personalities" (Ortiz 1947: 309).

Tobacco, the symbol of Cuban independence, of exceptional skill and unique natural factors, appears now as an increasingly homogenized mass product controlled by foreign interests, like sugar. But at this stage the issue is not to dissolve once again the sharp contrasts established earlier between tobacco and sugar, but to unmask these pretentious actors as mere creatures of human activity. The point is not so much that they are the products of machines, but of machines producing under specific social relations. At the end of the book, the owners of the machines emerge as the leading actors, for they dominate the structure and aims of production.

Similarly, at the conclusion of the first section, as the counterpoint of tobacco and sugar comes to the end, the pursuit of money and power emerges as a major force structuring the pattern of Cuban transculturations ever since the conquest. Ortiz approvingly quotes Ruiz's verses on the powers of money, the commodity that stands for all commodities, the universal fetish:

Throughout the world Sir Money is a most seditious man
Who makes a courtesan a slave, a slave a courtesan
And for his love all crimes are done since this old earth began. (1947: 81)

The chase after money and power in Cuba had helped fashion a social world that trapped them in subordinate relation to external conditions beyond their control. As Portell Vilá explains, "A difference of half a cent in the tariff on the sugar we export to the United States represents the difference between a national tragedy in which everything is cut, from the nation's budget to the most modest salary, even the alms handed to a beggar, and a so-called state of prosperity, whose benefits never reach the people as a whole or profit Cuba as a nation" (Ortiz 1947: xix). Just as money could "make a courtesan a slave," it made tobacco, the emblem of distinction, into a mass product like sugar. At the end, Cubans, with no control over the winds of history, appear as "birds of passage," transient creatures with fluid identities.

Without referring to parties, groups, or personalities, Ortiz depicts the dynamics of neocolonial Cuba, the malleable loyalties and identities of its major actors, the provisional character of its arrangements and institutions, the absence of control over its productive relations. He had seen how no political principle was secure; noninterventionists asked the U.S. ambassador to intervene, pro-civilians allied themselves with the military, advocates of honesty became masters of corruption. In Ortiz's narrative no names need to be mentioned, for tobacco and sugar act as a mirror in which one could see reflected familiar social identities.

By casting commodities as the main actors of his historical narrative, Ortiz at once displaces the conventional focus on human historical protagonists and revalorizes historical agency. Acting as both objects and subjects of history, commodities are shown to be not merely products of human activity, but active forces that constrain and empower it. Thus, historical agency comes to include the generative conditions of agency itself. As a critique of reification, Ortiz's counterfetishism questions both conservative interpretations that reduce history to the actions of external forces and humanist and liberal conceptions that ascribe historical agency exclusively to people. His counterfetishism encompasses a critique of Western humanism's essentialization of the individual and its hierarchization of cultures. As Paul Eiss argues, Ortiz enacts not only a counterfetishism, but a counterhumanism: "In addition to unmasking human social relations hidden in the apparent activity of commodities, Ortiz unmasks the agency of commodities which is hidden in apparently human agencies or characteristics. Ortiz's counterhumanism not only constitutes a brilliant spatial critique, but also challenges stable narratives and identities of colonial and neocolonial history" (Eiss 1994: 35). Transculturation thus breathes life into reified categories, bringing into the open concealed exchanges among peoples and releasing histories buried within fixed identities.

Counterpoints of Theory: Malinowski and Ortiz

Given Malinowski's international academic reputation, it is understandable that Ortiz, whose prestige was local, would welcome the opportunity to have Malinowski introduce his book. He regarded transculturation as a critical concept that countered prevailing anthropological theory by directing attention to the conflictual and creative history of colonial and neocolonial cultural formations; it offered the possibility of recasting not solely Cuban history, but that of "America in general." In all likelihood he felt that the endorsement of a metropolitan authority of Malinowski's stature would help gain him recognition.

Ortiz acknowledges, with a tone of formal correctness, Malinowski's "approbation" of his new term. At the close of his introduction to *Cuban Counterpoint's* second half, in which he presents his concept of transculturation, Ortiz adopts an impersonal tone and uses the passive voice when recounting the granting of approval by this intellectual authority: "When the proposed neologism, transculturation, was submitted to the unimpeachable authority of Bronisław Malinowski, the great figure in contemporary ethnography and sociology, it met with his instant approbation" (Ortiz 1947: 103). Resuming his characteristically direct narration, Ortiz explains that "under his eminent sponsorship, I have no qualms about putting the term in circulation." Yet he makes no further comment on Malinowski's introduction.

Malinowski is more explicit. He recounts in his introduction that he visited Cuba in 1939 and was pleased to meet Ortiz, whose work he had admired. He was enthusiastic about his plan to introduce the term "transculturation" as a replacement for the prevailing terms relating to cultural contact ("acculturation, diffusion; cultural exchange, migrations or osmosis of culture"). After stating that he promised Ortiz he would use it in the future, Malinowski recounts that "Dr. Ortiz then pleasantly invited me to write a few words with regard to my 'conversion' in terminology, which is the occasion for the following paragraphs" (1947: ix).

Just as it is reasonable to assume that Ortiz hoped to receive international validation through Malinowski's authority, we may surmise that Malinowski sought to consolidate his own reputation and that of functionalism by supporting while aligning with his own theoretical position the work of a noted anthropologist from the margins. The introduction reflects the tension between these two aims. At one level, Malinowski highlights the importance and originality of the book. He praises Ortiz's style and mastery of ethnographic materials, offers an appreciative exegesis of the book's argument, and recognizes the validity of the term "transculturation." Moreover, he supports plans for the creation in Cuba of an international research center. In brief, the introduction expresses strong support for the work of a peripheral ethnographer by a metropolitan anthropologist, an unusual and significant gesture.[20]

At another level, however, the introduction assimilates Ortiz's project into Malinowski's own, blunting its critical edge and diminishing its originality. This assimilation takes place through three related moves. First, Malinowski aligns Ortiz's transculturation with his own ideas concerning cultural contact; second, he defines Ortiz as a functionalist without evidence that this is the case; third, he reads *Cuban Counterpoint* literally as a book on tobacco and sugar, as material objects, without attending to their complex cultural structure as commodities and to the critical use Ortiz makes of this complexity. Let me explain these points further.

First, Malinowski presents as Ortiz's the notion that "the contact, clash and transformation of cultures cannot be conceived as the complete acceptance of a given culture by any one 'acculturated' group" (1947: xii) and supports it by quoting two statements from a 1938 article he wrote on cultural contact in Africa. These quotes, focusing on cultural "ingredients" and "typical phenomena of cultural exchanges"—"schools and mines, Negro places of worship and native courts of justice, grocery stores and country plantations"—present the idea that cultural contact affects both cultures and results in new cultural realities. While a sound idea, this formulation is well within the framework presented in the memorandum on "acculturation" by Robert Redfield, Ralph Linton, and Melville Herskovits (1936), considered the definitive statement on the subject at the time.[21]

During the 1930s, as the subjects of anthropological study could no longer be kept within the "slots" of the "primitive" and the "traditional" where they had been contained,[22] British and American anthropology renewed their theoretical concern with issues of cultural diffusion and contact. Through studies of culture contact in England and "acculturation" in the United States, anthropologists not only redefined the objects of anthropological study but also addressed issues of contemporary relevance. In a review of acculturation studies, Ralph Beals (1955: 622) remarks that "the obvious utility of acculturation studies for the solution of practical problems was also a factor in their early popularity." According to him, this sense of "utility" was not unrelated to the exercise of state power in the colonies and at home: "The beginnings of interest in contact situations in Great Britain, France, and Holland coincided with the rise of a new sense of responsibility toward colonial peoples, while in the United States the great development of acculturation studies coincided with the Depression era and its accompanying widespread concern with social problems" (Beals 1955: 622).

At this time British anthropology shifted its focus, geographically, from the Pacific to Africa and thematically from the study of pristine cultures to the study of "cultural contact." Malinowski was best known for his path-breaking *The Argonauts of the Western Pacific* (1922), a study of the Trobriand Islanders in which he defined anthropology as the study of culture as an integrated whole suspended in time. He adapted to this shift in focus, however, and defined as "the real subject-matter of field-work. . . . not the reconstruction of a pre-European native of some fifty or a hundred years ago," but "the changing Melanesian or African (Malinowski 1935: 480). His reason was the native's contact with the Western world: "He has already become a citizen of the world, is affected by contacts with the world-wide civilization, and his reality consists in the fact that he lives under the sway of more than one culture."

Malinowski had come to recognize not only that cultural contact entailed the transformation of both cultures leading to the formation of a new one, but also that colonial politics needed to be included in the ethnography of African societies. He had developed a three-column approach to the study of contact situations whereby data were placed in the appropriate column, thus mapping out the three phases of culture change: impinging culture; receiving culture; compromise and change. This model is refined in his book *The Dynamics of Cultural Change*, edited by Phyllis M. Kaberry and published posthumously in 1945.[23] Yet in this work, composed of notes and papers written between 1936 and his death in 1942, he continues to treat social change taxonomically, without attending to its historical or cultural depth. Malinowski's "Method of the Study of Culture Contact" in this book is evaluated by Beals as "a rather mechanical organization for analytical purposes." The three columns now have become five:

> (A) white influences, interests and intentions; (B) process of culture contact and change; (C) surviving forms of tradition; (D) reconstructed past; and (E) new forces of African spontaneous reintegration or reaction. The discussion and illustrations utilized adhere rigidly to Malinowski's classical functionalist approach save for a slight and grudging bow to time elements in the category of the "reconstructed past." The "method" is also focused directly upon Africa and upon administrative problems. (Beals 1955: 630)

This five-column approach was only a partial improvement over his previous scheme. The two new columns—"reconstructed past" and "new forces of spontaneous African reaction"—did little to add a historical dimension. According to Beals (1955: 631), "Malinowski, on the whole remained intransigent to the end concerning history, despite his inclusion of a column for the 'Reconstructed Past' in his outline tables. This indeed he really viewed not as a 'reconstructed past' but as a past remembered." His disciple Lucy Mair stated, "Of the specimen charts which are published in *The Dynamics of Culture Change*, only that on warfare contains entries under both of these heads and his comment on the reconstruction of the past is that, though of interest for the comparative study of warfare, it is 'of no relevance whatever for the application of anthropology'" (Mair 1957: 241).

Functionalism's attempt to address cultural change in colonial Africa did not lead to a reevaluation of its assumptions, but to the domestication of colonial history: conflict was contained within integration and transformation within reproduction. Thus, "savage" cultures remained safely subsumed by European civilization. We will never know what kind of book Malinowski would have written had he lived longer, but given his taxonomic treatment of change in the works that constitute *The Dynamics of Culture Change*, it is understandable that he did not engage Ortiz's work or even mention the term "transculturation."

Second, Malinowski, rather than distancing himself from Ortiz, sought to include him in his camp. In the introduction to *Cuban Counterpoint*, he refers to Ortiz as a functionalist three times. Given Malinowski's aversion to history, his insistence on casting Ortiz as a functionalist is telling, particularly since he presents Ortiz's extensive use of history as an expression of functionalist principles: "Like the good functionalist that he is, the author of this book resorts to history when it is really necessary" (1947: xiv).

Apparently, Malinowski believes history became "really necessary" for Ortiz as a tool to study changing patterns of tobacco and sugar production, independent of colonialism or imperialism. He construes these products as a source of pride for Ortiz, who,

> Cuban by birth and by citizenship, is justly proud of the role his country has played in the history of sugar, through the vast production of its centrals and in that of smoking, through having developed in its vegas the best tobacco in the world. . . . He describes the triumphal march of tobacco all over the face of the globe and determines the profound influence exerted by sugar on the civilization of Cuba, its principal effect having been, perhaps, to occasion the importation from Africa of the many and uninterrupted shiploads of black slave workers. (1947: xv)

Ortiz refers to tobacco and sugar as two sources of pride for Cuba, as "the country that produced sugar in the greatest quantity and tobacco in the finest quality" (1947: 92–93). Yet his analysis suggests how problematic the sense of national identification through these two commodities was. As we have seen, Ortiz had sought to find in the reflections of a sugar crystal a history of colonial domination. Ortiz's pride was not in the volume of sugar produced in Cuba but in the creation of a culture in Cuba that countered the degradation of this history; the quality of its tobacco served as a metaphor of Cuba's unique culture.

"Was Ortiz really a functionalist?" asks the Cuban historian Julio Le Riverend in an introduction to a Venezuelan edition of the book published in 1978.[24] He answers his own question by indicating that Ortiz repeatedly asserted that he was not. Le Riverend presents Ortiz as a thinker familiar with classical and contemporary social theory who had read Comte, Marx, and Durkheim, as well as many contemporary thinkers, among them Malinowski. According to Le Riverend (1978: xx–xxiii), Ortiz systematically avoided theoretical discourse and showed an increasing preference for a historical approach; he was an eclectic intellectual who resisted procrustean labels. Ortiz must have recognized the irony of accepting his public presentation as a functionalist in return for the intellectual acknowledgment of a book that sought to counter metropolitan anthropology and the imperial imposition of labels on Cuba.

Third, Malinowski's treatment of sugar and tobacco as mere things, divorced from their cultural and political significance, serves to obscure the metaphorical character of the book and blunt its critical edge. It must be remembered that Malinowski saw himself as no ordinary anthropologist, but as one who combined literary sensitivity with theoretical ambitions— he aspired to be the "Conrad of anthropology" (Stocking 1983: 104). Yet there is little indication that Malinowski appreciated the literary qualities of *Cuban Counterpoint*: its unconventional structure, its allegorical character, or its originality as an engaged ethnography produced by a native anthropologist involved in the political struggles of his nation. He reads "transculturation" as a technical term that expresses a certain dynamism in cultural exchanges, not as a critical category intended to reorient both the ethnography of the Americas and anthropological theory. In Malinowski's introduction there is little receptivity to a reading of *Cuban Counterpoint* as a critical intervention in Cuban historiography, or, least of all, as a text that could develop metropolitan anthropology.

Theoretical Transculturation:
Traveling Theory/Transcultural Theory

Many Cuban intellectuals have recognized Ortiz's wide range of accomplishments. Juan Marinello, echoing a term coined by Ortiz's secretary, Rubén Martínez Villena, called Ortiz "the third discoverer of Cuba" (after Columbus and Humboldt).[25] While many intellectuals have paid tribute to Ortiz,[26] few have directly engaged or developed his work outside Cuban circles. Perhaps the most remarkable exception is the Uruguayan literary critic Ángel Rama. His *Transculturación narrativa en la América Latina* (1982),[27] whose title pays tribute to Ortiz, begins with an appreciative discussion of his work and shows its relevance for Rama's own attempt to examine Latin American narratives from a Latin American perspective.[28] Using Ortiz's concept, Rama offers a critical examination of the anthropological and literary work of José Maria Arguedas, a Peruvian ethnologist and writer who committed suicide after dedicating his life to revalorizing and integrating the Quechua and Hispanic cultural traditions that make up his nation. For Rama, transculturation facilitates the historical examination of Latin American cultural production in the context of colonialism and imperialism. Perhaps through the influence of Rama's work, Ortiz's ideas have received some recognition in literary criticism and cultural studies.[29]

Among anthropologists, however, Ortiz's presence is marginal. Ralph Beals, in an overview of "acculturation studies," offers the following evaluation: "In his preface to the work [*Cuban Counterpoint*], Malinowski is enthusiastic about the new term, but one finds no serious consideration of the reciprocal aspects of culture contact in any of his own publications. 'Transculturation' has had some use by Latin American writers, and, were the term 'acculturation' not so widely in use, it might profitably be adopted" (Beals 1955: 628). Yet the Mexican anthropologist Gonzalo Aguirre Beltrán (1957: 11) criticizes the concept of transculturation on etymological grounds and argues that the term "created more confusion." The Brazilian anthropologist Darcy Ribeiro's monumental synthesis of Latin American cultural formations includes a critical discussion of the concept of acculturation in terms that resemble Ortiz's position, but despite Ribeiro's erudite references to a large number of authors, he does not mention Ortiz and retains the term "acculturation" (Ribeiro 1971: 24, 37–39).[30] Neither are Ortiz's books mentioned in the philosopher/anthropologist Nestor García Canclini's important work *Culturas híbridas* (1989). In a heated debate among prominent

Latin Americanists in the United States about approaches to the history of non-European peoples, Ortiz's ideas were not considered (Mintz and Wolf 1989; Taussig 1989). In a review of Caribbean anthropology, Michel-Rolph Trouillot (1992, 29), in contrast, mentions Ortiz's work in the context of his discussion about the development of a historically oriented anthropology and situates him in relation to the work of other Caribbean anthropologists, such as Jean Price-Mars in Haiti and Antonio Pedreira in Puerto Rico.

The 1944 and 1957 editions of the *International Encyclopedia of the Social Sciences*, edited by Edwin R. A. Seligman and Alvin Johnson, do not mention Ortiz. The 1968 edition, edited by David L. Sills, despite its proclaimed goal of being more international in practice, reproduces this silence. As a commentator states, "Despite the stated aim of the editors of the new encyclopedia to recognize the main international contributions to the development of anthropology and to overcome the Anglocentric character of the work produced by Seligman, the names of the founders of Afro-American studies, Nina Rodríguez and Fernando Ortiz, do not appear in the six hundred biographic entries: (Ibarra 1990: 1349, my translation).

Even as a marginal note, Ortiz's presence may be ephemeral. In the introduction to the first edition of Malinowski's *The Dynamics of Culture Change*, Phyllis Kaberry comments that Malinowski rarely used the term "acculturation" for he preferred the phrase "culture contact," but she also states that once he had "advocated the adoption of a term coined by Don Fernando Ortiz, namely, 'transculturation'" (Kaberry 1945: vii). Kaberry, in a footnote, gives the source of this reference as the introduction to *Cuban Counterpoint* and adds that "Malinowski also employed this term in his article 'The Pan-African Problem of Culture Contact.'" However, she does not elaborate. It is remarkable that in her introduction to the second edition of Malinowski's book, published a decade and a half later, she modified this section. Her reference to Fernando Ortiz is dropped without explanation, and together with it the reference to Malinowski's article in which he had used Ortiz's transculturation (Kaberry 1961). This may explain why Wendy James, in an informative assessment of Malinowski's increasingly critical opinion of colonial powers, strikingly titled "The Anthropologist as Reluctant Imperialist," makes no mention of this article (James 1973: 41–69).[31] Through these silences that appear in works analyzing the development of Malinowski's ideas, Ortiz's influence on his thoughts is erased. Emerging anthropological canons appear exclusively as Malinowski's own.

How are authors from the periphery recognized as the center? Edward Said's discussions of the complicity between imperialism and knowledge have played a pathbreaking role in unsettling Eurocentric representations and in valorizing the work of authors from the periphery. Paradoxically, his comments on nonmetropolitan anthropology reveal the intricate mechanisms through which its marginalization is often unwittingly reinscribed. In a talk delivered to a professional gathering of anthropologists in 1987, he considers the limits of peripheral anthropology and suggests that imperial power is so dominant in the periphery that anthropologists working at the center must recognize the special responsibility they have:

> To speak about the "other" in today's United States is, for the contemporary anthropologist here, quite a different thing than say for an Indian or Venezuelan anthropologist: the conclusion drawn by Jürgen Golte in a reflective essay on "the anthropology of conquest" is that even non-American and hence "indigenous" anthropology is "intimately tied to imperialism," so dominant is the global power radiating out from the great metropolitan center. To practice anthropology in the United States is therefore not just to be doing scholarly work investigating "otherness" and "difference" in a large country; it is to be discussing them in an enormously influential and powerful state whose global power is that of a superpower. (Said 1989: 213)

Indeed, Golte, a German anthropologist specializing in Andean studies, does not condemn anthropology in its entirety as a discipline bound to imperialism (Golte 1980). Rather, his argument implies that Latin American anthropology cannot escape from this complicity because it originates not in the European Enlightenment—presumably the foundations of metropolitan anthropology—but in European imperialism:

> Anthropology in Latin America is the instrument of the dominant classes in their relationship with the exploited classes. It forms part of a cultural context derived from bourgeois European thought which reifies potentially exploitable human groups. There are few indications that permit us to see a potential significance for anthropology in the context of the liberation of those who have been its objects, since Latin American Anthropology as a discipline had its origin not in the tradition of the European Enlightenment but in the tradition of European imperialism. (Golte 1980: 391)

Paradoxically, the epigraph of Golte's article is a quote from José María Arguedas, written in Quechua, in which Arguedas criticizes the colonial attitudes of the "doctors" working at the Instituto de Estudios Peruanos.

Instead of seeing in Arguedas an example of a different kind of anthropology, as Ángel Rama does, Golte treats his statement as a confirmation that no critical anthropology can exist in Latin America: "[Arguedas] learned anthropology in order to put his knowledge at the service of the Quechua peoples but failed to reach his goal. For him anthropology was not suitable for expressing and appreciating the Quechua worldview. Poetry, and the novel proved more valuable to him, but even with these he lost hope as the Quechua tradition and experience were being rapidly annihilated. He committed suicide in January 1970" (Golte 1980: 386–87).

Undoubtedly, Arguedas struggled with the tools he received and tried to adapt them to his own purposes, not always successfully. Like Ortiz, Arguedas rejected prevailing assumptions about progress and "acculturation," and sought instead to explore the dynamics of cultural transformation underpinning the formation of cultures in Latin America (Arguedas 1977). In a statement written before his death, on the occasion of receiving the literary prize "Inca Garcilasco de la Vega," Arguedas stated, "I am not an acculturated person; I am a Peruvian who proudly, as a happy devil, speaks in Christian and in Indian, in Spanish and in Quechua" (Arguedas 1971: 297, my translation). He explained that a principle guiding his life work was the effort to view Peru as an infinite source of creativity, a country endowed with such extraordinarily diverse and rich traditions, with such imaginative myths and poetry, that, "from here to imitate someone is quite scandalous" (Arguedas 1971: 298, my translation).[32]

While Golte evidently intends to demonstrate Latin American anthropologists' complicity with imperialism in order to critique it, his blanket dismissal unwittingly completes the scandal of imperialism. An examination of the relationship between anthropology and imperialism should make visible not only the complicity, but also the contrapuntal tension between the two. While Said does not distance himself from Golte's opinion, his plea for reading cultures contrapuntally in *Culture and Imperialism* (1993) opens a space for a more nuanced evaluation of cultural formations involving centers and peripheries. He argues for the interactional, or contrapuntal, constitution of cultural identities: "For it is the case that no identity can ever exist by itself and without an array of opposites, negatives, oppositions: Greeks always require barbarians and Europeans, Africans, Orientals, etc." (Said 1993: 52). He returns to this idea in his conclusion: "Imperialism consolidated the mixture of cultures and identities on a global scale. But its worst and most paradoxical gift was to allow people to believe that they were only, mainly, exclusively, white or Black, or Western, or Oriental" (1993: 336). Against this paradoxical gift, Said ends by offering, with a sense of urgency, a contrapuntal perspectivism: "Survival in fact is about the connections between things, in Eliot's phrase, reality cannot be deprived of the 'other echoes (that) inhabit the garden.' It is more rewarding—and more difficult—to think concretely and sympathetically contrapuntally about others than only about 'us'" (1993: 336). A contrapuntal perspective, by illuminating the complex interaction between the subaltern and the dominant, should make it difficult to absorb one into the other, completing, however unwittingly, the work of domination.

It is significant that the two critics of imperialism developed, independently of each other and fifty years apart, a contrapuntal perspective for analyzing the formation of cultures and identities. While Said derived his notion of counterpoint from Western classical music, Ortiz was inspired by Cuban musical and liturgical popular traditions. Perhaps a contrapuntal reading of Said and Ortiz points to a counterpoint between classical and popular music, and beyond that, to one between the cultures of Europe, Africa, and America.

Ortiz's presence as an echo in Said's garden, however, makes also more visible the need to understand the systemic and yet little known operations through which centers and margins are reproduced.[33] One may be tempted to see in the silences surrounding Ortiz, even as his ideas have had an impact on writing and analysis, a confirmation of Chakrabarty's argument that Third World histories are written with reference to First World theoretical canons and thus to regard this as yet another proof that social theory is an attribute of the center (Chakrabarty 1992). Yet Ortiz's work complicates this view. His understanding of the relational nature of cultural formations undermines the distinction between First and Third worlds that seems so central to authors related to the subaltern studies project.

For instance, Gyan Prakash's suggestive proposal for writing post-Orientalist histories depends on a fundamental distinction between First and Third worlds (Prakash 1990). While Prakash rejects foundationalist historiography, he ultimately brings "Third World positions" as a slippery strategic foundation that guarantees "engagement rather than insularity" (Prakash 1990: 403). By anchoring the writing of history in the "Third World," he thus hopes to counter the possibility that a postfoundational historiography may lead to the aestheticization of the politics of diversity (Prakash 1990: 407). Yet if the justification for this form of strategic foundationalism is its political efficacy, it must also account for the political consequences of categories that may polarize and obscure contests often fought on more varied terrains.

By examining how cultures shape each other contrapuntally, Ortiz shows the extent to which their fixed and separate boundaries are the artifice of unequal power relations. A contrapuntal perspective may permit us to see how the Three Worlds schema is underwritten by fetishized geohistorical categories that conceal their genesis in inequality and domination; more important, it may help develop nonimperial categories that challenge rather than confirm the work of domination.[34] The issue is not that the categories we have at our disposal, such as the "First" or "Third" world, should not be used, for it is evident that in certain contexts they are not only indispensable but also efficacious, but that their use should attend to their limits and effects. Arguments about theory production and subaltern historiography polarized in terms of the Three Worlds schema run the risk of reinscribing the hierarchical assumptions that underpin it.

In "Traveling Theory," Said discusses how theory travels through a study of the migration of Lukácsian Marxism after World War I to France and England and its transformation in the works of Lucien Goldmann and Raymond Williams (Said 1983). While James Clifford considers Said's essay to be "an indispensable starting place for an analysis of theory in terms of its location and displacements, its travels," he also states that "the essay needs modification when extended to a postcolonial context" (Clifford 1989: 184). He objects to Said's delineation of four stages of travel (origin; distance traversed; conditions for reception or acceptance; and transformation and incorporation in a new place and time), because, in his words, "these stages read like an all-too-familiar story of immigration and acculturation. Such a linear path cannot do justice to the feedback loops, the ambivalent appropriations and resistances that characterize the travels of theories, and theorists, between places in the 'First' and 'Third' worlds." Clifford complements Said's view of "linear" theoretical travel within Europe, with a conception of the "non-linear complexities" of theoretical itineraries between First and Third worlds (Clifford 1989: 184–85).

While there are significant differences in the way theory travels between different regions of the world, perhaps one may push Clifford's argument further and propose that all theoretical travel is defined by "nonlinear complexities," by processes of "transculturation" rather than "acculturation." The dichotomy between linear theoretical travel within Europe and nonlinear theoretical travel elsewhere anchors theory production at the center. Thus,

Clifford argues that Marx, who came from backward Germany, was "modernized" by moving to Paris and London. "Could Marx have produced Marxism in the Rhineland? Or even in Rome? Or in St. Petersburg? It is hard to imagine, and not merely because he needed the British Museum and its blue books. Marxism had to articulate the 'center' of the world—the historically and politically progressive source" (Clifford 1989: 181). From a different perspective one could ask: could Marx have produced Marxism if he had not grown up in the Rhineland and kept it close to his concerns? Could Smith or Proudhon have produced Marxism? Marxism entailed a nonlinear transculturation of intellectual formations involving not only "backward" and "modern" locations of European culture, but also dominant and subaltern perspectives within it. This suggests that all theoretical travel is inherently transcultural, but that the canonization of theory entails the retrospective erasure and "linearization" of traces and itineraries.

In my view, canons, not theories, are imperial attributes. While theoretical production—broadly understood as self-critical forms of knowledge—takes place in multiple forms and sites, disciplinary canons and the canonization of their creators largely remain the privilege of the powerful. Yet even canons, despite their hardness, are inhabited by subaltern echoes.[35] There is no reason to assume that theory travels whole from center to periphery, for in many cases it is formed as it travels through the interaction between different regions. The recognition of the existence of a dynamic exchange between subaltern and dominant cultures, including subaltern and metropolitan anthropologies, may lead to the realization that much of what today is called "cultural anthropology" may be more aptly addressed as "transcultural anthropology."

Transcultural Anthropology: Thinking Contrapuntally about Malinowski

If transculturation is a two-way process, could we find Ortiz's echo in Malinowski's growing acceptance of a more dynamic conception of culture change? Could it be that through his effort to contain *Cuban Counterpoint*, Malinowski was affected by Ortiz's ideas? Through a contrapuntal reading of Malinowski and Ortiz I wish to trace links between the changing geopolitics of empire and the politics of social theory and see the formation of theoretical canons as the product of transcultural exchanges. It is well established that Malinowski's ideas had changed on the basis of his experiences in Africa and that he shared, with many European intellectuals during the interwar period, a growing disillusion with notions of progress. I am not interested here in the impossible task of estimating the extent of Ortiz's influence on Malinowski, only in noting its presence.

In the care that Malinowski took to contain *Cuban Counterpoint* within functionalist anthropology I note a certain ambivalence, a veiled desire to domesticate its power. I read this ambivalence as a tension between denial and disavowal, between totally repressing and fleetingly recognizing Ortiz's originality as an ethnographer—an originality that countered metropolitan assumptions about "home" and "abroad," "science" and "fiction," "civilized" and "savage cultures." Three years earlier, Malinowski introduced *Facing Mt. Kenya*, written by his former student, the independence leader Jomo Kenyatta, stating, "Anthropology begins at home . . . we must start by knowing ourselves first, and only then proceed to the more exotic savageries" (Kenyatta 1965: vii). Clearly, in the case of Ortiz and Kenyatta, home and the exotic savageries coincided; as anthropologists, beginning at home entailed adopting a self-reflexive view from within and from without. In the case of Malinowski, for whom home and science coincided at the center, there was no privileged place outside the center on which to stand in order to begin at home; a self-reflexive view risked undermining the conceits of home and science alike.

In Malinowski's case, the absence of a totalizing perspective may be seen in relation to Perry Anderson's argument that British bourgeois culture is organized around an "absent center," the lack of a total theory of itself. The void at the center generated, according to Anderson, a "pseudo-center—the timeless ego . . . the prevalence of psychologism. . . . A culture which lacks the instruments to conceive the social totality inevitably falls back on the nuclear psych as a First Clause of society and history. This invariant substitute is explicit in Malinowski, Namier, Eysenck and Gombrich. It has a logical consequence. Time exists only as intermittence (Keynes), decline (Leavis), or oblivion (Wittgenstein). Ultimately, (Namier, Leavis, or Gombrich), the twentieth century itself becomes the impossible object" (Anderson 1968: 56).

Ortiz's totalizing historical narrative may have been particularly challenging to Malinowski, for *Cuban Counterpoint* constantly displaces and replaces home and exile, the national and the international, centers and peripheries and shows how they are formed historically through constant interplay. "Historicity," as Trouillot (1992: 33) argues in his review of Caribbean anthropology, "once introduced, is the nightmare of the ethnographer, the constant reminder that the groupings one needs to take for natural are human creations, changing results of past and ongoing processes." Ortiz's historical perspective sought not closure, but ruptures and openings. "Ortiz has never been able to encircle a subject of his study. In breaking the circle he seeks a problem's integral meaning, its significance in the world as a whole," according to a journalistic account titled "Mister Cuba" (Novás Calvo 1950). Ortiz's contrapuntal viewpoint also informed his practical concerns: "He has never thought of national affairs as separate from world affairs" (Novás Calvo 1950). Home and abroad, science and politics, self and other were intimately related in Ortiz's historical work.

In *The Argonauts of the Western Pacific*, Malinowski argues that an anthropological vision requires the perspective of a detached observer, capable of seeing the functioning of the whole society. "Exactly as a humble member of any modern institution, whether it be the state, or the church, or the army, is *of* it and *in* it, but has no vision of the resulting integral action of the whole, still less could furnish any account of its organization, so it would be futile to attempt questioning a native in abstract sociological terms" (Malinowski 1922: 12). Ortiz looks at Cuba, his "home," not from a detached Archimedean point, but from within; his integral vision of the whole was developed by being *in* it and *of* it. As an intellectual from the periphery, developing a critical perspective from within does not preclude, but rather is conditioned by, a view from without. Yet his critical distance entails a critique of distance and of the view from afar. This detachment is not the opposite of commitment but its necessary condition. Implicitly challenging the notion of the detached observer, Ortiz's work summons anthropologists, at the center or at the periphery, to recognize their positionality, the historicity of what Walter Mignolo (1993) has theorized as "the locus of enunciation." With particular urgency in postcolonial societies, this task involves taking a critical stance with respect to the available standpoints. Ortiz's work reflects a creative struggle to construct, rather than merely to occupy, a critical locus of enunciation.

It is difficult for me to imagine that Malinowski did not even glimpse the significance of Ortiz's achievement. If I am right in perceiving a tension in Malinowski's introduction between repressing and fleetingly seeing Ortiz's originality, perhaps we may see this tension on the two occasions when Malinowski used the term "transculturation."

The first appears in Malinowski's attempt to lay the foundations of functionalist anthropology in his *A Scientific Theory of Culture and Other Essays* (1944). In the second chapter, "A Minimum Definition of Science for the Humanist," he states that theory finds a source of inspiration and correction in practical concerns: "Finally, in all this the inspiration derived from practical problems—such as colonial policy, missionary work, the difficulties of culture contact, and transculturation—problems that legitimately belong to anthropology, is an invariable corrective of general theories" (Malinowski 1944: 14). Malinowski does not acknowledge the paternity of this concept or explain its significance.[36] While in later chapters he surveys developments in anthropological theory and identifies the authors related to them, he does not mention Fernando Ortiz or his work and ideas.

Ironically, on the basis of Malinowski's minimal use of the term "transculturation" in this book, the Oxford English Dictionary credits Malinowski as introducing the word; needless to say, it does not distinguish the term from "acculturation," which was Ortiz's intent in coining it:

> transculturation, n. (TRANS- prefix 3 + CULTURE n. + -ATION suffix) = ACCULTURATION, n.
>
> 1941 B. MALINOWSKI Sci. Theory of Culture (1944) ii. 14. Practical problems—such as . . . the difficulties of culture contact and transculturation—problems that legitimately belong to anthropology.
>
> 1949 Psychiatry XII. 184. This paper . . . has shown that the process of transculturation is not really a process of adaptation to a culture but to a political situation.
>
> 1970 R. STAVENHAGEN in I.L. Horowitz Masses in Lat. Amer. vii. 287. We use the terms "transculturation" and "acculturation" interchangeably.[37]

In striking contrast to Malinowski's minimal use of "transculturation" in this canon-setting book, in the last article he wrote before his death in 1942, "The Pan-African Problem of Culture Contact,"[38] he mentions the term several times, fully crediting Fernando Ortiz: "We shall, in a moment, have a closer look at the general principles of this cultural transformation—or transculturation, as we might call it—following the great Cuban scholar, Dr. Fernando Ortiz, whose name may well be mentioned here, for he is one of the most passionate friends of the Africans in the New World and a very effective spokesman of their cultural value and sponsor of their advancement" (Malinowski 1943: 650).

In this article Malinowski takes an unusually strong critical stance with respect to "the onslaught of white civilization on native cultures." In response to this onslaught, he states that "the anthropologist should immediately register that a great deal of African culture was destroyed or undermined in the process":

> The African lost a great deal of his cultural heritage, with all the natural privileges which it carried of political independence, of personal freedom of congenial pursuits in the wide, open spaces of his native land. He lost that partly through the predatory encroachment of white civilizations, but largely through the well-intentioned attempts of his real friends. At the same time, he did not gain any foothold in white citizenship in the social and cultural world of European settlers, officials, and even missionaries and educators—a foothold the promise of which was implicit in the very fundamental principles of Christianity and education alike. (Malinowski 1943: 651)

In response to the ravages of colonialism, Malinowski makes an extraordinary proposal: the establishment in Africa of "an equitable system of segregation, of independent autonomous development" (Malinowski 1943: 665).

How to explain Malinowski's exceptional use of Ortiz's "transculturation," his emotional denunciation of colonial destruction, his strong critique of white civilization, his proposal for empowering Africans at this time? We may find a clue to this puzzle in the way Malinowski justified his proposal for a system of "autonomous" African development:

> Speaking as a European, and a Pole at that, I should like to place here as a parallel and paradigm the aspirations of European nationality, though not of nationalism. In Europe we members of oppressed or subject nationalities—and Poland was in that category for one hundred and fifty years, since its first partition, and has again been put there through Hitler's invasion—do not desire anything like fusion with our conquerors and masters. Our strongest claim is for segregation in terms of full cultural autonomy which does not even need to imply political independence. We claim only to have the same scale of possibilities, the same right of decision as regards our destiny, our civilization, our careers, and our mode of enjoying life. (1943: 665)

In this unusual statement, Malinowski places himself in the text, but this time not as an impartial observer standing on an Archimedean point outside history, as in his early texts, or as a concerned anthropologist, as in some of his later writings, but as a positioned historical actor, a kindred victim of history's atrocities. A decentered and fragmented Europe seems to have enabled Malinowski to locate himself *in it*, to be *of it*, to speak *from it*. It is as if at the zenith of his life, the advance of fascism in Europe, the occupation of Poland, the destruction of his own "home," had made him receptive to the claims and experience of other oppressed groups. At that moment he was able to acknowledge Ortiz, to fulfill the promise he once made to him.

At a time when no place can be safe from history's horrors or innocent of its effects, we may wish to establish our affiliation with the Malinowski of 1942, rather than with the canonical figure of *Argonauts*. Malinowski's acknowledgment suggests how Ortiz's ideas helped him view cultural transformations from a nonimperial perspective and support the claims of subject peoples. In the spirit of Ortiz's work, we may honor his memory by suspending belief in his individual authorship and remembering *Cuban Counterpoint* as a text in which "cultural treasures," as Walter Benjamin and Ángel Rama recognized, cease to owe their existence exclusively to the work of elites and become, as products of a common history, the achievement of popular collectivities as well. Reflecting Ortiz's own counterpoint with these collectivities, *Cuban Counterpoint* celebrates the popular imagination and vitality that inspired this work: the "antiphonal prayer of the liturgies of both whites and blacks, the erotic controversy in dance measures of the rumba and . . . the versified counterpoint of the unlettered guajiros and the Afro-Cubans curros" (Ortiz 1947: 4).

Notes

Acknowledgments: I dedicate this essay to the memory of Oriol Bustamante and Sara Gómez, *amigos cubanos*. This essay incorporates comments of readers of a previous article on Ortiz (Coronil 1993): John Comaroff, Roberto Da Matta, Paul Friedrich, Roger Rouse, Rafael Sanchez, David Scobey, and Rebecca Scott. This version benefited from discussions after a lecture at Duke University and at the Affiliations faculty workshop, University of Michigan, and survived the scrutiny of participants in my Occidentalism graduate seminar: Marty Baker, Laurent Dubois, Paul Eiss, Javier Morillo, Colleen O'Neil, David Pedersen, and Norbert Ross. George Stocking provided perceptive comments concerning my argument about the links between Ortiz and Malinowski. Julie Skurski helped at every stage. My gratitude to all.

Notes on the epigraphs: The first epigraph can be translated as: "One tree does not make a forest." *Monte* has multiple meanings and associations in Cuba (e.g., "forest," "mountain," "bush"). See Lydia Cabrera's *El Monte* (1975), which is dedicated to Fernando Ortiz.

The third epigraph comes from Ángel Rama (1982: 19) and can be translated as: "Literary works do not exist outside of cultures, but crown them. To the degree that these cultures are the multitudinous creations of centuries, the writer becomes a producer, dealing with the work of innumerable others: a sort of compiler (Roa Bastos might have said), a brilliant weaver in the vast historical workshop of American society." My thanks to John Charles Chasteen for providing these translations.

1 For the 1963 edition of the book, published by the Consejo National de Cultura in Havana, Ortiz added twelve chapters (more than two hundred additional pages). He recognized the second part by dividing it into two sections, "Historia, etnografía y transculturación del tabaco habano," which discusses tobacco production in thirteen chapters (chaps. 3–10, 19–22, 25), and "Inicios del azúcar y de la esclavitud de negros en las Américas," which examines aspects of the evolution of sugar production in ten chapters (chaps. 11–18, 23–24). The section on tobacco includes (as chapter 2) the theoretical introduction to the second part, where Ortiz presents the term "transculturation." There is no indication that he regarded this addition as definitive; in some respects, it only highlights the open-ended character of the book. Except for a few modifications, he left the first section unchanged. The original Spanish and English editions included the prologue by Herminio Portell Vilá; in fact, Portell Vilá's name precedes Malinowski's in the Cuban edition (but not in the English version). In the 1963 edition, Portell Vilá's prologue is not included, but it appears again in an edition published by La Universidad de las Villas in 1983.

2 These comments only intend to suggest certain links between the work of Ortiz and that of other postcolonial intellectuals. Benita Perry (1987) discusses the role of binary oppositions in Frantz Fanon and other postcolonial thinkers in an illuminating discussion on colonial discourse. Homi Bhabha (1985) has brought up the important dimension of desire through a Lacanian reading of ambivalence in colonial situations.

3 For an illuminating discussion on Malinowski's impact on anthropology, see Stocking 1983.

4 It should be noted, however, that this temptation has not led to the inclusion of Ortiz in contemporary discussions about alternative forms of ethnographic writing. For references that defined this discussion, see Clifford and Marcus 1986; Marcus and Fisher 1986.

5 Ortiz's detailed examination of Afro-Cuban musical traditions in *Africanía de la música folkórica de Cuba* ([1950] 1965) and *Los bailes y el teatro de los negros en el folklore de Cuba* (1951) valorizes some aspects of the social dimensions of these musical forms (participative, improvisational, playful, democratic, etc.) without, however, paying sufficient attention to the gender inequalities reinscribed in them. These studies, more than his theoretical discussion, make evident the significance of his notion of "transculturation." They also develop this concept

in interesting directions. For example, Ortiz makes creative use of Marett's concept of "horizontal and vertical transvalorization" in his discussion of the transculturation of high and low music traditions (Ortiz [1950] 1965: ix, xix).

6 Many Caribbean writers have shown the connection between colonialism and the Caribbean (one can think here of writers as diverse as José Martí, C. L. R. James, Eric Williams, Nicolás Guillén, Frantz Fanon, Aimé Césaire, Alejo Carpentier, George Lamming, Michelle Cliff, etc.). For a perceptive discussion of this connection in relation to anthropology, see Trouillot 1992: 22. While the Caribbean offers a powerful vantage point from which to look at colonialism, it needs to be complemented with perspectives from societies in which native populations were not destroyed, and remain, through processes of transculturation necessarily different from those that have taken place in the Caribbean, active forces in the present.

7 These two sections draw freely from a previous article of mine (Coronil 1993).

8 His solution was to "keep Grau as a provisional president while changing the structure of the government so as to include representatives of all important political groups, this working toward a genuine 'national' government" (Aguilar 1972: 189). See also Pérez 1986.

9 For a discussion of Ortiz's frame of mind at this time, which shows the burden of evolutionary, positivist, and racist scientific ideologies on his thinking, see Helg 1990. Helg also argues that Ortiz's work at the beginning of the century helped consolidate dominant forms of racial prejudice (Helg 1990: 250). In an interesting discussion of "the conceptual horizon" within which Ortiz began his work in Cuba, Maria Poumier suggests that the race war of 1912, in which several thousand Afro-Cubans were massacred, helped consolidate certain silences about the discourse on race in Cuba at a time when Cuba's "whitening" was regarded as a necessary condition for its regeneration and unification as a nation. She situates Ortiz's silence with respect to this war as a sign of his ambiguous relationship with dominant views. Poumier also echoes the opinion of Cuban experts who believe, on the basis of extraordinary ethnographic information presented in Ortiz's works, that at one point he must have become an initiate of the Abakuá, an Afro-Cuban men's society, and that his obligations to its strict codes of secrecy may have constrained him from speaking on current issues of race (Poumier 1993). Helg's and Poumier's informative articles contribute to a fuller understanding of Ortiz's thought by specifying the context of its initial information. As their works make evident, an evaluation of Ortiz's entire corpus must avoid the danger both of deifying Ortiz as a "discoverer" of Cuba and a champion of liberal and socialist nationalist projects and of vilifying him as a ventriloquist of racial prejudice. These polarizing positions only simplify Ortiz's role in forming Cuban nationalist discourse and reduce the complex dynamic between his ideas and dominant ideologies to a few tenets. The challenge is to appreciate at once Ortiz's striking transformation *and* its

limits, given the origins of his work in racial ideologies and his position as an elite intellectual under changing political regimes. My thanks to Rebecca Scott for sharing these sources.

10 "No cerebro que llene el cráneo, sino ideas que lo inunden y limpien su modorra. . . . Sólo nos falta una cosa: civilización" (my translation).

11 I am indebted to Julie Skurski for this formulation.

12 Ironically, this denial of a "filial relation to Europe" took place through filial links to Europe, making these enduring ties shape the intellectual landscape on which Afro-Cubans were imagined as a source of culture, not an obstacle to it. This irony reminds me of a cartoon by Quinn, the Argentinian humorist, depicting a discussion between the Mafalda and Libertad, two politically concerned young girls, in which one of them asserts: "The problem with Latin Americans is that we always imitate others. We should be like North Americans, who don't imitate anyone."

13 The term *curros* referred to freed Afro-Cubans who roamed the streets of Havana during the first half of the nineteenth century and were considered part of the underworld. Ortiz examined this topic in *Los negros curros* (1986), a posthumous book.

14 On the ambiguities that marked this process, see Skurski 1994. On allegory in the literature of the periphery, see the exchange between Fredric Jameson (1986) and Aijaz Ahmad (1987).

15 Ortiz built on a tradition of thought, both popular and academic, that established connections between tobacco and sugar and the formation of Caribbean nations. H. Hoetink argues that Pedro F. Bonó, in an essay written in the 1880s about the Dominican Republic, was the first scholar in the Caribbean to evaluate the social impact of tobacco and to develop an argument about its "democratic character." He states that this argument was "repeated and elaborated with great literary and scientific erudition by the Cuban scientist, Fernando Ortiz" (Hoetink 1980: 5, my translation). Bonó argued that tobacco was the basis of democracy in the Dominican Republic because it promotes economic stability among agricultural workers and landholders (Bonó 1964: 199). My thanks to Robin Derby for these references.

16 I am indebted to Roxanna Duntley Matos and Norbert Otto Ross for this observation.

17 Ortiz's approach contrasts with that of other critics of the period. Ramiro Guerra y Sánchez, in the preface to the second edition of his *Azúcar y población en las Antillas* (1927), notes that his book had originally predicted the sugar crisis of 1930, which was determined by the "historical laws" that govern this industry, and had demonstrated how these events followed "with mathematical precision" from his account of Cuban history.

18 It is not clear who Ortiz had in mind, if Malinowski or some of his followers. Harriet de Onís translated "la escuela de Malinowski" as "Malinowski's

followers." I prefer the term "school." My preceding reference to the genetic union between individuals is also a more literal translation of Ortiz's text than Onís's "reproductive process." George Stocking has suggested that Ortiz may have read Malinowski's "Methods of Study of Cultural Contact" (1938) (personal correspondence).

19 There is vast literature on this subject. Most contemporary thinkers build upon the insights of Marx and Durkheim. For a discussion of anthropological perspectives on totemism and fetishism, see Turner 1985. See also discussions of commodities in Appadurai 1988; Ferguson 1988.

20 According to George Stocking, Malinowski was in the habit of co-opting both people and concepts for his functionalist movement. He perceptively notes that while "too 'strong' a reading of his preface runs the risk of making too much of small things . . . positively valued, this is precisely the point of de- or re-constructed readings (to make much of silences, or contradictions, or implications)" (personal communication).

21 They viewed acculturation as a two-way process mutually affecting the groups in contact: "Acculturation comprehends those phenomena which result when groups of individuals having different cultures come into continuous first hand contact, with subsequent changes in the original cultural patterns of either or both groups" (Redfield et al. 1936: 10). Malinowski's critique of Herskovit's "acculturation" shows not only their differences—which center on the role of applied anthropology, which Malinowski defended—but also on their shared understandings. Malinowski's agreement concerning the need to take into account the temporal or historical dimensions in the study of change shows how far he in fact is from Ortiz's position (Malinowski 1939).

22 See Trouillot's suggestive discussion of the "savage slot" in anthropological theory (Trouillot 1992); I am borrowing his term here.

23 Kaberry explains that this book is based on materials on this subject from Malinowski's 1936–38 seminars at the London School of Economics, his 1941 seminar at Yale University, and other papers and articles. Kaberry acknowledges that although she was familiar with Malinowski's ideas, the book she edited was "not the book that he would have written" (1961: vi).

24 This edition, published in 1978, was part of the Biblioteca Ayacucho series. Among the editors of this series was Ángel Rama, an admirer of Ortiz's work. The introduction by Julio Le Riverend is included in the 1983 edition of Ortiz's book published by the Editorial de Ciencias Sociales in Havana.

25 Marinello made this statement, which in certain respects highlights Ortiz's links to "outsiders" and to an outsider's perspective, in a section of *Casa de las Américas* dedicated to Ortiz after his death in 1969 (which included articles by Nicolás Guillén, José Luciano Franco, José Antonio Portuondo, and Miguel Barnet). I have mentioned the introduction to the 1940 edition by Herminio Portell Vilá and the introduction to the Venezuelan edition of *Cuban Counterpoint*

by Julio Le Riverend. Working within the context of U.S. universities, see the Cuban author Antonio Benítez-Rojo's book *The Repeating Island* (1992), dedicated to Ortiz on the occasion of *Cuban Counterpoint*'s fiftieth anniversary (Benítez-Rojo closely aligns Ortiz with postmodernism), and Gustavo Pérez Firmat's *The Cuban Condition* (1989). In an interesting critique of Tzvetan Todorov's and V. S. Naipaul's ideas, José Piedra (1989) uses the term "transculturation," without explicitly acknowledging Ortiz's work, to propose a transformative approach to colonial encounters. Coincidentally, Piedra supports his argument by comparing Malinowski's *The Argonauts of the Western Pacific* to his *A Diary in the Strict Sense of the Term*, noting that in the diary one can detect traces of transcultural exchanges between Malinowski and the Trobrianders that are suppressed in his monological scholarly text (Malinowski 1967: xx; for a discussion of this work, see Coronil 1989).

26 Ibarra refers to works by Alfred Métraux, Alfonso Reyes, Roger Bastide, Jean Price-Mars, Melville Herskovits (1938). C. L. R. James refers to Ortiz's work in glowing terms: "It is the first and only comprehensive study of the West Indian people. Ortiz ushered the Caribbean into the thought of the twentieth century and kept it there" (James 1963: 395).

27 [*Editors' note*: At the time, this book had not yet been translated. It has since been published in English as Ángel Rama, *Writing across Cultures: Narrative Transculturation in Latin America* (Durham, NC: Duke University Press, 2012).]

28 Rama appreciatively states that transculturation expresses "a Latin American perspectivism, including in that which it may incorrectly interpret" (Rama 1982: 33). The reference on "incorrect interpretation" concerns Gonzalo Aguirre Beltrán's etymological critique of Ortiz's term (Aguirre Beltrán 1957).

29 For example, Ortiz's ideas appear in the theoretical essays on cultural transformation by Bernardo Subercaseaux (1987) and George Yúdice (1992). Mary Louise Pratt's *Imperial Eyes: Travel Writing and Transculturation* (1992) credits Ortiz for the term "transculturation" and develops her conception of a linguistics of contact into a suggestive analysis of cultural transformation in "contact zones."

30 Ribeiro refers to Ortiz only in relation to specific aspects of Cuban ethnography.

31 I am grateful to Riyad Koya for bringing this article to my attention and for his helpful comments concerning Malinowski's affiliations and ideas.

32 "Imitar desde aquí a alguien resulta algo escandaloso" (my translation).

33 The reality of Ortiz's absence in contrast to the expectation of his presence became clearer when I delivered a version of this essay at Duke University. While Walter Mignolo had assumed before the talk that Said's contrapuntal perspectivism in *Culture and Imperialism* built upon Ortiz's ideas, Fredric Jameson believed that Claude Lévi-Strauss, given his *Mythologiques*, must have known and been influenced by Ortiz's work. After the lecture, Mignolo and I examined Said's book, and Jameson checked Lévi-Strauss's works; in neither case did we

find any reference to Ortiz. Yet Jameson conjectured that Lévi-Strauss must have known about *Cuban Counterpoint*, given Malinowski's introduction to the book, his own work in Brazil, and his travels and contact in South America. He exclaimed that if Malinowski's partial recognition of Ortiz's ideas is disturbing, Lévi-Strauss's silence is "thunderous."

34 I developed this idea in "Beyond Occidentalism: Towards Nonimperial Geohistorical Categories" (1996). [*Editor's note:* At the time, this work was not yet published.]

35 There are, of course, counter-canons and alternative modalities of establishing the significance of ideas and authors. This schematic formulation seeks to suggest a way of thinking about the role of power in the relationship between theory production and canon formation. In the Anglo-American world there is an important literature on canon formation. For broad-ranging discussions of the role of canons in literary theory that relativize Eurocentric standards from a Latin American perspective, see Mignolo 1991; Navarro 1985; Pastor 1988.

36 According to Huntington Cairns, the editor of this posthumous book, Malinowski had revised the first two hundred typed pages of the manuscript (1944: vii). Thus, it is clear that Malinowski not only wrote but revised the paragraph where he mentions transculturation.

37 *The Compact Oxford English Dictionary*, 2nd ed. (Oxford: Clarendon, 1989), 2096. I am grateful to Colleen O'Neal for bringing this reference to my attention. The OED does not consider translated texts, and thus *Cuban Counterpoint* could not figure as a source of the term. Thus, what may have been an isolated error reflects a systematic exclusion of the contribution of non-English writers to the English language. My thanks to Bruce Mannheim and Charles Bright for these observations.

38 This is the article that disappeared as a citation in Kaberry's introduction to the second edition of Malinowski's *The Dynamics of Culture Change* (1945).

References

Aguilar, Luis. 1972. *Cuba 1933: Prologue to Revolution*. Ithaca, NY: Cornell University Press.

Aguirre Beltrán, Gonzalo. 1957. *El proceso de aculturación*. Mexico City: Universidad National Autónoma de México.

Ahmad, Aijaz. 1987. "Jameson's Rhetoric of Otherness and the 'National Allegory.'" *Social Text* 17 (Fall): 3–25.

Anderson, Perry. 1968. "Components of the National Culture." *New Left Review* 50 (July–August): 3–57.

Appadurai, Arjun. ed. 1988. *The Social Life of Things: Commodities in Cultural Perspective*. Cambridge: Cambridge University Press.

Arguedas, José María. 1971. *El zorro de arriba y el zorro de abajo*. Buenos Aires: Losada.

Arguedas, José María. 1977. *Formación de una cultura national indoamericana*. Mexico City: Siglo Veintiuno.

Beals, Ralph. 1955. "Acculturation." In *Anthropology Today: An Encyclopedic Inventory*, ed. Alfred L. Kroeber, 621–41. Chicago: University of Chicago Press.

Benítez-Rojo, Antonio. 1992. *The Repeating Island: The Caribbean and the Postmodern Perspective*. Durham, NC: Duke University Press.

Bhabha, Homi K. 1985. "Signs Taken for Wonders: Questions of Ambivalence and Authority Under a Tree outside Delhi, May 1817." *Critical Inquiry* 12, no. 1: 144–45.

Bonó, P. F. 1964. "Apuntes sobre las clases trabajadoras dominicanas." In *Papels de Pedro F. Bonó*, ed. E. Rodríguez Demorizi. Santo Domingo: Editora del Caribe.

Cabrera, Lydia. 1975. *El monte*. Miami: Universal.

Canclini, Néstor García. 1989. *Culturas híbridas: Estrategias para entrar y salir de la modernidad*. Mexico City: Grijalbo.

Chakrabarty, Dipesh. 1992. "Postcoloniality and the Artifice of History: Who Speaks for 'Indian' Pasts?" *Representations* 37 (Winter): 1–26.

Clifford, James. 1989. "Notes on Travel and Theory." *Inscriptions* 5: 177–88.

Clifford, James, and George E. Marcus, eds. 1986. *The Poetics and Politics of Ethnography*. Berkeley: University of California Press.

Coronil, Fernando. 1989. "Discovering America—Again: The Politics of Selfhood in the Age of Postcolonial Empires." *Dispositio* 14, nos. 36–38: 315–31.

Coronil, Fernando. 1993. "Challenging Colonial Histories: Cuban Counterpoint/ Ortiz's Counterfetishism." In *Critical Theory, Cultural Politics, and Latin American Narrative*, ed. Steven M. Bell, Albert H. LeMay, and Leonard Orr, 61–82. Notre Dame, IN: University of Notre Dame Press.

Coronil, Fernando. 1996. "Beyond Occidentalism: Towards Nonimperial Geohistorical Categories." *Cultural Anthropology* 11, no. 1: 51–87.

Derrida, Jacques. 1974. *Of Grammatology*. Baltimore: Johns Hopkins University Press.

Eiss, Paul. 1994. "Politics of Space, or Political Emptiness?" Paper for the seminar "Occidentalism and Capitalism," University of Michigan, Ann Arbor.

Ferguson, James. 1988. "Cultural Exchange: New Developments in the Anthropology of Commodities." *Cultural Anthropology* 3, no. 4: 488–513.

Golte, Jürgen. 1980. "Latin America: The Anthropology of Conquest." In *Anthropology: Ancestors and Heirs*, ed. Stanley Diamond, 377–93. New York: Moulton.

González Echevarría, Roberto. 1977. *Alejo Carpentier: The Pilgrim at Home*. Ithaca, NY: Cornell University Press.

González Echevarría, Roberto. 1985. *The Voice of the Masters: Writing and Authority in Modern Latin American Literature*. Austin: University of Texas Press.

Guerra y Sánchez, Ramiro. 1927. *Azúcar y población en las Antillas*. Havana: Havana Cultural.

Helg, Aline. 1990. "Fernando Ortiz ou la pseudo-science contre la sorcellerie africaine á Cuba." In *La pensée métisse: Croyances africaines et rationalité occidentale en questions*, 241–50. Paris: Presses Universitaires de France.

Herskovits, Melville. 1938. *Acculturation: The Study of Culture Contact*. Locust Valley, NY: Augustin.

Hoetink, H. 1980. "El Cibao 1844–1900: Su aportación a la formación social de la República." *Eme Eme: Estudios Dominicanos* 8, no. 48: 3–19.

Ibarra, Jorge. 1990. "La herencia cientifica de Fernando Ortiz." *Revista Iberoamericana* 56, nos. 152–53: 1339–51.

James, C. L. R. 1963. *The Black Jacobins: Toussaint L'Ouverture and the San Domingo Revolution*. New York: Vintage.

James, Wendy. 1973. "The Anthropologist as Reluctant Imperialist." In *Anthropology and the Colonial Encounter*, ed. Talal Asad, 41–69. Atlantic Highlands, NJ: Humanities Press.

Jameson, Fredric. 1981. *The Political Unconscious*. Ithaca: Cornell University Press.

Jameson, Fredric. 1986. "Third-World Literature in the Era of Multinational Capital." *Social Text* 15 (Fall): 65–88.

Kaberry, Phyllis. 1945. "Introduction." In *The Dynamics of Culture Change*, by Bronisław Malinowski. New Haven, CT: Yale University Press.

Kaberry, Phyllis. 1961. "Introduction." In *The Dynamics of Culture Change*, 2nd ed., by Bronisław Malinowski. New Haven, CT: Yale University Press.

Kenyatta, Jomo. 1965. *Facing Mt. Kenya*. New York: Vintage.

Mair, Lucy. 1957. "Malinowski and the Study of Social Change." In *Man and Culture: An Evaluation of the Work of Bronisław Malinowski*, ed. Raymond Forth, 229–44. London: Routledge and Kegan Paul.

Malinowski, Bronisław. 1922. *The Argonauts of the Western Pacific*. London: Routledge.

Malinowski, Bronisław. 1935. *Coral Gardens and Their Magic*, 2 vols. London: G. Allen & Unwin.

Malinowski, Bronisław. 1938. "Methods of Study of Cultural Contact in Africa." *International African Institute Memorandum* 15: vi–xxxviii.

Malinowski, Bronisław. 1939. "The Present State of Studies in Culture Contact: Some Comments on an American Approach." *Africa* 12, no. 1: 27–48.

Malinowski, Bronisław. 1943. "The Pan-African Problem of Culture Contact." *American Journal of Sociology* 48, no. 6: 649–65.

Malinowski, Bronisław. 1944. *A Scientific Theory of Culture and Other Essays*. Chapel Hill: University of North Carolina Press.

Malinowski, Bronisław. 1945. *The Dynamics of Culture Change*, ed. Phyllis M. Kaberry. New Haven, CT: Yale University Press.

Malinowski, Bronisław. 1967. *A Diary in the Strict Sense of the Term*, ed. A. Valetta Malinowska. New York: Harcourt.

Marcus, George E., and Michael M. J. Fisher. 1986. *Anthropology as Cultural Critique.* Chicago: University of Chicago Press.

Marinello, Juan. 1969. Untitled article. *Casa de las Américas* 10, nos. 55–57: 4.

Marx, Karl. 1963. *The 18th Brumaire of Louis Bonaparte.* New York: International Publishers.

Marx, Karl. 1981. *Capital*, vol. 3. New York: Vintage.

Mignolo, Walter. 1991. "Canons A(nd)cross-Cultural Boundaries (Or, Whose Canon Are We Talking About?)." *Poetics Today* 12, no. 1: 1–28.

Mignolo, Walter. 1993. "Colonial and Postcolonial Discourse: Cultural Critique or Academic Colonialism." *Latin American Research Review* 28, no. 3: 120–34.

Mintz, Sidney, and Eric Wolf. 1989. "Reply to Michael Taussig." *Critique of Anthropology* 9: 1.

Navarro, Desiderio. 1985. "Otras reflexiones sobre eurocentrism y antieurocentrismo en la teoría literaria de la América Latina y Europa." *Casa de las Américas* 150 (May–June): 68–78.

Novás Calvo, Lino. 1950. "Mister Cuba." *The Americas* 12, no. 6: 6–8, 48.

Ortiz, Fernando. 1906. *Los negros brujos (apuntes para un estudio de etnología criminal).* Madrid: Librería Fernando Fé.

Ortiz, Fernando. 1910. *La reconquista de América: Reflexiones sobre el panhispanismo.* Paris: Sociedad de Ediciones Literarias y Artísticas.

Ortiz, Fernando. 1940. *Contrapunteo cubano del tabaco y el azúcar.* Havana: Jesús Montero. (New editions: New York, 1947, 1970: Las Villas, 1963; Barcelona, 1973; Caracas, 1978; Havana, 1983.)

Ortiz, Fernando. 1947. *Cuban Counterpoint: Tobacco and Sugar.* New York: Alfred A. Knopf.

Ortiz, Fernando. [1950] 1965. *Africania de la música folklórica de Cuba.* Havana: Editora Universitaria.

Ortiz, Fernando. 1951. *Los bailes y el teatro de los negros en el folklore de Cuba.* Havana: Ministerio de Educación.

Ortiz, Fernando. 1986. *Los negros curros.* Havana: Editorial de Ciencias Sociales.

Pastor, Beatriz. 1988. "Polémicas en torno al canon: Implicaciones filosóficas, pedagógicas y políticas." *Casa de las Américas* 171 (November–December): 78–87.

Pérez, Louis A. 1986. *Cuba under the Pratt Amendment, 1902–1934.* Pittsburgh: University of Pittsburgh Press.

Pérez Firmat, Gustavo. 1989. *The Cuban Condition: Translation and Identity in Modern Cuban Literature.* Cambridge: Cambridge University Press.

Perry, Benita. 1987. "Problems in Current Theories of Colonial Discourse." *Oxford Literary Review* 9: 27–58.

Piedra, José. 1989. "The Game of Critical Arrival." *Diacritics* 19, no. 1: 33–61.

Poumier, Maria. 1993. "Fernando Ortiz (1881–1969): Troisième découvreur de Cuba." *Espace caraïbe* 1: 81–93.

Prakash, Gyan. 1990. "Writing Post-Orientalist Histories of the Third World: Perspectives from Indian Historiography." *Comparative Studies in Society and History* 32, no. 2: 383–408.

Pratt, Mary Louise. 1992. *Imperial Eyes: Travel Writing and Transculturation*. London: Routledge.

Rama, Angel. 1982. *Transculturación narrativa en América Latina*. Mexico City: Siglo Veintiuno.

Redfield, Robert, Ralph Linton, and Melville H. Herskovits. 1936. "Memorandum for the Study of Acculturation." *American Anthropologist* 38: 230–33.

Ribeiro, Darcy. 1971. *The Americas and Civilization*. New York: E. P. Dutton.

Riverend, Julio Le. 1978. "Ortiz y sus contrapunteos." In *Contrapunteo Cubano del tabaco y el azúcar*, by Fernando Ortiz, ix–xxxii. Caracas: Biblioteca Ayacucho.

Sahlins, Marshall. 1993. "Good Bye Tristes Tropes: Ethnography in the Context of Modern World History." In *Assessing Cultural Anthropology*, ed. Robert Borofsky, 377–95. New York: McGraw-Hill.

Said, Edward. 1983. *The World, the Text and the Critic*. Cambridge, MA: Harvard University Press.

Said, Edward. 1989. "Representing the Colonized: Anthropology's Interlocutors." *Critical Inquiry* 15: 205–25.

Said, Edward. 1993. *Culture and Imperialism*. New York: Alfred A. Knopf.

Sills, David L., ed. 1968. *International Encyclopedia of the Social Sciences*. New York: Macmillan.

Skurski, Julie. 1994. "The Ambiguities of Authenticity in Latin America: Doña Bárbara and the Construction of National Identity." *Poetics Today* 14, no. 4: 59–81.

Sommer, Doris. 1991. *Foundational Fictions: The National Romances of Latin America*. Berkeley: University of California Press.

Spengler, Oswald. 1918. *The Decline of the West*. London: Allen and Unwin.

Spengler, Oswald. 1923. *La decadencia de occidente: Bosquejo de una morfología de la historia universal*. Madrid: Calpe.

Spivak, Gayatri Chakravorty. 1974. "Translator's Preface." In *Of Grammatology*, by Jacques Derrida, ix–xc. Baltimore, MD: Johns Hopkins University Press.

Stocking, George. 1983. "The Ethnographer's Magic: Fieldwork in British Anthropology from Tylor to Malinowski." In *Observers Observed: Essays on Ethnographic Fieldwork*, ed. George W. Stocking, Jr., 70–120. Washington, DC: American Anthropological Association.

Subercaseaux, Bernardo. 1987. "La appropriación cultural en el pensamiento latinoamericano." *Mundo* 1: 29–37.

Taussig, Michael. 1989. "History as Commodity in Some Recent American (Anthropological) Literature." *Critique of Anthropology* 9, no. 1: 7–23.

Trouillot, Michel-Rolph. 1992. "The Caribbean Region: An Open Frontier in Anthropological Theory." *Annual Review of Anthropology* 21: 19–42.

Turner, Terence. 1985. "Animal Symbolism, Totemism, and the Structure of Myth." In *Animal Myths and Metaphors in South America*, ed. Gary Urton, 49–107. Salt Lake City: University of Utah Press.

Yúdice, George. 1992. "Postmodernity and Transnational Capitalism in Latin America." In *On Edge: The Crisis of Contemporary Latin American Culture*, ed. George Yúdice, Jean Franco, and Juan Flores, 1–28. Minneapolis: University of Minnesota Press.

3   Foreword to *Close Encounters of Empire*

A pathbreaking study of U.S.-Latin American relations, *Close Encounters of Empire* is also a landmark of postcolonial studies in the Americas. The product of a conference at Yale University, this unusually coherent collection of essays reflects vigorous collective discussions, painstaking scholarship, and skilled editorial work. While the individual cases examine with sophistication a wide range of imperial encounters in the Americas, the introduction and the two concluding interpretive essays relate the studies to each other and discuss their collective achievements. I will exchange the opportunity to comment further on the case studies for the chance to discuss this volume's theoretical contribution to the broader field of postcolonial studies.

The authors of these essays treat postcolonial encounters in the Americas as complex affairs involving multiple agents, elaborate cultural constructs, and unforeseen outcomes. While evidently inspired by recent developments in social theory associated with cultural and feminist studies, as well as with poststructuralism and postcolonialism, the essays also build on a long tradition of Latin American scholarship on colonialism and imperialism. The book's theoretical importance results from the diverse ways in which its authors establish, often implicitly, a dialogue among these diverse bodies of scholarship.

In the introduction, Gil Joseph highlights the significance of this dialogue, noting that the collection is distinguished by the pioneering use of postmodern approaches to the analysis of U.S.-Latin American relations. As Joseph observes, while the essays are informed by a postmodern sensitivity to the formation of subaltern subjects, the ambiguities of power, and the multistranded character of historical processes, they do not abandon a more traditional concern with large-scale historical contexts and overarching political relations. Through the interplay of these approaches, the essays treat the "encounter" between the United States and Latin America as a complex interaction among unequal social actors, illuminating in new ways their modes of cooperation, subjection, and resistance under changing historical conditions.

This collection's engagement with modern and postmodern approaches is also underlined by Emily S. Rosenberg and William Roseberry in the two interpretive essays that close the book. Rosenberg contrasts the volume with studies that take a modernist perspective and emphasizes its affinity with postcolonial theory, postmodern studies of international relations, and culture-centered discussions of U.S. foreign relations. According to her, the recognition of the complexity and ambiguity of power systems has led to studies that reject the positivist conceits of the master narratives of modernism and that opt for the more modest goal of illuminating social reality through partial glimpses, attentiveness to localized context, and sensitivity to multiple stories and protean symbolic systems. For Roseberry, this volume's theoretical significance lies in its ability to draw on new perspectives while building on earlier modes of analysis. Seeking to bridge rather than to reinforce the gap between political economy and cultural studies that underwrites the modern-postmodern divide, Roseberry suggests that we read this book as affecting not so much a shift as a dialogue between these approaches.

Yet Latin America has been largely absent from the internal dialogue that has established the field of postcolonial studies in the metropolitan centers. Readers familiar with this field may be aware that it has been fundamentally defined by work produced about northern European colonialism in Asia and Africa and that its critique of dominant historiographies (whether imperial, nationalist, or Marxist) has led to a significant reconceptualization of the making and representation of colonial histories (perhaps best exemplified by the scholarship of India's Subaltern Studies Group). However, both postcolonial imperialism and Latin America (as an area of study and as a source of theoretical and empirical work) are fundamentally absent from postcolonial studies' canonical texts. This volume counters both absences.

The inclusion of the Americas expands the historical referents and theoretical scope of postcolonial studies. The Americas encompass a vast territory where, since the end of the fifteenth century, European imperial powers (not only Spain and Portugal but also England, France, Holland, and Germany) have imposed various modalities of colonial control learned from each other and transplanted this learning to other regions.

It is also the region where the United States has most forcefully practiced new modes of imperial domination as the world's major capitalist power. A lengthy postcolonial history has encouraged Latin American and Caribbean thinkers to confront imperialism's changing forms. From the perspective of the Americas, some of the pitfalls entailed by the *post of postcolonialism*, such as the notion that it denotes effective decolonization, are perhaps easier to avoid.

I will treat the encounter between modern and postmodern approaches that informs this collection on postcolonial encounters in the Americas as the opportunity to move beyond the limitations of either approach. The following five propositions, derived from my reading of this book, are but some tentative steps in this direction:

1. *Culture/Political Economy.* While the scholarship on U.S.-Latin American relations has traditionally centered on political economy (largely through works influenced by the dependency perspective), recent studies inspired by postcolonial theory tend to focus on the culture of imperial-subaltern encounters. Yet "political economy" and "culture" are ambiguous theoretical categories that refer both to concrete social domains and to abstract dimensions of any social domain. The traditional focus on political economy entails a neglect not only of domains outside the economy, but also of the cultural dimension of economic practices themselves. In postcolonial studies the current focus on culture has opened new areas of inquiry, yet has tended to neglect the study not only of economic and political relations, but also of the materiality of cultural practices. A recognition that the separation between culture and political economy is itself culturally constructed would help overcome this oversight.

2. *Metanarratives/Ministories.* One consequence of the various "turns" (discursive, linguistic) and "posts" (postmodernism, postcoloniality) has been the tendency to identify political economy with modernist master narratives and cultural studies with postmodern fragmented stories. While one approach typically generates unilineal plots, unified actors, and integrated systems, the other produces multistranded accounts, divided subjects, and fragmented social fields. Yet there is no reason why social analysis should be cast in terms that polarize determinism and contingency, the systemic and the fragmentary. The critique of modernist assumptions should lead to a more critical engagement with history's complexity, not to a proliferation of disjointed vignettes and stories.

3. *Fluid Subjects/Complex Wholes.* The field of postcolonial studies has focused on the range, inner complexity, and fluidity of the subjects and locations involved in imperial encounters. Yet the analytical inclusion of fluid subjects and unstable terrains must be complemented by the analysis of their articulation within encompassing social fields. These fields of power are internally ordered, and their systemic properties have effects that must be analyzed. Fragmentation, ambiguity, and disjuncture are features of complex systems, rather than their opposite. Lest we miss the forest for the trees, the task remains to understand the complex architecture of parts and wholes.

4. *Borders/Bodies.* Imperial encounters entail the transcultural interaction of the domestic and the foreign under changing historical conditions. This process does not involve the movement of discrete entities from one bounded body into another across fixed borders, but rather their reciprocal transformation. The borders between the dominant and the subaltern are multiple— from the physical frontiers that separate them to the "contact zones" where imperial and subaltern actors interact. In imperial-subaltern encounters, bodies and borders are mutually defined and transformed through asymmetrical processes of transculturation.

5. *Imperialism/Subalternity.* Imperial-subaltern encounters occur in social landscapes structured by differing modes of exploiting nature and labor. The social identities formed in these landscapes—constituted by such relations as nationality, class, ethnicity, gender, religion, race, and age—cannot be analyzed without reference to these forms of exploitation. A focus on the complex articulation of these asymmetrical relations avoids reductionist explanations that dismiss culture as a mere epiphenomenon, discursive accounts that disavow the material dimension of domination and essentialist interpretations that celebrate as resistance any form of subaltern response and adaptation. Studies of specific postcolonial encounters must address the encompassing landscapes of power in which they unfold and the persisting colonizing effects of (post)modern empires.

The Americas have always been a site of unexpected transfigurations. It would be a welcome irony if on the social terrain of the Americas—so saturated by a history of imperialism and by reflections on it—the turn to postmodern discursive approaches converged with or emerged as a material turn, understood as a move toward a fuller recognition of the complex wholeness of social reality. By bringing excluded objects of study into view and refining the way we view them, *Close Encounters of Empire* advances the project of developing a perspective on imperialism capable of confronting its ongoing colonizing effects on territories, peoples, and knowledges. This critical perspective will permit a fuller understanding of the colonial and postcolonial past, as well as more adequate responses to the new forms of subjection and inequality of the ever-changing postcolonial present.

Given the heated debates preceding its publication, the reception of Patrick Tierney's *Darkness in El Dorado* (2000) risks becoming entangled in sterile academic battles about turfs and personalities. This would be unfortunate, for the book offers a controversial account of the impact of Western research on an indigenous population that should urge us to think hard about our work. Even before its publication, *Darkness in El Dorado* became a Janus-faced text that in calling attention to methodological and ethical shortcomings of scientific research in the Amazon also brought attention to faults in its own production. This should not obscure its contribution or make us forget that the central issue in this drama, after all, should be the Yanomami. Far from worrying about the possible discredit this book may bring to anthropology, we ought to welcome the chance it offers to broaden its concern with the ethics and politics of knowledge production in the West.

Under what conditions does one produce knowledge? To what end does one produce knowledge? How can one produce meaningful knowledge? I draw these questions from Susan Sontag's reflections on her play *Alice in Bed*, about the life of Alice James (*New York Times*, October 29, 2000). Alice, Sontag says, finds it difficult to meet life's demands. How to respond to a beggar? "You can walk on, knowing you can't change a beggar's life by giving him money. Or you can give everything you have. Or you can give one warm coin. All three ways of acting seem wrong. Alice is constantly thinking about the question, the great question: How does one live? How ought one to live? How can one live better?"

Tierney's harrowing account forces us to ask how personal and professional ethical questions are defined and connected. His merit is to have brought together a vast amount of information about Western anthropological and medical practices carried out among the Yanomami and to have situated these practices within the network of institutional connections that made them possible and the ideologies of science and history that have rendered them so popular. At the book's heart is a two-stranded argument concerning the work among the Yanomami by the anthropologist Napoleon Chagnon and the geneticist James Neel. One strand follows their involvement in a complex set of medical practices centering on the collection of blood samples and a measles vaccination campaign. The other traces Chagnon's spectacular career as the creator of the Yanomami as anthropology's well-known "fierce people." While Tierney's focus is on individuals, his book locates them in two relevant contexts: the Cold War and the Vietnam War, during which currents of evolutionary genetics, sociobiology, and cultural anthropology claiming that aggression plays a positive role in human evolution found broad support, and the Venezuelan petro-state culture of clientelism, which fostered a network of corrupt politicians and businessmen with interests in the Yanomami and their territory for reasons of profit and power. His discussion argues that the work of Chagnon, Neel, and other scientists brought the Yanomami neither empowerment nor well-being but fragmentation and destruction.

The first strand of the book, which occupies less than one-tenth of Tierney's text but has received the most public attention, argues that Neel and Chagnon collected blood samples for the Atomic Energy Commission to compare mutation rates in populations contaminated by radiation with those in one uncontaminated by it and at the same time carried out an experiment on immunity formation among an isolated population involving a measles vaccination program. According to Tierney, although a safer and cheaper vaccine was already available, Neel chose the Edmonston B vaccine because it produced antibodies that would allow for comparison of European and Yanomami immune systems and prove the latter's ability to generate levels of antibodies similar to those of populations previously exposed to the disease. Tierney's most controversial and damaging charge is that these activities may have led to a deadly outbreak of measles. While medical experts agree that no vaccine could have caused an epidemic, it is still not clear why this outdated vaccine was chosen or what measures were taken to care for those affected by its known reaction.

The book's second and more significant strand centers on Chagnon's anthropological work. Tierney argues that Chagnon created the myth of the Yanomami as the "fierce people" through his own, personal brand of physical and symbolic violence against them. On the basis of extensive research, Tierney claims that Chagnon used his power and material resources to obtain information, often through bribes and coercion, about personal names and genealogies (which are taboo to reveal), created divisions by distributing valuable goods among different factions, promoted warfare for film performances, and misrepresented the Yanomami as an extraordinarily violent people. In numerous publications respected scholars (including Albert, da Cunha, Ferguson, Good, Jiménez, and Ramos) have long criticized Chagnon's practices, data, and essentialist and ahistorical arguments about such issues as Yanomami violence and its reproductive value. Scholars and activists in Venezuela and Brazil have argued that while Chagnon is entitled to have his views and is not responsible for the use others make of them, he is accountable for not having spoken against those who use his images to legitimize protecting "the Yanomami against themselves" by taking their territories and undermining their autonomy. Tierney reports that after Chagnon was barred from Yanomami territory by Venezuelan authorities he sought access to it through an alliance with two high-profile Venezuelans: Cecilia Matos, the mistress of then President Carlos Andrés Pérez (who was impeached for corruption), and Charles Brewer Carías, an ex-minister of youth-turned-mining entrepreneur. Had there not been a public uproar in Venezuela protesting their plan, they might have been able to establish a private biosphere in Yanomami territory, a sort of scientific hacienda where they would have had control over people and resources. This rejection by academic and political authorities in Venezuela had limited impact on the reception of Chagnon's work in the United States.

While the market value of Tierney's book undoubtedly comes from the sensational marriage of these two strands, its intellectual value has already suffered from their unfortunate union. As with a marriage, one may speculate whether this pair was brought together by bonds of conviction or of convenience. One may also wonder about the discrepancy between the rush to judgment that made possible the book's most marketable claim about the measles epidemic and the much more carefully supported discussion about Chagnon's work. The book's scholarly value may also be undermined by Tierney's propensity to explain social effects in terms of personal intentions and to personalize structural relations. This has already provoked defensive reactions that risk turning substantive discussions into proclamations about the intentions or integrity of individual scientists. A flurry of statements from leading institutions about Neel's personal and scholarly integrity has already served to cast a protective shadow over Chagnon's work. The simple fact that even an outdated vaccine cannot cause a measles epidemic has led some to dismiss the rather complex issues raised by the rest of the book. In the debate in the United States, so focused on the technical aspects of the epidemic, the concerns and information of scholars from Brazil and Venezuela about Chagnon's work have been fundamentally absent.

The controversy surrounding this book makes evident that in matters of knowledge, as in real estate, location is decisive. Most of the information Tierney presents has long been public knowledge in Venezuela and Brazil and has circulated in U.S. academic circles. Yet Tierney's book, by bringing this information together and by presenting it in the United States through a major commercial press, has shaken academic circles in this country and public opinion in Venezuela and Brazil. In Venezuela the government has already decided to create a high-level investigative commission whose work may have more than ornamental effects, given President Hugo Chávez's mandate to combat past corruption. There are also signs that in the United States this debate may evolve into a serious engagement with the politics of knowledge that acknowledges the special responsibility of those who work in a center of power that has profound impact on the rest of the world.

Like Sontag's Alice, we are constantly confronted with social suffering. When Jesús Cardozo, a Venezuelan anthropology student doing fieldwork in a Yanomami village under Chagnon's direction, asked his adviser to bring medical help to an acutely ill Yanomami girl, Chagnon reportedly replied that Cardozo would never be a scientist: "A scientist doesn't think of such things. A scientist just thinks of studying the people. . . . We didn't come to save the Indians. We came to study them" (quoted in Tierney 2000: 184). Though Chagnon refused this aid, he offered goods in exchange for information in the pursuit of science. As scholars, even as we may aid in particular situations, our privilege is to be able to respond to social suffering by producing knowledge that shows that isolated acts of assistance cannot undo the structures of domination that produce it. Our gift, our responsibility, is to work to produce forms of understanding that make intolerable the conditions that maintain injustice in any form, including our use of the privilege of science itself.

Bibliography

Albert, Bruce. 1985. "Temps du sang, temps des cendres: Représentations de la maladie, système ritual et espace politique chez les Yanomami du Sud-est (Amazonie Brésilienne)." Doctoral dissertation, University of Paris.

Albert, Bruce. 1989. "Yanomami 'Violence': Inclusive Fitness or Ethnographer's Representation?" *Current Anthropology* 30: 637–40.

Albert, Bruce. 1990. "On Yanomami Warfare: A Rejoinder." *Current Anthropology* 31: 558–62.

Albert, Bruce, and Alcida Rita Ramos. 1988. "O Extermínio 'acadêmico' dos Yanomami." *Humanidades* 18: 84–89.

Albert, Bruce, and Alcida Rita Ramos. 1989. "Yanomami Indians and Anthropological Ethics." *Science* 244: 632.

Carneiro da Cunha, Manuela. 1989. "Letter to the Committee on Ethics of the American Anthropological Association from the President of the Brazilian Anthropological Association." Anthropology Newsletter, January.

Ferguson, R. B. 1995. *Yanomami Warfare*. Santa Fe, NM: School of American Research Press.

Good, Kenneth, and David Chanof. 1991. *Into the Heart: One Man's Pursuit of Love and Knowledge among the Yanomama*. New York: Simon and Schuster.

Jiménez, Nelly Arvelo, and Andrew L. Cousins. 1992. "False Promises: Venezuela Appears to Have Protected the Yanomami, but Appearances Can Be Deceiving." *Cultural Survival Quarterly* (Winter): 10–14.

Ramos, Alcida Rita. 1987. "Reflecting on the Yanomami: Ethnographic Images and the Pursuit of the Exotic." *Cultural Anthropology* 2: 284–304.

Ramos, Alcida Rita. 1995. *Sanumá Memories: Yanomami Ethnography in Times of Crisis*. Madison: University of Wisconsin Press.

Tierney, Patrick. 2000. *Darkness in El Dorado: How Scientists and Journalists Devastated the Amazon*. New York: W. W. Norton.

5 The Future in Question:
History and Utopia in Latin America (1989–2010)

> A map of the world that does not include Utopia is not worth even
> glancing at, for it leaves out the one country at which Humanity
> is always landing. And when Humanity lands there, it looks out,
> and, seeing a better country, sets sail. Progress is the realisation
> of Utopias.
> —Oscar Wilde, "The Soul of Man under Socialism"

The year 1989, world historical for many reasons, marked the close of a long period of military dictatorships in Latin America. It also initiated novel approaches to progress through democratic procedures and the reconceptualization of democracy as not only a means to achieve progress but also one of its central ends. At that time, the defeat of Augusto Pinochet in a plebiscite brought to an end a dictatorship that had imposed on Chile a harsh neoliberal "shock treatment" that inaugurated neoliberalism's ascendancy in Latin America. Pinochet's victorious opponent in 1989 was the Concertación, an electoral alliance of seventeen political parties committed to promoting political democracy as well as social welfare and thus to binding together political and social rights. Only two decades later, several Latin American countries are governed by presidents who seek to deepen democracy by rejecting neoliberalism and proclaiming ideals commonly associated with socialist principles; more than three hundred million of the more than five hundred million people who live in Latin America are governed today, in 2010, by such leaders. To a large extent this change at the level of the state has been propelled by new social movements, indigenous communities, and political organizations that have struggled to construct a more equal and just society. Politics in Latin America during this period has veered from the familiar path. Despite visible as well as submerged continuities, novelty, apparent by the introduction of new actors, innovative agendas, and original ideals, has been its birthmark. Encompassing a wide range of heterogeneous processes in many of Latin America's twenty nations, this unprecedented transformation escapes conventional categories. What are we to make of this complex political change, one commonly referred to as Latin America's "turn to the left"?

In this chapter, I explore this broad question by focusing on a particular topic: the image of the ideal future that animates these changes. I examine this imagined future, the present-day future imaginary, not the Left's potential or likely future, however important these questions may be. While this is already a bounded topic, I draw even more precise boundaries around it. Given these nations' diversity and their internal heterogeneity, I limit my exploration by directing attention to the ways imaginaries of the future inhabit the state, the nation's central representative and main agent of "progress." This future imaginary can be glimpsed in everyday political actions and discourses as well as through concrete cultural artifacts such as plans, projects, and constitutions. Yet since fundamental conceptions of history—not their specific content but their framing temporal structure—are often implicit or taken for granted, I focus on how ineffable imaginaries of the future inhabit the present, how the "what is to be" saturates the "what is" or, in Reinhardt Koselleck's terms, how the "horizon of expectation" relates to the "space of experience during this leftward turn."[1]

The polemical notion of the "Left" has historically been given changing and contested meanings. Norberto Bobbio has provided a parsimonious conceptual grid for classifying political orientations in terms of the dual axis of equality-inequality and liberty-authoritarianism. According to him, "left" and "right" are not absolute but relative terms that represent shifting positions within an always historically specific political spectrum. For him, the Left is basically defined by a movement from inequality to equality; liberty can be associated with it, but it is not its defining criterion.[2] Building on his insightful discussion but avoiding its rather sharp separation between equality and liberty, I use the notion of "left" as a fluid sign to identify actions directed toward universal equality and well-being and thus toward forms of political life without which these goals cannot be achieved, including democracy, diversity, justice, and freedom. The meaning of each of these terms depends on the meanings of the others, so that they form a conceptual ensemble. Rather than being fixed or given, the particular significance of these terms individually and as an ensemble is the product of historical contests over their significance. Since left and right are relational categories defined through mutual interaction, the changing meanings of leftist projects have been produced by struggles to overcome the ever-changing relations of domination exerted by specific "rights." The Left stands in opposition to the Right because it pursues general well-being in ever more domains, ever more comprehensively. Conceptualizing it thus as an expansive democratizing political project, the "Left" can be identified with discrete achievements, such as the recognition of the rights of ethnic communities or of "nature" as a political actor, as established in Ecuador's 2008 constitution, as well as with the general process that encompasses them, such as the pursuit of an alternative social order guided by the indigenous concept of *el buen vivir*—living well (*sumak kawsay* in Kichwa).

As a political project, the pursuit of well-being for all—and all now includes nonhuman entities—is now less than ever the monopoly of the "West," of its dominant conceptions and logics. In effect, these struggles in Latin America are part of a decolonizing process that challenges the ethnocentrism of Western modernity and opens up spaces for other imaginaries based on different histories, epistemologies, aesthetics, and ethics. Since the Left-Right distinction is a Western scheme, it is understandable that its use has been contested in Latin America; current struggles entail defining what the "Left" is and whether it is still a relevant category. Perhaps more than in other periods (at least in Latin America), there are now multiple "leftist" ways of imagining an ideal society, entailing competing notions of well-being, justice, and rights. Some seek to expand material prosperity and individual rights to all, often entailing contests over the definition of collective and individual forms of property; others are based on conceptions of harmony among populations, with each other and with their common natural surroundings; "nature" is now represented in political discourse in some Andean nations not as an entity to be controlled or exploited by human beings but as a sentient being with rights of its own. For some, "right" and "left" are no longer relevant political categories. This proliferation of movements and positions erodes Western hegemony without necessarily entailing the rejection of the West or the establishment of an exclusive alternative hegemonic center. At this time, it no longer seems viable, or perhaps even desirable, to grant historical leadership to a privileged political agent or to postulate a universally valid political standpoint. Through exchanges among universalizing practices and ideals coming from within and outside the West, from centers as well as margins, these changes in Latin America have made it possible to question parochial universalisms and to pursue a more open universality.[3] Not without a sense of its inadequacy, in this essay I use the term "Left" to refer to these changes.

My central argument is that a puzzling paradox has marked this leftward turn. On the one hand, there is a proliferation of political activities inspired by socialist or communitarian ideals aiming at fundamentally changing society. On the other, there is a pervasive uncertainty with respect to the specific form of the ideal future. While there is an intense desire to change the nation, it is not clear what to desire—what are realistic aspirations, how to connect desire and reality. It has become common in Latin America to entertain the belief that actually existing capitalism is unviable for the long term while recognizing that socialism as it has actually existed offers no viable models for the future. Indeed, the project to build a "socialism of the twenty-first century," as proposed in Venezuela, Ecuador, and Bolivia, entails an implicit critique of the historical socialisms of the twentieth century, but its various national expressions thus far do not seem to have provided an alternative to them. Under the stewardship of leftist states, economic activity continues to unfold on the basis of capitalist relations, yet standing in tense relation to the expectation of an indefinitely deferred postcapitalist future. The entanglement between utopian aspirations and pragmatic or opportunistic accommodation has had tumultuous and contradictory effects on everyday life, personal relations, and national politics.

During this leftist turn, the present—the experience of the here and now—seems to be pulled by conflicting forces. On the one hand, it is animated by numerous struggles for a better society. On the other, it is trapped by formidable barriers that block these struggles. The hope of bringing about fundamental change is often displaced by the debilitating sense that human society cannot be improved. This double vision generates a split world, one that appears to oscillate between the malleable landscape of utopian imaginaries and the immutable ground of recalcitrant histories. From the fissure between these worlds there emanate contradictory dispositions and incentives that stretch the present forward and push the desired future toward an uncertain horizon. The Left pursues a just future, but its particular content eludes it. It has a sense of direction but no clear destination.

With the title "The Future in Question," this chapter seeks to evoke the distinctive presence of the future in Latin America during this turn to the left, the contradictory ways in which the coming time saturates the here and now and affects the current political imaginary. On the one hand, the future enters the public stage as an open horizon of expectation, as potentiality, offering a hopeful sense of possibility characteristic of liminal phases or revolutions. On the other, the future imposes its presence as a receding historical horizon, a future in doubt, inducing a sense of despondency typical of periods of decline or historical depression. I explore in two parts the question of this future. In the first, I discuss briefly the context in which the current Latin American Left has emerged. In the second, I examine the Left's future now, the paradoxical mode in which it has come to inhabit the present.

Emergence

I restrict my discussion of the rise of the Left to a brief outline of three conditions that affect its development at this time. These conditions have to do with the changing fate of the two major modernizing paradigms in the twentieth century, capitalism and socialism, and the crisis of neoliberalism, a model of capitalist development that at the end of the twentieth century promised to offer the key to progress.

The End of Socialism. The first condition is the global crisis and collapse of actually existing socialism at the end of the twentieth century (one could also say, the collapse of "actually nonexistent socialism"—or of various forms of state capitalism), symbolized by the fall of the Berlin Wall in 1989, the dissolution of the Soviet Union in 1991, and the rapid immersion of China in capitalist markets and logics. This collapse has been widely interpreted not just as the end of particular historical socialisms but as the historical end of socialism.

The Victory of Capitalism. The second condition is the apparent global triumph of capitalism. As soon as one of the two rivals in the twentieth-century struggle for world supremacy vanished, it seemed not just that the other antagonist was victorious but that its victory was permanent. Moreover, as if blinded by success, ideologues of capitalism also claimed that its promise of universal progress was soon to be universally realized. At the close of the century, neoliberalism had achieved globally the status of a sacred dogma. Conceptualized as the triumph of economic science over political ideologies, it proposed the dominion of technocracy in social affairs and the demotion of politics to the domain of the partisan and the emotional. In 1989, John Williamson coined the term "the Washington Consensus" to refer to a decalogue of policy prescriptions that would ensure that all nations that followed it, even those with serious economic problems, would achieve economic growth. These policies reflected the integration of geopolitical concerns with a technical version of neoclassical economics that reduces social life to an individualistic calculus of utilities or a game of expectations. This fantasy of universal progress was famously articulated in Francis Fukuyama's paradigmatic 1989 article (and 1992 book) in which he proclaimed the "end of history." In these texts, he argued that the worldwide generalization of the free market would dissolve ideological struggles, bring about progress, and create global harmony.

The Crisis of Neoliberalism. The third condition concerns the negative impact of free-market policies: growing polarization within and among nations, ecological destruction, exclusion of vast sectors of the population, the subordination of production to financial speculation, and pervasive individualism and consumerism. These effects have been felt in the capitalist system as a whole but earlier and more intensely in the Global South.

Because Latin American countries in most cases obtained their political independence in the first quarter of the nineteenth century—rather than after World War II, like most new nations in Africa and Asia—they have had extensive experience with various forms of modernization projects, from liberal ones in the nineteenth century, before the recent neoliberal phase, to state-centered ones during most of the twentieth century, ranging from state-promoted import substituting industrialization (ISI) to state-supported export promotion. Some Latin American countries sought to modernize through distinct models of socialism or of socialist-inspired political projects: Chile under Salvador Allende (1971–73), Nicaragua under the Sandinistas (1979–89), and Cuba under Fidel Castro and, since 2006, his brother Raúl (1959–current).

In response to the global hegemony of neoliberalism, during the last two decades of the twentieth century most states in Latin America reduced the role of the state in the economy, dismantled welfare institutions, deregulated the economy, and promoted the pursuit of comparative advantages according to free-market principles. These changes brought about aggregate economic growth but at the cost of a more polarized society and severe social dislocations. In response to these problems, the region saw the rise of a large variety of social and political movements focusing on specific demands, often inspired by socialist ideals, such as the Zapatistas in Mexico, the Landless Workers' Movement in Brazil (MST), the *piqueteros* (unemployed) in Argentina, and the indigenous movements in the Andean nations. In part because of neoliberalism's polarizing effects, but also as a result of the activism of social movements and political organizations, the ideological supremacy of neoliberalism did not last long in Latin America.

Even Fernando Henrique Cardoso, the acclaimed *dependentista* scholar who as president of Brazil (1995–2003) endorsed neoliberal policies and helped to integrate Brazil further into the structures of global capitalism, made it clear that he held no illusions about globalization's future: in his own lapidary expression, "Within globalization, no alternative, outside globalization, no salvation."[4]

Through regional meetings, the political organizations and social movements that opposed neoliberalism developed alliances and common projects. After a series of such meetings, representatives of these movements joined with kindred activists from all over the world in the World Social Forum, a gathering that met for the first time in 2001 in Porto Alegre, Brazil. Ever since, the World Social Forum has sought to articulate these disparate organizations in a common alliance against neoliberalism and for social justice and democracy. Indeed, for these movements and organizations, it has been clear that neoliberal globalization offers no real alternative. And yet, because "actually existing socialism" has not offered salvation, it has been easier for them to criticize neoliberalism than to articulate a viable alternative to it. Their concrete proposals typically address particularly harsh aspects of capitalism, not capitalism itself as a whole system.

With no visible redemption outside or within capitalism, utopian dreams have not so much vanished as taken the form of a rather raw hope for a remote future; the Left has centered its critique on acute forms of domination by capital rather than on capitalism. As the historian John French has perceptively noted, a focus on the critique of neoliberalism obscures an acceptance of capitalism. At the same time, it also serves to unite disparate sectors in the long-standing struggle for national development:

> If opposition to neoliberalism, not to capitalism, marks the fundamental boundary of the contemporary left, as I would argue, the terminology could be said to obscure the essential capitalist and imperialist enemy, if viewed in orthodox Marxist terms. Yet the emphasis on neoliberalism is especially appropriate to Latin America, where autonomous or semi-autonomous national development (be it capitalist or socialist) has long been a shared goal across the political spectrum. While anti-capitalism has had its place in the discourse of the region's left, the practical emphasis has more often been on the incapacity of capitalism to achieve the autonomous national development being sought, while the bourgeoisie has long been criticized for failing to spark a bourgeois democratic revolution or deliver prosperity to the masses.[5]

This insightful comment helps us see the current dilemmas of the Left in the context of Latin America's recurrent struggle to achieve some variant of Western progress. The region's long postcolonial experience has made it familiar with the shortcomings of different development projects and rather accustomed to the interplay between renewed promises and deferred achievements. At this time, however, the combination of widespread engagement in transformative politics with intensified uncertainty about the future has created particularly intense tensions between grand expectations and quotidian practices.

When neoliberalism was promoted as a reigning ideology in the United States and England, Latin America became the experimental ground for the implementation of neoliberal "shock treatments," most notably in Pinochet's Chile (1973–89) under the tutelage of the infamous "Chicago Boys" and during the ruthless rule of Argentina's military junta (1976–83). Through less repressive means, these policies were also implemented by democratic regimes, such as those of Carlos Andrés Pérez during his second presidency in Venezuela (1989–93) and Fernando de la Rúa in Argentina (1999–2001). In both cases, these presidents were removed from power largely as a result of the effects of these policies: Carlos Andrés Pérez in 1993; Fernando de la Rúa in 2001.

Given this history of truncated modernizing projects, it is understandable that Latin America became the region with some of the earliest and strongest protests against the current phase of neoliberal structural adjustments. Needless to say, the strongest opposition to them came as part of the struggles against the dictatorships in Chile and Argentina that had implemented these policies as a package, or "shock treatment," that was at once economic, cultural, and political. In other contexts, protests were largely a spontaneous response to a particular set of policies, such as Venezuela's 1989 Caracazo, the largest and most violently repressed anti-International Monetary Fund (IMF) uprising in the world, in reaction to food shortages and increased gasoline and transportation costs, or Argentina's massive movement in 2001 to oust President Fernando de la Rúa under the slogan *que se vayan todos* (away with them all), an unexpected protest in a country considered until then a model of the Washington Consensus but suddenly torn by a financial crisis and devastated productive structures resulting from the implementation of this model. In other cases, protests were carried out by social movements that had long organized toward this end, as during the 1994 Zapatista uprising in Chiapas, coinciding with the implementation by the Mexican state of NAFTA, the North American Free Trade Agreement.

As one would expect, despite neoliberalism's negative effects in the Global South, its limitations became globally visible only when they affected the North. When its policies did not work in the South, the dominant view attributed this failure not to the free market but to these backward nations, not to the cure but to "patients" unprepared to undergo the whole policy prescription. It was only as a result of the 2008 financial meltdown in the United States that the free market lost its sacred aura. As if a veil had been lifted, the whole world could now see the unregulated free market not as a self-regulating natural principle but as an all-too-human invention gone wild that needs to be disciplined and supported by the state. While the election of Barack Obama was to a large extent a response to the effects of neoliberalism in the United States—of the housing crisis and the financial meltdown resulting from deregulation—the election of many leftist presidents in Latin America was a much earlier response to the multiple effects of neoliberalism in the region.

Several genealogies and typologies have been produced to account for this leftward shift in Latin America. Most journalists and academics, despite their differing interpretations, see the election of Hugo Chávez in 1998 as the beginning of this shift, as his campaign was marked by an identification of democracy with the welfare state, a strong rejection of neoliberalism, and the promise of radical change. This makes sense, insofar as his election initiated a cycle of electoral victories of presidents who pledged to undertake fundamental social transformations. I prefer to mark the source of this shift with the electoral defeat of Pinochet in 1989 in order to highlight what I regard as central to this change: the value attached to democracy as the political form through which to pursue collective welfare and as a value in itself. But there is a difference. In Chile at that time, a society marked by intense political conflicts and torn by a brutal dictatorship, the establishment of political democracy was the major challenge faced by the multiparty alliance that sought to overturn the Pinochet regime; this alliance proposed to ameliorate the negative effects of neoliberalism, not to replace it. Now, in a period when neoliberalism has been in decline, if not in crisis, all leftist presidents elected after Chávez have promised to deepen democracy by limiting neoliberalism and implementing fundamental social welfare measures: in 2002, Lula da Silva in Brazil; in 2003, Nestor Kirchner in Argentina; in 2004, Tabaré Vázquez in Uruguay; in 2005, Evo Morales in Bolivia; in 2006, Michelle Bachelet in Chile, Daniel Ortega in Nicaragua, Rafael Correa in Ecuador, and Hugo Chávez reelected in Venezuela; in 2008, Fernando Lugo in Paraguay; in 2009, José Mujica in Uruguay; and in 2010,

Dilma Roussef in Brazil. Despite their differences, the pursuit of a deeper democracy has been their common ground.

Perhaps the most influential typology about these leftist regimes was a rather early scheme devised by the Mexican scholar and politician Jorge Castañeda, who divided their leaders into reasonable reformers and backward populists—implicitly, into the good and the bad Left. At one end he placed the "open-minded and modern left," represented by Brazil's Lula da Silva, and at the other end, the "closed-minded and populist left," represented by Venezuela's Hugo Chávez.[6] Even those who criticized Castañeda's argument have tended to repeat its dichotomous structure, often making opposite evaluations—Lula as the compromising reformist and Chávez as the true revolutionary. Of course, from conservative perspectives, often expressed through the mainstream media, all these leftist governments are seen in a negative light; in the United States, the media tends to oscillate between setting the "good" Left against the "bad" one or treating them all as an undifferentiated negative force.

Under leftist rulers, political contests over different visions of society have stimulated public debate but have also tended to polarize political discourse, turning often useful simplifications into flat caricatures that block rather than stimulate understanding. In the context of heated political confrontations, this flattening of reason and heightening of emotions have affected political representations both in Latin America and abroad, including those produced in academic and artistic circles. For instance, Oliver Stone's documentary on the rise of the Latin American Left, *South of the Border*, forcefully challenges blatant distortions produced by the U.S. media but presents an inverse mirror image of the Left that reproduces the media's flat vision of history. The demonization of the Left cannot be countered by its deification; the reduction of politics to a battle between Good and Evil must be challenged by accounts that develop the public's capacity to make sense of the world and of the history that produces it. If the mainstream media numbs people, we need accounts that help unnumb them.

Seeking to avoid flat dichotomies—or, at least, to turn them into meaningful distinctions—I offer a scheme that helps explore the Left's futures in Latin America by focusing on the conditions of possibility of historical change facing each nation. This scheme connects historical experience and political expectations by noting how distinct sets of economic and political conditions affect different modalities of leftist politics.

Political Conditions. In countries that have experienced recent dictatorships and severe political repression, the Left tends to underplay the notion of revolution or socialism, to emphasize formal democratic procedures, to establish broad alliances and political compromises, and to project socialist principles into the distant future. The tone of politics is moderate. Here the clearest examples are Chile, Argentina, Brazil, Uruguay, and Paraguay. On the other hand, in countries that come from conditions of economic and political turmoil and periods of political and social instability, involving the insurgency of excluded indigenous populations or popular sectors, the Left tends to promote basic constitutional changes, to be confrontational, and to take up openly the banner of revolution and socialism. The tone of their politics is radical (or immoderate). Here the paradigmatic examples are Venezuela, Bolivia, and Ecuador.[7]

Material Conditions. A twin set of core economic conditions fundamentally affects the relations between state and society during this shift to the left: how a nation's economic surplus is produced and how it obtains foreign exchange. While the generation of a surplus depends on the relation among capital, land, and labor (a central concern for both classical liberal and Marxist theories), the capture of foreign exchange depends on the relation between the national and international economies. When analyzed together, these two factors make visible the critical but insufficiently recognized role of ground rents in Latin America as "nature-intensive" or resource-based economies.[8] Agricultural and mineral rents play different roles and have distinct social implications as elements of specific ensembles of social relations. Whereas agricultural lands are typically privately owned and are thus the foundation of landowning classes that benefit directly from them, mines are generally controlled by the state, and their rents help give the state central political and economic importance. In the Latin American context, the dominance of agricultural rents at the national level generally goes together with a dispersion of economic power, a relatively diversified economy, a strong business sector, and a structural conflict between exporters and consumers over the allocation of agricultural goods either as sources of foreign exchange or as domestic consumer goods. Mineral rents, in contrast, tend to promote the concentration of power in the state, the creation of a subsidized and dependent business sector, and a structural conflict over the distribution of collective rents among citizens with equal rights over these rents but with unequal influence over the state that distributes them. Although ground rent is important in all societies, it plays a dominant role in nations in the Global South because of their subordinate position in the international division of labor and of nature. While I highlight the importance of natural resources, my argument counters the notion of the "resource curse," for resources do not do anything by themselves but through the social relations that make them significant.

During this leftward swing, where agricultural rents are central in a national economy, they have tended to support the forging of alliances between classes and interest groups, the negotiation of policies between the state and major sectors, and the promotion of a moderate political style, as occurs in Brazil, Argentina, and Chile. On the other hand, where mineral rents are the dominant locus of a national economy, they have promoted the concentration of power in the state, the dependence of the private sector on the state, and the development of a radical or immoderate political style that has intensified conflicts between classes and regions, as occurs in Venezuela, Ecuador, and Bolivia. In all Latin American nations, primary products (mineral or agricultural) remain the fundamental export commodities and sources of foreign exchange; in many countries, labor power, an unusual primary "export commodity," has increasingly become transformed into remittances, a major source of international currency. Despite the rejection of neoliberalism, the pursuit of comparative advantage in this domain continues to be the core economic policy of all Latin American states.

Of course, this simple scheme only begins to apprehend the complexity of each situation, not only because other factors also contribute to define each national context, but because these two conditioning factors may have complementary as well as conflicting effects. For instance, in Chile, even at the height of Pinochet's neoliberal project, the copper industry remained in the hands of the state, free from the free market, and copper income (and foreign exchange) granted the state extraordinary financial resources and domestic political leverage; this situation has not changed, except that the steady increase in copper prices in the past few years has given the state even more financial power. In this respect, Chile, despite its more diversified economy and post-Pinochet conciliatory political style, shares with mining countries the presence of a strong state. In Argentina, despite a tendency to establish alliances during the post-dictatorship turn to democracy, there has been historically a chronic conflict between agricultural producers interested in exporting their products in order to maximize their profits and consumers interested in keeping them in the domestic market in order to improve their welfare. The state must negotiate between these conflicting demands, which often become explosive, as was the case in 2008, during Cristina Fernández de Kirchner's presidency.

In addition, other forms of foreign currency must also be taken into account, such as international loans, which typically come together with coercive "collateral" political obligations. For instance, during the second presidency of Fernando Henrique Cardoso, when Brazil was facing severe financial needs and Lula was the likely candidate to win the 2002 presidential election, the IMF granted President Cardoso a $30 billion loan but stipulated that only $6 billion would be delivered to him and that the rest would be given to the new president under the agreement that all candidates would accept the IMF's prescriptions. Lula's Workers' Party (PT), through its "Letter to the Brazilian People," agreed to this condition.[9] This incident shows that the international financial community *no vota pero si veta* (does not vote, but it does veto).[10] Whether resulting from rents, profits, or loans, foreign exchange is a major force in the dynamics of what I have called "national" and "global" postcolonial imperialisms—modes of imperial dominion mostly exerted through economic control and political influence yet backed by the largest territorial and extraterritorial armed forces in human history.[11]

Since I find most labels commonly used to differentiate these leftist regimes inappropriate, I refer to the two groupings of this simple scheme by acronyms formed by the initials of three typical representatives of each: VEBo, for Venezuela, Ecuador, and Bolivia; and BrAC, for Brazil, Argentina, and Chile. Despite their differences, one thing is clear: far from facing the end of History, all these nations face its return; for them, History is back. But what kind of history is this, and what future inspires it?

The Left's Futures

It is remarkable but not exceptional that this leftward turn has entailed the return of History. National histories in Latin America have been typically represented as inscribed in a global historical journey toward Progress. What is rather exceptional about this juncture is not the reinscription of Latin America into History as a grand process but that now it is not clear where History is going.

Ever since the conquest and colonization of the Americas, the region's ruling elites have had a certain sense of its ideal future, or, perhaps more accurately, substantial models of ideal futures have heavily inhabited the region's quotidian life. Insofar as these elite imaginaries have been hegemonic, Latin America has lived the present under the shadow of the future; as Susana Rotker noted, "Latin America is . . . an action without past or present, only a future."[12] Under the burden of imperial futures, the present has appeared as a transitional period, a stage of history to be left behind, if not simply rejected as an embarrassing reality. These ideal futures have always already been known because they have always been the present of metropolitan centers: first, of the "civilized" colonial empires and, after independence, of the major modern industrial nations.

The legitimacy of elites in Latin America has depended on their ability to be messengers of the future. As political and cultural leaders, their task has been to be brokers between Latin America and the "civilized" or "modern" world, in effect, between past and future. In order to perform this historical alchemy, they have to become, in their very beings, embodiments of the future. They incarnate the future through myriad techniques of the self, including socialization at home, selective consumption, education, travel, and language learning. One could identify which "future" has been imagined by these elites by tracing their travels and, most of all, by noting in which nation they have been educated and what languages and literatures they read. Historically, their crucible for self-making was first Spain and Portugal, but soon afterward it was France and England, and since World War II it has been the United States. For some leaders of the Left, of course, the Soviet Union and East Germany played this civilizing function. In Latin America, the main languages of civilization have been Spanish for Spain's postcolonies, Portuguese for Brazilians, and for all, first French and now English.

This mode of historicity saturates political life with the syndrome of the "non-yet," a perspective that depicts some societies as always already not yet civilized, not yet industrial, not yet modern. It also classifies and ranks contemporary societies by transforming space into time, geographical contiguity into temporal distance, and cultural difference into evolutionary hierarchy. As a result, while existing at the same time in contiguous spaces, some societies are defined as civilized and others as primitive, representing an earlier and inferior stage of humanity. Given the dominance of this viewpoint, in Latin America's relation to the modern world simultaneity has not meant contemporaneity, for to be contemporaneous, as Ernst Bloch argued for other regions, is to be fully modern. The anthropologist Johannes Fabian has called this framing "the denial of coevalness"—that is, the construction of an "allochronic temporality" whereby simultaneously existing societies are given different evolutionary value and placed into different historical periods; while those treated as barbarous are displaced into the past, those viewed as civilized are kept in the present and presented as the apex of humanity.[13] When they are all placed on the same progressive arrow of time, non-Western societies are seen as representing the past of civilized societies and civilized ones as embodying the future of the non-West. When non-Western peoples are excluded from Western history, they are treated as radically other, more creatures of nature than creators of culture.

This historicist vision presents the West as the apex of civilization and the Rest as backward regions occupying a previous stage of development. In terms of this worldview, the area that has become Latin America has been variously depicted as both different and inferior at different times according to changing dominant typologies: as savage, primitive, backward, traditional, underdeveloped, developing, the Third World, emerging, failed—all different labels that identify it as less than, as living in what the historian Dipesh Chakrabarty has called, for other postcolonial societies, "the waiting room of History."[14] From this imperial perspective, Latin America is seen, and sees itself, as always catching up, never catching up, always not quite, permanently looking at history from the backstage, never sufficient, always never enough.[15]

In the twentieth century, particularly after the decolonization of European colonies in Africa, Asia, and the Caribbean following World War II, "modernization"—commonly understood as a process of development through industrialization, urbanization, democratization, and secularization—became the key to achieving the long-cherished ideal of civilization. Like most nations in the Third World—a category created at that time—Latin American countries continued to seek modernity, despite efforts at originality or at being nonaligned, by pursuing one of two established models: capitalism, the familiar track of the First World, or socialism, the experimental trajectory of the Second World. But after a long battle between these antagonistic models, neither one achieved a real victory. At the end of the twentieth century, although actually existing socialism had been defeated, capitalism's triumph has been shown to be pyrrhic. While this system has been a transformative historical force that has offered substantial benefits to large sectors and reduced poverty in some areas, it has done so at the expense of the exclusion of majorities and the degradation of the material foundations of humanity. Almost half the world's population is living under the poverty line; the wealthiest 20 percent consume 82.5 percent of all the riches on earth, while the poorest 20 percent live on 1.6 percent. Facing the bankruptcy of both models, Latin American cultural and political elites, as well as the population at large, long accustomed to viewing the present as a stage toward an ideal future, now confront the lack of guiding models; they face a crisis of futurity.

Now that History is back, the Left faces a similar future in all Latin American nations, even if embodied in different national dreams and under different political and economic conditions. Here I explore the gestalt of this future, this common "future form," through five interrelated themes.

Agitated Present, Spectral Future

I name this rubric "Agitated Present, Spectral Future" in order to evoke a modality of historicity, of being in the world, in which the future appears phantasmatic, as if it were a space inhabited by ghosts from the past and ideal dreams, and the present unfolds as a dense field of nervous agitation, constantly entangled in multiplying constraints, a conglomeration of contradictory tendencies and actions leading to no clear destination. Despite constant activity inspired by high hopes, despite even significant achievements, a nightmarish sensation of being trapped saturates the present, as if it were jammed or moved without advancing or in the wrong direction. Even when states manage to promote economic and public welfare, the ideal future remains elusive, threatened by chronic problems and newly emerging obstacles.

Under this modality of historicity, the present time seems not only agitated but expansive; it prolongs itself within lasting constraints. While it occupies the space-time of what may be measured as the chronological future, it does not become the Future itself, insofar as the future is imagined not just as the homogeneous time that lies ahead but as the anticipated epoch of historical fulfillment. As this historical future is identified not with empty calendric time but with the meaningful time of fulfilled history, it comes to embody both renewed hopes and repeated deferrals. As if held back by recalcitrant circumstances, this anticipated future keeps appearing and receding like a mirage, a haunting promise that threatens to always be a deferred presence.

Nationalist leaders in Latin America, including those on the left, have commonly defined the promised future as a "second independence": the achievement of economic and cultural autonomy of real, as opposed to formal, political independence. In the past, this goal typically had a specific historical foundation: the wars of independence, which broke the colonial link and established Latin American nations as formally independent republics (with significant exceptions, such as Brazil, whose independence was achieved by political means in 1822, when it became a monarchy, and Cuba, which became a U.S. protectorate in 1898 after thirty years of war against Spain and was finally granted conditioned independence in 1902).

Reflecting differences in political trajectories and goals, leftist regimes now have established more diverse foundational genealogies for the still heralded goal of "the second independence."

In an insightful discussion of the turn to the left in Latin America, Claudio Lomnitz notes the tendency for all leftist regimes now to establish a particular foundational past for their current struggles: Evo Morales places it in Bolivia's five hundred years of anticolonial resistance; Hugo Chávez defines it through the heroic leadership of Bolívar in the wars of independence (on occasion he looks to the sixteenth-century indigenous leader Guaicaipuro's battle against the Spanish colonizers); Cuauhtémoc Cárdenas sees himself as continuing the struggle of his uncle Lázaro Cárdenas for social justice in Mexico; Michelle Bachelet hails Allende's struggle for democratic socialism; Nestor Kirchner claims as his own Argentina's Peronist culture; Lula links himself to Brazil's transition democracy in 1983; and Tabaré Vázquez highlights Uruguay's social-democratic legacy of the 1920s. Juxtaposing temporal scales and historical epochs, Lomnitz states, "Bolivia, Venezuela, Mexico, Uruguay, Argentina, Brazil, Chile: 500 years, 200 years, 90 years, 80 years, 60 years, 40 years, 30 years. But also the pre-colonial era, the early republican moment, the popular regimes, and democratic socialism. These are some of the ghosts that haunt the new foundationalism."[16]

In the face of a history of partial achievements and constant deferrals, the ghosts of epic rebellions, revolutions, and republican nation building continue to animate the ongoing process of nation building—of constructing the nation and reconstructing its foundations. It is evident that the more varied repertoire of founding moments at this time reflects the Left's diverse nature. While the appeal to such founding moments may express an old political habit, its anxiously reiterative character reveals a distinctive anxiety concerning the future. In the past, claiming as foundational certain historical moments had served less to establish the basis for continuous development than to legitimate the ongoing pursuit of familiar goals in the face of continually deferred achievements. Despite more varied foundations now, a similar exchange between past glories and deferred triumphs is at work, except that now it is not just that the desired future remains unfulfilled but that its very being has become ethereal. Facing a groundless future, the Left must repeatedly ground itself in the past.

The invocation of a memorable past fixes certain times and places in the current national imaginary. This form of imagining the nation, by territorializing a history and historicizing a territory, helps frame the relation between past, present, and future.[17] As the uncertain long term shrinks, the short term expands, digging into the past to resurrect its icons and extending into the calendric future as it pushes the anticipated historical future beyond an ever receding horizon. In a lucid discussion of the current turn to the left in Latin America, Boaventura de Sousa Santos notes the peculiar relation assumed at this time in Latin America between the short and long terms. Whereas the long term has historically been the horizon of the Left, the overwhelming dominance of capitalism has now restricted the domain of the Latin American Left to the short term.[18] Without clear alternative images of the future, its struggles must focus on the here and now. According to him, this concentration on the short term also makes less relevant classical debates about reform and revolution. While he attributes this situation to a lack of integration between theory and praxis, I see it as reflecting also the extraordinary structural constraints within which the Left has emerged.[19]

In my view, these constraints have produced a rather peculiar articulation between practices and ideals in the short and long terms; while leftist governments proclaim socialist ideals for the long term, they promote capitalism in the short term. And while they promote capitalism in the short term, they regard capitalism as unviable for the long term. Thus, we have capitalism for a present without a future and socialism for a future without a present.

When these tensions prevail, they make quicksand of the present. We must keep moving to stay on top, torn between the desire to find a secure footing for all and the instinct of self-preservation that compels individuals to desert collective projects. The ever present talk of corruption within the current Left suggests that this tension leads many to use the language of the common good to conceal self-interested pursuits.

Of course, different countries embody this paradoxical historicity in different ways. Following my typology, while the VEBo countries (typified by Venezuela, Ecuador, and Bolivia) more openly endorse socialism and promote policies associated with it, such as the nationalization of enterprises and constitutional reforms, BrAC countries (exemplified by Brazil, Argentina, and Chile) take more moderate positions and focus on redistributive policies and social reforms. Since an original leftist economic project cannot be equated either with nationalizations (reducing it to a form of state capitalism) or with redistributive policies (reducing it to a version of a social-democratic state), the task remains to develop a viable project for the long term. While VEBo countries seem to have more innovative political projects and BrAC countries appear to be following a rather familiar track, both groupings are still seeking to define an original path toward a postcapitalist future.[20] While these leftist states may be moving in that direction, their reliance on the pursuit of comparative advantages suggests that so far they have not been able to meet this fundamental challenge.

Beyond Reform and Revolution

The rather familiar rhetoric of reform and revolution continues to be commonly employed in Latin America, even if it is increasingly unclear what these terms mean. In light of the typology I have proposed, it is evident that the VEBo countries—whose states control abundant mineral rents and are not the product of recent experiences of dictatorship—invoke more frequently the notions of revolution and of socialism. The BrAC nations—with diversified economies and coming from recent military dictatorships—follow the lead of Chile and Brazil in pursuing a politics of rhetorical moderation and class alliances.

During the twentieth century, "revolution" became the mantra of nationalist discourse. Revolution signified radical change. Most governments in Latin America, whether moderate or radical, claimed to be revolutionary. Often the label "revolution" was used not to promote but to contain radical change; the archetypical example of this usage is Mexico's PRI, the Partido Revolucionario Institucional (the Institutional Revolutionary Party), a party that took for itself the name of the Mexican revolution in order to domesticate its radical potential, making its oxymoronic name an apt descriptor of the party's normalizing ethos.

For the radical Left, "revolution" has historically meant the overturning of the capitalist system; it has claimed revolution for itself, reform for all others. But since overturning capitalism requires conquering the state, "revolution" came to identify two processes and to have two distinct meanings: taking over the state through armed struggle and unleashing radical change from the state. As the Cuban Revolution became the model of this view of "revolution," one that was emulated in many countries in the 1960s, these two meanings were seen as part of one process. The military victory of the Sandinistas against the Somoza dynasty in 1979 and the electoral defeat of the Sandinista revolutionary regime a decade later seem to have closed this cycle of armed revolutionary struggle.

The Chilean model, under Salvador Allende (1971–73), proposed an alternative view: "revolution" not as the violent seizure of state power, which should be captured by electoral means, but as the radical transformation of society. During the current leftward turn, this view has become dominant. As the World Social Forum proposes, revolution, including the sei-zure of power, should be carried out by democratic means. In Mexico, the Zapatista movement began an armed uprising of symbolic dimensions in 1994 but soon abandoned arms and made clear that its path was political struggle, in order not to seize the state but to create a space for a different kind of politics at the local and national level. On the basis of the Zapatista political project, which aims to change society by changing social relations without seizing the state, John Holloway has claimed that true revolution-ary politics involves creating a new world by changing society from within rather than through the state.

For most leftists, however, the state continues to be at the center of rev-olutionary politics. But even in this case, there is no common agreement about what makes politics radical. Chávez has converted the state into the main agent of the revolution, first through state-produced reforms in-spired by a sui generis model of the Third Way and after 2005 through what he has called "Socialism of the twenty-first century." But while the state is the main agent of revolutionary change in Venezuela, Chávez is the center of the state, unabashedly making its basic decisions and contradicting his own goal to promote "participatory democracy." Just as in 2005 he proudly declared in Porto Alegre that he alone decided that Venezuela should be socialist, in 2007 he boasted that he single-handedly wrote the socialist-inspired constitutional reform that he presented to the National Assembly, the product, as he said, of his *puño y letra* (written in his own hand).

At the other end of the left political spectrum, in Chile, the Concertación governments have sought to achieve consensus on basic developmental goals. José Insulza, who served the Concertación government for ten years, calls this approach, one that avoids ideological labels and focuses on partic-ular policies, "socialism by enumeration." As he explained to me, "We pre-fer to focus on housing, education, health, and so on. We don't need to use the label 'socialism.' We call this 'socialism by enumeration.'"[21] This helps explain why President Michelle Bachelet could not transfer her great popular-ity (84 percent) to Eduardo Frei, the Concertación's candidate, and why the election of conservative billionaire Sebastián Piñera in 2010 has been widely perceived as a more "efficient" way of continuing Chile's "modernization" rather than as a change of developmental models.

These differing strategies for change blur the boundaries between re-form and revolution. According to de Sousa Santos, in Latin America now "there are reformist processes that seem revolutionary" (his example is Ven-ezuela under Chávez), "revolutionary processes that seem reformist" (his example is the Zapatista movement), and "reformist processes that don't even seem reformist" (his example is Brazil's PT).[22] Independent of the validity of his examples, the point is that in the present context the concepts of reform and revolution, however indispensable in ideological struggles, have become increasingly inadequate as guides for action and as analytical categories.

One may read these circumstances as reflecting the closure of radical options but also as offering openings for new ways of imagining the ends and social logics of fundamental change. It is now less acceptable to justify questionable means in the name of superior ends. Instead, there is a growing demand to make everyday political actions correspond to ultimate values, to make the present prefigure the future. Democracy is increasingly valorized not as the protective shell of political life but as its foundation, not just as the means of revolution but as its end. In tension with historicist teleologies, it is now more possible to imagine the present not as a stage toward history's preordained future but as its necessary ground, if not as the history we want, then as the history we have.

Beyond the Single Revolutionary Project

The recent turn to the left in Latin America has taken place through the actions of a rather large diversity of actors who have become recognized as icons of the "Left." This contrasts with a historical tradition in which the Left was identified with political parties or organizations that claimed to represent workers and peasants as the main agents of revolutionary change. While this is true for all countries during this turn, in the VEBo countries certain sectors or individuals have assumed the main or sole leadership of the process, whereas in the BrAC countries the tendency has been to establish a politics of alliances among competing sectors.

In the past thirty years, as chronic and new problems proliferated in Latin America—in part resulting from the closing of protected enterprises, the expansion of informal economies, and severe migrations and displacements—there took place in Latin America a general disenchantment with traditional political parties and with politics itself. In this context, new social movements came to play a significant role in politics, such as the Zapatistas in Mexico; the Landless Workers' Movement (MST) in Brazil; the *piqueteros* (unemployed) in Argentina; and the indigenous and Afro-descendant movements in Ecuador, Bolivia, Colombia, and Peru. While these movements have struggled for specific demands, such as land, work, and recognition, and have reactivated the existing political system, they have also challenged politics as usual. At the same time, while most traditional political parties lost power, new parties became so important that in two cases they gained the national presidency through elections: the PT in Brazil and the Movement toward Socialism in Bolivia. Although these parties have at their core a particular social sector (workers and coca growers, respectively), they are socially heterogeneous and do not regard this core as a universal class. They have come to power through multiclass alliances in both regional and national politics; it should be remembered that before Lula won Brazil's presidential election in 2002 through alliances with business sectors, the PT had won important regional electoral victories through broad political alliances, as in São Paulo and Porto Alegre.

The new leftist presidents, elected with the support of these movements and organizations, represent a wide range of personalities, social origins, and political experiences. Including two women, an indigenous leader, a trade-union organizer, a former priest, and a lower-class and low-ranking military officer, this set of presidents reflects an exceptionally broad spectrum of the Latin American population. Their conceptions of rule vary, from the attempt by Chávez to create a uniform society through the monological voice of the state to the heteroglossic project announced by José Mujica, the new president of Uruguay. The product of a divided society, Chávez has built on this division and turned it into a chasm between *revolucionarios* and *escuálidos* (revolutionaries and "squalids," the term Chávez applies to his critics). Since 2005, he has turned this division into a struggle to the death between two systems: socialism and capitalism. His slogan for the revolution during this new phase is *patria, socialismo o muerte* (fatherland, socialism, or death).[23] In contrast, Uruguay's Mujica proclaimed in his inaugural speech the goal of *una patria para todos y con todos* (fatherland for all and with all), pointedly rejecting his earlier radical position as a Tupamaro leader (Tupamaros were an urban guerrilla organization active in the 1960s and 1970s) but maintaining the ideal of a just society.

While the search for a single revolutionary subject has declined, some leftists have transferred this role from the proletariat to the *pobretariado*, a concept developed by the Brazilian liberation theologist Frei Breto to refer to the largest sector of Latin America: the marginalized and excluded.[24] (*Pobretariado* is a clever play on words, as *pobre* in Spanish means "poor.") But the tendency in the region, particularly in the BrAC countries, is to recognize a plurality of agents of change, as if there were an implicit agreement that changing the world now requires an alliance among all those who suffer hardships in the world. In all countries, in a context where the majority of the population is excluded from the formal economy, the exploitation of labor is no longer considered the main factor in the formation of revolutionary subjects. Alliances are now sought among subjects affected by multiple forms of domination—not just economic exploitation but also cultural and political subordination and discrimination.

New political actors now participate in and even define public debate in Latin America. For Marisol de la Cadena, "what is unprecedented" in this turn to the left is "the presence of regional indigenous social movements as a constituent element of these transformations"; for her, these processes entail "plural politics in a political pluriverse."[25] Carlos de la Torre's lucid analysis of new populisms in Latin America has illuminated specific tensions inhering in this "plural politics," such as the conflict between the centralizing policies of Rafael Correa and the demands for autonomy of Ecuador's indigenous communities.[26]

Pluralizing the agents of change, particularly when they include indigenous sectors, has expanded conceptions of historical progress and eroded the hegemony of liberal conceptions of the nation as either a monocultural mestizo community or a multicultural polity. Now it has become possible to propose plurinationalism and interculturality as national ideals, particularly in Andean nations with large indigenous populations. These changes have expanded the domain of the political and brought into the public arena discussions about the legitimacy of cultural diversity that were previously confined to intellectual circles. The 2008 constitutions of Ecuador and Bolivia define these nations as plurinational societies, grant multiple rights to their diverse communities, recognize the value of intercultural dialogue, and, in the case of Ecuador, establish for the first time constitutional rights to nature as a political actor. During this turbulent period, competing principles and visions of life generate acute political tensions but also open politics to unprecedented possibilities.

Double Historical Discourse
It is common to think of double discourse in the political realm as involving duplicity and expressing a gap between claims and practices, between what is said and what is meant. Current leftist politics in Latin America are certainly not exempt from this rather common form of deceptive political discourse. In any historical context, principled claims are at times contradicted by self-seeking practices. In neocolonial contexts, however, there are specific forms of double discourse that reflect the tension between formal national independence and international dependence. This tension gener-

ates "a double discourse of national identity that expresses and organizes the split between the appearance of national sovereignty and the continuing hold of international subordination."[27] But what is distinctive now, in my view, is a peculiar modality of double discourse in which narratives about the present and the future produce accounts that are mutually contradictory but true, since they refer to different temporal horizons. Because it is constituted by the tension between the two temporal narratives of the short and long terms, I call this a double historical discourse.

My concern here is not the sincerity of beliefs or their relation to practices but the specific structural relations that make it possible for conflicting beliefs and practices to coexist without necessarily reflecting bad faith or deception. In an insightful analysis of the current turn to the left in Latin America, Atilio Borón notes a "disjunction" between the "consolidation of neoliberalism in the critical terrain of the economy and policy making" and its visible "weakening in the domains of culture, public awareness [conciencia pública] and politics."[28] He sees this disjunction as a reflection of the lack of an alternative economic program. I would modify this acute observation by suggesting that neoliberalism's "consolidation in the critical terrain of the economy" occurs mostly in the short term, for it is also rejected as an economic project for the future. This disjuncture is first between temporal frames and then between domains.

The perception that there is no immediate alternative to neoliberalism with respect to the economic core has led to the proliferation of this type of double discourse formed by narratives that contradict each other but are all true in terms of their respective historicities. The 2010 inaugural presidential speech of Uruguay's José Mujica clearly expresses this temporal disjuncture: "We'll be orthodox in macroeconomics. We'll compensate this extensively by being heterodox, innovative and daring in other aspects." In an earlier statement, he had asserted, "We have many things to do before socialism" (tenemos muchas cosas que hacer antes del socialismo).[29] Mujica was perhaps more candid than other leftist presidents who also claim that capitalism is ultimately unviable but who seek to maximize income through capitalist production in the here and now. This conflictual interplay between different temporal scales makes the present particularly agitated and murky; it is a space of creative undertakings but also of nefarious forms of duplicity and corruption. There is probably no more emblematic example of this mixture of immorality and deception than the discovery in Venezuela in June–July 2010 of about four thousand containers with more than one hundred thousand tons of imported food rotting all around the national ports, the result not just of ineptitude but of the profit-seeking actions of business networks operating at various levels of the Venezuelan state.

At the risk of simplifying a complex phenomenon, I suggest that the short and long terms are articulated differently in these countries. In the VEBo countries, where socialist ideals are constantly proclaimed, there is a close articulation between the short and long terms in the political domain but a sharp disjuncture between them in the economic realm. In the BrAC countries, where socialist ideals are understated, politics and economics tend to reinforce each other in the short term, pushing the long term toward an ever less visible future.

This double historical discourse expresses a perverse paradox. As I have already indicated, given the location of Latin America in the twin international division of labor and of nature, at the present time the pursuit of foreign exchange has meant that, in practice, all Latin American states— whether on the right or the left—promote comparative advantages within a neoliberal framework. Since the main comparative advantage of Latin America now is its vast natural resources, the maximization of foreign exchange places all Latin American states on the same economic plane—one of dependence on primary products.

This fundamental economic grounding threatens to erode the radical potential of the left turn and to make all states in Latin America, whether identified with the Left or the Right, converge around a set of rent-seeking economic policies. For example, Colombia, which had a relatively diversified export structure based on agricultural products, under conservative president Álvaro Uribe became a mining nation—oil and minerals now represent more than 60 percent of its total exports. While analysts generally place Brazil and Venezuela at opposite ends of the reformist and the revolutionary spectrum, these countries are equally intent on expanding oil production. Under Chávez, Venezuela has become ever more dependent on oil rents and on the importing of consumption goods. Under Lula, despite its rather dynamic economic structure, Brazil has continued to be a nation reliant on its vast natural resources, now magnified by newly discovered oil reserves. Chile, once the paradigmatic neoliberal model in Latin America, offers an instructive example: while the economy has indeed achieved significant rates of growth measured by conventional standards, this expansion has taken place at the cost of a skewed productive structure that relies on the exploitation of a few natural resources. As the 2010 election of Sebastián Piñera in Chile indicates, consensus among competing political parties around this economic foundation has diminished the difference between rightist and leftist policies. If this analysis is correct, in a perverse twist of fate, in pursuit of fortune, leftist states may be doing now the work of capital.

Still, since this double historical discourse is part of a plural discursive field, it is modified and challenged by other voices. This is a moment of heteroglossia. Some of these voices, including that of the state on occasion, propose models of the economy that are more ecologically sound and socially harmonious. While the proliferation of multiple voices in the political field may be confusing and conflictual, it offers the possibility of unexpected imaginings and original visions of the future.

Radical Democracy

In the past, equality has been the key word in global struggles for democracy: the pursuit of equality of citizens before the law. Marxists have criticized bourgeois democracy as being universal in form but partial in content. As Marx argued, it is not enough to be equal before the law—a universal law that posits that no one can sleep under a bridge only affects those who have no proper housing. Socialist democracy has sought to move from formal equality toward substantial social equality. Yet the socialist democracy of actually existing socialisms has produced its own state-centered inequalities and has imposed a single voice on society.

The current struggles in Latin America build on the global achievements and limitations of bourgeois and socialist democracies. In some respects, they represent a continuity of these past battles and reproduce familiar modes of power and conceptions of development. But it would be a mistake to reduce this complex period to politics as usual, to the familiar; politics now takes a range of forms in different locations. While their effects may be short-lived or be co-opted, the agency of new political actors and the force of new imaginaries have already changed the political scene in Latin America. This leftward turn has reactivated the public sphere and transformed politics itself.

Its most significant achievement, in my view, has been the value now placed on democracy as a political form that requires constant expansion and transformation; in different ways, this has been the joint accomplishment of the various Latin American Lefts in all countries, both through domestic struggles and regional initiatives and institutions, such as ALBA [the Bolivarian Alliance for the Peoples of Our America], an alliance that seeks to counter the free-trade association. As it has come to encompass ever new areas of social life, democracy names now a process rather than a political shell or set of institutions; as a "permanent democracy," it has displaced "revolution" as the key term for the Left at this time.[30] While this achievement is the result of many struggles, perhaps its most significant expression has been the recognition of difference as a political principle. In many countries, particularly in the VEBo nations, people now struggle for the recognition not only of citizens' equal rights before the law but of different conceptions of citizenship and of the law. These demands are often cast from different epistemological and cosmological positions and involve a critique not just of Western liberalism but also of Western modernity itself; as such, they involve the struggle not just over distinct sets of rights but over the right to have different conceptions of life. This has been the major contribution of the indigenous movements, from the Zapatistas in Mexico to those in the Andean nations. After a long century of homogenizing projects led by cultural and political elites who endorsed Western notions of progress, these movements have helped redefine the national imaginary, incorporating values of indigenous communities and conceptualizing the nation as plurinational community, as sanctioned in the new constitutions in Bolivia and Ecuador. Even in countries where the struggle for the recognition of difference has played a lesser role, as in Chile, Brazil, or Venezuela, the value of diversity has nevertheless changed the political field.

These struggles have expanded the agents, agendas, and conceptions of democracy. They draw strength from many local experiences. Just as no single social actor can now be represented as the agent of History without meeting significant resistance from other actors, no one conception of democracy can establish its hegemony without debate. The struggle *for* democracy now entails a struggle *about* democracy. As Boaventura de Sousa Santos has phrased it, political battles now pursue not an alternative to democracy but an alternative democracy.[31]

The Currency of the Current

If in the past the Left claimed to have a monopoly on the future; now it can offer but uncertain images of the future. Yet this very lack has opened spaces for the imagination and experimentation. Although the future is not open, it offers openings. And although the final destination may not be clear, the sense of direction is: toward justice, equality, freedom, diversity, and social and ecological harmony. The Left has no map, but it has a compass.

Latin America's crisis of futurity involves yet a more fundamental challenge. It is not just that the Left's imagined future is uncertain but that its real future existence is in question. This turn to the left already may turn out to be only temporary—a passing moment rather than a permanent achievement. At least at the level of the national state, the region seems to be shifting toward the right. A critical election suggests a change of direction: the victory of the billionaire Sebastián Piñera in Chile in 2010, despite Michelle Bachelet's 84 percent popularity. Even Fidel Castro, certainly an astute observer and one not prone to offer negative forecasts, stated that "before Obama completes his term there will be from six to eight right-wing governments in Latin America that will be allies of the empire."[32]

On the other hand, even if the Right may achieve electoral victories in the near future, my sense is that the Left has managed to redefine the terrain on which all political sectors must move. In Latin America, as in Europe, opponents of the Left now frequently endorse many of the Left's principles and policies. As Steven Erlander reported in the *New York Times*, "Europe's center-right parties have embraced many ideas of the left: generous welfare benefits, nationalized health care, sharp restrictions on carbon emissions, the ceding of some sovereignty to the European Union. But they have won votes by promising to deliver more efficiently than the left, while working to lower taxes, improve financial regulation, and grapple with aging populations." He cites the historian Michel Winockas, who argues that "the use of Socialist ideas . . . ha[s] become mainstream" by leaders, such as Nicolas Sarkozy of France and Germany's Angela Merkel, "who condemn the excesses of the 'Anglo-Saxon model' of capitalism while praising the protective power of the state."[33] In Latin America, the opposition to the Left now has also embraced its fundamental principles. While clearly there remain antagonistic poles in politics that reflect profound social inequalities and ideological differences, the boundaries between the traditional "Right" and "Left" are less sharp. In Latin America, it would be hard to be elected now—and to remain in power—without recognizing el pueblo as sovereign and paying more than nominal attention to the increasingly diverse demands of the popular sectors for which the Left has fought.

Some of these demands are very basic and could be addressed by governments of different political orientations, but others are quite radical. Although some of the most utopian demands may be unrealistic at this time, they express hopes and desires that affect the unfolding of current politics. As moderate a thinker as Max Weber recognized utopian strivings as indispensable in political life. As he said, "It is perfectly true, and confirmed by all historical experience, that the possible cannot be achieved without continually reaching out towards that which is impossible in this world."[34] Recently, the philosopher Alain Badiou has argued for the need to reach for what seems impossible. Given that capitalism, understood as a self-expanding system propelled by profit maximization, is globally unviable since it excludes majorities, degrades communal life, and erodes the natural habitat of humanity, fighting for an alternative world is absolutely indispensable. He responds to this need by proposing what he calls "the communist hypothesis." For him, this hypothesis is not a utopian ideal but a set of "intellectual practices always actualized in a different fashion" in diverse historical situations. In another register, he also presents this hypothesis as "what Kant called an idea with a regulatory function, not a programme."[35] It is significant that for Badiou this hypothesis has been present in fragmentary form in struggles for equality since antiquity but need not be identified with any model from the past, including those that have claimed to embody the communist ideal.

It is this historical dimension that Slavoj Žižek regards as essential. While enthusiastically endorsing Badiou's core argument, he rejects the notion of the communist hypothesis as a Kantian regulative idea and emphasizes its "precise reference to a set of actual social antagonisms which generate the need for communism."[36] As if echoing Weber, for Žižek this entails constant struggle, moving beyond models that have not worked and fighting to realize new ones, "again and again."[37] From a rather different theoretical perspective but following a similar radical impulse, David Harvey offers in the appendix to *Spaces of Hope* a boldly imaginative image of what one such model of a just and egalitarian society could look like based on cooperative forms of production and more flexible arrangements of work, family, and residence.[38]

Embers of the Past, Poetry of the Future

Throughout this chapter, I have argued that during this leftward turn the reiterative appeal to icons from the past is a symptom that reveals anxiety over an uncertain future and the desire to provide a stable foundation for an agitated present. Yet the appeal to past icons, when it arises organically from ongoing struggles toward a better world, may also express their lasting significance as vital embodiments of ideals of justice and equality. It is in this sense that Javier Sanjinés has used the notion of "embers of the past" to evoke history's capacity to energize and illuminate present struggles:

"'Embers' is, above all, a concept of sociocultural temporality: the persistence in the present of 'embers of the past,' buried, flickering, but still capable of igniting new conflagrations."[39] In the introduction to Sanjinés's book, Xavier Albó comments that the image offered by Sanjinés is more apt than Walter Benjamin's notion of "ruins," for "it refers to embers covered by ashes that never were really extinguished and which new winds will make burn again with vigor."[40] Although this is an acute observation, Benjamin viewed the past not just as ruins but as traditions that must be rescued, saved for present struggles. As Susan Buck-Morss argues, his conception of the dialectic involves not just the two familiar moments of negation and supercession (as the transcendence of negation in synthesis) but also the neglected notion of "saving." As she puts it, "The verb *aufheben* has a third meaning as well. It is the German expression for 'to keep, to save,' as in saving a material trace, a memento of the past. I would like for us to keep, to save this meaning. It bears affinities with Walter Benjamin's idea of *rescuing* the past."[41] In a similar spirit, the notion of "embers" is used by Sanjinés to recognize how the past can be awakened in the present in order to rescue the future.

Still, it is not clear how past flames can be made to endure and to illuminate present struggles. In a stern analysis of the crisis of modernity in the Global South, David Scott argues that the emancipatory struggles of the past provide inadequate models for the impasses of the postcolonial present.[42] In dialogue with Scott, Gary Wilder revisits the conceptual worlds of thinkers associated with the "Negritude" movement and demonstrates the value of inhabiting their untimely thoughts and exploring their ongoing relevance. Building on insights on "reified objects, emancipatory potentiality and historical temporality" in the work of Walter Benjamin, Theodor Adorno, and Ernst Bloch, Wilder makes a compelling case for examining "futures that were once imagined but never came to be, alternative futures that might have been and whose not yet realized emancipatory possibilities may now be recognized and reawakened as durable and vital legacies."[43]

The quest for sources of emancipatory imaginings was one of Marx's central concerns. While he was intent on freeing radical imaginings from the burden of the past, he recognized the past's capacity to illuminate present struggles. In his examination of the revolutions of the nineteenth century, his call for a poetry drawn from the future was not meant to discard the past, only to open the future to radical novelty. For him, the past could be brought to life if it was invoked to animate struggles to transform the world rather than to adorn its dramas. As he famously argued, while the bourgeois revolutions of the eighteenth century "awakened the dead" for "glorifying new struggles" and "magnifying the task in reality," the social revolutions of the nineteenth century did so for "parodying the old" and for "fleeing from [the task's] solution in reality."[44]

Carried along by winds of history that fan old flames and rouse new struggles, Latin America has become a diverse fabric of collective utopian dreams. The dialogue between past and future informing current struggles has, despite constraints, challenged place-bound, parochial conceptions of universality and has generated global exchanges about reimagined worlds. The search for equality goes beyond the struggle against forms of domination based on region, class, gender, ethnicity, religion, race, or age. Particularly in the Andean region, indigenous movements are proposing to move from anthropocentric struggles toward biocentrism as an expression of a planetary universality. As a result of recent struggles, it is now more possible in Latin America to value difference and to recognize that one does not dream the same in Spanish or in Aymara, as a woman or as a man, as an adult or as a child, from a bed or from under the bridge. Perhaps it has also become possible to engage different cosmologies, to recognize particulars in universals and universals in particulars, and to be open to the call "to see a World in a grain of sand, / And a Heaven in a wild flower."[45]

Of course, given the unequal structures of power within which this leftward turn has taken place, it is possible that its new imaginings may be co-opted or crushed. But given that these imaginaries now unite South and North in a politics that fuses the pursuit of well-being and sheer global survival, it is likely that a counterpoint between the embers of the past and the poetry of the future will continue to conjure up images of worlds free from the horrors of history.[46] Politics will remain a battle of desires waged on an uneven terrain. But as long as people find themselves without a safe and dignified home in the world, utopian dreams will continue to proliferate, energizing struggles to build a world made of many worlds, where people can dream their futures without fear of waking up.

Notes

Epigraph: Oscar Wilde, *The Soul of Man* (London: Arthur L. Humphreys, 1900), 40.

My gratitude to Julie Skurski, Genese Sodikoff, Katherine Verdery, John French, Talal Asad, Craig Calhoun, and students in my Spring 2010 seminar at the City University of New York's Graduate Center, as well as to an anonymous reader from the Social Science Research Council; their suggestions about content and form have considerably improved this chapter.

1 Reinhardt Koselleck, *Futures Past: On the Semantics of Historical Time* (New York: Columbia University Press, 2004), 259. By these terms, Koselleck explores the relationship between historical experience and expectations of the future. Scholars have shown that conceptions of history and cultural cosmologies are intimately connected to each other and are historically specific; in any given society, the relationship between present and future establishes distinctive temporalities and narratives of history. Despite persuasive critiques of Eurocentrism, canonical scholarly categories tend to reproduce Western assumptions about temporality and visions of history. While in sympathy with these critiques I deploy here the familiar trilogy of "past," "present," and "future" as it has been commonly used in studies about Latin America, as well as in Latin America itself, my use of this trilogy is largely descriptive, restricting my critical intent to making visible assumed or naturalized conceptions of history and of space and time.

2 Norberto Bobbio, *Left and Right: The Significance of a Political Distinction*, trans. Allan Cameron (Chicago: University of Chicago Press, 1996).

3 This comment reflects my own evaluation and position (and wishes) but is indebted to the fundamental work of members of a loose "decolonial" collective, or network, without a proper name or single position. For recent works on this topic by members of this collective, see the recent thoughtful texts of Arturo Escobar and Javier Sanjinés: Arturo Escobar, "Latin America at a Crossroads," *Cultural Studies* 24, no. 1 (2010): 1–65; Javier Sanjinés, *Rescoldos del pasado: Conflictos culturales en sociedades post-coloniales* (La Paz, Bolivia: Programa de Investigación Estratégica en Bolivia, 2009).

4 Atilio A. Borón, "Globalization: A Latin American Perspective," *Estudos Sociedade e Agricultura* 11 (1998): 164–80.

5 John French, "Understanding the Politics of Latin America's Plural Lefts (Chávez/Lula): Social Democracy, Populism and Convergence on the Path to a Post-Neoliberal World," *Third World Quarterly* 30, no. 2 (2009): 362.

6 Jorge Castañeda, "A Tale of Two Lefts," *Foreign Affairs* (May–June 2006): 28–43.

7 Arturo Escobar's discussion, in "Latin America at a Crossroads," of the turn to the left in Latin America focuses on these countries, in part because they seem to represent a more radical rupture from the past and a "decolonial" political project.

8 I discuss these concepts and issues in Fernando Coronil, *The Magical State: Nature, Money and Modernity in Venezuela* (Chicago: University of Chicago Press, 1997), 45–66.

9 Leonardo Avritzer, "El ascenso del Partido de los Trabajadores en Brasil," in *La nueva izquierda en América Latina: Sus orígenes y trayectoria futura*, ed. César A. Rodríguez Garavito, Patrick S. Barrett, and Daniel Chávez (Bogotá: Grupo Editorial Norma, 2004), 67–96.

10 César Rodríguez Garavito and Patrick Barrett, "La utopia revivida?" in Rodrí-guez Garavito et al., *La nueva izquierda en América Latina*, 40.

11 Fernando Coronil, "After Empire: Rethinking Imperialism from the Amer-icas," in *Imperial Formations and Their Discontents*, ed. Ann Stoler, Carole McGranahan, and Peter Purdue (Santa Fe, NM: School of American Research Press, 2007), 241–74.

12 Susana Rotker, *Bravo pueblo: Poder, utopia y violencia* (Caracas: Fondo Editorial La Nave Va, 2005), 85.

13 Johannes Fabian, *Time and the Other: How Anthropology Makes Its Object* (New York: Columbia University Press, 1983).

14 Dipesh Chakrabarty, *Provincialising Europe: Postcolonial Thought and Historical Differ-ence* (Princeton, NJ: Princeton University Press, 2000).

15 This mode of historicizing has been observed in Latin America by literary and political elites since the nineteenth century, including by such "founders" of Latin American nationalism as Simón Bolivar and José Martí. Chakrabarty has productively used the notion of the "not-yet" in his insightful critique of historicism: Chakrabarty, *Provincialising Europe*.

16 Claudio Lomnitz, "The Latin American Rebellion: Will the New Left Set a New Agenda?" *Boston Review*, September–October 2006.

17 I have discussed elsewhere Nicos Poulantzas's insight that nation formation involves the territorialization of a history and the historicization of a territory: Fernando Coronil, "Beyond Occidentalism: Towards Nonimperial Geohistori-cal Categories," *Cultural Anthropology* 11, no. 1 (1996): 51–87.

18 While this observation is accurate for recent periods in Latin American history, it must be noted that liberal thought has also claimed the future as its own. The very notion of the "long term" was created by Alfred Marshall in his *Principles of Economics* (London: Macmillan, 1890) to identify a time when the market would adjust all factors and define normal prices; for an elaboration of this point, see the interesting discussion of the public rhetoric of macroeconomics in Jane Guyer, "Prophecy and the Near Future: Thoughts on Macroeconomic, Evangeli-cal and Punctuated Time," *American Anthropologist* 34, no. 3 (2007): 409–21.

19 Boaventura de Sousa Santos, "Una izquierda con futuro," in Rodríguez Garavito et al., *La nueva izquierda en América Latina*, 437–57.

20 I use the notion of postcapitalism here as a rather vague term to evoke a hypo-thetical future society built on the foundations of capitalism but transcending its limitations.

21 José Insulza, interview with the author, University of Michigan, October 2006.

22 De Sousa Santos, "Una izquierda con futuro," 438–39, my translation.

23 It should be noted, however, that despite Chávez's division of the population into two antagonistic groups, he conceives of the revolutionary camp as plural, made up of many social sectors, as long as they agree with the goals of the revolution as articulated by the state.

24 Marcelo Colussi, "El pobretariado: Un nuevo sujeto revolucionario?" *Revista Amauta* (2009).

25 Marisol de la Cadena, "Indigenous Cosmopolitics in the Andes: Conceptual Reflections," *Cultural Anthropology* 25, no. 2 (2010): 334, 356.

26 Carlos de la Torre, "Correa y los Indios," *Diario Hoy*, March 6, 2010.

27 Julie Skurski and Fernando Coronil, "Country and City in a Colonial Land-scape: Double Discourse and the Geopolitics of Truth in Latin America," in *View from the Border: Essays in Honor of Raymond Williams*, ed. Dennis Dworkin and Leslie Roman (New York: Routledge, 1993), 25.

28 Borón, "Globalization."

29 Daniel Chávez, "Del frente amplio a la nueva mayoría," in Rodríguez Garavito et al., *La nueva izquierda en América Latina*, 172, my translation.

30 This concept, "permanent democracy," is borrowed by Juan Carlos Monedero from Boaventura de Sousa Santos in order to develop an argument about de-mocracy as an ever expanding and inclusive process: Juan Carlos Monedero, *El gobierno de las palabras: Política para tiempos de confusión* (México: Fondo de Cultura Económica, 2009), 221–75. Monedero's work reflects his engagement with con-temporary social theory as well as his recent experience in Venezuela as a key member of the Centro Miranda, a leftist think tank established under Chávez; he left this center after a rather unsuccessful attempt to develop constructive critiques of Chávez's Bolivarian "Revolution" from within.

31 De Sousa Santos, "Una izquierda con futuro."

32 Fidel Castro, "Reflections by Fidel Castro: [Obama] A Science Fiction Story," Caricom News Network, November 13, 2009.

33 Steven Erlander, "European Socialists Suffering Even in Downturn," *New York Times*, September 28, 2009.

34 Max Weber, "Politics as a Vocation," in *Weber: Selections in Translation*, ed. W. G. Runciman (Cambridge: Cambridge University Press, 1978), 225.

35 Alain Badiou, "The Communist Hypothesis," *New Left Review* 49 (2008): 29–42.

36 Slavoj Žižek, *First as Tragedy, Then as Farce* (New York: Verso, 2009), 87–88.

37 Žižek, *First as Tragedy, Then as Farce*, 86–104.

38 David Harvey, *Spaces of Hope* (Berkeley: University of California Press, 2000).

39 Javier Sanjinés, personal communication, May 1, 2010.

40 Xavier Albó, "Prólogo," in Sanjinés, *Rescoldos del pasado*, xiii, my translation.

41 Susan Buck-Morss, "The Second Time as Farce . . . Historical Pragmatics and the Untimely Present," unpublished ms., 2010, 16–17.

42 David Scott, *Conscripts of Modernity: The Tragedy of Colonial Enlightenment* (Durham, NC: Duke University Press, 2004).

43 Gary Wilder, "Untimely Vision: Aimé Césaire, Decolonization, Utopia," *Public Culture* 21, no. 1 (2009): 103.

44 Karl Marx, *The Eighteenth Brumaire of Louis Bonaparte* (New York: International Publishers, 1963), 17.

45 These are the first two lines from William Blake's "Auguries of Innocence."

46 The notion of a counterpoint between past and future is inspired by Fernando Ortiz's redemptive counterpoint between the Americas and Europe through the tropes of tobacco and sugar in *Cuban Counterpoint: Tobacco and Sugar* (Durham, NC: Duke University Press, 1995). "Poetry of the future" is my phrase drawn from Marx's argument that, unlike the bourgeois revolutions of the eighteenth century, the social revolutions of the nineteenth century must "draw their poetry from the future": Marx, *The Eighteenth Brumaire of Louis Bonaparte*, 18.

GEOHISTORICAL STATES

LATIN AMERICAN COUNTERPOINT

Part II. Geohistorical States: Latin American Counterpoint

Introduction EDWARD MURPHY

■ Fernando Coronil always returned to writing about Venezuela, the country that he regarded as his home, even as his path led him elsewhere. Using the provocative term that Jamaica Kincaid (1988) adopted to describe her own country, the Caribbean islands of Antigua and Barbuda, Coronil described Venezuela as a "small place." For both, "smallness" was far from being a mere description of population, geographic boundaries, or gross national product. It was instead indicative of a powerful imaginary that categorized the nations of the Global South as inconsequential. As Coronil insisted, moreover, a putatively small place such as Venezuela formed a constitutive part of the modern world, shaped in the crucible of ongoing processes of empire in the Americas. Circumstances in Venezuela were the tip of a moving "iceberg."

Coronil thus undertook the immense challenge of working through Venezuela's vast, labyrinthine connections and its troubled dynamics as a subaltern, poorly understood nation. Yet his effort to illuminate the country's unsettled, complex trajectory did not lead him to analytical despair. He never succumbed to postmodern resignation at the impossibility of developing meaningful and transformative knowledge. Referring to the coup against Hugo Chávez in 2002, an event shrouded in secrets, rumors, mistrust, and violence, Coronil wrote in his unfinished manuscript, *Crude Matters*, that he was committed to revealing what "*really* happened" (this volume, 281). While this included recovering silenced histories and overcoming misconceptions, it also expressed a provocative aspiration. For Coronil, revealing the dynamics behind such an event as the coup was grounded directly in his struggle to imagine a different kind of world—one that would be free of the secrecy and mystifications of power, the depredation of nature, and systemic forms of violence and subordination.

The urgency of this struggle often led Coronil to undertake work that directly engaged the crises of a given moment. He thus described *Crude Matters*, a book that he had not planned to write, as "an imperative demand" (this volume, 272). In the project, Coronil linked the failed 2002 coup to his longer-term understanding of the making of the Venezuelan state, taking advantage of his ability to interview key players in the event. In this crisis, he saw an opportunity to gain a deeper understanding of more general and entrenched dynamics. As he observed, "Because the normal order was un-settled, during these days much that is normally hidden was briefly uncov-ered" (this volume, 287).

Similarly, "Remembering and Dismembering the Nation," an article he co-wrote with Julie Skurski, was born in response to two state-promoted massacres in Venezuela that played important roles in the country's neolib-eral turn at the end of the 1980s. These events revealed central myths and deep fissures at the heart of Venezuela's nationalist project of modernity while also leaving enduring legacies. One of these events, the Caracazo, the term for the widespread popular uprising against the International Mon-etary Fund and military repression that encompassed Caracas and other cities in 1989, became for Hugo Chávez the massacre that helped to define his revolutionary trajectory. The Caracazo, for Chávez, symbolized the pro-found injustices and political failures that his movement would overcome.

While crises such as the Caracazo or the 2002 coup demanded Coronil's attention, they did so in a way that included a critical assessment of what it meant to have these events become defined as crises in the first place. Walter Benjamin's (1988: 257) insistence that "the tradition of the oppressed teaches us that the 'state of emergency' in which we live is not the exception but the rule" remained a guiding principle. In this, the challenge involved developing how the public recognition of emergencies or crises focused widespread attention on intolerable policies and actions while also eliding persistent forms of oppression and subordination. As in the case of Ven-ezuela's smallness, defining certain circumstances as crises and not others involves a hierarchical mapping of the world, masking structures of power and rendering particular peoples and experiences inconsequential and subordinate. A remapping of social categories and the relationships that undergird them was thus a constant, pressing need.

In Coronil's work on Venezuela, this remapping invariably led him back to the country's oil industry and to the notion of the future with which it became entwined. Beginning in the 1920s, Venezuela had been made into an "oil nation," a commonly used term that Coronil both questioned and imbued with a deeper meaning. Building on the work of the Latin American school of dependency theory and its analysis of enclave economies, he examined how oil has at once been central to Venezuelan capitalist accumulation and to its state and class formation. Yet Coronil criticized dependency scholars who viewed Venezuela's abundant foreign revenue as an exception to the dynamic of dependency and to its often attendant political instability. Instead, Coronil insisted, Venezuela shared crucial features with other nature-intensive exporting countries in Latin America and the Global South, all of which were also particularly prone to the negative effects of boom and bust cycles.

Coronil developed this insight during his involuntary return to Venezuela in the mid-1970s, a period of a spectacular oil boom, the inverse of the metropolitan oil crisis. This period quite naturally became one of the principal subjects of his book *The Magical State*. In it, Coronil examines the interwoven responses to the sudden "rivers" of international oil rents that flowed into the country, prompting a vision of "El Gran Venezuela" as modern, prosperous, and sovereign. Expansive state and consumer dreams were met by international bank promises, with offers of loans to construct a new Venezuela. Yet the petro-state simultaneously fueled imports in ways that undercut domestic forms of production. The rapid advent of a bust period, as oil prices and revenue fell, made the dreams of modernity and grand plans for transformation unattainable. Yet even in this failure, as Coronil also demonstrates, visions of a modern future persisted, fueled by the ongoing promise of oil revenues.

By establishing multilayered connections among policies, actors, money, and discourses, Coronil moved well beyond conventional political economic analysis. Yet rather than dismissing dependency theory as passé, he seriously engaged the theory's insights while participating in some of the foremost debates of the 1990s and 2000s about capitalism, state formation, and nationalist ideology. At the same time, his focus on nature, extraction, and ground rent anticipated more recent concerns with infrastructure and a "new materialism." His analysis of the oil economy and the oil state thus transcended conventional intellectual boundaries and disciplinary divides, ambitiously linking frameworks and objects of study that are typically treated in isolation from each other. As with the other elements of his work, elements of dependency theory were not mere building blocks. They were an active, interrelated presence, much like oil.

In Venezuela, Coronil argued, oil has ultimately shaped "politics at every level, defining the relation between citizens and nation, the formation of social classes, and the constitution of the state as the country's central political and economic agent" ("Venezuela's Wounded Bodies," this volume, 250). In the national imaginary, oil has acted as a kind of connective tissue that has brought the nation together. Yet as a volatile and intoxicating global commodity, oil has also torn the nation apart, fostering conflicts and fueling unfulfilled promises. In developing this perspective, Coronil claimed that Venezuela has two bodies: a natural body (territory and natural resources, including its oil) and a social body (people and citizens). In this conception, oil looms as the haunting and tantalizing promise of well-being and national redemption for the citizenry. As a solvent capable of reconciling the nation's two bodies, the state has maintained a powerful, even magical, hold on popular consciousness. It served as the custodian and developer of the nation's subsoil, promising to transform crude oil reserves into a changed landscape for the citizenry, "conjuring up the most fantastic dreams of progress" ([2000] 2016: 35). In this register, the state promises not only justice and effective governance but also national sovereignty and modernization. For Coronil, such promises take place in the powerful domain of what he termed "state fetishism."

Through oil production, the Venezuelan state became a landowner reliant on ground rent for profit, extracting surplus value from a nature-intensive industry. Given the volatile character of oil markets, the spectacular profit that oil can provide has also been unreliable and difficult to control. In analyzing the state's role as a landowner, Coronil built on Marx's (1981: 953) often overlooked argument that capitalism should be understood as a trinity form composed of capital-profit, labor-wages, and land-ground rent, each understood as an interactive bundle of social and spatial relations. While previous analysts examined how states mediated the relationship between capital and labor, they paid insufficient attention to the state's role in extracting and profiting from natural resource exports. But this mediation, Coronil demonstrated, is precisely what characterized Venezuela as an "oil nation."

Oil politics thus allowed Coronil to challenge the notion of Venezuela as a small or exceptional place. In Venezuela, as in many nations in the Global South, state-mediated ground rents from nature-intensive industries has been a critical, if overlooked, element in the making of global capitalism. The roots of this dynamic extend to the beginnings of colonialism in the Americas, as Spain and its colonies acted as rentier states in the production of such products as silver and sugar. Ultimately, Venezuela's trajectory as an oil nation has been forged in the inequitable and uneven processes of what Coronil insisted were the intertwined historical dynamics of capitalism *and* imperialism.

The Venezuelan state has occupied a critical and ambiguous space as a node and mediator in these global processes. As the caretaker of the nation's oil and its sovereignty, offering the appearance of autonomy, the state could promise, and at times deliver, wealth to the nation. But these promises and the state's ability to act on them were always circumscribed by its interactions with global forces. This long-term tension only deepened in the wake of Hugo Chávez's Bolivarian Revolution. As Coronil develops in "Oilpacity," the Chávez presidency actually intensified Venezuela's dependence on oil. This happened, in no small measure, because the regime sought to use oil income almost exclusively to address social problems. Resource dependency subsequently grew along with imports, while the business sector declined and shifted into financial and commercial activities. Following the coup, Chávez began to develop joint ventures with foreign companies, a process that helped both Chávez and the oil companies to consolidate their respective positions. As this unfolded, Chávez, a self-proclaimed anti-imperialist, came to rely ever more heavily on foreign oil companies and oil-export revenue. Like previous heads of state, then, Chávez maintained the vision of oil wealth as providing the promised future.

Coronil never shied away from confronting the contradictions of power or the power of contradictions. Throughout his work, he explored a troubled world of dominance, illusion, opacity, and mystification, shot through with silence, secrecy, violence, and inequity. Yet his analytical vision was never singularly bleak or without hope. For him, the very act of unveiling the labyrinthine histories of a seemingly small place such as Venezuela was a cause for optimism. By treating Venezuela not as a clearly delimited and isolated entity, but as a nation forged through intricate processes of transculturation within global relations of capitalism and imperialism, Coronil pursued what he called "a more democratic vision of history" ("Crude Matters," this volume, 286).

As with all of the terms he employed, Coronil critically assessed the use and effects of "democracy." In his essay "Transitions to Transitions," he recognized that "democracy" could itself be used in problematic ways, as when it was understood as an isolated set of practices or institutions that "developed" countries had and "developing" countries needed to obtain. He recognized democracy as a much broader concept, forming part of a shared inheritance from and beyond the Americas. He thus linked this concept to its shared pasts, presents, and possible futures. As Coronil insisted, the point is not simply to develop an exchange of ideas *about* democracy but, rather, to develop ideas *for* democracy ("Transitions to Transitions," this volume, 231). Concrete analyses of so-called small places in the Global South such as Venezuela were an integral part of this process. They were also a step toward realizing a more just and desirable world.

References

Benjamin, Walter. 1988. "Theses on the Philosophy of History." In *Illuminations: Essays and Reflections*, 253–64. New York: Schocken.

Coronil, Fernando. [2000] 2016. "Magical Illusions or Revolutionary Magic? Chávez in Historical Context." NACLA *Report on the Americas* 33, no. 6: 34–42.

Kincaid, Jamaica. 1988. *A Small Place*. New York: Farrar, Straus and Giroux.

Marx, Karl. 1981. *Capital*, vols. 1–3. New York: Vintage.

6   Dismembering and Remembering the Nation:
The Semantics of Political Violence in Venezuela

Coauthored with Julie Skurski

Y la muerte del pueblo fue como siempre ha sido:
como si no muriera nadie, nada,
como si fueran piedras las que caen
sobre la tierra, o agua sobre el agua.
—Pablo Neruda, *Canto General*

Violence and History

Although political violence has played a central part in the formation of nations, its historical constitution and its role in representing nations have
received scant attention. All too frequently the explanation of violence is
equated with the identification of its causes, its form is accounted for by its
function, and its function is seen in instrumental terms; violence is reduced
to a practical tool used by opposing social actors in pursuit of conflicting
ends. Whether treated as a cause, function, or instrument, violence is generally assumed rather than examined in its concreteness. Little attention is
paid to its specific manifestations, to the way its effects are inseparably related to the means through which it is exerted, and to the meanings that inform its deployment and interpretation. In contrast, typological approaches
that postulate a correspondence between types of societies and forms of violence often recognize the opacity of violence yet lose sight of the historical
depth and specificity of its manifestations.[1]

Moments of political violence may appear shatteringly similar in their
grim outcome and in the sheer physicality of the destruction they inflict.
Yet these moments, even those regarded as spontaneous outbursts, are
shaped by each society's particular history and myths of collective identity
and are energized by sedimented memories of threats to the collectivity.

In a critique of what he called the "spasmodic view of popular history," E. P. Thompson (1971) warned against viewing popular protest as a simple reaction to increasing prices, as if riots were the automatic response to economic stimuli, the result of compulsive rather than intentional historical agents. Just as riots are not a direct response to hunger, state repression is not simply a means to control popular unrest. Seemingly spontaneous popular action develops through the enactment of shared understandings and the enunciation of novel statements in a familiar idiom, while the state's use of force as a means to control unrest draws a vision of the natural ordering of society that is based on quotidian relations of domination. The immediacy and apparent naturalness of moments of collective violence may conceal their intentionality and socially constructed significance.

Violence is wielded and resisted in the idiom of a society's distinctive history. When it becomes a force in contending efforts to affirm or restructure a given vision of order, it simultaneously dis-orders and re-orders established understandings and arrangements. Aggression becomes inseparable from transgression, the rupture of conceptual and physical boundaries indivisible from the construction of new orders of significance. Violence pushes the limits of the permissible, opening up spaces where customary and unexpected meanings and practices are brought together in unprecedented ways, illuminating hidden historical landscapes in a flash, and leaving behind the opaque memory of ungraspable territories. In the crisis of meaning that violence conceives, the territoriality of nations and the corporeality of people become privileged mediums for reorganizing the body politic and for forcibly controlling the movement of people and ideas within the nation's material and cultural space. Statements to the collectivity are indelibly inscribed upon and made through the body, as it becomes a medium for searing assertions of power. The body is defiantly risked in the attempt to subvert ordinary restrictions and to avenge daily affronts. Individual biography and collective history seem momentarily united, as history and the body become each other's terrains.

Contending collective memories and differing accounts of an uncertain present shape these terrains. In this paper we examine two conflicts between the state and popular sectors in Venezuela and explore the making and representation of events regarded at the time as landmarks in that nation's history. We locate these conflicts in the context of their making, as they were conditioned at once by a colonial legacy and by a reordering of worldwide capitalist relations. As the hidden hand of finance capital and the visible hand of intellectual fashion etch the indeterminate boundaries of the postmodern map of the world, the contours of this landscape reveal the hold of transformed colonial relations in the age of postcolonial empires.[2]

History and the Massacres

The outbreaks of collective violence and civil unrest analyzed here were responses to social-economic transformations that in the past two decades have disrupted the bases of the populist political system based upon petroleum-rent distribution and have challenged the assumptions that had long sustained it. These conflicts became nodal points in the redefinition of the discourse of democracy, as dominant and opposition forces clashed over the interpretation of the events and their implications. The first conflict, a massacre that expressed the deepening crisis of the protectionist model of development and the hardening of the political system, occurred at the end of the 1988 presidential electoral campaign. It appeared far removed from the fanfare and display of politics, yet its message was directed to a national political audience. Fourteen villagers from the border town of Amparo were killed on October 29, 1988, on a remote cattle savanna on the Arauca River dividing southwestern Venezuela from Colombia. A government counterinsurgency brigade claimed the villagers were guerrillas killed by its troops in an armed encounter. Opponents contended that the government brigade had ambushed and disguised the innocent victims as a way of creating the appearance of a subversive threat to the nation. Electoral competition permitted these counterclaims to be amplified and validated within centers of power. As a result of sustained protest, the military encounter was publicly redefined as the Amparo massacre: an attack on innocent citizens who had no protection (*amparo*) against state violence and the manipulation of appearances.[3]

The second conflict, lasting from February 27 to March 3, 1989, was an urban social uprising in response to which the government used massive force: by official count, 277 people died (322 according to later studies[4]); by unofficial estimate, well over one thousand people were killed. This event reflected accumulated frustration with the nation's rapid economic decline and its political and economic corruption. It was detonated by the clash between the expectations of political and economic renewal raised by the electoral campaign and anger at newly elected President Carlos Andrés Pérez's abrupt adoption of a stringent International Monetary Fund (IMF) austerity program. In multiple unplanned protests over sharp price increases and food shortages, an estimated one million people spontaneously looted thousands of stores and factories in the capital and most major cities, in effect erasing state control of the street.[5] During five days the state responded to mass looting, redistribution, and destruction with containment, repression, and retaliation. It constituted by far the most massive and severely repressed such riots in the history of Latin America.[6]

The violent conflicts we discuss here shook assumptions concerning the relationship between civilization and barbarism, leader and *pueblo* (people), and state and citizen that have ordered populist discourse. In order to understand these unusual incidents of repression, protest, and revolt, we first look at the context in which they occurred. We then briefly examine dominant representations of the nation's history and promised future that articulate these relationships and became paradigms within populist discourse: the Bolivarian ideal of unity between leader and masses codified in official discourse and in the novel *Doña Bárbara*.[7]

The concept of democracy, which is the central term in Venezuela's dominant political discourse, draws on historical memories of autocratic rule and economic stagnation to validate the political party-led system of capitalist promotion. Dominant discourse holds democracy to be the nation's greatest achievement as well as the necessary condition for its progress. It closely links democracy to development, attributing Venezuela's rapid growth and prestige concerning political freedom and human rights to its multiparty system of government and construes the democratic regime to be the nation's guardian, entrusted with directing the flow of oil income to benefit the interests of the pueblo and the nation.[8] This conception of democracy builds implicitly on the memory of the nation's strife-filled history of *caudillo* rule and military strongmen, which lasted with brief interruptions until 1958; it rests as well on the memory of armed leftist opposition to the young democracy that occurred in the early 1960s. Populist discourse has linked internal threats to democracy from the right and the left to the presence of foreign threats to national sovereignty. In an effort to buttress its legitimacy and to strengthen its control of dissent, the democratic regime has kept alive the image of threats that reside concealed within the polity and at its borders, seeking the chance to return.[9]

The Venezuelan economy began a decline at the close of the 1970s into what became a crisis by the mid-1980s. It had experienced a short-lived euphoric oil boom, brought on by skyrocketing world oil prices, during President Pérez's first term of office (1974–79). His government launched an extraordinarily ambitious program to industrialize the economy, with the stated goal of freeing the nation from its dependence on oil exports.[10] The promise of rapid development, coupled with a protected economy in which state oil-rent distribution generously supported patronage-based political parties, raised expectations and defused opposition. But the program heightened tendencies within the rent-based system: a level of consumption that far outran production, concentration of power within the state and its allied economic groups, and corruption at the highest levels of the political and economic ruling elite. Moreover, the oil boom added a factor virtually absent from the Venezuelan economy since 1930: a large foreign debt.[11]

The unanticipated drop in world oil prices in the 1980s, the likelihood of which the country's leaders had ignored when they contracted the debt, propelled a downward slide of the economy.[12] In 1986, under President Jaime Lusinchi (1984–89), Venezuela signed a costly debt renegotiation agreement with the international banks.[13] It meant that repayment of the debt, rather than the state's promotion of development and social programs, received political priority. The financial sector and large economic groups with assets abroad and diversified investments at home profited; capital flight accelerated, as the wealthy deposited in foreign banks an estimated $60 billion, or twice the national debt, while domestic real income fell by 50 percent over this period. The debt service paid during Lusinchi's administration came to $30 billion and consumed 50 percent of the nation's foreign exchange, while the debt principal was only reduced from $35 billion to $32 billion. Although these changes undermined the basis of the protectionist model and powerful business organizations made gains in their promotion of free-market policies, the political elite maintained the rhetoric of populist nationalism. As the expectations this rhetoric fueled clashed with deteriorating conditions, political protest and disaffection with the nation's political leadership increased.

The rentier state's economic independence from a taxpayer base has permitted the Venezuelan political system, like the systems of other nations primarily dependent on exporting oil or other primary products, to become highly state-centered and unresponsive to demands from the public, thus discouraging the development of independent interests and organizations within civil society. Mechanisms of political reciprocity and accountability have remained restricted; elected officials obtain their position through their place in their party's hierarchy; and the expression of local demands is channeled through highly politicized structures.[14] Presidential campaigns, then, are the occasion for the promise of a dialogue between politicians and electorate to be momentarily constructed and consumed as an image.[15] Costly and lengthy, these campaigns orchestrate a national theater of democracy in which candidates seek to display mass support and their followers seek to position themselves favorably within the changing configuration of clientelistic ties.

The presidential election of 1988 prompted conflicting responses. The campaign brought to the fore a deep current of skepticism as regards electoral promises, yet it opened a space for opposition voices and raised hopes for economic improvement. It was a struggle not only between parties but within the ruling party, Acción Democrática (AD), as the Pérez and Lusinchi factions fought for control of its apparatus.[16] In the context of the campaign, fissures within AD facilitated public criticism of widespread administrative corruption and repression.

The election on December 4 brought two unprecedented results: for the first time in Venezuelan history, a former president was reelected, and voter abstention, previously below 10 percent, reached 20 percent. In addition, the left increased its representation in Congress, and Pérez's leading opponent made inroads in areas of AD allegiance. In comparison with Pérez's first victory (1973), which brought forth triumphant celebrations in the streets, this one was edged with skepticism and critique. Many wary voters had decided that Pérez might dare to bring about dramatic change, but they had weak allegiance to his party.[17]

It was widely believed that Pérez would bring an improvement in economic conditions. A leader of major initiatives during the oil boom of 1974–78, he had maintained his image as a decisive man of action who could defy domestic and international powers in defense of the nation and the pueblo.[18] His spectacular inaugural celebration on February 2, 1989, confirmed his image, for it convoked a wide spectrum of political leaders from 108 countries and issued a call to debtor nations to lobby against the oppressive policies of international banks and the IMF.[19] Yet unknown to the general public, Pérez was sending a quiet message to the banks at the negotiating table, where he offered to fulfill stringent conditions.

Within days of his inauguration, Pérez gravely announced the content of his inaugural promise to *sincerar* (to make truthful) the economy. The free market would cleanse it of monopolies and artificial practices, allowing it to become productive. The means consisted of a strict austerity program, administered rapidly and in a large dose, like a strong medicine.[20] He informed the public, which was largely unfamiliar with the consequences of such policies, that subsidies for basic goods would be eliminated, price controls ended, exchange rates unified and the currency allowed to fluctuate, tariffs lowered, interest rates freed, and the price of government services increased. Rejecting labor demands, he did not institute a wage raise, job freeze, or welfare measures. Instead, he offered the hope that international banks would quickly provide Venezuela with fresh money to tide it over its pressing situation and would forgive a significant percentage of its outstanding debt, making strict austerity a brief treatment on the path to economic recovery. His promise was to establish solid economic foundations for Venezuela's democracy. Just as protectionist import substituting industrialization had been established thirty years earlier in the name of strengthening democracy, it was now to be dismantled for the same reason.

The Bolivarian Ideal

Venezuelan nationalist discourse conceives of history as the uncertain advance of civilization over barbarism. In the struggle between these contending forces, the never fully achieved goal of locating the nation within the flow of world progress is felt to be constantly undermined by outside enemies and by the no less threatening savagery of the land and people within. Nationalist discourse has constructed history as the ongoing effort to conquer the natural and social geography, freeing the nation from the external and internal forces that undermine sovereignty and obstruct its progress. Accounts of foreign threats, rebellions, dictatorships, and industrialization campaigns chart a course of incomplete progress in which significant discontinuities and recurrent new beginnings mark the nation's spasmodic advance.

This view of history as conquest, represented spatially as the colonizing movement from the center toward the peripheral frontier, is embedded in numerous narratives recounting the nation's foundation. Official history has constructed certain events and figures as templates of the nation's civilizing project, embodiments of foundational relationships in terms of which the present is intended to be read and the future constructed. The epic tale of Simón Bolívar's battle to achieve South America's independence from Spain is the master narrative for nationalist discourse. It recounts Bolívar's victory against external forces, followed by incomplete success at home; this fusing of victory and defeat renders it particularly compelling as a model for projects that call for national unity to pursue an ever receding goal of modernity.

Official history presents Bolívar, a member of one of the largest land-holding families of the Creole oligarchy, as a providential leader empowered to represent the elite and speak for the unformed masses.[21] Depicted as a political and military genius with a unique capacity to communicate with and lead the common man, he brought over to the revolutionary cause the unruly llaneros, mestizo plainsmen who initially supported the Spanish crown during the Independence War (1811–21). At the outset, the llaneros and rebel slaves made devastating attacks on the families and estates of the landed oligarchy, turning the conflict into a civil war with racial dimensions.[22] Only after Bolívar allied with the llanero leader Jose Antonio Páez, promising the distribution of estate property to his troops and the manumission of slaves, could the patriots' side command broad support and defeat the royalists. The narrative of Bolívar's triumph depicts the patrician hero as having redirected the rebel masses' anarchic energies toward the construction of a liberal national order. This image has been encoded as a model of the union between civilizing force and barbarous energy that must be reproduced in the struggle to achieve historical progress.[23]

Nationalist discourse has suppressed from official history the oligarchy's prolonged resistance to slave abolition and its failure after the war to command broad allegiance from the population. Its attempts to govern throughout the turbulent nineteenth century were rent by caudillo-led revolts and defined by fear of the masses.[24] Throughout this period, contending regional caudillos offered their rural followers the opportunity to loot (saquear) the haciendas of the landed elite as recompense during their repeated assaults on power, and slave and peasant uprisings resulted in looting of the propertied. "Looting" (saqueo) also described in popular terminology the relationship of the caudillo victor to the state; his object of conquest was the state apparatus, which he could then loot by wielding his political power for personal enrichment.[25]

Only when foreign capital developed the petroleum industry in the 1920s did the economic elite—as it changed from an agrarian to a commercial base and allied politically with the middle class—offer a model of the national community that had broad social appeal. Popular and elite nationalism then found common ground in the project to democratize oil wealth and to modernize Venezuela through state protectionism (Coronil 1987). As the foundations of the state changed, the image of Bolívar as a tutelary leader of an unformed pueblo became a template for the construction of the nationalist development project. The Bolivarian ideal of the national community became elaborated and institutionalized within populist discourse and the democratic regime, linking the past to the hoped-for future and legitimizing the role of reformist parties. The massacres and the popular unrest we discuss here were intimately related forms of contestation and transformation of this ideal.

Populist Nationalism: Doña Bárbara

"A canoe travels up the Arauca River." This line opens the novel Doña Bárbara, written by Rómulo Gallegos during the regime of the caudillo autocrat Juan Vicente Gómez (1908–35),[26] quickly acclaimed by the dictator's supporters, as well as by his opponents, as the greatest literary expression of national identity. The novel's first line locates the reader on a journey inward in space and backward in time, at the social edges of the nation, where the Conquest is incomplete. The Arauca River crosses the Llanos in the state of Apure, marking Venezuela's southern frontier with Colombia. It traverses a sparsely populated region once inhabited by cattle hunters and contrabandists who were the troops for warring caudillos in the nineteenth century. To follow the river upstream, it is understood, is to enter a primitive social world, one that the novel constructs as an emblem of the backward nation.[27] The novel maps this space as the symbolic site for the construction of a new national identity. The establishment of the rule of law, private property, and legal marital union, it promises, will eliminate despotism and backwardness and domesticate savage man and untamed nature.

The boat carries Santos Luzardo (Holy Light), a lawyer from the capital who returns to his origins and faces challenges that make him complete as a man and as a historical agent. He confronts and tames the two sides of barbarism: the destructive (savage) dimension embodied by the powerful yet seductive mestiza (mixed race) horsewoman Doña Bárbara (a symbol of the dictator Gómez) and the innocent (wild) dimension embodied by her beautiful but primitive and untutored daughter Marisela (an emblem of the pueblo). Doña Bárbara (Lady Barbarian) rules despotically through her knowledge of primitive people and nature, using Indian sorcery and murderous henchmen to monopolize land and corrupt authority. Luzardo resolves to defeat her and to replace the rule of force by the rule of law. If he fails and succumbs to her temptations to act outside the law, he risks repeating the fate of her discarded alcoholic lover, Lorenzo Barquero, a once brilliant lawyer and Luzardo's cousin, whom she had seduced and made her pawn. In order to transform the Llanos, Santos Luzardo cannot simply eliminate Doña Bárbara. He must domesticate and instruct the helpless

Marisela, who is as innocent as untamed nature, in proper feminine speech and behavior. Once she becomes aware of her own backwardness and attempts to overcome it, Marisela is eligible for his love. Luzardo then courts her, and their promised union signals the end of Doña Bárbara's despotic rule. Their union marks as well the end of open-range cattle ranching and the beginning of modern production, as ranches are fenced to delimit their boundaries and cattle are raised in bounded spaces.

A foundational fiction that depicts the path to nation building through an allegorical romance,[28] the narrative charts the domestication of unconquered nature and uncivilized humans. The rule of law replaces the rule of violence, and the dominion of matrimonial love supplants the reign of sexual conquest. The relationship between energy and law, passion and love, the pueblo and the state is transformed from one of coercion and opposition into one of attraction and union. Marriage between the elite and the pueblo will create, it promises, national historical progress. The modern state, capitalism, and the bourgeois family will be harmoniously wed.[29]

An unacknowledged tension underlying this apparently linear tale of the triumph of progress organizes this myth's capacity to act as a template within the populist project. The novel closes with Doña Bárbara's disappearance but not her elimination. Overcome by her impossible love for Luzardo and by her newfound sentiment for her daughter, she renounces her power and returns downriver to her origins. A submerged presence, her reappearance is an unknown potential. She resides in the land and in the collective psyche. Luzardo and Marisela must struggle against the pull of savage barbarism, for ultimately it lies within themselves and the pueblo, requiring careful taming and containment.

This ambiguity, the sense of attraction and repulsion toward the repressed side of the popular, has structured the construction of the nation's populist discourse.[30] In his early writing, Gallegos (1954: 101) called for enlightened leaders to achieve the "containment of barbarism" whose "dark instinctual tendencies" were the energy that "rushes like a river overflowing its bed." In the allegorical romance Doña Bárbara, the river of instinctual energy represents the attraction and repulsion toward the repressed side of the people that is central to populist discourse.

As an allegorical tale of national, class, and family foundation, Doña Bárbara brings Bolívar back to earth, creating a powerful image of the modernizing leader who courts the untutored pueblo, ruling by consent rather than coercion. This hopeful view of national transformation became imaginable only with the growth of the oil industry in the 1920s and with the progress it promised. The emerging middle-class leaders of the 1930s and 1940s, many of whom were involved in clandestine political activities against the dictatorship and in the organization of nascent parties in the hinterland, saw themselves heroically reflected in the novel. For a certain social sector, it became a template for action, an image of the conquest of modernity.[31] As the AD party gained power in the 1940s, a formative period for the nation's present political leadership, the novel was canonized by populist discourse and educational curriculum. *Doña Bárbara* attained the status of nationalist myth, charting the nation's development as an ever present process of conquest.

The Amparo Massacre

The Theater of Violence

A canoe travels up the Arauca River. Thus began a drama on October 29, 1988—the beginning of a history that would be retold in opposing versions from competing sites of power and incorporated into alternative images of the nation. The boat with sixteen men entered a densely wooded branch of the river, the Caño Colorado, on a Saturday morning. Peasants far from the site heard massive outbursts of gunfire, followed by shooting from military helicopters. Within hours, reporters were flown to the scene by the military. General Humberto Antonio Camejo Arias, regional commander of the border counterinsurgency brigade CEJAP,[32] announced a successful encounter with fifty heavily armed members of Colombia's ELN (National Liberation Army) guerrilla organization, which had planned to sabotage oil pipes and kidnap ranchers within Venezuela. He stated that sixteen guerrillas had been killed, although the twenty-member security brigade reported no injuries.[33] Photos of bodies with ELN insignia and lying next to guns on the river shore quickly appeared in the press. President Lusinchi congratulated the general for controlling threats to Venezuela's borders and to its democracy.[34]

Two days later, voices challenging this version emerged in the press and were taken up by diverse sectors. The claims came from the outraged townspeople of Amparo located across the river from Colombia: the dead men were not Colombians but Venezuelans; they were not guerrillas but unarmed fishermen and workers, family men on a fishing expedition; they were preparing not the sabotage of oil pipes but the most popular weekend pastime of fishing and sharing a pot of soup (*sancocho*) and rum by the banks of the river. Above all, there were not sixteen dead men but fourteen. Two men had escaped by swimming through the swampy stream as helicopters searched for them overhead. With the aid of a neighboring rancher and the local police chief, they had returned to town in terror the next day to tell the story of the ambush. Fearing reprisals, they took refuge in the police station. When the National Guard and the DISIP asserted they were going to remove them from Amparo for questioning, a mass of angry townspeople impeded them from doing so, and the police chief, risking his life, threatened to shoot the DISIP officials if they insisted. Alarmed by the prospect of a civil disturbance, government authorities contacted Congressman Walter Márquez of the socialist party Movimiento al Socialismo (MAS), a well-known political activist in the border region, to mediate the situation.[35] The survivors were released into his custody, and he began what was to become a long campaign in their defense.

The government's effort to impose its version of reality began with the concealment of the victim's bodies and the discrediting of the towns-people's claims. The bodies, after being viewed by the press, were brought back to Amparo by the military and hastily buried, without the legally required autopsy, so that they could not reveal what had been done to them. Townspeople, Congressman Márquez, and journalists at the scene soon offered evidence that contradicted the government's claims. In response to growing denunciations, General Camejo Arias gave a televised declaration on November 4 in which he dismissed the veracity of the survivors' statements and claimed that intelligence reports confirmed that the men were linked to the ELN, had criminal and subversive records, and were on a sabotage mission.[36] They had offered armed resistance to the CEJAP brigade and were killed in action. President Lusinchi supported the general, insisting that these criminal guerrillas were part of a campaign to subvert democracy. He dismissed the denials of guerrilla ties by the people of Amparo, for the "golden rule of the clandestine struggle" is that you cannot tell "even those most closely related to you what you are doing" (El Nacional, November 5, 1988).

Investigation of the case began on two fronts: President Lusinchi assigned it to a military court, and a multiparty Congressional Commission began its own investigation shortly thereafter. By placing the case under military jurisdiction, the government shrouded it in the military's rules of secrecy and shielded it from the pressures of politicians and the press. Military judges, moreover, were likely to be personally and institutionally disposed in favor of the CEJAP. In effect, Judge Ricardo Pérez Gutiérrez, a close ally of General Camejo Arias, obstructed the investigation and maintained a hostile stance toward the survivors, José Augusto Arias and Wollmer Gregorio Pinilla.[37]

Congress named a five-man, multiparty commission on November 9, headed by a congressional ally of Carlos Andrés Pérez, to take testimony from officials and draw up an independent report.[38] Four days after the massacre, in direct disagreement with President Lusinchi, Pérez denied in a press conference that the villagers were subversives. He noted that many were members of AD who had supported his campaign, and he promised that justice would be applied.[39] His campaign rival, Eduardo Fernández of the Social Christian Party (Comité Organizador Partido Electoral Independiente, or COPEI), visited Amparo, an AD stronghold, and promised retribution for the victims' families.

In all likelihood, the massacre would have gained little national notice and the commission would not have been formed had it not occurred at the end of the electoral campaign. But the president's attempt to cast the deaths at Amparo in terms of the defense of democracy from external threat associated the concept of democracy with the narrow manipulation of power and appearances contrasted with the electoral campaign's effort to represent democracy in its most inclusive and popular terms. Lusinchi's stance brought to the fore the image of arbitrary rule established through coercion: it evoked the return of Doña Bárbara, devising and manipulating her own law.

The centrist presidential candidates, finding the regime's credibility threatened, hastened to defend democracy by demonstrating that the democratic system rested on the rule of law, not force, and that it defended national rather than particularistic interests. As opposition grew from outside the confines of the political elite, in the press and in leftist circles, Congress and the center parties sought to preempt the opposition, claiming for themselves the ability to uphold democracy's principles of legality and justice. Beyond their attempt to obtain electoral gain lay the effort to reproduce the moral-political bases on which the regime rested. In this process, dominant discourse created its own centrist opposition to the official line of argument, establishing a counterpoint between differing dimensions of democracy. Political leaders shifted the focus of appeal from the external threat to democracy, which Lusinchi evoked, to the submerged internal threat to democracy, which the collective lack of faith in democratic institutions would allegedly allow to reappear. Playing on the memory of civil strife and dictatorship, they cast the investigation as proof that the state, directed by the existing political elite, had the capacity to correct what they depicted as personalistic abuses of power, not structural problems.

Official, centrist, and opposition interpretations of the events emerged through many channels. The Congressional Commission called the directors of security agencies and the CEJAP brigade members to testify. These men reiterated the official claim that the fishermen were subversives and denounced Arias and Pinilla as guerrillas who were posing as innocent survivors. Although they cited unspecified intelligence reports, they primarily based their argument on the assumption that the dead men were the type of person—poor, uneducated border villagers of no means or reputation—who could be presumed to be allied with subversives.[40] General Camejo Arias asserted to the commission, "They are implicated in crime, because of that symbiosis that exists, that union that exists between crime and non-crime, in that mixture that exists between men from Colombia and men from Venezuela. . . . In those river areas there is practically nobody who is not involved in some kind of crime however small it might be, out there everyone is involved" (República de Venezuela 1989: 459). Barbarism still resides on the Llanos.

Cracks immediately appeared in this story, revealing a carelessly devised simulacrum. Government officials could not produce police records for the victims, and neither Venezuelan nor Colombian military intelligence agencies corroborated the claims of their records as subversives.[41] Reporters and congressmen visiting the site of the attack with the survivors filmed them on repeated occasions reenacting their escape (they swam skillfully through the waters, disproving their accusers' contentions) and found at the scene discarded cans of acid and clothes that were taken off the fishermen; the shell casings they found were only from M19 rifles, the DISIP's weapon.[42] They noted that the weapons displayed with the dead men were few and insignificant and that relatives of the victims had observed that the bodies were disfigured and had been shot in the head and back. The autopsy that the Colombian officials performed on the Colombian victim soon after his death stated that he had been shot in the back, his skull crushed by heavy blows, and his face burned with acid.

One month after the attack, due to delays imposed by Judge Pérez Gutiérrez, the Congressional Commission obtained an order for the bodies to be exhumed and an autopsy performed. In an open field, with congressmen, journalists, and family members looking on, forensic doctors found evidence that the men had been shot point-blank from behind, some tortured and mutilated, their bones crushed, and their tattoos and faces burned.[43] The judge prevented the release of the autopsy report, but news of what witnesses had observed was published, shocking the public. Evidence accumulated that the CEJAP's leaders had organized the ambush with General Camejo Arias's knowledge, were aware of the planned Saturday fishing outing, and were possibly instrumental in organizing it. They dressed several of the dead men in ELN uniforms (which lacked bullet holes) and had placed a few guns next to them.[44] This simulacrum of subversion was constructed for national, not local consumption, for it was clear that the townspeople of Amparo would recognize the victims. The assumption was that they were too powerless—and terrified—to counter the government's claims. Made more potent by the extremity and starkness of its elements, Amparo became a symbol because of the ways in which power and identity were constructed within the realm of everyday life. Explanations for the massacre's occurrence were incomplete, yet the issue of the massacre awoke broad public interest and the growing sentiment, outside of the conservative upper class, that the men had been victimized.

The fate of the survivors was emblematic of the inversion of order that the state could effect. After hearing testimony from the survivors and the CEJAP members, on November 14 Judge Pérez Gutiérrez ordered the arrest of Arias and Pinilla on charges of military rebellion, provoking protests at this conversion of the victims into the accused. Congressman Márquez had kept them in hiding, but they feared for their lives if they turned themselves in, as was expected. Márquez took the public by surprise by clandestinely obtaining refuge for them in the Mexican ambassador's house on November 21. On December 9, Arias and Pinilla were flown to Mexico after its government granted them political refuge. This international acknowledgment that their safety could not be assured undermined the official version of events and the government's image regarding human rights.

Once Pérez was elected president, the case appeared to reverse its direction. Pérez had promised to change its terms, and he sought to have Amparo removed as a point of political pressure by the time of his inauguration in February. An arrest order was issued for the CEJAP members on December 30 on charges of falsifying a crime, illicit use of arms, and homicide. After President-elect Pérez assured them of safe treatment, Arias and Pinilla returned to Venezuela on January 2 and turned themselves in. When a higher military court ruled there was no evidence against them, the charges were dropped, and they were freed on January 17. With their assailants now detained, they returned to Amparo amid celebrations, accompanied by representatives of a newly formed network of human rights activists, clergy, and political leaders. Critics noted, however, that the massacre's planners—in particular, Camejo Arias and Henry López Sisco—remained in power, and the pressures to obstruct the case were enormous.[45]

In this period of electoral transition, the Congressional Commission forged the emerging dominant version of events. Its report to Congress on January 18, 1989, concluded that an armed confrontation had not occurred and recommended that this "different event" be investigated judicially. It questioned that the victims were guerrillas and detailed the false and contradictory testimony given by the attack's planners and participants. While it criticized individual military officers, including General Camejo Arias and Judge Pérez Gutiérrez, it recommended that the DISIP be removed from the CEJAP and that military forces alone should direct a coordinated policy of development and defense of Venezuela's border.[46] Approved by the major parties, the report was portrayed as a validation of Venezuela's democratic processes. Acclaiming this achievement, Pérez promised to reorganize these security agencies and achieve justice for the victims as soon as he took office.

Alternative Representations

How did the opposition depict the massacre? In this seemingly open political system, issues of presidential and military credibility are hedged by unwritten rules bound by the mandate not to question the integrity of government institutions. Only after President Pérez was in office did opposition leaders offer fuller outlines of an alternative explanation, for they felt the threat of retaliation had lessened. The opposition version of events suggested that the Amparo massacre was carried out to further the interests of a highly placed set of intelligence, military, and business figures having strong economic interests in the border region. Backed by his documentation of this and previous cases of CEJAP violence obtained through confidential contacts, Márquez argued that powerful regional interests backed the counterinsurgency brigade's ascent as a "subversive manufacturing machine."[47] He stressed that the DISIP, whose commanders controlled the CEJAP, had become a politically privileged paramilitary organization involved in illicit activities in the western border area through which it expanded its power and buttressed that of its landowner and business allies. Ideologically fueled by extreme anticommunism, the foreign-trained commandos reputedly charged ranchers for protection from subversives; at the same time, in alliance with ranchers, the DISIP terrorized peasants and Indians so they would not defend their lands from encroachment by powerful landowners, many of whom were retired military men.

The Amparo attack, the opposition version claimed, had a history that included several prior DISIP and CEJAP massacres of alleged subversives.[48] The border brigade had manufactured subversives—generally undocumented Colombian workers who were lured into ambushes and brutally killed, their bodies then displayed as guerrillas. These supposed subversives were used to justify continuing government and rancher support for the DISIP and its autonomy in the region.[49] The previous massacres had not created a public outcry, in part because they involved Colombians or (in earlier years) Venezuelan leftists and because they did not take place during an electoral period. Each confrontation further justified the DISIP's power and augmented the president's image as the defender of a threatened democracy while spreading fear among different sectors of the population.

The subtext of the opposition account of men and their abuses was that a woman who epitomized the calculated manipulation of power connected this murky network of strongmen directly to President Lusinchi—his longtime mistress, Blanca Ibáñez. Her relationship to him and her extensive political influence could not be mentioned in the press (the secretary of the press exerted direct pressures on the media) but were widely recognized. Although she formally held the minor post of secretary to the president, she had become a central figure in his administration.[50] For those with power, she held the key to influencing decisions about government appointments and investments; for those without power, she was a distributor of presidential favors to the poor in charitable events and in the barrios, not unlike Eva Perón. Her distribution of patronage was tied closely to the securing of political control and the repression of dissent. She made the DISIP her special province, influencing the appointment of its directors and maintaining close links to its commander of operations, López Sisco, and his ally, General Camejo Arias. Critics maintained that through a combination of patronage and surveillance she had constructed a fiefdom of power that extended ties into the upper levels of economic and political activity, playing a role in Lusinchi's ability to silence dissent and to sustain the appearance of consent to his policies.

The opposition's accusations about responsibility for the Amparo massacre made unspoken reference to this reality. The sustained criticism of the Amparo massacre, seemingly focused on the abuses of an uncontrolled intelligence unit, implicated the specific forms through which power was exerted during this administration. Within the opposition, opinions differed as to whether these forms were limited to this administration or whether the relations of power that outlasted the tenure of the Lusinchi presidency were at stake.[51]

The Credibility of Power

Occurring at a time of political transition, the Amparo massacre jolted interpretive schemes, provoking a sense of indignation among sectors of the urban populace ordinarily uninterested in the fate of rural people and inclined to believe accusations of their criminality.[52] In protest against the government's cover-up, student-led demonstrations occurred during November in Caracas and other major cities, many of which ended in property destruction and police violence. A large demonstration in Caracas, the March for Life (November 10), brought together a wide spectrum of groups, using puppets and street theater to depict the massacre, in a march downtown to Congress. In the emerging contestatory interpretation, the government was the oppressor and the pueblo the innocent victim. A crescendo of protests, in which Christian base groups and activist clergy were vocal, created images of the Amparo fishermen as symbols of a martyred pueblo. They articulated a widely circulating opposition view: the Amparo victims stand for all of us. They are *desamparados*: forsaken, without legal protection, rights, or even identity. They are ordinary people, pawns in a system of inverted values. They are victims of government manipulation: deceived, used, and discarded.

The Amparo massacre resonated in the public imagination with the foundational tale of civilization and barbarism on the Llanos: the Arauca River in the state of Apure, the lawless frontier ruled by force, outbursts of savagery, and the helplessness of the pueblo in the face of personalized power. Many people were quick to relate the event to Gallegos's novel.[53] The drama of *Doña Bárbara* appeared to have been reenacted in Amparo, but who played what role in the tale? Was the CEJAP a representative of the law or a repressive tool like Doña Bárbara's henchmen? Were the men in the canoe barbarous subversives or innocent people of the pueblo, personifications of Marisela? Was Blanca Ibáñez the ruthless Doña Bárbara and President Lusinchi her submissive lover, Lorenzo Barquero? Or were they the representative of civilizing order, Santos Luzardo, in this drama? Or was Walter Márquez or Carlos Andrés Pérez the incarnation of Santos Luzardo? Or was he absent entirely?

Counterinterpretations of the massacre challenged not just the official version of events but the government's capacity to construct its own image. Throughout its tenure, the Lusinchi administration had relied on obscuring reality to maintain its public support. While it confronted the debt crisis by denying that a crisis existed, it financed state expenditures with Venezuela's international reserves, consuming them entirely by the end of his administration. Through polished propaganda focused on the president's affable personality, the administration reassured the public that the state's paternalistic role would remain unaltered, but a report by Amnesty International delivered to the government in July 1988, prior to the Amparo massacre, documented the administration's escalating suppression of political protest and its constant police and military violence against the poor (see Amnesty International 1987, 1988).[54] The state reproduced ever more overtly its official image as the protector of an anarchic pueblo while silencing its critics as "subversives."

By the end of Lusinchi's administration, dwindling resources made the illusion of abundance and progress increasingly tenuous. The Amparo massacre occurred not at the hopeful dawn of petrodollar-fueled growth when *Doña Bárbara* was written, but fifty years later, when credit and credibility were running out for the protectionist model of national development. Without projects to feed the promise of national development or the pacifying illusion of individual upward mobility, the political space of the nation shrank to a parochial arena. The threat of finding the path of historical progress blocked had become real for the citizens and for the nation.

Our interpretation of the Amparo massacre suggests that the Venezuelan state asserted its authority in a theatrical mode, constructing a drama whose plot reenacted the civilizing myth of the state as the scriptwriter. This simulacrum—the representation of the illusion of representing the real—rests on the controlled tension between fact and appearance, between attention to evidence and disregard for conflicting information, and thus on the willingness to allow cracks in the performance to reveal the arbitrariness of authority. Fear grows out of these cracks.[55] As in detective stories in which certain clues are left behind in order to induce a misreading, the visible marks of artifice in the misrepresentations of politics are not necessarily to be treated as faults but as signs to be deciphered.

El Masacrón

The Great Turn

When Carlos Andrés Pérez was elected on December 4, 1988, many, including opposition leaders, believed he would restore the tutelary bond between leader and pueblo and halt the nation's shrinkage and backward slide. His first term of office saw providential wealth raise living standards and establish Venezuela as a leader of Latin American economic integration. Thus, despite Pérez's links to corruption and to the debt, he represented for one current of collective memory the Bolivarian promise that the state would battle for social justice and economic independence. The electoral campaign had raised the hope that his presidency would signal an end to retrogression, a reopening of the nation to progress.

"The river overflowed its bed" (El río se salió de la madre) was the headline of an opinion article in the newspaper El Nacional on March 4, 1989, that described the outpouring of people into the streets of fourteen cities during five days of popular unrest and looting that shook Venezuela between February 27 and March 3, 1989.[56] These events constituted the most massive as well as the most violently suppressed urban protest in Venezuelan history. On February 27, 1989, masses of people took over the streets of most of the nation's major cities, particularly in the capital region, protesting increasing prices and looting stores.[57] Once the government recovered from its paralyzing shock, it responded with the suspension of constitutional guarantees and a storm of bullets. Thousands were wounded and arrested, and the official death toll reached 277. Unofficial estimates that observers from many fields circulated confidentially, however, estimated there were well over one thousand fatalities.[58]

No comparable social upheaval, in terms of the extent of the looting or the ferocity of the repression, had taken place in contemporary Latin America in response to an economic austerity plan. The total number of people reported killed in fifty different protest events occurring between 1976 and 1986 in thirteen countries was under two hundred; the most violent single incident had been the 1984 riots in the Dominican Republic, which claimed sixty lives (Walton 1989: 188). While the so-called IMF riots were frequent during this span, according to John Walton they generally grew out of organized protest, such as strikes and demonstrations, and they tended to select certain targets, both political and business. The Venezuelan riots, however, did not emerge from organized efforts, although they were preceded by years of sporadic conflicts in certain cities, and the looting was aimed at a broad range of businesses, encompassing street vendors and modern supermarkets, workshops and factories.

The events that shook state authority and fragmented the social territory also disrupted established interpretive schemes, resisting the efforts of official and opposition forces to fix them with a name. Official discourse neutrally labeled the conflict "27-F" and "the events" (los sucesos). The terms "the disturbances" and the "big jolt" (*el sacudón*), which suggest a passing disruption of the normal order, became widely accepted in the media. Opposition discourse introduced the terms social explosion, popular uprising (*poblada*), and the big massacre (*el masacrón*).[59] The stark label "the war" was common among professionals, expressing the social fracture that the middle class had experienced. It recalled as well the feared return of the civil wars that marked the nineteenth century whose memory has been kept present by government leaders. These differing classifications reflect the uncertain attempts to control the historical construction of events that overflowed traditional channels of contestation and categories of collective agency.

What had happened between February 2, when Pérez's spectacular inauguration took place, and February 27? On assuming the presidency, pressured by an acute shortage of funds, President Pérez took up the internationalist strand of Venezuela's Bolivarian nationalist ideology in an effort to refocus the state's civilizing mission.[60] He defined Venezuela as a leader of the debtor nations' battle against domination by international banks, a promoter of Latin America's unity against threats to its independence. This image built on the anticolonial component of nationalist discourse that equates national independence with equality and depicts the quest to free nations from foreign domination as a moral struggle. By evoking these shared assumptions, with their resonances of social justice, Pérez sought a legitimating link with official history for the government's policies.

On assuming the presidency, Pérez initiated his administration with an attack on the IMF and international lenders in the name of an imagined community of Latin American borrowers. Yet at the same time, his administration, committed to an IMF-inspired austerity economic program yet urgently needing new loans, sought to persuade the international banking community of its commitment to rationalizing the economy. Thus, Pérez criticized both the IMF and the domestic protectionist policies that had created a sick economy in need of emergency treatment. The prescription was the cleansing medicine of an austerity program. Through rhetorical jujitsu, the obligatory was made to appear desirable, the imposed to appear self-chosen.

The crucial task in the new economic strategy, and a condition the banks made for obtaining new loans, was to open the protective shell that had insulated the nation against international competition throughout most of this century. Ideologically constructed as a momentous historical change, this decision redefined Venezuela's place in history and in the world. From this perspective, the protected and subsidized market had fostered parasitical capitalists, inefficient industries, and corrupt politicians. But lacking the oxygen of abundant petrodollars, protectionism was asphyxiating the nation. Insulation from international competition had meant isolation from economic competence. Opening the nation to the world market meant building bridges to capitalism, allowing its rationality to flow into the nation. This new policy, which meant the decline of many small businesses, was suddenly presented as common sense. It received the strongest endorsement from wealthy businessmen and politicians able to retain power through the transition. This manner of pursuing modernity also made the nation vulnerable to world-market relations. The state had created an exceptionally sheltered domestic space—a fertile ground for cultivating hierarchical alliances and weaving illusions of social harmony. Opening this shell also meant tearing down this web of relations and shared understandings.

With the acceptance of the curative rationality of the free market, an important change occurred in the discourse of nationalist modernization. The achievement of a healthy economy became valorized as the nation's primary goal—above that of forming a developed pueblo. Although these goals had coexisted in parallel fashion in the discourse of protectionist modernization, arguments now openly privileged the economy's demands, subordinating those of the pueblo. The civilizing relationship that weds state and pueblo and engenders national progress no longer appeared as a protective bond. The dismembering of this bond was dramatically prefigured by the Amparo massacre. The border llaneros again became the emblems of the pueblo, but they were now transformed into a subversive threat to be silenced and written upon, evoking collective memories of the conquest.

With the ascent of a populist variant of free-market discourse under Pérez, the pueblo was presented as the undisciplined and lazy product of an unproductive economy, a symptom of the sickness caused by easy money obtained during years of abundant oil rents. The official effort to explain the crisis without seriously implicating the nation's ruling elite presented Venezuelans as wanton consumers. The assumption was that if the state's protectionist structures were dismantled, people would turn to productive work, for they needed the discipline and the instruction that the market could provide. The new administration introduced its adjustment program using a moral language of reform. Although it spoke of the need to reform individual behavior, it did not address social reform, which had long been central to protectionist discourse. The latter had promised to correct social inequities by intervening in the organization of the market. Instead, free-market discourse promised to correct economic distortions by reorienting individual behavior and perceptions.

In an oft-repeated lament, Pérez claimed that Venezuelans had been living in a world of illusion and false expectations. They must now face reality. On February 16, Pérez announced El gran viraje (The Great Turn): the move from artificial to real capitalism. The government would soon cut tariffs, remove price controls and subsidies, and unify the exchange rate at market levels, thus eliminating the preferential rates that had continued to subsidize imports subsequent to official devaluations. While these measures would take time to design and implement, the expectation of their advent, together with a shortage of foreign exchange, prompted a series of escalating processes.

The reality that consumers faced diverged wildly from one of market rationality. Confronted with the imminent dismantling of protectionism and the rising costs of imports, manufacturers cut back production, and businesses hoarded products. Several weeks before Pérez's inauguration, in an effort to drive prices up, businesses withheld government-regulated food and consumer items from the stores. Angry confrontations in markets and grocery stores between sellers and consumers escalated as consumers found that supplies of basic goods were rationed in stores, and they accused sellers of hoarding and of favoring their preferred customers. These confrontations occurred far from the large businesses that oligopolistically controlled commerce; they took place above all where the middle class and the poor shopped, in stores often run by Portuguese, Chinese, and Lebanese immigrants whom many thought to be avaricious and unscrupulous.

Commercial hoarding was met by consumer hoarding. Shortages and anticipated price hikes provoked consumer runs on products, a snowballing desire to stock up on necessities in preparation for the disruption of production or for some unknown eventuality. In uncertain times, hoarding provided a vague sense of protection, but only those with means could afford to hoard to any degree. Soon for the urban poor—for those who shopped daily and had no refrigerator and certainly no savings—the inability to purchase corn meal, bread, milk, oil, bread, flour, beans, sugar, coffee, salt, soap, and toilet paper with their money at the store; to be told at their neighborhood grocery no hay (there is none); and to search anxiously across the city for stores rumored to have the needed products fed a mounting anger. Their sense of affront at a deceptive political system reflected in the tyranny of profiteering businesses grew as supplies diminished.

As the austerity program's outlines became known, consumer anxiety changed to panic. Consumers learned from large press headlines and blaring radio programs that the price of such staples as bread, pasta, powdered milk, beans, and cooking oil would soon triple and quadruple. Wage earners felt threatened by rising prices and the prospect of unemployment in a shrinking economy, and the marginally employed felt unprotected. Confidence in progress turned into fear of sliding backward. The working classes no longer felt they shared a common space under the umbrella of the state, and the middle class saw its chance for ascent removed. Although some people hoped to hold their ground, and a few even to improve their lot, most realized they were left out and slipping down, a change of fate in a country where, during half a century, a significant segment of the urban population (which is 80 percent of the nation) had grown accustomed to rising living standards.

In this context, the government announced a doubling of gasoline prices, to take effect on February 26, as a first step toward reaching world prices. The government had decided to increase the state oil company's income by no longer subsidizing gasoline. In this oil-exporting nation, a hike in gas prices was not a simple mercantile decision. It implicated the bond that united the national community: an imagined shared ownership of the nation's petroleum resources based on its founding legal code. The state's legitimacy was intimately tied to its ability to control the nation's formerly foreign-owned oil industry in the name of the entire pueblo.[61] To equate oil with other commodities on the international market and to demand that people pay dearly for what was considered to be their national birthright was to rupture a moral bond established between the state and the pueblo.

This rupture was symbolized when the collective transport association, arguing that transportation fares had to reflect the increased costs of vehicles and parts, decided to raise bus and van fares by more than 100 percent on Monday, February 27, in defiance of the government's 30 percent ceiling.[62] Already resented by working-class commuters and students for their poor service, the privately owned transport companies' aggressive stance now provoked outrage. Passengers had no alternative transportation to the city and were down to their last change before receiving their pay at work at the end of the month. The abrupt doubling of bus fares crystallized the sense that people were being deceived and abused by the government and business, and it brought them together in the street, a place where both protest and the inversion of authority could occur. Before the battle in the streets began on February 27, the domestic space had already become a battleground between different moral and economic orders.

The Events/The War: Popular Expansion

Popular protest began at dawn on February 27 in the working-class town of Guarenas outside Caracas, as well as in the Caracas bus terminal, where workers and students congregated at an early hour.[63] The private owners of the varied buses, vans, and cars providing most urban transportation argued that escalating costs for the repair and replacement of vehicles made even a provisional ceiling intolerable. Drivers also refused to honor the student half-fare payments. The leaders of the bus association were affiliated with AD but refused to abide by a fare agreement, a symptom of AD's diminishing capacity to control its members. Protesters, some led by students chanting antigovernment slogans, initially blocked collective transport vehicles. Soon people turned against grocery stores and food markets. Leaders, generally young men who broke store locks with crowbars and smashed windows, emerged, urging people to take what was theirs. The people surging into the stores found to their outrage that stored deposits of subsidized basic food stuffs that had disappeared from the market were waiting to be sold at marked-up prices. Cases of powdered milk, cornmeal, pasta, and coffee were passed to the street and distributed as the outnumbered police looked on. Some policemen, themselves poorly paid, helped looting take place in an orderly fashion or took part in it as well.[64] A collective decision to occupy the streets and invade the stores, suspending the rules regulating public movement and commerce, took shape. The street became the site for the contestation of market and political controls widely regarded as immoral and oppressive.

Diffuse and decentered, the protest multiplied in commercial areas near working-class neighborhoods, following the city's principal streets. These avenues and freeways, the channels along which the news was quickly communicated to the major commercial centers by the city's numerous motorcycle messengers, were also vulnerable arteries that protesters blocked off with barriers, bringing traffic to a halt. Most public transportation ceased. Trapped delivery trucks were besieged, their goods carried off and distributed. By the end of the workday in Caracas, astonished downtown employees left their jobs to find the streets filled with people doing free shopping, calmly carting off food and even large appliances. A photograph of a man carrying a side of beef on his back in a burned-out street became one of the most reproduced images of the disturbances. The upheaval was soon disseminated throughout the vast barrio periphery, the lower-class residential areas of unplanned construction in which shanties, cinderblock houses, and housing projects crowd precariously on the hills surrounding the valley of Caracas and in the interstices of the city, in deep ravines that wind half-hidden near middle-class and wealthy neighborhoods.

In this *saqueo popular* (popular looting), people came down from the hills and up from the ravines, streaming toward local stores in the streets ringing the city. The term *saqueo popular* had a double meaning. The Venezuelan political and economic elite was widely accused of looting the national treasury, for it had engaged in notorious corruption and had taken twice the amount of the national debt out of the country in a massive flight of capital. Now it was the turn for the rest of the population to obtain things without working. Middle-class families in neighborhoods traversed by deep ravines, where looting had been initiated by slum dwellers, participated in the saqueo, driving their cars to the stores, in a few cases having their servants help with the heavier goods. At this early stage, when popular action had not encountered government repression and was limited in scope, observers of diverse social origins related with empathy to the call for saqueo popular.

In many barrios a loose organization within and among families emerged. Young men, risking serious injury from glass and metal, broke into new stores and processing plants and expanded the area of popular action. Women and children followed them into food and clothing stores, at times forming lines for the removal of groceries and shoes. Those who could not or dared not participate, such as the old and women with young children, received goods brought to their homes by others. People exchanged among themselves what they had obtained in quantity and carved up the sides of beef and pork they had carried away. As a woman later approvingly observed, "Money was no longer important. In a matter of hours we went back to the age of barter." In the industrial Antímano sector of Caracas, hillside residents attacked the Ronco pasta factory, loaded the large stores of pasta they found there onto the company's trucks, and distributed them throughout the area. "We made sure," a driver and father of several children said proudly, "that everybody got their package of pasta."[65] Enderson, an impoverished fourteen-year-old, said he broke into stores and threw food at the people outside, shouting, "¡Come, pueblo!" (Eat, people!). For him looting was not theft, for, he said, "It is not the people's fault that prices are going up, it is the government's fault. People have to eat. That morning there was nothing to eat at my mother's house."[66]

Looting dissolved momentarily money's ability to regulate collective life. The invasion of business establishments rendered meaningless the barriers that money normally imposes between commodities and consumers, between public and private space. In the midst of an uncertain and dangerous situation there were overtones of a village fiesta—a sudden abundance of liquor and grilled meat shared at impromptu gatherings in the poor neighborhoods on the hills circling Caracas. Bottles of champagne and brandy made a surprise appearance at parties now enlivened by dance music broadcast throughout the hills from newly acquired audio equipment. The smoke of barbecues mixed with that of burning stores. Against the "etiquette of equality" that ruled street behavior in this self-defined egalitarian society, the poor sought to assert, even if only momentarily, their image of real relations of equality.[67]

During this initial period, when rules were transgressed and categories confused, exhilaration and fear competed for control of the situation. Exhilaration followed from the collective assertion of popular understandings over official explanation. Through countless acts of defiance, which included burning some police stations and local AD offices, people spoke about their rejection of not only their immiseration, but the deceptive reasons routinely put forth to explain it and of the institutions supporting it.[68] On February 27, several hundred motorcycle delivery men, motorizados, surrounded the Fedecámaras building, the headquarters of the nation's largest business associations and a symbol of the business class that has benefited from government policies. Business leaders briefly caught inside spread rumors of alarm concerning attacks on the propertied. Some took their families out of the country, and many privately called on the president to act.

Looting, however, was the major means of protest. It was largely indiscriminate, as people generally looted areas close to where they resided. Many were drawn into looting out of concern to protect themselves against an uncertain future. At a moment perceived to be the onset of a crisis, they sought to obtain both expensive goods that had ceased to be attainable and food for their families. Raul, a young university-educated father from the barrio La Vega, watched in shock from his house as people rushed down the hill to loot the stores. When he looked at his little daughter, he said, "I saw her turn into a can of milk. All I could think of was, how was I going to feed her." That night he accepted cans of powdered milk taken from a neighboring store that a friend brought him.

"El pueblo tiene hambre" (The people are hungry), the slogan widely painted on walls, was the explanation most frequently offered by participants for the uprising. It imaged shared experiences uniting strangers who were anonymously joined in the simultaneous looting briefly televised to the country and the world. Hunger was regarded as a natural cause for revolt, but it was a shorthand expression referring, through the image of food, to what was regarded as unnecessary deprivation and insult in a country that had both wealth and democracy. With their revolt, people bluntly shattered the officially constructed illusion that the economy could be adjusted with popular acquiescence. Reflecting with surprise on their collective action, many observed, "We are no longer a passive pueblo." They expressed a sense of moral affront at the manipulation and silencing of popular demands that was the cumulative experience of this oil- and rent-based democracy. If, as Pérez demanded, it was time to face reality, this was what it looked like from the popular perspective.

The link between hunger and revolt connected notions about political action and rights, leaders and people, which were given blurred expression during the disturbances. In a striking gesture to appropriate the most hallowed official signs of nationhood, protesters in many instances sang, as they broke open stores, the opening line of the national anthem, "Gloria al bravo pueblo que el yugo lanzó" (Glory to the brave and angry people who threw off their yoke). They sang it both when they waved the national flag and when they faced the attack of the military in lines drawn in the streets between an unarmed people and occupying troops. This hymn to popular revolt linked anger to courage, political freedom to social justice. Invoked in official contexts, such as the state ceremonial occasion and the school salute to the flag, the hymn embalmed the bravo pueblo in the distant past; to sing it spontaneously in a popular assault on the street was to resuscitate it as a living critique, not a ratification of authority.

"El pueblo está bravo" (The people are angry), painted on walls and repeated by protesters, rebutted the official glorification of a silent pueblo. Popular anger was inseparable from indignation at being deceived. "Se han burlado de nosotros" (They have mocked us), "Basta del engaño" (An end to deception) declared looters and sympathetic observers (many from the middle class) at the outbreak of the disturbances. When in the polyphony of this mass upheaval, people asserted that "el pueblo habló" (the people have spoken), their actions indicated their refusal to remain passive.

Hunger initially rendered the looting understandable, even legitimate. A consensus in many sectors condoned the popular appropriation of food as being just. Given the anxiety over food shortages intensifying over weeks, a shared sensibility had begun to exist concerning market threats to survival.

Women were particularly adamant that people's right to food meant that the taking of food fell into a different moral category than other goods. For many women their participation in looting was their first public transgression of authority and was seen as an act of family defense. Looters also took clothes, appliances, furniture, hardware, and even unusable computers. Before the government intervened, on the afternoon of the second day, the television news showed live scenes of people (in the middle-class San Bernardino sector of Caracas), unhindered by authorities, calmly carrying audio equipment and videocassette recorders, and loading cars with furniture. Hunger for consumer commodities other than food violated elite and middle-class notions of what should rightfully be accessible to poor people. The idea took hold that not necessity but lust for material goods was fueling the looting. The terms "robbery" and "vandalism" spread, supplanting popular looting, as tales circulated of the destruction of stores, cars, and shopkeepers' houses. Attacks on property escalated as looters ripped out equipment and plumbing, hitting not only commerce and factories but medical and educational facilities. Many businesses were set on fire, spreading the sense that limits were no longer being respected.

Intense popular anger was directed at immigrant shopkeepers—the Portuguese, Chinese, and Lebanese merchants in daily contact with barrio residents who were long suspected of hoarding and overpricing clothing and food. Their threatening practices were symbolized by the fact that they did not extend credit, which was a tradition among Venezuelan small shopkeepers. For the urban poor, these businessmen were the visible face of cold capitalism and became the target of their rage. "No se fia" (We don't give credit) was the sign often displayed in their stores. Even the residences of many immigrant storekeepers who had long lived in the barrios were looted. Although they regarded themselves as part of the pueblo, the crowd attacked them as burgueses (bourgeois or the rich).[69] Venezuelan shopkeepers in some cases painted "I am Venezuelan" on the metal sheets covering their store windows in an effort to dissuade looters from attacking.

Fear set in, driving people to affix blame for the worsening course of events. The multilayered fear that emerged had two main sources: fear of uncontrolled popular criminality and fear of official repression. Both state action and state absence were cause for terror, compounded by the uncertainty as to whether the present government would be able to survive at all. In this seemingly solid democracy, no local system of political groupings was found to help reestablish order in the barrios, and no words of explanation were offered by the political leadership. As a resident of the devastated barrio

La Vega stated, "All of a sudden there were no more *adecos* [members of the ruling party AD] to be found anywhere. They took their pictures of Carlos Andres out of their windows and joined in the looting." Among the elite and the middle class, the fear that the disturbances were a threat to all private property and social order took hold. Some of the very wealthy left the country in their private jets. The middle class sought to band together to protect their property, often organizing armed defense groups among neighbors.

Gaps in the state's leadership and the coordination of its agencies became visible. Although the government's civilian leadership was hesitant, the military was suddenly decisive in the streets. On the morning of February 28, the military began to occupy the cities, ordering all businesses to close. By the end of the day, as assaults on businesses grew bolder and extended to small factories, troops cleared the streets by opening fire on the crowds of looters. People turned to the television for word from the government and found images of looting.

The president eventually spoke. He defined the disturbances as a protest of the poor that reflected long-standing social injustices (El *Nacional*, March 1, 1989). With this statement he placed responsibility on past policies and differentiated himself from those who blamed the upheaval on subversives, criminals, or illegal immigrants (though some members of Pérez's cabinet did so). With grim private sector leaders at his side, he declared a general wage raise and a four-month freeze on firings—both measures that business had until then opposed. However, Pérez offered no purpose around which to unite as a nation, no promise for the future; rather, he underlined, as on many occasions, the exceptional ties he had built in the international arena. The audience to which he was primarily speaking, in effect well outside the borders of the country, sat in the government and bank offices of Venezuela's creditors; he sought to communicate that Venezuela required concessions on its debt in order to avoid future upheavals, but that he was well in control of the present situation.[70] To his domestic audience he issued a demand for acquiescence. Pérez tersely announced that constitutional guarantees, including freedom of the press, were suspended and that a curfew, to begin within hours, would be in effect from 6 P.M. until 6 A.M. until further notice. His role as an international leader remained, but now it was one without a pueblo.

The suspension of guarantees led to a sharp escalation of state violence against the poor. When Minister of the Interior Alejandro Izaguirre, a seasoned AD leader (regarded as a man of the people and nicknamed "the

Policeman") appeared on television on March 1 to announce government measures, he was overcome by nervous exhaustion and rendered speechless on camera. Disney cartoons replaced him without explanation. The leadership of the party had been meeting since the previous day to discuss how to control the situation and was divided concerning the use of force. Although initially delayed, it had been used massively by the time of his television appearance. The traditional language of populism did not prepare Izaguirre to represent the state in this conjuncture.

The eruption of the pueblo into public view deeply troubled the Venezuelan political leadership. On March 1, at the height of government violence, AD's president and founder Gonzalo Barrios lamented that the international media had televised abroad "the horror, the primitive, the uncontrollable, from a civilized point of view, of the looting that took place in Caracas" (Sanín 1989: 143). He regretted that the events had shown "the entire world the other face of Venezuela, the face of slums, of the hungry masses, of marginal people" (El Nacional, March 4, 1989). This was the face that the government violently sought to conceal. Gonzalo Barrios cast the government's decision to use massive violence in terms that evoked the state's civilizing mission. In the congressional debate of March 1, the eighty-eight-year-old apostle of Venezuelan democracy, widely regarded for his wit and political acumen, concluded his speech by recounting a story that had "captivated" him because of its "implicit irony." The story concerned a British general who wanted to subdue one of the "less primitive tribes" of Africa. The general sent as his emissary a missionary who had lived among the indigenous people in order to convince them that British occupation would be to their benefit. The missionary told them of the hospitals, schools, means of communication, and laws they would receive from the British. The African chief recognized the value of this offer but rejected it, arguing that its acceptance would cause his people to lose their soul. The missionary, on reporting the chief's refusal to the general, suggested that the chief was right. "The general," Barrios said, "naturally paid no attention to the missionary and gave orders to blast the natives with gunfire (plomo cerrado), as often occurs in disputes among civilized nations." Barrios concluded, in a tone of ironic understatement, that if the congressmen decided to reject President Pérez's austerity program and the repressive measures taken to defend it, the nation would begin a backward slide: "I think that Venezuela would not necessarily return to loincloths and arrows, because we have well-grounded structures and progress, but we could go back to a situation in which luxuries like Rolls Royces and fancy televisions would disappear" (Sanín 1989: 155). This unabashed inscription of state policies within a colonial framework—the acceptance of massive state violence to oblige acquiescence and forestall greater decline and the identification of popular protesters as a "primitive tribe" and of congressmen as "civilizing generals"—went unnoticed, for the opposition shared its underlying premises.

The War/The Events: State Repression

The state's actions slowly took form, as it attempted to control, define, and conceal the events that were under way. Ten thousand troops were air-lifted into Caracas, which, because of its valley location, had been cut off by road from the rest of the country, interrupting its food supply. With a naturalness that stunned the barrio population, the military and police forces undertook to drive people out of the streets and to mark territorial boundaries delimiting the frontiers that the poor must not cross. Scenes of soldiers and police firing on looters in barrios were not televised nationally but were broadcast on U.S. and European news, bringing an unwelcome shock of recognition to Venezuelans with satellite dishes who discovered a disturbing new image of the nation through the eyes of the international media.

The militarization of the conflict under the suspension of most constitutional guarantees meant that "order" was reestablished in the barrios by means of massive violence, both indiscriminate and directed, despite the fact, as critics later argued, that the constitutional guarantee of the right to life had not been suspended. The military displayed its presence, stationing tanks to protect government and corporate offices, major shopping centers, and the borders of wealthy neighborhoods. But outside of a few shopping centers, these had not been targets of the looters. Rather, these outposts sig-naled the boundaries to be defended from the assault of the *marginales* (residents of the barrios).

Government repression brought to an end the expansive phase of the disturbances marked by the popular occupation of the street. Pockets of gunfire directed at government forces by so-called *antisociales* (antisocials) in certain barrios and housing projects became the focus of government attention. They were presented as revealing the true face of the disturbances: the anarchic and criminal effort to subvert democracy through violence. In the context of deep collective fear, the idea hardened that despite broad so-cial participation in the looting the disturbances emanated from the feared *cerros* (hillside barrios) ringing Caracas.

According to dominant notions, the very poor and the criminal, living in subhuman conditions in shanties and housing projects, lead a basically lawless existence in these zones. The cerros are regarded as the haven for various categories of antisociales: *malandros* (thugs), drug dealers, dark-skinned foreigners, and remnants of urban guerrilla groups. They allow the reproduction of those who occupy the margins of civilized life: the criminal, the subversive, and the alien. The dominant discourse soon constructed these disturbances as the unleashing of this primitive mass upon the city's center. At this moment of crisis, otherness was projected onto the city's barrios, as if the residents of these socially diverse areas in their entirety constituted a threat to the civilized order. As General Camejo Arias had said of the border region where the Amparo massacre occurred, "Everyone there is a criminal."

Collective fears fragmented the urban population along the lines they traced. Many barrio residents feared that marauding savagery might emerge within their midst. They believed that neighboring barrios, often situated higher up the hill and populated by recent immigrants, would attack their homes and property. The army and police, attempting to divide the poor through the spread of panic,[71] planted rumors that mobs of impoverished foreigners and criminals were leading night assaults on houses. Although the rumored assaults never materialized, barrio residents stood guard on their rooftops and in the streets, drawing gunfire from the troops. Although people in the barrios sought to defend themselves from their neighbors, people in wealthy districts armed themselves against the barrios. Residents of luxury apartments bordering on the barrios formed armed brigades with police approval, and Rambo-style groups of wealthy youths brandished sophisticated automatic weapons that the upper middle class had been bringing into the country for some time.

The government's armed agencies deployed violence in multiple forms, communicating in practice to the poor the distinct forms of otherness by which they could be encompassed. The military faced the barrio population as a military enemy; the police confronted it as a criminal gang; and the DISIP and other intelligence police treated it as a subversive agent. Their crosscutting attacks created confusion and panic, fragmenting the poor yet more. After the initial exhilaration of defiance, most of the population hoped for the reestablishment of order and for an end to uncertainty and destruction; and they often welcomed the young soldiers of rural origin who were posted in their neighborhood. But military officers responded to the subversion of order by defining the barrios as the source of that subversion. Their population became the enemy to be controlled, driven back, and broken. The death of an army officer leading a search for snipers was made the symbol of democracy under siege, one on which political and entertainment figures elaborated in televised statements and during the broadcast of his military funeral.

The battle lines were drawn in border areas at the edges of large barrios, particularly those with a reputation for criminality and subversion, from which encroachment by mobs of the poor was thought to be a threat to major commercial and government establishments. But government forces, ill prepared for civil conflict, did not carry out a strategically planned operation. The sound of supposed sniper fire provoked massive gunfire from nervous, inexperienced army troops who were rural recruits taught to fear urban subversives. The erratic and disproportionate character of their assault was their response to the menacing image of the popular threat. Claiming that heavily armed snipers were providing intense resistance, military officers ordered high-power automatic artillery fire to be directed at the exposed faces of the cerros and high-rise housing projects for hours at a time, perforating their thin walls.[72] A soldier warned Josefina, a working woman from Petare whose house overlooked a shopping center, "This hill has been taken. Stay inside. Anybody who moves will be shot." Stunned by this announcement, she and her family stayed on the floor for two days.

Police and security forces used the period of suspended legality to round up criminals, settle personal accounts, raid houses, and terrorize certain barrios. Policemen who knew the criminals and illegal aliens in a neighborhood sought them out in their houses and the streets, in some cases shooting them down or taking them away to unknown sites. For these operations some agents did not use their official weapon but an unregistered personal gun called the cochina (the dirty one; lit., the female pig).[73] Security forces also used a tactic developed in demonstrations and on the university campus to provoke incidents and turn public opinion: masked gunmen known as encapuchados (hooded ones) in civilian clothes shot at people, often from motorcycles, creating panic. It was impossible to determine whether they were police, criminals, or subversives. Terror became faceless.

Intelligence forces put into effect counterinsurgency measures. They detained and in some cases tortured activists from barrio cultural organizations and from student and political groups. The only cases to cause a public outcry were those of university student leaders and prominent Jesuit priests residing in the barrio La Vega, one of whom was Luis Ugalde, the vice rector of the prestigious Andres Bello Catholic University and an editor of the magazine SIC.[74] The intention was to identify publicly members of the leftist intelligentsia with subversion and to define them for the future as an alien threat.

The identities of casualties from the barrios were rapidly erased. Their massive number and the places and circumstances in which they occurred rendered them subversive. In understaffed hospitals and morgues overrun with corpses, norms and procedures were suspended in chaotic streets where unidentified armed authorities ruled.[75] Records that could substantiate the widely circulating estimates of a high death toll were not maintained, and bodies disappeared from the streets. The minister of defense calmly insisted, even as gunfire continued through the nights, that order had been restored and the death toll was low. The media soon ceased reporting news of casualties. Death was the occasion to imprint upon the poor their marginality to civilized society.

The morgue was the site for the encounter between the poor and their own invisibility, as people sought in vain to recover the bodies of their relatives and friends. Some knew that a person's body had been sent there after witnessing their death. Others arrived after fruitless quests at overflowing jails and hospitals. Unclaimed decomposing bodies were stacked in the morgue hallways where, defying rules and the stench, relatives searched among them. The city's supply of coffins ran out. Eventually many family members were told by indifferent morgue workers to end their vigil. Loads of cadavers, they said, had been taken en masse to an unmarked mass grave in the Caracas public cemetery—in garbage bags.

The geography of the sprawling old Cementerio del Sur replicates that of Caracas. Past the crypts and statues in the center area that belong to families with names and means, there rises a crowded periphery of untended hillsides with rough-hewn paths and barely visible crosses. Cemetery workers confirmed that a mass grave had been opened in an elevated area named La Nueva Peste (The New Plague), the successor to a mass grave for victims of an epidemic in the past. It was visited at night by trucks, and an unknown number of bodies in bags unregistered in the records had been covered there.

Images of bodies picked up and tossed into trucks, dumped in garbage bags, and buried in unknown sites by tractors took hold of the collective imagination. Repeated and magnified in the barrios, they objectified for the poor their own erasure, the futility of attempting to establish their individual claims. A month after the massacre, Yvonne Pirela, a textile worker, vainly sought an order to exhume the body of her son from La Nueva Peste. The court official impatiently told her, "But Señora, the bags they were in are broken. Everything has become one mass by now. Forget it."[76]

Just as many bodies were erased, so were the figures of the casualties. After initial estimates of several hundred dead in Caracas, the media quickly stopped giving information on the number of fatalities. The government, denying unofficial estimates of more than one thousand dead and hundreds wounded and maimed, has maintained that 277 people died.[77] Because conditions were chaotic and people alarmed, the tendency at the moment for many people was to hold exaggerated notions of the deaths involved, which rumors placed in the thousands. However, the government has not released the names of the dead and has refused repeated legal efforts by newly formed groups of the victims' families, such as the Committee against Forgetting and the Committee of Relatives of the Innocent Victims of February–March, to obtain the exhumation of the mass graves.

The Revelation: The Nation's Primitivity

The startling suddenness of the popular protest brought often candid commentary, yet its complexity and newness defied description. Uncertain on a changing ground, commentators sought the stable footing of established foundations. One such premise, concealed in normal times, concerned the intrinsic backwardness of the country. It was as if by overflowing the riverbed, the masses had uncovered the hidden but familiar bedrock of the nation's identity: its primitivity. The evaluation of the nature, source, and significance of the nation's backwardness had been the obscure object of literary and political attention, distinguishing oligarchic and populist views of the nation. For the elite, the upheaval brought repressed understandings of this troublesome issue to the surface. At the height of the crisis, when people gained control of the streets, submerged populist assumptions converged with the oligarchic conception of the pueblo as backward masses. While under ordinary conditions populist rhetoric depicts the pueblo in positive terms, as virtuous, albeit ignorant and therefore in need of guidance, during this crisis the element of ignorance was brought to the foreground in order to present the pueblo as savage: prone to lose control if not adequately harnessed and ready to plunge the nation into chaos if not swiftly repressed. It is not surprising, therefore, that on March 4 an outspoken journalist such as Alfredo Peña would employ without qualms the image of the pueblo as an uncontrolled river.

Ambivalence toward the pueblo did not disappear but was displaced. According to Peña, popular protest had been justified. The problem arose because the masses, without adequate political or trade union organizations, had no adequate means of expressing themselves. Although the economic crisis in Venezuela was less serious than in Argentina and Uruguay, the masses in those countries remained controlled because they had representative parties and trade unions: "Without leadership they (the masses) become anarchic or overcome their leadership, overflow the riverbed—and the unruly come to lead the movement" (El Nacional, March 4, 1989). The masses were right in being upset, he reasoned, but wrong in their form of protest.

In the congressional debate of March 6, Teodoro Petkoff, the leader of the moderate left party MAS, suggested that the protesters were not organized workers but people pushed to the edges of society—to prostitution, drugs, and alcoholism. Petkoff argued that the Venezuela that "erupted like a volcano" on February 27 was not "the Venezuela of workers organized in trade unions or associations. No, it was another Venezuela, it was the non-organized Venezuela, the Venezuela that has been piling up in a huge bag of wretched poverty." According to him, the Venezuela that "came down from the hills or up from the ravines" was "a Venezuela of hungry people, of people who are not part of the conventional organization of society." This Venezuela had produced "the roar of a wounded animal." He blamed the politicians of the ruling parties for having created this other Venezuela, labeling them Doctor Frankensteins: "They created a monster, and this monster came out to complain, came out to demand its share of the immense petroleum booty of all these years."[78]

As hidden assumptions surfaced during the riots, they took on novel meanings and were recast by changing conditions. The opposition between civilization and barbarism now equated rationality with the free market—the domain of the modernizing elite—and backwardness with state protection—the province of the needy masses, corrupt politicians, and inefficient businessmen. This division became graphically imaged in the layout of the cities, as the borders between rich and poor neighborhoods became military and moral battlegrounds, frontiers separating different kinds of people. In ever more binding ways, the ruling elite established its fraternity across international lines, for its overriding concern was with international financial flows rather than with the organization of the domestic market. It interpreted popular protest as a reaction against capitalist rationality, denying the multilayered critique of injustice it contained—a protest at once against new free-market measures and against a politically constructed economy characterized by corruption, inflation, scarcity, and the hoarding of basic goods.[79]

Bodily Inscriptions and the Body Politic

Having represented the pueblo as a barbarous mass blind to the force of reason, the governing elite found justification for using blinding force against it. The ferocious deployment of state violence at the center stage of national politics blocked from view the significance of popular protest as a critique of the social order. Through the display of force, the government represented the protesting pueblo as a multiheaded monstrous threat that assumed the form of subversives, foreigners, drug dealers, Cuban agents, guerrillas, and common criminals—all dangerously invisible.[80] In this light, the mass killings were a way of constructing the pueblo as an irrational mass and the government as the sole defender of reason. Through the massacre, the logic of the Spanish Conquest was reinscribed on new bodies. For this conquest, government leadership endorsed the civilizing mission of heavy gunfire (plomo cerrado), modeled itself after representatives of the imperialist English state, and imaged the popular sectors as African natives. The nation was split in two.

The uprising of the pueblo changed the anatomy of the nation. From the perspective of the elite, the masses now embodied the menace of barbarism surfacing anywhere in the body politic, not just at its frontiers. Borders were no longer solely located at the nation's outer edges but had become internalized, turning into the arteries that irrigate the country with poor people. Wherever there were people at the margins—the marginales—a threat was seen. Caracas, once the showcase of modernity, appeared fragmented by the slums that surround it, as well as by those that grow like wild grass in the multiple ravines that crosscut the city.

The elite confronted the fractured body politic by enunciating its own contradictory relationship to the pueblo, deepening national divisions while calling for the restoration of unity. The defense minister directed the removal of alien elements at the same time that politicians called for renewed communication with the pueblo. Employing the paternalistic terms of elite discourse, the leader of the Christian Democratic Party, former President Rafael Caldera, reprimanded the national political leadership for having distanced itself "from the pueblo who feel, who live, who sometimes express themselves in an improper fashion, and sometimes look for forms of expression that border on barbarism, but that must be understood. We have to reestablish communication with them" (Sanín 1989: 138).

As violence provoked a crescendo of fear, Defense Minister General Italo Alliegro became the public hero in the reestablishment of order. His capacity to express a combination of authority and sympathetic concern and to invoke democratic principles as the reason for military action made him the personification of the ideal leader for the moment of crisis. By the time troops were withdrawn and the media had defined the riots as vandalism and resistance as subversion, suppressing initial reports of military and police abuses, Alliegro's smiling face appeared on magazine covers and his name topped public opinion polls in popularity.[81] As in Barrios's colonial allegory, conquest was a time for generals, not politicians—but generals of a populist mold.[82]

At the moment officially construed as a historical crossroads in the nation's ascent to modernity, threatening images of the people as savages— overflowing rivers that undermine order, primitive force that blocks national progress, barbarous masses that assault property and reason—made violence against them seem acceptable, necessary. The death of the pueblo was made to appear inconsequential, inscribed in the collective imagination through images of the poor as an anonymous mass of savages, as refuse to be discarded in garbage bags, as if the poor, in death as in life, were one mass.

The Barbarism of Civilization

> Discovered by our men, . . . the natives' obstinance was such that, unwilling to surrender, although assured of their lives, they resorted to arrows, shooting the entire supply in their quivers from above. When all had been used, in desperation they pulled out from their own bodies those the Spaniards' Indian allies had fired from below. They placed them in their bows with pieces of flesh still clinging to the tips and fired them again on their original owners. The Spaniards, appalled at such barbarity, at length brought them down with bullets, impaled them and left their corpses on the hill as a lesson in terror for others.
> —José Oviedo y Baños, *The Conquest and Settlement of Venezuela*

> Twelve Indians, two of whom were children, were massacred . . . in the Rómulo Gallegos District of the state of Apure, a few kilometers from the Colombian border. The bodies of the Indians were found in a lake. All of them had been stabbed to death, and their bodies had been quartered. . . . Murders of indigenous people are constantly denounced in this area, but on this occasion it could be proved

because the cadavers were found. The crime was committed during Easter, but a
survivor only now made public this information.

—El Diario de Caracas

The corporeality of people has served as a privileged medium for the political imagination in Latin America as states that have but partial control over populations and territories have inscribed on the bodies of their subjects assertions of power directed to collective audiences. These inscriptions encode not only the reasons of state but the unquestioned foundations of these reasons, the bedrock of common sense that makes a social landscape seem natural. In this respect, physical violence, not unlike printing, is a vehicle for making and encoding history whose specific form and significance cannot be understood outside that history. Times of crisis show more clearly that these assumptions are reinterpreted and transformed from the standpoint of the present rather than being reproduced unchanged. In making history, people remake their history, recasting the past through a contemporary optic. The waking terrors of the living are the nightmare through which the past is imagined.

A colonial history that engraved upon bodies the denunciation of the victim's crimes informed the Amparo massacre.[83] Similarly, a tradition of conquest weighed upon the state's treatment of the masacrón victims as an anonymous mass. But if both instances reconfigured the present in terms of the past, they also reconstructed the past in terms of the present, making salient suppressed conceptions of the poor as disposable savages. In accord with shifts in domestic and international conditions, the terms of nationalist discourse acquired new accents. "I would have killed all those savages, as I am sure they would have killed us if they had a chance. They hate us," Sofía, a wealthy young lawyer and Harvard-trained businesswoman, told us as she shaped her arm into a machine gun and pointed her finger toward the slums that surrounded her office in a skyscraper overlooking the hills from which looters had descended.

For the past half-century, state affluence held social conflict in check. During this time, petroleum abundance and torrential money flows brought rapid social and geographical mobility and helped redraw social identities. But as petroleum money dried up, the social world built upon the fluid foundations of this easy money began to crack. With the crisis of credit came a crisis of credibility. Not surprisingly, the poor were to be the victims and the demons of the ensuing social reordering. In the turmoil of meaning provoked by the mass uprising, dominant discourse transformed the pueblo from the virtuous foundation of democracy into a savage threat to its existence—a barbaric presence.

As the debt crisis has set the stage for the civilizing advance of the free market, the pueblo is being redefined as an aggregate of citizens at the same time that the meaning of citizenship is being recast through practice. With the ascent of free-market ideology and the displacement of the moral economy of protectionism by the morality of capital, a rupture of customary bonds uniting leaders and masses, state and people, has pushed the poor to the border of the body politic. In this new configuration of social relations, boundaries are transformed into frontiers that separate the civilized from the barbarous. Without state protection, people are being left free to choose progress. Hand in hand, the logics of conquest and of the free market converge to impress upon people the changing meaning of their social anonymity.

State power was exercised, in characteristic fashion in a dramaturgical mode by means of performances designed to establish an account of reality through the persuasiveness of power; they intended less to convince than to produce acquiescence. When the reproduction of state authority is so deeply intertwined with the construction of its representation, politics centers on the artifice of its making. The makeshift or contrived character of certain political representations, visible in the theatrical display of state violence during both massacres, may actually express a form of constructing power rather than a deficiency in its organization.[84]

In each massacre, the state attempted not simply to represent reality but to show that it had the power to write the plot, to decide who belongs at center stage, who is at the margins, who is in the audience, and who is shut outside. When people dared to act, transgressing spatial and conceptual boundaries, the state counteracted by turning them into actors of different dramas. By transforming peasants into guerrillas and protesters into savages, the state sought simultaneously to control their actions and to reconstitute the pueblo as the usual chorus in the wings of the theater of populism. At the margins of this official drama, however, people spoke lines of their own making, challenging the plot of a modernizing project that was based on their silence. Less than four weeks after Pérez's inauguration as president, in response to the state's attempt to make commodities reflect the unmediated rationality of the free market, people responded with fury by "spontaneously" freeing commodities from the market. This spontaneity at once revealed the hidden activity of sedimented memories and experiences and made explicit a popular critique of relations of rule that was embedded in quotidian life. Through their actions, people pried open a space through which to glimpse a different social imaginary by ignoring the state's drama (which they called the farce) and attacking for a moment the theater itself.

While popular violence was circumscribed, centering on material barriers between things and people, state violence was unbounded, as if its aim were to trap popular will; with heavy gunfire it cast a net around streets and slums, targeting the poor and their homes. The planning and execution of the Amparo massacre assumed an implicit definition of the pueblo as passive and disposable, and the February–March massacre was presented as a natural government reaction to an explosion of popular savagery. As with apparently spontaneous popular action, the very naturalness of state activity revealed the invisible work of historical memory through which not only the governing elite but large sectors of the population interpreted the sources of danger and the meaning of rights.

It will be as difficult to remember as it is hard to forget just how order was reimposed. While people inscribed with their bodies their presence upon the state, the state inscribed its power upon their bodies.[85] To achieve the reestablishment of stability, the state can no longer assume that there are compliant actors or a passive audience; it must modulate its actions in accord with its memory and with its altered perception of what the pueblo might do. As the state continues to present the drama of modernization on stage, people murmur in the aisles, walk out, and talk outside. We may be able to hear these voices questioning the assumption that the death of the pueblo may take place "as if no one, nothing had died, as if they were stones falling on the ground, or water on the water."

Violence and Modernity

Are the events we discuss here, then, just further exotic tales about the violent character of distant others, a confirmation of the premodern character of contemporary Latin American states? A myth central to modernity, whose paternity can be traced to G. W. F. Hegel and Michel Foucault (1979), contends that as heirs to the Enlightenment, modern states establish their authority by embodying not divine will or force but reason. The modern state, it asserts, having domesticated the bloody theater of violence of the ancien régime, replaces publicly inflicted physical punishment with myriad disciplinary procedures that permeate the body politic and engender the modern soul. From this perspective, state violence as a reason of state marks the premodern domain, in which the state writes its texts on the bodies of its citizens, presumably because premodern souls grasp its reasons concretely.

Our analysis questions a viewpoint that divides history into neat ascending stages and is blind to the violence through which modern states secure their hegemony. The forms of state violence may indeed vary in different societies, in part reflecting how their mechanisms of social control—what Antonio Gramsci called their "trench systems"[86]—protect states from political and economic threats. State violence is thus inseparable from other forms of social violence, the exceptional deployment of state force from the quotidian practice of social domination. But whenever states violently reproduce the conditions of their existence by imposing the standards of their rule through force, we may glimpse how myths of authority are grounded on the terrain of history and how, as Walter Benjamin (1969: 256) suggests, documents of civilization are at the same time documents of barbarism.

In this discussion we have sought to advance an argument for understanding political violence as an opaque historical artifact—that is, as a set of practices and cultural forms whose meanings can only be deciphered by understanding the historical memory and the social relations of the society within which it arises, takes form, and achieves effects. As violence becomes embodied in practices and objectified in institutions, technologies, and icons, it becomes modular; commoditized and taught in multiple forms, it circulates in markets that cross boundaries.[87] "I only wish I could have been trained in Israel like López Sisco, for there they teach you to be a killer machine," a DISIP member assigned to guard the Amparo survivors told us as he caressed his favorite weapon, a Magnum, and praised its superiority over his revolver and submachine gun. The irony that his idol had led the massacre of the Amparo fishermen whom he was guarding highlights another historical irony: the barbarity attributed to the periphery has been historically forged in conjunction with the barbarity of the centers of civilization, where it parades in the guise of reason, morality, and technique.[88] Because history is the offspring of such ironies, we must seek the specific historical character of violence behind the outward similarity of its mechanisms and consequences. By situating these massacres within the history of their making, we have tried to observe how they were represented, to decode the semantics of violence, and to listen to what was said.

Listening to violence entails exploring a terrain in which the construction of meaning is contested through the deployment of competing modes of meaning making. If, building on Michel de Certeau's work, we view society as being constituted by "heterogeneous places" in which a "forest of narrativities" (de Certeau 1984: 183, 201) engenders multiple conceptions of reality, we may hear a multitude of submerged voices speaking through a variety of semantic fields. Narratives of violence form a dense forest with deceptively homogeneous contours. While Foucault posits the existence of a clear correlation between types of society and forms of state violence, our analysis suggests that these typological correspondences may be partial and shifting, for the surface similarity of the elements composing the forest of violence obscures how the power of these forms derives from their complex articulation with each other on heterogeneous social terrains.

In the Amparo and February massacres, state violence took place at once as a spectacular theatrical performance and a hidden technical operation. Neocolonial societies, by making particularly visible the ongoing imbrication of heterogeneous historical forms, also illuminate the emerging landscape of the postcolonial world. At a moment in history when the globalization of space is being achieved through simultaneous integration and fracture, inclusion and exclusion, transmuted colonial relations remain dynamic forces within processes of global change. The events we analyze in this essay are moments in this worldwide reordering of body politics. Through them we may glimpse the movement from a world organized by what Tom Nairn (1981: 356) calls the uniformed imperialism of direct political control and territorially fixed markets to one shaped by what we call the multiform imperial controls of fluid finance capital, a world of increasingly deterritorialized markets and shifting political, economic, and cultural boundaries. The Venezuelan riots and massacres, as people who lived through them know, are inseparable from the hidden violence of postmodern empires.

Notes

Research for this paper was supported by the Michigan Society of Fellows and the Spencer Foundation. In Venezuela we were affiliated with the Centro de Estudios Latinamericanos Rómulo Gallegos; we thank all of these institutions for their interest and support. Our research at the time of the Amparo massacre and the February riots involved extensive observation and interviews with a wide range of people. They included the presidential candidates and their campaign organizers, members of the business community, the Amparo survivors and relatives of victims, members of the human rights community, people participating in and affected by the February riots, clergy, opposition activists, and security agents. Our statements about collective states or agencies reflect a necessarily simplified assessment of extremely complex and contradictory realities, the further discussion of which we are developing in a longer work. Versions of this essay have been presented at the Annual Meeting of the American Anthropology Association, Washington, DC, November 1989, and the Annual Meeting of the American Ethnological Association, Atlanta, April 1990. At the University of Michigan, versions were presented to the Michigan Society of Fellows, the Program for the Study of Social Transformations, the Graduate Student Association for Latin American Studies, and the Program in History and Anthropology; a version was presented at the University of Chicago to the Workshop on Comparative Nationalism. We express our gratitude for the constructive comments we received. In addition, we thank Roger Rouse for many helpful discussions and John Comaroff, Raymond Grew, Richard Turits, Tom Wolfe, and an anonymous reviewer for their valuable insights. Finally, we acknowledge the cooperation of many people in Venezuela who shared with us their understanding of these conflicts.

Notes on the epigraphs: The verses from the opening epigraph are from Neruda 1978: 174. They refer to a massacre of Chilean workers in 1946. The English translation (Neruda 1991: 186–87) reads:

> And the death of the people was as it has always been:
> As if no one, nothing had died,
> As if they were stones falling
> On the ground, or water on the water

The second epigraph is from Oviedo y Baños 1987: 196. *The Conquest and Settlement of Venezuela* is an eighteenth-century account of the Conquest based on original records and written from the perspective of the colonial elite. The third epigraph is from "Twelve Indians Were Massacred," *El Diario de Caracas*, April 27, 1989.

1   In contrast to predominant approaches to this subject, the works by Silvio R. Duncan Baretta and John Markoff (1978), Michael Taussig (1987), and E. P. Thompson (1971) illustrate attempts to examine the historical construction and cultural forms of violence.

2   This issue is addressed in Coronil 1989, in a critique of postmodern discourses on colonialism.

3   Ironically, the word *amparo* means protection or shelter and is also a judicial measure affording defendants legal protection. In a society in which personal fortune is closely tied to one's patronage relations, to be *desamparado*, or unprotected, is to be socially alone and vulnerable.

4   *Editors' note:* This later figure was published in 1999; see Centro de Estudios para la Paz 1999.

5 This figure is necessarily tentative. The journalist Jack Sweeny calculates that in Caracas alone, between 500,000 and 750,000 people participated in the riots (*VenEconomía*, March 1989).

6 For a careful comparative analysis of protests in Latin America against debt related austerity programs, see Walton 1989.

7 First published in 1929, *Doña Bárbara* was written by Rómulo Gallegos (1959), a pedagogue and author of several noted novels, and a founder of Acción Democrática Party (AD). He became Venezuela's first freely elected president in 1948.

8 The nation's petroleum-export industry began under the autocratic rule of General Juan Vicente Gómez (1908–35) and buttressed his monopolistic hold over wealth and power. During the transition toward pluralism after 1936, AD governed briefly (1945–48) but was overthrown by the military. Marcos Pérez Jiménez headed a repressive military regime (1948–58) during which oil wealth benefited a growing commercial bourgeoisie.

9 Leftist guerrillas were active in the early 1960s in opposition to the alliances that President Rómulo Betancourt (the founder of AD and mentor of Carlos Andrés Pérez) made with domestic and foreign capital. The government launched a successful, but costly in terms of rights and lives, counterinsurgency campaign directed by Minister of the Interior Carlos Andrés Pérez. The guerrillas failed to win support among the peasants who were loyal to AD but found some backing in the capital's large working-class periphery (*barrios*). The defeated guerrilla groups were formally pacified in 1970, but the barrios have remained the base for occasional small radical groups and continue to be seen as the primary site of subversive threats to democratic order: see Ellner 1980.

10 World oil prices quadrupled in late 1973 and remained high until the close of the decade, when they again doubled. Government income from oil (which ranges from 60 percent to 75 percent of its total income and accounts for more than 90 percent of export earnings) quadrupled just before the newly elected Carlos Andrés Pérez took office. Pérez's program, which claimed it would bring about Venezuela's Second Independence, emphasized capital-intensive heavy industry (petrochemicals, steel, aluminum, hydroelectric power). Although it ignored the social impact of these projects, it directed large sums of money into subsidizing popular consumption and services. Together with the increase in construction and luxury consumption, this created an illusion of prosperity. For the "appearance of development" created through borrowing in Latin America, see Walton 1989.

11 With a foreign debt of $33 billion and a population of approximately twenty million, Venezuela has a per capita foreign debt that is the highest in Latin America. A number of sources discuss the oil boom and its consequences. For an analysis of the petroleum boom and the effects it had on cultural forms and institutional practices, see Coronil 1987. For the impact of the oil boom on

industrial policy, see Coronil and Skurski 1982. Bernard Mommer's innovative work analyzes the historical development and the logic of the rent-based economy (see Mommer 1983, 1988). For examples of critical evaluations of the administrations of Pérez and his successors, see Hellinger 1985; Malavé Mata 1987; Proceso Político 1978.

12 The president who followed Pérez, Luis Herrera Campins of the Social Christian Party (COPEI), also contracted large debts, encouraged once again by a brief rebound of oil prices in 1979. But the nation's finances worsened rapidly, and the currency, the bolívar (basically stable since the 1920s), was abruptly devalued in 1983.

13 Pérez and Lusinchi are leaders of the centrist-reformist party Acción Democrática (founded in 1941). Longtime party leaders and former allies, they are both powerful national figures and now head rival factions within the party. The AD, the nation's leading party, is historically associated with populist reform and a nationalist oil policy. It relies heavily on making pacts with political and economic elites, rests on patronage distribution rather than mobilization, and exerts political control over the major labor and peasant federations. There are few good analyses of AD: see Blank 1973; Ellner 1982; Martz 1966; Moleiro 1978. For the rhetoric and imagery utilized by the AD, see Britto García 1988. For theoretical discussions of Latin American populism, see Hennessy 1976; Laclau 1977.

14 An electoral reform program began to take effect in 1990, but structural constraints, both financial and administrative, limit the autonomy of local officials. See the magazine SIC for analysis of changes in the electoral system. On the political party system, see Arroyo Talavera 1988; Hein and Stenzel 1973; Hellinger 1985; Levine 1973; Magallanes 1986, 1987; Romero 1986.

15 Venezuela's electoral democracy was established in 1958, and power has changed hands peacefully every five years since 1959. The Social Christian Party governed twice in this period—1969–74 under Caldera and 1979–84 under Herrera Campins—but AD governed during the remaining terms. Given the political stability of Venezuela's multiparty system in an era marked by violent military takeovers in much of the continent, its elections have been much studied: see Lubrano and Sánchez 1987; Marta Sosa 1984; Martz and Baloyra 1977; Martz and Myers 1977; Rangel 1973, 1982; Rangel and Duno 1979; Silva Michelena and Sonntag 1979.

16 Lusinchi had backed his ally, Senator Lepage, for the party's nomination during its primary. Pérez mobilized support from the labor sector to win the nomination.

17 Pérez ("the man with energy") defeated his leading opponent, Eduardo Fernandez ("the Tiger") of COPEI, by a 13 percent margin, receiving an unusually high 53 percent of the 7,321,281 votes cast. Teodoro Petkoff, the candidate of the allied socialist parties MAS (Movimiento al Socialismo) and MIR (Movimiento

de Izquierda Revolucionaria), received 2.7 percent of the vote; these parties received 10 percent of the congressional vote, depriving AD of its majority. Lusinchi's administration had been marked by parochialism, paternalistic clientelism, and increasing repression, directed on occasion against highly placed critics of his policies. In contrast to Lusinchi, Pérez had a cosmopolitan image, international experience, and a record of incorporating rather than excluding critics. His electoral victory aided the chances that his supporter would gain positions of control in the party apparatus.

18 The term *pueblo* has a dual set of meanings. On the one hand, it encompasses the entire citizenry of Venezuela and is invoked in relation to the nation's defense and the memory of its independence. On the other hand, the term refers to people who have lower-class (popular) origins and is widely used as a substitute for social class categories when referring to the poor, who are the majority of the population. Its connotations, charged with ambiguity, vary with context, speaker, and audience.

19 Twenty-two heads of state attended the inauguration, which had an international and elite style. Various proponents of revising the terms of Third World debt attended, among them Germany's Willy Brandt, Spain's Felipe González, and the United States' Jimmy Carter. Vice President Dan Quayle of the United States was present on his first official international trip. Nicaragua's Daniel Ortega and Cuba's Fidel Castro (his first trip to Venezuela since 1959) drew great attention; their presence augmented Pérez's image as a leader willing to challenge foreign and conservative pressures.

20 The program was the standard package of measures that the IMF requires of debtor nations in order for them to qualify for new loans. Variants of it have been applied in many countries and have often provoked violent protests. While Pérez continued to criticize the IMF, his team of negotiators, with international reserves alarmingly low and interest payments on the debt suspended, agreed to meet IMF conditions to obtain new loans.

21 For a study of the cult of Bolívar as a civic religion, see Carrera Damas 1972.

22 On the extreme polarization of colonial society and the social content of the war, see Carrera Damas 1968; Izard 1981; Lynch 1973. On the piecemeal abolition of slavery and the racial dimension to social conflict in the postindependence period, see Fundación John Boulton 1976; Lombardi 1971; Matthews 1977.

23 On the construction of categories of high and low as an element in class formation, see Stallybrass and White 1986.

24 The wars of the nineteenth century were fought largely with plainsmen from the cattle frontier, the Llanos, and the threat of anarchy became closely identified with this population formed at the social margins. See Baretta and Markoff's (1978) comparative analysis of violence and cattle frontiers.

25 The right to loot was established practice during the Independence War on the part of Bolívar, as well as his llanero opponent, Boves. It was a necessity, given

the lack of supplies and money to support the troops. The looting of the national treasury, now a common image in contemporary politics, was seen in the nineteenth century as part of the spoils a political leader offered his followers. This was acknowledged in a saying of the time: "I don't ask to be given anything, I just ask to be placed where there is something." Baretta and Markoff (1978: 606) suggest the foundations of looting in the practice of cattle rustling on the Llanos, governed by notions of social justice and common property. For the practice of *saqueo*, see Brito Figueroa 1966; Britto García 1988; Carrera Damas 1972; Gilmore 1964; Matthews 1977.

26   Under Gómez, who rose to power under Cipriano Castro (1899–1908), Andeans monopolized control of the state and of choice property. Gómez put an end to *caudillismo*, a system of regional strongmen vying to control the state, and centralized state power. He ruled as a *hacendado* patriarch, with personal mystique and the ability to use repression without hesitation and used state power to achieve the greatest accumulation of wealth in land and industry in Latin America. He continues to be a controversial and historically opaque figure: see Pino Iturrieta 1985; Segnini 1982; Sosa 1985; Velásquez ed. 1986.

27   Critics canonized it as a "novel of the land" and only recently have located it in relation to nationalist discourse: see Howard 1976; Dessau 1980; Scharer-Nussberger 1979; Skurski 1993; Sommer 1991.

28   For an innovative study of foundational fictions, Latin American novels that allegorically link national integration and family romance, see Sommer 1991.

29   On the construction of the colonized subject and the National Symbolic, see Berlant 1988, 1991.

30   For an analysis of *Doña Bárbara* as a nationalist myth that incorporates the Bolivarian model within the populist project, see Skurski 1993.

31   Our interviews with political figures of this era confirm the impact of *Doña Bárbara* on the emerging political leadership's self-conception and vision of progress. See also Dessau 1980; Howard 1976.

32   The Comando Específico "General en Jefe José Antonio Páez" (CEJAP) was named after the llanero caudillo hero of the Independence War. It brought together members of the army, the Policía Técnica Judicial (PTJ), and the Dirección de los Servicios de Inteligencia y Prevención (DISIP), a paramilitary intelligence police specializing in counterinsurgency. Created on October 28, 1987, under the Border Law, the CEJAP had broad powers to act against suspected subversives and contrabandists. General Camejo Arias was its regional commander, but the chief of operations of the DISIP, Henry López Sisco, was its leader. López Sisco, trained abroad in counterinsurgency, had previously gained notoriety as the leader of DISIP's armed attacks on so-called subversives.

33   López Sisco, the brigade's commander, was not present, as he had been injured days earlier during preparations for the attack. Nine DISIP members, seven PTJ members, and four soldiers participated in the attack.

34 This event depicted Lusinchi as a defender of the national territory at a time when Carlos Andrés Pérez was accused by opposition candidates as having reached a secret agreement with Colombia about a long-standing border dispute on the oil-rich coast.

35 Márquez is locally known for his battles against landowner and military abuses in the border region. Trained as a historian, he has backed peasant land claims with research into obscure land titles. From a modest family in a small Andean town and disabled since infancy by a crippling disease, Márquez has acquired a hero's status in the region as a defender of the powerless.

36 One of the victims was a Colombian from the town of Arauca, across the river from Amparo. The residents of the border area move freely between Venezuela and Colombia, and intermarriage and dual citizenship are common. Commerce between the two towns is heavy, and goods are often carried across the river in both directions by fishing boat owners, depending on fluctuations in currency values and the prices of goods. Residents regard most of this movement as trade rather than contraband.

37 Arias, thirty-five, and Pinilla, twenty-six, are both natives of Amparo, single, and irregularly employed. Arias, who served in the army, works for a land surveying company. Pinilla, who has close family in Colombia, works on fishing boats during the Arauca River's flood season. Neither had known political or religious affiliations. Prior to the attack they were acquaintances, but they became close over the following months of obligatory companionship.

38 Three members were added to the commission. They included Walter Márquez and Congressman Raul Esté, elected on the Communist Party slate. Esté had investigated earlier DISIP massacres, led by López Sisco, against claimed subversives: see Esté 1986.

39 Pérez remained closely tied to the military leadership, and his assertions were seen as more than campaign rhetoric.

40 Guerrilla forces are linked to contraband, robbery, and kidnapping activities, and thus a criminal record was used as presumption of possible guerrilla ties. In the border regions especially, guerrilla identification carried no necessary assumption of ideological affiliation.

41 A few had been jailed for drunkenness and fights. Officials of Venezuela's and Colombia's military intelligence agencies (the director of the Dirección de Administración Social [DAS] in Arauca, Colombia, Francisco Alberto González, and the national director of the Dirección General Sectorial de Inteligencia Militar [DIM] in Venezuela, German Rodríguez Citraro) denied Camejo Arias's claim that the men had a record for criminal or subversive acts. The DIM director's testimony undermined the official account and indicated opposition by military intelligence to the autonomy granted the DISIP (a civilian police agency) under Lusinchi. A sign of this tension is the DIM's offer to bring Walter Márquez and the survivors to Caracas in its airplane.

42 El Diario de Caracas, November 15, 1988, 8.

43 The official autopsy was not released, on the grounds that the legal case had
not been concluded. However, the journalist Fabricio Ojeda reported details of
its findings, including evidence of the torture of seven men and the castra-
tion of one. "En una 'orgía de sangre' mataron a los pescadores" [Fishermen
killed in "orgy of blood"], El Nacional, March 24–25, 1989, D10–11. A Colombian
informer also participated in the attack but remained hidden until December.
Fragments of his confession to the DIM leaked to the press describe the assault's organization and how a DISIP member, Hipólito, forced him to shoot
a wounded survivor as a "test of courage": "La confesión de Yaruro" [Yaruro's
confession], El Nacional, April 10, 1989, D17.

44 A locally feared DISIP member of the CEJAP (César Rincones, or Hipólito) who
resided in Amparo was seen before the ambush with the owner of the fishing
boat. Some speculate he promoted the outing by offering the boat's owner
money to carry contraband. After the attack, he attempted to force the release
of the survivors from the local jail, but the police chief resisted.

45 Nevertheless, conflicts continued between different factions. On their return,
the survivors were again under the control of Judge Pérez Gutiérrez (backed
by Camejo Arias and Lusinchi), who jailed them for two weeks and treated
the jailed CEJAP members with open friendliness. He was instrumental in the
reversal of the case that occurred after the president's inauguration, resulting
in the freedom of the attackers and the accusation of the survivors.

46 It called for an investigation of Judge Pérez Gutiérrez's obstructionist behavior. For the text of the report, widely reported in the press, see República de
Venezuela 1989.

47 The leftist members of the commission were guarded in revealing their information to the press about the powerful landed, military, and political interests
that supported the CEJAP. They also took care not to be seen as maligning
the military as an institution. Márquez quietly received support from military
intelligence officials, who were critical of DISIP incursions into their field and
of DISIP-led attacks tarnishing the army's reputation (personal interviews with
Walter Márquez, January 1989). The backers of the DISIP issued death threats to
Márquez and in order to discredit him organized a costly right-wing advertising
campaign that was paid for by a branch of Lyndon LaRouche's party based in
the United States. It portrayed the Gnostic church to which Márquez belongs as
a satanic sect and a guerrilla front: El Nacional, January 28–February 3, 1989.

48 Congressman Márquez compiled information placing the Amparo massacre
within the context of previous massacres, all of which involved General Camejo
Arias, the DISIP's López Sisco, and Judge Pérez Gutiérrez, carried out in 1988
by the CEJAP: Cotufí (ten dead) in January, Las Gaviotas (two dead) in April,
Los Totumitos (five dead) in July, El Vallado (three dead) in October (El Nacional
February 1, 1989; El Diario de Caracas, March 18, 1989; personal interviews with

Márquez, 1989). This information matches that of Congressman Raul Esté concerning earlier DISIP massacres at Cantaura and Yumare. Esté stresses the ideological intentions of the attacks to quell dissent (personal interviews with Esté, November 1988, January and July 1989).

49 These death factories have been documented in detail by U.S. journalist Ralph Schusler in investigative reports in *El Diario de Caracas*, December 22–23, 1988, and *El Nacional*, May 1–3, 1989. Schusler was fired from his job at the English-language *Daily Journal* after he questioned Carlos Andrés Pérez concerning the Amparo massacre at a press conference. His articles, based on interviews with survivors, describe how Colombians were brought across the border by DISIP agents on the promise of ranch work, only to be killed, often after torture.

50 Lusinchi was the first president to bring his mistress, Blanca Ibáñez, into a position of power. He broke another unofficial political rule by bringing divorce proceedings against his wife of many years, the pediatrician Gladys Lusinchi, while he was in office, moving into quarters at his executive office with Ibáñez. Most critics focused on Ibáñez, defining her as exerting sinister control over the easygoing Lusinchi. Criticism of her power, which was backed by use of the DISIP, entered the national press in August 1988, when the elder AD leader Luis Piñerúa opposed the party's effort to slate her for a congressional seat (see *New York Times*, January 23, 1988). Piñerúa (1988) and Agustín Beroes (1990) refer to her intromission in political, police, and military affairs.

51 Two months after Pérez took office, military and political pressure began to reverse the Amparo case. On April 6, a military court headed by a *compadre* of Camejo Arias ordered the CEJAP members released on a legal technicality. The survivors, fearing for their lives with their assailants free, sought sanctuary from the church; they spent one month in Caracas in a church in a working-class area of Petare. Clergy active in human rights, particularly Fathers Matías Camuñas and Antonio García and Sister Lali Lacarra, placed them in contact with barrio Christian base groups. In a cruel irony, the government kept them guarded by members of the DISIP under the guise of protecting them. Underlining the deep relations of complicity involved in the Amparo massacre, the Supreme Court refused to hear the case, and the Martial Court declared on April 25, 1990, that the incident at Amparo had in fact been an armed encounter and that Arias and Pinilla were guerrillas posing as survivors; simultaneously, President Pérez ordered the investigation of Judge Pérez Gutiérrez to be dropped (*El Nacional*, April 26, 1990). In a shift reflecting internal disagreement, the Supreme Court then rejected the military court's ruling in August 1990 and agreed that it would hear the case. See the magazine SIC and the human rights newsletter *Provea* for accounts of developments.

52 For an excellent discussion of the negative associations historically attached to the Venezuelan peasantry, see Roseberry 1986.

53 The Spanish news magazine *Cambio 16* opened its November 11, 1988, article on the Amparo massacre by making reference to the novel's setting.

54 Prominent media and political figures had been attacked through loss of their jobs, by physical assault, or censorship for having criticized government corruption, particularly in relation to Ibáñez. The report on human rights connects DISIP and police attacks on prominent figures to the abuse and deaths of numerous ordinary citizens, many of whom were labeled criminals.

55 This mode of exercising state power relies on techniques for forming political subjects and gaining their conformity to political rule analogous to those which supported the culture of the baroque in seventeenth-century Spain. The baroque, José Antonio Maravall (1986) argues, was a culture of state building in a time of crisis that arose as part of the state's effort to move and to control a mass of anonymous, potentially disruptive subjects. Its theatrical character grew from the orchestration of appearances by the combination of terror and propaganda, the excessive use of force, and the overproduction of rational formulas. For the quotidian theater of the civilizing process, see Comaroff 1989.

56 The author, Alfredo Peña, is an influential political commentator.

57 For factual reporting and analysis of the events of the week, see *VenEconomía*, March 1989, and SIC, April 1989.

58 The estimate of 1,000–1,200 deaths is based on our interviews with highly placed figures in the media, the military, the political arena, and the health field. The U.S. State Department (1990) acknowledges this estimate and details the military's deliberate armed attack on the population.

59 "The big massacre" is the phrase used in the African context by human rights groups and protest singers.

60 President Pérez suddenly learned that the total amount of Venezuela's international reserves was only $200 million, which necessitated an abrupt change of policy.

61 Venezuelan legislation continued the Spanish colonial legal definition of the subsoil, and thus of petroleum, as the property of the state. In 1976, President Pérez nationalized the oil industry with generous compensation.

62 The private owners of the varied buses, vans, and cars providing most urban transportation argued that escalating costs for the repair and replacement of vehicles made even a provisional ceiling intolerable. Drivers also refused to honor the student half-fare payments. The leaders of the bus association were affiliated with AD but refused to abide by a fare agreement, a symptom of AD's diminishing capacity to control its members.

63 For vivid descriptions and photos of the outbreak and spread of the riots in the Caracas area by journalists on the scene, see the photo essays in El Nacional (1989–90) and Catalá 1989. For analysis of the riots, see *Cuadernos del CENDES* 1989; Tierra Firme 1989; Sanín 1989.

64 The Metropolitan Police, like the looters, have low wages, are of lower-class origins, and generally live in the barrios. Outnumbered by looters, they interfered
little or actively cooperated at the outset, although in some cases they shot at
looters. Observers have stated that the government issued orders initially to
respond with minimal violence to the protests.

65 This section draws on personal interviews conducted with residents of barrios
in Antímano, La Vega, El Valle, El Cementerio, and Petare in the days immediately following the riots. See El Nacional (1989) for an account of the situation in
Antímano and the role of the police in negotiating women's orderly looting of
groceries, which was termed shopping, while men were kept at a distance.

66 Personal interview, August 29, 1990.

67 We are indebted to Roger Rouse for this expression "etiquette of equality" and
for his observations concerning behavior in the street.

68 The information concerning attacks on small factories and on police and party
centers was kept out of the media, while news of sniper fire on troops and
police was amplified.

69 There was much variation in these situations. In many cases, neighbors banded
together to defend a neighborhood store owned by immigrants from attack by
looters from outside the barrio.

70 On February 28, the commission negotiating the restructuring of the debt
signed a letter of intent with the IMF in New York, committing the government
to the austerity program despite the outbreak of the riots. For its contents, see
SIC, April 1989.

71 Interview with a reporter who investigated the sources of such rumors and El
Nacional 1989. This tactic was also used in Chile in 1973 by the forces opposed to
President Allende: see Provea 1989).

72 In Caracas, certain sectors were the object of particularly heavy gunfire: the 23
de Enero housing projects, located near the capitol building and a perennial
site of political and criminal resistance; barrios in El Valle, near the wholesale
food market and a military deposit; and barrios in Petare, near market and
military sites and bordering on upper-middle-class residential zones.

73 Personal interview with a member of a security force, July 27, 1989. Many
relatives of such victims were later afraid to denounce deaths that occurred in
this way because of their own illegal status or activities and their daily fear of
police retaliation (personal interviews with members of the Committee for the
Disappeared).

74 For an account of the detention of six Jesuit priests who live in the barrio La
Vega, see "Carta al Director de la DIM," SIC 52, no. 516 (July 1989), 274–75. For
an account of the torture of a student activist, see Roland Denis, "El encuen-
tro," Punto, February 15, 1990, 10.

75 Personal interview with a forensic doctor who worked in the Bello Monte
Morgue of Caracas continuously for three days during the riots (April 1989).

76 Personal interviews with cemetery employees, journalists, and relatives of victims.

77 The actual number of those killed nationwide is unknown and is very difficult to ascertain. Many more were injured; some were disabled for life. Two policemen and two members of the army were reported killed. Undoubtedly, considerable time will pass before reliable confirmation of these estimates can be obtained. See also note 4 above.

78 Petkoff is a leader of the left known for his role as a guerrilla leader in the 1960s and for having led the division of the Communist Party of Venezuela after the Soviet invasion of Czechoslovakia. A proponent of social democracy, he received 2.6 percent of the presidential vote in 1988.

79 Even coins were scarce as speculators melted them for their nickel content, making the Venezuelan currency's loss of value poignantly visible.

80 Among the conservative elite, the rumor circulated and was published in the press that Fidel Castro, after attending the inauguration, had left behind three hundred trained agents who had organized the riots.

81 Indicative of his political star quality, Alliegro exerted the erotic attraction characteristic of the successful male populist leader. Newspapers noted that he was besieged by lovely young female reporters, and women often commented he would make an attractive president.

82 Alliegro's appointment as the minister of defense expired in June 1989 (he began under Lusinchi) and was not renewed. It was rumored that the AD leadership feared the effects of Alliegro's popularity if he were to remain. Only after his obligatory retirement from the military could Alliegro speak to the press about his opinions. In a televised interview on the anniversary of the riots, Alliegro criticized the Pérez government for having applied its program too rapidly and without measures to aid the poor. He expressed interest in becoming the representative of a new "independent" political coalition: El Diario de Caracas, February 28, 1990.

83 The brief article "Twelve Indians Were Massacred" was buried in the middle of El Diario de Caracas. Unlike in the reporting of the Amparo massacre, the victims were not identified, and the incident went unnoticed. For a prior Indian massacre in this region, see Coppens 1975.

84 For a discussion of the double discourse of nationalism as it negotiates the ambiguous bases of authority in postcolonial societies, see Coronil and Skurski 1991.

85 We are indebted to Kathleen Canning, William Sewell, and Jane Burbank for their comments concerning the impact of popular action on the body politic. Although we do not see the emergence of a counterhegemonic discourse, the events we discuss here indicate that the demobilizing promise of the modernization project has lost some of its hold. In the municipal elections of December 1989, held for the first time under a new electoral law, 80 percent of the

electorate abstained; the media label it was given, the electoral jolt (*el sacudon electoral*), drew a parallel to the riots.

86 Gramsci's conception of the fluid and shifting relationship between the state and civil society whereby "state functions" are sometimes taken up by civil society suggests a nonessentialist view of state power: see Forgacs 1989.

87 This formulation draws on Benedict Anderson's (1983) discussion of nationalism as a "cultural artifact" that has become "modular." In highlighting the opaque and historical character of violence, however, we want to underline both its multivocal semantic structure and its historically specific significance. While the modular character of violence leads to a process of standardization, even of commodification, its significance always remains specific and must be ascertained by locating it within a particular field of social forces; no cultural analysis of violence detached from specific historical contexts can account for its meaning.

88 Taussig (1987) examines the mutual constitution of colonizer and colonized through histories and stories of terror and wildness.

References

Periodicals
Daily Journal
El Diario de Caracas
El Nacional
El Universal
NOTIcrítica
Provea
Punto
Referencias
SIC
Ultimas Noticias
VenEconomía

Other Sources
Amnesty International. 1987. "Political Prisoners in Venezuela." London: Amnesty International.
Amnesty International. 1988. "Memorandum al gobierno de Venezuela." London: Amnesty International.
Anderson, Benedict. 1983. *Imagined Communities*. London: Verso.
Arroyo Talavera, Eduardo. 1988. *Elecciones y negociaciones: los límites de la democracia en Venezuela*. Caracas: Fondo Editorial CONICIT.
Baretta, Silvio R. Duncan, and John Markoff. 1978. "Civilization and Barbarism: Cattle Frontiers in Latin America." *Comparative Studies in Society and History* 20, no. 4: 587–605.

Benjamin, Walter. 1969. *Illuminations*. New York: Schocken.

Berlant, Lauren. 1988. "Race, Gender, and Nation in *The Color Purple.*" *Critical Inquiry* 14 (Summer): 831–59.

Berlant, Lauren. 1991. *The Anatomy of National Fantasy: Hawthorne, Utopia, and Everyday Life*. Chicago: University of Chicago Press.

Beroes, Agustín. 1990. RECADI: *La gran estafa*. Caracas: Planeta.

Blank, David Eugene. 1973. *Politics in Venezuela*. Boston: Little, Brown.

Brito Figueroa, Federico, 1966. *Historia económica y social de Venezuela*. Caracas: Universidad Central de Venezuela.

Britto García, Luis. 1988. *La máscara del poder: Del gendarme necesario al demócrata necesario*. Caracas: Alfadil.

Carrera Damas, Germán. 1968. *Boves: Aspectos socioeconómicos de la Guerra de Independencia*. Caracas: Ediciones de la Biblioteca de la Universidad Central.

Carrera Damas, Germán. 1972. *El culto a Bolívar*. Caracas: Universidad Central de Venezuela.

Catalá, José Agustín. 1989. *El estallido de febrero*. Caracas: Centauro.

Centro de Estudios para la Paz de la Universidad Central de Venezuela. 1999. "Caracterización de las muertes violentas en Caracas, 1986–1988." Caracas: Base de Datos, Universidad Central de Venezuela.

Comaroff, John L. 1989. "Images of Empire, Contests of Conscience: Models of Colonial Domination in South Africa." *American Ethnologist* 16, no. 4: 661–85.

Coppens, Walter. 1975. *Los Cuiva de San Estéban de Capanaparo*. Caracas: Fundación La Salle de Ciencias Naturales.

Coronil, Fernando. 1987. "The Black El Dorado: Money, Fetishism, Democracy and Capitalism in Venezuela." Ph.D. diss., University of Chicago.

Coronil, Fernando. 1989. "Discovering America—Again: The Politics of Self-hood in the Age of Postcolonial Empires." *Dispositio* 14, nos. 36–39: 315–31.

Coronil, Fernando, and Julie Skurski. 1982. "Reproducing Dependency: Auto Industry Policy and Petrodollar Circulation in Venezuela." *International Organization* 36, no. 1 (Winter): 61–94.

Cuadernos del CENDES. 1989. No. 10.

De Certeau, Michel. 1984. *The Practice of Everyday Life*, trans. Steven Rendall. Berkeley: University of California Press.

Dessau, A. 1980. "Realidad social, dimensión histórica y método artístico en Doña Bárbara, de Rómulo Gallegos." In *Relectura de Rómulo Gallegos*, by the Instituto Internacional de Literatura Iberoamericana. Caracas: Ediciones del Centro de Estudios Latinoamericanos Rómulo Gallegos.

Ellner, Steven. 1980. "Political Party Dynamics in Venezuela and the Outbreak of Guerrilla Warfare." *Inter-American Economic Affairs* 34, no. 2 (Autumn): 3–24.

Ellner, Steven. 1982. "Populism in Venezuela, 1935–48: Betancourt and 'Acción Democrática.'" In *Latin American Populism in Comparative Perspective*, ed. Michael L. Conniff, 135–50. Albuquerque: University of New Mexico Press.

Esté, Raul. 1987. *La masacre de Yumare*. Caracas: Fondo Editorial "Carlos Aponte."

Forgacs, David. 1989. "Gramsci and Marxism in Britain." *New Left Review* I/176 (July–August): 70–88.

Foucault, Michel. 1979. *Discipline and Punish: Birth of the Prison*. New York: Vintage.

Fundación John Boulton. 1976. *Política y economía en Venezuela, 1810–1976*. Caracas: Fundación John Boulton.

Gallegos, Rómulo. 1954. *Una posición en la vida*. Mexico City: Ediciones Humanismo.

Gallegos, Rómulo. 1959. *Doña Bárbara*. In *Obras Completas*, by Rómulo Gallegos, vol. 1. Madrid: Aguilar.

Gilmore, Robert L. 1964. *Caudillism and Militarism in Venezuela, 1810–1910*. Athens: Ohio University Press.

Hein, Wolfgang, and Conrad Stenzel. 1973. "The Capitalist State and Underdevelopment in Latin America: The Case of Venezuela." *Kapitalistate* 2: 31–48.

Hellinger, Daniel. 1985. "Democracy in Venezuela." *Latin American Perspectives*, no. 12: 75–82.

Hennessy, Alistair. 1969. "Latin America." In *Populism: Its Meaning and National Characteristics*, ed. Ghita Ionescu and Ernest Gellner, 28–61. London: Macmillan.

Howard, Harrison Sabin. 1976. *Rómulo Gallegos y la revolución burguesa de Venezuela*. Caracas: Monte Avila Editores.

Izard, Miguel. 1981. *El miedo a la revolución*. Madrid: Universal.

Laclau, Ernest. 1977. *Nationalism, Populism, and Ideology*. London: Verso.

Levine, Daniel H. 1973. *Conflict and Political Change in Venezuela*. Princeton, NJ: Princeton University Press.

Lombardi, John V. 1971. *The Decline and Abolition of Negro Slavery in Venezuela, 1820–1854*. Westport, CT: Greenwood.

Lubrano, Aldo, and Rosa Haydee Sánchez. 1987. *Del hombre completo a Jaime es como tú: Recuento de un proceso electoral venezolano*. Caracas: Vadell Hermanos.

Lynch, John. 1973. *The Spanish-American Revolutions, 1808–1826*. New York: W. W. Norton.

Magallanes, Manuel Vicente, ed. 1986. *Reformas electorales y partidos políticos*. Caracas: Publicaciones del Consejo Supremo Electoral.

Magallanes, Manuel Vicente. 1987. *Sistemas electorales, acceso al sistema político, y sistema de partidos*. Caracas: Publicaciones del Consejo Supremo Electoral.

Malavé Mata, Hector. 1987. *Los extravíos del poder*. Caracas: Universidad Central de Venezuela.

Maravall, José Antonio. 1986. *Culture of the Baroque: Analysis of a Historical Structure*, trans. Terry Cochran. Minneapolis: University of Minnesota Press.

Marta Sosa, Joaquín. 1984. *Venezuela: Elecciones y transformación social*. Caracas: Ediciones Centauro.

Martz, John. 1966. *Acción Democrática: Evolution of a Modern Political Party in Venezuela*. Princeton, NJ: Princeton University Press.

Martz, John, and Enrique Baloyra. 1977. *Electoral Mobilization and Public Opinion: The Venezuelan Campaign of 1973*. Chapel Hill: University of North Carolina Press.

Martz, John, and David J. Myers, eds. 1977. *Venezuela: The Democratic Experience*. New York: Praeger.

Matthews, Robert D., Jr. 1977. *Violencia rural en Venezuela, 1840–1858*. Caracas: Editorial Ateneo de Caracas.

Moleiro, Moisés. 1978. *El partido del pueblo*. Valencia, Venezuela: Vadell Hermanos.

Mommer, Bernard. 1983. *Petróleo, renta del suelo e historia*. Mérida, Venezuela: Universidad de los Andes.

Mommer, Bernard. 1988. *La cuestión petrolera*. Caracas: Fondo Editorial Trópikos.

El Nacional. 1989. *El día que bajaron los cerros*. Caracas: Editorial Ateneo de Caracas.

El Nacional. 1990. *27 de Febrero: Cuando la muerte tomó las calles*. Caracas: Editorial Ateneo de Caracas.

Nairn, Tom. 1981. *The Break-up of Britain*. London: Verso.

Neruda, Pablo. 1978. *Canto General*. Caracas: Biblioteca Ayacucho.

Neruda, Pablo. 1991. *Canto General*, trans. Jack Schmitt. Berkeley: University of California Press.

Oviedo y Baños, José. 1987. *The Conquest and Settlement of Venezuela*. Berkeley: University of California Press.

Piñerúa, Luis. 1988. *Luis Piñerúa: Enfrentamiento con el poder*. Caracas: Ediciones Centauro.

Pino Iturrieta, Elías, ed. 1985. *Juan Vicente Gómez y su época*. Caracas: Monte Avila.

Proceso Político. 1978. *CAP: 5 años*. Caracas: Equipo Proceso Político.

Rangel, Domingo Alberto. 1973. *Los mercaderes del voto*. Valencia, Venezuela: Vadell Hermanos.

Rangel, Domingo Alberto. 1982. *Fin de fiesta*. Valencia, Venezuela: Vadell Hermanos.

Rangel, Domingo, and Pedro Duno. 1979. *La pipa rota: Las elecciones de 1978*. Caracas: Vadell Hermanos.

República de Venezuela. 1989. *Gaceta del Congreso*, vol. 18, no. 1 (March–January).

Romero, Aníbal. 1986. *La miseria del populismo*. Caracas: Ediciones Centauro.

Roseberry, William. 1986. "Images of the Peasant in the Consciousness of the Venezuelan Proletariat." In *Proletarians and Protest*, ed. Michael Hanagan and Charles Stephenson, 149–69. Westport, CT: Greenwood.

Sanín. 1989. *Los muertos de la deuda*. Caracas: Ediciones Centauro.

Scharer-Nussberger, Maya. 1979. *Rómulo Gallegos: El mundo inconcluso*. Caracas: Monte Avila.

Segnini, Yolanda. 1982. *La consolidación del régimen de Juan Vicente Gómez.* Caracas: Biblioteca de la Academia Nacional de la Historia.

Silva Michelena, José Agustín, and Heinz Rudolf Sonntag. 1979. *El proceso electoral de 1978.* Caracas: Editorial Ateneo de Caracas.

Skurski, Julie. 1993. "The Leader and the 'People': Representing the Nation in Postcolonial Venezuela." Ph.D. diss., University of Chicago.

Skurski, Julie, and Fernando Coronil. 1991. "Country and City in a Colonial Landscape: Double Discourse and the Geopolitics of Truth in Latin America." In *View from the Border: Essays in Honor of Raymond Williams,* ed. Dennis Dworkin and Leslie Roman, 231–59. New York: Routledge.

Sommer, Doris. 1991. *Foundational Fictions: When History Was Romance.* Berkeley: University of California Press.

Sosa, Arturo A., ed. 1985. *Ensayos sobre el pensamiento político positivista venezolano.* Caracas: Ediciones Centauro.

Stallybrass, Peter, and Allon White. 1986. *The Politics and Poetics of Transgression.* Ithaca, NY: Cornell University Press.

Taussig, Michael. 1987. *Shamanism, Colonialism, and the Wild Man.* Chicago: University of Chicago Press.

Thompson, E. P. 1971. "The Moral Economy of the English Crowd in the Eighteenth Century." *Past and Present* 50: 76–136.

Tierra Firme. 1989. *Revista Tierra Firme: Revista de historia y ciencias sociales* 7, no. 28.

U.S. State Department. 1990. "Report to Congress on Principal Human Rights Concerns in Venezuela" (February).

Velásquez, Ramón J., ed. 1986. *Juan Vicente Gómez ante la historia.* San Cristóbal, Venezuela: Biblioteca de Autories y Temas Tachirenses.

Walton, John. 1989. "Debt, Protest, and the State in Latin America." In *Power and Popular Protest,* ed. Susan Eckstein, 299–328. Berkeley: University of California Press.

7   Transitions to Transitions:
Democracy and Nation in Latin America

By Way of Introduction: Latin America in South Africa

This reflection on "transitions to democracy in Latin America" was delivered at the opening session of the conference "Democracy and Difference"
organized in celebration of the first democratic elections in South Africa in
May 1994. The conference took place the week before Nelson Mandela's inauguration as the first elected president of South Africa. The participants
included academics and political figures, many of whom had limited familiarity with Latin American politics. The conference organizers suggested that
my comments be cast at a general level. In this version I have made only
minor changes in the essay in order to preserve its spirit as an intervention
in a public discussion about the politics of democracy at a critical historical
juncture.

Transitions to Democracy in Latin America

While it would be instructive to examine in detail the historical production of democracy in particular Latin American countries or to evaluate
the evolution of democracy in the region as a whole, I think it is more
useful at this exceptional moment to reflect more generally about some
of the central assumptions that have framed the understanding of Latin
American democracy in academic and political circles. Since these assumptions reflect also rather widespread notions about democracy elsewhere, my hope is that this discussion may contribute to an exchange of
ideas *about* democracy at a time when ideas may indeed make a difference
for democracy.

It indeed makes sense to think of Latin America when one approaches the topic of "transitions to democracy" because many Latin American nations have, in fact, adopted democratic institutions during this century, particularly in the past fifteen years. This recent trend toward democratization was preceded by an earlier one toward militarization; in some cases, therefore, it would be more accurate to talk about re-democratization. Between 1964 and 1976, the democratic regimes of Brazil, Ecuador, Peru, Uruguay, Chile, and Argentina fell to the military. From 1979, when in Ecuador the military returned to the barracks until the present moment, a dozen Latin American and Caribbean nations have replaced dictatorial regimes with elected governments. This is an ongoing process—think of the efforts made to reinstate J. Bertrand Aristide as Haiti's legitimate president.

This "transition" has affected states of all sizes: small ones, such as El Salvador, and large ones, such as Brazil. It has taken place through a great variety of means and under very different conditions: from planned insurrection from below (as the Sandinista revolution against the dictatorship of Anastasio Somoza in Nicaragua) to intraelite conflict at the top (as the palace revolt against the even lengthier dictatorship of Alfredo Stroessner in Paraguay). Democratic institutions have been restored or inaugurated as a result of the breakdown of authoritarian regimes (as in Argentina, whose ruling military junta collapsed after being defeated in the Malvinas/Falklands war in 1982), as well as through negotiated arrangements among representatives of competing political sectors (as in Brazil after 1982, where a gradual process of liberalization within the authoritarian military regime has led to the reestablishment of civilian democratic rule). The military foundation of dictatorial states may be dismantled and radically reconstituted (as in Nicaragua under the Sandinistas), partially transformed (as in Argentina under Raúl Alfonsín and Carlos Menem), or maintained as a source of support of the new regime (as in Chile, where Augusto Pinochet gave up his position as head of state after being defeated in the presidential elections of 1989 but maintained his command of the military).

A common feature of these recent transitions, however, is what a scholar of Latin America aptly called "the Venezuelan syndrome"—that is, "restored legitimacy for bourgeois politicians, elite consensus, the definition of democracy in procedural terms, the shelving of conflictive issues, the marginalization of the left, and the deliberate strengthening of the executives over legislatures, and leaders over parties." There is a discernible trend, according to this analyst, toward "self limiting democracy of the Venezuelan type" (Cammack 1985: 1944).

In this century, some of these transitions to democracy have led to relatively stable regimes, as in the case of Costa Rica and Venezuela, the Latin American countries that currently have the longest-lasting democracies. In other situations, the transition has been short-lived, as in Argentina, which has experienced shifting cycles of dictatorship and democracy. Yet in other instances, as in Chile, the transitions have involved a return to long-standing democratic institutions following an exceptional period of military rule. Thus, while they share some attributes, these "transitions" are not a unitary phenomenon. They entail different types of transformations and durations: stages in the construction of democratic stability, periods in oscillating cycles of democracy and dictatorship, and phases in the re-democratization of societies that experienced exceptional episodes of military rule. Some analysts distinguish between *transitions to* democracy and *consolidations of* democracy. While they have focused on the period of transition itself, because they regard it as more open to the play of politics and therefore as a crucial arena for scholarly and political intervention (O'Donnell et al. 1986), they have also examined the process of "democratic consolidation" (Mainwaring et al. 1992).[1] Others disagree with this distinction and suggest that the study of transitions must be rooted in the analysis of democracy itself as a system of rule (Levine 1988).

The Politics of Democracy and the Scholarship of Transitions

Democracy, both as a political project and as a scholarly issue, has been discussed in Latin America for a long time. However, it is mostly in this recent period—the past fifteen years or so—that debate about it has become a central scholarly problem, and it is from the perspective of these recent transitions that older processes of democratization are now being examined or reevaluated. A whole academic cottage industry has burgeoned around the study of these transitions as social scientists have sought to ascertain their causes, evaluate the conditions that made them possible, describe their structural features, and investigate the political processes that distinguish them. "Transitionology" has become a subfield mined by experts. Since the 1960s, when Latin Americans developed the dependency paradigm (through the outstanding works of Fernando Henrique Cardoso, Enzo Faletto, Theotônio dos Santos, Aníbal Quijano, and others), Latin American scholarship had not produced another body of work unified by a common theme and perspective. This subfield has been energized by authors committed to the defense of democratic values who make rather direct links between descriptive and prescriptive propositions in their studies. Far from limiting their conclusions to Latin America, they have sought to draw general lessons—about causes, conditions, mechanisms—that can be applied to other societies.

This concern with general lessons and with the practical uses of social-science knowledge is salutary, particularly at a time when in other scholarly fields there is a retreat from political engagement and a penchant for abstract and esoteric formulations. The recent upsurge of scholarly work on transitions to democracy in Latin America has been produced in response to emerging political demands within Latin America. In the 1960s, the Latin American Left widely dismissed electoral or procedural democracy as being seriously limited, merely political rather than social, concerned with rules rather than with outcomes. "Revolution" was then the galvanizing concept. In the 1970s, however, a general shift of public opinion toward the valorization of democratic forms and procedures as such began to occur. "Democracy" has now become the keyword.

A number of interrelated factors have been crucial in this shift. I will note five, which I believe help us understand the new meanings attached to democracy in Latin America. The first is the devastating effects of the wave of military rule that swept over Latin America in the 1960s and '70s. The second is a widespread disenchantment with Cuban socialism, together with the realization that its limitations are related to the excessive concentration of political power in few institutional sites and hands. The third is the overthrow of the elected socialist government of Salvador Allende in Chile in 1973 and the recognition that the construction of socialist democracy depends on the establishment of strategic alliances with heterogeneous social sectors. These three factors intensified interest in the role of formal democratic procedures both in socialist and capitalist societies. A fourth factor that contributes to the growing interest in bourgeois democracy is the breakdown of socialist regimes in Eastern Europe and the Soviet Union. To these strictly political transformations I would add a changed intellectual climate related to the international impact of poststructuralism, the crisis of Marxism, and the appeal of the individualistic perspectives of neoliberal economics, rational choice, and game theory. In the social sciences, this climate has encouraged a critique of systemic and modernist teleologies of history as well as an approach to the political as a relatively autonomous domain.

These factors have inflected discussions about democracy. For those who continue to embrace socialism even as actually existing socialism either vanishes or ceases to embody emancipatory hopes, the tragic fate of socialism on earth signals not its defeat but a call to forge stronger connections between socialism and democracy. For those whose utopian horizon is confined to the reformation of capitalism, the struggle to deepen bourgeois democracy acquires singular importance. Thus, to the extent that capitalism and socialism continue to be major contestants in the utopian imaginary as alternative models for constructing a society with a "human face," the pursuit of democracy provides a common referent, even when the "face" of humanity embodied in these models reflects not just different human physiognomies, but contrasting images of humanity. Underlying a common concern with democracy may lie radically different understandings of its meaning, which in subterranean ways configure and energize democratic struggles as well as academic discussions about democracy.

After two decades of intense political contests in which revolutionary hopes crashed against harsh historical realities throughout the continent, the scholarship on transitions to democracy in Latin America is characterized by a sense of urgency and a practical interest in securing democracy within existing capitalist societies, even among authors who still hold socialism as an ideal standard. This in part explains the existence of a strong current within this literature that seeks to ascertain, through comparative and taxonomic approaches, modalities of transition to democracy and types of democratic regimes within capitalist nations. Rather than present a synthesis of the major formulation of this vast literature, I think it is more useful on this occasion to explore some of its basic assumptions, for they reflect widespread understandings about democracy. I present my discussion under six interrelated headings.[2]

The Conceptual Landscape of the Discourse on
Transitions to Democracy

1. An Emphasis on the Political as an Independent Domain
As I have suggested, there is a tendency in this field to treat politics or "the political" as an independent domain. Ironically, this focus on the political in isolation from economic and other constraints contrasts sharply with previous attempts to examine the rise of authoritarian regimes in Latin America. Reflecting on the development of several authoritarian regimes in South America since the late 1960s, Guillermo O'Donnell (1973), an Argentine political scientist, developed the argument that the "deepening" of capitalism (the movement from the production of consumer goods to the production of intermediate and capital goods) required in Latin America the development

of bureaucratic-authoritarian regimes—that is, repressive states managed by an alliance of military and technocratic elites, which reduced the cost of labor and controlled dissent. His argument questioned Seymour Martin Lipset's (1959) optimistic formula about the rise of democracy in the West, according to which there is a positive correlation between the level of capitalist development and the development of democracy. While his specific argument about authoritarianism and industrialization proved to be more accurate for Argentina than for other Latin American nations, his work stimulated important discussions in Latin America about the relationship between economic change and political development (Collier 1979).

Unlike these earlier approaches to the study of democracy and authoritarianism, which in contrasting ways posit the existence of a correlation between a specific regime of economic accumulation and a particular type of political system, the recent literature on transitions to democracy, including O'Donnell's important work in this area, tends to focus on political factors (O'Donnell et al. 1986; Baloyra 1987; Diamond et al. 1989). This scholarship has made invaluable contributions to our understanding of democracy, in particular because it has paid close attention to a wide range of political phenomena through intensive studies of particular countries as well as through comparative analysis. Yet to the extent that it focuses exclusively on political variables, its propositions about the dynamics of transitions tend to be either so bound up with the details of particular situations or so abstract that they do not readily provide illuminating insights into patterns of democratic transformation.

In the work of some Latin American scholars one may notice an attempt to bring back the economic dimension that was critical to the older scholarly tradition that sought to make connections between economic and political domains. Thus, in an article significantly entitled "Beyond Transitions to Democracy in Latin America," Marcelo Cavarozzi argues that the analysis of democracy should be placed within the context of the crisis of the political and economic model of development established in several Latin American nations after 1930. According to him, attention should shift from the short-term prerequisites of the "transition paradigm" to the "long-term historical process, which began long before the emergence of the recent military regimes" and which affects as well the construction of democratic regimes. According to Cavarozzi (1992: 684), the examination of this deeper context requires facing the problem of the "relationship between economic and political variables."

Other Latin American scholars are paying special attention to the role of political culture in the construction of democracy in the context of a pervasive economic crisis. Thus, in a collection of essays edited by Norbert Lechner and sponsored by the Consejo Latinoamericano de Ciencias Sociales (CLACSO), Facultad Latinoamericana de Ciencias Sociales (FLACSO), and Instituto de Cooperación Iberoamericano (ICI), Lechner (1987: 9) notes that efforts to construct democratic institutions in Latin America have been linked to attempts to develop a democratic culture. Yet the essays point to the difficulty of building a democratic culture in the context of an economic and social crisis that undermines trust in the institutions of the past and in the viability of the country's future. Paradoxically, as Lechner (1987: 253–62) notes, the valorization of democracy coincides with a loss of faith in politics, in parties, and in political projects.

Francisco Weffort makes a similar point in his evaluation of Brazilian democratization. After years of political terror, Brazilians believe in democracy despite being pessimistic about the economic future of their nation; they have come to value democracy as an end in itself, not just as a means: "The discovery of the value of democracy is inseparable, within the opposition, from the discovery of civil society as a political space" (Weffort 1989: 345). The experience of political terror undermined the traditional focus on the state as the locus of the political. According to Weffort (1989: 345), by valorizing civil society, it placed the "concept of politics on its true foundations."

The discussion about transitions to democracy in Latin America reflects a focus on politics but, at the same time, a growing awareness of the limits of this focus. Democracy cannot respond only to the (political) terrors of the past, but also to the (economic) terrors of the present. If the political, as Weffort suggests, encompasses civil society as well as the state, both state and society must be seen as complex ensembles of multiple social relations that cannot be reduced to political variables.

2. A Procedural Focus on Democracy

For reasons I have suggested, in progressive circles in Latin America in the 1960s bourgeois democracy was often treated as an epiphenomenon of more fundamental socioeconomic relations—a brittle shell that conceals unacceptable social inequalities. Since the mid-1970s, bourgeois democracy has been increasingly valorized as the embodiment of liberal values—a fundamental framework that sustains basic human rights. Democracy has been equated with liberal institutions. Formal procedures have now acquired a valued content.

This shift has entailed an emphasis on politics as a domain encompassed by state-civil society relations. Statecraft—by which political scientists mean intentional political action relatively disengaged from structural constraints—has become a central focus of studies of transition to democracy in Latin America. This disengagement from structural constraints has also implied the pragmatic acceptance of existing conditions as defining the field of political action. The shift from revolution to reform has been represented in political discourse as a change from the rhetoric of illusion to the language of reality. In the name of realism, reform has become the pragmatic imperative, even within the limited circles that still pursue radical change. Compromise, rather than rupture, marks the tone of most transitions. In countries that underwent the terrors of authoritarian rule, the construction of democracy has entailed a compromise between the necessity of social reconciliation and the demands for justice and truth. The politics of historical memory remains a critical site of struggles in Argentina and Chile, which provide different models of relating past and present in the process of creating a democratic future.

The scholarship on transitions reflects the political interests as well as the ideological horizons that have defined major political struggles in Latin America in the past two decades.

3. The Modernist Teleology of the Rhetoric of Transition

My third and central point concerns the theoretical status of the concept of "transition." Even a limited knowledge of contemporary Latin American history points to a historical irony. Despite the great number of transitions to democracy throughout this century in Latin America, it is generally understood that no country in the region has completed its transition to democracy. All Latin American democracies are seen, in one way or another, as being "transitional." Even countries such as Venezuela and Costa Rica, which have had long-standing democratic regimes, are typically cast as incomplete or truncated democracies.

Revealingly, in the scholarship on transitions to democracy in Latin America, these older democracies are presented as models for democratization only with respect to their initial, transitional stages toward democracy, not in relation to their present condition. For instance, what is found noteworthy and exemplary in the Venezuelan case is its political experience immediately after the fall of the dictatorship of General Marcos Pérez Jiménez in 1958, characterized by pact making and compromise among competing political sectors. The subsequent evolution of Venezuelan democracy has not been considered particularly relevant in these discussions.

Since the 1980s, however, a deepening economic and political crisis has polarized the Venezuelan population and seriously eroded support for the political system. In 1989, popular protests were met by brutal state repression; in 1992, two attempted military coups almost toppled the government; in 1993, Congress removed the president from office for corruption, and only half the population voted in the following presidential election (a sharp decline from previous elections). The "evolution" of Venezuelan democracy makes starkly visible the conceptual blinders of the modernist teleology underpinning much of the discussion of "transitions to democracy" in Latin America.

The notion of "transition" refers to the passage from a point of departure to a point of arrival or to the transformation from one state to another. In Latin America, the points of origin of these transitions to democracy are relatively unambiguous. They refer to actual political systems that have affected all countries in the region: the familiar authoritarian or dictatorial regimes of one form or another. The end point or the transformed state, in contrast, tends to be seen, implicitly or explicitly, as the idealized political reality of other societies—that is, the remote democracies of the United States and northern Europe. The political and epistemological effect of this geographical and historical displacement, of this shift from one's familiar reality to another's ideal one, has been to construct Latin American nations in terms of a lack—that is, as inferior societies. Accordingly, projects of development or modernization typically depict Latin American nations as countries that temporarily occupy a lower, transitional stage in an evolutionary scheme whose higher positions are occupied by "modern" nations.

The notion of a lack is often part of a larger ideological field that attributes this inferiority to domestic deficiencies and roots it in internal aspects of these societies—the culture, the people, the economy, the climate, or what have you. While in the nineteenth century Domingo F. Sarmiento, the Argentine politician and writer, made the development of Argentina contingent on the whitening of its population by importing Europeans and culturally eradicating Blacks and Indians, a century later the ideas of David McClelland, the Harvard social psychologist, inspired development projects designed to inject "achievement motivation" into the minds and hearts of Latin Americans in order to make them work enthusiastically toward modernity. These two examples illustrate the continuing hold of Eurocentric understandings of Latin American realities. Whether from the perspective of the ideologies of conquest in the sixteenth century or those of modernization today, Latin America has been typically defined as inferior in relation to Anglo-European "civilized" centers.

In the context of the history of Third World nations, the notion of "transition" is saturated with colonial associations. As an element in visions of historical development, this notion shows an uncanny kinship with Western mythologies of progress. While works in this field are often self-consciously critical of teleological conceptions of history, the rhetoric of "transitions" typically conjures up images of projects of national "development" that purportedly connect backward pasts to modern futures in a preordained chain of historical evolution.

4. Beyond "Democracy": Democratizing Democracy

My fourth point grows out of the previous one and concerns the notion of "democracy" as an ideal achieved in advanced Western nations. Not always clearly defined, and most often implied, the concept of "democracy" typically brings to mind the image of a fully constituted democracy, of democracy fulfilled. The content of this image is a finite set of institutions identical to those that characterize existing democracies in advanced capitalist societies today. These institutions, extricated from their history, are turned into reified emblems of democracy. From a means for constructing democracy, these institutions become democracy itself.

Perhaps as scholars we may promote the deepening of democracy by historicizing these institutional and political features, showing how they are the temporary embodiment of democratic struggles and compromises rather than democracy's essential and eternal characteristics. In political as well as in scholarly circles, democracy is too often treated as a thing—a set of institutions—possessed by certain nations, rather than as a contested process. Possessing this fetish-thing means possessing democracy. From this vantage point the struggle for democracy is limited to the acquisition of its emblems. To the extent that we treat democracy as a finished product, we reproduce rather than examine these widespread assumptions.

I think that we all can contribute to democratizing democracy by treating it as a substantive process, not a thing, by regarding the institutionalization of democratic ideals in specific contexts not as their fulfillment, but as their always contested and temporary crystallization. Turning these historical achievements into fetish-things inhibits the struggles that have made of democracy such a compelling and progressive historical force. Recognizing how the concept of democracy takes on new meanings and flows in response to emergent social demands may permit us to contribute to the ongoing invention of democracy.

Through a wide range of political struggles worldwide, emergent meanings or criteria are being attached to the pursuit of democracy. "Democracy" is being made to refer not just to a set of electoral procedures, but also to effective political institutions—for example, fair judicial systems, powerful legislatures, civilian control of the military, or even more basically, the drastic reduction of the use of force in social affairs. These criteria are also being expanded to domains not previously associated with political institutions, such as the realms of culture, the economy, sexuality, or the family.

These struggles show that the boundaries containing democracy are also the limits of our political imagination. Democracy is being imagined as centering not just on issues of political representation but also of power over decisions and outcomes, as involving not only the regulation of rights and duties, but also the satisfaction of needs, not just the representation of political subjects and of their interests, but the constitution of subjects and of their desires in contexts of social equality. The struggle for democracy may broaden the political field in order to include children and youth as political agents. Its horizons can also be expanded to include the rights and welfare not only of human beings, but also of other living creatures.

The democracies of advanced industrial nations represent a collective historical achievement of extraordinary value that provides exemplary lessons to peoples in other societies. However, the notion of democracy as a fulfilled ideal modeled after the existing political regimes of these societies helps to legitimate their power hierarchies, to freeze history, and to inhibit the further development of the democratic imagination. As scholars we should question, rather than endorse, the sense of completeness evoked by prevailing images of advanced democracies. What standards are employed in the definition of a democracy? Who has the power to define its limits? Whose interests are served by restrictive definitions of democracy?

5. *The Historical Construction of Democracy:*
Democracy as a Transnational Achievement

My fifth comment also follows from the previous discussion and concerns the historical construction of democracy. To the extent that democracy is treated as a set of institutional arrangements, their specific form is commonly associated with the political systems of the most economically advanced nations of the West. The key institution in these regimes—which include parties, trade unions, free press, and a complex governmental apparatus divided into various branches—is universal suffrage. Universal suffrage is usually understood as the process through which most adults participate in the electoral process under conditions of secrecy and freedom of expression, with no restrictions in terms of property, class, gender, race, religion, or ethnic affiliation; people younger than eighteen are not considered political actors when it comes to voting, although they often participate in political struggles. Generally missing from this common view of democracy, however, is an understanding of its historical construction. I would like to comment on three aspects of this history.[3]

First, democracy understood in terms of universal suffrage as defined earlier is a recent phenomenon. Democracy did not come whole to any of the countries that now serve as its exemplary models. The various components of universal suffrage came together in Western nations only after a long and uneven history—a history of ongoing transitions to democracy (Therborn 1977). If we take universal suffrage as commonly understood today as the defining standard of democracy, by 1914 only Australia, New Zealand, and Norway could be regarded as democratic nations. Switzerland was a pioneer in establishing universal male suffrage and in abolishing property qualifications but was the last Western country to fully enfranchise women, in 1971. The United States was one of the earlier Western nations to establish rules and a constitution explicitly designed to build democratic institutions, but only in the 1960s were African Americans fully enfranchised in the South.

Second, conventional—that is, Eurocentric—wisdom suggests that democracy was institutionalized first in metropolitan centers and that it has been exported or diffused to the periphery. In reality, the invention of democracy, as John Markoff (1993) has argued, has been a global process; its institutional mechanisms have been invented in many different countries, and very often in countries that occupied peripheral positions in the international order when these forms were created. As he has highlighted, women's suffrage was first universalized in New Zealand. Australia probably developed the secret ballot. The first Western nations to enact a deliberate set of basic rules to construct democratic institutions were probably the United States and Poland. The recent elections in South Africa included an exemplary innovation (as far as I know) that may make possible a broader participation of the population in the electoral process: various days for voting, with one day allocated to the old and infirm, and provisions made for voting by the incarcerated.

Third, while democracy, as we understand it, today develops within national domains, its conditions of possibility are necessarily transnational. Given the formation of nations under regimes of colonial imperial and neocolonial subjection, it makes little analytical sense to treat nations as independent entities and to see the task of constructing democracy as an exclusively national undertaking. It is within the context of hierarchically constructed global relations that democracy is constructed within nations. Thus, as we look at the construction of democracy within nations, we must keep in mind not only domestic factors or the interaction among nations as bounded units, but also the vast ensemble of formal and informal circuits through which goods, ideas, and people circulate worldwide and redefine national boundaries. The study of transition to democracy must shift attention from an exclusive focus on domestic factors to an analysis of the global conditions of democratization.

6. The Disjuncture between Market and Nation

The recognition that the conditions of possibility of national democracies are transnational leads to my sixth and last comment on assumptions that inform the scholarship on transitions. This literature tends to focus on domestic factors. Historically, however, the disjuncture between the domestic requirements of political legitimacy and the international conditions of capital accumulation has had profound consequences in Latin America. During the present transitions to democracy in Latin America, this disjuncture between market and nation has created an unprecedented crisis of the nation as a viable political entity. More urgently than ever before, the analysis of democratization in Latin America must take into account the transnational conditions within which national democracies are being constructed.

The adoption of neoliberal policies has led to a radical reorganization of polities and markets in Latin America. Even in the few countries where these policies have promoted significant economic growth, the distribution of benefits has been highly skewed. In every country free-market policies have socially polarized the population and fractured domestic economies, widening dramatically the income gap between rich and poor. In Latin America, public sector spending (in health, education, housing) has declined by more than 50 percent in the past decade. In 1990, approximately 44 percent of the continent's population (close to two hundred million out of five hundred million people) were living below the poverty line—an increase of 112 million over 1970. Almost half of this group, or 88 million people, live in conditions of extreme or critical poverty.

During this period, foreign and local capital benefited greatly. Although figures are hard to determine with precision, close to $300 billion in profits left Latin America in the past decade. Neoliberal policies help create a dual and fragmented economy: they generate upward mobility and prosperity for the top 10–20 percent of the population linked to transnational circuits of accumulation while forcing downward mobility upon the vast majority tied to the domestic economy. Under these conditions, the construction of social order entails a significant degree of repression; democratic states have to contain social dissent and repress the poor and marginalized, often through violent means.

This paradox points to a tragic irony. In Latin America as well as elsewhere, states are being reconstituted as more representative and democratic at the *national* level at a time when their policies are defined in response to *international* market forces, beyond domestic control, which have profoundly exclusionary and undemocratic effects. The split between national political sovereignty and international economic subjection, between formal and substantive democracy, between representation and participation has seldom been so deep and serious in its implications.

In the context of a highly internationalized economy and polarized society, the old connection between nation, state, economy, and people has been unfastened. As a result of these conditions, the class alliances and political identities that have sustained national projects are breaking down or being redefined in many countries. In Latin America, ruling national elites are increasingly integrated into global circuits of accumulation, consumption, and leisure. In response to the social crisis, the wealthy are increasingly insulated in domestic fortresses. They vacation and shop overseas or in domestic enclaves. Their children go to private schools and foreign universities; as professionals, they seek employment in transnational organizations or stay overseas. In effect, in many countries, these conditions are producing a sort of social apartheid.

Since the internationalization of the domestic economy takes place through the expansion of selected economic sectors that have a "comparative advantage," the leading sectors of the local elites are more interested in promoting regional and transnational markets than integrated national markets. The emphasis has shifted from the protection of domestic production to the regulation of international trade. The promise is that national markets and domestic production will develop through competitive international trade. The reality has been that local production has been restricted to limited areas, and a broad range of productive sectors, whose existence depended upon generous state protection, have suffered under international competition.

The fracture of the market has profound social effects. From the perspective of leading segments of the transnationalized local elites, their nations have become local bases of operation within a global arena. To the extent that the domestic market ceases to have much economic importance for these elites, large sectors of the domestic population of their nations become economically and socially dispensable. If these conditions do not change, the growing disjuncture between nation and market may indeed define Latin American democracies as stuck in a historical limbo, as permanently "transitional."

New Communal Imaginings: Democracy in Different Spaces

While in this discussion I have emphasized some troublesome effects of the internationalization of national economies, there are also hopeful signs. The same processes that have disrupted the old project of national unity have created spaces for liberatory collective imaginings. Among the five hundred million people who live and toil in Latin America there is a resurgence of new social movements: ecological, residential, feminist, human rights, Christian, Afro-American, indigenous (Alvarez 1990; Calderón 1986; Eckstein 1989). Some of these groups are becoming increasingly organized. The forty million to sixty million indigenous people in Latin America constitute majorities in Guatemala and Bolivia; close to half the population in Peru and Ecuador; and are large minorities in Mexico, El Salvador, and other countries. They are beginning to link economic demands to cultural and political rights.[4] In some cases, the defense of indigenous culture has taken place through strategically deployed technologies and forms of knowledge associated with the West. For instance, the Kayapo, an Amazonian indigenous group of Brazil, have utilized their royalties from gold mines to control their territory by hiring Brazilian lawyers, recording their meetings and communicating with each other through video tapes, and overseeing their land from their private airplanes (Turner 1991). Needless to say, in this as in other cases, it is not easy to evaluate how the particular strategies of these movements will affect their development and their impact upon national politics.

In Latin America, political identities are being imagined and defended in unprecedented ways by new actors. There is a decline in what up to now has been, to use Charles Tilly's expression, "state-led nationalism." Yet these grassroots initiatives do not necessarily correspond to what Tilly

(1993) calls "state-seeking nationalism." In many cases, struggles are taking place outside the usual domain of the state, at the margins of normal politics. Issues of class, ethnicity, and nation play a role, but in new ways, as these issues are no longer defined within the political space dominated by states that in many countries have lost moral authority and practical efficacy. "The nation," a construction of community whose commanding power rests on the illusion of eternity it conjures up (Anderson 1983), is showing its age. In some cases, nations are being deserted from above and challenged from below. It is not clear, however, whether these new collective imaginings will achieve the kind of organization and power necessary to gain control of ruling political institutions or to create alternative political formations. As in other parts of the world, the social crisis may also produce intensified forms of nationalism that will reassert the centrality of the nation as the source of communal imaginings.

With the globalization of political and economic relations, the democratic imagination is also being displaced from its usual space within the "traditional" national territory. In agreement with Eric Hobsbawm (1990), Charles Tilly (1993), John Comaroff and Paul Stern (1993), I believe that new forms of ethnic and nationalist struggles are the expression not of the strength of nationalisms as we have known them, but of their transformation. The struggles for democratization in Latin America are taking place through both traditional and novel channels, through old and reformed political parties, as well as through new social movements. Thus, the implementation of universal suffrage and the establishment of constitutional democracies also involve efforts to construct new spaces for political participation that push democracy beyond its usual institutional boundaries. Democracy, as a political shell that protects but also that conceals hierarchies of class, gender, age, and ethnicity, is being simultaneously defended and challenged.

As in the past, now democracy is being invented or imagined in novel ways in the peripheries of the West. I learned in a paper by Henry Chipeya, prepared for this conference, that Nelson Mandela wanted to lower to fourteen the voting age of South Africans; Chipeya predicts that this electoral innovation will take place in the next elections in South Africa. I do not know whether this is a wise innovation, but at least it raises the issue of the political rights of youth and children. It may be more accurate and also more enabling to think of transitions to democracy in South Africa, Latin America, and elsewhere not just as moving toward a known end point—the consolidated democracies of the West—but as creating as well new conceptions of democracy.

The election of Nelson Mandela, which was made possible by the struggles of South Africans and the solidarity of people throughout the world, represents an extraordinary global victory. This collective achievement, and the energy unleashed in this historical turning point, rubs against the grain of postmodern disenchantment. Transitions to democracy at the periphery may make us think of all existing democracies as transitional and strengthen our interest in the possibility and trajectory of progressive historical transformations. The establishment of constitutional democracies within nations may then be seen as a condition for deepening democracy in other domains—from the "private" domain of the family and personal relations to the "public" realm of global markets and cultures. With the winds of history in their sails, perhaps these democratic transitions will inspire yet more liberatory democratic imaginings and struggles everywhere.

Notes

1 O'Donnell's view of a consolidated democracy follows the Schumpeterian model of democracy. He considers democracy "consolidated" when civilian rule has been established and its basic requirements are fulfilled, as identified by Robert Dahl (1971): freedom of association, freedom of expression, right to vote and to be elected, political competition, multiple sources of information, universal elections.

2 As I have indicated, there is a vast literature on this topic. For reviews of some of the major works in this area, see Karl 1990; Mainwaring 1992.

3 There is an ample bibliography on this topic. My comments here draw mostly from Markoff 1996 and Therborn 1977.

4 For an interesting discussion of some of these indigenous movements, see The First Nations: 1492–1992, special issue, NACLA Report on the Americas 25, no. 3 (1991).

References

Alvarez, Sonia. 1990. Engendering Democracy: Women's Movements in Transition Politics. Princeton, NJ: Princeton University Press.

Anderson, Benedict. 1983. Imagined Communities. London: Verso.

Baloyra, Enrique. 1987. "Democratic Transition in Comparative Perspective." In Comparing New Democracies: Transition and Consolidation in Mediterranean and the Southern Cone, ed. Enrique Baloyra, 9–52. Boulder, CO: Westview Press.

Calderón, Fernando. 1986. *Los movimientos sociales ante la crisis*. Buenos Aires: Consejo Latinoamericano de Ciencias Sociales.

Cammack, Paul. 1985. "Democratisation: A Review of the Issues." *Bulletin of Latin American Research* 2: 39–46.

Cavarozzi, Marcelo. 1992. "Beyond Transitions to Democracy in Latin America." *Journal of Latin American Studies* 24: 665–84.

Collier, David, ed. 1979. *The New Authoritarianism in Latin America*. Princeton, NJ: Princeton University Press.

Comaroff, John L., and Paul C. Stern, eds. 1993. *Perspectives on Nationalism and War*. Working Paper no. 163. New York: Center for Studies of Social Change, New School for Social Research.

Dahl, Robert A. 1971. *Polyarchy: Participation and Opposition*. New Haven, CT: Yale University Press.

Diamond, Larry, Juan J. Linz and Seymour Martin, eds. 1989. *Democracy in Developing Countries*. Boulder, CO: Lynne Rienner.

Eckstein, Susan, ed. 1989. *Power and Popular Protest: Latin American Social Movements*. Berkeley: University of California Press.

Hobsbawm, Eric. 1990. *Nations and Nationalism since 1780: Programme, Myth, Reality*. Cambridge: Cambridge University Press.

Karl, Terry. 1990. "Dilemmas of Democratization in Latin America." *Comparative Politics* 22 (October): 1–21.

Lechner, Norbert. 1987. *Cultura política y democratización*. Buenos Aires: Consejo Latinoamericano de Ciencias Sociales.

Levine, Daniel. 1988. "Paradigm Lost: Dependence to Democracy." *World Politics* 40 (April): 377–84.

Lipset, Seymour Martin. 1959. "Some Social Requisites of Democracy: Economic Development and Political Legitimacy." *American Political Science Review* 53: 69–105.

Mainwaring, Scott. 1992. "Transitions to Democracy and Democratic Consolidation: Theoretical and Comparative Issues." In *Issues in Democratic Consolidation*, ed. Scott Mainwaring, Guillermo O'Donnell, and J. Samuel Valenzuela, 294–341. Notre Dame, IN: University of Notre Dame Press.

Mainwaring, Scott, Guillermo O'Donnell, and J. Samuel Valenzuela, eds. 1992. *Issues in Democratic Consolidation*. Notre Dame, IN: University of Notre Dame Press.

Markoff, John. 1996. *Waves of Democracy: Social Movements and Political Change*. Thousand Oaks, CA: Pine Forge.

Munk, Ronalda. 1989. *Latin America: The Transition to Democracy*. London: Zed.

O'Donnell, Guillermo. 1973. *Modernization and Bureaucratic-Authoritarianism: Studies in Latin American Politics*. Berkeley: University of California Press.

O'Donnell, Guillermo, Philippe Schmitter, and Lawrence Whitehead, eds. 1986. *Transitions from Authoritarian Rule: Prospects for Democracy*. Baltimore: Johns Hopkins University Press.

Therborn, Göran. 1977. "The Rule of Capital and the Rise of Democracy." *New Left Review* 103: 3–41.

Tilly, Charles. 1993. "States and Nationalism in Europe since 1600." In *Perspectives on Nationalism and War*, ed. John L. Comaroff and Paul C. Stern, 187–204. Working Paper no. 163. New York: Center for Studies of Social Change, New School for Social Research.

Turner, Terence. 1991. "'The Social Dynamics of Video Media in an Indigenous Society: The Cultural Meaning and the Personal Politics of Video-Making in Kayapo Communities." *Visual Anthropology Review* 7, no. 2: 69–76.

Weffort, Francisco. 1989. "Why Democracy?" In *Democratizing Brazil*, ed. Alfred Stepan, 327–50. New York: Oxford University Press.

8   Venezuela's Wounded Bodies:
Nation and Imagination during the 2002 Coup

During Latin America's political "left turn" each progressive government in the region has followed its own distinctive historical trajectory.[1] Common to all, however, have been intense struggles over the development and control of natural resources. This is not surprising in a part of the world dominated by processes of capitalist accumulation based on nature-intensive indus-tries. Despite regional governments' attempts to diversify their economies, such industries as large-scale agriculture, mining, and hydrocarbons remain Latin America's international comparative advantage and main productive activity. In the case of Venezuela—where President Hugo Chávez ignited the left turn with his election in 1998—control of the state-run oil industry has long been at the center of power struggles.

Ever since Venezuela became a major oil producer in the 1920s, these struggles over oil have shaped national politics at every level, defining the relation between citizens and nation, the formation of social classes, and the constitution of the state as the country's central political and eco-nomic agent. Elsewhere I have argued that as a result of these contests, the Venezuelan nation has been imagined as consisting of "two bodies": its social body (citizens, people) and its natural body (territory and natural resources, especially oil, which by law belongs to all Venezuelans).[2] As a result of efforts to influence policy decisions and gain access to oil wealth, "democracy" has been understood in Venezuela as the participation of all citizens in the nation's two bodies; it has meant the generalization not just of political rights but also of the right to benefit from the nation's wealth.

Opposition to the state, whether dictatorial or democratic, has been typically cast as a critique of the private or partisan appropriation of the nation's wealth. As these notions took root as taken-for-granted premises of social life, it became commonsensical in Venezuela to believe that the state's primary duty is to establish a harmonious relationship between the nation's two bodies. And it fell to the president, as the embodiment of the rich petro-state, to play the role of the savior who protects and unifies them. Thus, in political contests, leaders' claims to legitimately represent the nation have come to depend on their ability to present credible national development projects to the collectivity. They typically promise one version or another of "progress." Opposing the regimes that preceded them, all potential saviors claim that under their rule, the nation's collective wealth will finally be safeguarded and used for the common good. These conceptions of state, nation, and the presidency have animated much of recent Venezuelan history, achieving during historical junctures the power of a material force capable of influencing outcomes.

This was the case in 2002, when the imaginary of "two bodies" informed the actions that led to the ousting of Chávez at dawn on Friday, April 12, followed by his return to power the following Sunday, April 14. Yet these conceptions of the Venezuelan state not only affected events but were resignified by them. Three critical moments during the April days reveal recent transformations in Venezuelan social relations and collective imaginaries: the anti-Chávez opposition march of April 11; the media representation of the Llaguno Bridge Massacre, which took place during the march; and the self-proclamation of business leader Pedro Carmona as president on April 12.

With the promise of his Bolivarian Revolution, Chávez was elected in 1998 with 56 percent of the national vote. Supported by the country's poor majority, he also enjoyed the support of many sectors that thought he would continue the traditional politics of alliances and compromises. But by the end of 2001, it was clear that Chávez was breaking the rules of the game. Without consulting influential economic and political actors, he used his legal powers to implement a controversial set of policies—forty-nine decrees affecting a variety of areas, including the energy sector, agricultural lands, and seas and rivers.

By early 2002 Chávez's approval rating had fallen to about 30 percent from a soaring 80 percent the previous year. The opposition had taken form as a political bloc that feared Chávez was either an authoritarian ruler, a socialist in disguise, or both, and opposed his attempt to control the state oil company, Petróleos de Venezuela, S.A. (PDVSA). In a country accustomed to celebrating its social harmony, however illusory, people split furiously into two factions, each more passionate than the other and convinced that only it possessed the Truth. Chávez's opponents came out against not only the management that the state wanted to impose on PDVSA but its entire oil policy. Most favored returning to the policy of the former PDVSA president Luis Giusti, who had sought to make Venezuela a major oil power by maximizing production rather than increasing prices, and thus distancing Venezuela from the Organization of Petroleum Exporting Countries (OPEC) and its regulations. Perhaps the most publicly criticized Chávez measure in the oil sector was an oil subsidy to Cuba.

But it was Chávez's appointment of a partisan managerial board to PDVSA during the first weekend of April 2002 that set in motion the events leading to the coup. Chávez rudely announced on his nationally broadcast TV show *Aló Presidente* (Hello, President) that he was firing a handful of PDVSA executives and replacing them with close supporters who would bypass the promotion ladder normally required to reach such leadership positions. As PDVSA president he named Gastón Parra Luzardo, an academic with theoretical expertise on petroleum but without managerial experience in the industry. Opposition leaders used this breach of meritocratic procedure as a banner to rally people against the administration. They called for a protest march under the familiar political slogan "Not one step back" (*Ni un paso atrás*), intended to establish kinship between their movement and other historically significant struggles for democracy, including Chile's protests against the authoritarian rule of Augusto Pinochet.

From the opposition's point of view, the nation's natural body was endangered by Chávez, whom they viewed as an autocrat threatening to monopolize power and mismanage Venezuela's precious resources. From an opposite perspective, the Chavistas viewed the opposition's meritocracy discourse as a smoke screen—a "mythocracy," as Chávez frequently called it—meant to hide their intention of ousting the government and taking over the national oil industry. According to official spokesmen, the new board of directors was composed of known and respected career petroleum experts, each with more than twenty years of experience in petroleum affairs; they had only skipped over a few merit levels to reach the directorship (between four and seven levels out of a total of thirty-six); and similar changes had occurred in the past without arousing any protest. The fundamental problem was one of politics, not management norms, according to Chávez and his supporters. Convinced that the country was being led adrift, the opposition sought to rid Venezuela of Chávez. Now the same discourse that had helped propel Chávez to power—the defense of the nation's wealth on behalf of the people—would be used against him. Although the opposition's public efforts to oust him took the form of a legal public gathering, certain powerful, backstage sectors sought to be rid of Chávez by any means necessary. On April 11, the opposition mobilized the largest protest march in the country's history up to that point from its base in eastern Caracas. An ardent crowd gathered in the recently baptized Meritocracy Square in front of PDVSA headquarters, where they had a permit to assemble. Although the march was cast as a protest against the breach of meritocracy in the oil industry, for many, including some who were involved in conspiracies at that time, its goal from the beginning was to oust Chávez.

Moved by their own desires as well as instigated by those who had a preconceived plan, the protesters quickly radicalized their aims. By midmorning, they went from defending meritocracy to demanding Chávez's resignation. At noon leaders redirected the march toward the Miraflores Palace, the president's office and residence. As it moved from eastern to western Caracas, traversing about seven miles to Miraflores, the march expanded, reaching several hundred thousand (estimates range from three hundred thousand to one million). The extraordinary size of the march strengthened the opposition's perception that the whole country was with them and that history was on their side. On that day, chanting slogans from other historic struggles—for example, "The people, united, will never be defeated"—the marchers came to believe that their collective action could wrest control of the state, save the country from misrule, and change the course of history. As the opposition newspaper El Nacional put it in an article commemorating the third anniversary of the April 11 march: "The feeling of power of these masses of humanity was absolute."[3]

Although the goal of ousting Chávez, however premeditated, was publicly presented as a pressing political demand in the early hours of the demonstration, the afternoon's bloody events made it possible to present his ouster as an urgent moral necessity. In several areas around Miraflores Palace and the Llaguno Bridge over Baralt Avenue, nineteen people were shot dead. Soon afterward, widely watched news on private networks reported that the government had carried out these killings. The video, produced by Venevisión, a network owned by Gustavo Cisneros, a major opposition leader, showed images of people wearing the signature Chavista red shirts firing from the bridge, while a voice-over asserted that these were government officers and sympathizers firing on "peaceful demonstrators." The repeated airing of this video magnified its significance and sense of truth.

The Llaguno Bridge Massacre, as it came to be known, quickly transformed a civil rejection into an open military rebellion against Chávez. The image of government representatives and supporters firing from Llaguno Bridge, together with images of dead or wounded bodies, were repeatedly shown to demonstrate the absolute illegitimacy of a government that had killed "innocent people." Major civilian figures insisted that it was no longer possible to tolerate a government that had "soiled its hands with the blood of the people," as the veteran leader and Chávez's political mentor Luis Miquilena proclaimed on the evening of April 11. They were joined in the evening by the top military commanders of the four armed forces, who one after the other announced their rejection of Chávez; their objection to the president's controversial order to contain the demonstration using Plan Ávila, a military contingency plan to maintain order in Caracas, had already created a ground for their rebellion.

The video images of the Llaguno massacre were shown to officers at military bases to legitimize the demand for Chávez's renunciation. They were also circulated by the media in the United States, Europe, and other Latin American countries, where they were used to back up official declarations, such as that of the Bush administration's press secretary, Ari Fleischer, whose statement on April 12 emphasized that Chávez had provoked his own downfall for having attacked protesters: "We know that the action encouraged by the Chávez government provoked this crisis." Fleischer added: "According to the best information available, the Chávez government suppressed peaceful demonstrations. Government supporters, on orders from the Chávez government, fired on unarmed, peaceful protesters, resulting in 10 killed and 100 wounded."[4]

Never before had an attack on the nation's social body inspired such an outpouring of sympathy from the country's elite and media. It is instructive to compare it with the massacre that took place in 1989 during the uprising in Caracas known as the Caracazo, in which the state forcibly suppressed a massive protest against declining economic conditions and structural adjustment policies imposed by the International Monetary Fund. The National Army killed almost four hundred protesters, whose deaths, in contrast to those nineteen in April 2002, were accepted by the political elite and the media as a necessary measure to safeguard the social order in a period of neoliberal restructuring. No major leaders, parties, or civil society organizations protested the massacre; COFAVIC [the Comité de Familiares de Victimas], the nongovernmental organization that took it upon itself to help the victims and their families, worked practically alone and against the current. In contrast, on April 11 and 12, the Llaguno massacre was repeatedly presented by the opposition as proof that Chávez had lost all legitimacy to rule the nation.

The massacre remains a controversial event. But while it is possible that Chavistas fired at the marchers from the bridge or elsewhere at one point or another, there is no doubt that the Venevisión video misrepresents what happened at that specific time. The wounded and the dead shown on the Venevisión video were not people on Baralt Avenue, as the voice-over reported, but on the bridge itself; the video had no angle of vision over Baralt Avenue. Another video taken at exactly the same time with a view of both Baralt Avenue and the Llaguno Bridge shows Metropolitan Police officers on foot and from armored vehicles shooting at the Chavistas on the Llaguno Bridge (the police force was under the command of the opposition leader Alfredo Peña, the mayor of Caracas). At that time, the government TV station was taken over by opposition forces and so could not present an alternative view. At this critical juncture, opposite ideas were in battle, not in dialogue; the power of evidence became drowned by the evidence of power. Those who controlled the media managed to define public truths.

Accounts of the events that followed also remain controversial and confusing to this day. The official story is that Chávez, seeking to avoid a bloodbath, followed the advice of his domestic and international advisers (mainly Fidel Castro) and agreed to let General Lucas Rincón—his only three-star general, the highest military rank—announce his resignation in the early morning of April 12, as long as certain precautions were taken regarding his departure from the country. Nevertheless, minutes after this announcement, the officers at Fort Tiuna (an army base near downtown Caracas) changed the condition that had been negotiated. They objected to letting Chávez flee to Cuba, demanding instead that he be tried in Venezuela for the killings of the previous day. Chávez then refused to sign the text of his resignation that had been faxed to him. Still, seeking to avoid a bloody confrontation and to negotiate with those who seemed to hold the power of arms in those confusing times, he agreed to be held under arrest.

The opposition's various versions of the story share the notion that Rincón announced Chávez's resignation, either in recognition that the president had lost power (and this is the most widespread belief) or as a trick to gain time so that Chávez could find out who was really against him. In either case, and despite the constitution's provisions governing the chain of command, according to the opposition this situation created a de facto power vacuum on April 12. Many in the opposition, in fact, still argue that there was no coup; Chávez abandoned the seat of power, and the opposition took a place that had remained empty.

Early on the morning of April 12, with Chávez in custody, Vice President Diosdado Cabello in hiding, and the National Assembly disbanded, the Chavista state, so centered on the figure of the president, was in effect suddenly decapitated. A group of officers and civilians at Fort Tiuna took up the functions of the state with no more legitimacy than the might of power. Far from public scrutiny, this small group, clearly acting on the basis of predesigned plans, however incoherent, and with the apparent aid of high military commanders and other key national and international actors, put the final touches on previously elaborated decrees and on the terms of the transition. As planned, they named an interim president, Pedro Carmona. At dawn on April 12, through a televised announcement, they presented the new president to the nation.

In a ceremony that aspired to be spectacularly historical, Carmona inaugurated himself as president in Ayacucho Hall at Miraflores Palace on the afternoon of April 12. In that solemn ceremony, he also named some members of his cabinet; summarily dismissed the National Assembly, the state governors, and municipal leaders (all of them democratically elected); disbanded the Supreme Court; and fired the attorney-general and the people's defender. He annulled Chávez's forty-nine decrees. Finally, he changed the country's official name back from the Bolivarian Republic of Venezuela to simply Venezuela, and he suspended the agreement to provide subsidized oil to Cuba.

Carmona's inauguration included two highly symbolic actions that implicitly evoked, at a historically crucial juncture, the imagery of a wounded nation and its new guardian state. As if to communicate his desire to heal the wounds in the nation's social body, Carmona began his speech by asking for a moment of silence in honor of the fallen from the previous day and offered to help the victims' families. And in a gesture that indicated his intention of safeguarding the nation's natural body, Carmona took special care to name General Guaicaipuro Lameda as the new president of PDVSA. Illustrating the importance of PDVSA in the whole drama, Carmona called Lameda to offer him the state oil company's directorship at about 6:30 A.M. on April 12, right after he was chosen as interim president. In a way, it was Carmona's first act as president. Lameda, a competent engineer, had demonstrated that he admired the opposition's corporate model of PDVSA and agreed with the views of its former president, Luis Giusti, who was at that time a senior adviser at the Center for Strategic and International Studies in

Washington, DC, and an informal energy consultant to President George Bush.

Yet restoring the Giusti agenda at PDVSA was not enough to sustain the Carmona government. Carmona's unilateral liquidation of democratically established government institutions alarmed many of his own supporters. In the historical contingency of that moment, other options seemed possible. Carmona could have gone through the National Assembly to be named interim president, as many advised him to do. Or, even within the political framework that he chose, he could have included a wider swath of society. His failure to organize a more inclusive and representative administration—in the context of an opposition that consisted of various factions operating as a coalition—amounted to breaking the opposition's implicit pact. If Carmona had not committed the political transgression of excluding elements of his own coalition, the legal violation of liquidating government institutions would likely have been accepted.

What certainly did happen, though, is that a wide range of Venezuelan society immediately rejected Carmona's actions. Many felt that instead of changing the country's course and entering into history as the nation's savior, he had derailed the opposition; the repression against Chavista leaders and activists confirmed fears among some that the new regime might be far from democratic. Commenting on these events in their aftermath, sharp observers such as the political analyst Carlos Blanco argued that the popular mobilization against Chávez did in fact force him from power on April 11, whereas the "real coup" was carried out against the opposition on April 12, when Carmona took power for himself. Other commentators, including reporters from *Newsweek*, presented Carmona's taking office as a "hijacking" of the coup, or as "a coup within a coup," an interpretation I believe is more accurate, since it recognizes not just the coup against the opposition on April 12, but also the coup against Chávez on April 11.[5]

The head of the military, General Efraín Vásquez Velasco, who resented Carmona for having failed to name him defense minister, forced Carmona to set things straight—or at least less crooked. Heeding Vásquez, Carmona called for a session of the National Assembly to select the provisional president on the afternoon of Saturday, April 13. As a solution, it was a perfectly logical proposal: aside from offering a mantle of legality, it signaled that Carmona was willing to include a variety of social groups and to engage in political negotiations; power would be shared, not concentrated. But as a course correction, not only was it too little, too late; it was far too blatant. Carmona convened the assembly with little credibility, having dissolved the body the previous day with the stroke of a pen. But more importantly, he had already lost power.

At Miraflores, the Presidential Guard, which surprisingly had not been replaced by the insurgents and had feigned to support and serve Carmona, retook the presidential palace and arrested the members of his cabinet who were there for their swearing-in ceremony planned for Saturday afternoon and had not managed to escape. In an inverted replay of the events of Friday, when insurgent officers threatened Chávez that they would attack Miraflores if he did not resign, the officers supporting Chávez now threatened, through their spokesman General Raúl Baduel, commander of the paratroopers stationed in the nearby city of Maracay, to shell the insurgents if they did not support the constitutional order.

The opposition forces quickly folded. The streets that they had occupied so massively and dramatically on April 11 were populated after April 12 only by growing numbers of Chávez's followers. In contrast to the military officers supporting constitutional rule, who had gained the firm loyalty of midlevel officers in direct command of the troops, the high-ranking officers who rebelled against Chávez, having no true control over any troops, had little choice but to surrender, flee, or be arrested. When the National Assembly finally made its appearance on the political scene late on that confused Saturday afternoon, it was not to legitimate Carmona, as he had proposed under the pressure of changing circumstances, but to show that the constitution was still in effect and to return the Chávez administration to power. Television viewers could see the National Assembly president swearing in the vice president, Diosdado Cabello, as president; in this spectacle of state power, they could not see that the National Assembly in fact had not convened—it was a ceremony performed by two men. Hours later, at 4 A.M. on Sunday, April 14, the television news broadcast Chávez's return to the presidential palace in the midst of an emotional crowd, where he was recognized as the president he had legally never ceased to be.

During the Chávez period, basic images of the nation and the state, formed throughout the course of the twentieth century and already modified by the country's economic crisis of the 1980s, have been significantly transformed. The myth of the political system in place before Chávez, known as the Fourth Republic, was that of a modernizing capitalist project led by the state on behalf of the nation as a whole. In contrast, the foundational myth of Chávez's Fifth Republic is a project of social justice on behalf of the majority in the context of an uncertain modernity in a world dominated by U.S. imperialism. Earlier presidents promised to bring the material and cultural accomplishments of advanced capitalist nations to all in a nation imagined as a united society; Chávez has promised justice and improved living conditions to the majority of a nation divided into the rich and the poor. For Chávez, "justice" means creating a new moral community: previously it was a matter of catching up with History; now it is a matter of creating a new History. The events of April 2002 expressed but also intensified the nation's social polarization, as well as the consolidation of these two alternative national imaginaries.

This ideological polarization shaped the April events as well as their ongoing public representations in terms of two contrasting narratives. For the opposition, Chávez lost all legitimacy by wounding the nation's two bodies: its population and the core of its economy, the oil industry. For his supporters, Chávez had protected the nation from a privileged group that wanted to regain the benefits they had enjoyed in the past. The coup encouraged Chávez to concentrate further powers in the presidency. Stimulated in part by winning the referendum on his rule in August 2004 (after regaining popularity through the social service "missions" he began to create in 2003), Chávez increased his control of every branch of the state and of society. The fear of his critics seemed to have been validated early in 2005, when Chávez proclaimed that Venezuela would be a socialist nation.

After winning his reelection in 2006, Chávez further intensified efforts to exert state control over society, to turn the armed forces into a defender of the "socialist" fatherland, to integrate the parties that supported him into a unified socialist party, and to promote various forms of popular participation in production and decision making. However, after the defeat of his constitutional reform in the referendum of December 2007 (his first major electoral setback), he was forced to modify his program of socialist change—not so much to abandon it as to try to implement it through other means. On February 15, 2009, he won a referendum that modifies the constitution so as to allow the indefinite reelection of the president. For the opposition, all of these developments confirmed long-held fears, as Chávez concentrated power in his person and sought to move the country toward a form of socialism whose closest model, despite claims to novelty, seems to be Cuba.

There are significant differences among "leftist" governments in Latin America. Yet even socialist-inspired presidents must govern societies that depend on financial resources generated by the capitalist economy. This includes Chávez, who criticizes the inequities and irrationality of capitalism—and who seeks to reduce these inequities, to democratize social services, and even to develop at the margins collective forms of ownership—but who is constrained to promote national development through capitalist accumulation. Ironically, their attempt to maximize national income continues a long colonial tradition of relying on developing the region's comparative advantages in cheap labor and, more importantly, natural resources.

In the last decade under Chávez, Venezuela has become even more dependent on oil and ever more entangled in capitalist markets and long-term associations, including with China, today's global capitalist factory. While a torrential oil income (often calculated as more than $900 billion in ten years) provided benefits in health, education, and subsidized food to large sectors of the population, Venezuela is facing an escalating foreign debt, a significant decline in industrial and agricultural production, the highest inflation rate in Latin America, alarming insecurity and criminality, and, ironically in a country with abundant energy and rivers, severe shortcomings in the provision of water and electricity. After more than a decade of Chávez's rule, the widening gap between the regime's claims and its accomplishments has become increasingly visible and onerous.

For those who believe in Chávez, he still embodies public virtue itself, which he has come to identify with socialism; in a country where socialism, as represented by socialist or communist parties, has historically had a minuscule ideological presence, socialism for many of the president's supporters means not so much a particular doctrine as whatever Chávez stands for. For those who oppose him, he appears typically disguised as a socialist donning the mask of a "socialism of the twenty-first century" yet following the models of the bureaucratic socialisms of the twentieth century. Or, worse, he is perceived as an authoritarian ruler wearing a democratic mask who cares only about power and creating a state-capitalist regime that has promoted the emergence of a new privileged class, the boliburguesia (Bolivarian bourgeoisie)—a nouveau riche sector of parasitical capitalists dressed in revolutionary costume. Removing Chávez's mask has become the task of the opposition. From the Chavistas' perspective, the opposition's defense of democracy is voiced by leaders who had no qualms about overthrowing democratic institutions and ignoring legality in 2002 by violent means; their call for democracy and critique of Chavismo hides their partisan ambitions and oligarchic interests.

Yet there is an emerging common ground. Despite these dramatically polarized imaginaries, the pursuit of political change on behalf of the majority through democratic elections has become a deeply rooted ideal shared both by the opposition and the government. This is largely attributable to lessons derived from the 2002 coup, which helped to delegitimate coups as political weapons and to value democratic procedures. In a political culture characterized by grand promises, there are now growing pressures to make actions match words. Almost a decade after the coup, the legitimacy and power of both the Chávez government and the opposition increasingly depend on their ability to make their proclaimed ideals correspond to effective political practices.

Notes

1 This article is based on a chapter in Jonathan Eastwood and Thomas Ponniah, eds., *The Revolution in Venezuela: Social and Political Change under Chávez* (Cambridge, MA: Harvard University Press, 2011). My gratitude to Pablo Morales for his helpful editorial suggestions. [*Editors' note:* When this article was originally published, the chapter cited here was still forthcoming.]

2 For more on this, see Fernando Coronil, *The Magical State: Nature, Money, and Modernity in Venezuela* (Chicago: University of Chicago Press, 1997).

3 "El sentimiento de poder de esas masas humanas era total," *El Nacional* (Caracas), April 11, 2005.

4 Quoted in a White House press release dated April 12, 2002.

5 Joseph Contreras and Michael Isikoff, "Hugo's Close Call," *Newsweek*, international ed., April 29, 2002. The "coup within a coup" phrase comes from Omar G. Encarnación, "Venezuela's 'Civil Society Coup,'" *World Policy Journal* 19, no. 2 (June 2002): 38.

9 Oilpacity:
Secrets of History in the Coup
against Hugo Chávez

Venezuela's President Hugo Chávez was overthrown on April 11, 2002, and was returned to power three days later. He had also almost been ousted from power through an oil lockout that lasted from December 2001 until January 2002. The oil industry's role in these events and how Chávez responded to them remain largely secret. As another step in my long-standing examination of the Venezuelan "magical state," I examine here one of the most puzzling aspects of Chávez's oil policy after these events: how Chávez turned oil joint ventures into icons of nationalism.

Since 1936, Venezuela's long-standing goal of "sowing the petroleum" (*sembrar el petróleo*) has been interpreted as the transfer of oil resources into permanent agricultural and industrial production. In contrast to previous governments that used oil to diversify the economy, Chávez has employed oil resources to address social problems ranging from public healthcare to food distribution. Decreased state support and a growing number of nationalizations and expropriations have intensified businessmen's fears that the state seeks to reduce the private sector's role. As a result, businessmen have shifted their industrial and agricultural investments to financial and commercial activities or decided to invest their capital abroad. This has led to a port economy sustained by oil income.

Shift to Joint Ventures

As the country's dependency on oil has grown, the expansion of oil income has become a government target. While respecting its commitment to OPEC's quotas, Venezuela has set increased oil production as a goal. The 2006–12 plan, "Siembra Petrolera," has a target of five million barrels a day, up from three million today. To achieve this goal, the government has devised an oil policy that secures stable access to foreign technology and capital and grants transnational corporations significant benefits. This perhaps explains Chávez's puzzling shift from oil operating agreements and service contracts—which were to end in less than a decade—to joint ventures.

These service contracts and operating agreements with transnational corporations drew away massive resources from the nation; transnational corporations circumvented tax laws and operated as if they owned the oil. Between 2006 and 2007, the government began an alleged process of renationalization, intended to secure tighter industry control: no longer could the private sector operate alone in oil projects, and existing service and operating agreements would be rescinded.

The government decided to force transnational companies to become minority partners (40 percent) with the state in joint ventures, migrating previous contracts into partnerships. The new joint companies would last at least twenty-five years, with the possibility of extending them to forty. In a few months, thirty-two contracts were rescinded and twenty-three joint ventures were formed. The government presented this change as a nationalist triumph—a second nationalization that secured oil sovereignty.

This alternative, however, remains puzzling. Joint ventures have been seen as threats to national sovereignty and were chosen without public discussion. Oil experts have criticized it as an unnecessary denationalization. They argue that as the owner of a resource without which the oil companies are worthless, the state has the power to negotiate better service contracts and operating agreements, gaining access to foreign technological assistance and financial participation without making any company a partner in the oil business.

Historically, there has been public concern in Venezuela about establishing joint ventures in the oil sector with private companies, so it is surprising that these associations with foreign capital are presented now as a nationalist corporate form. Debates about the 1975 nationalization law centered precisely on this issue and was finally approved with the explicit requirement that ventures with private companies could only occur in special cases and with congressional approval.

It is evident that by turning foreign oil companies into minority partners in joint ventures, the state has secured powerful economic and political allies, as well as a stable income stream. In exchange it has granted foreign oil companies significant influence over the management of the industry and reliable access to oil. By forcing them to become owners of 40 percent of the industry, including their proportional share of the oil produced, the state has in fact partially privatized Venezuelan oil; it has placed oil in foreign hands, even if these hands are constrained by significant regulations.

Evaluation of Joint Ventures

To understand this issue, I asked major participants of the state and oil industry to evaluate the decision to create joint ventures. While ideologically opposite, Luis Giusti and Alí Rodríguez Araque both circumvented my question. In contrast, Alberto Quiróz Corradi, former chief executive officer of Shell Oil of Venezuela and former president of Maraven and Lagoven, two oil subsidiaries of PDVSA, provided a succinct explanation of the difference between the two options at hand:

> Service contracts were agreements between PDVSA and oil companies whereby the latter would invest, develop and produce some oil fields only marginally attractive to PDVSA. The oil companies recovered their investments and made a profit for their troubles through a pricing formula. The oil produced was the property of PDVSA, which was solely responsible for its export sales. Joint ventures, on the other hand, made the oil companies partners in the exploitation of those fields with property rights over their share of the oil produced. Thus PDVSA transformed a contractor into a full-fledged partner and opened the door for future, more mature partnerships between the state and the private oil companies. Although somewhat battered by being forced unceremoniously out of previous agreements, the oil companies should be delighted with the outcome, which gives them reasonable expectations of a more permanent presence in the Venezuelan oil industry. (Coronil 2008: 27)

Permanence in a country with abundant oil reserves is what oil companies most need. Permanence in power is also Chávez's cherished goal. This arrangement offers stability by forming a tight, long-term economic alliance with powerful actors that otherwise might undermine his regime. Even if the state could have obtained similar economic results, it is unlikely that the service contracts would have had the binding force of a joint venture. The fact that Chávez renegotiated previous contracts made their instability evident. Despite political tensions and mutually hostile rhetorical claims, major foreign transnational corporations are his central economic allies and partners.

I believe that Alberto Quiróz Corradi's speculation regarding the position of the U.S. government after the April 2002 coup applies to U.S. oil companies more generally: "Others think that the U.S. Government was indeed concerned with 'the day after Chávez' and was quite happy to see him back in the presidential chair" (Coronil 2008: 26). Similar views were expressed when Chávez won the 2004 referendum. Perhaps worry about "the day after" helped cement an alliance between the Venezuelan state and oil companies.

Chávez has renegotiated his relationship with the private energy sector, dividing it into the foreign and the domestic. From seeking conciliation with domestic oil actors immediately after the 2002 coup and the December–January 2002 PDVSA lockout, Chávez has sought to ally the state with foreign corporations and undermine the power of private domestic energy actors. As economic allies in the oil business, foreign corporations provide Chávez with reliable financial resources and political support without the threat of becoming domestic political rivals. As foreign agents that are also illegitimate local political actors, they cannot properly challenge his rule, particularly since anti-imperialism is a powerful force in Venezuelan political culture. While in Cuba the economic alliance of state and foreign corporations intentionally inhibits the growth of domestic private capital, in Venezuela it undermines its large presence. The Chávez state has extraordinary control over its share of expanding oil resources. The joint-venture arrangement helps grant the Chavista regime as well as the oil corporations one of their most frequently stated goals: permanence.

Reference

Coronil, Fernando. 2008. "Oil and Revolution: Viewpoints." *ReVista: Harvard Review of Latin America* 8, no. 1 (Fall): 21–33.

10   Crude Matters: Seizing the Venezuelan Petro-state
in Times of Chávez

Editors' note: The following excerpts from *Crude Matters* were recovered after
Coronil's death, and we believe them to be the most updated version of
these chapters. He had not completed the references and footnotes, and
we have done our best to incorporate those into this version. In order to
better situate and contextualize the piece, we begin with a reflection from
Andrea Coronil, who accompanied her father while he was doing research
for the book in Venezuela.

During the time that my father carried out research for *Crude Matters* over
the course of several trips, I was living in Caracas and studying at the public
arts university (UNEARTE; previously IUESAPAR, renamed under Chávez).
I do not know exactly what the deciding factor was that prompted my
father to take up writing about the coup. I do know, however, that he initially thought it would be a much more contained and manageable project than it turned out to be. The framework for it was a stark departure
from *The Magical State*; for this new book he intended to solely focus on the
three-and-a-half days over which the coup occurred. He had written about
crime and scandal before; chapter 8 of *The Magical State*, on the murder of a
lawyer, had all the features of a dramatic movie. I remember that he often
suggested to me to start with that chapter. It seemed to me that with this
project he was taking his own advice.

He was especially concerned with understanding how and why nineteen people had been murdered during the march of April 11, when the
streets were taken over by an outpouring of people—both opponents and
supporters of Chávez. In order to analyze what had happened, my father
closely studied the televised video footage of the protests, which showed

gunmen shooting from behind a wall on Puente Llaguno [Llaguno Bridge], a pedestrian overpass crossing over a busy avenue.

One of the most enduring memories I have is of him in his rented furnished studio apartment watching the videos of the protest march and shootings that were broadcast on TV, taking notes, pacing, and rewatching the footage. I think of this period as a time when he was very energized by the project, just beginning to grapple with the reality of its complexity. Returning home one evening, he mentioned what a friend of his in the business world had just told him: his colleagues had asked him who this meddling Coronil guy was, adding that they should just get rid of *ese pendejo* (that fool). My father did not express any concern about this news; if anything, I think he took it to be an indication that he was getting somewhere and that there was more work to be done. The following day I went to meet up with him at his apartment, and he was not there (yet). I imagined my father imitating his friend's voice mocking his own colleague's suggestion to get rid of Coronil. Now I was the one pacing, knowing that my father was most likely just running late, which he was. I still have a vivid image of him finally bounding through the doorway, looking like his mind was bustling with ideas. He had carried on with his work, hardly remembering the cause for my concern when I brought it up; there were notes to jot down and interviews to schedule. And it was time to go out and meet up with friends for dinner.

Whenever my father met with friends, he was always also conducting work, assessing their take on the situation—and learning from their reactions to his. He published an article on his analysis of what happened on April 11. Shortly afterward, we were out and encountered a couple who were longtime friends of his. The wife approached my father, deeply upset with him for calling into question the opposition's account that Chávez supporters were responsible for the shootings—so angry that she threatened to end their friendship. This was something my father was not quick to dismiss; unlike the comment that his business friend shared from his colleagues, he took this as a sign of caution, seeing just how deeply polarizing accounts of this particular event could be. I think that for my dad and many of his friends, the telling of stories was part of a political commitment to delve into what was not being publicly aired. In many ways, his friends, across affiliations and social classes, were his audience and those to whom he kept himself accountable. His work, while solitary at times, was not a solo venture. It seemed to me that part of what complicated matters was that both political parties were enmeshed in experiencing and reproducing forms of violence, to one degree or another. I remember the look of certainty on this friend's face and her outrage as she recalled witnessing the fatal gunshots that tore through the protest in which she took part. There seemed to be no space for ambiguity in this narrative—the experience cut too deep.

We traveled to Ramo Verde, a military prison in the mountains outside Caracas, where my father conducted interviews with political prisoners. The coup marked a shift within the military in terms of allegiances and possible covert ties to the dueling powers of Cuba's intelligence and U.S. agencies. While my father interviewed those who had fallen out of favor with Chávez, he also worked to cultivate connections with those who were part of his government.

Over the years I remember my father meeting with members of the government, but what he really wanted was the opportunity to interview Chávez himself. Celebrities and filmmakers from the United States had met with Chávez and were given official tours of the country, yet although my father met with some of his advisers and aides, and it is safe to say that Chávez had a copy of his book, the closest he managed to get to speak with him was at a public event. I remember the look of excitement on my father's face as he recounted how, in the midst of a crowd, he got up close enough to shout a question to Chávez. Despite being quite critical of Chávez, he was truly curious and eager to speak to him. It did not occur to me to inquire what he would have asked him. What he hungered for, it seemed to me, was dialogue—a chance to create space for nuance. There was no shortage of ready-made declarations, narratives, gestures, and reactions relating to the state of national affairs. However, these images and declarations were highly polarized; they met only to clash in confrontation—not unlike the supporters and protesters on April 11.

This dynamic seemed to saturate everyday life with violence, fed by increasingly nationalist rule and economic uncertainty. I remember my father visiting Elsa Morales, a sister-like friend of my parents' who had been physically attacked by protesters during the strike. She was not a government supporter, but her attackers assumed that she was a Chavista; as an indigenous woman with dark skin, she fit into their profile. Elsa had come to Caracas when she was young, working cleaning houses, and later became a renowned self-taught artist. Laughing, she recounted that when visitors at the hospital asked how she was doing, she muttered, "Que viva Chávez!"—parodying how she had been stereotyped. She, like my father, demonstrated a resistance to being consumed by the bitterness that fueled the rhetoric of political allegiances.

The difficulty, it seemed to me, was to carry out such work without feeding into the prevailing declarations of blame and allegiance—despite the consequences. A close friend of my father's since high school was a journalist who was outspoken against the current government and, as a result, had problems finding work. She hosted a get-together of high school classmates, and they all reminisced and broke out chanting leftist political songs from when they served together in the student government. Many, if not most, of my father's lifelong friends with whom he shared political commitments were critical of Chávez's government because of the very obstacles my father was confronting. Since he did not celebrate the government, my father never was given access to interview Chávez, constraining his research. When The Magical State was translated into Spanish, my father proudly chose Monte Ávila Editores to publish it. As a federally funded company it had a long history of making classic and contemporary works widely available for a low price. However, copies of the book ran out, and the company claimed that they could not republish it because they "lost" the manuscript. While my father did not express any ill view toward the publishers, with time I came to view this as a possible casualty of the increasing controls placed by the government's strictly pro-Chávez interests.

There were very real challenges for broadening the terms of the conversation and seeing past perceived differences. During this period, my dad and I visited a New York Times journalist living in Caracas; his laptop and research materials had been stolen from his home. He had moved to another place but continued to work, now with heightened home security. I remember walking along the street with my father as he pointed out the security devices: cameras and barbed wire installed atop walls separating the sidewalks from the residences they protected. Every home necessarily had its own variation of elaborate gates and security watchmen, or, in low-income areas, broken glass bottles atop cinderblock walls. Thinking aloud, or maybe suggesting it to me, he played with the idea of studying the aesthetics of security that increasingly shaped the cityscape. There seemed to be parallels between the words that were being hurled and the technologies and ways of occupying space that were being promoted.

I remember when my father and I passed the building where his father used to have a modest clinic that served low-income people, off a busy avenue near his high school. The paint was chipped; the walls were crumbling; and the space had been taken over by squatters. A young man sat in the front doorway selling burned CDs with what looked like makeshift beds behind him. According to government decree, any space that was not being used could legally be taken over. I do not remember my father saying much; however, his look of sadness and palpable sense of grief has remained with me. It was not just that the space where his father had lovingly tended to an underserved population was no longer being used in this spirit, but that this change did not represent transformation so much as it entailed living in ruins.

Fortunately, he also encountered spaces that brought unexpected relief from the weight of political rhetoric. My father knew and had great respect for Antonieta Sosa, a conceptual artist who was leading an art critique class that I attended. I invited him to come for my presentation and, seeing him there, she asked him to share some thoughts as an anthropologist. As was the class practice, all of the students had offered their feedback on the work, relating it to the artist. To my surprise, my father got choked up. What I remember is the gratitude he expressed to the class; he was moved by the level of thoughtfulness of their responses. My sense is that their openness and dialogue deeply resonated with him and offered a dose of hope.

Despite the heaviness of the everyday tensions and difficult questions of truth embedded in his work, my father managed to stay open and to savor the complexity of the situation. He got up early each morning and would go down to the kiosk, which was right in front of the apartment building, and buy a copy of every newspaper. He seemed to have a special appreciation for newspaper vendors, often chatting with them about the latest headlines. Returning upstairs, sometimes with a *cafecito*, he would read the newspapers, strewing them around him as he worked from his hammock; he created a form of total immersion in the headlines, at once surrounded by newspapers, switching between television news programs and checking online sources on his laptop. It seemed that as much as my father became disturbed by his research, his resolve to work on it strengthened. He somehow managed to navigate across very contentious inner circles without necessarily subscribing to their views. Among those he deeply respected were a group of leftist experts on oil production who were very critical of the government's management of oil resources. I remember he told me that he invited a friend from the financial sector to a meeting they held, saying that he could come with him on the condition that he be there (silent) like a *piedrita*—a little rock.

I got the sense that for my father, part of conducting fieldwork involved including others, mutually broadening each other's scope of reference. I consider myself fortunate to have been among those with whom he shared his ventures as a mentor and a friend. In facing challenges, he would advise me, "Usa la mano izquierda," an expression that conveyed what I imagine was his mother's disposition: "to use one's left hand"—that is, to take care and not force matters but to proceed attentively, as one might do with the slight discomfort of employing your less used muscles. With this older generation's refrain, I believe he was suggesting that one should tend to even difficult—or crude—matters with kindness and care.

—Andrea Coronil

Preface to *Crude Matters*

"You'll be found dead if you ever find the *la verdad verdadera* (the real truth) about those days and have the courage to tell it," Dietmar Dismoner, director of Nueva Sociedad and editor of my previous book on Venezuela, *The Magical State*, told me. Yolanda Salas, one of Venezuela's finest cultural analysts, commented in reply: "Don't worry, Fernando, you'll live. The truth is too well hidden; you'll only be able to tell stories about the truth, urban legends. You're safe." An economist familiar with the workings of power in Venezuela asserted what many told me: "You must be crazy to have gotten involved in this venture; it is an impossible project." Grimacing, he said, "There is so much dirt in this. It is like getting inside a huger sewer! It makes me nauseous even to think of researching this." But Fausto Masó, a veteran Venezuelan journalist, was a bit more optimistic; he saw exile in my future: "If your book manages even to come close to telling the truth, you'll have to leave Venezuela." In contrast to the reaction of my Venezuelan friends, my colleagues in the United States, including Latin Americans, encouraged me to carry out what they viewed as an important and viable project. Claudio Lomnitz, a leading Mexican anthropologist, said, "You have to do this. You're in an exceptional position to make sense of what happened in Venezuela during those days."

In effect, rather than choosing this undertaking, I felt that it chose me. In 2002 I had begun a research project concerning the relation between aesthetics and politics in the visual representation of Cuban history. On April 12, a phone call from the PBS *NewsHour* brought me to U.S. national television, turning me briefly into an actor in the narration of the events taking place in Venezuela. Later I learned that media representations had played a critical role in the shaping of events in Venezuela. Although I didn't know it at the time, this event also spurred a reorientation of my plans.

Initially, I rejected the PBS invitation. At that time, I was in Washington, DC, at a meeting of the Darkness in El Dorado Task Force of the American Anthropological Association to evaluate the allegations of scientific misconduct by researchers among the Yanomami that Patrick Tierney made in *Darkness in El Dorado*. My mind was in the Amazon, not in Caracas. However, PBS insisted. The news directors offered me access to my colleagues from its offices. I accepted.

At the PBS office, I rushed through emails and documents. I was still trying to make sense of these materials when I was called to the makeup room, where I met Michael Shifter (then senior fellow at the Inter-American Dialogue), also scheduled by PBS to talk about these events. He seemed to know what he would say. As they sprinkled makeup on our faces, we chatted about what was happening until we stopped to watch the introduction to our interview by PBS. The headline announcing the film clip about the events of that day said, "Coup in Venezuela." The person from PBS in charge of our appearance exclaimed, "Ha! We're calling it a coup!" Shifter showed displeasure at this choice of words.

In response to Ray Suarez's questions, I argued that no matter what one thought of Chávez's leadership, overthrowing him represented a serious violation of constitutional norms and had foreboding implications for Latin American democracy. Michael Shifter, in contrast, presented the argument of the U.S. government and of Venezuela's opposition forces: under Chávez, Venezuela had become "ungovernable," and thus ousting Chávez signified not a rupture of democracy but, rather, its defense. His removal, according to Shifter, showed that "democratic principles are still going to be protected and that people are still going to respond and defend democracy." I interjected at the program's close: "It's very hard to do that if democratic principles are violated."

Although I continued to work on my project on political representations in Cuba, the upheaval in Venezuela haunted me. One day while working at home in Ann Arbor, what had begun as a crude impulse for me suddenly felt like an imperative demand. I decided to reorient my research and work on the events in Venezuela. To my amazement, a few minutes after this decision William Lara, then president of the Venezuelan National Assembly, whom I had never met, phoned me from Caracas. Lara told me that he and other members of the National Assembly were impressed by my analysis in *The Magical State* of the pre-Chávez era, and he wanted to know if I had written anything on the Chávez period. Startled by the coincidence, I told him I hadn't, but that I had decided to work on the April events. "The National Assembly will sponsor your research," he replied. After thanking him, I declined, telling him that my project had to be independent, but I did request that he help me obtain information. Further encouraged by this convergence, I changed course and began doing research on this project.

Through Lara, I obtained publicly available information from the National Assembly and valuable contacts with politicians and upper level officers in the armed forces. My work was financed by research funds from the University of Michigan. I also benefited from a year at Harvard University, where I was invited to teach in the History Department, with a fellowship from the David Rockefeller Center of Latin American Studies to study the April events. When I was offered the opportunity to choose among four sponsors of the center's fellowships—three prominent U.S. businessmen and Gustavo Cisneros, a Venezuelan magnate—I chose the Cisneros Fellowship. Cisneros has frequently been linked to the April events; according to *Newsweek*, he was "the mastermind behind the coup," a charge that Cisneros strongly denied. I believed that being a Cisneros Fellow would facilitate access to him and the Cisneros organization—as, indeed, proved to be the case. I also could not resist what a prominent Latin Americanist at Harvard called the "delicious irony" of researching the April events as a Cisneros Fellow.

At least as important as these professional links with U.S. academia were my Venezuelan family connections resulting from the chance of birth. The fact that I am the son of two prominent medical doctors who were members of respected families opened many doors. Most people I interviewed were well disposed toward me because they respected my family, knew a relative of mine, or saw me as continuing a family tradition of professional service. Of course, the fact that some viewed me as a middle-class academic incapable of betraying his social class or family friends was a mixed blessing: it opened some doors but closed others.

Thus, there were tensions that derived from my privileged position. People who had been involved in the April events had powerful reasons to be concerned about my research, in part because the government began prosecuting leaders of the coup. I was surprised to learn that some highly placed individuals believed that my real aim was to discover "dirt" in order to sell a sanitized account or to extort them; some speculated they could scare me away from this project by "beating the shit out of me." But more typically participants assumed I was linked to some intelligence agency, whether the U.S. Central Intelligence Agency (CIA), the Cuban G2 or the Chávez Ministry of the Interior.

I frequently felt surrounded by an invisible barrier, an aura of suspicion.

The gift of trust through personal connections entailed the expectation of reciprocity—of solidarity and loyalty. A journalist actively involved in the April events offered me some insider information while confiding, "I'm telling you this because I trust a Coronil; a Coronil *no nos va a echar una vaina* (won't screw us)." Three generals who had led the movement against Chávez talked to me fairly candidly in an interview arranged by a mutual friend. Yet one of them placed two magnums on the table next to the second bottle of Johnny Walker Black Label we were consuming, warning me: "We are talking to you openly, but if we don't like what you write, we'll know where to find you."

"Have you already found out what happened?" or "Have you discovered who did it?" I was often asked while I was carrying out this project. I typically responded by joking that being alive was proof that I was still far from *la verdad verdadera*. My joke, of course, reflected a truth. The pursuit of knowledge about sensitive matters entails risks not just for the subjects researched, but for researchers and the project itself.

While I do not claim to have found the truth, this work is not a *Rashomon*-like portrait of various accounts of a single event, or a postmodern ensemble of multiple stories that asserts the impossibility of ever finding the truth. This is indeed about what happened in Venezuela during those three-and-a-half fateful days. It treats interpretations of what happened as part of what happened, but it also evaluates their truth claims against all the evidence I could gather. It seeks to distinguish claims to truth from the truth, not by reducing the real to interpretations of it, but by treating it as distinct from them, and keeping them in tension.

"Your project is impossible," many people told me. This is true only if the task is to provide definitive answers to specific questions. This book responds to this impossibility with another understanding of the possible: to seize the chance to advance knowledge about the present by examining how it is cloaked, to pierce through its opacity, to tell the truths it can tell, and to counter claims that we cannot know what happened that unquestioningly uphold the powerful.

In the end, all my friends, from North and South, were right. They captured different aspects of my double position as a respected Venezuelan scholar with the support of prestigious U.S. academic institutions researching a highly sensitive matter in Venezuela.

As was the case with *The Magical State*, this book was written for my daughters, Mariana and Andrea, only that now that we all are older, they have made me wiser. When they were babies I was blinded by my love for them; now I see that through them I have come to understand much that I didn't understand about my own parents, about all parents, and perhaps about all children. Perhaps love in particular is a path to love in general.

Chapter 1. Events in Question

> En el cajón de los secretos hay muchos secretos. Si revelas uno,
> corres el riesgo de revelarlos todo.
> —Laura Restrepo, *Delirio*

Events

Sometime during the night of April 11, 2002, Lieutenant-Colonel Hugo Chávez, the president of Venezuela who was elected in December 1998 with 56 percent of the votes, was ousted. Two days later, he returned to power. Never before anywhere has the elected president of a nation been overthrown and brought back to power within such a brief span under such bizarre circumstances. What happened during those days has remained covered in secrecy.

The morning of April 11, a massive protest in Caracas against Chávez, the largest in Venezuela's history up to that time (estimates range from 300,000 to 1.3 million people), marched toward the city's center. It ended in the afternoon with the massacre of around twenty demonstrators and bystanders, igniting the rebellion of almost one hundred top-ranking military officers who blamed Chávez for the killings, demanded his resignation, and forced him out of office. In what remains a particularly puzzling episode, at 3:20 A.M. on April 12, General Lucas Rincón, Chávez's highest-ranking and most trusted general, announced that Chávez had "accepted" the demand that he resign. Yet half an hour later, Chávez presented himself to the rebellion's leaders as a "prisoner president" in Fort Tiuna, Caracas's military garrison. He claimed later that the military had changed the conditions for his resignation and that he had turned himself in to avoid a bloodbath, refusing to respond with violence to the threat of an attack against the presidential palace.

Imprisoned in Fort Tiuna under the custody of the military police, Chávez was flown first to a nearby military base in the town of Turiamo in order to distance him from his supporters in Caracas, crowds of whom had begun to surround the presidential palace and Fort Tiuna, and then to the island of La Orchila, as a step toward taking him to Cuba, Puerto Rico, or his death. We will never know what destination awaited him at that point. An abrupt shift of events on mainland Venezuela dramatically changed his, and the nation's, destiny.

With Chávez out of sight, in the afternoon of April 12, Pedro Carmona, head of the conservative business federation Fedecámaras, swore himself in as the new president of the nation in a televised ceremony at the presidential palace, evidently with the backing of an alliance of powerful yet only partially visible actors. As part of this state act, Carmona immediately began reconfiguring the state and governing the nation. With the stroke of a pen, he cancelled Chávez's forty-nine recent economic decrees, dissolved the National Assembly and the Supreme Court of Justice, dismissed governors and other elected officials, appointed his cabinet and a new director of the national oil company PDVSA, and, in a deeply symbolic act, restored the name of the nation to "Venezuela"—erasing Chávez's renamed "Bolivarian Republic of Venezuela." Several hundred people in attendance erupted in cheers as Carmona baptized the nation anew and chanted "Democracy, democracy!" as he dissolved state institutions in the name of a new state.

Overthrowing a government typically entails breaking the law in the name of the law. In this case, despite its legal façade, this event violated not just the laws of the nation—even if Chávez had resigned, the constitution establishes procedures for presidential succession—but the laws of power, for key sectors were excluded from the new government. Viewers of this ceremony found the absence of the labor leader Carlos Ortega particularly disturbing, for as the president of the major trade union (CTV), he had allied with the business leader Carmona of Fedecámaras to head the broad opposition against Chávez that had organized the April 11 march. In the preceding months, given the weakness of traditional political parties, this unusual alliance of organizations representing sectors of capital and labor provided an institutional focus to the heterogeneous opposition against Chávez. Also noteworthy was Carmona's choice of Vice Admiral Hector Ramírez Pérez from the Navy as his defense minister rather than Efraín Vásquez Velasco, the general commander of the armed forces, who had played a key role in overthrowing Chávez.

From the outset, despite this ceremony's formal staging, flaws in its script—legal violations and abrupt changes of state policies, but perhaps more important, blunders in its casting—the exclusion of key actors—made it difficult for the public at large to suspend disbelief and accept this performance at face value. Suspending disbelief was even more difficult for influential figures who had imagined themselves at center stage or at least in the select audience, rather than as ordinary citizens at home watching this ceremony on TV. For them, this act was not just an implausible "act" but a personal affront and a sign that they were being left out just when they thought they were reconquering the state. Still, at the end of this ceremony, there was no way to discern that its outcome would not be lasting. Its solemnity, despite its flaws, made it seem conclusive; the euphoria of Chávez's opponents along with the dejection of his supporters confirmed this impression.

Yet influential actors from differing positions, disturbed by what came to be called "the Carmonazo" (a wry reference to the Caracazo popular uprising of 1989), quickly moved to correct or challenge it. Even before it occurred, as it was hurriedly orchestrated behind closed doors, the political deals that brought forth this state act on the basis of a previous rough design had become the object of intense infighting. Even minutes before the ceremony took place, prominent individuals who met with Carmona at Miraflores begged him to revise his plan and suggested to him an alternative—working through the National Assembly rather than dissolving it. But after consulting with key advisers and making a phone call to an unknown prominent figure, he rejected their proposal, affirming emphatically, "This is already decided."

Beyond intraelite disputes whose significance was restricted to a limited audience, the ceremony made tangibly real for the public at large the brazenly exclusionary character of this event. Carmona's appointees and the euphoric audience at the palace looked glaringly upper class in terms of dress, skin color, and body language—a suitable group for a country club reception, but an inappropriate look for this political occasion. Soon the jagged edges of the performance prompted questions about its making and meaning. The image of this ceremony acquired powerful force, even as seen through differing lenses; this led to its undoing.

Questions about it spread like fire. Was Carmona's new governing group representative of the "civil society" alliance that had opposed Chávez? Had "civil society," the category the opposition claimed for itself, become a façade that concealed a privileged elite resentful of having been displaced from the state and access to oil income? Was the Carmonazo the result of hurried decisions by inexperienced actors whose errors could be corrected in time, or was it the outcome of a meticulously planned right-wing conspiracy that had hijacked the broad movement against Chávez, auguring poorly for Venezuelan democracy? Or was the whole thing an *auto-golpe* gone wrong, a coup planned by Chávez against himself to discover his enemies? This latter version reflects how for some the long-term satanization of Chávez had magnified his powers.

However, there were other accounts that carried political weight. Notably, one of them questions the very logic of interpretations that assume the coherence of plans and existing capacity to implement them. Some believed (and still do) that there was no causal explanation for the overthrow, only a contingent convergence of ill-designed plots and improvised decisions. As a person who participated in these events said to me, "En nuestra Venezuela tropical no se puede planificar nada, y mucho menos un golpe de estado" (In our tropical Venezuela, nothing can be planned, and least of all a coup d'état). Yet it is striking that those who make this belittling argument were often themselves involved in the conspiracies. Yet there are also people who were not involved in the conspiracies who believe there was no coup. As a political analyst told me, in Venezuela one can apply an old saying about the belief in witches to beliefs about coups: "Yo no creo en brujas, pero de que vuelan, vuelan" (I don't believe in witches, but that they fly, they fly).

While it may be true that there was no single master plan, arguing that Venezuelans are unable to plot a coup entails forgetting or minimizing the significance of a tradition of coups, both successful (in that they led to changes in government, as in 1945, 1948, 1952, and 1958) and failed (including the aborted coups by Chávez and his supporters in February and November 1992). Despite almost five decades of democratic stability, a history of conspiracies still haunts the Venezuelan political imaginary, not the least because this stability has been maintained by paying close attention to recurrent conspiracies. Ever since Chávez was elected there was talk of conspiracies and coups. In the months preceding the April days, the ghost of a coup d'état was given life not just by Chávez's opponents but by Chávez himself. In some circles, people claimed that in February 2002 Chávez promoted a coup against himself in order to discover his enemies. In effect, those who were alerted to this fake coup and deactivated it came to play an active role in the April events that overthrew Chávez. They defused a fake coup but plotted a real one. The U.S. government supported both the countercoup and the later coup.

At that time, these and other accounts—which continue to define the interpretation of these events—reinforced divisions that shattered the attempt to impose a new government and grant it support and legitimacy.

In less than twenty-four hours, the challenges to Carmona coming both from Chavistas and those opposed to Chávez yet critical of the Carmonazo forced Carmona to abandon the presidential palace and seek refuge in Fort Tiuna. In a desperate last measure to appease his opponents, Carmona sought to convene the National Assembly he had dissolved the day before. But this belated and transparently opportunistic attempt to broaden his base of support and restore a semblance of legality fell flat. Realizing that he had in fact lost power, he formally renounced it in a televised ceremony on April 13 that was a largely forgotten formality.

Yet it is significant that this ceremony took place, because it highlights the hold of ritualized state forms in Venezuela even when they appear to lack substantial content. They confirm the power of forms, particularly when they break down or are being revised. Forms may create a sense of order that allows people to move in and out of exceptional and chaotic situations with less risk and more dignity. Carmona's resignation lacked the power to become memorable, but it somewhat tamed power. It helped construct a sense of civility when some forms of civility had broken down and there was no certainty that others would not follow suit.

Since the breakdown of state power on April 11, behind the scenes of the public stage violent actions were auguring a dark future: the Cuban Embassy was attacked by supporters of the coup; the newly named state leaders arrested Chavista leaders and community activists; and many people (probably two or three times [the number of] those killed on April 11) were killed. While the twenty deaths of April 11 have been the object of memorialization and investigation by both sides, the more numerous and still largely faceless deaths of April 12 and 13 remain in shameful silence.

The shifting sands of the newly made markers of state power crumbled as quickly as they had been erected, bringing down the leaders who stood on their pedestals. Carmona's presidential inauguration of April 12 underwent a rapid transfiguration. As it became clear that his ceremonial ascension to power would not signal a reordering of national history, what had been cast as a dramatic historical event on April 12 soon became recast as a farce or, for his vanishing sympathizers, as a tragedy, a brave act fated to fail by the power of entrenched interests. On April 12, Carmona, a short man, had suddenly appeared tall by standing on the presidential stage as the leader of a wounded nation, a savior bringing into being a new national order. Yet unable to secure the backing of a broad civilian alliance supported by military officers willing or able to consolidate power by using violence, he rapidly lost status and stature. Without the support of either the weapons of politics or the politics of weapons, by the next day the Napoleon-like hero he sought to incarnate deflated into a rather pedestrian figure with an ordinary first name. People appended a sarcastic last name referring to his ephemeral appearance on history's stage: Pedro Carmona became known as *Pedro el breve* (Pedro the Brief) after his defeat. By April 13 a space was opened that other actors sought to occupy.

In response to the void left by Carmona's resignation and Chávez's public absence, Diosdado Cabello, former military officer and the vice president, was named president of the nation in another state act—but in this case, it was presented as a return to Chávez's government. This was a made-for-television political ceremony, hastily designed to defuse the sense that no one was in command. The camera did not show the meeting of the National Assembly because its delegates were still dispersed or in hiding. What the public did see was the National Assembly's president, William Lara, with a bound copy of the constitution in hand, naming Diosdado Cabello president. Since for his supporters Chávez had never ceased to be the president, it was not clear why Cabello was sworn in, except, as some believed, to make evident that power remained in the hands of Chávez's supporters, or, more ominously, as a sign of internal realignments, as a step toward Chavismo without Chávez—possibly as a coup within the coup. Independently of what transpired behind the façade of power, subsequent events gave public meaning to this event as a critical step in Chávez's return to power.

During the dawn of April 14, Chávez was brought back to the presidential palace by Navy helicopters, which fetched him from the tiny island of La Orchila just seconds before he was to be taken away to an unknown destination—or to be killed. Before sunrise he descended from the dark sky to land at the capitol building, Miraflores, illuminated by television lights, as if an apparition. Thousands of his supporters, who had surrounded the palace since Carmona had usurped power two days earlier, euphorically welcomed him. For them, their leader was back; the violated constitution was restored; legitimacy was defended; and their faith was confirmed. Shortly after, in another ceremony, Cabello transferred to Chávez the presidency that formally had never ceased to be his. Thus, in a bizarre chain of events, Venezuela ceremonially had three presidents at four moments: Hugo Chávez, Pedro Carmona, Diosdado Cabello, and Hugo Chávez.

These were disorienting days at many levels. As Chávez emerged from the helicopter at dawn of April 14 he greeted an anti-Chavista photographer, a tall *criollo* who was taking photos for an opposition newspaper. Embracing him, Chávez said, "*Hermano* (brother), it's great that you're taking photos for History." The photographer later told me: "As Chávez almost lifted me from the ground, I hugged him back, with tears in my eyes. Then, as he walked away toward the entrance of the presidential palace, I asked myself: What on earth am I doing? In the heat of the moment I forgot I was against him!"

Some confusing events are innocent and may be acknowledged with laughter. But these days witnessed many shifts of loyalties—people did not just forget whom they were for or against but accommodated to the changing currents of history. Others took an active role in redirecting these currents. Many factors conspire to maintain a shroud of secrecy over these days. To ask questions about them is dangerous. Truthful answers may place people in danger—and elicit retaliatory responses that put others in danger. Some questions touch on particularly sensitive issues. Were the April 11 demonstrators who died killed by Chávez's forces or by the conspirators to justify their planned coup? Did Chávez's trusted generals turn against him, horrified by the massacre attributed to him, or did they betray him as part of a long-planned conspiracy that included the massacre itself? When General Lucas Rincón announced Chávez's resignation, did he act on Chávez's behalf or in complicity with the rebellious generals? Did Carmona represent the coalition that opposed Chávez or a reactionary clique? Why didn't the insurgent generals use violence to obtain their goal, as General Augusto Pinochet had done in Chile when Dr. Salvador Allende was overthrown? Crucially, what was the role of foreign powers in these events?

Even when events were still too "hot" to have become "past," looking backward to understand what had happened was essential for knowing what to do next. Yet in the heat of the moment, it was also essential to look ahead, even without really understanding these turbulent days or seeking to understand too much. How to recompose power after these traumatic events? How to know what should be understood, what should be kept in the dark? Who should be prosecuted, forgiven, or simply left outside public scrutiny? Should the state revise its oil policies and compromise (as Fidel Castro reportedly advised Chávez by phone on the night of April 11) or charge ahead with renewed commitment? Whom could Chávez trust? Like the politics of memory, the politics of understanding responds to imperceptible operations that take place behind understanding itself. If nations appear as eternal and immemorial as much through collective amnesia as through shared memories, their vitality as ongoing concerns also results from collectively leaving beyond understanding certain things as well as by understanding collectively many others. History's closet is crowded with repressed memories, covered secrets, and silenced understandings.

Back as the head of state, Chávez appeared powerful again. Behind the rhetoric of national conciliation, power began to be negotiated anew on an uncertain and unstable terrain. Voicing the position of major economic groups, the media that had shortly before demonized Chávez now presented him as a powerful leader who must be contended with. There was a tacit agreement to move ahead without fully accounting for the still too present past.

Since then much has happened, but the April days remain obstinate events, the entangled object of crude politics, of battles over power and memory that resist resolution. Attempts to forget or bury them in the past compete with efforts to control them by turning them into epic stories of the opposition vs. the government. In response to changing circumstances, the government and the opposition continue to oscillate between remembering and forgetting.

Much of what has happened has been shaped, often unrecognizably, by those three-and-a-half days. In part as unsettled mysteries they continue to haunt the living, and as unhealed wounds they continue to hurt, remaining a force in the present. There are many accounts and images of this history, including spectacular footage of the only ousting of a president filmed live from within the presidential palace at the time it was happening, as well as several films about the April 11 massacre.[1] But whose history do they depict?

The many scripts that have represented the chain of events between April 11 and 14 offer contrasting plots: a civil rebellion, a reactionary coup against the democratic movement of civil society, a civilian-military coup against Chávez, a constitutional "vacuum of power," an *auto-golpe* gone awry, the contingent outcome of several disorganized plots and conspiracies, a "coup within the coup," or an imperial oil coup supported by one or more Western powers (the United States, England, Spain, and Israel).

These interpretations still cloud the April events; while they are largely incompatible, many of their elements are complementary and could be integrated into a more complete and accurate account. Yet new scandals or political dramas tend to push these days into the past, or at least place them out of public sight. Attempts to resolve or clarify aspects of those April days are commonly interpreted as politically motivated; new accounts about them, or judicial actions against the alleged perpetrators of the coup, are assumed to be guided by hidden agendas, casting doubt on the truthfulness of their claims. Rather than clarifying it, they tend to thicken the murky opacity that surrounds what happened.

Given the mantle of secrecy and obscurity covering these events, how can one discern among competing accounts or come up with a more satisfactory one? How can any interpretation avoid being subjected to the play of interests and passions? I take these obstacles as the ground for my own interpretation. I explore what *really* happened during these days—both the mantle that covered over what happened and what it covered, how and why. I inquire into what happens when events are obscured by secrecy and ambiguity and some questions remain—or are kept—without satisfactory answer. Is the opacity of these exceptional days also exceptional, or does it throw some light upon the ordinary exercise of power everywhere? Is secrecy the secret of power?

Chapter 2. Matters at Stake

Crude: 1. In an unrefined or natural state, raw: crude oil. 2. *Archaic.* Unripe or immature. 3. Lacking tack refinement or taste. 4. Not carefully or completely made; rough. 5. Displaying a lack of knowledge or skill. 6. Undisguised or unadorned, blunt: *must face the crude truth.*
—American Heritage Dictionary

At Heart

Crude Matters is about events that happened in Venezuela between April 11 and April 14, 2002, when the state was suddenly up for grabs and Venezuela came to have, or so it appeared, four changes of the president in three days. Insofar as it deals with what happened a while ago, it is indeed about a certain "past," about events that are buried and perhaps should rest in peace. Yet it is also about an ongoing "present," not just because these days are still so close in time, but because they remain largely unresolved and their specters continue to haunt what has happened since. In many respects, those days involved matters that were and remain *crude*: blunt, rough, unprocessed, and unfinished. They also entailed at their inner core battles over the Venezuelan state and the vast oil wealth it controls.

As an exploration of an unsettled history, this book is also a reflection on history itself, in its twin reference to an object and to knowledge about it—to events produced, remembered, and narrated by those who participated in them, as well as to a scholarly genre practiced by historians (professional or not) at a temporal or spatial remove from its original actors. Obstinate events such as the April days of 2002—crude events that find only partial narrative closure, that resist being cooked into finished narratives—remain open as unhealed wounds, as persistent sites of struggle over history both as a process and as stories about it, raising questions about its construction by its multiple doers, tellers, and listeners.

How are past and present distinguished? Are they separated only by degrees of temporal distance, or also by different modes of experience and distinct narrative forms? Is the present the domain of politicians, who create history, and the past the realm of historians, who re-create it, as the historian Lewis Ranke proposed? Is the present defined not so much by *chronos*, clock time, as by *kairos*, momentous opportunity, as the philosopher Martin Heidegger noted? How is history transformed from "crude" or "raw" events into processed narratives or, since any event is always already narrated, from rough narratives into more polished ones? Is "history" about the past, as the dominant Anglo-American paradigm tends to assume, or is it also about ongoing and anticipated developments, as a Germanic tradition has it? How is history lived and constructed in the Américas, where processes of transculturation have involved not only mutually constitutive encounters among different societies, but also original modes of confronting history and reflecting about it? Given my focus on a recent moment in Venezuelan history, I am interested in particular in the question of the present—or, rather, of the relation between the present and the past. What is the present, how is it narrated, when, and how, does it become "past" or "history"? Or, is the present also "history"?[2]

As a study of events that took place in Venezuela, *Crude Matters* is also on the face of it a book about a marginal "national" history—a topic typically considered parochial if the nation in question belongs to the "South," and is thus seen as having only local or regional significance. How can a history of such a nation—or of just a few of its days—be of interest to people who know little about it and who may not even be able to place it on a map? Of course, this is a common problem faced by those of us who write about "small places"—to borrow Jamaica Kincaid's provocative expression—in the South for a broad public and often have to establish their importance by claiming their significance for metropolitan histories. In contrast, the history of metropolitan nations envelops us, not only as familiar as the air we breathe, but as an indispensable standard for any other history.[3]

One solution is to go with the grain and give texture to familiar images of the postcolonial South, making them all the more compelling if authorized by an insider's intimate familiarity, as the Trinidadian novelist V. S. Naipaul has done with superior but twisted eloquence. Yet it is precisely the Occidentalist perspectives that depict our regions as emblems of difference—no matter if it is of the backward or incomplete or of the magical or authentic—that turn them into small places where nothing really consequential happens except their difference, the smallness ("irrationality," "barbarity," "enchantment") that makes others big ("rational," "developed," "civilized"). The challenge is to appreciate their specificity without either belittling or idealizing them.

Treating the West not as a fixed geopolitical region but as the shifting apex of modernity, I seek to counter the "imperial eyes" that classify the world's populations in terms of hierarchies on the basis of the West's assumed superiority. Building on works that have examined how Western political dominance and modes of knowledge have affected the representation of different societies (including their self-representation), here I continue to engage the ongoing complicity between power and knowledge that I have treated, in dialogue with Edward Said's "Orientalism," as "Occidentalism" and "globalcentrism." By illuminating how the histories of different peoples are mutually constituted and draw together a changing international landscape, I seek to develop a perspective that overcomes representations that depict history in terms of bounded units and envision the global from the parochial universalism of the West's commanding heights, whereby those placed below, their internal and external "others," are depicted as deficient, if not plainly inferior.[4]

Under the shadows cast by the West's blinding light, I seek to recognize an emerging landscape of power as well as a different understanding of historical difference. Dominant understandings and cartographies of modernity are particularly misleading when, as in this case, struggles in the South over power and resources are intensely global in their making and consequences and bring out unexpected protagonists who challenge the existing order of things by their actions or even by their style and appearance. I look at these events through their interconnections, in light of intellectual traditions that conceptualize social reality as an inherently relational field of forces rather than as a composite of bounded units in which nations, states or the globe appear as "billiard balls" bouncing off each other, in the anthropologist Eric Wolf's felicitous image.[5] Just as their appearance as separate entities is a condition of their mystifying power, recognizing their mutual historical constitution already offers a more democratic vision of history and of struggles for more just forms of society.

Revealing how geohistorical units that display themselves as self-made are actually the product of global exchanges serves not just to provincialize the West—to show how Europe made its provincial history into universal history, a pathbreaking achievement of postcolonial critics and South Asian historians—but also to globalize its margins, to discern how colonized histories have formed universal history, a major contribution of Latin American scholarship. Building on this collective work, my aim is to reach a form of knowledge that acknowledges the varied participation of all regions and peoples in the making of world history without either privileging the allegedly universal view of those powerful and arrogant enough to define others and speak for them or accepting what appears as the inevitable indispensability of their categories. Far from undoing real differences by conceptual fiat, this perspective seeks to recognize them for what they are: historical distinctions changeable by historical action. It recognizes the global, transcultural formation of utopian visions as well as of persisting forms of domination.

This perspective reveals how central aspects of these visions—such as ideals of democracy and justice—as well as persisting obstacles to their realization, are formed through global exchanges within naturalized hierarchies within and among societies that function as sites of power to obscure their formative processes; depict differences as inherent rather than historical; and rank them in terms of the alleged universality of parochial standards, which are typically northern European and Anglo-American, male, white, and elite.[6]

The intensely politicized debate in Venezuela under Chávez has magnified polarized stereotypes of all sorts—about Venezuela, about its people, about politics in the tropics. Images of Chávez (and his allies) as gorillas are as common as those of him as Simón Bolívar's incarnation. Long-standing and contingent complicities tying knowledge to power have shaped the Manichaean optic that organizes political discourse about Venezuela. As if caught in the act that we watch, as a public we are pushed to join the chorus of one or another drama: the epic of an original socialist revolution or the reprise of authoritarian military populism; the heroic saga of astute revolutionaries or the banal farce of mimic men (or of monkeys rather than people). Independent observers have no easy place in this theater.

The history of April has been obscured by forces that remain obscure—and by obscure forces. Taking this pervasive obscurity as part of my analysis, I seek to offer an accurate interpretation of what happened, one respectful of all available evidence. I want not just to counter, but also to account for, a culture of ambiguous opacity that covers over these days. By looking into stories and viewpoints that have shaped the memory and historical narratives of these events, I seek to understand how a public sense of the real is constructed from positions that reflect various forms of power and influence. My own position claims no special privilege. *Crude Matters* is still a crude, unfinished interpretation, one rendered less so not by disinterested detachment, but by a commitment to free understanding, all the more rigorous for being, at heart, a personal response to the ethical and political urgency of creating a sense of the real that makes more, and better, sense.

Power

These were, indeed, three and a half very bizarre days. Yet the extraordinary often offers insights into the ordinary. During this turbulent period, political battles were enacted at center stage in terms of competing visions of democracy, legality, and justice and alternative images of the nation's development. But through the cracks of the fractured state, the pursuit of rival lofty ideals became openly entangled with the struggle over mundane, usually occult, ambitions and positions. Because the normal order was unsettled, during these days much that is normally hidden became briefly uncovered—and swiftly covered over again.

Routinely, *el poder* (power), the vague name commonly given in Venezuela, as in many countries, to the prized object of political struggles, conjures up the image of a concrete institutional body or force, typically incarnated in governmental entities and individuals authorized to speak on the state's behalf. Yet in times of crisis, when the legitimacy of those in command is in question, others may feel powerful enough to claim that they embody the nation's will. In April battles over the state brought forth actors with the power to make this claim, fusing and confusing power struggles with struggles over power—contests not just over who represents the state, but over the state itself, not just over its embodiment, but over its very body. As if a fantastic storm had suddenly opened up the ocean, *el poder* fleetingly appeared as an iceberg of unfathomable enormity whose visible tip could no longer keep down, by the weight of its authoritative public face, the rough body that sustains it atop.

A central if submerged portion of this invisible mass has been the nation's valuable material body, its vast but imperceptible oil deposits. As a rich "gift of nature" and the largest source of Venezuela's foreign exchange since the early twentieth century, oil rapidly became the assumed ground of the nation's political landscape, the taken-for-granted foundation of its identity as an "oil nation." As if honoring its subterranean existence, oil has made its presence felt largely invisibly, not primarily as a crude substance or its derived products, but in its most refined and insubstantial form: through its dematerialized transfiguration into money—as petrodollars.

When taking the form of the universal equivalent, oil abandons its earthly origins and ascends to the heavenly sphere of the global market, where it comes to embody pure exchangeability. Incarnating the polymorphous potentiality of endless exchange, petrodollars become transfigured into a fountain of desire, a dreamed pathway toward the future. As crude substance or as transformed into petrodollars, oil comes to embody the future, to hold within itself the cherished anticipation of things or times to come—particular commodities as well as projects of development, concrete materializations as well as intangible illusions.

Much before "oil futures" became a hot commodity in metropolitan commodity markets at the end of the twentieth century, in the Venezuelan political arena oil morphed into a sort of "political futures" that filled the present with its anticipated unfolding. From the outset, the polymorphous potentiality of petrodollars helped fuse the lines separating present and future, what is and what is yet to be. But it also confused right and might, what is and what ought to be. Through the many forms it came to assume, oil wealth fueled the state's sense of power over history while it undermined the moral trenches created to channel it toward collective historical ends. Through myriad paths, access to public wealth opened doorways to private power, blurring the lines between public and private domains.

This capacity to incarnate the promise of fulfilled desire is, of course, intrinsic to all forms of money, but it takes distinct form when it is intimately bound up with a natural resource, when this resource is controlled by the state, and when its abundance manifests itself not as the incremental result of steady work, but as an unexpected gift, as in a casino jackpot or a lottery prize. Particularly for countries in the South, a sudden windfall of publicly owned foreign exchange, as if it were history's jackpot, heightens the political significance of money's potential exchangeability. Even more so in states relatively accountable to their subjects, this money is typically charged with the mission of healing the wounds of a colonial history and bringing about, at last, the cherished future that had never quite arrived.

During oil booms, oil's materiality, however, is often brought back to public awareness, as its abundance overflows the customary channels through which money circulates. Then oil is often renaturalized in public imagery, but not as its earthly reality as crude matter but as a mysterious substance, as "showers" or "rivers" of wealth. If used productively, this substance is seen as a gift from heaven, nourishment that fertilizes the nation's soil and fuels development projects. But if consumed improperly, then oil is seen as a negative force, the "devil's excrement" (a term rendered popular by Juan Pablo Pérez Alfonso, Venezuela's leading oil expert during the 1970s oil boom), an indigestible substance that corrupts national bodies and souls and brings ruin to the nation.

The inflow of abundant foreign exchange magnifies the risk of "contracting" the "Dutch Disease," which I have rebaptized as "the Neocolonial Disease," since the negative effects of windfall profits affect mono-exporters from the South more severely than metropolitan nations with resilient and diversified economies. (The Netherlands actually survived well the discovery of gas in the North Sea.) As if it were an uncontrollable virus, this money erodes incentives to invest in productive enterprises, promotes spectacular undertakings, stimulates financial and commercial speculation, and turns state-dependent ventures into the main channel for obtaining political and economic power.

Whether invested by the state in development plans or improperly appropriated by private individuals, in Venezuela this public money is typically treated as a bridge to the future. The future has appeared in the image of the North's present—yet primarily as a cornucopia of its material embodiments rather than as the social capacity to produce them. As a nation having a long postcolonial history of frustrated development plans, the persisting gap between the ideal future and the recalcitrant present has created a fertile terrain on which public money's polymorphous power comes to fuel ever renewed projects of national development as well as private schemes for individual enrichment—and to blur the line between them.

In Venezuela, oil was politicized from the beginning of its transformation into the nation's main source of foreign exchange. Venezuela became an early oil producer and the world's major oil exporter in 1928, during the long dictatorship of Juan Vicente Gómez (1908–35). From the outset, the struggle for political democracy developed in tandem with the struggle to democratize public wealth. Political battles over the dictatorial state helped establish oil as Venezuela's national patrimony. The state was constituted as a petro-state through its institutional expansion and transformation into the agent in charge of propelling the "backward" country toward "progress" by "sowing the oil"—that is, by transforming nonrenewable natural riches into permanent social wealth.

"Sowing the oil," a phrase coined in 1928 to argue that ephemeral mineral riches should be invested in productive agricultural and industrial activities, has guided the development projects of all governments in Venezuela, whether democratic or dictatorial. Despite Chávez's claim to have broken from the past, he has used this slogan, slightly shifting it from *sembrar el petroleo* to *la siembra del petroleo* (from sowing the oil to the sowing of oil). Once again under Chávez, oil was imagined as the bridge to the future.

Whether seen as dreadful nightmare or as desired reality, the future weighed heavily upon the April days. As Chávez's government took actions and made claims that were considered radical, Venezuela came to be deeply divided into two camps, each inhabiting a different future. While for his supporters Chávez embodied the will of the nation, or at least of its nonprivileged majority, for the opposition he incarnated the dangerous privatization of the state on behalf of either partisan or foreign interests. (The specter of Cuba weighed heavily on the opposition's imaginary.)

The April events became a grand stage for the expression of oil's boundless potentiality. At that time, when the petro-state openly became the object of political struggles, oil imperceptibly energized collective and individual actions, fusing and confusing obstinate realities and fantastic illusions, public virtues and private vices. Amid a global energy crisis, oil in the crude form of vast deposits became an obscure object of foreign desire, a battlefield for global politics. What happened during those days in Venezuela concerned not only its citizens but also outsiders—those hungry for its oil and powerful enough to believe they could control its destiny.

During April, oil emerged at center stage yet suitably masked as one of the forms it takes in Venezuela. The march organized by opposition forces on April 11 was ostensibly a protest against Chávez's recent selection of a new executive board for PDVSA. Claiming that the government's appointments were based on politics rather than on merit, opposition leaders argued that this violation of *la meritocracia petrolera* (oil meritocracy) threatened the integrity of the oil industry and thus the future of the nation. Yet it was widely understood, and openly acknowledged by its leaders, that the march against the real or alleged politicization of PDVSA was primarily a means to mount a general protest against Chávez's rule—and thence to force him out of office.

Through its control of the media, the opposition placed oil at center stage, but as embodied in the institution that managed its extraction. By confining the critique of Chávez's oil policy to the violation of bureaucratic rationality and projecting onto the future the specter of a mismanaged company and a bankrupted nation, this focus concealed from view the substantive content of Chávez's oil industry strategy at that time and thus silenced open debate about it. It depicted the battle for *meritocracia* as a struggle against an inept and autocratic government, not as a means to engage the content of the oil policies themselves. Reduced to a sign of bureaucratic incompetence, oil—and the political economy of oil—remained masked as a secondary supporting actor in a grand plot about the struggle for "democracy." Revealingly, many of the people I interviewed, including leading political analysts, insisted that the April events "had nothing to do with oil."

Yet from another perspective, including that of the Chávez government, oil's marginal role onstage was a disguise that covered its central place in the plot. Control over Venezuela's vast oil resources was the prize of the epic struggle over the state, and the political drama on public view was but its theatrical staging. From this perspective, foreign actors bent on having influence over Venezuela's oil were major actors—in alliance with local sectors—in the ousting of Chávez.

Among the many accounts that circulate in Venezuela, these two rival scripts continue to be central, each claiming a different role for oil and for foreign actors during the April days. For the opposition, the ousting of Chávez resulted from a mass democratic movement that sought to counter a turn to leftist authoritarian rule under the influence of, or even directed by, communist Cuba. The neighboring island and political ally had benefited from Chávez's policies, which provided it with nearly one hundred thousand barrels of oil a day at a highly discounted price and employed large numbers of its professionals.

However, for the Chávez regime and its supporters, the coup was the outcome of a right-wing conspiracy orchestrated by an alliance among Venezuelan conservative sectors and U.S., British, Spanish, and Israeli forces interested in restoring elite rule in Venezuela, undermining Venezuela's leadership in the Organization of Petroleum Exporting Countries (OPEC), and seizing control over Venezuela's vast oil resources by changing state polities.

These rival scripts offered two different accounts of a central legal and political aspect of Pedro Carmona's brief presidency: Carmona had legally filled the political space left vacant by a "vacuum of power" resulting from a democratic protest that forced Chávez's resignation; or, Carmona illegally seized the presidency as a result of a carefully planned coup d'état. While according to the opposition Chávez had resigned, creating *un vacío constitucional* (a constitutional vacuum) that Carmona temporarily filled, according to the Chávez forces the opposition had created a fiction based on Chávez's nonexistent resignation in order to dress in legal costume what in reality was an elite-orchestrated *golpe petrolero*—an "oil coup."

These events remain covered by an ambiguous opacity, not so much despite as because of the multiple accounts that claim to be truthful but only partially disclose their supporting evidence. Yet these competing stories make evident the intertwined phantom presence of oil and foreign actors in Venezuela. Their real or imagined role in the April events reflects a longstanding widespread assumption that struggles over the Venezuelan state are not strictly domestic affairs, but are forged with and through global connections. Particularly concerning oil policies, it has become a habit to assume that it is impossible to draw clear lines between the national and the foreign. Ironically, the resulting sense of historical national vulnerability has helped overproduce forms of patriotism, magnifying the significance of national frontiers in the defense of sovereignty. Yet the practice of politics frequently turns these imaginary fences into porous borders, tracings on the map, that act not as barriers but as legal disguises that conceal illicit traffic across them.

Given a widespread sense that the United States has frequently had a hand in Venezuelan politics, it was hard to conceive in Venezuela that the attempt to overthrow Chávez could even be imagined without some degree of U.S. involvement or, at least, tacit endorsement. The commonsense perception that the United States must have been involved in one way or another made it more difficult, even unnecessary, to stipulate the specific manner of its involvement. At the same time that Chávez's "Bolivarian Revolution"—using petroleum as a tool of domestic and foreign policy—sought to relocate Venezuela's place in the world and even to redefine global politics, it became common for people to believe that other nations had a stake in what happened locally. Perceived as ghostly agents, foreign forces participated in intimate association with local actors in the unfolding of the April events, blurring national boundaries and helping draw an international landscape of power. A global iceberg of power, its outlines barely visible, began to emerge.

Empire

Months earlier, another dramatic rupture of normal time in another land had permitted a glimpse of this global iceberg. On September 11, 2001, passenger-filled airplanes redirected as deadly missiles attacked the Twin Towers in New York and the Pentagon in Washington, DC. This shocking blow to the financial and political heart of the United States exposed two interrelated realities. One was disconcertingly novel: the vulnerability of the United States to nonstate foreign enemies using nonconventional weapons. The other was uncannily familiar: the imperial vocation of the United States. The visibility of these realities has had enormous global consequences. While it is now known that before these attacks the Bush administration had planned to invade Iraq in order to gain more control over the oil-rich Middle East, the attacks legitimated the United States' proclamation as the guardian of global civilization. President George Bush's crusade against an invisible and amoral enemy waging endless terror in a borderless world produced the United States as its counterimage: a moral empire waging an endless war in a borderless world—a war in which all forms of struggle were valid.

Historically, the United States has presented two faces: a publicly democratic republic at home (despite the destruction and displacement of Native Americans, the enslavement and disenfranchisement of Africans and African-descendants, and the marginalization of various "minorities"), on the one hand, and a semiconcealed empire abroad, on the other. Before September 11, the democratic face had largely covered the imperial one or had made it appear as an extension of democracy. While the denial of empire had characterized the historiography of the United States (Williams) and become a central aspect of its imperial culture (Kaplan), after September 11 the affirmation of empire has fused its two faces.[7] It has become possible to recognize openly the United States as an empire, even if only "lite," "reluctant," or "benevolent." The growing acceptance of its new imperial image has even made it possible to criticize the U.S. government not for being imperial, but for not being imperial enough.

Yet the recognition and even celebration of the United States as a republican empire has also been countered by a profusion of critiques that have revealed its normally hidden imperial face. No longer confined to leftist critics, a growing number of journalists and academics have examined the concentration and abuse of power exerted from the "chain of command" of a government increasingly controlled by a self-possessed elite (Hersch);

the "sorrows" of an empire subjected to the expanding demands of its global military establishment (Johnson); the formation of a theocratic ruling sector that has eroded democracy at home and abroad (Philips); the occult "deep politics" intrinsic to a vast network linking the U.S. state to the hidden commerce of drugs, arms, and oil (Scott); the power exerted by the U.S. Treasury Department over the globally destructive policies of the International Monetary Fund (IMF; Stiglitz); the determining centrality for global politics of backstage struggles over the control of oil and other strategic resources (Yergin and Klare); the remarkable continuity of imperial policies through different administrations and periods (Bacevich); the centrality of Latin America as the United States' imperial "workshop" (Grandin), as well as many other studies of no less important aspects of its imperial face. Growing understanding of the United States' imperial role has also resulted from the expansion of alternative media, including scholarly websites, independent news networks, and television satirists.[8]

Building on this body of critiques as well as on a long-standing Latin American tradition of reflections on its postcolonial history, this study seeks to illuminate an aspect of this global iceberg that has been largely submerged or relegated to the past: imperialism. While focusing on a few days in the present, I situate those days within a longer historical arc in order to explore this history and imperialism in light of each other. My purpose is double: to make sense of this history through more adequate theories, and to use this history to develop more adequate theories to understand history.

Mainstream discussions conceptualize imperialism as a superior stage of capitalism propelled by the internal dynamics of advanced capitalist nations, and capitalism as a European phenomenon dependent on the generalization of free wage labor during the industrial revolution. As I have argued elsewhere, a more illuminating view may be gained by considering imperialism not as a stage of capitalism, but as coeval with it, and placing capitalism's origins not in industrial Europe, but in the eighteenth century with the entangled exchanges between Europe and the colonial world that initiated the integration of the globe through the expansion of commodity circulation in the sixteenth century.

Since then the commodification of labor power has taken multiple forms, of which free labor constitutes capitalism's dominant but not exclusive modality. The encounter between Europe and America provided Europe (at the time on the margins of the world's Chinese and Middle Eastern civilizations) with resources and ideas through which it fashioned itself as the new center of the world. The development of plantations, large agroindustrial capitalist units integrating slave labor in the fields and in the mills, contributed to the formation of the modern world not just as models of large-scale commodity production, but as means to cheapen the cost of reproducing laboring classes worldwide and as "economic" institutions dependent on "political" alliances and institutional arrangements between ruling classes and states across territorial boundaries. The growth of modern empires and their subsequent dissolution led to the formation of nation-states. As during previous periods, but in novel form, since the sixteenth century colonial empires and then metropolitan nation-states have incorporated and subjected peoples through multiple modalities of control, including differing ways of articulating formal and informal aspects of "the market" and the "state."

Based on their analysis of nineteenth-century British imperial rule, the historians of the British empire John Gallagher and Ronald Robinson argue for a unified view of imperialism as a complex totality premised on the integration of informal economic control in certain regions ("whenever possible") and formal political rule in others ("whenever necessary").[9] In my view, the pair of binaries political-formal and economic-informal is most helpful if these distinctions are treated as historically variable and specific dimensions of relational entities rather than as the defining and unchanging features of bounded units. Modern empires always integrate states and markets; markets and states always entail formal and informal aspects. Just as states and markets are variable and changing social institutions that help define imperial formations, imperial formations help form states and markets. Since the sixteenth century, states and markets have led an intertwined existence. The expansion of global commodity production, the growth of transcontinental empires culminating in the scramble for Africa at the turn of the nineteenth century, the struggle over insurgent colonial possessions during the first half of the twentieth century, and the dissolution of northern European colonial empires after anticolonial movements following World War II intensified the apparent separation between "states" and "markets." These processes are the condition for the emergence of the "economy" as the dominant foundation of imperial control among formally independent but unevenly dependent nation-states.

From the outset, the Americas were the global crucible of modern imperial formations. As a region subjected to Iberian empires, the Americas came to model northern European as well as U.S. imperialism. As a region that, since the American and Haitian revolutions, gave birth to a diverse group of postcolonial nations, the Américas have a long tradition of non-colonial, imperial subjection. Those regions once colonies of the Spanish and Portuguese empires (though some continued as French, Dutch, Spanish, and British colonies), became part of the British "informal empire" as independent nations until the end of the nineteenth century, when they came under the aegis of U.S. hegemonic dominance over the Western Hemisphere. When the United States became the hemisphere's major power after the Spanish-Cuban-American War of 1898, the United States came to exert control of the Américas through a combination of policies that centered on economic domination but included a vast range of mechanisms of subjection, from direct military force to psychological warfare, political propaganda, and commercial appeal. As a laboratory of policies that have come to be deployed by the United States throughout the world, Latin America was, and has remained, in Greg Grandin's apt phrase, the "empire's workshop."[10]

In this long historical arc from the Conquest to the present, the locus of imperial formations has moved from territorially defined units to transterritorial networks. The shift from British to U.S. dominance in the Américas redefined the significance of the formal-informal distinction as modes of imperial control. In Latin America, the category of informal imperialism has been largely restricted to historians of the nineteenth century concerned with British influence in the region. Because the British had a formal empire elsewhere, Latin America could be imagined as part of its informal empire. Revealingly, informal imperialism is seldom used to describe U.S. influence in the region. After Latin America became subject to U.S. imperial power after 1898, informal control did not need to be recognized as such, for it became not the exception but the rule.

Like Gallagher and Robinson, I think it is essential to see imperial formations as complex totalities. But these totalities are made up of the articulation of states and markets not as separate, thing-like units, but as mutually constituted entities. The entwined unfolding of capitalism and imperialism has always entailed not just the articulation between states and markets, but their construction as separate domains. For these authors, imperialism is a process "of integrating new regions into an expanding economy"; its "sufficient" function is political, while its "necessary" function" is economic.[11] Yet as colonial empires have given way to national and global empires and the economy has become the dominant political structure of imperial subjection, it is increasingly difficult to sustain the appearance of politics and economics as separate realms, with one or the other being the "sufficient" or "necessary" function of integrating new regions. The modes of integration of new imperial formations make more evident what was true earlier: the unity of the formal and informal, the political and the economic within the totality of imperial formations. It also shows that this unity involves the mutual transformation of constituent elements and constituted totalities; just as imperial formations are transformed by changes in states and markets, states and markets take new form with the transformation of imperial formations.

These intertwined changes reveal the complex unity of capitalism and imperialism as mutually constituted manifestations of an open-ended process. Capitalism and imperialism are two sides of one coin; they are each other's coeval condition of possibility. Just as without capitalism there would be no modern imperialism, without modern imperialism there would be no capitalism. And just as imperialism makes evident the political dimension of capitalism, capitalism makes visible the economic dimension of imperialism. The challenge is to observe how specific imperial formations take form under changing historical conditions.

The April days in Venezuela were the expression of changes in both national and international relations that reveal the ongoing transformation of imperial formations. This book is also an exploration of this changing global landscape of power, constantly redrawn by intertwined local and foreign forces acting across national boundaries. By examining those three-and-a-half days in light of a larger history, it offers insights into the specific form of current struggles—at once national and global—over peoples, power, ideas, and scarce resources.

Poetics

For many reasons—because the stakes were and remain so high, because so many of the main protagonists were and continue to be so influential, because many of them are facing or may confront the force of legal or political sanctions, because unspeakable acts were committed in the name of lofty principles, because of a chasm dividing the epic presented at center stage and the machinations orchestrated backstage—these days continue to be covered by torrents of secrets and rumors that feed clashing versions of the truth. Perhaps for these reasons, historians and social scientists have avoided engaging these events in depth, although there are numerous books, reports, and articles about them, often based on limited evidence. The proliferation of competing but inconclusive "true stories" has stifled confidence in truth itself. "Nadie cree nada" (Nobody believes anything), the title of a magazine article on a still unexplained helicopter crash on April 20, 2002, that killed officers who had been involved in the April 11–14 events, reflects a deepening erosion of trust in the truth about the April days.

If there is a common ground emerging about these competing accounts, it is not about the facts of the matter, but about the matter of facts. There is an acknowledgment—often signaled in conversations by a knowing wink or by shifting register to a whisper—that the facts about those murky days will long remain dark. Hope for the emergence of a definitive truthful account has been placed in the future—when the present has safely become past. A book whose title announces that it will answer "100 questions" about Chávez's Venezuela nevertheless asserts, "No one will ever know all of the plans involved in the coup plot."[12] I was often told that if "la verdad verdadera" (the real truth) about those days ever comes forth, it would happen after the leading protagonists are long dead.

Is there something peculiar about the limited knowledge we have about those April days, or is this sort of partiality common to all knowledge about history? It has long been understood that our knowledge of history is filled with gaps. This understanding has been compellingly expanded through the insights of literary theory, deconstruction, and postcolonial and feminist critiques that show how thoroughly our accounts are social constructions; how truth claims necessarily rely on unproven premises; how narratives are inherently selective; how perspectives are unavoidably shaped by specific cultures; how such fundamental categories as gender, class, race, and ethnicity influence records and recordings; how silences punctuate and puncture archives and narratives; how subaltern subjects generally do not write themselves into history but are written about or written off. From different fields—whether the matter at hand is the ancient past explored by archeologists through scant material evidence; ancient or modern societies studied by historians through a complex range of textual sources; or ethnographic units defined by anthropologists through fieldwork using oral sources and the observation of multiple activities and material records—there is increasing awareness that the facts of history are historical artifacts, that human beings are the creators and creatures of their history, and that the history they re-create in their minds cannot stand outside the history that creates them.

These discussions have raised anew old questions about evidence and truth, making clearer the inadequacy of the extreme positions of positivists

who claim to pursue truths that directly reflect social reality, or deconstruc-
tionists who, with no less certainty, proclaim that all we can have are interpretations and claims to truth about an unknowable reality. As the
historian Carlo Ginzburg argues, the recognition that there is a difference
"between representations and the reality they depict or represent" requires
that we explore them together in their difference and yet intimate unity;
while we must interpret truth claims, we must also evaluate their veracity.[13]
As Luise White has shown, stories about vampires are facts whose study
can make "for better, more comprehensive histories." It is not a matter
of opposing reality and fiction: "The imaginary makes the real, just as it
makes more imaginings; it is the inclusion of both that gives depth to historical analysis, and if not some certainty, at least solid grounds on which
to assess motivations, causes and ideas."[14] Just as White makes sense of
vampire stories by placing them in specific times and locations, we should
make sense of our thoughts about history by addressing specificities of
context. It is ironic, therefore, how frequently our theorizations about history dehistoricize it and assume that its object is a homogenous "past."

In reflections about their craft, historians are fond of mentioning approvingly Benedetto Croce's felicitous expression, "All history is contemporary history." Part of this dictum's power derives from its ability
to capture in a nutshell an obvious truth: since history can only be alive
for the living and current concerns affect the telling of past events, "all"
history is always being re-created from the standpoint of the present. But
perhaps its force also derives from its ability to draw on widely accepted
assumptions. This phrase's two references to "history"—"all history" and
"contemporary history"—take for granted and refer to the ambiguous
dual meanings associated with this term: what happened and accounts of
what happened. On the basis of these premises, Croce prompts us to take
as a matter of fact that we should understand "all history" to mean what
happened in the past, and "contemporary history" to mean knowledge
about the past. If this is so, who studies contemporary history as *process*
and as *knowledge* of this process? In Croce's phrase, contemporary history
is directly present only as *knowledge* of the past. Implicitly left out as a contemporary process and as knowledge about it, history vanishes from this
evocative phrase, leaving its aura to haunt us.[15]

It is revealing that neither Croce nor his commentators have remarked
on the ambiguity of this proposition and its erasure of "contemporary history," in the sense noted earlier. What if we were to reverse this statement
and claim, "All contemporary history is history"? Would "contemporary

history" be considered history in the same way as the past is treated as history? Or, more fundamentally, what is "it"? Is it equivalent to "the present"? If contemporary concerns affect accounts of the past, making all history contemporary, how do they affect the telling of contemporary history? If we view the present as an open-ended process (that is, history as what is happening) does it take time to develop a perspective that would allow us to know which aspects or events are significant enough to become history (that is, history as knowledge)? If so, should we see the present as "history" only as an object, as a process, but not yet as knowledge of this process, or only crudely so—a sort of "proto-history"? Still, in some respects we seem to have a better sense of the present, at least of some aspects of it, because we participate in it and are of it, as witnesses and actors. Do we have more access to the present because we are part of it, or must we remain blind to it, presumably like fish are to the water?

While philosophers of history have examined basic questions about history and interrogated common assumptions, historians and social scientists who seek to reach a broad public tend to cast our work in terms of given premises, even as we seek to refine them or take advantage of their elasticity. In common understanding, past and present are not sharply defined, flowing in and out of each other without clear boundaries or breaks. Yet the notion of archive, so central to historical practice, evokes the image of enclosures, of containers with boundaries that keep some things in and some out. If so, what are or where can we locate the archives of the present? According to the historian Arnold Toynbee, "Very recent historical evidence is apt to be very uneven in quantity and quality, and therefore very difficult to assess." For Toynbee, who wrote grand narratives about epochs, what is "recent" is probably different than what it is for historical anthropologists engaged in fieldwork about sensitive ongoing events. They face directly the limits of what we may know and thus, in David W. Cohen's evocative phrase, the "risks of knowledge."[16] The nature of historical evidence, the knowledge it makes possible, and the silences it creates vary depending on location, time, and circumstances.

Historical anthropologists, who often write about both the past and the present, are particularly well situated to reflect upon the production of history under different circumstances. In *Silencing the Past*, Michel-Rolph Trouillot uses key moments in the history of Haiti, his nation of birth, to reflect on how the past has been reconstructed from positions of power. Building on his analysis of specific case studies, he notes four operations through which power influences the writing of history, from the moment of the making of facts ("sources"), of assembling them ("archives"), of retrieving them ("narratives"), and of retrospective significance ("history"). His detailed studies show why certain events that would trouble official views and mainstream understandings are muted or excluded from historical narratives. Thus, just as Haitian nationalist historiography effaces intraelite conflicts that divided major leaders of the war against French colonialism and cast dark shadows upon nationalist heroes, French historiography erases the presence and significance of a major revolution that took place in a faraway small island and was therefore "unthinkable" from the standpoint of a Europe that saw itself as the center of the world.[17]

Around the time of the Haitian Revolution, Hegel claimed that all that was historically important happened in Europe and in his own examination of master-slave relations as a trope to discuss the unfolding of Western history, he silenced the Haitian Revolution, although it evidently affected his thinking.[18] In *The Writing of History*, Michel de Certeau argues that history as a Western discipline was formed in tandem with the development of European states in the context of the colonization of the Americas.[19] Trouillot's imaginative discussion of silences of the past reveals the complicity between history and the state. The silences he examines are mainly *of history* as a Western form of knowledge, not of other modes of accounting for the past. And they are indeed silences *of the past*—of events that took place a long time ago, centuries ago, that have been constantly re-created through the present. But what about the silences of the present, or of what may be called the "contemporary past"—that is, events that have taken place rather recently, by which I mean within a decade or so?

In a thoughtful study of the mysterious murder of Kenya's Foreign Minister Robert Ouko, Cohen recognizes that the fresh past-ness of this event creates unfolding conditions that affect how it is recounted. The passage of time, even of only a few years, opens new sources and offers changing perspectives upon these events. As he says, "By the circumstance of time," our position to evaluate these events changes. We are able not just to assess the expanding records of what happened, but the changing field within which these records are produced: "The details of what others knew and did not know are what become, in all their 'incomplete dialectics,' critical to an understanding of Ouko's death."[20] Are there specific factors that make for an incomplete dialectics of knowledge about current events? Who can write about the silences of the present?

It is commonly understood, even taken for granted, that much of what happens in the here and now is shrouded by secrecy and protected by political and legal walls. Observers of current events comment frequently about the secrecy of the military establishment, of large corporations and financial institutions, of the apex of political power, of international agencies such as the IMF and World Bank. Major archives are kept from the public for several decades, some forever. Intense debates concern the opening of these archives. While the public knows of the existence of notorious intelligence agencies, such as the CIA, we are largely unaware of the vast network of institutions, public and private, that constantly gather information, often through illegal means, including torture and blackmail, but make it available only to restricted circles. The Nobel Prize–winner Joseph Stiglitz, on the basis of his experience in the World Bank and at the White House, has documented how the extensive use of secrecy in public and private institutions gives "discretion" to officials, protects "private interests," "hides mistakes," and "undermines democracy."[21] Examining the hidden networks linking the domain of oil, drugs, and war, the Canadian diplomat and Berkeley Professor Peter Dale Scott coins the terms "deep politics" to refer to any form of unacknowledged form of political influence, and "para-politics" to refer to conduct carried out by "indirection, collusion and deceit." The more closely we observe the centers of power, the more these terms, which may suggest exceptional states, in fact describe common practices. The openly exceptional often reveals the hidden rule. In response to September 11, 2001, U.S. Vice President Dick Cheney announced that from now on, the state had to work "on the dark side."

Cheney's comment signals not a novel practice but the intensification of business as usual, except, perhaps a more unabashed openness about the United States' imperial policies. And these practices, although more consequential in powerful centers, are typical of all bureaucracies. As Max Weber observed long ago, "The concept of the 'official secret' is the invention of bureaucracy." According to Weber, "Every bureaucracy seeks to increase the superiority of the professionally informed by keeping their knowledge and intentions secret."[22] While Weber discussed secrets as the willful action of individuals, Karl Marx treated them as inherent to the ordinary workings of society; secrets happen, as it were, behind people's back.

Marx's *Capital* can be seen as a code to decipher "the official secrets" of capitalism. The ordinary working of capitalist societies entails the formation of a culture—of representations of social life—that obscures social contradictions and gaps between ideals and realities. "Economic mystifications," Marx claims, legitimate the production of wealth by misrepresenting in myriad ways its operations—at the core, by concealing how labor power produces more value than the exchange value it receives in the form of wages. In order to discover the "secret of profit making," Marx tells us, we must turn away from the public sphere, the stage of deceiving appearances, and enter the backstage, where the appearance of the real is produced. He leads us into this journey, bringing along also the two main protagonists (in his view) of capitalist society: capital and labor. "Accompanied by Mr. Moneybags and by the possessor of labor-power," he writes, "we therefore take leave for a time of this noisy sphere, where everything takes place on the surface and in view of all men, and follow them both into the hidden abode of production." Acting as a witty guide, Marx makes us notice that on the "threshold" of this "hidden abode" there is a warning sign designed to exclude those who do not belong there: "No admittance except on business." But, of course, his "business" is to trespass this barrier and to reveal the secret of business—or, rather, to show how we can extract it by intense intellectual labor (as exemplified in *Capital*): "Here we shall see, not only how capital produces, but how capital is produced. We shall at last force the secret of profit making."[23]

Although Marx also wrote insightfully about politics, his work centered on the hidden abode of production, leaving largely out of sight the hidden abode of politics—a task that remains still unrealized, despite significant achievements by Marxists and non-Marxists alike. How to force the secret of power making? Even if one were to circumscribe the abode of politics to the state, it may not prove easy to define its limits. In my previous work, the more closely I looked into it, the more I realized that the state was not a bounded site but a "mystifying complex of practices and beliefs," the unity of particular embodiments of general power. Thus, one of the difficulties of studying politics is that, unlike the production of profits, the production of power—or whatever general term one chooses to represent the object of politics—takes place in many sites; the abode of politics is as diverse as its products. Another difficulty is that unlike profits, these "products," if we may even call them that, do not lend themselves to quantification, despite the conceit of the proponents of rational choice, game theory, or even analytical Marxism who believe that social life can be rendered as a calculus of utilities of one sort or another, as if society were a market and politics could be reduced to the choices and preferences of individuals. But if politics concerns not just the choices and actions of subjects but their formation as subjects, then the abode of politics turns out to be society at large.

There is yet another major hurdle to analysis. Even if we were to treat the abode of production as a loose metaphor to explore the abode of politics, we would soon discover the limits of this metaphor not just for the production of power, but for the production of production as well—at least as Marx presented it. Nations of the Global South, particularly primary product exporters in which states control mineral and other natural resources, make particularly evident that politics is inseparably linked to economics—and vice versa. Even in cases when it is directed at creating a free market, politics involves the definition of "the economy," as illustrated by the extreme brutal exertion of power that was necessary to create a free market in Chile under Augusto Pinochet.

If we wished to enter the abode of production in these nations, we could not forget, as Marx did, to bring along the owners of land—the rentiers who in one way or another own or control the earth's riches. Bringing this protagonist would not only expand our understanding of the cast of characters involved in production—including the state as well as multinational corporations—but would change our understanding of the character of production itself. It would help us see that if profits are indeed made through the exploitation of labor, they also depend on the extraction of riches through the exploitation of nature. By observing this unified process, we would see how lines separating states and markets merge, how the frontiers dividing the national and the international dissolve. We could then see more clearly the secret of the wealth of nations under capitalism everywhere: it results from the unity of the value produced by labor and the riches provided by nature.

It would be difficult then not to recognize the importance of the struggle over natural resources in the past two centuries. The April events were part of this long history, even if this history was kept largely secret. There is importance in truth, but even more in ethics.

Notes

Notes on the epigraphs: The epigraph for chapter 1 is from Laura Restrepo, *Delirio* (Bogotá, Colombia: Alfaguara, 2004), 143. The epigraph for chapter 2 is from the *American Heritage Dictionary.*

1 See, e.g., "The Revolution Will Not Be Televised—Chávez: Inside the Coup," posted November 5, 2009, https://www.youtube.com/watch?v=Id--ZFtjR5c.
2 While the Anglo-American historical tradition is associated with British individualism and empiricism, the German historical tradition is linked to Hegel's

idealistic philosophy and romantic thought. Ranke made this distinction in his inaugural lecture as Ordinary Professor in Berlin in 1872. In his early lectures, Heidegger distinguished between *chronos* and *kairos* on the basis of ideas developed by Kierkegaard and Schopenhauer. In *Being and Time*, the present occupies a fundamental place as home. On the German historical tradition and colonialism, see Susanne Zantop, *Colonial Fantasies: Conquest, Family and Nation in Precolonial Germany, 1770–1870* (Durham, NC: Duke University Press, 1997). For a discussion of Ortiz's concept of transculturation, see my introduction (this volume) to the new edition of his work *Cuban Counterpoint: Tobacco and Sugar* (Durham, NC: Duke University Press, 1995).

3 The reference is to Jamaica Kincaid, *A Small Place* (New York: Penguin, 1988). In the book, she makes smallness stand as a metaphor for the inconsequential history of postcolonial nations. (Venezuela, I should note, is twice the size of France.) Dipesh Chakrabarty lucidly argues about the indispensability of European history for historians of the non-West in *Provincializing Europe: Postcolonial Thought and Historical Difference* (Princeton: Princeton University Press, 2008).

4 Focusing on literary works and travel accounts about the Americas, Mary Louise Pratt unveils an imperial way of seeing in *Imperial Eyes: Travel Writing and Transculturation* (London: Routledge, 1992). The reference to Said is to his classic *Orientalism* (New York, Vintage: 1978), but also to *Culture and Imperialism* (New York: Alfred A. Knopf, 1993). [Editor's note: For Coronil's critique of "Occidentalism," see chapters 10 and 11 in this volume.]

5 Eric Wolf, *Europe and the People without History* (Berkeley: University of California Press, 1982), 6.

6 See the historical and theoretical work produced by scholars associated with two subaltern studies groups: the South Asian and the Latin American. In *Provincializing Europe*, Chakrabarty developed the notion of "provincializing" Europe, as well as a compelling argument concerning the "inadequacy" but also "indispensability" of Western categories. For an attempt to establish a dialogue between the positions held by Chakrabarty and myself, see Walter Mignolo, *Local Histories/Global Designs: Coloniality, Subaltern Knowledges, and Border Thinking* (Princeton, NJ: Princeton University Press, 2000), chap. 4.

7 William Appleman Williams, *Empire as a Way of Life* (Oxford: Oxford University Press, 1982); Amy Kaplan, *The Anarchy of Empire in the Making of U.S. Culture* (Cambridge, MA: Harvard University Press, 2005).

8 Seymour Hersch, *Chain of Command: The Road From 9/11 to Abu Ghraib* (New York: Harper, 2004); Chalmers Johnson, *The Sorrows of Empire: Militarism, Secrecy and the End of the Republic* (New York: Metropolitan, 2004); Kevin Philips, *American Theocracy: The Peril and Politics of Radical Religion, Oil and Borrowed Money in the 21st Century* (New York: Viking, 2006); Peter Dale Scott, *The Road to 9/11: Wealth, Empire and the Future of America* (Berkeley: University of California Press, 2007); Joseph E. Stiglitz, *Globalization and Its Discontents* (New York: W. W. Norton,

2002); Daniel Yergin, *The Quest: Energy, Security and the Remaking of the Modern World* (New York: Penguin, 2011); Michael T. Klare, *Resource Wars: The New Landscape of Global Conflict* (New York: Henry Holt, 2001); Andrew Bacevich, *American Empire: The Realities and Consequences of U.S. Diplomacy* (Cambridge, MA: Harvard University Press, 2002); Greg Grandin, *Empire's Workshop: Latin America, the United States, and the Rise of the New Imperialism* (New York: Metropolitan, 2006).

9 John Gallagher and Ronald Robinson, "The Imperialism of Free Trade," *Economic History Review*, new series, 6, no. 1 (1953): 1015. See also John Gallagher and Ronald Robinson, *Imperialism: The Robinson and Gallagher Controversy* (New York: New Viewpoints, 1976).

10 Grandin, *Empire's Workshop*.

11 Gallagher and Robinson, "The Imperialism of Free Trade," 5–6.

12 Chesa Boudin, Gabriel Gonzalez, and Wilmer Rumbos, *The Venezuelan Revolution: 100 Questions—100 Answers* (New York: Avalon, 2006), 83.

13 Carlo Ginzburg, *The Judge and the Historian: Marginal Notes on a Late-Twentieth-Century Miscarriage of Justice*, trans. Anthony Shugaar (London: Verso 1999), 17.

14 Luise White, *Speaking with Vampires: Rumor and History in Colonial Africa* (Berkeley: University of California Press, 2000), 307.

15 The reference to Benedetto Croce is classical. Arnold J. Toynbee quotes the statement in "The Writing of Contemporary History for Chatham House," *Royal Institute of International Affairs* 219, no. 2 (April 1944): 137–40.

16 David W. Cohen, *The Risks of Knowledge* (Athens: Ohio University Press, 2004).

17 Michel-Rolph Trouillot, *Silencing the Past: Power and the Production of History* (Boston: Beacon, 1997).

18 Susan Buck-Morss, "Hegel and Haiti," *Critical Inquiry* 26, no. 4 (July 2000): 821–65.

19 Michel de Certeau, *The Writing of History* (New York: Columbia University Press, 1988).

20 Cohen, *The Risks of Knowledge*, 261.

21 Stiglitz, *Globalization and Its Discontents*; Scott, *The Road to 9/11*.

22 Max Weber, *From Max Weber: Essays in Sociology* (London: Routledge, 2009), 233.

23 Karl Marx, *Capital: A Critique of Political Economy*, vol. 1, pt. 1 (New York: Cosimo Classics, 2007), 195.

BEYOND OCCIDENTALISM,

BEYOND EMPIRE

Part III. Beyond Occidentalism, Beyond Empire

Introduction PAUL EISS

■   The essays gathered here under the rubric "Beyond Occidentalism, Beyond Empire" were published over a period of a decade, from
the mid-1990s through the early years of the 2000s. While they were deeply
engaged with debates of the times of their original publication, taken individually and as a group the essays retain great currency, even urgency,
for contemporary discussions of their central subjects. While originally
composed as a response to Edward Said's discussion of Orientalism, for
instance, Coronil's analysis of "Occidentalism" raises critical questions
about the epistemological formation that he considered Orientalism's dark
side. His discussion of the constructions of Western selfhood that underwrite Western representations of the otherness of subjected populations
makes clear that such representations were and are intimately connected to
global and asymmetrical relations of power and exploitation. In veiled
form, such an epistemology remains characteristic of power relations, and
associated forms of othering, under the contemporary neoliberal global
order. In "Listening to the Subaltern," Coronil poses a timely rejoinder to
Gayatri Spivak's now classic discussion of subaltern speech but also moves
substantially beyond its terms. He expands the scope of the concept of
subalternity to embrace representatives of neocolonial states as they endeavor to speak for, about, or to sovereign, collective entities, such as "the
people." In "Smelling Like a Market," a critique of James Scott's 1998 treatise on authoritarian high modernism, Coronil signals some substantial
limitations of a work that excluded market-based schemes of social intervention to focus only on policies of modernizing states. But more than
that, he sketches the outlines of a more expansive study of the state that
remains compelling, suggesting that static and scopic approaches to state

power be replaced by a dialogic, performative, and processual approach to representations of state and market.

The last two essays in part III provide trenchant contributions to discussions of postcolonialism and empire across multiple fields—fields whose regional and disciplinary boundaries Coronil constantly urges us to cross, or transgress. In "Latin American Postcolonial Studies and Global Decolonization," he calls attention to the problematic nature of "Latin American Postcolonial Studies" as an assumed rubric. Despite many shared subjects of critical concern relating to colonialism and its entailments, he notes areas of remarkable disconnection between the fields of postcolonial studies and Latin American studies. He concludes by making an argument against regionalist parochialism and advocating for a kind of "tactical postcolonialism" that would bring about a truly "global circulation of postcolonial studies as a potent intellectual currency for the exchange and development of perspectives on colonialism and its legacies from different regions and intellectual traditions" (this volume, 419).[1] In "After Empire," Coronil proposes to recast the study of empire and imperialism in several ways. He stresses the importance of recognizing the critical role of the Spanish and Portuguese in laying the groundwork for later imperial regimes and highlights the coeval formation of capitalism and imperialism in the unfolding history of relations between metropoles and colonies. Most important, and based on a definition of imperialism that privileges the perspective of populations subjected to a system of naturalized difference under hierarchical structures, Coronil argues for the recognition of the neoliberal global order as an imperial formation. While according to Coronil "globalcentrism" has superseded the Eurocentrism of earlier imperial forms, practices of othering and subjection are no less systematic and, in fact, all the more pernicious due to their masking by a rhetoric of formal, market-based global equality.

Such contributions to discussions and debates around empire, postcolonialism, and subalternity remain salient for scholars working in those fields. Just as important, though—and perhaps posing even deeper challenges for contemporary readers—are other aspects of Coronil's analysis and his intellectual and political commitments. Throughout these essays, as in his other works, Coronil insistently emphasizes the relationality of social and historical processes and particularly of the social, political, and analytical categories that tend to obscure that relationality. In his work on Occidentalism, he expresses an antiessentialist perspective that is surely informed by his engagements with postcolonial studies; he states the importance of recognizing cultural difference but also stresses the contrapuntal relationship between presumably distinct, and bounded, cultures. He levels an unrelenting critique of the ways European selves and their presumed others are generally construed, arguing instead, memorably, that "difference be historicized rather than essentialized, and that . . . boundaries and homogeneity be determined, not assumed" (350). Similarly, in "Listening to the Subaltern," Coronil seeks to transcend the polar opposition between dominator and dominated, or between unified modern and dispersed and fragmented postmodern subjects, to argue for a nonessentialist conception of subalternity. If, as he argues, both dominance and subalternity are relational rather than inherent qualities, then subalternity might extend, at moments, to encompass even social elites, or the state itself. Indeed, such a relational critique is the basis, in his comments on Scott, for Coronil's challenge to Manichaean analytical oppositions between state and market and the forms of power associated with them; it resides at the core of his analysis of Venezuelan political economy in The Magical State, and it informs his discussions of the relationship between imperialism and capitalism, in which states and markets are "dual facets of a unitary process," and imperialism figures as "capitalism's coeval condition of possibility" (442).

In his essays on postcolonialism and Latin American studies, and on empire, Coronil makes clear how a relational approach to historical processes might pose trenchant challenges to those fields. This informs Coronil's call to pluralize colonialism ("Latin American Postcolonial Studies," this volume, 399–424), to avoid privileging one empire—that is, the British empire—as a standard for colonial or postcolonial histories and experiences but instead to recognize multiple forms of Western empire and their global interrelation. It also drives his incitement to "globalize the periphery" by recognizing the mutual formation of metropoles and peripheries and, most important, the relational formation of dominant and subaltern subjects within the hierarchical and naturalized structures of difference characteristic of imperial and neoimperial regimes of power. Throughout his published work, and most explicitly in his discussions of postcolonialism and imperialism, Coronil faults recent scholars for their failure to reckon with the important work of Latin American dependency theorists and analysts. In his view, the importance of that work resides particularly in its relational understanding of metropoles and peripheries in imperial systems and its critical systemic analysis of wholes that could complement the postcolonialist emphasis—informed by the critique of modernity and its narratives—on the fragmentary study of parts. A thoroughgoing, even radical relationality was thus intrinsic to Coronil's call, in "Latin American Postcolonial Studies," for a "bifocal perspective" (403) that might marry the insights of both fields.

Such relationality is central to a second feature of Coronil's work: a politics of knowledge that is both dialectical and reflexive. This feature is suggested by his repeated use of chiasmic formulations at key points of his analysis. Hence, at stake in his conception of Occidentalism, Coronil writes, is the "politics of epistemology and the epistemology of politics" (350)—the "representation of power and the power to represent" (352). Subalternity figures, in his essay on that topic, as "not the being of a subject, but a subjected state of being" (374). As Coronil goes on to demonstrate in his discussion of subaltern state speech, the "locus of enunciation is inseparable from the enunciation of a locus," both related dimensions of a "single historical process" (382). A story Jorge Luis Borges wrote about an imperial map, Coronil writes in "Smelling Like a Market," is "not just about the truth of scientific representations but about the representation of truth, about power's representations and the power to represent, about the truth of power" (347).

More than rhetorical or poetic turns of phrase, such chiasmic formulations index a profoundly important approach to the knowledge of power—and the powers of knowledge not just to represent the world, but to change it. In his discussion of subalternity, Coronil sets the stakes high for his call to listen to silences and voices in the "cracks of dominant histories and narratives; to do so is to begin to overcome the "conditions that make subalternity possible" (369). In his critique of Scott, Coronil denounces the complicity of established ways of understanding the state with forms of imperial hubris and violence; he calls instead for the drawing of a new conceptual map that "would recognize the marks of human daring, a map that would dare our imagination, that would show new vistas and make us desire to mold the existing order into a different, dignified landscape for humankind" (398). Similarly, while exploring the relationship between Latin American studies and postcolonial studies, Coronil suggests the two might find dialogue and common cause in a "tactical postcolonialism"— one defined perhaps less by the history or intellectual program of either field, and more by a kind of conceptual work that is both deconstructive and political, thus contributing to struggles to "decolonize knowledge and build a genuinely democratic world" (420). In "After Empire," Coronil declares his intention to be that of making historical and contemporary forms of domination "at once more intelligible and more intolerable" (450); in "Beyond Occidentalism," he calls for us to sunder the connections between Western knowledge and Western power via a "decentered poetics that may help us imagine geohistorical categories for a nonimperial world" (324).

In a short essay of literary criticism entitled "Partial Enchantments of the Quixote," Borges—whom Coronil often cited—commented on several works that included depictions of those very works within their pages. Volume 2 of *Don Quixote*, for instance, includes a depiction of protagonists reading volume 1. Similarly, according to Borges, Shakespeare's *Hamlet* includes a scene in which actors onstage perform a tragedy very similar to *Hamlet*, and in one of the nights recounted in the 1001 *Nights*, the sultana, recounting her nightly tales to the sultan, tells him his own story, triggering dizzying fears of infinite regress. Borges compares such literary devices to an imaginary map proposed by the American philosopher Josiah Royce in 1899. Royce evokes a map of England that is so exact as to represent the very slightest detail of the country's terrain on its surface. As the map is itself produced in England, it would then have to contain an image of itself of its own surface, which if it were to be exact, would then have to contain another image of the map within itself—and so on and so forth. What is so disquieting about such a thought experiment, according to Borges, is not the possibilities of infinite regress in Quixote's or Royce's map. Rather, it is that "those inversions suggest that if the characters in a story can be readers or spectators, then we, their readers or spectators, can be fictitious."[2]

In a similar way, the essays included in part III—particularly, "Beyond Occidentalism"—are strongly marked by a kind of dialectical reflexivity. They are maps *of* the world whose rigor extends to a reckoning of themselves as maps *in* the world. Yet at the same time they draw attention to what Borges called the fictitious nature of author and readers, particularly if we understand fiction, by one of its uses, to draw attention to the aspects of crafting or making that are intrinsic to any account, or any map. Ultimately, the poetic quality of "Beyond Occidentalism," and that of Coronil's other writings, derives from a realization that is as simple as it is radical: if power and knowledge are so intimately bound, then to conceive the world differently is to begin a process of change. As Fernando Coronil tells us, to write the poetry of the present is not only to represent the world, but to remake it.

Notes

1 Unless otherwise noted, parenthetical citations given in this introduction refer to page numbers in the current volume.
2 Jorge Luis Borges, *Other Inquisitions: 1937–1952*, trans. Ruth L. C. Simms (Austin: University of Texas Press, 1965), 46.

11 Occidentalism

As an inherently fluid geohistorical category that expresses varying understandings of the "West," "Occidentalism" is a polysemic "conceptual monster" (Latouche 1996: 7) that conjures up a sense of unity out of shifting geographical and historical referents. In light of the West's role as a colonial and imperial power, renderings of Occidentalism are inherently normative and comparative and are thus exceptionally susceptible to political positioning and ideological perspective. In ordinary use, "Occidentalism" refers to the "customs, institutions, characteristics, ways of thinking etc. of Western Nations" (Oxford English Dictionary). In scholarly works influenced by critiques of Eurocentrism and of Orientalism, "Occidentalism" refers to the West's self-representation, to other societies' representations of the expanding West, or to representations of cultural difference framed in terms of Western political epistemologies. "Occidentalism" is thus an imprecise term that denotes a wide range of representations of the West as well as Occidentalist modalities of representation.

The Rising West and Its Hegemonic Representation

Westernization, Colonialism, and European Hegemony
Occidentalism's multiple renderings have reflected the West's imperial history and sustained or contested its rise to global dominance. Hegemonic accounts locate the West's origins in ancient Greek civilization, even if some interpretations extend its roots deeper into Egyptian and Mesopotamian cultures. They present Rome's assimilation of Greek culture and the expansion of the Roman empire—its project to create "one world"—as initiating a process of Westernization or Occidentalization.

Through the rise and fall of the Holy Roman Empire and until the end of the Middle Ages, Westernization and the West meant Christianization and Christendom. Concentrated in Western Europe, Christendom was overshadowed by the dynamic expansion of Islam after the seventh century, and it had no influence over the empires and civilizations of Asia, Africa, and what came to be known as the Americas. Occidentalism thus designated a rather confined political and ideological formation.

The colonization of the Americas was a turning point in the making of the modern West and in the Occidentalization of the world (O'Gorman 1958; Dussel 1995). When Columbus landed in what Spain called the "Occidental Indies," Europe was still on the margins of the world's major civilizations in the Middle East and China, and Islam was the most expansive of the major religions. The Spanish and Portuguese colonization of the Americas made it possible to think for the first time in global terms and to represent Europe as the center of the world. Supported by the labor and wealth of the Americas, the Habsburgs constructed the most extensive empire the world had ever known, "the empire where the sun never sets," stretching from the Americas to Eastern Europe. This period of Iberian dominance saw the rise of Occidentalism as a legitimating discourse of imperial rule that concerned at once the evangelization and assimilation of America's native populations and the making of Spain and Portugal as imperial powers.

The process of transculturation (Ortiz 1940, 1995) involving Europe, America, and Africa shifted power in the old world toward the Mediterranean and eventually to the Atlantic. Following the lead of Spain and Portugal, England, France, and Holland competed for control of the Americas, participating in the subjugation and conversion of its native populations as well as in the massive enslavement of African peoples and their forced relocation to the New World. Between the sixteenth and eighteenth centuries, through momentous transformations in politics (the English, U.S., French and Haitian revolutions), in culture (the Enlightenment), and economic relations (the expansion of global trade and production), power shifted within Europe toward its northwestern nations. By the end of the nineteenth century, their development as nation-states and their colonial expansion in Asia and Africa, conditioned by their earlier European colonial experience in the Americas, consolidated Europe's position as the world's dominant capitalist center.

During its rise as a global power, Europe fashioned itself as the apex of civilization in opposition to its overseas territories. It organized its rule both at home and abroad through taxonomies of cultures intimately linked with gender, class, and racial hierarchies. Since the nineteenth century and up to World War I, Occidentalism's core referent was northern Europe, even as it included the United States as an emerging capitalist power with imperial interests in the Caribbean, Latin America, and the Pacific. During this period of capitalist expansion, nation-state formation, and high colonialism, dominant renderings of Occidentalism were framed in terms of evolutionary schemes drawn from the natural and social sciences. The Occident, which during the early colonial period had fashioned itself in relation to "savages" located in distant lands, was now defined in relation to "primitives" who were projected backward into the distant past (Fabian 1983; Mignolo 1998; Trouillot 1991).

Westernization, U.S. Hegemony, and Neoliberal Globalization

European global hegemony came to a crisis in the twentieth century as a result of two world wars, decolonization, and the consolidation of the United States as the dominant world power and new icon of the West. After World War II, the pursuit of competing visions of independent national *development* turned colonial and postcolonial areas, designated as the "Third World," into a battlefield in a global struggle between the major socialist nations, or "Second World," and the advanced capitalist powers, or "First World." In the context of the Cold War, the West (the First World), which came to include ascendant Japan, referred centrally to the "free (capitalist) world" led by the United States, and the East, whose basic referent had been the "exotic" cultures of the Orient, designated the "totalitarian (socialist) world" behind the "iron curtain." This "three-world scheme" (Pletsch 1981) has ceased to reflect the power relations resulting from the fall of Soviet socialism in 1989 and the widespread acceptance of the capitalist market as the foundation of social rationality and the source of new transnational political and economic entities. While the fluid boundaries that had defined the West in relation to the rest of the world have been further detached from their customary geographical referents, Western economic and political power has become more concentrated and centralized through transnational networks that link dominant sectors across the globe. In this more abstract political cartography, the West has been variously identified as a cultural formation involved in a "clash of civilizations" in an era of attenuated political conflicts and renewed ancestral cultural hostilities (Huntington 1993), or as the less visible imperial center of subtle modalities of Westernization disguised as globalization (Amin 1997).

After Orientalism: Occidentalism within Academia

The West's rise to global dominance has entailed the hegemony of Western social thought. It placed "Europe" or "the West" not just at the center of history, but also as the source of the theories and academic disciplines in terms of which global and local histories have been narrated (Chakrabarty 1992; Wallerstein et al. 1996). A variety of oppositional Occidentalisms, reflecting different conceptions of the expanding West, have contested Western supremacy. For example, at the turn of the nineteenth century, for German romantics, Occidentalism designated the soulless cultures of England and France, and for Latin American Arielistas, it referred to the crass materialism of the United States. After World War II, for many Third World intellectuals and activists, decolonization entailed the rejection of Occidentalism as the expression of an imperial culture. At the close of the twentieth century, for Middle Eastern fundamentalists, Occidentalism means the decadent culture of a political rival, and for nationalist Japanese modernizers, it denotes a civilization to be both emulated and counter-poised to their own valued traditions. From different locations, struggles against Western supremacy have provided critical visions of the West and drawn attention to the connection between the West's political central-ity and the Eurocentric disposition of its epistemological order. Informed by this critique and conditioned by the worldwide erosion of modernist projects in the last quarter of the twentieth century, the examination of Western epistemologies and conceptions of historical progress has been reflected in developments in social theory associated with poststructural-ism, postmodernism, and the linguistic turn.

Occidentalism and Orientalism: Inversion, Self-Reflection, Critique
Since the 1970s in intellectual circles influenced by these transforma-tions, critics of Eurocentrism have described in relational terms the mode of representation the West exerts on the East. Through the influence of Edward Said's (1978) pathbreaking discussion of Orientalism as a form of discourse about the Orient rooted in Western epistemologies and political dominance, Orientalism has come to refer to Eurocentric and stereotypical representations of any culture.

Reversing the gaze, scholars have generally used Occidentalism as the inverse of Orientalism to designate the study of the West (Hanafi 1991) as well as simplified or stereotypical renderings of the West by non-Western societies. In one of the earliest uses of Occidentalism understood as the opposite of Orientalism, Laura Nader (1989) discusses how Muslim men deploy Western conceptions of women to subjugate women in their own societies. Along similar lines, Xiaomei Chen (1992: 691) distinguishes "official Occidentalism," by which he means a negative image of the West used by the Chinese socialist government to control its own populations, from "anti-official" Occidentalism, which refers to counterdiscourses of Western superiority used by the Chinese intelligentsia to support their political opposition to the government. (For a related oppositional use of Occidentalism, see Findley 1998.)

James Carrier coins the category "ethno-Occidentalism" to refer to "the essentialist rendering of the West by members of alien societies," and reserves the term "Occidentalism" for "the essentialist rendering of the West by Westerners." Regarding the "essentialization" of concepts as inherent to "the way Westerners and probably most people think," he argues that relating representations of otherness to those of the West would lead to a better understanding of cultural representations of difference (Carrier 1992: 198–207). Nancy Armstrong (1990) uses "Occidentalism" to refer to the formation of specific forms of racialized and gendered Western selves as the effect of Orientalist representations upon Western societies. Reflecting on its use in scholarly works, Wang Ning (1997: 62) suggests that "Occidentalism," understood as the counterpart of Orientalism, is an even more imprecise and indeterminate term, a "quasi-theoretical concept" that has not led to an independent discipline like Oriental studies. In a discussion that focuses on the genealogy of "Occidentalism" in the Americas, Walter Mignolo (1998) shows how Latin American thinkers have used the term as a critical category to refer to Western imperial culture as well as to the project to transcend it, as in Roberto Fernández Retamar's (1976) concept of "post-Occidentalism" and Coronil's (1996) call to go "beyond Occidentalism."

Occidentalism as Imperial Epistemology
Treating the partiality of imperial representations of cultural difference as the effect of historically specific unequal power relations, Coronil (1996: 56–58) argues that Occidentalism is an imperial epistemology that expresses a constitutive relationship between Western constructions of difference and Western worldwide dominance. He develops Occidentalism as an analytical category that links the production of Western representations of alterity to the implicit constructions of selfhood that underwrite them. As an ensemble of representation practices, Occidentalism consists of accounts

that produce polarized and hierarchical conceptions of the West and its others and makes them central figures in narratives of global and local histories that separate the world's components into bounded units; disaggregate their relational histories; turn difference into hierarchy; naturalize these representations; and thus participate in the reproduction of asymmetrical power relations. These operations are apparent in three dominant Occidentalist modalities of representation: the dissolution of the other into the self; the incorporation of the other into the self; and the destabilization of the self by the other. The subordination of geography to history in these modes of representing modernity contributes to the narration of local histories in terms of the West's alleged universal history and thus to obscuring the participation of non-Western societies in the making of the modern world. In this usage, Occidentalism is an analytical category that refers to representations of cultural difference framed in terms of Western political epistemologies rather than a term that designates characterizations of the West; it refers to the conditions of possibility of Orientalism, not to its symmetrical counterpart.

Occidentalism and Globalization

The conditions that have enabled Western representations of cultural difference in the modern world in terms of radical alterity, subordination, and exoticism include colonialism and imperialism; a hierarchical system of nation-states; capitalism as a global mode of production of regions, persons, and things; a division of the person into private individual and public citizen; faith in secular science; and an expansive *universalism* supported by the sciences and by ideologies of progress. At the onset of a new millennium, these conditions are being modified by transformations epitomized by the hegemony of neoliberal globalization. The intensified commodification of social life and the breakdown of commodities into bundles of risk spread across space and time have heightened the significance of the market as an organizing principle of geopolitical and cultural differences. Critical accounts of globalization treat it as both a unifying and divisive process that involves a dialectic of globalization and localization, universalization and particularization, spatialization and temporalization, and cultural homogenization and ethnic diversification. In contrast, hegemonic discourses of globalization emphasize unity over difference and produce an image of an increasingly integrated globe no longer radically divided between the West and its others, thus masking persisting operations of othering that continue to take place through various forms of naturalization such as the racialization of class distinctions and the essentialization of cultural differences.

Insofar as discourses of neoliberal globalization emphasize the potential equality and universality of humankind through the market, they imply a shift of focus in the representation of cultural difference from alien subjects located outside Western centers to subordinated populations dispersed across the globe. As the West seems to dissolve into the market and Westernization appears as globalization, political projects to civilize alien others are being recast as self-induced processes of incorporation by willing citizens-consumers. In contrast to Occidentalist modalities of representation based upon a binary opposition between a superior Western self and its subordinate others, prevailing discourses of globalization appear as a compelling but circuitous form of Occidentalism whose power derives from its capacity to obscure the presence of the West and the operations through which it constitutes itself in opposition to others. Its mode of constructing cultural difference through subalterity rather than alterity reflects conditions that continue to contradict ideals of equality and universality, and yet open up the possibility for their fuller realization (Coronil 2000).

References

Amin, Samir. 1997. *Capitalism in the Age of Globalization: The Management of Contemporary Society*. London: Zed.

Armstrong, Nancy. 1990. "The Occidental Alice." *Differences* 2, no. 2: 3–40.

Carrier, James G. 1992. "Occidentalism: The World Turned Upside-down." *American Ethnologist* 19, no. 2: 195–212.

Chakrabarty, Dipesh. 1992. "Postcoloniality and the Artifice of History: Who Speaks for 'Indian' Pasts?" *Representations* 37: 1–37.

Chen, Xiaomei. 1992. "Occidentalism as Counterdiscourse: 'He Shang' in Post-Mao China." *Critical Inquiry* 18, no. 4: 686–712.

Coronil, Fernando. 1996. "Beyond Occidentalism: Toward Nonimperial Geohistorical Categories." *Cultural Anthropology* 11, no. 1: 51–87.

Coronil, Fernando. 2000. "Towards a Critique of Globalcentrism: Speculations on Capitalism's Nature." *Public Culture* 12: 351–74.

Dussel, Enrique. 1995. *El encubrimiento del otro: Hacia el orígen del mito de la modernidad*. Madrid: Nueva Utopia.

Fabian, Johannes. 1983. *Time and the Other: How Anthropology Makes Its Object*. New York: Columbia University Press.

Fernández Retamar, Roberto. 1976. "Nuestra América y Occidente." *Casa de la Américas* 98: 36–57.

Findley, Carter V, 1998. "An Ottoman Occidentalist in Europe: Ahmed Midhat Meets Madame Gulnar, 1889." *American Historical Review* 103, no. 1: 15–49.

Hanafi, Hassan. 1991. *Muqaddimah fi 'Ilm al-Istighrab*. Cairo: Dar al-Fanniyah.

Huntington, Samuel P. 1993. "The Clash of Civilizations?" *Foreign Affairs* 72, no. 3: 28–48.

Latouche, Serge. 1996. *The Westernization of the World*. Cambridge: Polity.

Mignolo, Walter. 1998. "Postoccidentalismo: El argumento desde la América Latina." In *Teorías sin disciplinas: Latinoamericanismo, poscolonialidad y globalización en debate*, ed. Santiago Castro-Gómez and Eduardo Mendieta, 31–58. Mexico City: Miguel Angel Porrúa.

Nader, Laura. 1989. "Orientalism, Occidentalism, and the Control of Women." *Cultural Dynamics* 2: 323–55.

Ning, Wang. 1997. "Orientalism versus Occidentalism?" *New Literary History* 28, no. 1: 57–67.

O'Gorman, Edmundo. 1958. *La invención de América: La universalización de la cultura occidental*. Mexico City: Universidad Nacional Autónoma de México.

Ortiz, Fernando. 1940. *Contrapunteo cubano del tabaco y el azúcar*. Havana: Jesús Montero.

Ortiz, Fernando. 1995. *Cuban Counterpoint: Tobacco and Sugar*. Durham, NC: Duke University Press.

Pletsch, Carl E. 1981. "The Three Worlds, or the Division of Social Scientific Labor, circa 1950–1975." *Comparative Studies in Society and History* 23, no. 4: 565–90.

Said, Edward W. 1978. *Orientalism*. New York: Pantheon.

Trouillot, Michel-Rolph. 1991. "Anthropology and the Savage Slot." In *Recapturing Anthropology: Working in the Present*, ed. Richard G. Fox, 17–44. Santa Fe, NM: School of American Research Press.

Wallerstein, Immanuel, et al. 1996. *Open the Social Sciences: Report of the Gulbenkian Commission on the Restructuring of the Social Sciences*. Stanford, CA: Stanford University Press.

12 Beyond Occidentalism:
Toward Nonimperial
Geohistorical Categories

Are you sure it is my name?
Have you got all my particulars?
Do you already know my navigable blood,
my geography full of dark mountains,
of deep and bitter valleys that are not on the map?
—Nicolás Guillén, "My Last Name"

A place on the map is also a place in history.
—Adrienne Rich, "Notes toward a Politics of Location"

Frantz Fanon begins the conclusion of *Black Skins, White Masks* with the following epigraph taken from Marx's *The Eighteenth Brumaire of Louis Bonaparte*:

The social revolution . . . cannot draw its poetry from the past, but only from the future. It cannot begin with itself before it has stripped itself of all its superstitions concerning the past. Earlier revolutions relied on memories out of world history in order to drug themselves against their own content. In order to find their own content, the revolutions of the nineteenth century have to let the dead bury the dead. Before, the expression exceeded the content; now the content exceeds the expression. (Fanon 1967: 223)

Imagining a future that builds on the past but is not imprisoned by its horror, Fanon visualized the making of a magnificent monument: "On the field of battle, its four corners marked by scores of Negroes hanged by their testicles, a monument is slowly built that promises to be majestic. And, at the top of this monument, I can already see a white man and a black man hand in hand" (Fanon 1967: 222).[1] Drawing his poetry from the future, Fanon sought to counter the deforming burden of racialist categories and to unsettle the desire to root identity in tradition in order to liberate both colonizer and colonized from the nightmare of their violent history.

In a shared utopian spirit, here I explore representational practices that portray non-Western peoples as the Other of a Western Self. By examining how these practices shape works of cultural criticism produced in metropolitan centers and subtly bind them to the object of their critique, I seek room for a decentered poetics that may help us imagine geohistorical categories for a nonimperial world.[2]

Imperial Maps

How to represent the contemporary world? Maps have often served as a medium for representing the world as well as for problematizing its representation. From Jorge Luis Borges's many mind-twisting stories involving maps, I remember the image of a map, produced under imperial command, that replicates the empire it represents. The map is of the same scale as the empire and coincides with it point for point. In this exact double of the empire's domain, each mountain, each castle, each person, and each grain of sand finds its precise copy. The map itself is thus included in the representation of the empire, leading to an infinite series of maps within maps. The unwieldy map is eventually abandoned and is worn away by the corrosive force of time even before the decline of the empire itself. Thus, history makes the map no longer accurate, or perhaps turns it into a hyperreal representation that prefigures the empire's dissolution.

Unlike cartographers' maps produced under imperial orders, the representations I wish to examine are discursive, not graphic, and seem to be the product of invisible hands laboring independently according to standards of scholarly practice and common sense. Yet they involve the use of a shared spatial imagery and have the strange effect of producing a remarkably consistent mental picture or map of the world. In everyday speech as much as in scholarly works, terms such as the "West," the "Occident," the "center," the "First World," the "East," the "Orient," the "periphery," and the "Third World" are commonly used to classify and identify areas of the world. Although it is not always clear to what these terms refer, they are used as if there existed a distinct external reality to which they corresponded, or at least they have the effect of creating such an illusion.

This effect is achieved in part by the associations they conjure up as a group of terms. Often combined into binary sets, these sets forge links in a paradigmatic chain of conceptions of geography, history, and personhood that reinforces each link and produces an almost tangible and inescapable image of the world. For instance, the West is often identified with Europe, the United States, us, or with that enigmatic entity, the modern Self. In practice, these paradigmatic elements are frequently interchangeable or synonymous, so that such terms as "We" or "Self" are often employed to mean Europe, the United States, or the West—and vice versa. The term "Third World," used since its creation during World War II to define the "underdeveloped" areas caught between the First (capitalist) and Second (socialist) worlds, has remained the preferred home for the Other.[3] Although many of these categories are of only recent origin, they have gained such widespread acceptance that they seem almost unavoidable. Drawing on the naturalizing imagery of geography, they have become second nature.

Despite the apparent fixity of their geographic referents, these categories have historically possessed remarkable fluidity. With postmodern élan, they have taken on various identities and have come to identify places and peoples far removed from their original territorial homes. Japan, until recently an emblem of the East, has increasingly been accepted as a member of the West in international organizations as well as in popular culture. Raymond Williams, in a discussion tracing the origins of the West-East distinction to the Roman Empire and to the separation between the Christian and Muslim worlds, argues that the West "has so far lost its geographical reference as to allow description of, for example, Japan as Western or Western-type society" (Williams 1983: 333). Noam Chomsky (1991: 13), in turn, explains, "I'm using the phrase 'Europe,' of course, as a metaphor. Europe includes and in fact is led by the former European colonies in the Western Hemisphere and Asia. And of course Europe now includes Japan, which we may regard as honorary European." Historians of Europe are still of many minds about the birth of "Europe" as a meaningful category and warn against the habit of reading history backward, extending the existence of present-day Europe into the past beyond a time when one could reasonably recognize its presence. The "Third World," for years firmly anchored in the "periphery"—that is, in Asia, Africa, and Latin America—seems now to be moving toward the United States, where the term is being applied not just to areas populated by migrants from the original "Third World" but to spaces inhabited by old domestic "minorities" such as "women of color" and to "underprivileged" ethnic and social groups. Los Angeles is increasingly referred to as "the capital of the Third World," a designation that also serves as the title of a recent book (Rieff 1991).

While one may wish to question the imperial conceit that lies behind this move to elect as the capital of the "Third World" a metropolitan city located within the territorial boundaries of the old First World, this ironic twist raises even more basic questions about the stability and meaning of these categories. If, like Chomsky's "Europe," these terms are used as metaphors, what are their original referents? Were they ever not metaphors? Yet, aren't these terms unavoidable precisely because they seem to designate tangible entities in the world, because they appear to be as natural as nature itself? In the face of their slippery fluidity, should our task be, as in the case of Borges's imperial map, to construct a perfect map by finding words that faithfully match reality "out there" point for point? And if we managed to freeze history and replicate geography in a map, wouldn't this representation be ephemeral? Since space too is located in time and is changing constantly, how could a map represent geography without apprehending its movement? But perhaps this shows that maps do not mirror reality but depict it from partial perspectives, figuring it in accordance with particular standpoints and specific aims.

Within academia, the growing awareness of the limitations and ideological bias of the three worlds schema as a "primitive system of classification" (Pletsch 1981) has not stopped or significantly altered its almost inescapable use. The common practice among some scholars of indicating discomfort with the categories of this classificatory scheme by means of quotes or explicit caveats only confirms its stability and the lack of an alternative taxonomy. If we were to choose not to employ the term "Third World," would we be better served by such categories as "the underdeveloped world," "backward areas," or the euphemism "developing nations"? As soon as new conceptions are constructed, as in the case of the call by the South Commission presided over by Julius Nyerere to promote a "new world order," they seem to be resituated within the semantic field defined by the old binary structure, as was the case when George Bush appropriated this phrase months after it was formulated to create his own version of a "new world order" during the rhetorical war that preceded the Gulf War (Chomsky 1991: 13). The shrinking of the Second World has not dissolved the three world scheme, only realigned its terms. Thus, a noted journalist can say straightforwardly that the "Evil Empire turned out to be a collection of third-world countries" (Quindlen 1994).

With the consolidation of U.S. hegemony as a world power after 1945, the "West" shifted its center of gravity from Europe to "America," and the United States became the dominant referent for the "West." Because of this recentering of Western powers, "America," ironically, is at times a metaphor for "Europe." Perhaps one day Japan, today's "honorary European," will become the center of the West. In this string of historical turns, it is another historic irony, as well as a pun, that what began as an accident—the discovery of America as the "Eastern Indies"—gave birth to the Occident. Columbus, sailing from the west to reach the east, ended up founding the West. Perhaps if one day Japan becomes the West, and today's West recedes to the East, it will turn out that Columbus indeed reached, as he insisted, the East.

Given the intimate association between Europe and Empire, it is significant that in colonial and postcolonial studies Europe is primarily equated with the nations of its northwestern region. This exclusion of southern Europe is accompanied by the analytical neglect of Spain and Portugal as pioneering colonial powers that profoundly transformed practices of rule and established modular forms of empire that influenced the imperial expansion of Holland, England, and France. So ingrained has the association between European colonialism and northern Europe become that some analysts identify colonialism with its northern European expression (Klor de Alva 1992), thus excluding the first centuries of Spanish and Portuguese control in the Americas.

The Politics of Epistemology:
From Orientalism to Occidentalism

The problem of evaluating the categories with which the world is represented was compellingly faced by Edward Said in *Orientalism* (1979), a pathbreaking work that raised to a higher level the discussion of colonial discourse in the United States. I propose to advance a related argument concerning Western representations of cultural difference that focuses on the politics of geohistorical categories.

In *Orientalism*, Said defines Orientalism as taking three interdependent forms: the study of the Orient; a "style of thought based upon an epistemological and ontological distinction made between the 'Orient' and (most of the time) the 'Occident'"; and a corporate institution dealing with the Orient (Said 1979: 2–3). While Said's discussion of each of these forms relates Orientalism to the exercise of power, his major concern is the connection between modern Orientalism and colonialism. Yet at times Said's discussion ambiguously moves between an abstract conception of the inevitable partiality of any representation and a historically situated critique of the limits of specific representations as the effect of unequal power relations. This unresolved tension may create the impulse to approach the gap between Western representations of the Orient and the "real" Orient by searching for more complete maps without inquiring into the sources of partiality of Orientalist representations.

Said confronted the ambiguity of his formulation in "Orientalism Reconsidered" (1986), written in response to the persistence of Orientalist representations in works produced by critics of imperialism. He called for an inclusion of "Orientalists" as part of the study of Orientalism, "because the social world includes the person or subject doing the studying as well as the object or realm being studied, it is imperative to include them both in any consideration of Orientalism" (Said 1986: 211).

For Said, the inclusion of the Orientalists entails a fundamental critique of the forms of Western knowledge informing their works in the following terms:

> What, in other words, has never taken place is an epistemological critique at the most fundamental level of the connection between the development of a historicism which has expanded and developed enough to include antithetical attitudes such as ideologies of western imperialism and critiques of imperialism on the one hand and, on the other, the actual practice of imperialism by which the accumulation of territories and population, the control of economies, and the incorporation and homogenization of histories are maintained. If we keep this in mind we will remark, for example, that in the methodological assumptions and practice of world history—which is ideologically anti-imperialist— little or no attention is given to those cultural practices like Orientalism or ethnography affiliated with imperialism, which in genealogical fact fathered world history itself; hence the emphasis in world history as a discipline has been on economic and political practices, defined by the processes of world historical writing, as in a sense separate and different from, as well as unaffected by, the knowledge of them which world history produces. The curious result is that the theories of accumulation on a world scale, or the capitalist world state, or lineages of absolutism depend (a) on the same displaced percipient and historicist observer who had been an Orientalist or colonial traveler three generations ago; (b) they depend also on a homogenizing and incorporating world historical scheme that assimilated non-synchronous developments, histories, cultures and peoples to it; and (c) they block and keep

down latent epistemological critiques of the institutional, cultural and disciplinary instruments linking the incorporative practice of world history with partial knowledges like Orientalism on the one hand and, on the other, with continued western hegemony of the non-European, peripheral world. (Said 1986: 223–24)

This provocative challenge invites multiple responses. Here I propose to move beyond a predominantly epistemological critique of Western knowledge cast in its own terms toward a political understanding of the constitution of the "West" that encompasses an examination of its categorical system. To the extent that "the West" remains assumed in Said's work, I believe that Said's challenge, and the ambiguity in his discussion of Orientalism, may be creatively approached by problematizing and linking the two entities that lie at the center of his analysis: the West's Orientalist representations and the West itself.

I wish to take a step in this direction by relating Western representations of "Otherness" to the implicit constructions of "Selfhood" that underwrite them. This move entails reorienting our attention from the problematic of "Orientalism," which focuses on the deficiencies of the West's representations of the Orient, to that of "Occidentalism," which refers to the conceptions of the West animating these representations. It entails relating the observed to the observers, products to production, knowledge to its sites of formation. I would then welcome Said's call to include "Orientalists" in our examination, but I will refer to them as "Occidentalists" in order to emphasize that I am primarily interested in the concerns and images of the Occident that underwrite their representations of non-Western societies, whether in the Orient or elsewhere. This perspective does not involve a reversal of focus from Orient to Occident, from Other to Self. Rather, by guiding our understanding toward the relational nature of representations of human collectivities, it brings out into the open their genesis in asymmetrical relations of power, including the power to obscure their genesis in inequality, to sever their historical connections, and thus to present as the internal and separate attributes of bounded entities what are in fact historical outcomes of connected peoples.

Occidentalism, as I define it here, is thus not the reverse of Orientalism but its condition of possibility, its dark side (as in a mirror). A simple reversal would be possible only in the context of symmetrical relations between "Self" and "Other"—but then who would be the "Other"? In the context of equal relations, difference would not be cast as Otherness. The study of how "Others" represent the "Occident" is an interesting enterprise in itself that may help counter the West's dominance of publicly circulating images of difference. Calling these representations "Occidentalist" serves to restore some balance and has relativizing effects.[4] Given Western hegemony, however, opposing this notion of "Occidentalism" to "Orientalism" runs the risk of creating the illusion that the terms can be equalized and reversed, as if the complicity of power and knowledge entailed in Orientalism could be countered by an inversion.

What is unique about Occidentalism, as I define it here, is not that it mobilizes stereotypical representations of non-Western societies, for the ethnocentric hierarchization of cultural difference is certainly not a Western privilege, but that this privilege is intimately connected to the deployment of global power. In a broad-ranging discussion of constructions of cultural difference, John Comaroff defines ethnicity, in contrast to totemism, as a classificatory system founded on asymmetrical relations among unequal groups and reminds us that "classification, the meaningful construction of the world, is a necessary condition of social existence," yet the "marking of identities" is always the product of history and expresses particular modes of establishing cultural and economic difference (Comaroff 1987: 303–5). As a system of classification that expresses forms of cultural and economic difference in the modern world, Occidentalism is inseparably tied to the constitution of international asymmetries underwritten by global capitalism. Linking Eurocentrism to capitalism, Samir Amin (1989: vii) argues that "Eurocentrism is thus not a banal ethnocentrism testifying simply to the limited horizons beyond which no people on this planet has truly been able to go. Eurocentrism is a specifically modern phenomenon."[5]

While classificatory systems may construct the relations among their terms as unidirectional, in effect they always entail different forms of mutuality. Noting that Said has not analyzed the impact of Orientalist images upon the people who use them, Nancy Armstrong has shown how Occidentalism involves the formation of specific forms of racialized and gendered Western Selves as the effect of Orientalist representations of non-Western Others.[6] In my view, Occidentalism is inseparable from Western hegemony not only because as a form of knowledge it expresses Western power, but because it establishes a specific bond between knowledge and power in the West. Occidentalism is thus the expression of a constitutive relationship between Western representations of cultural difference and worldwide Western dominance.

Challenging Orientalism, I believe, requires that Occidentalism be unsettled as a style of representation that produces polarized and hierarchical conceptions of the West and its Others and makes them central figures in accounts of global and local histories. In other words, by "Occidentalism" I refer to the ensemble of representational practices that participate in the production of conceptions of the world, which (1) separate the world's components into bounded units; (2) disaggregate their relational histories; (3) turn difference into hierarchy; (4) naturalize these representations; and thus (5) intervene, however unwittingly, in the reproduction of existing asymmetrical power relations.

Three Occidentalist Representational Modalities

In response to Said's call to deepen the critique of Orientalism, I discuss three modes of Occidentalist representation and illustrate my argument with examples taken from texts that have played a significant role in the contemporary critique of imperialism. I do not set these examples against ideal non-Occidentalist texts, for my argument concerns implicit assumptions that influence intellectual agendas and cultural habits everywhere, whether in the center or the periphery. At the risk of simplifying their arguments, I select certain elements of these works in order to discuss three Occidentalist representational modalities: the dissolution of the Other by the Self; the incorporation of the Other into the Self; and the destabilization of the Self by the Other.[7]

The Dissolution of the Other by the Self

In this modality of representation, Western and non-Western cultures are opposed to each other as radically different entities, and their opposition is resolved by absorbing non-Western peoples into an expanding and victorious West. I discuss this mode by analyzing the transformation of Hegel's dialectic between Master and Slave into Tzvetan Todorov's interaction between Self and Other in *The Conquest of America: The Question of the Other* ([1974] 1984).

Perhaps more than any other body of thought, Hegel's philosophy of history has influenced the entire political gamut of modern Western interpretations of world development. For the purposes of this essay, I sketch the geopolitics of Hegel's thought so as to relate his discussion of the dialectic between Master (Self) and Slave (Other) in *The Phenomenology of Mind*

(1967) to his ideas concerning the historical place of Europe, America, Africa, and Asia that he put forth in *Lectures on the Philosophy of History* (1975). In these writings, we can see the emergence of a map of the world that continues to define the Western political imaginary.

In *The Phenomenology of Mind*, Hegel argues that the "World Spirit" is realized through the dialectic between Self and Other. Consciousness of Self, achieved through recognition by the Other, makes possible the movement of the World Spirit by means of dialectical transformations through which distinct forms of consciousness mutually constitute each other as spiritual forms and as historical objectifications. Europe, or the Old World, as Hegel (1975: 171) makes clear in *Lectures on the Philosophy of History*, is "the setting of world history," the stage upon which the embodiment of the universal spirit is objectified as History. "The world," he says, "is divided into the Old and the New." America is "new" not only because it has "recently come to be known by Europeans." Rather, "The New World is not just relatively new, but absolutely so, by virtue of its wholly peculiar character in both physical and political respects" (Hegel 1975: 162). America's fauna, he argues, following Buffon, was primitive and weak: "Even the animals show the same inferiority as the human beings. The fauna of America includes lions, tigers, and crocodiles, but although they are otherwise similar to their equivalents in the Old World, they are in every respect smaller, weaker, and less powerful" (Hegel 1975: 163). Because of America's immaturity, its civilizations, as in Mexico and Peru, had no lasting significance, for its culture was "purely natural which had to perish as soon as the spirit approached it" (Hegel 1975: 162). According to Hegel, "America has always shown itself physically and spiritually impotent, and it does so to this day. For after the Europeans had landed there, the natives were gradually destroyed by the breath of European activity" (Hegel 1975: 163).

Hegel classifies the three continents of the Old World according to cultural principles drawn from distinctions attributed to three geographical areas: uplands regions, broad river valleys, and coastal lands. Since for him these geographical distinctions characterize the three continents of the Old World, he feels he can "classify these according to which of the three principles are dominant within them":

> Africa, generally speaking, is the continent in which the upland principle, the principle of cultural backwardness, predominates. Asia, on the other hand, is the continent in which the great antitheses come into conflict, although its distinguishing feature is the second principle,

that of the broad river valleys; these support a culture which broods for ever within itself. The totality consists in the union of all three principles, and this is to be found in Europe, the continent in which the spirit is united with itself, and which, while retaining its own solid substance, has embarked upon that infinite process whereby culture is realised in practice. (Hegel 1975: 172)

Hegel recognizes that Asia is older than Europe and presents it as the continent where "the ethical world of political consciousness first arose." It is, he argues, "the continent of sunrise and of origins in general" where "the light of the spirit, the consciousness of a universal, first emerged, and with it the process of world history" (Hegel 1975: 191). He also acknowledges that the cardinal points are relative: "Admittedly, every country is both east and west in relation to others, so that Asia is the western continent from the point of view of America" (Hegel 1975: 190–91). Yet he asserts the centrality of Europe as the heir and apex of ancient civilization: "But just as Europe is the centre and end of the Old World—i.e. absolutely the west—so also is Asia absolutely the east" (Hegel 1975: 190–91). While geography makes cardinal distinctions relative, history renders them absolute: "World history has an absolute east, although the term east in itself is wholly relative; for although the earth is a sphere, history does not move in a circle around it, but has a definite eastern extremity, i.e. Asia" (Hegel 1975: 197). East and West are thus defined by the convergence of the geographical and the historical, the natural and the moral. While the east is "where the external and physical sun rises" and the west is where "it sets," it is in the west "that the inner sun of self-consciousness, which emits a higher radiance, makes its further ascent. World history imposes a discipline on the unrestrained natural will, guiding it towards universality and subjective freedom" (Hegel 1975: 197). Through Hegel's pen, the Spirit draws a map that produces a now familiar image of the world: "World history travels from east to west; for Europe is the absolute end of history, just as Asia is the beginning" (Hegel 1975: 197).

Although Hegel's dialectic engages Master and Slave in intimate reciprocity, one of the consequences of Hegel's Eurocentric view of history is that the unfolding of the dialectic is confined to the West; the non-West remains fundamentally external to it. This regional focus is reproduced, although in attenuated form, in the most influential elaboration of Hegel's model, Marx's vision of the universal movement of capitalism. Thus, in Marx's view of history, the emancipatory dialectical relationship between capitalist and worker also unfolds within the advanced capitalist nations of Europe.

But whereas for Marx non-European societies underwrite the development of European nations through colonialism, primitive accumulation, and world trade, for Hegel these peripheral societies have limited significance for the moment of history. Fanon perceptively noted how the Hegelian dialectic loses its generative power as it leaves Europe and embraces peoples of darker complexion. According to Fanon, Hegel's dialectical understanding of the Master-Slave relation does not apply to race relations as defined in center-periphery interactions, for in colonial slavery "the master differs basically from the master described by Hegel. For Hegel there is reciprocity: here the master laughs at the consciousness of the slave. What he wants from the slave is not recognition, but work" (Fanon 1967: 220).

Ever since Hegel cast his Eurocentric conception of the evolution of universal history in terms of a struggle between Master and Slave, there have been numerous attempts to sociologize his philosophical categories and historicize his ontology of history. Most works that transpose the Master-Slave scheme to historical situations preserve Hegel's Eurocentric bias while vulgarizing his dialectic and essentializing his philosophical categories. In this vulgarized sense of the dialectic, Todorov's The Conquest of America is implicitly a Hegelian work. It recounts how European Selves (presented as universal Selves) learn to deal with Otherness through the experience of the conquest, destruction, and domination of Mesoamericans.

Seen as a normative injunction, this learning has a seemingly laudable end: confronting Otherness should mean that Others are treated as different but equal. However, this norm takes for granted the imperial categories of Selfhood and Otherness that are the preconditions of this learning. In Hegel, this learning takes place through the long movement of history, and its lessons are internal to the "West." In Todorov's account of the relationship between Self and Other, there is no dialectic in the Hegelian sense, only an interaction between discrete actors. He presents Mesoamericans as a homogeneous mass, incapable of reacting to novelty and trapped in an oral culture. Their monological existence is defined by immutable codes that condemn them to the mere reproduction of their world until rescued into history by Western intervention. He presents Europeans, in contrast, as history's agents. Capable of historical action, innovation, and self-transformation, their dialogical self-identities are constantly transformed on expanding historical terrains. Through the experience of dominating others and learning about their cultures, Europeans learn about themselves and become capable of relativizing their perspective. Through this interaction between knowledge and conquest, they become capable of turning violence into love and domination into communication. In Todorov's account, Selfhood is an attribute that identifies history's victors; the West is the space they occupy.

Todorov, like Hegel, celebrates the Self-Other polarity because it is through the clash of its poles that historical progress takes place. But while for Hegel the struggle between Self and Other entails their mutual transformation, for Todorov the confrontation between Europeans and Mesoamericans must lead to the destruction or Westernization of native Americans. The "hybridization" of Mesoamericans means in reality their Europeanization, the abandonment and destruction of their original cultures. The "hybridization" of Europeans, in contrast, means the evolution of Western culture through its encompassment of other cultures. The West is a name for history's victors. "There is an odd double standard here which in effect makes it impossible for the West to lose or the Other to win which is built into the logic of the West" (Hayden 1991: 21). Europeans need Mesoamericans in order to discover who they are. Thus, the discovery and conquest of America is fundamentally the discovery and making of "Europe" and of the Western "Self." Historical progress takes place not with, but at the expense of, others.

Although Todorov's intent is to analyze European reactions to Mesoamericans, his work is subtitled *The Question of the Other*. The question of the Other is presented as a problem *for* the Self, not *of* the Self or for the Other. In this modality of Occidentalism, the Self is assumed. Analysis centers on the problems the Self confronts but does not include the constitution of the Self as a problem. The other question is not asked: the question of the Self.

In this representational modality, America becomes but the territorial stage for the expansion of the West, and its diverse cultures the object to be absorbed. Since the Self is identified with history's victors, it is understandable that the increasingly powerful United States was identified with America and became a metaphor for Europe. In contrast, in Latin America the term "America" refers first to the entire continent and "Americans" to its inhabitants, although those continuing to be identified as members of native societies are often dismissed as "indios" and excluded from this geocultural category. In the United States, this exclusion of native populations takes no less insidious forms. President Ronald Reagan's historical reflection on Native Americans places the benevolent modern Self on the side of history, willing to incorporate those who are not: "Maybe we made a mistake. Maybe we should not have humored them in that—wanting to stay in that kind of primitive life style. Maybe we should have said, 'no, come join us. Be citizens along with the rest of us'" (quoted in "Moscow Summit" 1988).

The Incorporation of the Other into the Self

In this second modality of Occidentalism, a critical focus on Western development unwittingly obscures the role of non-Western peoples in the making of the modern world, subtly reiterating the distinction between Other and Self that underwrites Europe's imperial expansion. I develop this argument through a discussion of Eric Wolf's *Europe and the People without History* (1982), which presents Western capitalism as a transformative process that originates in the center and engulfs non-Western peoples, and Sidney Mintz's *Sweetness and Power: The Place of Sugar in Modern History* (1985), which analyzes sugar's place in the modern world in terms of the interplay between commodity production in the colonies and consumption in the imperial center.

While Todorov excludes Mesoamericans from history, Wolf brings non-Western peoples into the Self's history. His important book ambitiously traces the evolution of mercantile and capitalist development from the fifteenth century to the twentieth century, focusing on the production of a number of key primary products throughout the world. Against the atomistic view of the world as an aggregate of independent, thing-like entities, reinforced by the reified categories of conventional social science, Wolf proposes a historical perspective that seeks to represent the unitary character of world history. The central metaphor informing his critique of prevailing conceptions of global history is the image of the world as a pool table in which isolated units bounce against each other without being affected internally by their collision:

> By turning names into things we create false models of reality. By endowing nations, societies, or cultures with the qualities of internally homogeneous and externally distinctive and bounded objects, we create a model of the world as a global pool hall in which the entities spin off each other like so many hard and round billiard balls. Thus it becomes easy to sort the world into differently colored balls, to declare that "East is East, and West is West, and never the twain shall meet." In this way a quintessential West is counterposed to an equally quintessential East,

where life was cheap and slavish multitudes groveled under a variety of despotisms. (Wolf 1982: 6–7)

Wolf's alternative interpretation seeks to make visible the interaction between worldwide structural transformations and local changes. Since his book presents capitalism as a global system engendered by the metropolitan centers, the interaction between macro- and micro-levels is presented as equivalent to that between cause and effect. In Wolf's words, he "hopes to delineate the general processes at work in mercantile and capitalist development, while at the same time following their effects on the micro-populations studied by the ethnohistorians and anthropologists" (Wolf 1982: 23).

Following this provocative introduction, Wolf's analysis proceeds as an account of the inexorable movement of capitalism from center to periphery. Capitalism, understood as a process of production of commodities in which labor itself becomes a commodity, originates in Europe and moves to other territories, transforming them into colonies or outposts for the production of a few primary goods. As capitalism expands, various precapitalist societies are transformed and rearranged in order to fulfill the requirements of capitalist production. One by one, the production of specific commodities—wheat, sugar, coffee, gold, diamonds, meat, and so on—comes to reorder and determine the fate of precapitalist societies. Their incorporation into the capitalist market means their entrance into history.

In this analysis, the interaction between Europe and its Others is largely restricted to the transformation of precapitalist societies under the impact of capitalist production. While Wolf starkly depicts its fundamental asymmetry, his account of this interaction gives the impression that agency is located predominantly at one end. "If the world is a 'global pool hall,' the European billiard ball is composed of solid steel while those of non-Europeans are of the flimsiest papier-mâché; in the aftermath of collision, Europe continues on course unscathed, while the other party is utterly transformed (or brutalized)" (Herron 1991: 2). There is little mutuality in this conception of interaction; the capitalist steel ball stamps its mark upon the places it traverses without being significantly affected by them. As the capitalist steel ball moves toward new territories, commodity production takes place in predictable patterns.

Perhaps because of his zeal to critique the power of capitalism, Wolf focuses his discussion on the global impact of commodity production. Yet the peoples and societies producing these commodities or affected by their production are largely absent, save as another commodity, labor power. In contrast to works in which Wolf has compellingly analyzed the cultural transformations of colonized societies, in this book the narrative focuses on the inexorable movement of capitalism as a system of production of things, obscuring how capitalism itself is the product of human activity. Thus, the history of the peoples without history appears as the story of a history without people. Not even Europe seems populated, for in this account "Europe" is a metaphor for capitalism. The story of capitalism as a self-expanding system becomes history.

Like Wolf, Mintz, in *Sweetness and Power*, examines capitalism as a system of production of commodities for the market. Mintz focuses on one product, sugar, and two processes, production and consumption. The book neatly moves from sugar production in the West Indies to its consumption in England. In certain respects, this narrowing of focus gives this work a particularly deep scope, for Mintz is able to show how England itself was affected by developments in its colonies. By carefully examining changing patterns of colonial sugar production and imperial sugar consumption, he provides a textured image of how the increasing availability of sugar in Europe as a result of the development of plantation economies in the colonies affected changing patterns of metropolitan consumption, including the cultural understandings attached to sugar as it ceased to be an elite product and became a staple for the laboring classes. He also points out that plantation sugar production set a model for the organization of factory production in England. This suggests that the development of industrial capitalism in England could be reconceptualized not only as the result of domestic transformation of production and of the division of labor (the classic story of the internal breakdown of feudalism, the evolution of the putting out system first into manufacture, then into machinofacture, and so on) but also as the expression of the spatially separate but historically related process of colonial domination.

While Mintz's discussion of sugar production and consumption offers a compelling view of the interaction between colonies and metropolitan centers, he does not justify the basic theoretical and organizational scheme that informs his account: production in the colonies, consumption in the center. This division is taken for granted, as if the colonies' relation to sugar could be reduced to their role as producers for the imperial center, or as if the consumption of sugar would take place only in England. What happened to sugar in the colonies? How was it consumed, both by the elites and the laboring classes? What meanings were attached to the commodity upon which the life of the colony depended? Why do we see pictures in the book of a variety of candied treats in Europe—for instance, such imperial "sweets" as a bust of George V, a replica of the royal state coach, the cathedral of Notre Dame, even a life-size chocolate female nude lying on a bed of six hundred sugar roses—but only one picture of sweets in the colonies, the photograph of fantastic candy skulls, tombs, and wreaths prepared in Mexico for El Día de los Muertos (All Saints' Day, or "the Day of the Dead"). In a brief explanation of that photograph, Mintz (1985: 185) tells us that "the artistic and ritual association between sugar and death is not a Mexican monopoly; in much of Europe, candied funeral treats are popular." Throughout the book, Mintz only occasionally notes the place of sugar in the colonies as an item of consumption. For instance, he comments that sugar consumption in old sugar colonies such as Jamaica was substantial, for "slaves were given sugar, molasses and even rum as part of their rations" (Mintz 1985: 72). Yet these brief references only create a desire for a more extended discussion of the local consumption of sugar. Given this lack, it is difficult to understand the multiple meanings of sugar in Caribbean societies, to sense its evocatory power, such as when Celia Cruz, the great Cuban singer who popularized Caribbean music throughout the world, punctuates her songs with her inimitable exclamation "¡Azúcar!" (Sugar!). But since sugar was fundamentally produced for export, it is particularly important to ask: was sugar consumed in the colonies only as sugar?

Sugar was also consumed as money. Given the double character of commodities as use values and exchange values, it may thus be helpful, particularly in colonial and neocolonial contexts, not to restrict the analysis of commodities to their use value—that is, to their consumption as sensuous things endowed with particular attributes and utility. What would happen if sugar and other commodities were analyzed also as exchange values, as material vehicles for capturing "hard" metropolitan currencies—that is, as export commodities whose dominant function is to serve as means of exchange? The examination of their "consumption" would entail an analysis of how they are transformed into money, and specifically into international currency. If we analyze the process by which the value of these colonial commodities is realized through their transformation into money, we could then take another step and see how these commodities circulate as money in both metropolitan and colonial societies. Since the value of money is realized through its transformation into other commodities, we could extend this analysis further and include as well the uses to which sugar money is put.

In this expanded sense of the consumption of commodities, sugar, as sugar money, was "consumed" in multiple forms: it purchased the accoutrements of social status for an emerging class; it supported, through taxation and other means, the imperial state and its outposts in the colonies; and, as capital (that is, transformed into means of production), it contributed to the expansion of capitalism at home and abroad. Its consumption as capital is most significant, because as self-expanding value it had a multiplier effect. Sugar money fueled the slave trade, turning millions of people into commodities, carving the path for their forced migration, creating conditions for the formation of plantation societies built around the massive production of a single product, and making the fortunes of these people depend upon the shifting demand and volatile price sugar commanded in changing world markets.

Given this emphasis on sugar's exchange value, it becomes necessary to discern how the price of sugar is determined. A common view, of course, is that the price of commodities results from the play of supply and demand. Yet there are additional social and political dimensions that intervene in the formation of price, for "price" is a complex category that reflects struggle and competition among the many social actors involved in the production and exchange of commodities. The effort to see the mechanisms of price formation as unfolding not just in the market, regarded as a separate domain, but within society as a whole distinguishes a Marxist perspective. Taking this perspective, we may see how "sugar money," as the expression of the metamorphosis of sugar into value, is an index of multiple social relationships.

As is well known, Marx, in response to certain ambiguities in Adam Smith's theory of value, argued that total surplus value, as the exclusive product of labor power, is divided among profits for capitalists, rents for landowners, and wages for workers (in the case of slaves, the cost of their reproduction). According to his analysis, profits and rents do not reflect the proportional contribution of capital and land to the price of commodities, as Smith suggested, but the social power of capitalists and landowners. Marx argued that the competition among different forms of capital and the struggle among opposing social classes affect not only the distribution of surplus value but also the level of market prices. Landowners, by demanding a rent, influence the level of prices. By directing our attention to land-ground rent, we may link readily observable and quantifiable measures, such as the level of supply and demand, to the more opaque but no less significant worldwide power relations affecting the determination of commodity prices.

I believe that our understanding of colonial histories would be enhanced by taking fuller advantage of the category of "land-ground rent." Marx (1981: 953) felt that this category together with "capital-profit" and "labor-wages" formed the "trinity" that "holds in itself all the mysteries of the social production process," a strong claim even for Marx, yet one that he supported with laborious scholarship.[8] Given the intellectual and political climate of our postmodern times, few may wish to accompany me in regarding these tools as useful. Yet I believe that what is at stake is not a trivial technical matter but the possibility of analyzing capitalist production as a totalizing social process that involves the increasing commodification of social life and the simultaneous production of things and of social relations. Of course, the danger in using tools that claim to have such general applicability is that they may homogenize and flatten what are distinct historical terrains. However, if these tools are used flexibly—as a broom rather than a hammer—they may clear the ground and reveal how each society is affected by particular forms of commodification.

The recognition of the centrality of ground rent for capitalism should lead to a different view of colonial and imperial histories and of capitalism itself. It entails the inclusion of "land" (by which Marx meant all the powers of nature) as well as of the social agents identified with it, in particular the state as the sovereign representative of a national territory. As Henri Lefebvre has argued, a focus on the commodification of land together with that of labor and capital—Marx's "trinity" formula—should displace the capital-labor relation from the ossified centrality it has been made to occupy by Marxist theory (Lefebvre 1974). This shift from a binary to a triadic dialectic expands the geographical and social referents of capitalism and decenters Eurocentric conceptions that reduce its development to a dialectic of capital and labor originating in advanced "centers" and engulfing a passive "periphery." Rather than homogenizing capitalism, this global perspective should bring out its contradictions and complexity, showing how its totalizing impulse is only partially fulfilled and making visible the social spaces that lie outside its control.[9]

Few anthropologists have contributed as much as Wolf and Mintz to the understanding of the links between colonial and imperial histories. With respect to the books discussed here, whereas Wolf's broad vision reveals patterns in the global movement of capitalist expansion, Mintz's concentrated focus makes visible the dynamic interaction between colonial production and metropolitan consumption. As much by what they accomplish as by what they leave uncharted, their works show that if we examine commodities in their double life as objects of utility and sources of exchange, we can see how their multiple transfigurations are part of a wider social metamorphosis that necessarily involves the production of social relations. Since the agents involved in commodity production do not appear ready-made on history's stage but are constituted by their activity, a comprehensive study of colonial commodities must address as well the production of the social agents that participate in their production.

In this respect, we may find instructive *Cuban Counterpoint: Tobacco and Sugar* ([1940] 1995), written by the Cuban anthropologist Fernando Ortiz, a pioneering work that sees sugar and tobacco as windows into Cuban history. Ortiz develops the concept of "transculturation" in order to grasp the reciprocally transformative character of cultural encounters under colonialism, as opposed to the unidirectional concepts of "acculturation" and "cultural contact" prevailing in British and U.S. anthropology in the 1930s.[10] Weaving together various theoretical perspectives and narrative modalities, Ortiz shows how sugar and tobacco are elements in an ongoing interaction across cultural boundaries that involves the mutual production of commodities and society. His treatment of commodities offers an unusual understanding of the intimate links between colonial commodity production and the making of colonial societies.

Treating commodities as complex hieroglyphs, Marx focused on the mystery of exchange value and dealt but tangentially with the complexities of use value. For some years now, there has been a move away from Marx's concern with the relationship between exchange value and value. Some steps in this reorientation have been taken by Jean Baudrillard, who has insisted on the need to problematize use value as part of a more sweeping critique of Marxist epistemology, and by the cultural studies approach, which has brought the study of consumption to the foreground. Perhaps the strongest departure, however, has come from the field of economics. Treating the labor theory of value as either wrong or irrelevant, neoclassical as well as some Marxist economists have reduced exchange value to price and have treated price as a measure that can be readily derived from quantitative data concerning supply, demand, and technology.[11] It is worth remembering, however, that just as "use" is not a natural but a cultural category, "price" is not merely an "economic" but a political measure, and neither term can be understood independently of the other or outside their common involvement in the history of capitalism's global expansion.

The expansive, boundary-crossing impulse of capitalist production struck thinkers who witnessed the early period of British colonial domination.

John Stuart Mill recognized, from an imperial perspective, the intimate connection between England and its colonies:

> These are hardly to be looked upon as countries, carrying on an exchange of commodities with other countries, but more properly, as outlying agricultural or manufacturing estates belonging to a larger community. Our West Indian colonies, for example, cannot be regarded as countries with a productive capital of their own [but are, rather,] the place where England finds it convenient to carry on the production of sugar, coffee and a few other tropical commodities. All the capital employed is English capital; almost all the industry is carried on for English uses; there is little production of anything except for staple commodities, and these are sent to England, not to be exchanged for things exported to the colony and consumed by its inhabitants, but to be sold in England for the benefit of proprietors there. The trade with the West Indies is hardly to be considered an external trade, but more resembles the traffic between town and country. (Quoted in Mintz 1985: 42)

Mill illuminates certain aspects of the relations between empire and colony ("the traffic between town and country") yet obscures not only the violent nature of these connections but also many of their specific manifestations. This treatment of colonies as the empire's "hinterland," according to Raymond Williams, is an ideological transposition to the international level of the mystifying country and city model. In his pathbreaking *The Country and the City* (1973), Williams argues that the representation of the divisions between country and city should be seen as the result of a unified process by which social practices and forms of consciousness are at once mutually constituted and become separated and opposed. The cultural construction of urban and rural sectors tends to abstract their features and to give them a metaphysical status, presenting domains that are social and interrelated as if they were natural and autonomous. Williams's work suggests that we examine the historical encodings of country and city so that we may trace the hidden connections that reside within these concepts. His observation that "one of the last models of the 'city and the country' is the system we now know as imperialism" (Williams 1973: 279) directs our attention to the links between colonial centers and colonized peripheries. "At the global level we may observe the same ideological concealment that operates domestically: a tendency to obscure the mutually constitutive relationship between center ('city') and periphery ('country') and to represent them as separate entities whose characteristics appear as the consequence of intrinsic attributes" (Skurski and Coronil 1992: 233). Just as viewing England's colonies as its "countryside" was for Mill a natural fact of empire building, treating Latin America as the United States' "backyard" is a ruling assumption of official ideology and political practice, as when President Bill Clinton, in describing U.S. vital interests in Haiti, stated, "First of all, it's in our backyard."[12]

So pervasive was the impact of colonial production on the international division of labor and on the constitution of colonial societies that even after independence these nations have continued to depend on primary export production. As independent republics, most of these ex-colonies have instituted projects of national development designed to promote economic diversification. But since these modernizing projects are typically financed by foreign exchange obtained through the export of primary products, they often have the paradoxical effect of intensifying the production of traditional export commodities, thereby recasting the old colonial role of these societies in the international division of labor as primary producers. Neocolonialism thus follows postcolonialism. In this respect, the "post" of postcolonialism is not a sign of the overcoming but of the reproduction of colonialism.

It is thus understandable that the present worldwide turn toward free market economics, with its command to erect the market as the source of the natural and the rational, has led to the reprimarization of many economies whose partial diversification had been achieved through state protectionism, which is now seen as the locus of the artificial and irrational. It is being rediscovered, with a convenient mixture of historical amnesia and imperial nostalgia, that the comparative advantage of the ex-colonies lies in their colonial role as sources of cheap labor and raw materials. These neoliberal policies assume a view of nations as independent units, whose transformation and historical progress depend on internal "adjustments."

Focusing on the dynamic exchange between metropolitan and (neo)colonial societies would lead to a less dichotomous view of their identities and to a unifying conception of capitalism. Rather than the West molding its Others, the emerging image would reveal hidden connections obscured within these imperial dichotomies.

The Destabilization of Self by Other

While in the previous two modalities of Occidentalism non-Western peoples are either dissolved or incorporated by the West, in this third form they are presented as a privileged source of knowledge for the West. This knowledge becomes available, as in the first modality, by opposing Western and non-Western peoples as contrasting entities, but in this case the depiction of radical Otherness is used to unsettle Western culture. By examining Michael Taussig's *The Devil and Commodity Fetishism in South America* (1980) and Timothy Mitchell's *Colonising Egypt* (1988), I wish to show how the use of polarized contrasts between cultures that are historically interrelated has the effect of exalting their difference, erasing their historical links, and homogenizing their internal features, unwittingly reinscribing an imperial Self-Other duality even as it seeks to unsettle colonial representations.[13]

In *The Devil and Commodity Fetishism in South America*, Taussig examines fantastic devil beliefs in South America as critical responses to encroaching capitalism by peoples unaccustomed to its objectifying logic and argues that capitalism's naturalized assumptions are also fantastic constructs that only our long familiarity has made appear commonsensical. In his book, ethnography is inseparable from cultural critique. Taussig (1980: 13) has objected to accounts that reproduce capitalism's phantom objectivity by reinscribing its forms of knowledge, arguing that "critique sustained in conventional terms sustains conventions." Evidently, he seeks to find critical counterconventions in the beliefs of peoples not yet subjected to capitalism's all-encompassing logic.

The bearers of precapitalist culture in Taussig's *The Devil and Commodity Fetishism in South America* are Colombian peasants and Bolivian miners. In my view, the heart of this book is its analysis of a set of beliefs concerning two rituals for obtaining money, the baptism of the bill and the devil contract, which Taussig interprets as expressing peasant reactions to capitalist commodification in Colombia's Cauca valley. Taussig offers a brief description of these beliefs and an extensive interpretation of their meaning. The ethnographic account seems to be intentionally thin; we are told little about the place of devil beliefs within a larger ensemble of beliefs and practices, believers and practitioners. Questions such as who accepts them and how belief relates to practice seem to be out of place. In fact, Taussig (1980: 95) argues that it does not matter whether these rituals are practiced; what matters is that people believe that they are sustained, because he is concerned "with a collective belief."

Taussig believes, however, that devil contracts really do take place, and he supports this claim by stating that he knows two folk healers who arrange such contracts and by giving one example. His example, a story he was told by a close friend, departs considerably from his original formulaic description of devil contracts (Taussig 1980: 95). The story tells of a man born on the Pacific coast who came to the Cauca valley as a young boy. He worked intermittently on the plantation, and frequently visited his father on the Pacific coast, where he acquired knowledge of magic. Increasingly resentful of plantation work, he decided to make a pact with the devil. To this end he bought several books of magic that are sold in the plantation town marketplace. Drawing on their instructions, he performed the following ritual: "One day he went to the sugarcane field and eviscerated the palpitating heart of a black cat over which he cast his spell (oración, or prayer). No sooner had he done so than a tremendous wind came roaring through the sugarcane. Terrified, he ran away. 'He did it in order to sell his soul to the devil, so that he could get money without working,' said my informant" (Taussig 1980: 96).

This individual example of a "collective belief" raises many questions concerning a variety of issues: the role of individual creativity and agency (of the informant, if this was but a tale; of the ritual performer, if the event took place); the existence of a flexible repertoire of devil contracts (if this particular ritual is part of a larger set of beliefs or practices); the rigidity of the devil contract (if the moral of this story is that modifications of formulaic rituals will lead to disastrous results); and the role of books of magic in the development of peasants' responses to capitalism. More fundamentally, this example suggests the importance of relating ritual belief to ritual performance and relating talk about rituals to beliefs in rituals. But since Taussig uses this illustration as an example of the devil contract, its place in the text raises an even more basic question: what is this example an example of?

In the narrative, Taussig depicts Colombian peasants as the subjects of a natural economy ruled by use value and of a precapitalist culture organized by the logic of analogical reason. In my view, this story of the devil contract is an example of the precapitalist Other. That is, this illustration works as an example of an example in a paradigmatic chain of examples of Otherness. It is an example of the devil contract in the same sense that the devil contract is an example of peasant consciousness, and peasant consciousness is an example of natural economy, and natural economy is an example of noncapitalist society, and noncapitalist society is an example of analogical versus causal rationality, and each, in turn, exemplifies the Other. In each case, ethnographic contextualization is relinquished for the sake of a higher purpose: to construct an image of Otherness that, by standing in opposition to "our" capitalist culture, can help us demystify its underlying assumptions. If the peasants are models of Otherness, any one of their beliefs may stand for them. Given this paradigmatic structure, what seems important in this narrative is to conjure up an image of an alternative culture and to avoid producing a conventional ethnographic account that reproduces the West's objectifying gaze. At stake is a conception of ethnography as a particular kind of cultural critique. Instead of risking objectifying others along conventional lines, Taussig provides a suggestive portrait of peasant cultures, but one drawn less as a means to understand "other" societies in their unique complexity than as a way to gain a critical vantage point to critique "our" own.

Taussig's exceptional contribution to the ethnography of Latin America lies precisely in his having opened up an imaginative space for understanding fundamental cultural differences. Yet his own analysis permits one to interrogate his manner of constructing difference and to ask, who are "they" and who are "we"? Ironically, Taussig constructs these peasants into Others by leaving to one side his examination of "their" history, and in so doing mystifies as well what appears as "our" history. In two informative historical chapters that precede his analysis of these rituals, he shows how the peasants in the Cauca valley are the offspring of a long process of slavery, colonial domination, and market involvement. That some of these peasants managed to create relatively isolated communities during the nineteenth century only heightens the significance of their centuries-long engagement with market forces and forms of capitalist commodification. Yet, so that they might defamiliarize our understanding of capitalism, he constructs them as pure emblems of precapitalism and places them on an island of Otherness, untouched by commodity fetishism. By his own account, however, these peasants are in fact co-authors of the history of Western capitalism and should be seen as part of the Western world. Just as their slave ancestors contributed to the making of the Occident, these peasants are engaged today in reproducing Western capitalism. The books of magic that some of them read include codified responses to market forces whose roots may be traced back to the European Middle Ages and beyond. As if by a hidden historical affinity, their devil beliefs involve a transformation and adaptation of these European beliefs to their own conditions and traditions.

In an increasingly interrelated world, it is to be expected that books and beliefs participate in complex global circuits of exchange across time and space. In effect, while Taussig claims that only from the precapitalist margins can one demystify the all-encompassing phantom objectivity of capitalist culture, he sees the peasants' responses to capitalism in South

America through the prism of his previous understanding of capitalist culture derived from the defamiliarizing writings of Marx, Benjamin, Lukács, and Adorno. Their books, like the books of magic available to the Colombian peasants, codify various responses to commodity culture. The very existence of these books and of the critical traditions they represent shows that commodity culture is not of one piece or all-encompassing, that its phantom objectivity has been resisted by popular and intellectual traditions both in Colombia and in Europe, and that its conventions include counterconventions. One could perhaps imagine the occurrence of a hidden transcultural exchange between devil beliefs and European critical theory. It is by resituating and rearticulating these interconnected beliefs and traditions that Colombian peasants, as well as Taussig, make sense of their world.

Mitchell's splendid works *Colonising Egypt* and "The World as an Exhibition" (1989) illustrate an interesting variation of this modality of Occidentalism. His provocative analysis of colonialism is also based on a sharp distinction between Self (Occident) and Other (Orient). Instead of focusing on the Other in order to destabilize the Self, however, Mitchell focuses on the Self's expansion into the Other—the European colonization of Egypt—as a process that illuminates the Self. For him, the colonization of Egypt involved "the spread of a political order that inscribes in the social world a new conception of space, new forms of personhood, and a new means for manufacturing the experience of the real" (Mitchell 1988: ix). Since colonialism implied the attempt to impose a Western metaphysics on an Oriental one, the analysis of colonialism entails the examination of the ontological and epistemological assumptions underwriting Western metaphysics. Drawing on Heidegger's view of modernity, Mitchell views the metaphysics of modernity as entailing the splitting up of the world into "representation" and "reality." Following the logic of the world's seeming division into two, Mitchell (1988: 32) argues that this distinction corresponds to another division of the world, into the West and the non-West. Thus, the colonization of Egypt is simultaneously the construction of the West by means of this foundational metaphysical principle: the separation between reality and representation. Mitchell's discussion of Western metaphysics is further illuminated by his fascinating account of the complementary perspective offered by Oriental visitors to the Occident.

While Mitchell's book focuses on Western metaphysics, his argument requires that it be opposed to an alternative conception of order—an Oriental metaphysics. In order to highlight the contrast between Western and Eastern modes of manufacturing a sense of the real he offers Pierre Bourdieu's description of the Kabyle house. This house, like Taussig's Colombian peasants, stands in his narrative as an example of a radically different order of things, an instance of "Otherness." Interestingly, Mitchell recognizes this similarity in a comment that shows his awareness of the risks entailed in the use of polarized totalities that come to be inhabited by collective prejudices and anxieties:

> Because the purpose of such examples is to make visible our own assumptions about the nature of order by contrasting them with a kind of order whose assumptions are different, I run the risk of setting up this other as the very opposite of ourselves. Such an opposite, moreover, would appear inevitably as a self-contained totality, and its encounter with the modern West would appear, again inevitably, as its rupturing and disintegration. These sorts of self-contained, precapitalist totalities acquire the awful handicap, as Taussig has remarked, of having to satisfy our yearning for a lost age of innocence. Such consequences, though perhaps inevitable, are undesired and unintended. (Mitchell 1988: 49)

Despite Mitchell's recognition of the undesirable consequences of polarized typologies, he constructs Egypt as a self-contained, precapitalist totality in order to make visible the assumptions underpinning capitalist culture. Building on Bourdieu's account of the Kabyle house in Algeria, Mitchell (1988: 49) provides a detailed exegesis of it as an expression of a radically different conception of the world. The logic governing its spatial organization reveals the relational character of its various components, viewed as forces, not objects. His conclusion is that the house defines "a way of dwelling that did not reduce order to a question of the relationship between things and their plan, between the world and a map." The house is an emblem of an order in which there is no split between reality and representation. It is not the case that in this order the relationship between objects and people, meanings and practice, is differently articulated, that objectification and representation have come to assume different forms. Rather, here there are no representations and no symbols, only contextual relations and associations:

> Such relations are not the relations between an object and its meaning, as we would say, or between a symbol and the idea for which it stands. There is nothing symbolic in this world. . . . These associations, in consequence, should not be explained in terms of any symbolic or

cultural "code," the separate realm to which we imagine such signs to belong. They arise entirely from their particular context, in the difference and similarity that produces context, and are as many and as varied as such contexts might be. (Mitchell 1988: 60–61)

It is against this Eastern world of immanent meanings that the West appears as a world split by the separation between reality and representation. Mitchell's book is structured in terms of the binary opposition between two historical actors who stand for, or are constituted by, these different metaphysics. Each actor appears as a bounded homogeneous totality, without fractures or contradictions, without long-term historical connections, without people—classes or categories of people—taking different positions or responding in distinct ways to their respective worlds or to the often violent collision among them. Mitchell's didactics of polarized contrasts reveals much about Western colonialism. Yet perhaps one of the undesired and unintended consequences of the contrasting opposition that structures this study of colonialism is that its innovative examination of the underlying metaphysics of the modern West ends up producing West and East, and colonialism itself, as metaphysical entities.

In my view, the call to question the epistemological assumptions underpinning Orientalist representations entails interrogating modes of constructing cultural diversity that mystify the connections between Western and non-Western peoples, either inflate or erase their distinctive differences, and thus risk stabilizing a hegemonic categorical order. Just as Orientalist accounts are partial not because of their inherent incompleteness, representations of non-Western cultures have colonizing effects not because they depict diversity. What makes a difference is not the inscription of difference but the kind of difference it makes.

In other words, there is no such thing as an immaculate representation. Since all representations are saturated with history, the issue is to recognize the implications of their involvement in history. At stake is the accountability of our accounts, a matter of politics rather than of metaphysics, of alterable historical consequences rather than of unavoidable transhistorical effects or, more precisely, of the politics of epistemology and of the epistemology of politics. In my view, challenging an imperial order requires overturning the Self-Other polarity that has served as one of its foundational premises. This requires that cultures be seen, as Ortiz and Said propose, in contrapuntal relation to each other rather than taken to be autonomous units, that their difference be historicized rather than essentialized, and that their boundaries and homogeneity be determined, not assumed.[14] This contrapuntal perspective may encourage the development of a decentered "transcultural anthropology" (Coronil 1995: xiii) that avoids confirming a Self-centered standpoint from which difference is turned into Otherness either through Self-confirming objectification or Self-questioning exoticization.

Labyrinths of the Imagination: The Truth of Power

In his discussion of the 1889 Parisian Oriental exhibition, Mitchell remarks on the continuity between the exhibition and a world outside which looked like an "extended exhibition": "This extended exhibition continued to present itself as a series of mere representations, representing a reality beyond" (Mitchell 1988: 10). Borrowing an image from Jacques Derrida, he suggests that we may think of it less as an exhibition than as a kind of labyrinth that "includes in itself its own exits." Like Derrida, who once said that all of his subsequent writings "are only a commentary on the sentence about a labyrinth," Mitchell (1989: 224) tells us that his own essay also "should be read as a short additional comment on that sentence."

There is an affinity between the idea of a labyrinth that includes not only the maze but the exits leading beyond it and the idea of a map that represents not only geography but history. Or, to offer an alternative reading, there is an affinity between a labyrinth without real exits to the world, which dissolves the distinction between the inside and the outside, and a map without real difference from the world, which erases the distinction between representation and reality. Indeed, Derrida acknowledges his intellectual debt to Borges, who plays with epistemological paradoxes in his writings. Let us now return to Borges's story of the imperial map.

It is in the nature of paradoxes to elicit multiple readings. Baudrillard begins *Simulations* (1983) with a reading of the Borges map story as a parable about simulation. He uses the story to argue that our age involves an epochal break in the relationship between reality and representation. If previously maps were taken as representations of reality, now they are a means to generate reality. Thus, Borges's image of the tattered map may be read as a prefiguration of the empire's decay. As Baudrillard (1983: 2) puts it, "Simulation is no longer that of a territory, a referential being or a substance. It is the generation by models of a real without origin or reality: a hyperreal. The territory no longer precedes the map, nor survives it. Henceforth it is the map that precedes the territory." Baudrillard portrays

Marx as a thinker still caught up in a world divided by a distinction between reality and representation. Following his lead, Mitchell argues that Marx held the illusion that by lifting the veil of mystification produced by commodity fetishism one would find naked reality ready to be represented. "Marx opposed to the imaginary productive processes represented by these misunderstood hieroglyphics the 'transparent and rational form' in which the practical relations of everyday life should present themselves" (Mitchell 1988: 180). This means, for Mitchell (1988: 18), that "to the mechanisms of misrepresentation by which power operates, Marx opposed a representation of the ways things intrinsically are, in their transparent and rational reality." Thus, Marx's theory of commodity fetishism was flawed, because in "revealing power to work through misrepresentations, it left representation itself unquestioned" (Mitchell 1988: 18). The crucial problem is that it expressed what for Mitchell is a central tenet of Western metaphysics: "It accepted absolutely the distinction between a realm of representation and the 'external reality' which such representations promise, rather than examining the novelty of continually creating the effect of an 'external reality' as itself a mechanism of power" (Mitchell 1988: 18–19).

For Mitchell, power seems to be epochal rather than historical; it is the expression of an age, not of a particular society. Insofar as it has a specific social referent, it works in Foucauldian fashion through capillary effects dispersed throughout society rather than being enacted as well by competing forms of organized human agency. In his concern "to question representation," Mitchell draws on Heidegger's examination of objectification in the modern world, cast in terms of epochal and existential categories, and cites him in his book's opening epigraph: "The fundamental event of the modern age is the conquest of the world as picture" (Mitchell 1988: v). It is as "picture" that Baudrillard reads Borges's map.[15]

Borges's story, however, could also be read as an allegory of power. From this perspective it is about imperial power—the power to constitute the Empire through the exercise of power and the ability to determine the terms in which reality should be defined. It is not only about the truth of representation but about the representation of truth. It is about the representation of power and the power to represent, about the truth of power. In other words, it is about the connection between knowledge and power and, more specifically, about the relationship between imperial power and imperial knowledge.

This reading permits us to approach the unresolved ambiguity in Said's critique of Orientalism—that is, the tension between the limits of Orientalist constructs as necessarily incomplete representations or as misrepresentations that reflect unequal power relations under colonialism and imperialism. If one abandons the pursuit of the complete map—a map that coincides with reality point for point—the fundamental issue becomes not the existence of an unavoidable gap between reality and representation but the consequences of specific representations, or, in other words, the relationship between the representation and constitution of social relations in specific societies. Marx's (1981: 956) statement that "all science would be superfluous if the form of appearance of things directly coincided with their essence" calls attention not to a reality outside representation that analysis can apprehend directly, but to the need to evaluate the effects of existing representations and to contribute to developing more enabling ones.

By deconstructing the categories through which European (primarily British) capitalist society imagined itself, Marx intended to understand them but did not hold the illusion that in so doing he could dispel their power. Their hold over people's consciousness could not be changed by reinterpreting the world, only by transforming it. These categories, he argued, are necessary mystifications because they are both true, in that they enter into the constitution of social relations in capitalist society, and false, in that they obscure their character. For example, the idea that money "begets" money, that money "grows" or "produces" interest in banks, is a fetishistic mystification in that money does not in fact expand by itself. Yet it is an accurate depiction of what happens in capitalist society when money is placed as capital in banks, where it is used as a means to capture value produced elsewhere. Thus, money does appear to grow in banks. This appearance, as well as the obscuring of the actual source of money's "growth," is necessary for the constitution and legitimation of capitalist society.

For Marx, social life could be apprehended as a "transparent and rational form" not through an epistemic act but through social revolution: the overcoming of relations of domination. Transparency works in Marx's narrative as a utopian standard by which one can evaluate existing forms of mystification on the basis of their role in obscuring relations of power: "The religious reflections of the real world can, in any case, vanish only when the practical relations of everyday life between man and man, and man and nature, generally present themselves to him in a transparent and rational form. The veil is not removed from the countenance of the social life-process, i.e. the process of material production, until it becomes production by freely associated men, and stands under their conscious and planned control" (Marx 1981: 173).

Assuming that the social world has largely been defined from the perspective of the powerful, Marx aspires to illuminate it from a less partial—or more universal—standpoint. The humility of this epistemological aspiration is the other side of its radical political ambition to create grounds of social equality as the condition for the endless unfolding of universality. In my view, the aim is not to create a transparent social world but to overcome conditions that lead to the systemic obscuring of inequality and mystification of privilege in specific social domains and that thus constrain the free development of all. Perry Anderson (1988: 336) comments that "a whole utopian tradition . . . assumes that a free and equal society would be transparent. . . . If you actually had a socialist society in which production, power, and culture were genuinely democratic, you would have an enormous multiplication of different ways of living." By being able to choose to live in ways that are suppressed under capitalism, Anderson suggests, people would live in a complex, but accessible and intelligible, social world.

There is no exit from the lived world, only views from different positions within it. It is as if the world were a labyrinth whose exits were entrances into an expanding labyrinth and our maps not only modeled these labyrinths but also created them. Thus, maps embody the imagination of the future, not only that of the past. The destiny of our journey also defines its trajectory.

History and the Fetishization of Geography

Borges's cartographers produced maps for the emperor. Here I have discussed the often implicit maps of empire produced by invisible hands and reproduced, with varying degrees of critical distance, by critics of colonialism for the metropolitan academic community and the public at large. I have focused on how certain representational practices assume a privileged center—the Occident, the First World, the West, the Self—from which difference continues to be defined as Otherness. Whether Otherness is dissolved in the service of the Self, subsumed within the Self, or celebrated in opposition to the Self, as in the three modalities discussed here, is in this respect less significant than its ongoing definition as a counterimage to a Self in need of confirmation, critique, or destabilization.

If in this discussion I have called attention to the way these maps reinscribe certain imperial boundaries, it is because, as Nicolás Guillén's poem suggests, they do not sufficiently educate us to see forms of humanity "that are not on the map." If Occidentalism is an imperial malady, one of its major symptoms is the ongoing reproduction of a colonial Self-Other polarity that mystifies the present as much as the past and obscures its potential for transformation.

In his last book, *State, Power, Socialism*, Nicos Poulantzas (1978: 114) argued that states establish a "peculiar relationship between history and territory, between the spatial and the temporal matrix." Taking the nation as his fundamental unit, he characterized the unity of modernity in terms of the intersection of temporal and spatial dimensions: "National unity or modern unity becomes a historicity of a territory and territorialization of a history" (Poulantzas 1978: 114). Before his death, Poulantzas was building on Lefebvre's pathbreaking work *La production de l'espace* (1974), which attempts to integrate the study of geography with that of history and has inspired an important body of work by contemporary thinkers who have also reacted against the historicist conception of space as the static stage where time dynamically unfolds.[16] I wish now to bring this literature to bear on Occidentalism through a brief commentary on Poulantzas's insight.

Poulantzas's notion that modernity entails the territorialization of a history and the historicization of a territory does not indicate how this interaction works, but his wording gives the impression of a symmetrical exchange. Yet, the prevailing understanding of history as fluid, intangible, and dynamic and of geography as fixed, tangible, and static suggests that modernity is constituted by an asymmetrical integration of space and time. A telling example is Ernesto Laclau's argument, in *New Reflections on the Revolution of Our Time* (1990), that space is fundamentally static while time is dynamic.[17] Paradoxically, therefore, the historicization of territories takes place through the obscuring of their history; territories are largely assumed as the fixed, natural ground of local histories. The territorialization of histories, in turn, occurs through their fixation in nonhistorical, naturalized territories. As a consequence, the histories of interrelated peoples become territorialized into bounded spaces. Since these spaces appear as being produced naturally, not historically, they serve to root the histories of connected peoples in separate territories and to sever the links between them. Thus, the illusion is created that their identities are the result of independent histories rather than the outcome of historical relations. There is a dual obscuring. The histories of various spaces are hidden,[18] and the historical relations among social actors or units are severed.[19]

In other words, history and geography are fetishized. As with commodities, the results of social-historical relations among peoples appear as intrinsic attributes of naturalized, spatialized, bounded units. Although Poulantzas focused on nations, we could consider these units to be groups of nations or supranational entities: the West, the Occident, the Third World, the East, the South, as well as localized intranational subunits, such as peasants, ethnic "minorities," "slum dwellers," the "homeless," forms of "communalism," and so forth. With the generalization of commodity relations, modes of reification involved in commodity fetishism radiate from the realm of the production of things to the production of social identities. Typical markers of collective identities, such as "territory," "culture," "history," or "religion," appear as autonomous entities. Identified by these markers, interconnected peoples come to lead separate lives whose defining properties appear to emerge from the intrinsic attributes of their "histories," "cultures," or "motherlands." As commodity fetishism becomes deeply rooted in society, it works as a cultural schema that permeates other sociocultural domains. As with commodities, the material, thing-like, tangible form of geographical entities becomes a privileged medium to represent the less tangible historical relations among peoples. Through geographic fetishism, space is naturalized and history is territorialized. Thus, the West is constituted as an imperial fetish, the imagined home of history's victors, the embodiment of their power.

Every society represents other societies as part of the process of constructing its own collective identity, but each does so in ways that reflect its unique historical trajectory and cultural traditions. What distinguishes Occidentalism as an ethnocentric style of representation is that it is linked to the West's effective global dominance. While this linkage raises a number of questions concerning the relationship between Western knowledge about the world and power over it, it must be noted that this dominance is always partial and that it takes place through processes of transculturation which also transform the West. Westernization entails not the homogenization of the world's societies under the force of capitalism but their reciprocal transformation under diverse historical conditions. In this light, capitalism appears not as a self-identical system that emanates from the West and expands to the periphery but as a changing ensemble of worldwide relations that assumes different forms in specific regional and national contexts.

Modernity and Occidentalism

The nineteenth-century thinkers who insightfully examined the making of the modern world before its categories became second nature initiated a polemical discussion of the relationship between modernity and capitalism. Yet it is striking that even divergent ideological positions often coincide in their assumption that the West is the source and locus of modernity. If we expand our focus so as to bring the West and the non-West within a unified field of vision that encompasses the historical terrain of their mutual formation (see, e.g., Cooper and Stoler 1989), the modern world appears larger and more complex, formed by universalizing and innovating impulses that continuously redefine geographical and cultural boundaries and set new against old, Self against Other. If the West is involved in the creation of its obverse and the modern is unimaginable without the traditional, the West's preoccupation with alterity can be seen as being constitutive of modernity itself rather than as an incidental byproduct of Western expansionism. The examination of Western representations of Otherness, from the perspective of a critique of Occidentalism, could then be encompassed within an interrogation of why Otherness has become such a peculiarly modern concern.

Bourgeois modernity is torn by contradictory tendencies. Its universalizing force is inseparably linked to expansive and yet exclusionary movements of capital that polarize nations across the globe as well as people within societies. Spurred by the pursuit of profit, capital's continuous transformation of economic relations dissolves established customs and makes obsolete the new, yet its innovative force is constrained by the structures of privilege within which novelty itself is produced. Commodities come to occupy a central place in the formation of individual and collective life projects, generating forms of power that rely on the possession and consumption of things. Through the medium of things, modernity promises abundance and endless progress. This promise is fulfilled within conditions of inequality that redefine its meaning and is constrained by powerful interests that confine and condition its fulfillment. "Progress" is thus constituted through a contradictory movement that erodes and establishes boundaries, that releases and contains energies. The future, as a modern construct, is rent by these tensions. The expansion of capital across space and time entails the dissolution of barriers to "development" but also the construction of walls against "disorder." While capital's expansion is the condition of its stability, stability is the condition of its expansion.

In the modern world, as Marx and Engels observed, "all that is solid melts into air," but air itself is rendered solid, turned into another object.

Premised on a teleology of progress, capitalist development is embodied in reified institutions and categories. Cultural constructs such as the West and the Third World come to acquire, like a commercial brand, an independent objective existence as well as the semblance of a subjective life. As part of their social intercourse, these forms feed the collective imagination and participate in the making of desires and needs, circulating as objects of libidinal attraction (Bhabha 1986) and as subjects of political action that define the terms of political intercourse. As fetishes of modernity, these cultural formations stand for social powers by alienating them; parts replace wholes. The West comes to be identified with leading capitalist nations, the economy with the market, democracy with universal elections, difference with Otherness. Embodying the contradictions of capitalist society, these formations help shape the landscape within which, with mesmerizing allure despite its disruptive social consequences, capitalist arrested development parades as modern progress.

This map of modernity is being redrawn by global changes in culture, aesthetics, and exchange that are commonly associated with the emergence of postmodernity. These transformations have multiple determinants and expressions, of which I can register only a few: the simultaneous integration and fragmentation of social space through new forms of communication; the globalization of market relations and financial networks; the shift from Fordism to flexible accumulation; the increasing tension between the national basis of states and the global connections of national economies; and the growing polarization of social classes both domestically and internationally.[20] As a result of these changes, familiar spatial categories are uprooted from their original sites and attached to new locations. As space becomes fluid, history can no longer be easily anchored in fixed territories. While deterritorialization entails reterritorialization, this process only makes more visible the social constructedness of space, for this "melting" of space is met partly with the "freezing" of history. With the generalization of the commodity form, as Lukács (1971: 90) noted, "time sheds its qualitative, variable, flowing nature; it freezes into an exactly delimited, quantifiable continuum filled with quantifiable 'things.' . . . [I]n short, it becomes space." This spatialization of time serves as the location of new social movements, as well as of new targets of imperial control; it expands the realm of imperial subjection but also of political contestation.

As a result of these transformations, contemporary empires must now confront subaltern subjects within reconfigured spaces at home and abroad, as the Other, once maintained on distant continents or confined to bounded locations at home, simultaneously multiplies and dissolves. Collective identities are being defined in fragmented places that cannot be mapped with antiquated categories. The emergence of a new relationship between history and geography may permit us to develop a critical cartography and to abandon worn imperial maps shaded in black and white. Perhaps one day "their tattered fragments will be found in the western Deserts, sheltering an occasional Beast or beggar" (Borges 1970: 90) or, in a world without beggars, an archaeologist of modernity.

Toward Nonimperial Geohistorical Categories

> DAUGHTER: Mom, why did all those people lose their jobs? Will we be poor too?
>
> MOTHER: Because the factories where they worked were moved to places where it's cheaper to make cars, as often happens when capitalists compete to make more money. If we worked for GM we would have a hard time now.
>
> DAUGHTER: Why can't we just say no to capitalism? Do you think in a few years human beings are going to be extinct? Is the world going to be so polluted that if there is a God, God will say, "I'm tired of all this"? But if that happens, there won't be any Santa Claus. I just can't imagine there never being any more people in the world, never ever.
>
> —Dialogue between Andrea Coronil, 10, and Julie Skurski, following the televised announcement that 74,000 General Motors employees would lose their jobs, Ann Arbor, December 18, 1991

How can we articulate the future historically? In seeking to prefigure an emancipatory future, we may track down its marks in the tensions of the present. As Terry Eagleton argues, "A utopian thought that does not risk simply making us ill is one able to trace within the present that secret lack of identity with itself which is the spot where a feasible future might germinate—the place where the future overshadows and hollows out the present's spurious repleteness" (Eagleton et al. 1990: 25). Walter Benjamin, who sought to understand the past in order to find within the present the seeds of a desirable future, asserted that

> to articulate the past historically does not mean to recognize it "the way it really was" (Ranke). It means to seize hold of a memory as it flashes up at a moment of danger. . . . Only that historian will have the gift of

fanning the spark of hope in the past who is firmly convinced that even the dead will not be safe from the enemy if he wins. And this enemy has not ceased to be victorious. (Benjamin 1969: 255)

It may be that only that historian who is convinced that the living cannot be safe as long as the dead remain unburied will have the gift of fanning the spark of hope in the future. "If you can write this," said a relative of peasants massacred in the town of Amparo, Venezuela, on the pretext that they were Colombian guerrillas, "tell them that despite all the lies they [the powerful] will tell, they won't be able to hide the truth. Sooner or later, the truth will be known. . . . Even though those people may not believe it, the dead also speak" (personal communication, July 17, 1989). The dead speak in many ways. In February 1989 another massacre took place in Venezuela in which several hundred people were killed following rioting against an International Monetary Fund austerity program. The effort to exhume the secret mass graves of the army's victims became the focus of popular struggle around the massacre, as the government sought to prevent the bodies of the victims from speaking of how they had met death. When the stakes of history are high, the safety of the living rests on the voices of the dead who speak through the actions of the living. Establishing this link across time, the Maya rebels of the contemporary Zapatista movement in Mexico define their opposition through a collective history, proclaiming, "Zapata lives, the struggle continues!" while their spokesperson, Subcomandante Marcos, underlines that the people who now speak "are the dead people of always, those who have to die in order to live" (quoted in Poniatowska 1994).

The interaction between geography and history thus involves an exchange not only between past and present but between present and future. Fanon, like Marx, drew on the poetry of the future to imagine a world in which the dead may bury the dead so that the living may be freed from the nightmare of the past. Reflecting on his position as an African American, Henry Louis Gates expresses the tension energizing an aspiration to identity informed by history and yet unconstrained by the past: "So I'm divided. I want to be black, to know black, to luxuriate in whatever I might be calling blackness at any particular time—but to do so in order to come out the other side, to experience a humanity that is neither colorless, nor reducible to color" (Gates 1994: xv). It is also in the spirit of freeing the living into the future that Carolyn Steedman concludes her powerful analysis of working-class longing, in which after illuminating everyday formations of desire within working-class culture she calls "for a structure of political thought that will take all of this, all these secret and impossible stories, recognize what has been made out on the margins; and then, recognizing it, refuse to celebrate it; a politics that will, watching this past, say 'So What?' and consign it to the dark" (Steedman 1987: 144).

As the future flashes up to a child in the form of a disenchanted, inhospitable, and depopulated world, the safety of those who follow us comes to depend as well on the poetry of the present.

Notes

This essay is the product of a seminar I taught on Occidentalism in the fall of 1991 and has benefited from discussions in many other contexts—the Power Conference, University of Michigan (1992); the Department of Anthropology, University of Chicago (1993); American Anthropological Association (1993)—and, above all, in two other seminars I taught at the University of Michigan, one in conjunction with Walter Mignolo. In these contexts I have been offered more helpful suggestions than I could include in the essay or acknowledge here. I thank in particular my students at the University of Michigan and Arjun Appadurai, Lauren Berlant, John Comaroff, Paul Eiss, Raymond Grew, David Hollinger, Brink Messick, Walter Mignolo, Colleen O'Neal, Sherry Ortner, Seteney Shami, Carolyn Steedman, and Gary Wilder for their comments, and Julie Skurski, who shared in the production of this article.

Epigraphs: Guillén (2003), 73; Rich (1994), 212.

1 The gender bias of this utopian image shows that utopian visions, however universal in their intent, are necessarily saturated by the history they seek to overcome and limited by the local position from which they are enunciated.

2 Like Mignolo's "pluritopical" and Ella Shohat and Robert Stam's "polycentric," I use here "decentered" as a sign of relationality and differentiation among human communities (Mignolo 1995; Shohat and Stam 1994).

3 Carl Pletsch (1981) insightfully discusses the genesis of the three worlds taxonomy and its ideological character as a primitive system of classification.

4 After I presented this paper at the Power Conference, Michigan (January 1992), I read an article by Carrier where he makes various useful distinctions: "ethno-Orientalism," by which he means "essentialist renderings of alien societies by members of those societies themselves"; "ethno-Occidentalism," which refers to "essentialist renderings of the West by members of alien societies"; and "Occidentalism," by which he means "the essentialistic rendering of the West by Westerners" (Carrier 1992: 198–99). Carrier's classification helps us recognize various approaches to this general topic, such as Chen 1992; Keesing 1982; Nader 1989. Carrier's attempt to analyze the process of producing of Orientalist

representations, and to relate dialectically representations of Otherness to representations of the West, parallels my own aims in this article.

5 Amin (1989: ix, xii–xiii) defines Eurocentrism as "an essential dimension of the ideology of capitalism" and explains his choice of this term over others, including "occidentalocentrism."

6 Armstrong (1990) uses the term "Occidentalism" to refer to the "effects" of Orientalism on Western selves. I see these effects as one dimension of Occidentalism, as I define it here.

7 For discussions that highlight the contributions of some of the works I examine in this section, see the reviews of Wolf's work by Talal Asad (1987) and William Roseberry (1989). The reader may find instructive the caustic exchange between Taussig (1989) and Mintz and Wolf (1989), as well as that between Taussig (1987a) and his critics in "Capitalism and the Peasantry in South America" (1986). For my discussion of Todorov's book, see Coronil 1989.

8 The excellent reviews by Asad (1987) and Roseberry (1989), although in dialogue with a Marxist tradition, do not note this absence.

9 This perspective informs my work on state formation in Venezuela, an oil exporting nation (Coronil and Skurski 1982, 1991). I discuss elsewhere the significance of the shift from a binary to a triadic dialectic that I have outlined here (Coronil in press) [Editor's note: here Coronil was referring to his forthcoming book *The Magical State*].

10 Ortiz integrated poetic and historical narratives in *Cuban Counterpoint* ([1940] 1995) in order to evoke the presence of Cuba's major export products throughout Cuban history. For a discussion of his treatment of commodities and of the relevance of his book for postcolonial critique, see Coronil 1995.

11 Given neoclassic economics' selective construction of its ancestry, it may be useful to remember that an approach to price formation grounded in the production of value occupied a central place in Smith 1976: chaps. 4–6; Ricardo 1983: chaps. 1–5.

12 Quoted in Rother 1994. It should be noted that in consulting the United Nations prior to invading Haiti, Clinton was the first U.S. president to seek international approval in advance for intervening in the nation's strategically defined periphery. He thus implicitly recognized that the U.S. does not have exclusive rights over the Western Hemisphere, as long defined by the Monroe doctrine. Gaddis Smith, author of *The Last Years of the Monroe Doctrine*, sees in this remark a sharp reversal of policy. "The United States has recognized that threats to peace and security in the Western Hemisphere are as much for consideration by the Security Council as threats to peace and security in Korea or the Balkans" (quoted in Sciolino 1994). This change shows how an imperial map of the modern world, in which metropolitan centers had their well-defined "backyards," is being redrawn by newer imperial forces which are compressing global space and reconfiguring the spatial referents of "postmodern" empires.

13 Taussig is critical of the works by Mintz and Wolf I discuss here, for in his opinion they reproduce, rather than counter by conjuring up an alternative reality, capitalism's "phantom objectivity" (Taussig 1989: 11). His *Shamanism, Colonialism, and the Wild Man* (1987b) unsettles the dichotomy that informs his analysis in *The Devil and Commodity Fetishism in South America* (1980) by showing how "civilizing" conquerors and "wild" conquered have woven a web of mutually defining relations and representations. For a fuller discussion, see Coronil 1988.

14 Said argues for a "contrapuntal perspectivism" in *Culture and Imperialism* (1993). For an earlier expression of this perspective that pays particular attention to the play of power in economic and cultural relations, see Ortiz [1940] 1995.

15 Interestingly, Baudrillard (1983: 2) also suggests that this story could be interpreted as "an allegory of the Empire." But he does little with this insight, except to relate it to the "imperialism" of present day simulators who try to make the real coincide with their simulation models. Essentially, the map remains a trope with which to discuss epistemological rather than political questions, although this distinction, of course, is one of degree.

16 See, e.g., works produced by political geographers (Entrikin 1991; Harvey 1989; Smith 1990; Soja 1989), literary critics (Jameson 1984), and social philosophers (de Certeau 1988; Foucault 1980).

17 Doreen Massey (1992) offers a persuasive critique of Laclau's conservative understanding of space and develops an important argument concerning the relationship between time and space.

18 For this discussion, I find useful de Certeau's (1988: 117) conception of "space" as a "practiced place."

19 This point is supported by the pioneering work of African and African American scholars who have discussed the erasure of links between Greece and Africa in dominant historiography (see, e.g., Diop 1974) as well as by Martin Bernal's forceful argument in *Black Athena* (1987).

20 For a lucid discussion of central issues in the study of globalization and transnationalism, see Rouse 1995.

References

Amin, Samir. 1989. *Eurocentrism*. New York: Monthly Review.

Anderson, Perry. 1988. "Modernity and Revolution." In *Marxism and the Interpretation of Culture*, ed. Cary Nelson and Lawrence Grossberg, 317–33. Urbana: University of Illinois Press.

Armstrong, Nancy. 1990. "The Occidental Alice." *Differences* 2, no. 2: 3–40.

Asad, Talal. 1987. "Are There Histories of Peoples without Europe?" *Comparative Studies in Society and History* 29: 594–607.

Baudrillard, Jean. 1983. *Simulations*. New York: Semiotext(e).

Benjamin, Walter. 1969. *Illuminations*. New York: Schocken.

Bernal, Martin. 1987. *Black Athena: The Afroasiatic Roots Classical Civilization*, 3 vols. New Brunswick, NJ: Rutgers University Press.

Bhabha, Homi. 1986. "The Other Question: Difference, Discrimination and the Discourse of Colonialism." In *Literature, Politics and Theory*, ed. Francis Barker, Peter Hulme, Margaret Iversen, and Diana Loxley, 148–72. London: Methuen.

Borges, Jorge Luis. 1970. *Dreamtigers*. Austin: University of Texas Press.

"Capitalism and the Peasantry in South America: The Chevalier-Taussig Controversy: A Critical Review Symposium." 1986. *Social Analysis* 19: 57–119.

Carrier, James G. 1992. "Occidentalism: The World Turned Upside-down." *American Ethnologist* 19, no. 2: 195–212.

Chen, Xiaomei. 1992. "Occidentalism as Counterdiscourse: 'He Shang' in Post-Mao China." *Critical Inquiry* 18: 686–712.

Chomsky, Noam. 1991. "The New World Order." *Agenda* 62: 13–15.

Comaroff, John L. 1987. "Of Totemism and Ethnicity: Consciousness, Practice, and the Signs of Inequality." *Ethos* 52: 301–23.

Cooper, Fred, and Ann Laura Stoler. 1989. "Introduction: Tensions of Empire: Colonial Control and Visions of Rule." *American Ethnologist* 16: 609–21.

Coronil, Fernando. 1988. "Review of Michael Taussig's *Shamanism, Colonialism and the Wild Man*." *American Journal of Sociology* 94, no. 1: 1524–27.

Coronil, Fernando. 1989. "Discovering America Again: The Politics of Selfhood in the Age of Post-Colonial Empires." *Dispositio* 14: 315–31.

Coronil, Fernando. 1995. "Transculturation and the Politics of Theory: Countering the Center, Cuban Counterpoint." Introduction in *Cuban Counterpoint: Tobacco and Sugar*, by Fernando Ortiz, ix–lvi. Durham, NC: Duke University Press.

Coronil, Fernando. In press. *The Magical State: Black Gold and the Appearance of Modernity in Venezuela*. Chicago: University of Chicago Press. [Editors' note: This was the original title of the work that was ultimately published in 1997 as *The Magical State: Nature, Money and Modernity in Venezuela*.]

Coronil, Fernando, and Julie Skurski. 1982. "Reproducing Dependency: Auto Policy and Petrodollar Circulation in Venezuela." *International Organization* 36, no. 1: 61–94.

Coronil, Fernando, and Julie Skurski. 1991. "Dismembering and Remembering the Nation: The Semantics of Political Violence in Venezuela." *Comparative Studies in Society and History* 33, no. 2: 288–337.

de Certeau, Michel. 1988. *The Practice of Everyday Life*. Berkeley: University of California Press.

Diop, Cheikh Anta. 1974. *The African Origin of Civilization: Myth or Reality?* Westport, CT: L. Hill.

Eagleton, Terry, Fredric Jameson, and Edward Said. 1990. *Nationalism, Colonialism, and Literature*. Minneapolis: University of Minnesota Press.

Entrikin, J. Nicholas 1991. *The Betweenness of Place: Towards a Geography of Modernity*. Baltimore: Johns Hopkins University Press.

Fanon, Frantz. 1967. *Black Skins, White Masks*. New York: Grove.

Foucault, Michel. 1980. "Questions of Geography." In *Power/Knowledge: Selected Interviews and Other Writings*, ed. Colin Gordon, 63–77. New York: Pantheon.

Gates, Henry Louis, Jr. 1994. *Colored People: A Memoir*. New York: Alfred A. Knopf.

Guillén, Nicolás. 2003. "My Last Name." In *Man-Making Words: Selected Poems of Nicolás Guillén*, 2nd ed., trans. Roberto Márquez and David Arthur McMurray, 73–78. Boston: University of Massachusetts Press.

Harvey, David. 1989. *The Condition of Postmodernity*. Cambridge: Basil Blackwell.

Hayden, Bridget. 1991. "The West as Self-Representation." Paper presented at the seminar Beyond Occidentalism: Rethinking Imperial Representations, University of Michigan, Ann Arbor.

Hegel, G. W. F. 1967. *The Phenomenology of Mind*. New York: Harper Torchbooks.

Hegel, G. W. F. 1975. *Lectures on the Philosophy of History*. Cambridge: Cambridge University Press.

Herron, James. 1991. "Europe and the People Soon to Be 'Europeans.'" Paper presented at the seminar Beyond Occidentalism: Rethinking Imperial Representations, University of Michigan, Ann Arbor.

Jameson, Fredric. 1984. "Postmodernism, or, The Cultural Logic of Late Capitalism." *New Left Review* 146: 53–92.

Keesing, Roger. 1982. "Kastom in Melanesia: An Overview." *Mankind* 13: 297–301.

Klor de Alva, Jorge. 1992. "Colonialism and Postcolonialism as (Latin) American Mirages." *Colonial Latin American Review* 1, nos. 1–2: 3–23.

Laclau, Ernesto. 1990. *New Reflections on the Revolution of Our Time*. London: Verso.

Lefebvre, Henri. 1974. *La production de l'espace*. Paris: Anthropos.

Lukács, Georg. 1971. *History and Class Consciousness*. Cambridge, MA: MIT Press.

Marx, Karl. 1981. *Capital*, vol. 3. New York: Vintage.

Massey, Doreen. 1992. "Politics and Space/Time." *New Left Review* 196: 65–84.

Mignolo, Walter. 1995. *The Darker Side of the Renaissance*. Ann Arbor: University of Michigan Press.

Mintz, Sidney W. 1985. *Sweetness and Power: The Place of Sugar in Modern History*. New York: Penguin.

Mintz, Sidney W., and Eric R. Wolf. 1989. "Reply to Michael Taussig." *Critique of Anthropology* 9: 25–31.

Mitchell, Timothy. 1988. *Colonising Egypt*. Cambridge: Cambridge University Press.

Mitchell, Timothy. 1989. "The World as an Exhibition." *Comparative Studies in Society and History* 31, no. 2: 217–36.

"Moscow Summit: Excerpts from the President's Talks to Artists and Students." 1988. *New York Times*, June 1, A12.

Nader, Laura. 1989. "Orientalism, Occidentalism, and the Control of Women." *Cultural Dynamics* 2: 233–355.

Ortiz, Fernando. [1940] 1995. *Cuban Counterpoint: Tobacco and Sugar*. Durham, NC: Duke University Press.

Pletsch, Carl. 1981. "The Three Worlds, or the Division of Social Scientific Labor, circa 1950–1975. *Comparative Studies in Society and History* 23, no. 4: 565–90.

Poniatowska, Elena. 1994. "El Pais." *La Jornada*, August 16, 19.

Poulantzas, Nicos. 1978. *State, Power, Socialism*. London: New Left.

Quindlen, Anna. 1994. "Public and Private: Game Time." *New York Times*, June 25, A23.

Ricardo, David. 1983. *On the Principles of Political Economy and Taxation*. Cambridge: Cambridge University Press.

Rich, Adrienne. 1994. "Notes Towards a Politics of Location." In *Blood, Bread and Poetry: Selected Prose, 1979–1985*, 210–31. New York: W. W. Norton.

Rieff, David. 1991. *Los Angeles: Capital of the Third World*. New York: Simon Schuster.

Roseberry, William. 1989. "Review of Eric Wolf, Europe and the People without History." *Dialectical Anthropology* 10: 141–53.

Rother, Larry. 1994. "Close to Home: Remembering the Past; Repeating It Anyway." *New York Times*, July 24, 4.

Rouse, Roger. 1995. "Thinking through Transnationalism." *Public Culture* 7, no. 2: 353–402.

Said, Edward W. 1979. *Orientalism*. New York: Vintage.

Said, Edward W. 1986. "Orientalism Reconsidered." In *Literature, Politics, and Theory*, ed. Francis Barker, Peter Hulme, Margaret Iversen, and Diana Loxley, 210–29. London: Methuen.

Said, Edward W. 1993. *Culture and Imperialism*. New York: Alfred A. Knopf.

Sciolino, Elaine. 1994. "Monroe's Doctrine Takes another Knock." *New York Times*, August 9, E6.

Shohat, Ella, and Robert Stam. 1994. *Unthinking Eurocentrism*. New York: Routledge.

Skurski, Julie, and Fernando Coronil. 1992. "Country and City in a Colonial Landscape: Double Discourse and the Geopolitics of Truth in Latin America." In *View from the Border: Essays in Honor of Raymond Williams*, ed. Dennis Dworkin and Leslie Roman, 231–59. New York: Routledge.

Smith, Adam. 1976. *The Wealth of Nations*. Chicago: University of Chicago Press.

Smith, Neil. 1990. *Uneven Development*. Cambridge: Basil Blackwell.

Soja, Edward. 1989. *Postmodern Geographies*. London: Verso.

Steedman, Carolyn Kay. 1987. *Landscape for a Good Woman: A Story of Two Lives*. New Brunswick, NJ: Rutgers University Press.

Taussig, Michael. 1980. *The Devil and Commodity Fetishism in South America*. Chapel Hill: University of North Carolina Press.

Taussig, Michael. 1987a. "The Rise and Fall of Marxist Anthropology." *Social Analysis* 21: 101–13.

Taussig, Michael. 1987b. *Shamanism, Colonialism, and the Wild Man*. Chicago: University of Chicago Press.

Taussig, Michael. 1989. "History as Commodity in Some Recent American (Anthropological) Literature." *Critique of Anthropology* 9, no. 1: 7–23.

Todorov, Tzvetan. [1974] 1984. *The Conquest of America: The Question of the Other*. New York: Harper and Row.

Williams, Raymond. 1973. *The Country and the City*. New York: Oxford University Press.

Williams, Raymond. 1983. *Keywords: A Vocabulary of Culture and Society*. New York: Oxford University Press.

Wolf, Eric. 1982. *Europe and the People without History*. Berkeley: University of California Press.

13   Listening to the Subaltern:
The Poetics of Neocolonial States

Rethinking the Subaltern

Beginning at dawn on February 27, 1989, a large number of people took to the streets and began rioting and looting in Venezuela's major cities in protest against worsening economic conditions. By the end of the day, several hundred thousand people in Caracas had participated in street protests. Popular anger was triggered by a 100 percent price increase in state-owned gasoline, which led to the doubling of fares for public transportation. This step, taken to bring the price of domestic gasoline in line with world-market gasoline prices, was one of the initial measures implemented by the three-week-old government of President Carlos Andrés Pérez as part of a state policy shift from protectionism—a deeply entrenched distributionist system fueled by abundant petrodollars—toward a free-market economic model designed in accordance with International Monetary Fund (IMF) requirements for debtor nations. After thirty years of oil-supported democratic stability and party control over popular mobilization, the popular sectors were believed to be incapable of such an independent expression of will. Having erroneously assumed the passivity of the popular sectors, the startled government reacted to their activism with unprecedented repression. Ten thousand soldiers were airlifted to Caracas from the interior. The armed forces of the state opened fire on people in the barrios and on the streets, killing several hundred.[1] Lasting five days, this episode was the largest and most severely repressed protest against austerity measures not only in Venezuelan history, but in contemporary Latin America.[2]

On March 1, during the third day of rioting, the public waited anxiously for the government to make a long-delayed televised announcement to the nation. Minister of Interior Alejandro Izaguirre, a seasoned politician who has frequently served as the acting head of state, appeared before the cameras. Much to the public's shock, he muttered, "I can't, I can't," and stopped speaking. Radio and television stations immediately interrupted the broadcast without explanation. (One of the networks aired Disney cartoons for the remaining time that had been reserved by the government.) The state, ordinarily the central source of authoritative public speech, suddenly appeared speechless. This incident reveals in a flash that state speech—not only its form or content, but its very conditions of possibility—cannot be taken for granted.

More fundamentally, this moment of state speechlessness makes dramatically visible the problematic nature of its obverse—subaltern political speech—and raises questions about subalternity in general: the nature of its agents, the forms of their expression, and the possibility of representing their actions and voices. By calling attention to the complex exchange between subaltern agency and speech, in their multiple forms of expression, and neocolonialism, in its many modalities of domination, I wish to explore modes of listening to and of conceptualizing the subaltern that may counter rather than confirm the silencing effect of domination. In her influential article "Can the Subaltern Speak?" Gayatri Spivak (1988a) problematizes the production and retrieval of subaltern speech in light of its dependence on dominant discursive fields, which constitute subaltern subjects, define their modalities of expression, and structure the positions from which they speak and are heard. I want to address the problem Spivak has so provocatively and productively raised in order to take advantage of the space she has opened up, but also to advance a different approach to subalternity. Spivak's aim is, in her words, "to learn to speak to (rather than listen to or speak for) the historically muted subject of the non-elite" (Spivak 1988a: 271). As part of a larger exchange, I seek to learn to listen to subaltern subjects and to interpret what I hear. This exchange also involves my learning to speak to a variety of publics, not only to subaltern subjects, but to any who share an interest in overcoming the conditions that make subalternity possible. The interpretation I offer here is an instance of this engagement, in which I participate as a Venezuelan citizen working as an anthropologist in the United States.

Spivak, by means of an extended discussion of sati (or suttee)—the practice of self-immolation by Indian widows on their husbands' pyres—presents as emblematic of the subaltern the case of a political activist who sought to communicate her personal predicament through her suicide but whose communication was foiled by the codes of patriarchy and colonialism in which her actions were inevitably inscribed. Spivak depicts her situation in the following terms:

> A young woman of sixteen or seventeen, Bhuvaneswari Bhaduri, hanged herself in her father's modest apartment in North Calcutta in 1926. The suicide was a puzzle since, as Bhuvaneswari was menstruating at the time, it was clearly not a case of illicit pregnancy. Nearly a decade later, it was discovered that she was a member of one of the many groups involved in the armed struggle for Indian independence. She had finally been entrusted with a political assassination. Unable to confront the task and yet aware of the practical need for trust, she killed herself. . . . Bhuvaneswari had known that her death would be diagnosed as the outcome of illegitimate passion. She had therefore waited for the onset of menstruation. While waiting, Bhuvaneswari, the brahmacarini who was no doubt looking forward to a good wifehood, perhaps rewrote the social text of sati-suicide in an interventionist way. (Spivak 1988a: 307)

Despite Bhaduri's precautions, her death is remembered by her relatives (her nieces) as "a case of illicit love," and the meaning of her act thus seems to have been lost to history, although it is not clear, given the nature of the evidence provided, whether Spivak was uniquely able to retrieve it (Spivak 1988a: 308). Since Bhaduri's actions are not only inscribed but read in terms of the dominant codes of British imperialism and Indian patriarchy, Spivak concludes, provocatively, that "the subaltern cannot speak" (Spivak 1988a: 308).

Her conclusion is preceded by a discussion of Antonio Gramsci's and Ranajit Guha's treatments of subalternity, in which her main focus is Guha's analysis of the social structure of neocolonial societies by means of a "dynamic stratification grid":

Elite:
1. Dominant foreign groups.
2. Dominant indigenous groups on the all-India level.
3. Dominant indigenous groups at the regional and local levels.
4. The terms "people" and "subaltern classes" have been used as synonymous throughout this note. The social groups and elements included in this category represent *the demographic difference between the total Indian population and all those whom we have described as the "elite."* (Spivak 1988a: 284 [Guha's emphases])

Guha's grid is built upon the assumption that subalternity resides in "the people," taken as an undifferentiated subject. In terms of this grid, the intermediate groups between the elite and the people, the "dominant indigenous groups at the regional and local levels" (number 3), are particularly problematic because they can be either dominant or dominated, depending on situational considerations. As Guha says, "The same class or element which was dominant in one area . . . could be among the dominated in another. This could and did create many ambiguities and contradictions in attitudes and alliances, especially among the lowest strata of the rural gentry, impoverished landlords, rich peasants and upper-middle-class peasants all of whom belonged, *ideally speaking*, to the category of people or subaltern classes" (Spivak 1988a: 284 [Guha's emphases]). Given this conceptualization of the intermediate groups within the project of studying the subaltern, Spivak notes that for Guha the "task of research" is "to investigate, identify, and measure the *specific* nature and degree of the *deviation* of [the] elements [constituting item 3] from the ideal and situate it historically" (Spivak 1988a: 285 [Guha's emphases]).

Noting the essentialist and taxonomic character of this program, Spivak emphasizes the fact that "the object of the group's investigation, in this case not even of the people as such but of the floating buffer zone of the regional elite-subaltern, is a *deviation* from an *ideal*—the people or subaltern—which is itself defined as a difference from the elite" (Spivak 1988a: 285 [Spivak's emphases]). After making these observations, Spivak leaves the problematic "buffer zone" group behind and moves on to problematize the research of item 4: "the people," or "subaltern classes," the *ideal* itself. In her provocative but complicated discussion of the subaltern as female, she seems to be arguing that the subaltern's voice/consciousness cannot be retrieved and that analysis should indicate this impossibility by charting the positions from which the subaltern speaks but "cannot be heard or read" (Spivak 1988a: 308). As one of Spivak's interpreters has argued,

> Rather than speak for a lost consciousness that cannot be recovered, a paternalistic activity at best, the critic can point to the place of woman's disappearance as an *aporia*, a blind-spot where understanding and knowledge is blocked. Complicating the assumption that the gendered subaltern is a homogeneous entity whose voice can be simply retrieved, Spivak demonstrates the paradoxical contradictions of the discourses which produce such *aporia* in the place of subject-positions,

showing that the *sati* herself is at best presented with the non-choice of the robber's "your money or your life!" "Voice" is of little use in this situation. (Young 1990: 164)

Spivak's assertion that the subaltern cannot speak "has been pervasively read as an expression of terminal epistemological and political pessimism" (Lowe et al. 1990: 83). Yet in a recent interview, saying that she had been misunderstood, Spivak claimed that her purpose had been to counter the impulse to solve the problem of political subjectivity by romanticizing the subaltern. Instead of treating the subaltern as an unproblematic unified subject, she would apply to the subaltern "all the complications of 'subject production' which are applied to us" (Spivak 1990: 90). While this seems eminently reasonable—except that she presupposes and reproduces a questionable polarity between "we" (dominant) and "they" (subaltern)— her next proposal is disconcerting. Spivak suggests using the term "subaltern for everything that is different from organized resistance" and justifies this usage by building on Guha in the following terms:

Because I use the word difference, it's seen as me talking Derrida. Derrida is not my prophet. I'm not talking Derrida, I'm talking about the introduction to the first volume of Ranajit Guha's *Subaltern Studies* where he is making an analysis of how a colonial society is structured, and what space can be spoken of as the subaltern space. There is a space in post-imperial arenas which is displaced from empire-nation exchange. Where one sees the "emancipated bourgeoisie," "organized labor," "organized left movements," "urban radicalism," the disenfranchised "women's arena" (these words are all used in quotes), all of this is constituted within that empire-nation exchange, reversing it in many different kinds of ways. But in post-imperialist societies there is a vast arena which is not necessarily accessible to that kind of exchange. It is that space that one calls subaltern. The romantic notion that the subaltern as subaltern can speak is totally undermined by the fact that the real effort is to pull them into national agency with the sanctions that are already there. (Spivak 1990: 90–91)

It seems to me that with this move, Spivak has in effect homogenized and pushed the subaltern out of the realm of political exchange, beyond "national agency." The ambiguities and contradictions in the notion of the subaltern, which were sharply visible in Guha's intermediate category (the "dominant indigenous groups at the regional and local levels"), seem resolved here by the subaltern's relegation to the margins and transformation into an outsider, an other. Thus, building on Michel Foucault's approval of nominalism in *The History of Sexuality*, Spivak says, "To that extent, the subaltern is the name of the place which is so displaced from what made me and the organized resister, that to have it speak is like Godot arriving on a bus. We want it to disappear as a name so that we can all speak" (Spivak 1990: 91). Making it "disappear as a name" entails creating a democratic society—a society without dominance and subalternity—but this process presupposes the recognition of the subaltern as an agent of historical transformation not just despite, but because of, its subalternity at this time. Yet, with this topographic conception, Spivak seems to reconstitute the subaltern not only as a unified subject which cannot speak, but as a mute object—positioned outside agency.

Spivak conceptualizes the subaltern differently in commenting on her own position during her evaluation of the historiographic work of the Subaltern Studies Group in India. She says that she is "progressively inclined . . . to read the retrieval of subaltern consciousness as the charting of what in post-structuralist language [would] be called the subaltern subject-effect." From this perspective, the subject is metaleptic—an effect substituted for a cause. Her invocation of the strategic use of positivist essentialism appears to be a necessary but theoretically unsatisfactory response to the poststructuralist dissolution of the subject (Spivak 1988b: 12–15). In my view, the problems associated with structuralist conceptions of sovereign, unified subjects who operate as causes of historical effects are only mirrored by the poststructuralist conception of dispersed subjects who operate as effects; a more fruitful conceptualization would be one that overcame the polarization of terms in which this debate is being cast.[3]

As a step in this direction, I propose that we view the subaltern neither as a sovereign-subject that actively occupies a bounded place nor as a vassal-subject that results from the dispersed effects of multiple external determinations, but as an agent of identity construction that participates, under determinate conditions within a field of power relations, in the organization of its multiple positionality and subjectivity. In my view, subalternity is a relational and a relative concept; there are times and places where subjects appear on the social stage as subaltern actors, just as there are times or places in which they play dominant roles. Moreover, at any given time or place, an actor may be subaltern in relation to another, yet dominant in relation to a third. And, of course, there are contexts in which these categories may simply not be relevant. Dominance and subalternity are not inherent but relational characterizations. Subalternity defines not the being of a subject, but a subjected state of being. This relational and situational view of the subaltern may help anticolonial intellectuals avoid the we-they polarity underlying Spivak's analysis and listen to subaltern voices that speak from variously marginalized places.

From this perspective, I wish next to discuss subaltern speech as it is articulated at the very center of neocolonial societies. Drawing my examples from a larger investigation in which I have sought to listen to dominant as well as subaltern neocolonial discourses by contextualizing them within a historical and cultural field (Coronil and Skurski 1991), here I will focus exclusively on speech articulated by representatives of the state, who are generally seen as "dominant" actors. In what form, if any, is subalternity expressed in the speech of the neocolonial state, the institution that must constitute and represent itself as the locus of sovereignty and autonomy?

State Speech

Like metropolitan states, subaltern states "speak"—literally and metaphorically—through the languages that constitute them as central sites of authority, and their multiple forms of speech impact the daily lives of people within their societies. As states, they must continually authorize themselves by producing binding statements (regulations, laws, policies, etc.) whose authority over citizens within a bounded territory rests on a combination of consent and coercion. Underlying Max Weber's understanding of the state as the institution that holds a monopoly on legitimate violence is the fact that the state can not only back up its statements with force but can deploy violence as its legitimate statement.

Indeed, on March 1, 1989, the Venezuelan state's speechlessness was only partial. Minister Izaguirre's collapse before the cameras was a response to the state's "speech" in the streets: he fainted when he heard a burst of gunfire outside and realized that the armed forces were shooting at people—the *pueblo*—the foundation of Venezuelan populist nationalism. The minister had spent long, sleepless hours analyzing the situation with other leaders and coming to terms with the decision he had been about to announce: the state had brought in the army to restore public order. The following day, at a different center of power, another state representative was quite able to speak of the need to use violence to ensure order and progress. Gonzalo Barrios, eighty-eight years old, a founding figure of Venezuelan democracy; leader of the ruling party, Acción Democrática; and president of the National Congress, made an important speech to Congress. The day before, the Christian Democrat Rafael Caldera, former president of Venezuela, had delivered an impassioned address to Congress, urging the nation's leadership to recognize the existence of serious problems and to restore national unity. Barrios's speech was both a response to this call and a justification of the measures the government had resolved to take to enforce public order.

The contrast between Minister Izaguirre's and Senator Barrios's responses to the crisis highlights not only the opposition between speech and speechlessness but also their location on a shared discursive terrain. It is within the context of Izaguirre's silence that I wish to examine Barrios's speech, so as to illuminate the dynamic relationship between speech and its "locus of enunciation" (Mignolo 1989) during changing historical conditions. At this critical juncture in Venezuelan history, the outlines of a reconfigured relationship between state and nation, government and citizenry, became visible. The different responses by these officials to the crisis represent two distinct interventions in this redrawing of Venezuela's conflicting identities.

Representing the State

At first glance, Barrios's speech seems like just one more instance of the usual intraelite dispute over everyday politics. It is difficult to discern from its tone or content that a crisis is under way, that several hundred people have already been killed, or that the army is at that very moment shooting people down in the streets. As Barrios's discourse unfolds, what seems to matter is preventing Caldera from using the crisis to elevate himself and to be recognized as the authoritative interpreter of these events.

Senator Barrios starts by noting that he was glad to have had the opportunity to read Caldera's speech instead of responding to it as he heard it the previous day, for "it is not the same thing to listen to a speech and to experience the collective emotion that it unleashes as it is to be able to judge it quietly in one's study, reading and rereading some concepts in order to see their hidden intent" (Barrios 1989: 143).[4] Speaking as the tempered voice of reason, Barrios then proceeds to set the record straight by presenting his own interpretation of events. Thus, in the midst of a crisis characterized by the massive, independent intervention of popular sectors in national politics, what is foregrounded is an intraelite difference of opinion. In its failure to focus either on the actions and voices in the street or even on their armed repression, Barrios's speech embodies the silencing and denial of popular claims on the nation.

This exclusion of the popular sectors is reproduced throughout the speech. In the face of an independent mass action, former President Caldera emphasized the need for "leaders to reach out to the *pueblo* in order to channel their feelings toward civic attitudes, toward orderly protest, toward [making] their presence [felt] within the framework of the Constitution and the laws" (Caldera 1989: 136). In his response, Barrios minimizes the importance of popular mobilization by attributing it to the influence of political agitators. Distancing himself from Caldera, he condemns interpretations that explain the recourse to violent action by appeal to the growing frustrations of people faced with worsening living conditions. Just as the command "thou shall not kill" allows no exceptions, Barrios argues, people should not be permitted to engage in violent actions. Revealingly, Barrios appears not to notice the irony in this case—namely, that the command "thou shall not kill" is being violated in the streets and barrios by the government as the army escalates its attack and the death toll reaches several hundred (fewer than ten casualties among government forces resulted from the week of conflict). For Barrios, the popular sectors remain fundamentally faceless.

At this moment of crisis, the public that concerns Barrios is to be found outside Venezuela, in the United States and Europe. He observes that "it is very rare for the television of these countries to take note of our countries, particularly if it is a question of reporting happy incidents or facts that elevate us, but it would seem that they rejoice in presenting any event, any manifestation, that tends to show us as depressed countries, as primitive cultures" (Barrios 1989: 144). He expresses his regret that these events have shown "the horror, the primitive, the uncontrollable, from a civilized point of view, of the looting that took place in Caracas" (Barrios 1989: 144). According to Barrios, this has happened at a time when Venezuela has been demanding more attention from these nations and has managed to overcome "the prejudices that exist in the developed nations with respect to ourselves" (Barrios 1989: 144). The day before, Caldera had expressed a similar concern over Venezuela's shattered image in a much-quoted passage of his speech: "Venezuela has been a kind of pilot country. At this moment it is what North Americans call a 'showcase,' the display case of Latin American democracy. . . . This display case was destroyed by the blows and rocks of the starving people from the Caracas barrios who are being subjected to the iron chains imposed, directly or indirectly, by the IMF"

(Caldera 1989: 137). Building on a distinction between "developed nations" and "our countries," both Caldera and Barrios express regret at the negative image of Venezuela now being projected to the developed world.

Caldera's metaphor of Venezuela as a showcase, with its Madison Avenue overtones, had wide appeal partly because it conjured up the familiar image of a gap between the façade of national progress and the lived reality of chronic problems. Caldera's speech observed the typical conventions of nationalist rhetoric, including a grandiloquent call to repair the tarnished image of Venezuela as a united nation coupled with a denunciation of outside interference by such powers as the IMF. In contrast, Barrios's response was cast in the colloquial style of intra-elite conversation and addressed, with ironic understatement, the all-too-familiar reality behind the embellished images constructed for outside consumption. He appealed to the elite by publicly using its private language and by expressing, through self-parody that verged on self-denial, its unflattering view of Venezuela.

This view of Venezuela comes across in Barrios's discussion of the country's relations with the International Monetary Fund. Barrios chooses to open this discussion by attacking Caldera for presenting himself as a nationalist leader who, unlike others, would not leave Venezuela even if the IMF policy package failed to achieve its aims. Barrios sarcastically congratulates Caldera, but declares his certainty that other respectable people, including himself, would not abandon the ship even if it threatened to sink. He then proceeds to counter Caldera's condemnation of the IMF by matter-of-factly noting that the IMF is just a capitalist institution whose business it is to serve the interests of capitalism. He describes the IMF in terms targeted to the elite, not to the masses, calling it "a tremendously nasty, disagreeable institution (*una institución tremendamente antipática, muy desagradable*) whose purpose is not simply to help bankrupt nations" (Barrios 1989: 146). He contrasts the IMF with the Red Cross, whose objective is to help countries with specific problems. The IMF's resources, Barrios emphasizes, are intended to promote capitalism, not "to finance the corruption, waste, and administrative vices of developing nations." We could go along with Caldera and protest against the IMF's requirement that we behave in ways contrary to our own culture, Barrios says, but then adds, "I don't think we have the right to tell the IMF: 'My culture of a tropical, underdeveloped country requires a certain *guachafita* [disorder, mess] in public administration'" (Barrios 1989: 147).

Barrios then gives substance to this image of a "tropical, underdeveloped country" by listing a set of features that paint a dark picture of Venezuela and its elite: individual, group, and class favoritism; wasted public resources; poorly invested public funds, and so on. Barrios concludes this discussion of Venezuela's relationship to the IMF on a note of sarcasm: "It would be nice if there were an international institution with enough funds to help those who commit crimes in this fashion . . . , but such an institution does not exist. As I said before, the International Red Cross serves other purposes and does not have the resources for these causes" (Barrios 1989: 147).

Throughout this speech, Barrios avoids the elevated rhetoric of grand transformations. He chooses instead to use the elite's private language of mundane complicity in order to elicit support for the government's program, which he defines simply as making Venezuela a "modern state." By adopting these (IMF-mandated) measures, Barrios argues, Venezuela would get the resources it needs now and would learn to behave as a well-organized country in the future. There is no talk here of great transformations.

Noting that no one has come up with a workable alternative to the government's policies, Barrios argues that the only other possibility is to go backward. He concludes his speech by dismissing this alternative and by justifying state violence against the popular sectors with a story that "captivated" him because of its "implicit irony." The story concerns a British general who wanted to subdue one of the "less primitive tribes" of Africa. The general sent as his emissary a missionary who had lived among the indigenous people and who might convince them that British occupation would be to their benefit. The missionary told them of the hospitals, schools, means of communication, and laws they would receive from the British. The African chief recognized the value of this offer but rejected it, arguing that its acceptance would cause his people to lose their soul. The missionary, on reporting the chief's refusal to the general, suggested that the chief was right. "The general," Barrios says, "naturally paid no attention to the missionary and gave orders to blast the natives with heavy gunfire [plomo cerrado], as often occurs in disputes among civilized nations." Barrios then adds, in a tone of ironic understatement, that if Congress decides to reject President Pérez's austerity program and the repressive measures taken to enforce it, the nation will begin a backward slide: "I think that Venezuela would not necessarily return to loincloths and arrows because we have well-grounded structures and [have made] progress, but we could go back to a situation in which Rolls-Royces and fancy televisions with satellite dishes would disappear" (Barrios 1989: 148).

The Poetics of Neocolonialism

Barrios unabashedly legitimates the new policies by passing off an old colonial framework as his own, transmuting the Venezuelan people into a "primitive" African tribe, converting congressmen into civilizing British generals, and reformulating state violence against the people as a tool of civilization. Given the Venezuelan elite's view of England as the crucible of Western capitalism, and of Africa as the dark land of primitivism, the brand of colonialism conjured up in Barrios's speech establishes a stark contrast between civilization and barbarism in which the ambiguities associated with the Spanish imperial experience in America are elided. By choosing this remote, paradigmatic colonial model, Barrios offers the local political elite an image of itself as an agent of civilization. Within the simplistic terms of this idealized model, violence against "the primitive" can be articulated in elite-coded language, without sentimentality or grandiosity, as a necessary condition of historical progress. *Plomo cerrado* (approximately, "heavy gunfire"), with its colloquial, laconic overtones, mimics the language of violence on the streets; it forecloses discussion.

In this speech, the movement from barbarism to civilization can be charted by four emblematic objects. "Loincloths and arrows" bring to mind the figure of a primitive order that lies not too far in the past and that manifests itself in the present through the Venezuelan "Indian," who is widely regarded as ignorant. Saved from this backward world by the existence of "well-grounded structures" and "progress," the desired realm of superior civilization is conjured up by two commodities that, ironically, represent what is well beyond even the elite. A "Rolls-Royce," given high domestic taxes and limited service, is a vehicle that is out of reach for most members of the upper class. As an emblem of unattainable luxury for an elite that prides itself on being able to purchase and even surround itself with such external tokens of "civilization," it is a reminder of a distance from the metropolitan centers that not even money can entirely bridge. "Fancy televisions with satellite dishes," on the other hand, are available to relatively large segments of the upper middle class (particularly since one satellite dish can serve many apartments in a high-rise), but access to them only emphasizes the contrast between Venezuelan and U.S. television programs and the different societies they reflect. For those who have access to U.S. TV shows, they are a daily reminder of the gap between the two worlds, as well as a means of partially bridging it; they mark both the connection and the separation between these worlds. Since, from the second day of rioting, Venezuelan television stations were not allowed to show what was occurring in the streets, it was through these "fancy televisions" that the elite, including Barrios, found itself in the odd position of watching Venezuela being watched by foreign journalists, as the international news showed "the horror, the primitive, the uncontrollable, from a civilized point of view, of the looting that took place in Caracas."

Thus, through the language of objects and commodities, Barrios conjures up the image of a country suspended in an endless middle passage, eternally stranded in a transition between the threat of encroaching backwardness and the vision of receding modernity. Since he is speaking to his fellow political leaders, not to the masses, Barrios can acknowledge the limited nature of the state's goals. It is no longer a case, as with other opportunities, of proposing to take great strides toward "modernity," but of simply putting one's house in order, of making this "tropical capitalism" less corrupt so as to give these politicians and the economic elite linked to them continued access to the worldly goods of the metropolitan centers. The price this ruling stratum must pay is giving up a model of protectionism that is no longer viable. But abandoning protectionism entails a violent rupture of identities that Barrios's distancing allegory cannot completely conceal. His colonial story does violence not only to the representation of the popular sectors, who must abruptly be seen as a disposable primitive mass, but also to that of the governing elite itself, to its self-image as the anti-imperialist defender of the interests of the pueblo and as the builder of Venezuelan democracy. All of a sudden, this political group, with its long populist history, finds itself cast in the role of an imperial general. Minister Izaguirre's speechlessness reveals the dissonance with which the elite must cope in taking up this role.

With the adoption of free-market policies and a shift of profitmaking opportunities from local to international markets, the social and political elite increasingly had to identify with its international counterparts and to sever its links with the popular sectors. The popular image of the people as the virtuous foundation of democracy in need of tutelary guidance had given way to a revised conception of them as backward masses in need of control. The formation of this emergent social landscape fractured the customary bonds tying state to citizens, parties to people, and leaders to masses.

Barrios's colonial allegory must be understood within the context of a society in which political speech serves the ongoing construction of public images that conceal relations of power through the artful interplay of irony and deceit, simulation and artifice. The attention paid by Barrios to Venezuela's external image is not narcissistic but strategic: it is from the standpoint of civilization that backwardness is constructed and that the local elite constitutes itself as a mediator between these states. In Venezuela, the political elite remains situated in an unstable neocolonial landscape which continually undermines national sources of identity and knowledge. This instability is articulated through a "double discourse" of national identity that "expresses and organizes the split between the appearance of national sovereignty and the continuing hold of international subordination, a split inscribed in the truncated character of domestic productive relations as well as in the mimetic form of consumption values, in the production of political knowledge as well as in the formation of collective identities" (Skurski and Coronil 1993: 25).

Enunciating a Locus of Enunciation

As this brief discussion suggests, the transformation in Venezuela's social anatomy has entailed a crisis of representation, which is inevitably a crisis of self-representation as well. The shift from protectionist to free-market policies in Venezuela has been a violent process, with state violence not only repressing the political activism of the popular sectors, but also their representation in discourse. The growing dissonance between the discourse of traditional populist nationalism and the emergent free-market discourse of economic globalization has made shaky ground of the terrain on which social actors must now stand. The state, the locus of authoritative public speech, has been caught off-balance in this ideological struggle among conflicting positions. If Izaguirre's speechlessness speaks of the state's state of crisis, Barrios's speech speaks of its character. In the course of mutating and mutilating the identities of both the people and their representatives, Barrios included, his speech shapes the contours of Venezuela's emerging neocolonial landscape. In the fault lines of this landscape we may recognize a common ground on which variously positioned subaltern subjects—and I would include here the agents of the neocolonial state in certain relational contexts—must now stand and speak.

This ground, however, should not be seen as a place beyond agency and consciousness. If, as Nicos Poulantzas (1978: 114) suggests, national unity involves the "historicity of a territory and the territorialization of a history," then the new social geography emerging in Venezuela is a new social anatomy as well. Treating space and time as mutually constitutive dimensions of social reality may permit us to see how postcolonial topographies are historically formed or reformed through human agency and how these forms are *informed* by the meanings attached to this agency.[5] Such a space and time perspective should also help us to get beyond the analytical dichotomies that rupture the complex unity of social life; thus, the oppositions that Spivak posits between subject position and voice, space and consciousness, may be usefully reconceptualized as relationships rather than polarized positions, thereby avoiding the need to choose between them in our analyses.

The locus of enunciation is inseparable from the enunciation of a locus; analysis must comprehend them as interrelated dimensions of a single historical process. A subject position, therefore, is not only a structural locus of enunciation but a topos partially defined by a positioned subject through speech, which in turn makes speech possible. At the height of the Venezuelan crisis, when a complex set of international and domestic forces shifted the ground on which all social actors stood, a new terrain was mapped not only by these forces, but by their representation in state speech. While in the midst of the crisis Minister Izaguirre lost his voice as well as his footing, Senator Barrios staked his claim on this new terrain by enunciating the new locus of state speech. Although I sympathize with Spivak's efforts to counter the conceit that intellectuals can directly represent subaltern voices or consciousness, I believe that restricting analysis to the study of mute subject positions continues a history of silencing such voices. Engaging with subaltern subjects entails responding to their presence within silenced histories, listening for voices—and to silences—within the cracks of dominant histories, if only to widen them.

Notes

This essay is based on research supported by the Spencer Foundation and the Rackham School of Graduate Studies, University of Michigan. My gratitude goes to these institutions and to Julie Skurski, who has participated in every aspect of this research; to Rebecca Scott, who encouraged me to clarify my discussion of the subaltern subject; and to my students at the University of Michigan, whose insights have deepened my understanding of these issues.

1   The official figure is 277. Definitive figures are difficult to establish. Unofficial estimates of the death toll made by journalists and human rights organizations have been reduced from around one thousand (at the time of the riots) to five hundred.

2 For a detailed examination of these events, see Coronil and Skurski 1991. For an interesting taxonomic discussion of fifty instances of protest and repression in Latin America associated with the implementation of free-market policies from 1976 to 1986, see Walton 1989.

3 Spivak's discussion of the "subaltern" is developed in yet other directions (which I cannot discuss here) in her response (Spivak 1989) to Benita Parry's (1987) helpful critique of her work. This exchange suggests that a critical awareness of the complicity between imperialism and anthropology should lead not to a rejection of the representation of "native" voices but to a critical transformation of anthropology's modes of representing (and of conceptualizing) itself and its objects of study.

4 All translations from Spanish are mine.

5 I have sought to develop some of the implications of Poulantzas's insight into the interplay between geography and history, in Coronil 1996. [*Editors' note*: At the time this article was written, "Beyond Occidentalism" had not yet been published and therefore was described here as "forthcoming."]

References

Barrios, Gonzalo. 1989. Untitled speech. *Diario de Debates del Senado, República de Venezuela XIX*, January–June 1989, vol. 1, 143–48. Caracas: Imprenta del Congreso de la República.

Caldera, Rafael. 1989. Untitled speech. *Diario de Debates del Senado, República de Venezuela XIX*, January–June 1989, vol. 1, 135–40. Caracas: Imprenta del Congreso de la República.

Coronil, Fernando. 1996. "Beyond Occidentalism: Towards Nonimperial Geohistorical Categories." *Cultural Anthropology* 11, no. 1 (February): 51–87.

Coronil, Fernando, and Julie Skurski. 1991. "Dismembering and Remembering the Nation: The Semantics of Political Violence in Venezuela." *Comparative Studies in Society and History* 33, no. 2: 288–337.

Lowe, Donald, Michael Rosenthal, and Ron Silliman. 1990. "Introduction," in "Gayatri Spivak on the Politics of the Subaltern (an Interview with Howard Winant)." *Socialist Review* 20, no. 3: 81–97.

Mignolo, Walter. 1989. "Afterword: From Colonial Discourse to Colonial Semiosis." *Dispositio* 14: 36–38.

Mignolo, Walter. 1995. *The Darker Side of the Renaissance: Literacy, Territoriality and Colonization*. Ann Arbor: University of Michigan Press.

Parry, Benita. 1987. "Problems in Current Theories of Colonial Discourse." *Oxford Literary Review* 9: 27–58.

Poulantzas, Nicos. 1978. *Power, State, Socialism*. London: New Left Books.

Skurski, Julie, and Fernando Coronil. 1993. "Country and City in a Colonial Landscape: Double Discourse and the Geopolitics of Truth in Latin America."

In *View from the Border: Essays in Honor of Raymond Williams*, ed. Dennis Dworkin and Leslie Roman, 231–59. New York: Routledge.

Spivak, Gayatri Chakravorty. 1988a. "Can the Subaltern Speak?" In *Marxism and the Interpretation of Culture*, ed. Cary Nelson and Lawrence Grossberg, 271–313. Urbana: University of Illinois Press.

Spivak, Gayatri Chakravorty. 1988b. "Subaltern Studies: Deconstructing Historiography." In *Selected Subaltern Studies*, ed. Ranajit Guha and Gayatri Chakravorty Spivak, 3–32. New York: Oxford University Press.

Spivak, Gayatri Chakravorty. 1989. "Naming Gayatri Spivak (an Interview with Maria Koundoura)." *Stanford Humanities Review* 1: 84–97.

Spivak, Gayatri Chakravorty. 1990. "Gayatri Spivak on the Politics of the Subaltern (an Interview with Howard Winant)." *Socialist Review* 3: 81–97.

Walton, John. 1989. "Debt, Protest, and the State in Latin America." In *Power and Popular Protest*, ed. Susan Eckstein, 299–328. Berkeley: University of California Press.

Young, Robert. 1990. *White Mythologies: Writing History and the West*. New York: Routledge.

14   Smelling Like a Market

I remember some markets as worldly celebrations of labor and sociality, their busy exchanges and careful presentation of goods and crafts a feast of abundance, colors, and smells. One of my favorite markets in the United States is Philadelphia's Italian market, which combines the buzz of a major city with the intimate feel of certain regional markets in Latin America, where goods have to do with local production and uses. Of course, there are also less appealing markets, like some in the barrios of Latin American cities, where no effort can dispel a sense of disorder and lack, the stink of abjection. In some markets, one can "smell" fear: one has to be careful not to be robbed by either the vendors or the clients. Others communicate calm, like my local farmer's market, a place for socializing and shopping in an atmosphere of cordial and safe exchange. There are also markets, alien to me, like the New York Stock Exchange, defined by the high-energy movements of betting on the shifting risks of corporate values, transacted in anonymous exchanges. The chain supermarket where I shop, homogenizing and impersonal, also qualifies as a market, as do the West's new temples, the malls, those commodity shrines whose excess, social control, and rarefied air so quickly disorient my senses. The markets of socialist Cuba have an estranging atmosphere all their own, one that smells of desires and social divisions defined by the boundaries of the dollar's circulation. While ordinary stores carry but a limited array of inexpensive local goods sold for Cuban pesos, new supermarkets and malls offer diverse imported goods at inflated state-set prices for U.S. dollars.

Markets not only have smells, they are also apparently able to smell. Advocates of the capitalist market tell us that it can smell a successful product, a crisis, or a consumer need. For those who imagine it as an invisible hand that turns selfish individual choices into harmonious collective ends, the market seems to operate as a hidden nervous system: it senses people's desires, monitors their private decisions, and directs their conduct toward the production and consumption of goods that satisfy ever more differentiated needs. For its critics, the capitalist market is an all-too-earthly invention, rather than a benevolent transcendent force, blind to human needs and aimlessly propelled by the short-sighted pursuit of filthy money.

Clearly, markets vary immensely in their purposes, organization, state relations, and social norms. Given not only its widely varying historical forms and attributes but also the divergent theories directed at explaining it, is there such a thing as smelling like a market?

These thoughts came to my mind as I read James C. Scott's thought-provoking book *Seeing Like a State: How Certain Schemes to Improve the Human Condition Have Failed*, which proposes that the modern state has a distinctive way of "seeing" that constitutes a form of political power. In order to control and establish its authority over society through plans to improve it, Scott argues, the modern state strives to make society "legible" by means of homogenizing operations such as censuses and maps. It is these "simplifying" systems of representation, measurement, and naming that define the modern state's short-sighted way of seeing. The flatness of the modern state's vision concerns Scott not only because of its epistemic shortcomings but also because of its political effects: it shapes flawed and costly plans and molds the subjects it seeks to control. Critical of the belief that society can be improved through overarching rational designs—which he calls "high modernism"—Scott centers his discussion on large-scale state plans that embody this dangerous conceit. "Seeing like a state," the suggestive title of this book, refers to a simplifying mode of vision Scott attributes to the state that has been instrumental in effecting sweeping social transformations at considerable human cost since the end of the eighteenth century.

According to Scott, high-modernist plans to improve the human condition tend to go awry independently of the intentions or skills of planners, for they are based on "thin simplifications" that misrepresent society's dense interplay of interdependencies and ignore people's practical knowledge. While Scott recognizes that the state is not the exclusive agent of grand schemes of social engineering and that these plans have on occasion been successful, this recognition does not alter his sole focus on the state and his critique of its blinding vision. His concern with failed high-modernist plans to change society is limited to a critique of the state and its utopian designs.

Scott presents this general argument by means of an imaginative but problematic selection of failed schemes of large-scale state engineering. His cases proceed from state-led attempts to reorder "nature" through scientific forestry in order to increase productivity to efforts to reorganize "society" through state planning in capitalist and socialist societies with the goal of improving life and even human nature. The cases cover more than two hundred years, advance chronologically from the second half of the eighteenth century to the late twentieth century, and move from a critique of designs to transform specific areas of capitalist societies to a sustained censure of attempts to reshape society under socialist rule. The main target of his critique is the radical utopian vision. He contrasts the top-down totalizing views of progressive reformers such as Le Corbusier and revolutionaries such as Vladimir I. Lenin to the more practical perspectives of radical thinkers such as Rosa Luxemburg and critics of modern urbanism such as Jane Jacobs. He attributes Jacobs's sensitivity to the microsociology of urban orders to her "woman's eye," an eye trained to observe ordinary activities such as taking a walk or window shopping that "have no single purpose or that have no conscious purpose in the narrow sense."[1]

His first case concerns the rise of state-directed projects of scientific forestry in Prussia and Saxony in the late eighteenth and early nineteenth centuries, a fascinating study of the unintended effects of large-scale plans. The effort to maximize timber production and revenues by creating stripped-down, timber-producing forests led instead to the destruction of the complex ecosystem on which the very growth of timber depends. Rather than maximizing long-term production, this state-led plan resulted in the destruction of the social and natural fabric of the forests and to a sharp decline in production after the first generation of rationalized tree planting.

Scott presents this case as paradigmatic of the processes he critiques, frequently evoking the "forest" as a metaphor for "society." He shows how the same mode of vision associated with state "simplifications" designed to make the forest more productive has informed a number of efforts to improve society, leading to the violent disruption of the historical fabric of society like that inflicted on the natural fabric of the forest. While the object of planning is significantly different from that of scientific forestry, the planning logic and its devastating effects are similar. The progression of his narrative, as it spirals from state-led plans to reorder nature to the ever more ambitious designs to reshape society, makes clear that his central target is "authoritarian high modernism"—that is, the "aspiration to the administrative ordering of nature and society," which he presents as an extension of scientific forestry to the social domain.

His main case studies include the construction of Brasília, the Brazilian state's modernization project inspired by Le Corbusier's vision of a total urban environment; the Soviet collectivization of agriculture, an expression of Lenin's centralized bureaucratic aim to build socialism in one country; and the forced "villagization" of Tanzania from 1973 to 1976, an instance of Julius Nyerere's effort to settle a largely nomadic population in administrative villages and create a modern and productive peasantry. All these plans "failed" because they were based on "state simplifications" that did not reflect the actual complexity of society but, rather, a will to render it manageable and to redesign it according to the state's utopian vision. Making an explicit analogy with scientific forestry, he argues that the "modern state, through its officials, attempts with varying success to create a terrain and a population with precisely those standardized characteristics that will be easiest to monitor, count, assess, and manage."[2]

To the possible objection that some plans failed not just because they were grand but because they were ill conceived or because of unpredictable changes in political or environmental conditions, Scott's book seems to provide a ready reply: it is precisely because no plan can account for life's contingencies that any plan aspiring to more than cautious reforms is doomed to failure. His suggestions make a reasoned argument for gradualism (but I see no reason why they could not orient the implementation of large-scale plans as well): "take small steps," "favor reversibility," "plan on surprises," and "plan on human inventiveness."[3] While it is evident that his position reinforces both the conservative and liberal opposition to radical plans for societal change, it is less obvious that it may undermine the political ground of reformism itself. On the basis of his discussion of the unintended effects of high-modernist designs, Scott proposes that thin simplifications cannot apprehend the dense complexity of social interdependencies—the removal of unsightly scrubs may thwart the growth of useful pine trees. But what of the possibility that without the threat of radical movements, as the historical evidence suggests, moderate reforms would find a less propitious political terrain? Scott would probably agree that utopian visions sometimes provide a necessary sense of direction for social reforms; he does not object to radical visions per se but to top-down grand designs that seek to change society without taking into account local particularities and practical knowledge. But since it is not always possible to separate utopian visions from the designs they inspire, the political feasibility of Scott's "thin" recipe for gradual reform may well depend, ironically, on the existence of the utopian schemes he warns against.

Scott's often brilliant insights concerning the individual cases contribute to our understanding of specific state practices and warn against the modernist hubris that rational schemes are capable of redesigning society. Yet as a study of the unplanned consequences of high-modernist plans, his book makes a limited contribution to the growing body of scholarship on the effects of partial interventions in complex systems. Since it examines only cases of failure, it provides thin support for his general argument about high modernism. His sample does not help us understand the conditions that lead to the failure or success of high-modernist designs or to the outcome of plans by nonstate actors that also use "simplifications" to reorder society and that, if we accept his categories, "see like a state." Why did Oscar Niemeyer's Brasília "fail" rather miserably while Baron Haussmann's redesign of Paris famously succeeded? Why did the Marshall Plan work while the "villagization" of Tanzania did not? How to compare the public health systems of England or Spain to the health services available in the United States? Scott's limited sample supports only the rather obvious point that some ill-conceived modernist plans indeed had ill consequences, or the more general but truistic claim that bad plans generally lead to bad results. But even these assertions assume a number of unexamined premises about standards for evaluating historical outcomes and for isolating the factors that determined them.

Any book necessarily focuses on certain problems and cannot be faulted for excluding other questions. Yet Scott's general claims about high modernism require a consideration, however partial, of a number of issues. Among these, I would list the following: the criteria used to judge historical outcomes in terms of "failure" or "success"; the factors external to planning that affect its results; "successful" instances of modernist designs, of which there are examples in a range of counties and fields; nonstate designs to transform society, particularly by market institutions; "simplifications" that have enabled the development of complex social formations in the modern world; the interplay of "realism" and "utopia" in political struggles and in defining the horizon of social expectations; the existence within modernism of philosophical, aesthetic, and political currents of thought that questioned the flat vision of formalized "normal" science (which Scott identifies with modernism) and provided a more dynamic view of modernity; and the appropriateness of a reflectionist or scopic framework for analyzing the state's sign systems, instead of a dialogic or performative model that examines representational systems as processual practices within fields of power.

Scott's focus on the state grows out of his conviction that the state has been responsible for the failure of the major twentieth-century designs to improve the human condition. The tragic failure of these plans can be explained, according to him, by a combination of four conditions: the state's efforts to order nature and society by administrative means, a high-modernist ideology according to which science is capable of improving both society and human beings, the deployment of authoritarian state power to implement large-scale transformations, and a weak civil society unable to resist these measures of control. In this set of conditions, Scott presents the state as the only actor that incarnates high-modernist ideology. In contrast, he portrays civil society not as a terrain where this ideology could be produced or take root but only as a potential site of resistance against it, particularly when it is "strong" and can repel state interventionism.

His lack of attention to the designs of nonstate actors that have also had tragic effects is remarkable, particularly since Scott acknowledges that market institutions have been fundamental bearers of high modernism and are today perhaps one of its principal agents. Scott recognizes this lack in his book's introduction:

> As I finished this book, I realized that its critique of certain forms of state action might seem, from the post-1989 perspective of capitalist triumphalism, like a kind of quaint archeology. States, with the pretensions and power that I criticize, have for the most part vanished or have drastically curbed their ambitions. And yet, as I make clear in examining scientific farming, industrial agriculture, and capitalist markets in general, large-scale capitalism is just as much an agency of homogenization, uniformity, grids, and heroic simplification as the state is, with the difference being that, for capitalists, simplification must pay. A market necessarily reduces quality to quantity via the price mechanism and promotes standardization; in markets, money talks, not people. Today, global capitalism is perhaps the most powerful force for homogenization, whereas the state may in some instances be the defender of local difference and variety.[4]

It is striking that Scott's awareness of the role of the capitalist market in high modernism did not oblige him to modify his focus on the state, except by stating that his book is also a critique of the market through his examination of "scientific farming, industrial agriculture, and capitalist markets in general." His discussion of scientific forestry, however, did not lead him to develop an argument about the role of the market as an agent of high-modernist designs but instead to build a paradigmatic model of state planning for the rest of the book. If Scott's argument is that high modernism entails a simplifying, abstracting, and homogenizing mode of vision that can be deployed by state and nonstate social actors (since "large-scale capitalism is just as much an agency of homogenization, uniformity, grids, and heroic simplification as the state"), then why attribute this way of seeing to the state and restrict analysis to state designs without justifying this partial focus? If the claim is that abstractions and simplifications of the state, given its political power, are unlike those of the market or have different effects, why not develop this argument? Nowhere in the book is there a sustained discussion of the capitalist market as an institution that has redesigned societies through no less costly modalities of social engineering than the ones Scott examines in the book. The current faith in the free market and the impact of neoliberal policies throughout the world only make it more urgent to examine the role of the market in intensifying ecological destruction and worldwide social inequalities amid unprecedented plenty. One is left to wonder about the role of a clarification that does not modify the overall narrative that required making it in the first place.

As I see it, the issue is not that the capitalist market should be included solely because it has been a major agent of high modernism or because it plays an even larger role as a homogenizing force now that many socialist states have collapsed but because the opposition between state and market that structures the book is itself a thin simplification that obscures the mutual historical constitution of "state" and "market," their close interaction, and their ongoing transformation. The modes of objectification, homogenization, and abstraction that Scott attributes to the state are inseparable from conceptual, technological, and social transformations linked not just to the constitution of modern state bureaucracies but to the development of global capitalism and the generalized commodification of social life. That Scott sees scientific forestry as an example not only of state planning but also of market rationality shows that the opposition between state and market may be misleading and that some designs are best seen as the joint result of a high-modernist vision shared by states and markets. In this century, states that sought to build socialism often relied on conceptual schemes generated within capitalist society, such as the notion of "scientific management" or conceptions of industrialization as the motor of progress. If after 1989 "global capitalism is the most powerful force for homogenization," it is not just in opposition to some states that resist it, as Scott says, but in alliance with major states that help define the shifting legal, cultural, and political parameters that shape capitalism. While Weberian and Marxist discussions of the state have been premised on a separation between the state and society (or the economy), new approaches suggest the inseparability of the political and the social, particularly now that it is easier to see how the capitalist market has imposed its logic on society and become a "political" force of its own.

Scott's treatment of the state and society as separate entities is reinforced by his discussion of two different modalities of knowledge: abstract and practical. He poses a stark contrast between scientific planning from above, based on fixed designs geared to grand transformations, and practical knowledge from below, stored in habits and traditions attuned to the complexity of reality and open to the play of contingency. While restricting his critique of high-modernist knowledge to state-led exercises in social engineering, Scott turns to civil society as the locus of an alternative mode of knowledge: the practical knowledge the ancient Greeks called *metis*, exemplified by the flexible intelligence that guided Odysseus's quest through unexpected situations. This binary contrast between abstract and practical knowledge, treated not so much as different modalities of knowledge that any social actor or institution can deploy but as rooted in the state and society as separate social domains, helps consolidate the opposition between state and society that underwrites his argument about the way the modern state sees.

Scott's critique of the abstract knowledge informing large-scale state designs and his celebration of the practical knowledge stored in civil society resonates with liberal rejections of state planning and endorsement of the free market. Although Scott clarifies that "his bill of particulars against a certain kind of state is not a case for politically unfettered market coordination as urged by Friedrich Hayek and Milton Friedman," he endorses Hayek's critique of state planning, approvingly citing his claim that a "command economy, however sophisticated and legible, cannot begin to replace the myriad, rapid, mutual adjustments of functioning markets and the price system."[5] Like Scott, but with more theoretical rigor, Hayek forcefully argued against what he called the "constructivist fallacy," by which he meant the notion that social institutions can be the object of successful rational design. Similarly, Michael Oakeshott, Karl Polanyi, and Gilbert Ryle warned against institutions that seek to make decisions for their intended beneficiaries, the bearers of the practical knowledge that these institutions cannot systematize or control. While he shares the liberal critique of the state, Scott warns that market designs, just as much as state planning, may deny the practical knowledge of common people, but he does not show how this may be the case.

Scott's generous desire to empower the individual against external constraints is flawed by his murky treatment of the source of these constraints. His insistence that his critique of the state as an agent of high modernism is not a "case for the invisible hand of market coordination as opposed to centralized economies" is cast in terms that show that, in effect, it is a limited critique of the market that upholds its basic principle. He objects to the market because it "is itself an instituted, formal system of coordination, despite the elbow room that it provides to its participants, and it is therefore dependent on a larger system of social relations which its own calculus does not acknowledge and which it can neither create nor maintain."[6] Yet any complex social institution is constituted through processes of formalization and is dependent on larger fields of social relations; the market is not unique in this respect. As Émile Durkheim showed, social facts constrain and empower; as Karl Marx argued, the issue is to discern the particular manner in which specific social facts alienate or enable differentially distinct sectors of society. While on the one hand, Scott objects to the market as a coercive formal structure, on the other, he endorses Thomas Jefferson's celebration of yeomanry, which he calls a "training ground of democratic citizenship."[7] This combined focus helps cast the institution of private ownership of the means of production, the material foundation of Jeffersonian yeomanry as well as of the capitalist market, not as a source of profound inequalities in the real world but as the foundation of an implausible democracy of small property owners in an ideal world.

Given his slippery treatment of capitalism, it is hard not to smell something fishy in Scott's exclusive focus on the state and his inattention to the market and its ways of seeing, a partial view all the more odd given his criticism of the capitalist market in this and previous books. Would a book critical of modernist visions titled *Seeing Like a Market* be likely to be produced or to gain wide acceptance at this time? It is as if neoliberal hegemony had worked in this text to present capitalism's complex contradictions as a Manichaean opposition between the state and society. Authorial intentions aside, *Seeing Like a State* turns the state into the leading agent of ill-conceived modernist fantasies and construes society as the potential site of a Panglossian vision of capitalism (or precapitalism)—a bucolic community of small property owners without dispossessed proletarians or giant conglomerates, unhampered by institutional constraints, where everyone freely cultivates his or her own capital garden.

A similar tension between abstract critique and concrete celebration appears in his discussion of language as an example of both rigid simplification and fluid metis. In his early discussion of the relationship between language and the state, Scott states that "of all state institutions, then, the imposition of a single, official language may be the most powerful, and it is the precondition of many other simplifications." Yet in the concluding pages of the book, he treats language as the "best model" of a metis-friendly institution; the book's last sentence refers to language as "a structure of meaning and continuity that is never still and ever open to the improvisation of all its speakers."[8] This tension between language as an instrument of the powerful and language as an empowering institution for all speakers remains unresolved; it is difficult to see how language is "open to the improvisation of all its speakers" when some speakers (through institutions they control) not only have more say than others but can define the language in which everyone must speak. Juan Marinello, the Cuban essayist, incisively captured the dilemma of colonized populations condemned to use the colonizer's language: "The American writer is a prisoner. Firstly of his language." Arguing that colonial language has been "the most powerful obstacle to a vernacular idiom," Marinello explains why it has made it difficult for the (Latin) American writer to improvise: "Language has a life of its own. We struggle to secrete creolisms onto the mother tongue, and when we make a serious effort to innovate our speech, we come up with forms that lived a youthful existence centuries ago in Andalusia or Extremadura. Or that could have had such an existence."[9]

Just as the "democratic" figure of yeomanry serves to occlude the presence of power in the market, the homogenizing trope of "all speakers" evacuates power from language. As power vanishes from our sight, we are left with a vision of a world of property owners and speakers with equal shares of material and symbolic capital. Independently of Scott's intentions, his abstract critique of the market as a formal institution and endorsement of the myth of individual ownership of the means of production ends up lending support to the really existing market.

Since Scott restricts his attention to state designs, his pair of binary oppositions between state and society and abstract knowledge and metis unfolds as a compound opposition between state-abstract knowledge and society-metis. This opposition has the unintended effect of confirming current neo-liberal prejudices against the state. The contemporary religion of the free market transforms the market into society's best organizational form. It also turns the market into the locus of individuality and common sense in opposition to the state as the domain of authoritarian practices and impractical designs. Within this charged ideological landscape it is difficult not to smell the hegemonic presence of the market behind Scott's critique of the state and celebration of metis.

It is also difficult not to see the state as the embodiment of a threat against society's "normal" functioning, despite the fact that any such "normality" presupposes power relations mediated by specific states. States, like societies, come in many forms, and their changing configurations reflect ongoing social struggles over different conceptions of the normal and the desirable. While Scott says a great deal about the way some state plans work, nowhere does he offer a conceptualization of the state. The modern state emerges from his narrative as a unified actor endowed with a single mode of vision. The immense variety of states and their no less varied internal heterogeneity and complexity is flattened into a unique type that stands in opposition to society.

From a Latin American perspective, the conception of the state as a unified actor having a single mode of vision is particularly problematic. States in Latin America have been formed within complex hierarchical processes of institutionalization and codification. During colonial times, local state officials knew that imperial orders were to be obeyed but also violated. "Obedezco pero no cumplo" (I obey, but I do not comply) expressed the conventional response of state officials in the Americas to commands from imperial Spain, a veiled effort to adjust plans to local conditions and power relations. Colonial officials learned when to apply, ignore, or flexibly interpret laws and designs.

In this ability to combine abstract and practical knowledge, "modern" states are not significantly different. In my own study of state planning in twentieth-century Venezuela, I showed how plans are formulated by the state but are not plans of the state, for they are produced in conjunction with other powerful actors that shape the state and are modified by the ongoing play of politics.[10] Diverse state institutions, as well as individuals within the same institution, play different roles with respect to state planning. Plans to create "the Great Venezuela" after the 1974 oil boom were devised by state technocrats but were typically transgressed by upper-level state officials less concerned with the coherence of the plans than with their political effects. States embody both the abstract logic Scott associates with high modernism and the practical knowledge he identifies with metis. No state in Latin America—or anywhere, for that matter—would be able to function without being adept at combining multiple modalities of knowledge. As a form of "practical" knowledge, "metis" is a term that aptly describes a required mode of operation of any complex social institution. Modern states, like markets, "see" and "smell" in many ways. Instead of using maps that reproduce common illusions, in order to orient ourselves within the labyrinthine boardrooms and halls of mirrors of modern states we need to develop a critical cartography of modernity.

Maps have often been used as a trope to reflect on the relationship between representations and reality and on the uses of knowledge. Scott opens his discussion of state simplifications in the area of urban planning in chapter 2 with the following epigraph about a map: "And the Colleges of the Cartographers set up a Map of the Empire which had the size of the Empire itself and coincided with it point by point . . . Succeeding generations understood that this Widespread Map was Useless, and not without Impiety they abandoned it to the Inclemencies of the Sun and the Winters." He attributes this text to Suárez Miranda's *Viajes de varones prudentes* (1658). As far as I know, however, this book was never written, and its author did not exist. Nevertheless, the text Scott quotes does exist, but only as part of a slightly longer fictional story written by Jorge Luis Borges titled "On Exactitude in Science." (A footnote in the following chapter reveals that Scott has not read the story but knows through a colleague that Borges wrote one about maps.) Borges's story is written as a citation that he attributes to Miranda's *Viajes de varones prudentes*; he gives a fuller reference: fourth book, chap. 45, Lérida. Borges's story at once tells a tale about maps that exposes the imperial conceit that the empire's cartographers can represent the empire as a geographical and historical reality "point by point" and enacts a related conceit by creating a replica of a text written in the literary style of seventeenth-century Spain.

Borges's story is immensely suggestive. I have interpreted it as his attempt to problematize the relationship between reality, representation, and power.[11] I see it as an allegory not just of science but of power—or, rather, of the connection between knowledge and power. As a story about the power to determine the terms in which the empire should be represented, it addresses the relationship between imperial power and imperial knowledge.

It is therefore a story not just about the truth of scientific representations but about the representation of truth, about power's representations and the power to represent, about the truth of power. Through it, Borges calls our attention to the conditions of production of knowledge, its politics and uses.

By seeing Borges's literary replica as a literary original, Scott adds an unexpected but corroborating wrinkle to Borges's concern with the limits and (mis)uses of knowledge. Following a long-standing Latin American concern with the relation between image and reality, Borges tricks us, but his trick is a playful invitation to think about the belief that as scientists we are free to reproduce or interpret the world as it is rather than under specific cultural constraints and political conditions. He also invites us to think of a map, or any interpretation, as an inexact model, which reveals not just its inevitable partiality as an incomplete representation but also its inescapable partiality as a design of power. As such, any representation must be evaluated by its uses and effects.

Seeing Like a State is in this sense an imperial map of the modern world. From a lofty position, it gazes on a wide geographical and historical terrain, recounts imaginatively a number of themes and problems, and offers a set of recommendations for social reform. Like most maps, the book helps us see some things and occludes others from view. At the end, one is left with a striking irony. Scott's map of what he calls high modernism seems to be produced from the same all-seeing standpoint he identifies with high modernism—an imperial way of seeing for which Mary Louise Pratt has persuasively established a longer, colonial genealogy.[12] As a high-modernist critique of high modernism, it reinscribes the hubris he has so aptly discerned and ends up producing a simplified account of high modernism and of the state and its way of seeing.

My concern is not that this map does not show us all of reality, for no map can do this. Rather, it is that its significant but one-sided illumination of a complex social landscape leaves obscured much of the terrain we have traversed, directs us to an impoverished destiny, and blocks alternative pathways. Scott invites us to keep our eyes so close to the ground, to take such small steps, that we may become blind to the violence of familiar paths and never risk to step out of the capitalist dystopia that surrounds us. I wish to have a map that would ask us to proceed with caution, as Scott does, but that would recognize the marks of human daring, a map that would dare our imagination, that would show new vistas and make us desire to mold the existing order into a different, dignified landscape for humankind. As Borges's story suggests, the truth of a map lies in its use. A map of history is not simply its model but its figuration. Our journey's desired destiny also defines the way we depict its trajectory.

Notes

1 James C. Scott, *Seeing Like a State: How Certain Schemes to Improve the Human Condition Have Failed* (New Haven, CT: Yale University Press, 1998), 138.
2 Scott, *Seeing Like a State*, 81–82.
3 Scott, *Seeing Like a State*, 345.
4 Scott, *Seeing Like a State*, 7–8.
5 Scott, *Seeing Like a State*, 8, 256.
6 Scott, *Seeing Like a State*, 351.
7 Scott, *Seeing Like a State*, 355.
8 Scott, *Seeing Like a State*, 72, 357.
9 Juan Marinello, "Americanismo y cubanismo literarios" (1932), in *Ensayos*, by Juan Marinello (Havana: Editorial Arte y Literatura, 1977), 48–49.
10 Fernando Coronil, *The Magical State: Money, Nature and Modernity in Venezuela* (Chicago: University of Chicago Press, 1997).
11 Fernando Coronil, "Beyond Occidentalism: Towards Nonimperial Geohistorical Categories," *Cultural Anthropology* 11 (1996): 51–87.
12 Mary Louise Pratt, *Imperial Eyes: Travel Writing and Transculturation* (London: Routledge, 1992).

15 Latin American Postcolonial Studies and Global Decolonization

Given the curiously rapid rise to prominence of "postcolonial studies" as an academic field in Western metropolitan centers since the late 1980s, it is to be expected that its further development would involve efforts, like this one, to take stock of its regional expressions. Yet, while the rubric "Latin American postcolonial studies" suggests the existence of a regional body of knowledge under that name, in reality it points to a problem: there is no corpus of work on Latin America commonly recognized as "postcolonial." This problem is magnified by the multiple and often diverging meanings attributed to the signifier "postcolonial," by the heterogeneity of nations and peoples encompassed by the problematical term "Latin America," by the thoughtful critiques that have questioned the relevance of postcolonial studies for Latin America, and by the diversity and richness of reflections on Latin America's colonial and postcolonial history, many of which, like most nations in this region, long predate the field of postcolonial studies as it was developed in the 1980s. How then to identify and examine a body of work that in reality does not appear to exist? How to define it without arbitrarily inventing or confining it? How to treat it as "postcolonial" without framing it in terms of the existing postcolonial canon and thus inevitably colonizing it?

These challenging questions do not yield easy answers. Yet they call attention to the character of "postcolonial studies" as one among a diverse set of regional reflections on the forms and legacies of colonialism—or, rather, colonialisms. In light of the worldwide diversity of critical thought on colonialism and its ongoing aftermath, the absence of a corpus of Latin American postcolonial studies is a problem not of studies on Latin America but between postcolonial and Latin American studies. I thus approach this discussion of Latin American postcolonial studies—or, as I prefer to see it, of postcolonial studies in the Americas—by reflecting on the relationship between these two bodies of knowledge.

While its indisputable achievements have turned postcolonial studies into an indispensable point of reference in discussions about old and new colonialisms, this field can be seen as a general standard or canon only if one forgets that it is a regional corpus of knowledge whose global influence cannot be separated from its grounding in powerful metropolitan universities; difference, not deference, orients this discussion. Rather than subordinating Latin American studies to postcolonial studies and selecting texts and authors that may meet its standards and qualify as "postcolonial," I seek to establish a dialogue between them on the basis of their shared concerns and distinctive contributions. This dialogue, as with any genuine exchange even among unequal partners, should serve not just to add participants to the "postcolonial discussion," but also to clarify its assumptions and transform its terms.

My discussion is divided into four sections: (1) the formation of the field of postcolonial studies; (2) the place of Latin America in postcolonial studies; (3) responses to postcolonial studies from Latin Americanists; and (4) open-ended suggestions for deepening the dialogue between postcolonial and Latin American studies. By focusing on exchanges between these fields, I have traded the option of offering close readings of selected texts and problems for the option of engaging texts that have addressed the postcolonial debate in terms of how they shape or define the fields of postcolonial and Latin American studies.

Postcolonial Studies

Despite a long history of critical reflections on modern colonialism originating in reactions to the conquest and colonization of the Americas, "postcolonialism" as a term and as a conceptual category originates in discussions about the decolonization of African and Asian colonies after World War II. At that time, "postcolonial" was used mostly as an adjective by sociologists and political scientists to characterize changes in the states and economies of former colonies of the "Third World," a category that was also created at that time. This regional focus was already present in the French sociologist George Balandier's (1951) analysis of "the colonial situation" as well as in later debates about the "colonial" and "postcolonial state" (Alavi 1972; Chandra 1980), the "colonial mode of production" (Alavi and Shanin 1982), or the "articulation of modes of production" (Berman and Lonsdale 1992; Wolpe 1980). Although Latin America was considered part of the Third World, because most of its nations had achieved political independence during the first quarter of the nineteenth century, it was only tangentially addressed in these discussions about decolonization that centered on the newly independent nations of Africa and Asia.

As "old" postcolonial nations that had faced the problem of national development for a long time, the key word in Latin American social thought during this period was not colonialism or postcolonialism but "dependency." This term identified a formidable body of work developed by leftist scholars in the 1960s, designed to understand Latin America's distinct historical trajectory and to counter modernization theory. Riding atop the wave of economic growth that followed World War II, modernization theory presented capitalism as an alternative to socialism and argued that achieving modernity would overcome obstacles inhering in the economies, cultures, and subjective motivations of the peoples of the "traditional" societies of the Third World. W. W. Rostow's *The Stages of Economic Growth* (1960), revealingly subtitled *A Non-Communist Manifesto*, was a particularly clear example of modernization theory's unilineal historicism, ideological investment in capitalism, and teleological view of progress.

In sharp contrast, dependency theorists argued that development and underdevelopment are the mutually dependent outcomes of capitalist accumulation on a world scale. In their view, since underdevelopment is the product of development, the periphery cannot be modernized by unregulated capitalism but through an alteration of its polarizing dynamics. This basic insight into the mutual constitution of centers and peripheries was rooted in the Argentinian economist Raúl Prebisch's demonstration that unequal trade among nations leads to their unequal development. Formulated in the 1940s, Prebisch's critique of unequal exchange has been considered "the most influential idea about economy and society ever to come out of Latin America" (Love 1980: 46). His insights were integrated into "structural" reinterpretations of social and historical transformation in Latin America by Fernando Enrique Cardoso, Enzo Faletto, Aníbal Quijano, Theotônio dos Santos, Ruy Mauro Marini, and many other "dependency" theorists; as Cardoso (1977) noted, their work was "consumed" in the United States as "dependency theory" associated with the work of Andre Gunder Frank.

The worldwide influence of dependency declined after the 1970s. Dependency theory was criticized for its one-dimensional structuralism and displaced by the postmodern emphasis on the textual, fragmentary, and indeterminate; its Eurocentric focus on state-centered development and disregard of racial and ethnic divisions in Latin American nations has been a focus of a recent critique (Grosfoguel 2000). Despite its shortcomings, in my view the dependency school represents one of Latin America's most significant contributions to postcolonial thought within this period, auguring the postcolonial critique of historicism and providing conceptual tools for a much needed postcolonial critique of contemporary imperialism. As a fundamental critique of Eurocentric conceptions of history and of capitalist development, dependency theory undermined historicist narratives of the "traditional," "transitional," and "modern," making it necessary to examine postcolonial and metropolitan nations in relation to each other through categories appropriate to specific situations of dependency.

Starting around three decades after World War II, the second usage of the term "postcolonial" developed in the Anglophone world in connection with critical studies of colonialism and colonial literature under the influence of postmodern perspectives. This change took place during a historical juncture formed by four intertwined worldwide processes: the increasingly evident shortcomings of Third World national development projects; the breakdown of really existing socialism; the ascendance of conservative politics in Britain (Thatcherism) and the United States (Reaganism); and the overwhelming appearance of neoliberal capitalism as the only visible—or, at least, seemingly viable—historical horizon. During this period, postcolonial studies acquired a distinctive identity as an academic field, marked by the unusual marriage between the metropolitan location of its production and the anti-imperial stance of its authors, many of whom were linked to the Third World by personal ties and political choice.

In this second phase, while historical work has centered on British colonialism, literary criticism has focused on Anglophone texts, including those from Australia and the English-speaking Caribbean. The use of postmodern and poststructuralist perspectives in these works became so intimately associated with postcolonialism that the "post" of postcolonialism has become identified with the "post" of postmodernism and poststructuralism. For instance, a major postcolonial reader argues that "postcolonial studies is a decidedly new field of scholarship arising in Western universities as the application of post-modern thought to the long history of colonising practices" (Schwarz 2000: 6).

In my view, equally central to postcolonialism has been the critical application of Marxism to a broad spectrum of practices of social and cultural domination not reducible to the category of "class." While marked by idiosyncratic traces, its identifying signature has been the convergence of these theoretical currents—Marxist and postmodern/poststructuralist—in studies that address the complicity between knowledge and power. Edward W. Said's integration of Gramscian and Foucauldian perspectives in his path-breaking critique of Orientalism (Said 1978) has been widely recognized as foundational for the field. A similar tension between Marxism and poststructuralism animates the evolving work of the group of South Asian historians associated with subaltern studies, the strongest historiographical current of postcolonial studies.

Postcolonial critique now encompasses problems as different as the formation of minorities in the United States and African philosophy. But while it has expanded to new areas, it has retreated from analyzing their relations within a unified field; the fragmentary study of parts has taken precedence over the systemic analysis of wholes. Its critique of the grand narratives of modernity has led to skepticism toward any grand narrative, not always discriminating between Eurocentric claims to universality and the necessary universalism arising from struggles against worldwide capitalist domination (Amin 1989; Lazarus 1999).

As the offspring of a tense marriage between anti-imperial critique and metropolitan privilege, postcolonial studies is permeated by tensions that also affect its reception, provoking sharply different evaluations of its significance and political implications. While some analysts see it as an academic commodity that serves the interests of global capital and benefits its privileged practitioners (Dirlik 1994), others regard it as a paradigmatic intellectual shift that redefines the relationship between knowledge and emancipatory politics (Young 2001). This debate helps identify what in my view is the central intellectual challenge postcolonial studies has raised: to develop a bifocal perspective that allows one, on the one hand, to view colonialism as a fundamental process in the formation of the modern world without reducing history to colonialism as an all-encompassing process and, on the other hand, to contest modernity and its Eurocentric forms of knowledge without presuming to view history from a privileged epistemological standpoint.

In this light, the apparently simple grammatical juxtaposition of "post" and "colonial" in "postcolonial studies" serves as a sign to address the murky entanglement of knowledge and power. The "post" functions both as a temporal marker to refer to the problem of classifying societies in historical time and as an epistemological sign to evoke the problem of producing knowledge of history and society in the context of imperial relations.

Postcolonial Studies and Latin America

Given this genealogy, it is remarkable but understandable that debates and texts on or from Latin America do not figure significantly in the field of postcolonial studies as it has been defined since the 1980s. As Peter Hulme (1996) has noted, Said's canonical *Culture and Imperialism* (1993) is emblematic of this tendency: it centers on British and French imperialism from the late nineteenth century to the present; its geographical focus is limited to an area stretching from Algeria to India; and the role of the United States is restricted to the World War II period, disregarding this nation's origin as a colonial settlement of Britain, Spain, and France, the processes of internal colonialism through which Native Americans were subjected within its territory, and its imperial designs in the Americas and elsewhere from the nineteenth century to the present.

The major readers and discussions on postcolonial studies barely take Latin America into account. One of the earliest attempts to discuss postcolonial literatures as a comprehensive field, *The Empire Writes Back: Theory and Practice in Post-Colonial Literatures* (Ashcroft et al. 1989), acknowledges a focus on Anglophone literatures. Even so, its extensive sixteen-page bibliography, including "all the works cited in the text, and some additional useful publications" (Ashcroft et al. 1989: 224), fails to mention even a single text written on Latin America or by a Latin American author. The book treats Anglophone literatures, including those produced in the Caribbean, as if these literatures were not cross-fertilized by the travel of ideas and authors across regions and cultures—or at least as if the literatures resulting from the Iberian colonization of the Americas had not participated in this exchange.

This exclusion of Latin America was clearly reflected in the first general anthology of postcolonial texts, *Colonial Discourse and Postcolonial Theory* (Williams and Chrisman 1993), whose thirty-one articles include no author from Iberoamerica. Published two years later, *The Post-colonial Studies Reader* (Ashcroft et al. 1995) reproduces the Anglocentric perspective that characterizes their earlier *The Empire Writes Back*, but this time without the justification of a topical focus on English literatures. The reader features eighty-six texts divided into fourteen thematic sections, including topics such as nationalism and hybridity, which have long concerned Latin American thinkers. While some authors are repeated under different topics (Bhabha appears three times; Spivak, twice), the only author associated with Latin America is José Rabasa, whose contribution is a critical reading of Mercator's Atlas, a topic relevant but not specific to Latin America.

The marginalization of Latin America is reproduced in most works on postcolonialism published since then. For example, Leela Gandhi's *Postcolonial Theory: A Critical Introduction* (1998) does not discuss Latin American critical reflections or include even a single reference to Latin American thinkers in its extensive bibliography. While *Relocating Postcolonialism* (Goldberg and Quayson 2002) "relocates" the postcolonial through the inclusion of such topics as the cultural politics of the French radical right and the construction of Korean American identities, it maintains the exclusion of Latin America by having no articles or authors associated with this area. This taken-for-granted exclusion appears as well in a dialogue between John Comaroff and Homi Bhabha that introduces the book. Following Comaroff's suggestion, they provide a historical frame for "postcoloniality" in terms of two periods: the decolonization of the Third World marked by India's independence in 1947 and the hegemony of neoliberal capitalism signaled by the end of the Cold War in 1989 (Goldberg and Quayson 2002: 15).

In contrast, two recent works on postcolonialism include Latin America within the postcolonial field, yet their sharply different criteria highlight the problem of discerning the boundaries of this field. In an article for a book on the postcolonial debate in Latin America, Bill Ashcroft (whose co-edited book, as mentioned earlier, basically excludes Latin America) presents Latin America as "modernity's first born" (Ashcroft 1999) and thus as a region that has participated since its inception in the production of postcolonial discourses. He defines postcolonial discourse comprehensively as "the discourse of the colonized" produced in colonial contexts; as such, it does not have be "anticolonial" (Ashcroft 1999: 14–15). He presents Rigoberta Menchú's *I, Rigoberta Menchú* and Juan Rulfo's *Pedro Páramo* as examples that reveal "the transformative strategies of postcolonial discourse, strategies which engage the deepest disruptions of modernity, are not limited to the recent colonized" (Ashcroft 1999: 28). While his comprehensive definition of the field includes Latin American discourses from the conquest onward, his examples suggest a narrower field defined by more discriminating but unexamined criteria.

The second text is Robert Young's *Postcolonialism: An Historical Introduction* (2001). While Young (like Ashcroft) had not discussed Latin America in a previous work (*White Mythologies* [1990]) that had served to sacralize Said, Homi Bhabha, and Gayatri Spivak as the foundational trinity of postcolonial studies, in his new book he gives such foundational importance to Latin America and to the Third World that he prefers to name the field "tricontinentalism," after the Tricontinental Conference held in Havana in 1966 (Young 2001: 57). Young recognizes that postcolonialism has long and varied genealogies, but he finds it necessary to restrict it to anticolonial thought developed after formal political independence has been achieved: "Many of the problems raised can be resolved if the postcolonial is defined as coming after colonialism and imperialism, in their original meaning of direct-rule domination" (Young 2001: 57). Yet Young distinguishes further between the anticolonial thought of the periphery and the more theoretical thought formed at the heart of empires "when the political and cultural experience of the marginalised periphery developed into a more general theoretical position that could be set against western political, intellectual and academic hegemony and its protocols of objective knowledge" (Young 2001: 65). Thus, even successful anticolonial movements "did not fully establish the equal value of the cultures of the decolonised nations. . . . To do that," Young argues, "it was necessary to take the struggle into the heartlands of the former colonial powers."

Young's suggestive discussion of Latin American postcolonial thought leaves unclear the extent to which its anticolonialism is also "critical" in the sense he ascribes to metropolitan reflections. Young discusses Latin American postcolonial thought in two brief chapters. The first, "Latin America I: Mariátegui, Transculturation and Cultural Dependency," is divided into four sections: "Marxism in Latin America," an account of the development of communist parties and Marxist thinkers in the twentieth century, leading to the Cuban Revolution; "Mexico 1910," a presentation of the Mexican revolution as precursor of tricontinental insurrections against colonial or neocolonial exploitation; "Mariátegui," a discussion of Mariátegui's role as one of Latin America's most original thinkers, highlighting his innovative interpretation of Peruvian reality; and "Cultural Dependency," an overview of the ideas of some cultural critics that, for brevity's sake, I will reduce to a few names and to the key concepts associated with their work: the Brazilian Oswald de Andrade's "anthropophagy" (the formation of Latin American identity through the "digestion" of worldwide cultural formations); the Cuban Fernando Ortiz's "transculturation" (the transformative creation of cultures out of colonial confrontations); the Brazilian Roberto Schwarz's "misplaced ideas" (the juxtaposition in the Americas of ideas from different times and societies); and the Argentinian Nestor García Canclini's "hybrid cultures" (the negotiation of the traditional and the modern in Latin American cultural formations).

Young's second chapter, "Latin America II: Cuba: Guevara, Castro, and the Tricontinental," organized around the centrality of Cuba in the development of postcolonial thought, is divided into three sections: "Compañero: Che Guevara," focuses on Guevara's antiracism and radical humanism; "New Man" relates Guevara's concept of "the new man" to José Martí's proposal of cultural and political independence for "Our America" and to Roberto Fernández Retamar's Calibanesque vision of *mestizaje*; and "The Tricontinental," which presents the "Tricontinental Conference of Solidarity of the Peoples of Africa, Asia and Latin America" held in Havana in 1966 as the founding moment of postcolonial thought; in Young's (2001: 213) words, "Postcolonialism was born with the *Tricontinental*."

While Young's selection is comprehensive and reasonable, its organizing criteria are not sufficiently clear; one can easily imagine a different selection involving other thinkers and anticolonial struggles in Latin America. Despite the significance he attaches to theoretical reflections from metropolitan centers, Young makes no mention of the many Latin Americanists who, working from those centers or from shifting locations between them and Latin America, have produced monumental critiques of colonialism during the same period as Said, Bhabha, and Spivak—for example, Enrique Dussel, Aníbal Quijano, and Walter Mignolo, among others.

The contrasting positions of Bill Ashcroft and Robert Young reveal the difficulty of defining postcolonial studies in Latin America. At one extreme, we encounter a comprehensive discursive field whose virtue is also its failing, for it must be subdivided to be useful. At the other extreme, we encounter a restricted domain that includes an appreciative and impressive selection of authors but that needs to be organized through less discretionary criteria. Whether one adopts an open or a restricted definition of Latin American postcolonial studies, however, what is fundamental is to treat alike, with the same intellectual earnestness, all the thinkers and discourses included in the general field of postcolonial studies, whether they are produced in the metropolitan centers or in the various peripheries, writing or speaking in English or in other imperial and subaltern languages. Otherwise, the evaluation of postcolonial thought risks reproducing within its midst the subalternization of peoples and cultures it claims to oppose.

Latin American Studies and Postcolonial Studies

It is understandable that the reception of postcolonial studies among Latin Americanists should have been mixed. Many thinkers have doubted the appropriateness of postcolonial studies to Latin America, claiming that postcolonial studies responds to the academic concerns of metropolitan universities, to the specific realities of Asia and Africa, or to the position of academics who write about, not from, Latin America and disregard its own cultural traditions (Achúgar 1998; Colas 1995; Klor de Alva 1992, 1995; Moraña 1997; Pérez 1999; Yúdice 1996). Jorge Klor de Alva has presented the most extreme critique, arguing that colonialism and postcolonialism are "(Latin) American mirages," for these terms, "as they are used in the relevant literature" or "as commonly understood today," properly apply only to marginal populations of indigenes, not to the major non-Indian core that has formed the largely European and Christian societies of the American territories since the sixteenth century. For him, its wars of independence were not anticolonial wars, but elite struggles inspired in European models that maintained colonial inequalities.

This argument, in my view, has several problems: it takes as given the standard set by discussions of the Asian and African colonial and postcolonial experiences; it assumes too sharp a separation between indigenous and nonindigenous peoples in America; it adopts a restricted conception of colonialism derived from a homogenized reading of Northern European colonialism and an idealized image of the effectiveness of its rule; it disregards the importance of the colonial control of territories in Iberian colonialism; it pays insufficient attention to the colonial control of populations in the high-density indigenous societies of Mexico, Peru, and Central America and in plantations run by imported slave labor in the Caribbean and Brazil; and it fails to see the similarity between the wars of independence and the decolonizing processes of Asia and Africa, which also involved the preservation of elite privilege and the reproduction of internal inequalities (what Pablo Gonzalez Casanova [1965] and Rodolfo Stavenhagen [1965] have theorized for Latin America as "internal colonialism"). Rather than presenting one set of colonial experiences as its exclusive standard, a more productive option would be to pluralize colonialism—to recognize its multiple forms as the product of a common historical process of Western expansion.

An influential debate on colonial and postcolonial studies in a major journal of Latin American studies was initiated by Patricia Seed, a historian of colonial Latin America, who presented the methods and concepts of colonial and postcolonial discourse as a significant breakthrough in social analysis. According to Seed (1991), postcolonial studies' critique of conceptions of the subject as unitary and sovereign, and of meaning as transparently expressed through language, recasts discussions of colonial domination that are simplistically polarized as resistance versus accommodation by autonomous subjects. Two years later in the same journal, three literary critics questioned her argument from different angles. Hernán Vidal (1993: 117) expressed misgivings about "the presumption that when a new analytic and interpretative approach is being introduced, the accumulation of similar efforts in the past is left superseded and nullified," which he called "technocratic literary criticism." Rolena Adorno (1993), echoing Klor de Alva's argument, argued for the need to recognize the distinctiveness of Latin America's historical experience, suggesting that colonial and postcolonial discourse may more properly apply to the historical experience of Asia and Africa. Walter Mignolo (1993), for his part, argued for the need to distinguish among three critiques of modernity: postmodernism (its internal expression), postcolonialism (its Asian and African modality), and post-Occidentalism (its Latin American manifestation). Yet far from regarding postcolonialism as irrelevant for Latin America, he suggested that we treat the former as liminal space for developing knowledge from our various loci of enunciation. Mignolo has developed his ideas of "post-Occidentalism" (building on its original conception by Fernández Retamar [1974] and on my own critique of "Occidentalism" [Coronil 1996]) in his pathbreaking *Local Histories/Global Designs* (2000), a discussion of the production of nonimperial knowledge that draws on wide-ranging Latin American reflections, in particular Quijano's (2000) notion of the "coloniality of power" and Enrique Dussel's (1995) critique of Eurocentrism.

Subaltern studies has been widely recognized as a major current in the postcolonial field. While historians developed subaltern studies in South Asia, literary theorists have played a major role in the formation of subaltern studies in the Latin American context. Around the time of the Seed debate, the Latin American Subaltern Studies Group was founded at a meeting of the Latin American Studies Association in 1992. Unlike its South Asian counterpart, after which it was named, it was initially composed of literary critics, with the exception of Seed and two anthropologists who soon thereafter left the group. Its "Founding Statement" offered a sweeping overview of major stages of Latin American studies, rejecting their common modernist foundations and celebrating the South Asian critique of elitist representations of the subaltern. However, unlike the South Asian group, formed by a small group of historians organized around a coherent historiographical and editorial project centered on rewriting the history of India, this group, mostly composed of literary critics, was characterized by its diverse and shifting membership and the heterogeneity of their disciplinary concerns and research agendas. While the publications of its members have not fitted within traditional disciplinary boundaries, they have privileged the interpretation of texts over the analysis of historical transformations. The group's attempt to represent the subaltern has typically taken the form of readings of texts produced by authors considered subaltern or dealing with the issue of subalternity. In its decade-long life (I myself participated in the second half of it), the group stimulated efforts to rethink the intellectual and political engagements that had defined the field of Latin American studies.

While centered on literary studies, subaltern studies has been considered a major source of postcolonial historiography in Latin America. In a thoughtful discussion entitled "The Promise and Dilemma of Subaltern Studies: Perspectives from Latin American History," published in a forum on subaltern studies in a major history journal, the historian Florencia Mallon (1994) examines the consumption and production of subaltern studies in Latin America and evaluates the tensions and prospects of this field. Her account focuses on historical works, making explicit reference to the contributions of scholars based in the United States who have made significant use of the categories or methods associated with Subaltern Studies. She highlights Gilbert Joseph's pioneering use of Ranajit Guha's work on India's peasantry in his examination of banditry in Latin America (Joseph 1990), noting that it moved discussion beyond simplistic oppositions that reduced bandits to either resisters or reproducers of given social orders.

In her review, Mallon does not address subaltern studies in literary and cultural criticism (perhaps because she does not find this work properly historical), but she does offer a critique of the Latin American Subaltern Studies Group's "Founding Statement," noting its ungrounded dismissal of historiographical work on subaltern sectors in Latin America. She makes a similar critique of the more substantial article by Seed, the one historian of the group (already discussed here). Objecting to Seed's presentation of members of the "subaltern studies movement" as leaders of the "postcolonial discourse movement," Mallon offers ample references to recent historical work on politics, ethnicity, and the state from the early colonial period to the twentieth century that "had begun to show that all subaltern communities were internally differentiated and conflictual and that sub-alterns forged political unity or consensus in painfully contingent ways" (Mallon 1994: 1500).

Mallon's erudite discussion expands the scope of subaltern studies, but it does not sufficiently clarify why certain historical works should be considered part of the "subaltern" or "postcolonial" movement. Since studies on the social and cultural history of subaltern sectors ("history from below") and subaltern/postcolonial studies share subalternity as a subject matter and employ similar theories and methods, the lines sepa-rating them are sometimes difficult to define. Yet South Asian subaltern historiography has sought to distinguish itself from social and cultural history by attaching singular significance to the critique of historicist and Eurocentric assumptions, problematizing the role of power in field-work and in the construction of archives and interrogating such central historiographic categories as the "nation," the "state," "consciousness," and "social actors." The historiographical subaltern project has been marked by the tension between its constructivist aim, which necessarily involves the use of representational strategies not unlike those of so-cial and cultural history, and its deconstructivist strategy, which entails questioning the central categories of historical research and interrupt-ing the narratives of the powerful with those expressed by subaltern actors.

Mallon casts the "dilemma" of Latin American subaltern studies in terms of the tension between (Gramscian) Marxist and postmodern per-spectives (a tension frequently noted in discussions about South Asian subaltern studies). She proposes to solve this dilemma by placing the Fou-cauldian and Derridean currents of postmodern criticism "at the service of a Gramscian project" (Mallon 1994: 1515). Perhaps her subordination of deconstruction, so central to subaltern history, to the Gramscian project, so fundamental to social and cultural history, helps account for her insuf-ficient attention to the difference between these fields.

This difference is central for John Beverley (1993, 1999, 2000), one of the founders of the Latin American Subaltern Studies Group, who in his writings argues for the superiority of subaltern perspectives over non-subalternist ones of the subaltern. Deploying criteria that for him define a subalternist perspective, he criticizes Mallon's *Peasant and Nation: The Making of Postcolonial Mexico and Peru* (1995), arguing that, despite her in-tentions, Mallon appears as an omniscient narrator engaged in a positivist representational project that uses subaltern accounts to consolidate rather than interrupt the biographies of the nation, reinscribing rather than deconstructing the official biographies of these nations.

In a sophisticated discussion of subaltern studies and Latin American history, the Ecuadorian historian Guillermo Bustos (2002) uses Mallon and Beverley as a focal point to assess the relation between these two bodies of knowledge. While sympathetic to Mallon's discussion of this topic in "The Promise and Dilemma of Subaltern Studies" (1994), Bustos notes the Anglocentric and metropolitan focus of her discussion and suggests the inclusion of a more representative sample of work produced in Latin America; her only reference is to the Andeanist historian Flores Galindo, which Bustos complements by mentioning three related Andeanists: Carlos Sempat Assadourian, Julio Silvia Colmenares, and Silvia Rivera Cusicanqui. Like Beverley, Bustos recognizes the need to distinguish between social history and subalternist perspectives. While Beverley, however, uses this distinction to evaluate Mallon's work in terms of the standards of subaltern studies, Bustos uses it to caution against assuming the superiority of a subaltern perspective, recalling Vidal's (1993) critique of "technocratic literary criticism."

Bustos's proposal is to turn claims about the theoretical and political superiority of any perspective into questions answerable through concrete analysis. He exemplifies this option through a subtle reading of Mallon's *Peasant and Nation* (1995) that demonstrates the complexity of her narrative, including her attempt to engage in dialogical relation with her informants and fellow historians. While distancing himself from Beverley's critique, Bustos endorses Tulio Halperin Donghi's observation that Mallon's presentation of other perspectives does not prevent her from assuming (as in common practice) the superiority of her own professional account. His point is thus neither to criticize nor to defend Mallon's work, but to refine the dialogue between subaltern studies and Latin American historiography. He develops his argument by discussing other texts, including related attempts to break away from accounts organized as "the biography of the nation-state," based on the critical use of multiple voices and sources (Chiaramonti 1997; Coronil 1997; Thurner 1997). In agreement with the Italian historian Carlo Ginzburg, Bustos proposes that we meet the postmodern challenge not by making "evidence" impossibly suspect, but by following, as Paul Ricoeur suggests, the "traces that left from the past, take its place and represent it" (Bustos 2002: 15). Needless to say, the challenge remains how to retrieve and interpret these traces.

Postcolonial historical studies also received attention in Latin America in a book published in Bolivia, *Debates postcoloniales: Una introducción a los estudios de la subalternidad* (Postcolonial Debates: An Introduction to Studies of Subalternity [1999]), edited by the historians Silvia Rivera Cusicanqui and Rossana Barragán and composed of translations of a selection of nine essays by South Asian authors. In their introduction, Rivera Cusicanqui and Barragán make only tangential reference to the Latin American Subaltern Studies Group and none to the work of its members. They are critical of its "Founding Statement" for reducing the contributions of the South Asian Group to an assortment of ethnographic cases that "exemplify from the South the theory and the broad conceptual guidelines produced in the North" (Rivera Cusicanqui and Barragán 1999: 13). They also criticize Mallon's article on subaltern studies both for its inattention to a long Latin American tradition of critical work on colonialism and postcolonialism and for reducing South Asian subaltern studies "to a questionable Gramscian project on behalf of which one should place the whole postmodern and poststructuralist debate" (Rivera Cusicanqui and Barragán 1999: 13).

Their own interpretative effort is centered on underlining the significance of South Asian subaltern studies for Latin American historiography, emphasizing the innovative importance of the poststructuralist perspectives informing the South Asian scholarship. Their brief discussion of Latin American work highlights three critical currents: the Argentinian school of economic history represented by Enrique Tandeter, Carlos Sempat Assadourian, and Juan Carlos Garavaglia, distinguished by its transformation of Marxist and Gramscian categories through a confrontation with the specificities of Indian labor in the Potosí area; the studies of peasant insurgency and oligarchic rule carried out by the Taller de Historia Oral Andina (Workshop of Andean Oral History) and by such influential scholars as Alberto Flores Galindo and Rene Zavaleta; and the studies of "internal colonialism" initiated by the Mexican sociologist Pablo González Casanova in the 1960s (and, I should add, Rodolfo Stavenhagen). Their call for a "South-South" dialogue at the same time avoids a dismissal of the "North," warning against the danger present in "certain academic Latin American circles" of adopting new theories and discarding "our own intellectual traditions— and Marxism is one of them—for this impoverishes and fragments the Latin American debate" (Rivera Cusicanqui and Barragán 1999: 19). Their horizontal dialogue establishes a common ground between postcolonial studies and Latin American historiography on colonialism and postcolonialism yet presents subaltern studies as the product of an "epistemological and methodological rupture" (Rivera Cusicanqui and Barragán 1999: 17). If subaltern studies is postcolonial, its "post" is the post of postmodernism and poststructuralism.

A variant of this view is presented by the philosophers Santiago Castro-Gómez and Eduardo Mendieta in their thoughtful introduction to an important book of essays written by Latin Americanists published in Mexico under the title *Teorías sin disciplina: Latinoamericanismo, postcolonialidad y globalización en debate* (Theories without Discipline: Latin Americanism, Postcoloniality and Globalization in Debate [1998]). Focusing on the relationship between critical thought and the historical context of its production, Castro-Gómez and Mendieta seek to determine the specific character of postcolonial studies. They draw a distinction between "anticolonial discourse," as produced in Latin America by Bartolomé de Las Casas, Felipe Guamán Poma de Ayala, Francisco Bilbao, and José Enrique Rodó, and "postcolonial discourse," as articulated by Said, Spivak, and Bhabha. For them, anticolonial discourse is produced in "traditional spaces of action"—that is, "in situations where subjects formed their identities in predominantly local contexts not yet subjected to intensive processes of rationalization" (as described by Max Weber and Jürgen Habermas). They argue that postcolonial theories, in contrast, are produced in "post-traditional contexts of action"—that is, "in localities where social subjects configure their identities interacting with processes of global rationality and where, for this reason, cultural borders become porous" (Castro-Gómez and Mendieta 1998: 16–17). For them, this distinction has political implications: while anticolonialist discourse claims to speak for others and seeks to dismantle colonialism deploying colonial categories, postcolonial discourse historicizes its own position, not to discover a truth outside interpretation, but to produce truth effects that unsettle the field of political action. It follows that radical politics lies not in anticolonial work that defines struggles with the categories at hand, thus confirming the established order, but in intellectual work that deconstructs them in order to broaden the scope of politics. From this perspective, the "post" of postcolonialism turns out to be an anti-anticolonial "post" at the service of decolonizing decolonization.

This position has the merit of offering a clear definition of postcolonialism. In my view, it raises several questions. Its distinction between anticolonial and postcolonial discourse risks reproducing the tradition-modernity dichotomy of modernization theory, turning the convulsed and rapidly changing social worlds of Las Casas, Guamán Poma, or Bilbao into stable "traditional" societies of limited rationality, in contrast to the globally rational worlds that engender postcolonial theorists and their superior discourses. By treating deconstruction as a theoretical breakthrough that supersedes previous critical efforts—now relegated to less rational traditional contexts—this position also risks becoming an expression of Vidal's "technocratic literary criticism." Spivak's dictum that "Latin America has *not* participated in decolonization" (1993: 57) is perhaps an extreme expression of this risk. While Castro-Gómez and Mendieta (1998: 20) acknowledge the "irritation" of those who recognize that Latin American thinkers have "long shown interest in the examination of colonialism," they seem to accept this risk as an inevitable consequence of the radical theoretical and methodological novelty of postcolonial studies.

By contrast, the Cuban public intellectual Roberto Fernández Retamar's discussion of Latin American decolonizing struggles, originally offered as a lecture for a course on Latin American thought in Havana, can be seen in part as a response to Spivak's dictum, which, according to him, wins the prize for epitomizing the problem of Latin America's exclusion from postcolonial studies (Fernández Retamar 1996). It is impossible to summarize his already tight synthesis, organized around thirteen interrelated themes identified by key phrases or ideas that embody political and intellectual movements, such as "independence or death." Suffice it here to indicate that his presentation links together political struggles and intellectual reflections as part of a single process of decolonization. Thus, he joins the Haitian Revolution, wars of independence, the Mexican revolution, the Cuban revolution, and the movements of the Zapatistas and the Madres de la Plaza de Mayo with such diverse intellectual struggles as literary modernism, theology and philosophy of liberation, dependency theory, pedagogy of the oppressed, Latin American historiography, and *testimonio*. His wide selection of authors and texts celebrates the originality and heterogeneous sources informing self-critical reflections from the Americas. His examples are too numerous to mention here, but they include the Venezuelans Simón Rodríguez and Andrés Bello, the Mexicans Leopoldo Zea and Octavio Paz, the Brazilians Oswald de Andrade and Darcy Ribeiro, and the Cubans José Martí and Fernando Ortiz. He highlights the contemporary importance of Rigoberta Menchú and Subcomandante Marcos as articulating in new ways the decolonizing projects of indigenous and national sectors in Guatemala and Mexico. Fernández Retamar is not concerned with defining or erasing the boundaries between Latin American and postcolonial critical thought but with appreciating their shared engagement with decolonization.

The difference between Castro-Gómez and Mendieta and Fernández Retamar, like that between Ashcroft and Young, reveals the difficulty of defining the relation between postcolonial and Latin American reflections on colonialism and its aftermath. As in Bustos's discussion of the Mallon-Beverley exchange, a dialogue between these intellectual traditions requires not only clearer classificatory efforts, but also closer reading of texts, in order to refine the criteria that define these fields. A treatment of authors who are not considered part of the postcolonial canon as postcolonial thinkers may help us appreciate different modalities of critical reflexivity, as Sara Castro-Klarén (1999, 2001) has done through her subtle reading of Guamán Poma and of the Inca Garcilaso de la Vega. Or perhaps, as Hulme (1996: 6) suggests, "The real advantage of considering distant figures like Ralph Waldo Emerson or Andres Bello as postcolonial writers is that this leads us to read them as if they were new." A particularly productive option is to engage the postcolonial debate through studies of specific postcolonial encounters, as in the pioneering integration of theoretical reflection and detailed historical case studies of U.S.–Latin American relations in the collection edited by Joseph, Catherine Legrand, and Ricardo Salvatore (1998).

Elephants in the Americas?

This discussion has made evident how difficult it is to define "Latin American postcolonial studies." As in the well-known parable of the elephant and the wise blind scholars (each of whom visualizes the elephant as a different creature by the part he or she feels), this field, like the wider field of postcolonial studies itself, can be represented in as varied a manner as there are different perspectives from which it can be "seen." If this parable shows that knowledge of reality is always partial and inconclusive, its use to reflect on Latin American postcolonial studies raises two more fundamental points.

First, the peculiar object of postcolonial studies is not a natural entity, like an elephant, or even a social subject regarded as sharing the cultural world of the observer, but one formed as a colonized object, an inferior and alien "other" to be studied by a superior and central "self." Since the "elephant" can speak, the problem is not just to represent it but to create conditions that would enable it to represent itself. From the perspective of postcolonial studies, analysis should involve not just self-reflection (an inherent dimension of any serious intellectual enterprise), or granting subjectivity to the social subject studied (as anthropologists and cultural historians have typically sought to do), but the integration of these two analytical endeavors into one unified intellectual project directed at countering this unequal, colonizing relationship. Its epistemology is not just representational but transformative; it uses representational strategies to counter the hierarchies and assumptions that turn some subjects into objects of knowledge for allegedly superior subjects.

Second, insofar as postcolonial studies appears as the most evolved critique of colonialism, it tends to invalidate or diminish the significance of reflections on colonialism developed from other locations and perspectives. If the wise scholars were to act wisely, they would not privilege their respective views of the elephant or isolate it from other creatures. As a reflection on the relationship between postcolonial and Latin American studies, the parable appears as a literal story, the absence of indigenous elephants in the Americas justifying the identification of postcolonial studies with scholarship on Africa and Asia.

If we take the parable literally, since the only elephants that exist in the Americas are imported ones, artificially confined in zoos or circuses so as to protect them from an inhospitable terrain, we may have the desire to see only those rare creatures who have managed to mimic their Asian or African counterparts—our Latin American "elephants." Refusal is another option. Following thinkers who justifiably object to the ease with which metropolitan ideas become dominant in Latin America, or who unjustifiably see Latin America as a self-fashioned and bounded region and argue in defense of its autochthonous intellectual productions (but doing so typically in metropolitan languages and with arguments supported by theories that were once considered "foreign"), one could reject the attempt to define Latin American postcolonial studies, restricting postcolonial studies to other continents and regarding it as an imperial "import" that devalues "local" Latin American knowledge.

In my opinion, the view that restricts postcolonial reflexivity to certain currents of Western intellectual theory, as well as the position that treats postcolonial studies as another foreign fad that undermines local knowledge, reinforces both the field's theoretical and ethnographic provincialism and its de facto exclusion of Latin America. These two sides of a protected parochial coin prevent us from taking advantage of the global circulation of postcolonial studies as a potent intellectual currency for the exchange and development of perspectives on colonialism and its legacies from different regions and intellectual traditions.

The problem is not simply, as some Latin American critics of postcolonialism have suggested, that Latin Americanists should be drawing on Rodolfo Kusch or Jorge Luis Borges as much as on Said or Jacques Derrida, but that knowledge should be global and acknowledge the worldwide conditions of its production. Just as Kusch drew on Heidegger, and Derrida was inspired by Borges, Said and Ortiz developed independently of each other, fifty years apart, a contrapuntal view of the historical formation of cultures and identities that disrupts the West-rest dichotomy (Coronil 1995). Critical responses to colonialism from different locations take different but complementary forms. While from an Asian perspective it has become necessary to "provincialize" European thought (Chakrabarty 2000), from a Latin American perspective it has become indispensable to globalize the periphery: to recognize the worldwide formation of what appear to be self-generated modern metropolitan centers and backward peripheries.

As it has been defined so far, the field of postcolonial studies tends to neglect the study of contemporary forms of political domination and economic exploitation. Recognized by many as one of the field's founders, Edward Said (2002: 2) has distanced himself from it, saying that he does not "belong to that" and arguing that "postcolonialism is really a misnomer" that does not sufficiently recognize the persistence of neocolonialism, imperialism, and "structures of dependency." Said's concerns, so central to Latin American thought, highlight the importance of expanding postcolonial studies by building on Latin American critical traditions.

If the relationship between colonialism and modernity is the core problem for both postcolonial and Latin American studies, the fundamental contribution of Latin American studies is to recast this problem by setting it in a wider historical context. The inclusion of Latin America in the field of postcolonial studies expands its geographical scope and also its temporal depth. A wider focus, spanning from Asia and Africa to the Americas, yields a deeper view, revealing the links between the development of modern colonialism by northern European powers and its foundation in the colonization of the Americas by Spain and Portugal. This larger frame modifies prevailing understandings of modern history. Capitalism and modernity, so often assumed both in mainstream and in postcolonial studies to be a European process marked by the Enlightenment, the dawning of industrialization, and the forging of nations in the eighteenth century, can be seen instead as a global process involving the expansion of Christendom, the formation of a global market, and the creation of transcontinental empires since the sixteenth century. A dialogue between Latin American and postcolonial studies ought not to be polarizing and might range over local histories and global designs, texts and their material contexts, and subjective formations and structures of domination.

This dialogue should bring to the forefront two interrelated areas of significant political relevance today: the study of postcolonialism itself, strictly understood as historical transformations after political independence, and the analysis of contemporary imperialism. Ironically, these two areas, so central to Latin American thought, have been neglected by postcolonial studies. At the juncture of colonialism's historical dusk and the dawn of new forms of imperial domination, the field tends to recollect colonialism rather than its eventualities. Building on a long tradition of work on postindependence Latin America, I have argued for the need to distinguish "global" from "national" and "colonial" imperialism as a phase characterized by the growing abstraction and generalization of imperial modes of political and economic control (Coronil 2003). Drawing on postcolonial studies, I have proposed to understand what I call "Occidentalist" representations of cultural difference under global imperialism as involving a shift from "Eurocentrism" to "globalcentrism." I see globalcentrism as entailing representational operations that (1) dissolve the "West" into the market and crystallize it in less visible transnational nodules of concentrated financial and political power; (1) lessen cultural antagonisms through the integration of distant cultures into a common global space; and (3) emphasize subalternity rather than alterity in the construction of cultural difference. In an increasingly globalized world, U.S. and European dominance is achieved through the occlusion rather than the affirmation of radical differences between the West and its others (Coronil 2000: 354).

This dialogue should also redefine the terms of postcolonial studies. Postcolonialism is a fluid and polysemic category whose power derives in part from its ability to condense multiple meanings and refer to different locations. Rather than fix its meaning through formal definitions, I have argued that it is more productive to develop its significance through research into and analysis of the historical trajectory of societies and populations subjected to diverse modalities of imperial power (Coronil 1992: 101). In the spirit of a long tradition of Latin American transcultural responses to colonialism and "digestive" appropriation of imperial cultures, I thus opt for what I call "tactical postcolonialism." While Spivak's notion of "strategic essentialism" serves to fix socially constructed identities in order to advance political ends, tactical postcolonialism serves to open up established academic knowledge toward open-ended liberatory possibilities. It conceives "postcolonialism" not as a fenced territory but as an expanding field for struggles against colonial and other forms of subjection. We may then work not so much *within* this field as *with* it, treating it with Ortiz as a "transcultural" zone of creative engagements, "digesting it" as Andrade may playfully do, approaching it as a liminal locus of enunciation as Mignolo suggests in order to decolonize knowledge and build a genuinely democratic world, "a world which would include many worlds," as Subcomandante Marcos and the Zapatistas propose.

Note

This chapter reflects the lively discussions of a postgraduate seminar on postcolonialism and Latin American thought that I taught during the summer of 2002 at the Universidad Andina Simón Bolivar, Ecuador. My gratitude to all. Thanks also to Genese Sodikoff and Julie Skurski for help with the editing of this chapter.

References

Achúgar, Hugo. 1998. "Leones, cazadores e historiadores: A propósito de las políticas de la memoria y del conocimiento." In *Teorías sin disciplina: Postcolonialidad y globalización en debate*, ed. Santiago Castro-Gómez and Eduardo Mendieta, 271–85. Mexico City: Miguel Angel Porrúa.

Adorno, Rolena. 1993. "Reconsidering Colonial Discourse for Sixteenth- and Seventeenth-Century Spanish America." *Latin American Research Review* 28, no. 3: 135–52.

Alavi, Hamza. 1972. "The State in Post-Colonial Societies: Pakistan and Bangladesh." *New Left Review* 74: 59–81.

Alavi, Hamza, and Teodor Shanin, eds. 1982. *Introduction to the Sociology of Developing Societies*. London: Macmillan.

Amin, Samir. 1989. *Eurocentrism*, trans. Russell Moore. New York: Monthly Review.

Ashcroft, Bill. 1999. "Modernity's First Born: Latin America and Postcolonial Transformation." In *El debate de la postcolonialidad en Latinoamérica*, ed. Alfonso de Toro and Fernando de Toro, 13–30. Madrid: Iberoamericana.

Ashcroft, Bill, Gareth Griffiths, and Helen Tiffin. 1989. *The Empire Writes Back: Theory and Practice in Post-Colonial Literatures*. London: Routledge.

Ashcroft, Bill, Gareth Griffiths and Helen Tiffin, eds. 1995. *The Postcolonial Studies Reader*. London: Routledge.

Balandier, George. 1951. "La situation coloniale: Approache théorique." *Cahiers Internationaux de Sociologie* 11, no. 51: 44–79.

Barker, Francis, Peter Hulme, and Margaret Iversen, eds. 1994. *Colonial Discourse/Postcolonial Theory*. Manchester: Manchester University Press.

Berman, Bruce, and John Lonsdale. 1992. *Unhappy Valley: Conflict in Kenya and Africa*, book 2. London: James Currey.

Beverley, John. 1993. *Against Literature*. Minneapolis: University of Minnesota Press.

Beverley, John. 1999. *Subalternity and Representation: Arguments in Cultural Theory*. Durham, NC: Duke University Press.

Beverley, John. 2000. "The Dilemma of Subaltern Studies at Duke." *Nepantla* 1, no. 1: 33–44.

Bustos, Guillermo. 2002. "Enfoque subalterno e historia latinoamericana: Nación y escritura de la historia en el debate Mallon-Beverley." Unpublished ms.

Cardoso, Fernando Henrique. 1977. "The Consumption of Dependency Theory in the United States." *Latin American Research Review* 12, no. 3: 7–24.

Castro-Gómez, Santiago, and Eduardo Mendieta, eds. 1998. *Teorías sin disciplina: Latinoamericanismo, postcolonialidad y globalización en debate*. Mexico City: Miguel Angel Porrúa.

Castro-Klarén, Sara. 1999. "Mimicry Revisited: Latin America, Post-colonial Theory and the Location of Knowledge." In *El debate de la postcolonialidad en Latinoamérica*, ed. Alfonso de Toro and Fernando de Toro, 137–64. Madrid: Iberoamericana.

Castro-Klarén, Sara. 2001. "Historiography on the Ground: The Toledo Circle and Guamán Poma." In *The Latin American Subaltern Studies Reader*, ed. Ileana Rodríguez, 143–71. Durham, NC: Duke University Press.

Chakrabarty, Dipesh. 2000. *Provincializing Europe: Postcolonial Thought and Historical Difference*. Princeton, NJ: Princeton University Press.

Chandra, Bipan. 1980. "Karl Marx, His Theories of Asian Societies and Colonial Rule." In *Sociological Theories: Race and Colonialism*, 383–452. Paris: United Nations Educational, Scientific, and Cultural Organization.

Chiaramonte, José Carlos. 1997. "La formación de los Estados nacionales en Iberoamérica." *Boletín del Instituto de Historia Argentina y Americana "Dr. Emilio Ravignani*," 3rd series, no. 15: 143–65.

Colas, Santiago. 1995. "Of Creole Symptoms, Cuban Fantasies, and Other Latin American Postcolonial Ideologies." *Publications of the Modern Language Association of America* 110, no. 3 (May): 382–96.

Coronil, Fernando. 1992. "Can Postcoloniality Be Decolonized? Imperial Banality and Postcolonial Power." *Public Culture* 5, no. 1: 89–108.

Coronil, Fernando. 1995. "Transculturation and the Politics of Theory: Countering the Center, Cuban Counterpoint." Introduction in *Cuban Counterpoint: Tobacco and Sugar*, by Fernando Ortiz, ix–lvi. Durham, NC: Duke University Press.

Coronil, Fernando. 1996. "Beyond Occidentalism: Towards Nonimperial Geohistorical Categories." *Cultural Anthropology* 11, no. 1: 52–87.

Coronil, Fernando. 1997. *The Magical State: Nature, Money, and Modernity in Venezuela*. Chicago: University of Chicago Press.

Coronil, Fernando. 2000. "Towards a Critique of Globalcentrism: Speculations on Capitalism's Nature." *Public Culture* 12, no. 2: 351–74.

Coronil, Fernando. 2004. "Globalización liberal o imperalismo global: Cinco piezas para armar el rompecabezas del presente." *Comentario Internacional* 5: 103–32.

Dirlik, Arif. 1994. "The Postcolonial Aura: Third World Criticism in the Age of Global Capitalism." *Critical Inquiry* 20, no. 2: 328–56.

Dussel, Enrique. 1995. *The Invention of the Americas*, trans. Michael D. Barber. New York: Continuum.

Dussel, Enrique. 1998. "Beyond Eurocentrism: The World-System and the Limits of Modernity." In *The Cultures of Globalization*, ed. Fredric Jameson and Masao Miyoshi, 3–31. Durham, NC: Duke University Press.

Fanon, Frantz. [1961] 1965. *The Wretched of the Earth*, trans. Constance Farrington. New York: Grove.

Fernández Retamar, Roberto. 1974. "Nuestra América y el Occidente." *Casa de las Américas* 16, no. 98: 36–57.

Fernández Retamar, Roberto. 1996. "Pensamiento de nuestra América: Autorreflexiones y propuestas." *Casa de las Américas* 37, no. 204: 41–56.

Gandhi, Leela. 1998. *Postcolonial Theory: A Critical Introduction*. New York: Columbia University Press.

Goldberg, Theo, and Ato Quayson, eds. 2002. *Relocating Postcolonialism*. Oxford: Blackwell.

González Casanova, Pablo. 1965. "Internal Colonialism and National Development." *Studies in Comparative International Development* 1, no. 4: 27–37.

Grosfoguel, Ramón. 2000. "Developmentalism, Modernity and Dependency in Latin America." *Nepantla* 1, no. 2: 347–74.

Hulme, Peter. 1996. "La teoría postcolonial y la representación de la cultura en las Américas." *Revista de la Casa de las Américas* 36, no. 202 (March): 3–8.

Joseph, Gilbert. 1990. "On the Trail of the Latin American Bandits: A Reexamination of Peasant Resistance." *Latin American Research Review* 25, no. 3: 7–54.

Joseph, Gilbert, Catherine Legrand and Ricardo Salvatore, eds. 1998. *Close Encounters of Empire: Writing the Cultural History of U.S.-Latin American Relations*. Durham, NC: Duke University Press.

Klor de Alva, Jorge. 1992. "Colonialism and Postcolonialism as (Latin) American Mirages." *Colonial Latin American Review* 1, nos. 1–2: 3–23.

Klor de Alva, Jorge. 1995. "The Postcolonization of the (Latin) American Experience: A Reconsideration of 'Colonialism,' 'Postcolonialism,' and 'Mestizaje.'" In *After Colonialism: Imperial Histories and Postcolonial Predicaments*, ed. Gyan Prakash, 240–75. Princeton, NJ: Princeton University Press.

Lazarus, Neil. 1999. *Nationalism and Cultural Practice in the Postcolonial World.* Cambridge: Cambridge University Press.

Love, Joseph L. 1980. "Raúl Prebisch and the Origins of the Doctrine of Unequal Exchange." *Latin American Research Review* 15, no. 3, 45–72.

Mallon, Florencia. 1994. "The Promise and Dilemma of Subaltern Studies: Perspectives from Latin American History." *American Historical Review* 99, no. 5: 1491–1515.

Mallon, Florencia. 1995. *Peasant and Nation: The Making of Postcolonial Mexico and Peru.* Berkeley: University of California Press.

Mignolo, Walter D. 1993. "Colonial and Postcolonial Discourse: Cultural Critique or Academic Colonialism?" *Latin American Research Review* 28, no. 3: 120–34.

Mignolo, Walter D. 2000. *Local Histories/Global Designs: Coloniality, Subaltern Knowledges, and Border Thinking.* Princeton, NJ: Princeton University Press.

Moraña, Mabel. 1997. "El boom del subalterno." *Revista de Crítica Cultural* 15: 48–53.

Nkrumah, Kwame. 1965. *Neo-Colonialism: The Last Stage of Imperialism.* London: Thomas Nelson.

Pérez, Alberto Julián. 1999. "El poscolonialismo y la inmadurez de los pensadores hispanoamericanos." In *El debate de la postcolonialidad en Latinoamérica*, ed. Alfonso de Toro and Fernando de Toro, 199–213. Madrid: Iberoamericana.

Quayson, Ato. 2000. *Postcolonialism: Theory, Practice or Process?* Cambridge: Polity.

Quijano, Aníbal. 2000. "Colonialidad del poder, eurocentrismo y América Latina." In *La colonialidad del saber: Eurocentrismo y ciencias sociales. Perspectivas latinoamericanas*, ed. Edgardo Lander, 201–46. Buenos Aires: Consejo Latinoamericano de Ciencias Sociales.

Rivera Cusicanqui, Silvia, and Rossana Barragán, eds. 1999. *Debates postcoloniales: Una introducción a las estudios subalternos.* La Paz, Bolivia: Sephis/Aruwiyri.

Rodriguez, Ileana, ed. 2001. *The Latin American Subaltern Studies Reader.* Durham, NC: Duke University Press.

Rostow, Walt Whitman. 1960. *The Stages of Economic Growth: A Non-Communist Manifesto.* Cambridge: Cambridge University Press.

Said, Edward W. 1978. *Orientalism.* New York: Random House.

Said, Edward W. 1993. *Culture and Imperialism.* New York: Alfred A. Knopf.

Said, Edward W. 2002. "A Conversation with Neeldari Bhattacharya, Suvir Kaul and Ania Loomba." In *Relocating Postcolonialism*, ed. Theo Goldberg and Ato Quayson, 1–14. Oxford: Blackwell.

Salih, Tayeb. 1969. *Season of Migration from the North*, trans. Denys Johnson-Davies. London: Heinemann.

Sangari, Kumkum. 1990. "The Politics of the Possible." In *The Nature and Context of Minority Discourse*, ed. Abdul JanMohamed and David Lloyd, 216–45. New York: Oxford University Press.

San Juan, Epifanio. 1998. *Beyond Postcolonial Theory*. New York: St. Martin's.

Schwarz, Henry. 2000. "Mission Impossible: Introducing Postcolonial Studies in the U.S. Academy." In *A Companion to Postcolonial Studies*, ed. Henry Schwarz and Sangeeta Ray, 1–20. Oxford: Blackwell.

Seed, Patricia. 1991. "Colonial and Postcolonial Discourse." *Latin American Research Review* 26, no. 3: 181–200.

Spivak, Gayatri Chakravorty. 1993. "Marginality in the Teaching Machine." In *Outside in the Teaching Machine*, 53–76. New York: Routledge.

Stavenhagen, Rodolfo. 1965. "Classes, Colonialism and Acculturation: Essay on a System of Inter-Ethnic Relations in Mesoamerica." *Studies in Comparative International Development* 1, no. 6: 53–77.

Thurner, Mark. 1997. *From Two Republics to One Divided: Contradictions of Postcolonial Nationmaking in Andean Peru*. Durham, NC: Duke University Press.

Vidal, Hernan. 1993. "The Concept of Colonial and Postcolonial Discourse: A Perspective from Literary Criticism." *Latin American Research Review* 28, no. 3: 113–19.

Williams, Patrick, and Laura Chrisman, eds. 1994. *Colonial Discourse and Post-Colonial Theory: A Reader*. New York: Columbia University Press.

Wolpe, Harold, ed. 1980. *The Articulation of Modes of Production*. London: Routledge and Kegan Paul.

Young, Robert. 1990. *White Mythologies: Writing History and the West*. London: Routledge.

Young, Robert. 2001. *Postcolonialism: An Historical Introduction*. Cambridge: Blackwell.

Yúdice, George. 1996. "Puede hablarse de la postmodernidad en América Latina." *Revista Crítica Literaria Latinoamericana* 15, no. 29: 105–28.

16   After Empire:
         Reflections on Imperialism
         from the Américas

> Imperialism, like any word which refers to fundamental social
> and political conflicts, cannot be reduced, semantically, to a single
> proper meaning. Its important historical variations of meaning
> point to real processes which have to be studied in their own terms.
> —Raymond Williams, *Keywords*

The subject of empire, an old-fashioned and respected scholarly issue usually confined to erudite rumination in ivory towers, has recently become a public concern in the United States as well as abroad. Tossed around and accented with new meanings by competing parties at the onset of this new millennium, "empire" has been brought from its seclusion as a relic of the past and turned into a hot term of current political discourse. No doubt, its present salience as a word and as an issue is largely due to the more explicit and forceful role the U.S. state assumed as the self-proclaimed defender of "civilization" after September 11, 2001. Although it may not always be clear what is meant by this expression, the United States is now increasingly addressed as an empire—whether a "lite," "reluctant," "benevolent," or simply less concealed one. Now that empire looms large before our eyes, how are we to look at this dusty relic? How useful is it as an analytical category for understanding not only colonialism or postcolonialism but also noncolonial geopolitical dominance, past or present?

  This essay is a response to a timely invitation to look at empire beyond its usual European location, to explore its varied historical expressions, and to discern its usefulness as an analytical construct for engaging contemporary politics. Recognizing that "from the literal to the metaphorical to the contemporary, empire and anthropology have long and entwined careers," I welcome the call "to take the anthropological study of empire to the next level, specifically to look beyond the European empires upon which we have overwhelmingly focused."[1] I also take this call as an invitation to counter the complicity between imperial histories and anthropology, history, and other social sciences.

My turn to "other" empires entails a shift not just of place but also in time. Situating "empire" within an expanded spatial and temporal landscape makes it easier to overview its varied historical forms. This larger frame places the study of European colonial empires, which have been the prominent object of colonial and postcolonial scholarship in the modern era, alongside that of empires without colonies, whose diverse forms have been commonly seen as belonging to the past and yet, in my view, are of singular relevance for considering the present. Some of these forms were already highlighted by Hans Kohn in the 1950s, who considered colonialism as only one of five modalities of imperial control. Focusing on past empires, his other four modalities of "imperial but noncolonial solutions" are, at opposite extremes, political formations that accord subjects full autonomy within an imperial framework (Hungary under Austria), those that annihilate or expel original inhabitants (Native Americans under U.S. settlers), and, in between, "solutions" that keep indigenes on their land but as inferior subjects (India or South Africa under British rule), or grant citizenship to natives but submerge their nation within a larger nation (the Kurds under the Turkish empire).[2]

This expanded landscape also allows exploration of the connection between new and old imperialisms, a distinction made by Hamza Alavi in a pioneering article, written more than forty years ago, in which he argued that in the "new imperialism" informal economic control is as effective as the direct political control of old imperialism.[3] One of the earliest and potentially most productive uses of a distinction between the formal and informal dimensions of imperialism was proposed by John Gallagher and Ronald Robinson in 1953 and taken up by scholars of the British empire.[4] While it does not build on the formal-informal distinction, the concept of "imperialism without colonies" also recognizes that imperial control can be predominantly exerted by economic influence, rather than by direct political control.[5]

This expanded temporal and spatial frame facilitates, more significantly, a shift in viewpoint. Rather than being confined to given imperial genealogies, so intimately linked both to the self-images of empires and to sharp distinctions between "the market" and the "state," the "political" and the "economic," or the "formal" and the "informal," which have been so central in their self-representation as well as in academic discussions, I wish to observe what may be termed "imperial effects." While a focus on effects is associated with postmodern critiques of unitary subjects and grand narratives, I intend here to develop a subalternist perspective to tackle the consequences of domination for those who are subjected to it. By observing these consequences, I seek to bring into view particular power formations within general processes, without assuming, but also without assuming away, their systemic structures, inner logics, or identifying boundaries. My attention to effects is at once conceptual and practical; the aim is to recognize systems of domination by their significance for subjected populations, rather than solely by their institutional form or self-definition.

Since dominance—however one understands this elusive concept—is a rather regular dimension of interregional or international life, specifying the criteria used to define its specific character is a condition for analysis. Lest we let these criteria be established by convention—so often the expression of dominant perspectives—they ought to specify the object of our analysis only by becoming its object. For my purposes here, I argue for the usefulness of the concept of empire to engage relatively large geopolitical formations that establish dominion by hierarchically differentiating populations across transregional boundaries. (For other purposes, one may find this notion either too boundless or too bounded.) Always concerned with the lived experiences of those at the margins, Edward Said insisted that "the historical experience of imperialism for the imperialized entailed subservience and subjection."[6] I seek to develop a perspective that pluralizes empires and provincializes their European forms, but most importantly, that counters the effacing of those subjected to imperializing powers, regardless of their apparent forms.

Empires "Beyond Europe"

I will "move beyond Europe" not by leaving Europe behind, but by moving toward other literal and metaphorical "Europes." One of my most vivid childhood memories concerns my first trip to Spain. I remember that when we crossed the Pyrenees by car, as we left France and entered Spain, my relatives remarked, as if these mountains stood as an invisible sign that identified and contained a "real" Europe: "*Dicen* [they say] that Europe ends at the Pyrenees; we are leaving it now." I did not understand then who was the "they" who said this, but it was clear to me that this phrase did not express the views of either my relatives or Spaniards. As a Latin American in Spain, it was impossible for me not to feel that I was in Europe, at the heart of what had been a vast empire, whose allegedly superior civilization had legitimated the conquest and colonization of the Americas. I have since learned that from the vantage point of the dominant centers of Europe, Spain appeared then as "non-Europe," or at least as "not Europe yet," a region that, like my home country and the rest of Latin America, needed to "catch up" in order to become fully modern. Now I see that by "Europe" is meant the shifting apex of modernity.

It is ironic that southern Europe, seen then as marginal to Europe, was the birthplace of the modern empires of Portugal and Spain and the crucible of modern colonialism. During the early modern period, Portugal and Spain established not only model empires but also the conditions for the emergence of the empires that stand now as canonical in colonial studies: those of England and France. Such shifts in the location of imperial centers have become familiar in Latin America, a region whose populations have been subjected to various regimes of control by many political centers. Before the Iberian conquest, the Aztec and Inca empires subjected and integrated large regions and populations; these empires provided persisting structures of rule upon which Spain built its own empire in the Americas. After the conquest, the area of the Americas under Iberian control became colonies of Spain and Portugal until independence in the nineteenth century. As independent nations, Latin American countries were subjected to the informal imperial control of England and France until well into the twentieth century, and their ethnic minorities to various forms of internal colonialism by local elites. Of course, since its emergence as the hemispheric power at the end of the nineteenth century until its position now as a global hegemon, the fundamental imperial force in the region has been the United States.

The recognition that it is now common to exclude Spain and Portugal from Europe and to place the United States at Europe's center makes evident that "Europe" is an imaginary construct that blurs the boundaries between literal and metaphorical frontiers. As a hyper-real construct, "Europe"—or its more general embodiment, "the West"—is a geohistorical sign that points to the apex of modernity and contains it within limits no less constraining for being shifting and imaginary.

The view from the apex obscures what lies below, the larger whole of which it is but a part, particularly since the apex's self-fashioning as such involves disavowing its connections to the rest. As a fetish that embodies powers not of its own, the West is construed as superior through Occidentalist modalities of representation that associate it with the rest of the world through dissociations—by separating relational histories, reifying cultural difference, and turning difference into hierarchy. It is by looking at this apex from the perspective of the obscured transcultural histories that sustain it that I seek to explore European empires beyond Europe.

September 11: Naming History

It is a privilege of empires to make their histories appear as History. September 11 has become an evocative sign that points not just to a singular instance when the United States was deeply wounded within its borders by foreign attack, but to an open-ended historical phase construed by the United States as an endless global war against terror; this date names a bounded moment as well as a momentous era. I will use September 11 as "clue" (à la Carlo Ginzburg) to examine the imperial character of this era.

It is generally assumed that 9/11 names this, and not any other time in any other place. Not unlike naming famous people only by their first names "9/11" identifies its September 11. Its "surname," 2001, is assumed. Yet if one moves south and gives this date a year, 9/11 names a different history. In 1973, on another September 11, an elected socialist president and many of his supporters died defending a democratically established government in a coup organized by the local opposition with the support of the U.S. government and U.S.-based transnational corporations. As a result of the coup, which included the bombing of La Moneda, the presidential palace in which Dr. Salvador Allende died defending his government, a regime of terror was established, also supported by the United States, which was responsible for the death of more than three thousand and torture of more than twenty-eight thousand Chileans and the exile of many more over many years.

A brief look at the historical arc that joins these two dates, pieces of a much longer historical process, offers a different view of the significance of each event and of the common history that forged them. While the U.S. September 11 has brought into the open the subject of empire, I will use the memory of Chile's September 11 to resurrect the subject of imperialism, a topic buried in the Global North for more than a quarter-century, but whose specter has always hovered around the Global South. From the vantage point of this historical arc, I ask the following: How useful is it to think of the present not just in terms of empire but in terms of imperialism? Are there significant continuities between both dates, or are we facing an altogether new configuration of power that makes these concepts irrelevant?

Entwining Empire and Imperialism

The attack against Salvador Allende on 1973's September 11 must be placed within a long tradition of U.S. interventions in the hemisphere—ranging from the direct use of force to various forms of influence—that began with its conquest of native territories before it became an independent nation. While after its independence the United States used force of arms many times in Latin America during the nineteenth century, one intervention stands as major landmark: U.S. participation in the Spanish-Cuban-American War in 1898. This intervention was followed by the U.S. occupation of Puerto Rico and Cuba in the Caribbean and of Guam and the Philippines in the Pacific. A major turning point in global relations, 1898 signified a transfer of imperial control over the hemisphere from England and Spain to the United States. While Puerto Rico acquired an ambiguous colonial status, Cuba, whose long struggle against Spain (1868–98) made it more resistant to direct imperial control, first became a protectorate (1901) and then an independent republic (1902). As an independent republic, Cuba remained subjected to various forms of U.S. control and influence, including several direct armed interventions. It was not the direct possession of territories and populations, however, but the indirect control over Cuba that came to define U.S. relations with Latin America during the twentieth century.

The Monroe Doctrine, proclaimed in 1823 to defend the Americas from foreign intervention, came to be interpreted after 1898 as a chart to justify U.S. influence over the region. The mechanism for this change was the 1905 Roosevelt Corollary to the Monroe Doctrine, signed in the aftermath of the Spanish-Cuban-American war, through which the United States authorized itself to intervene in Latin America whenever it considered intervention necessary. According to Walter LaFeber, with the ascendance of the United States as the hegemonic power in the region, "the Doctrine itself shifted to mean that Latin Americans should now be controlled by outside (that is, North American) intervention if necessary."[7] The Roosevelt Corollary became the principal political device to justify the new role of the United States as an agent of "order" in the region.

After 1898, the United States became a Janus-faced entity for Latin America, a dominant empire, but also a model postcolonial nation. As the

Mexican novelist Carlos Fuentes notes, "Spain, our old empire, was defeated and dismantled by the United States, our new empire, in 1898; the Philippines and Puerto Rico became North American colonies, Cuba a subject state. Our sympathies shifted to the defeated empire: the United States desatanized Spain while satanizing itself." This satanization, however, came together with the idealization of its republican democracy. Fuentes aptly expresses the double character the United States came to have in Latin America, particularly among its political and intellectual elites: "The United States became the Jekyll and Hyde of our wildest continental dreams: a democracy inside, an empire outside."[8] Although it was not clear in 1898 what kind of empire it was going to be, it became evident that the United States would exert control following not the Puerto Rican but the Cuban model. Indirect control, however, did not preclude the direct exercise of force.

The U.S. empire became the invention of Latin America, just as Europe, as Frantz Fanon famously put it, was the invention of America.[9] Latin America "invented" the U.S. empire as its primordial imperialized subject in a similar way as earlier it had invented European empires as their major colony. Given their mutual formation, the reverse, of course, is also true—Europe also invented America—but under asymmetrical conditions that require reversing mainstream currents that efface their mutual engagement. As the region became not only the object of imperial policies, but also an active agent of responses to them, it became a crucible of empire that often produced imperial policies or "modular" reactions transportable to other imperial contexts.

The heterogeneity of the region made it necessary for the United States to develop different forms of control. In areas geographically closer, the United States would be more inclined to use rather open military might, while in those farther away, the United States would rely more on economic pressure, diplomatic influence, and concealed force. For example, the United States took half of Mexico in the mid-nineteenth century (it acquired the territories and populations of the current states of Texas, New Mexico, Arizona, Colorado, Nevada, California, and parts of Oregon and Utah); under U.S. influence, Colombia lost its northern region of Panama in 1903, and Panama as an independent nation only gained control over the canal built in 1914 (a project that had given birth to Panama as a nation) at the end of the twentieth century. While as the United States' "backyard" Central America and the Caribbean became the main field of its armed interventions in the region, the rest of South America became its favored ground for dominion through a vast network of alliances and economic investments in ever expanding and more diversified areas of the economy. In all cases, the United States sought to protect its interests in the area by actively supporting, or helping place at their head, suitable rulers, including ruthless dictators, whether in Central America, the Caribbean, or South America.

Needless to say, there were differences between the aggressive expansionism of Theodore Roosevelt's Big Stick policy and Taft's Dollar Diplomacy, at the outset of the twentieth century, and the quiet imperialism of Franklin D. Roosevelt's Good Neighbor Policy during the 1930s, or between the outwardly progressive Democratic policies of John F. Kennedy's Alliance for Progress and Jimmy Carter's human rights, and the more overtly aggressive stance of the Republican administrations of Richard Nixon, Ronald Reagan, or George Bush father and son. Despite the differences among these different administrations, they established a consistent position in Latin America characterized by the establishment of strategic alliances with local allies, cemented by common economic interests and ultimately backed by armed force.

Most of the United States' direct armed interventions in Latin America and the Caribbean took place during the first half of the twentieth century; these interventions were generally brief and intended to achieve specific political or economic outcomes, not direct and permanent political dominion. Yet there were also a number of lengthier occupations: Cuba (1906–1909), Nicaragua (1912–33), Haiti (1915–34), the Dominican Republic (1916–24), Cuba (1917–22), Mexico (1918–19), and Panama (1918–20). These examples are only the tip of an iceberg. Between 1898 and 1920 U.S. armed forces intervened twenty times in the Caribbean.[10] A report of the Foreign Affairs Division of the Congressional Research Service lists seventy-three instances of use of the U.S. armed forces in Latin America between 1798 and 1945, more than half after 1898.[11] According to the Harvard historian John Coatsworth, between 1898 and 1994 the U.S. government "intervened successfully to change governments in Latin America a total of at least 41 times. That amounts to once every 28 months for an entire century."[12]

As a leader of the free world during the post–World War II Cold War (in reality, a hot war carried out in many areas of the Third World), the United States increasingly exerted force indirectly through alliances with local actors. A paradigmatic example is the U.S.-orchestrated coup against Guatemala's President Jacobo Árbenz in 1954, which involved a gamut of activities, from diplomatic influence to cultural warfare and military intervention. A wide range of actors took part in the coup, including the U.S. State Department; the Central Intelligence Agency (CIA); United Fruit Company; the U.S. Information Agency (which led a propaganda war); local and U.S.-based churches; Guatemalan armed forces; and the neighboring governments of Nicaragua, Panama, and Honduras. From Honduras, Carlos Castillo Armas led the CIA-supported army invasion that eventually toppled Árbenz. "Success" in Guatemala served to model another invasion that turned out to be what Fidel Castro has often called the "first defeat of U.S. imperialism" in Latin America: the Bay of Pigs fiasco of 1961. President Dwight Eisenhower's plan to overthrow Fidel Castro through a CIA-organized invasion carried out by an army of exiles failed partly because of determined resistance in Cuba, but also because President Kennedy's concern to avoid identifying the invasion with the United States and his decision to suspend the use of U.S. airplanes to support it. What had become "formal" in Latin America was for the United States to act "informally."

Still, even after World War II there were several instances of outright U.S. military intervention in the area, such as the 1965 invasion of the Dominican Republic, involving an extraordinary force of twenty-two thousand marines, ostensibly to prevent the return to power of Juan Bosch,[13] and the invasion of Grenada (1983) in order to control forces sympathetic to Maurice Bishop's People's Revolutionary Government, despite the fact that Grenada was a member of the Commonwealth. But in most cases, as in the overthrow of Chile's Allende, U.S. participation was covert. While there has been evidence that major U.S. corporations and the U.S. government had endorsed a regime change in Chile, it took years to obtain declassified materials that demonstrate more conclusively their complicity in supporting the advent and consolidation of the Pinochet regime.[14] It may also take years to determine how deeply the United States was involved in the April 11, 2002, coup that toppled Venezuela's President Hugo Chávez in the span of forty-eight hours.[15]

Although not always its last resort, the United States' deployment of military forces has certainly not been its favored option. Indeed, U.S. policy toward Latin America seems to have been guided by the principle of extending control through domestic forces whenever possible and by external force whenever necessary. With this notion I am paraphrasing Gallagher and Robinson's argument that British policy in the nineteenth century "followed the principle of extending control informally if possible and formally if necessary."[16] Their larger argument about the need to relate the formal and informal aspects of empire has particular relevance for understanding U.S. involvement in Latin America in the twentieth century.

According to Gallagher and Robinson, "The usual summing up of the policy of the free trade empire as 'trade, not rule' should read 'trade with informal control if possible; trade with rule when necessary.'"[17] But rather than separate free trade from imperial trade, or informal from formal empire, they argue for the need to see these as part of a unitary process, marked not by fundamental differences of kind, but by shifting degrees of control. They ask to approach history through the "concept of the totality of British expansion." As they put it, "A concept of informal empire which fails to bring out the underlying unity between it and the formal empire is sterile. Only within the total framework of expansion is nineteenth-century empire intelligible."[18] While critical of totalizing narratives that assume the character and direction of historical change, my argument here also seeks to develop a holistic framework for the study of empire.

The scholarship on imperial relations in Latin America, mostly concerned with U.S. influence in the region, has only occasionally employed the notion of informal empire to explore U.S. expansion in the region. This may seem puzzling since it makes sense to treat the United States' involvement in the region as mostly "informal." Yet perhaps the recognition that U.S. influence was mostly "indirect" or "informal" made the distinction less useful; in the U.S. case, the "informal" *was* indeed the "formal." With a few exceptions, the concept of "informal imperialism" has been largely confined to studies that examine specific aspects of the British "informal empire" in the region, which contrasted with its large formal empire elsewhere.[19]

In Latin America the presence of imperialism has often been assumed as part of a commonsense understanding of reality, often not even naming it as such. Scholars writing not just about but from Latin America have developed structuralist perspectives to examine processes of uneven development, emphasizing skewed patterns of accumulation and foreign control over key economic sectors in the domains of production, finance, and commerce, in conjunction with associated forms of class relations, state formation, and political culture.[20]

This structuralist perspective views imperial domination as a two-way process rather than as a one-sided external imposition. Working within the *dependentista* perspective, Andre Gunder Frank's notion of the "development of underdevelopment," even as it emphasizes movement in one direction, calls attention to the reciprocal formation of centers and peripheries.[21] Similarly, Fernando Henrique Cardoso and Enzo Faletto's notion of "associated dependent development" shows that U.S. influence does not involve an external imposition but a triple alliance among foreign, domestic, and state capital within national formations.[22] As with Gallagher and Robinson's concern with developing a "total framework" for examining imperial expansion, these structuralist perspectives argue for a holistic view of historical transformations in Latin America in the context of imperial relations.

These works make evident shifts in modes of U.S. influence in the region. From a focus on controlling productive enclaves through direct investment in mining and agriculture during the first half of the twentieth century, the United States diversified investments in all areas of the economy, often participating as a "domiciliated" corporate citizen in joint ventures in industry, banking, services, and commerce.[23] While U.S. influence in its various modalities is more dominant in countries closer to its borders (Mexico, Central America, and the Caribbean), the United States' presence as an industrial investor, trading partner, and financial center is strong in all countries, including Brazil, despite diversified trading partnerships. Heavy debt burdens, slow economic growth, and the need of foreign capital have made most countries in the region heavily dependent on U.S. industrial and financial capital, as well as on institutions over which the United States exerts dominant control, such as the International Monetary Fund (IMF). After 1973, with U.S. support and the guidance of the "Chicago Boys" (economists following the University of Chicago's liberal economic doctrine), Chile's free market program was imposed and hailed as a model of development for Latin America and the rest of the world.

In retrospect, then, Chile's September 11 stands as a landmark of three facets and phases of the United States' imperial role: its long-standing economic and political involvement in the hemisphere, its political leadership in the struggle against socialism during the Cold War, and its emerging hegemonic role as the center of a globalized market organized around neoliberal principles.

Yet several decades after its initial "exemplary" implementation in Chile, even advocates of the free market are concerned with its disruptive effects, both globally and in Latin America. International organizations such as the World Bank and the International Labor Organization (ILO) have singled out growing worldwide poverty as a central problem of the global economy. According to the latest report of the ILO, half of the world's 2.8

billion workers earn less than $2 per day, leaving them and their families with "few prospects to escape from grinding poverty." Metropolitan centers, with 21 percent of the world population, consume 78 percent of global goods and services and 75 percent of the world energy. Wages for equivalent work are twenty times higher in the North. Today there are probably three times as many slaves than the approximately twelve million people who worked as slaves in the Americas for more than three centuries; the claim that "an overseas woman can be bought for about the same price as a kitchen blender—$40" seems hard to believe in a world accustomed to the idea that slavery is a matter of the past or that the value of slaves today would be higher.[24] The unrestrained expansion of the market is undermining not just its own material foundations, but the natural conditions of life for everyone. As rampant deforestation continues, it will be a pyrrhic market victory when water becomes, as predicted by many, a precious commodity.

In Latin America the social and ecological effects of market reforms are particularly pronounced. The implementation of free market policies (including the dismantling of the welfare state, privatization and denationalization of key economic sectors, deregulation of the financial sector, and exploitation of forests and mines) has intensified fractures in already divided societies, further polarizing income inequalities (the highest in the world), expanding the informal sector (that now employs the majority of the population), undermining already weak public services, intensifying quotidian personal and criminal violence, eroding their natural foundations, and developing new forms of racism, ethnic discrimination, and class conflict.

While formal equality before the market creates a universalistic framework that can serve to uphold egalitarian claims beyond the market, market practices are creating deep inequalities that undermine their realization. In highly polarized societies with limited prospects of collective improvement, social and economic boundaries are becoming also moral and cultural frontiers. Amid the promise of equality among different peoples promoted by the market, these cleavages are naturalizing difference within hierarchical structures and conjuring up images of superior and inferior peoples, as in colonial empires.

The Subject of Empire

A creative promiscuity of criteria has made it possible to bring together under the rubric of "empire" such vastly different geohistorical formations as the Roman, the Aztec, the Incan, the Russian, and the "American." In the modern period, in part because of the association between empires and overseas expansion, the treatment of the Russian and U.S. political systems as empires has been marked by deep ambivalence. Russia, despite its huge land conquests in Asia, has not been recognized as an empire like the maritime empires of the Spanish or the British. The United States did see itself as an empire in the eighteenth century, but the more it expanded across land and seas, the more it presented itself as a leading democratic republic and the less inclined it was to see itself as an empire.

Empire as a category has a long history, yet its meaning shifted significantly when it was used to refer to modern political systems.[25] When used in relation to premodern social formations, "empire" refers to a variety of centralized forms of rule involving differing degrees and forms of political control over populations typically spread over adjacent territories. The Latin *imperium* was used to refer to systems of authority of strong political centers over peoples generally located in contiguous territories. In the modern period, empire came to be associated with European political systems based on strong states that exerted control over distant populations, propelled in part by the expansion of trade and industry.

The scholarship on modern colonial empires makes evident that their fundamental political problem has been the differential incorporation of colonizers and colonized into a common and yet exclusionary system. The extensive racialization of difference after the eighteenth century, so commonly associated with northern European colonialism, was built upon previous classifications of American people in terms of variable combinations of natural and cultural factors (which in turn drew from biocultural classifications of Christians, Moors, and Jews during the Spanish Reconquista). Racial formations entail the making of identities through the fusion and confusion of visible and invisible markers. Certain sensorial facets, such as skin color or facial features, signifying descent serve to define social identities, naturalizing what is social. As a form of fetishism, racial thinking turns the social into the natural, wholes into parts, faces into facets, and attributes to these elements powers and significance that lie elsewhere. The essential analytical premise is that imperial formations, whether colonial or not, involve variable systems of difference between dominant and subaltern subjects; discerning *what* these differences are, and *how* they are constituted under specific imperial situations serves to establish a comparative reference, rather than exclusive standards for the study of imperial formations. What makes a difference is not specific differences but the systematic production of unequal difference. Since the differences that imperial powers claim as foundational are historical rather than inherent, what seems constant is constantly made, the object of ongoing and conflictual social making, whose object is their re-creation or transformation.

Empires encompass distinct populations, whether contiguous or not, of the same or different ethnic or racial identification. Whatever their particular form, empires involve hierarchical relations that do not just rank but differentiate subjects, making differences of degree into differences in kind, whether in principle, as in colonial empires, or in practice, as in postcolonial empires. They are structures of domination that bring different populations under one encompassing formation as different and unequal subjects. Whether subjects are exploited economically, exterminated or segregated racially or ethnically, granted partial autonomy, offered equality of rights, or assimilated, they are subjected and turned into others by making the different unequal, the unequal different. In Latin America, the current crisis has created a cultural chasm between social classes that has often led to the racialization of class differences and of social spaces, turning the poor, from dominant perspectives, into an internal "other." Otherness is only a universal human condition if one forgets the particular conditions that make some selves inferior to others. Empires are thus embodiments of the tension between the incorporation of subjects and their subjection.

The Subject of Imperialism

Imperialism as a category emerged in northern Europe in contests over its colonial rule; in contrast to empire, imperialism thus has a recent history. It was first used in France as a critical term (imperialiste) to refer to a partisan of the Napoleonic empire; it was later employed to criticize the Caesarist ambitions of Louis Napoleon. From this rather domestic origin in critiques of the French imperial policies of uncle and nephew, it evolved during British expansionism in the second half of the nineteenth century, first as an invective to criticize Benjamin Disraeli's policies, and then as a positive term to refer to the project of establishing a "Greater Britain" through the expansion of England into an "imperial federation" that would include Britain, its overseas settlements, and India. Although increasingly associated with British colonialism, the term came to refer to the expansionist drives of any European state.

Imperialism gained theoretical status when it was used to explain the underlying factors that cause European expansionism. This critical use characterized its deployment in debates over the Boer War and Europe's further entanglement in Asia and Africa. During this period, imperialism developed as a category to explain the political and economic dimensions of European colonialism.[26] In *Imperialism: A Study* (1902), John Atkinson Hobson argued that imperialism was driven by the need of states to find external markets because of the limits of consumption at home.[27] Building on this argument, a number of Marxist writers developed a more systemic theory of the links between capitalism and imperialism.[28] While Rosa Luxemburg developed Hobson's notion of underconsumption into a theory of the necessary limits of capitalist accumulation within one country, and Karl Kautsky developed the concept of ultraimperialism to argue that the exploitation of poorer nations led to the alliance of imperial powers, Lenin's classical analysis of imperialism as the highest phase of capitalism emphasized the necessity of interimperial rivalry during a phase of capitalist expansion based on the monopolization of production, the merger of financial and industrial capital, and the export of capital.

While I recognize limitations of the concept and its association with stale debates and teleological narratives, I think "imperialism" is out in the streets as an indispensable political term. Despite its shortcomings, it continues to have currency in political discourse among peoples subjected to the devastating effects of global powers, evoking memories and affects and making sense of current experiences of inequality, exploitation, and domination. Particularly after September 11, 2001, some scholars have offered strong arguments for considering its ongoing relevance.[29] In my view, if we want to engage contemporary politics beyond the high walls of academia, the question is not so much whether to use this term or not but to recast it to make it useful.

Recasting Imperialism

Most discussions of imperialism tend to reproduce the provincial Eurocentric focus that marked its original framing. Ironically, although the scope of imperialism is global, Europe has been its main, if not only, active subject. As non-Europe, the rest of the world participates in these discussions as the object of imperial subjection, not as an agent in imperial formations. On the basis of the Latin American historical experience, I seek to decenter this concept and reconsider its validity in light of different assumptions.

Three interrelated premises have framed discussions of imperialism. First, capitalism is seen as a European phenomenon. Second, European capitalist nations are viewed as the basic agents of imperialist expansion, even if it is recognized that these nations interact in a global market. Third, imperialism has been seen as following capitalism, even if it is not always regarded as caused by capitalism or as its higher phase. Rather than entering the discussion on imperialism in these terms, I wish to recast them by looking at "empires beyond Europe" on the basis of different premises, building on work that has already questioned them.

Dependency, world systems, and a number of colonial and postcolonial scholars have argued for the need to view capitalism as a global rather than as a national or regional process. Debates on the origins of capitalism tend to focus on specific relations within Europe itself. A global perspective redefines the discussion of its origins by framing it within a different scale. This perspective does not deny the role of local relations; rather, it places them within global interactions. The issue is not to choose to locate the origins of capitalism, as in a famous debate, in class relations of the European countryside or in urban trade,[30] but to place Europe itself in the context of global relations. Through a discussion of just one commodity, Sidney Mintz offers a glimpse into this worldwide process, showing how Caribbean sugar came to sustain not just the British state and ruling sectors, but also its laboring classes, transforming eating habits, desires, and individual and collective identities and possibilities.[31] As other scholars have shown, Caribbean slaves did not just give sugar to Europe or provide a major source of earnings to states, traders, and industrialists, but contributed to changing global understandings of humanity and citizenship. For example, slaves in Saint-Domingue forced French revolutionaries to abolish slavery and make more universal their provincial universalism.[32] The abolition of slavery in Haiti also created conditions for the generalization of "free labor" everywhere, which has always been supported by forms of "unfree" and poorly remunerated labor, such as highly gendered housework or work in subsistence agriculture.

If labor, capital, and land are the "trinity form" that "holds all the mysteries of the social production process,"[33] this trinity form helps explain the mystery of its historical development. Not just capital and labor but also land (as the socially mediated powers of nature) have been engaged in the worldwide production of capitalism. The Iberian colonial experience in the Americas provided Europe with immense wealth in the form of riches extracted from American soil as well as surplus value exploited through many forms of coerced labor. It also provided other European powers with models of rule and of production. Spanish jurisprudence, largely developed on the basis of debates resulting from the colonial encounter, established the foundation for international law.[34] Caribbean and Brazilian plantations, integrating agriculture and industry in large-scale productive structures, were early forms of agribusiness that served as templates for industrial production in Europe.[35] As Fernando Ortiz shows through his evocative "counterpoint" of American tobacco and European sugar, the modern world is best seen not as originating in one isolated European region, but as the result of "transcultural" engagements among metropolitan and colonial societies and cultures.[36]

From this perspective, capitalism did not originate in Manchester, Liverpool, or the British countryside and then spread to the tropics. It developed between colonial and metropolitan regions in the expanding world economy of the sixteenth century. Its origins thus lie not in one region, but *between* regions in the processes that formed them. Free labor is the dominant as well as the most disguised form of coerced labor under capitalism, not its defining criterion. Capitalist development is not just uneven but unequal, its multiple regional forms reflecting its polarizing dynamics and the shifting worldwide power relations within which it unfolds. Increasingly defined by networks of capital and labor that transcend national boundaries, capitalist divisions of both labor and nature continue now to divide humanity, separating it between zones that concentrate knowledge and skilled labor and areas that produce labor-intensive and nature-intensive commodities.

The formation of nation-states has been intimately linked to the worldwide development of capitalism. As political centers, empires promoted the expansion of capitalist trade and industry even before nations were constituted as independent states. Spain as a nation was formed in the longue durée that included both the constitution and dissolution of its empire. During the colonial period, Spain was composed of separate principalities ruled by the Castilian king. "Spain" represented a unitary ideal that encompassed the peninsula but also extended to the colonial relation. As Irene Silverblatt has argued, "Spain's two referents—national ideal and colonial power—developed in tandem."[37] Latin American independence struggles, Benedict Anderson has insisted, pioneered modern nationalism.[38] The dissolution of the Spanish empire led not only to the formation of independent nations in the Americas, but of Spain itself as a nation-state. As Fred Cooper shows, the entity called France, referring to an empire-state and also to a nation-state, became strictly "national" after the dissolution of its empire in the second half of the twentieth century.[39] Nations have been formed in tandem with empires through different forms of defining, incorporating, and differentiating their distinct subject populations.

From this perspective, imperialism does not result from the expansive dynamics of advanced capitalist nations. Rather, imperialism is capitalism's coeval condition of possibility. Capitalism and imperialism developed together as twin forces in the creation of a world market beginning in the sixteenth century; they are the cause and effect of the interactions between imperial centers and colonial peripheries. The export of capital, the search for markets, the interaction between financial and productive capital, and inter-state rivalries and alliances—factors highlighted by theorists of imperialism as taking place at a particular phase of metropolitan national capitalisms—have been at work in different form from the colonization of the Americas to the present; their specific configuration at any specific moment (as in Lenin's classical formulation) defines a modality of imperialism, not its defining manifestation. Just as imperialism makes evident the political dimension of capitalism, capitalism makes visible the economic dimension of imperialism, revealing "states" and "markets" as dual facets of a unitary process. Without capitalism there would be no modern imperialism, but equally, without modern imperialism there would be no capitalism.

Writing during the first half of the twentieth century (1936), the Peruvian political leader Victor Haya de la Torre argued that in Latin America imperialism is not the highest stage of capitalism, but the first phase of its capitalist development (Kwame Nkrumah made a related argument in *Neocolonialism: The Last Stage of Imperialism*).[40] Here I extend Haya de la Torre's argument. What he says about Latin America is true of all capitalist development. Yet, I do not mean to reverse Lenin's dictum and say that capitalism follows imperialism in the periphery or elsewhere, but to argue that in the modern world capitalism and imperialism are coeval processes that mutually condition each other in historically variable contexts. Just as there were empires before there was capitalism, there were (and there might be) forms of imperialism without capitalism, but modern imperialism is intimately bound up with capitalism (including imperial socialist states that are integrated to the capitalist world economy and control rather directly their domestic capital and markets).

Based on this broad conception of modern imperialism, I wish to distinguish three of its dominant modalities. At the risk of reducing complex processes to flat distinctions, I define "colonial imperialism" as the formal dominion of a political center over its colonies; "national imperialism" as the informal dominion of a nation-state over independent nations; and "global imperialism" as the informal dominion by a network of capital and states over an increasingly integrated worldwide system. Each of these modalities may involve different forms of "internal colonialism," a category developed to analyze the subjection of marginalized populations within a territory by domestic elites. Needless to say, any form of imperialism also articulates with related forms of subjection based on other principles of difference, such as gender, age, and religion.

This scheme of modes and phases of domination allows for historically variable expressions of their relation to each other in specific contexts, without assuming that they are linked in a teleological progression of universal stages. Thus, while colonial imperialism preceded and made possible national and global imperialisms, it may coexist with them. For instance, the British empire combined colonial and nationalist imperialist modalities; it involved a formal empire in Africa and Asia as well as an informal empire in Latin America. The current period encompasses the three modalities of imperialism, but it is defined by the articulation of its national and global forms. Since World War II the United States has been the major national imperial power, but in the past two decades it has also increasingly been at the center of an emerging system of internationalized capital, states, and culture, leading some thinkers, such as Antonio Negri and Michael Hardt, to argue for the emergence of a global "empire."[41] To the extent that globalization has led to the appearance of a unified world despite its internal fractures, Eurocentrism gives way to globalcentrism as a mode of constructing difference, creating a common ground for potential equality but also redefining the spaces and meanings of different forms of alterity and subalternity. Yet the U.S. reaction to the attacks of September 11, 2001, has made evident the persistent national foundational of transnational networks and alliances. Rather than consolidating global networks, the current crisis seems to be stimulating the more open development of the dual character of the United States as a nation-state and an empire-state. This development also has intensified the deployment of cultural and religious factors as markers of hierarchical difference between the United States and its opponents.

This scheme may help us observe features and changes of imperial formations. The movement from national to global imperialism seems to be related to a generalization and growing abstraction of the main forms of capital (land/ground rent, labor/wages, and capital/profits and its de-rived mode, money/interest). Financial markets have expanded dramati-cally, affecting a "real economy" that involves the commodification of ever more domains across space and time (by 1997 derivatives were exchanged for $360 trillion, twelve times the value of world economic production). Labor has become more globally integrated and specialized, giving tan-gible support to Marx's notions of "abstract" labor, of the collective "social worker," and of expanded units of production beyond traditional factories. Since wealth derives from the union of value produced by labor and riches gifted by nature, the relentless pursuit of wealth under global imperialism propels the international division of both labor and nature into ever wider domains, dividing time and space ever more minutely and fragmenting na-tions and markets ever more mindlessly.[42]

These transformations are inseparable from the changing articulation of states and markets. Current modes of global capital accumulation place new strains upon the reproduction of state legitimacy at the national level. States and capitals vary in their capacity to negotiate this tension. While metropoli-tan nations orchestrate this process through such institutions as the IMF, World Trade Organization, General Agreement on Tariffs and Trade, and Group of 7, nations from the "South" find themselves increasingly subjected to directives from international organizations and to the pressures of trans-national capital (including their own transnationalized capital). The wid-ening gap among and within nations affects more severely populations of nations in the South. The joint unfolding of capitalism and imperialism, in tandem with the formation of nations and empires, has always entailed not just the articulation, but the construction of "economics" and "politics" as separate domains or functions. For Gallagher and Robinson, imperialism is a process "of integrating new regions into an expanding economy"; its "suf-ficient" function is political; its "necessary function" is economic.[43] Yet under current forms of "national" and "global imperialism" it becomes increasingly difficult to separate politics and economics and argue that one or the other is the "sufficient" or the "necessary" function of integrating new regions into an imperial domain. As the "economic" becomes ever more evidently "political" in its effects, analysis should make increasingly clear what was opaque before: the unity of the formal and informal, the political and the economic within the open-ended and ever changing totality of imperial formations.

Nation-State and Empire-State: The United States
and National and Global Imperialism

In the 1950s, William Appleman Williams noted that while a dominant theme of U.S. historiography is that the United States is not an empire, historians, "if pressed," would admit that the United States once had an empire and speak persistently of the United States as a "World Power."[44] Building on Williams's work, the cultural critic Amy Kaplan four decades later treated the "absence of empire in the study of American culture" as a central aspect of its imperial culture.[45]

Current debate about the United States' international role reenacts the old ambivalence about casting it as imperial, yet it also exhibits a growing inclination to recognize it as such. For example, a recent *New York Times Book Review* issue that includes several book reviews on the subject of empire features an article reporting a dialogue between two Yale historians revealingly titled "Kill the Empire! (Or Not)." While the title dramatically captures the entrenched ambivalence about identifying the United States as an empire, the dialogue shows that empire, however unpalatable, must now be accepted as common sense, a fact about America. As John Lewis Gaddis puts it, the notion of empire has been present from the birth of the United States as a nation: "We've always had an empire. The thinking of the founding fathers was we were going to be an empire. Empire is as American as apple pie, in that sense. The question is, what kind of an empire do we have?"[46]

Before September 11, the significance of imperialism for the present was debated within very restricted scholarly circles. Scholars were divided. Some asserted imperialism's persisting centrality, others were ambivalent about it, and still others affirmed that imperialism has ceased to be a relevant category, as it has been replaced by the notion of a global empire.[47] Yet since September 11, 2001, many radical critics have argued more insistently that imperialism has validity as a concept for the present. For Jonathan Schell, imperialism is even a more fundamental category than empire; for him, we now face "imperialism without empire" since the United States is unable to exert sufficient worldwide control.[48] Others prefer to recognize novel forms of empires and imperialism that involve fundamental changes in the forms and spaces of imperial domination.[49]

In his incisive critique of Hardt and Negri's *Empire*, George Steinmetz offers a forceful argument for the relevance of imperialism today. According to him, after September 11, 2001, imperialism became an explicit element of U.S. politics. Integrating insights from regulation and world system theories, he argues that a "structural" change took place after September 11, 2001. This involved continuity at the level of the core framework for regulating post-Fordist imperial globalization but discontinuity at the level of its ideological legitimation, characterized by a "more imperialistic politics and a more authoritarian interior order."[50] For Steinmetz, "September 11th was the shock that allowed an explicitly imperialist and authoritarian rethinking of the model of regulation to come to the fore. . . . This emergent framework is still post-Fordist with respect to the core model of industrial production, but the state model is domestically authoritarian and geopolitically imperialistic."[51]

While for Steinmetz September 11 turned imperialism into an explicit state ideology, for Leo Panitch and Sam Gindin it revealed what had until then been hidden: "the American empire is no longer concealed."[52] Building on Nico Poulantzas's argument that the U.S. state is the center of an "imperialist chain" that has established hegemony over other societies by "generalizing its relations of production and domination inside other metropolises," Panitch argues that U.S. dominance involves a new type of "non-territorial imperialism maintained not through direct rule by the metropolis, nor even through political subordination of a neo-colonial type, but rather through the 'induced reproduction of the form of the dominant imperialist power within each national formation and its state.'"[53] What is needed, according to Panitch and Gindin, is not to dismiss the relevance of imperialism because the market is now globalized, but to "transcend the limitations of the old Marxist 'stagist' theory of inter-imperial rivalry, and allow for a full appreciation of the historical factors that have led to the formation of a unique American informal empire. This will involve understanding how the American state developed the capacity to eventually incorporate its capitalist rivals, and oversee and police 'globalization'—i.e. the spread of capitalist social relations to every corner of the world."[54] This need becomes even more urgent now that the United States encounters increasing difficulties in ruling a "truly global informal empire" in alliance with states subjected to ever more intense domestic pressures.[55]

Imperial Effects

If a focus on imperial effects may serve to recognize empires, it may also be used to endorse them. Thus, for Niall Ferguson, since the United States functions like an empire, it should more fully behave like one. According to him, "If you do not recognize that you are essentially performing the functions of an empire, you are incapable of learning from the mistakes of past empires." Asked why he calls the United States an empire despite the fact that "most Americans don't think of their country that way," Ferguson offers a revealing answer:

> Well, it functions like an empire, in the sense that it projects its military power globally, its economic interests are global, its cultural reach is global. In many ways, it's a more impressive empire than any empire has ever been. The only strange thing about it is that its citizens don't recognize the fact. That's odd, because the Founding Fathers quite openly called the United States an empire. Jefferson, Hamilton, Madison, Washington all used the e-word to describe the United States.[56]

Even before September 11 there were calls for the United States to assume an imperial role, but based on the extension of informal influence. In 2000, Richard Haass, as director of foreign policy studies and chair in international security at the Brookings Institution, proposed that Americans "re-conceive their role from one of a traditional nation-state to an imperial power." As he explained, "An imperial foreign policy is not to be confused with imperialism. The latter is a concept that connotes exploitation, normally for commercial ends, often requiring territorial control. It is grounded in a world that no longer exists."

Revealingly, Haass proposes an imperial (but not imperialist) role for the United States through a misreading of Gallagher and Robinson. Arguing for the relevance for the United States of their axiom that "the British followed the principle of extending control informally if possible, and formally if necessary," he proposes that the United States should be an informal empire so as not to be an imperialistic one: "Indeed, an American empire would have to be informal if it were to succeed if only because American democracy could not underwrite an imperial order that required constant, costly applications of military power."[57] How are we to interpret the United States' extraordinary military presence throughout the world—which includes more than seven hundred conventional military bases, not to mention those under leaseholds, concealed, or under other arrangements[58]—and its costs to democracy at home and abroad? Was Haass asking for the dismantling of this huge military establishment? Should we believe, like Haass, that by becoming an informal empire—by avoiding "the constant, costly applications of military power"—the United States can avoid being an imperialist one?

Haass wrote this before September 11, 2001, when post-1989 globalization had made war seem unnecessary. As Andrew Bacevich has noted, "Before September 11, the conventional wisdom had been that globalization was fast making war obsolete; after September 11, the conventional wisdom was that globalization was making war an all but permanent and inescapable part of life in the 21st century."[59] Since September 11, 2001, terror has been presented as an enemy without national boundaries or centers, a diffuse force that blurs the boundaries between military and civilian agents, between armies and "the people." The elusiveness of terror makes it increasingly untenable for the United States to separate central from collateral damage, political from military targets, external from internal enemies, severely restricting civil rights at home. Now that an endless war against terror defines the United States' domestic and foreign policy, how are we to think of its imperial role?

According to Gallagher and Robinson, Britain's informal empire was no less imperialistic than its formal empire; rather, the informal imperialism of free trade was Britain's preferable modality of imperialism. Their main argument is that imperialism is a total process that includes formal and informal dimensions; these dimensions do not entail essential differences, but rather varying degrees and modes of control. More than the term "empire," "imperialism" helps show that imperial control is achieved through the joining and transformation of distinct communities brought together by the force of the market as well as by armed force—whether actively deployed or kept as threat.

After Empire

The war against terror has forcefully brought "home" the imperial problem of rule over others. In a remarkable article in the *New York Times* titled "What Does the Pentagon See in 'Battle of Algiers'?" strangely presented under "film studies," the author reports on a screening in the Pentagon of Gillo Pontecorvo's classical anticolonial film *The Battle of Algiers*.[60] The idea of showing and discussing the movie came from the Directorate for Special Operations and Low-Intensity Conflict, a civilian-led group entrusted with responsibility "for thinking aggressively and creatively" on issues of guerrilla warfare. Forty officers and civilians were invited to consider "the problematic but alluring efficacy of brutal and repressive means in fighting clandestine terrorists."

The *New York Times* article gives us an unusual glimpse into an intraelite debate about the war occurring not just in the Pentagon, but, evidently, through the U.S. media. The flier inviting the selected guests to the Pentagon screening framed their viewing of the film in the following terms: "how to win a battle against terrorism and lose the war of ideas. Children shoot soldiers at point-blank range. Women plant bombs in cafes. Soon the entire Arab population builds to a mad fervor. Sound familiar? The French have a plan. It succeeds tactically, but fails strategically. To understand why, come to a rare showing of the film." This article on "film studies" concludes as follows: "If indeed the government is currently analyzing or even weighing the tactical choices reflected in the 'Battle of Algiers,' presumably that is being done at a higher level of secrecy than an open discussion following a screening of the Pontecorvo film. Still, by showing the movie within the Pentagon and by announcing that publicly, somebody seems to be raising issues that have remained obscured throughout the war against terror."

What are "these issues"? Is there a link between the Pentagon's screening and the *New York Times*'s reporting? If tactics following the French victory in the battle of Algiers in 1957 led to its loss of Algeria in 1962, what is the danger to be avoided now? What strategic victory should follow the United States' tactical victory in Iraq in 2003? Clearly, somebody is trying to tell somebody else something, but we—the general readers of the *New York Times*—do not really know who is speaking to whom or what is being said. What has happened since the article was published—public revelation of widespread torture and growing resistance in Iraq—makes this exchange about tactics at elite circles all the more significant. This exchange reveals—even without knowing more about it—that for people with the power to stand at the apex of the world and to make decisions that affect the lives of people below, the battle over Iraq is not unlike the battle over colonial Algeria. For them, the U.S. republican state, whatever we call it, has much to learn from the French imperial state.

In effect, as Neil Macmaster has shown in his analysis of torture from Algiers to Abu Ghraib, French colonial officials involved in Algiers taught the United States practices of torture it has used in Iraq.[61] But, then, the United States has deployed globally a gamut of imperial practices—from torture to subtle forms of cultural influence—that it either learned from other imperial experiences or developed on its own, and that in most instances it first practiced in Latin America. From the vantage point of Latin American history it is difficult not to see the presence of the United States in the region as imperial. But whether we call the United States an empire, an imperialist state, or a republic, in the end what matters is how the concepts we use help us understand and counter formations of domination. Attending to these effects, this essay has sought to make domination in the modern world—whether in Algeria or in Iraq, in the name of the French empire or the U.S. republic—at once more intelligible and more intolerable.

Notes

This paper has benefited from the advice of many. I thank my SAR colleagues and friends; my Harvard students from a seminar on globalization and imperialism (Fall 2004); and Genese Sodikoff, Edward Murphy, and David Pedersen for their invaluable comments.

Epigraph: Raymond Williams, *Keywords* (London: Fontana, 1983), 160.

1 Carole McGranahan and Ann Laura Stoler, "Empires: Thinking Colonial Studies beyond Europe," proposal for a School of American Research Advanced Seminar, April 2002, unpublished ms.

2 Hans Kohn, "Reflections on Colonialism," in *The Idea of Colonialism*, ed. Robert Strausz-Hupé and Harry W. Hazard (New York: Frederick A. Praeger, 1958), 3–4.

3 Hamza Alavi, "Imperialism Old and New," *Socialist Register* 1 (1964): 105–26.

4 John Gallagher and Ronald Robinson, "The Imperialism of Free Trade," *Economic History Review* 6, no. 1 (1953): 1–15.

5 See, e.g., Harry Magdoff, *Imperialism: From the Colonial Age to the Present* (New York: Monthly Review, 1978); Prasenjit Duara, "The Imperialism of 'Free Nations': Japan, Manchukuo, and the History of the Present," in *Imperial Formations and Their Discontents*, ed. Ann Stoler, Carole McGranahan, and Peter Perdue (Santa Fe, NM: School for Advanced Research Press, 2007).

6 Edward Said, *Reflections on Exile and Other Essays* (Cambridge, MA: Harvard University Press, 2000), xxviii.

7 Walter LaFeber, *Inevitable Revolutions: The United States in Central America* (New York: W. W. Norton, 1992), 38.

8 Carlos Fuentes, "Prologue," in *Ariel*, by José Enrique Rodó (Austin: University of Texas Press, 1988), 16.

9 See Frantz Fanon, *The Wretched of the Earth* (New York: Grove, 1965), 102.

10 See Robert Freeman Smith, *The United States and the Latin American Sphere of Influence* (Malabar, FL: Krieger, 1981), 152; Bryce Wood, *The Making of the Good Neighbor Policy* (New York: Columbia University Press: 1961), 5; Alexander DeConde, *A History of American Foreign Policy* (New York: Scribner, 1971), 536.

11 William Blum, *Killing Hope: U.S. Military and CIA Interventions since World War II* Monroe, ME: Common Courage, 1995), 444–51.

12 John H. Coatsworth, "United States Interventions: What For?" *ReVista: Harvard Review of Latin America* (Spring 2005): 6–9.

13 In an illuminating discussion of the causes of U.S. intervention in Latin America, Coatsworth argues that the Santo Domingo invasion was the result of domestic politics, not of external threats. President Lyndon B. Johnson "felt threatened by Republicans in Congress": Coatsworth, "United States Interventions," 8.

14 Peter Kornbluth, *The Pinochet File: A Declassified Dossier on Atrocity and Accountability* (New York: Free Press, 2003); Kenneth Maxwell, "The Case of the Missing Letter in Foreign Affairs: Kissinger, Pinochet and Operation Condor," working paper, David Rockefeller Center of Latin American Studies, Harvard University, Cambridge, MA, 2004.

15 For a discussion of U.S. involvement in the coup based on U.S. government declassified documents, see Eva Golinger, *El Código Chávez: Descifrando la intervención de los Estados Unidos en Venezuela* (Caracas: Melvin, 2005). The United States immediately endorsed the interim government of Pedro Carmona and blamed President Chávez for his downturn. While the U.S. government denies it was involved in the coup, Chávez's government claims that it was carried out with U.S. support. I am currently writing a book on the coup; for a discussion of other aspects of the coup, see Fernando Coronil, "Nación y estado durante el golpe contra Hugo Chávez," *Anuario de Estudios Americanos* 62, no. 1 (2005): 87–112.

16 Gallagher and Robinson, "The Imperialism of Free Trade," 13.

17 Gallagher and Robinson, "The Imperialism of Free Trade," 13.

18 Gallagher and Robinson, "The Imperialism of Free Trade," 7.

19 One exception is Ricardo Salvatore, who uses the notion of "informal empire" to examine the "representational machinery" of empire, yet in his work this term does not really build on the work of Gallagher and Robinson; rather, it serves to address mostly cultural productions in the area: see Ricardo Salvatore, "The Enterprise of Knowledge: Representational Machines of Informal Empire," in *Close Encounters of Empire: Writing the Cultural History of U.S.–Latin American Relations*, ed. Gilbert Joseph, Catherine C. Legrand, and Ricardo D. Salvatore (Durham, NC: Duke University Press, 1998), 69–106. Following Gallagher and Robinson more closely are works that examine the British empire in Latin America: see, e.g., Richard Graham, *Britain and the Onset of Modernization in Brazil, 1850–1914* (London: Cambridge University Press, 1968); Michael Monteón, "The British in the Atacama Desert: The Cultural Bases of Economic Imperialism," *Journal of Economic History* 25, no. 1 (March 1975): 117–33; Peter Winn, "Britain's Informal Empire in Uruguay during the Nineteenth Century," *Past and Present* 73 (November 1976): 100–26; George Edmund Carl, "First among

Equals: Great Britain and Venezuela, 1810–1910," *American Historical Review* 86, no. 2 (April 1981): 483–84; Roger Gravil, *The Anglo-Argentine Connection, 1900–1939* (Boulder, CO: Westview, 1985).

20 For a discussion of the place of Latin American scholarship within the field of postcolonial studies that highlights the significance of the deep temporal experience of colonialism and imperialism in Latin America, see Fernando Coronil, "Latin American Postcolonial Studies and Global Decolonisation," in *Postcolonial Literary Studies*, ed. Neil Lazarus (London: Cambridge University Press, 2004), 221–41.

21 Andre Gunder Frank's concept is developed in his pamphlet "The Development of Underdevelopment," *Monthly Review* 18, no. 4 (1966): 17–31.

22 See their classical book Fernando Henrique Cardoso and Enzo Faletto, *Dependency and Development in Latin America* (Berkeley: University of California Press, 1979). Peter Evans developed this idea in *Dependent Development: The Alliance of Multinational, State, and Local Capital in Brazil* (Princeton, NJ: Princeton University Press, 1979).

23 On the basis of Richard L. Sklar's "doctrine of domicile," I use the notion of "domiciliated corporate citizen" to refer to the sector of foreign capital that becomes rooted socially and politically in dependent nations: Richard L. Sklar, *Corporate Power in an African State: The Political Impact of Multinational Mining Companies in Zambia* (Berkeley: University of California Press, 1975), 186.

24 Paul M. Weyrich, "Contemporary Slavery," commentary, CNSNews.com, January 16, 2004, http://www.enterstageright.com/archive/articles/0104/0104slavery.htm. The United Nations defines slavery as a variety of human rights violations. In addition to traditional slavery and the slave trade, these abuses include the sale of children, child prostitution, child pornography, the exploitation of child labor, the sexual mutilation of female children, the use of children in armed conflicts, debt bondage, the traffic in people and in the sale of human organs, the exploitation of prostitution, and certain practices under apartheid and colonial regimes.

25 Schmuel Eisenstadt offers a useful discussion of the problem of incorporating subject populations in premodern and modern empires: Schmuel N. Eisenstadt, "Empire," in *International Encyclopedia of the Social Sciences*, 17 vols., ed. David Sills (New York: Macmillan, 1968), 5:41–48. Of course, the "modern-premodern" distinction is problematic; while aware of its pitfalls, I follow here those who roughly place its temporal divide around the sixteenth century and associate modernity with the colonization of the Americas and the rise of capitalism as a global social and cultural formation.

26 Hans Daalder, "Imperialism," in Sills, *International Encyclopedia of the Social Sciences*, 7:101–9.

27 John Atkinson Hobson, *Imperialism: A Study* (London: George Allen and Unwin, [1902] 1961).

28 See, e.g., Rudolf Hilferding, *Finance Capital: A Study of the Latest Phase Capitalist Development* (London: Routledge and Kegan Paul, [1910] 1981); Rosa Luxemburg, *The Accumulation of Capital* (New York: Monthly Review, [1913] 1964); Karl Kautsky, *Die Internationalität und der Krieg* (Berlin: Vorwärts, 1915); Vladimir I. Lenin, *Imperialism: The Highest Stage of Capitalism* (New York: International Publishers, [1917] 1947); Nikolai I. Bukharin, *Imperialism and World Economy* (New York: International Publishers, [1918] 1929); Leonard Woolf, *Economic Imperialism* (London: Swarthmore, 1920); Maurice Dobb, *Studies in the Development of Capitalism* (New York: International Publishers, 1946); Paul Sweezy, *The Theory of Capitalist Development* (Oxford: Oxford University Press, 1946); Paul Sweezy and Paul Baran, *Monopoly Capital: An Essay on the American Economic and Social Order* (New York: Monthly Review, 1966).

29 See, e.g., the Cuban journal *Temas*, nos. 33–34 (April–September 2003), and *Socialist Register* (2004).

30 Dobb, *Studies in the Development of Capitalism*; Robert Brenner, "The Origins of Capitalist Development: A Critique of Neo-Smithian Marxism," *New Left Review* 1, no. 104 (July–August 1977): 25–92; Sweezy, *The Theory of Capitalist Development*.

31 Sidney Mintz, *Sweetness and Power: The Place of Sugar in the Modern World* (New York: Penguin, 1985).

32 C. L. R. James, *The Black Jacobins: Toussaint L'Ouverture and the San Domingo Revolution* (New York: Vintage, [1963] 1989); Laurent Dubois, *A Colony of Citizens: Revolution and Slave Emancipation in the French Caribbean, 1787–1804* (Chapel Hill: University of North Carolina Press, 2004).

33 Karl Marx, *Capital, Volume III* (New York: Vintage, 1981), 953.

34 Carl Schmitt, *The Nomos of the Earth in the International Law of the "Jus Publicum Europaeum"* (New York: Telos, 2003).

35 Eric Williams, *Capitalism and Slavery* (Chapel Hill: University of North Carolina Press, 1961); Mintz, *Sweetness and Power*.

36 Fernando Ortiz, *Cuban Counterpoint: Tobacco and Sugar* (Durham, NC: Duke University Press, 1995). See also Fernando Coronil, "Transculturation and the Politics of Theory: Countering the Center, Cuban Counterpoint," in Ortiz, *Cuban Counterpoint*, ix–lvi; Fernando Coronil, *The Magical State: Nature, Money and Modernity in Venezuela* (Chicago: University of Chicago Press, 1997).

37 Irene Silverblatt, *Modern Inquisitions: Peru and the Colonial Origins of the Modern World* (Durham, NC: Duke University Press, 2004), 137.

38 Benedict Anderson, *Imagined Communities: Reflections on the Origins and Spread of Nationalism* (London: Verso, 1991).

39 Frederick Cooper, "Provincializing France," in *Imperial Formations and Their Discontents*, ed. Ann Laura Stoler, Carole McGranahan, and Peter C. Perdue (Santa Fe, NM: School for Advanced Research Press, 2007), 341–77.

40 Victor Haya de la Torre, *El imperialismo y el Apra* (Santiago de Chile: Ercilla, 1936); Kwame Nkrumah, *Neo-colonialism: The Last Stage of Imperialism* (New York: International Publishers, 1965).

41 Michael Hardt and Antonio Negri, *Empire* (Cambridge, MA: Harvard University Press, 2000).

42 See Fernando Coronil, "Towards a Critique of Globalcentrism: Speculations on Capitalism's Nature," *Public Culture* 12, no. 2 (Spring 2000): 351–74.

43 Gallagher and Robinson, "The Imperialism of Free Trade," 5–6.

44 William Appleman Williams, *Empire as a Way of Life: An Essay on the Causes and Character of America's Present Predicament, along with a Few Thoughts about an Alternative* (New York: Oxford University Press, 1980).

45 Amy Kaplan, "Left Alone with America: The Absence of Empire in the Study of American Culture," in *Cultures of United States Imperialism*, ed. Amy Kaplan and Donald E. Pease (Durham, NC: Duke University Press, 1993), 3–21.

46 John Lewis Gaddis and Paul Kennedy, "Kill the Empire! (Or Not)," *New York Times Book Review*, July 25, 2004.

47 See, respectively, Magdoff, *Imperialism*; Eric Hobsbawm, "Addressing the Questions," *Radical History Review* 57 (Fall 1993): 73–75; Hardt and Negri, *Empire*.

48 Jonathan Schell, "Imperialism without Empire," Global Policy Forum, August 26, 2004, https://www.globalpolicy.org/component/content/article/154/25704.html.

49 Neil Smith, *American Empire: Roosevelt's Geographer and the Prelude to Globalization* (Berkeley: University of California Press, 2003).

50 George Steinmetz, "State of Emergency and the Revival of American Imperialism: Towards an Authoritarian Post-Fordism," *Public Culture* 15, no. 2 (2003): 327.

51 Steinmetz, "State of Emergency and the Revival of American Imperialism," 341.

52 Leo Panitch and Sam Gindin, "Global Capitalism and American Empire," *Socialist Register* (2004): 1.

53 Poulantzas quoted in Leo Panitch, "The New Imperial State," *New Left Review* 2 (March–April 2000): 9.

54 Panitch and Gindin, "Global Capitalism and American Empire," 4.

55 Panitch and Gindin, "Global Capitalism and American Empire," 30.

56 Niall Ferguson, "Imperial Denial," interview by Nonna Gorilovskaya, *Mother Jones*, May–June, 2004, http://www.motherjones.com/politics/2004/05/imperial-denial.

57 Richard N. Haass, "Imperial America," paper presented at the Atlanta Conference, November 11, 2000, https://monthlyreview.org/wp-content/uploads/2003/05/Imperial_America_Richard_N_Haass.pdf.

58 Chalmers Johnson, *The Sorrows of Empire: Militarism, Secrecy, and the End of the Republic* (New York: Metropolitan, 2004).

59 Andrew Bacevich, *American Empire: The Realities and Consequences of U.S. Diplomacy* (Cambridge, MA: Harvard University Press, 2002), 225.

60 Michael T. Kaufman, "What Does the Pentagon See in 'Battle of Algiers'?" *New York Times*, September 7, 2003, 3.

61 See Neil Macmaster, "Torture: From Algiers to Abu Ghraib," *Race and Class* 46, no. 2 (October 2004): 1–21. I am grateful to an anonymous reviewer of this article for this reference.

Chapter 1, "Pieces for Anthrohistory: A Puzzle to Be Assembled Together," first appeared in *Anthrohistory: Unsettling Knowledge, Questioning Discipline*, ed. Edward Murphy, David Cohen, Chandra Bhimull, Fernando Coronil, Monica Patterson, and Julie Skurski (Ann Arbor: University of Michigan Press, 2011), 301–316.

Chapter 2, "Transculturation and the Politics of Theory: Countering the Center, Cuban Counterpoint," first appeared in Fernando Ortiz, *Cuban Counterpoint: Tobacco and Sugar* (Durham, NC: Duke University Press, 1995), ix–lvi.

Chapter 3, "Foreword to *Close Encounters of Empire*," first appeared in *Close Encounters of Empire: Writing the Cultural History of U.S.–Latin American Relations*, ed. Gilbert Joseph, Catherine LeGrand, and Ricardo Salvatore (Durham, NC: Duke University Press, 1998), ix–xii.

Chapter 4, "Perspectives on Tierney's *Darkness in El Dorado*," first appeared in *Current Anthropology* 42, no. 2 (April 2001): 265–276.

Chapter 5, "The Future in Question: History and Utopia in Latin America (1989–2010)," first appeared in *Business as Usual: The Roots of the Global Financial Meltdown*, ed. Craig Calhoun and Georgi Derluguian (New York: NYU Press, 2011), 231–264.

Chapter 6, "Dismembering and Remembering the Nation: The Semantics of Political Violence in Venezuela," first appeared in *Comparative Studies in Society and History* 33, no. 2 (April, 1991): 288–337.

Chapter 8, "Venezuela's Wounded Bodies: Nation and Imagination during the 2002 Coup," first appeared in NACLA *Report on the Americas* 44, no. 1 (2011): 33–39.

Chapter 9, "Oilpacity: Secrets of History in the Coup against Hugo Chávez," first appeared in *Anthropology News* 52, no. 5 (2011): 6.

Chapter 12, "Beyond Occidentalism: Toward Nonimperial Geohistorical Categories," first appeared in *Cultural Anthropology* 11, no. 1 (1996): 51–87.

Chapter 13, "Listening to the Subaltern: The Poetics of Neocolonial States," first appeared in *Poetics Today* 15, no. 4 (1994): 643–658.

Chapter 14, "Smelling Like a Market," first appeared in *American Historical Review* 106, no. 1 (2001): 119–129.

Chapter 15, "Latin American Postcolonial Studies and Global Decolonization," first appeared in *Postcolonial Studies: An Anthology*, ed. Pramod Nayar (Chichester, UK: Wiley-Blackwell, 2015), 175–192.

Chapter 16, "After Empire: Reflections on Imperialism from the Américas," first appeared in *Imperial Formations*, ed. Ann Laura Stoler, Carole McGranahan, and Peter Perdue (Santa Fe, NM: School for Advanced Research Press, 2007).

Adorno, Theodor, 157, 348

Allende, Salvador, 133, 144, 146, 234, 281, 429–30

American Anthropological Association, 31–32, 272

Amparo Massacre, 173, 181–89, 192, 203, 210, 212

anthrohistory, 29–30, 33, 36, 47–49, 53–68

Arbenz, Jacobo, 11, 432–33

Argentina, 133, 135–36, 138–40, 144, 145, 148, 207, 232–33, 236, 238–39

Aristide, Jean Bertrand, 232

Arnal, Rafael Castillo, 28

authoritarianism, 37, 129, 232, 235–36, 238–39, 260, 291, 390, 395, 446

Batista, Fulgencio, 11, 14, 71, 76, 77

Baudrillard, Jean, 342, 351

Bay of Pigs Invasion, 14, 433

Benjamin, Walter, 30, 60n3.2, 60n5.2, 69, 87, 106, 157, 166, 213, 348, 359–60; "Theses on the Philosophy of History," 53, 56–57, 59–63

Betancourt, Rómulo, 11, 14, 21, 216n9

Bishop, Maurice, 433

Blake, William, 55, 61n7.4

Bolivia, 131, 136, 138–40, 144–45, 148–50, 154, 245, 345, 413

Borges, Jorge Luis, 1, 48, 50, 53, 55, 60n4.1, 61n6.1, 312, 313, 351, 396–98,

418; and maps, 324, 326, 351–52, 354, 359

Brazil, 32, 95, 125–26, 133–34, 141, 143–46, 148–49, 154, 232, 237, 245, 388, 408, 435, 441; presidency of Luiz Inácio Lula da Silva, 136–40, 152

Bustos, Guillermo, 412

Canclini, Nestor García, 95, 406

Caracazo, 29, 135, 166, 189–206, 254, 277

Cardoso, Fernando Henrique, 134, 140, 233, 401, 435

Carmona, Pedro, 251, 256–58, 276–77, 279–81, 292

Carpentier, Alejo, 1, 79, 108n6; The Kingdom of This World, 55, 57n1.1, 61n7.1

Carter, Jimmy, 25, 218n19, 432

Castro, Fidel, 11, 18–19, 39n26, 133, 407, 433; 1959 visit to Venezuela, 14, 218n19; and Hugo Chavez, 225n80, 255, 281; and Barack Obama, 155

Castro-Gómez, Santiago, 414–16

Chagnon, Napoleon, 31–33, 124–26

Chakrabarty, Dipesh, 65n9.4, 99, 142, 305n3, 318, 418

Chile, 138–40, 145–47, 152, 154–55, 215, 224n71, 233, 238; and the Salvador Allende government, 133, 144, 146, 234, 281, 429–30, 433; and the "Chicago Boys," 435; and the Augusto Pinochet regime, 4, 128, 135–36, 139, 232, 252, 281, 304, 433

Cohen, David William, 58n1.3, 301, 306n16

Cohn, Bernard, 17, 29

Colombia, 148, 152, 345–49, 360, 431; and the Amparo Massacre, 173, 179, 181–87

Coronil, Domingo Antonio, 10

Coronil, Fernando Rubén, 9–10

Coronil, María Elena, 10

Correa, Rafael, 136, 150

de la Cruz, Sor Juana Inés, 55, 61

Derrida, Jacques, 55, 61n7.2, 71, 351, 372, 418

Doña Bárbara (Gallegos), 174, 179–81, 183, 189

Durkheim, Emile, 94, 393

Dussel, Enrique, 32

Ecuador, 130–31, 136, 138–40, 145, 148, 150, 154, 232, 245

El Dorado Task Force, 31–32, 272

Fanon, Frantz, 20, 74, 107n2, 323–24, 334, 360, 431

Fernández Retamar, Roberto, 319, 407, 409, 415–16

Foucault, Michel, 16, 212, 214, 352, 373

Fuentes, Carlos, 19, 431

functionalism, 16, 70, 93

García Márquez, Gabriel, 19

globalcentrism, 419

Gómez, Juan Vicente, 9–10, 179, 216n8, 219n26, 289–90

Gómez, Sara, 19–20, 40n32

Gramsci, Antonio, 19–20, 30, 72, 75, 213, 226n86, 403, 411, 413; and definition of subalternity, 370

Grenada, 433

ground rent, 5, 30, 138, 167–68, 340–41, 444

Guatemala, 11, 245, 415, 432–33

Guayasamín, Oswaldo, 4

Guha, Ranajit, 370–72, 410

Guillén, Nicolás, 1, 108n6, 110n25, 325, 355

Haiti, 11, 55, 61, 96, 232, 300–301, 344, 362n12, 432, 440

Haitian Revolution, 295, 301, 316, 415

Hall, Stuart, 7, 30

Hausmann, Georges-Eugène, 389

Heidegger, Martin, 55, 284, 305n2, 348, 352, 418

Hegel, Georg Wilhelm Friedrich, 55, 212, 301, 331–35

Hulme, Peter, 416

Ímber, Lya, 8–10, 21, 24, 29, 38n11, 58n1.1

International Monetary Fund (IMF), 29, 166, 254, 294, 377, 435; austerity measures imposed by, 173, 191; protests against, 135, 190, 360, 368

Izaguirre, Alejandro, 200–201, 368, 374–75, 380–82

Joseph, Gilbert, 410

Kant, Immanuel, 55, 156, 64n9.1

Kincaid, Jamaica, 165, 284, 305n3

Lander, Edgardo, 32

Left, Latin American, 5, 6, 37, 130–31, 135, 137, 148, 152–53, 155

Lévi-Strauss, Claude, 55, 61, 63, 111n33

Lewis, Oscar, 19

Lukács, György, 100, 348, 358

Lula da Silva, Luiz Inácio, 136–37, 144, 149, 152

Lunar, Emerio Darío, 27

Lusinchi, Jaime, 175–76, 181–83, 187–89

Malinowski, Bronisław, 50, 70, 75–76, 86, 89–96, 101–6
Mallon, Florencia, 410–11, 413
Marcos, Subcomandante, 60n4.1, 360, 415, 420
Marinello, Juan, 95, 394
Marx, Karl, 57, 302, 393
Marxism, 4, 7, 31, 101, 234, 303, 406; and Antonio Gramsci, 19, 72; in Cuba, 19, 75; and György Lukács, 100; in Latin America, 406, 413; and postcolonialism, 402–3
Mendieta, Eduardo, 414–16
Meneses, Guillermo, 11
Mexico, 16–17, 144, 146, 185, 332, 339, 406, 414, 431–32, 435; indigenous people in, 245, 408; Zapatista movement in, 133, 147–48, 154, 360, 415, 420
Mignolo, Walter, 32, 58, 103, 111n.33, 319, 361n2, 375, 407, 409, 420
Mintz, Sidney, 96, 336, 338–41, 440
Mitchell, Timothy, 345, 348–52
Morales, Elsa, 27, 268
Morales, Evo, 136, 144

Naipaul, V. S., 285
nature, 31, 34, 121, 138, 150, 165–68, 179–80, 304, 387–90, 440–41, 444; and oil, 168, 250, 288
neocolonialism, 76, 344, 369, 379, 418
Neruda, Pablo, 66n10, 171, 215
Nicaragua, 133, 136, 232, 432, 433
Nixon, Richard, 11, 432

Occidentalism, 32, 285, 309–10, 312, 315–21, 335–36, 344, 348, 355–57, 409; definition of, 329–31
Organization of Petroleum Exporting Countries (OPEC), 252, 262, 291
Orientalism, 285, 309, 315, 318–20, 327–31, 352, 361n4, 403

Ortiz, Fernando, 50–51, 57, 62n8.2, 69–112, 342, 350, 362n10, 406, 415, 418, 420, 441

Padilla, Herberto, 19, 40n28
Paris, 11, 16, 19, 21, 55, 101, 351, 389
Pérez, Carlos Andrés, 173–74, 176, 182–93, 198, 200–201, 211, 368, 378
Pinochet, Augusto, 4, 128, 135–36, 139, 232, 252, 281, 304, 433
Portell Vilá, Herminio, 70, 88,
postcolonialism, 4, 6, 32, 118, 120, 344, 425; and Latin America, 310–12, 404–20
poststructuralism, 55, 72, 118, 234, 318, 402
Prakash, Gyan, 99
Price-Mars, Jean, 96
Puerto Rico, 96, 276, 430–31

Quijano, Aníbal, 32, 409

Rama, Ángel, 69, 95, 98, 106–7
Reagan, Ronald, 335, 402, 432
Rincón, Lucas, 255, 275, 281

Sahlins, Marshall, 64, 75
Said, Edward, 16, 60, 62, 96–100, 111n33, 285, 311, 318, 327, 418, 427
Sandinistas, 133, 146, 232
Sartre, Jean-Paul, 19, 55, 61, 64
Scott, James, 309, 311–12, 385–98
Seeger, Anthony, 16
Somoza, Anastasio, 146, 232
Sosa, Antonieta, 270
South Africa, 231, 242, 246–47, 426
Spivak, Gayatri, 71, 309, 369–74, 382, 383n3, 404, 405, 407, 414–15, 419
Stanford University, 15
Steinmetz, George, 445–46
subaltern, 309, 311, 368–74, 408–11

Taussig, Michael, 345–49, 363n13

Tierney, Patrick, 32, 51, 123–26, 272

Todorov, Tzvetan, 331, 334–36

transculturation, 21, 50–51, 121, 169, 284, 316, 356, 406; coining of term by Fernando Ortiz, 70, 73–75, 84–86, 88–89; use of term by Bronisław Malinowski, 70, 75–76, 86, 89–94, 101–6

Tricontinental Conference, 17, 406–7

Trouillot, Michel-Rolph, 60n3.1, 63n8.5, 96, 102, 110n22, 300–301

Turner, Terence, 15–16, 23, 29, 39n22

Turner, Victor, 15–16, 39n22, 63

University of Chicago, 16–17, 22, 23, 25, 29, 435

University of Michigan, 29, 32–35, 57, 273

Uruguay, 95, 136, 138, 144, 149, 151, 207, 232

utopia, 1, 6, 7, 8, 34, 37, 324, 361

Vargas, Rafael, 26

Venceremos Brigade, 18–19, 21

Vietnam War, 16, 18, 21, 124

Walcott, Derek, 2, 62

Williams, Raymond, 30, 64, 100, 325, 343, 425

Wolf, Eric, 65, 286, 336–38

Yanomami, 32–33, 123–26, 272